introduction to
marketing

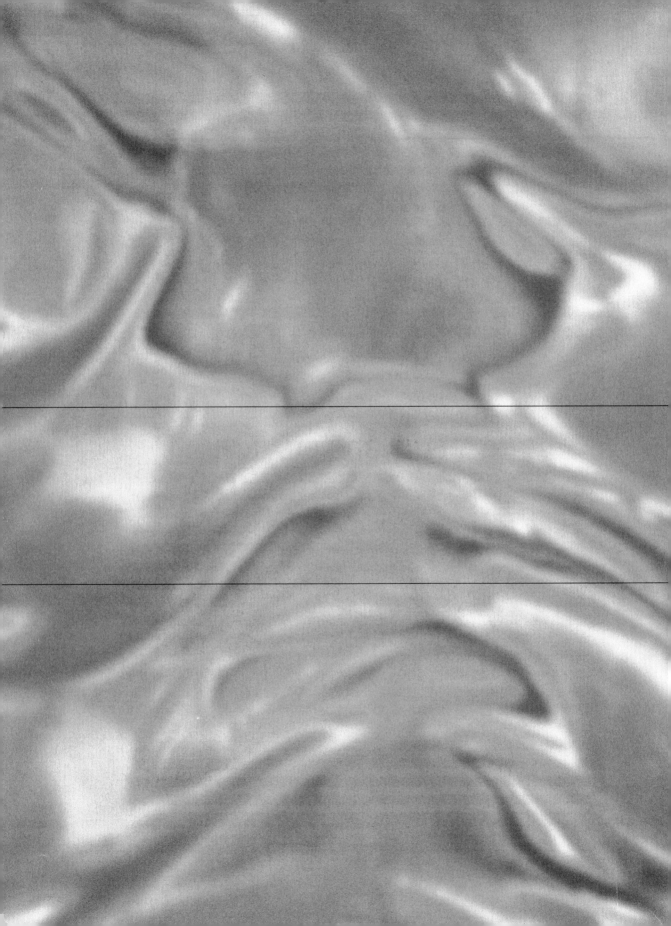

introduction to
marketing

theory and practice

Adrian Palmer

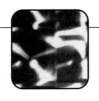

OXFORD
UNIVERSITY PRESS

OXFORD
UNIVERSITY PRESS

Great Clarendon Street, Oxford OX2 6DP

Oxford University Press is a department of the University of Oxford.
It furthers the University's objective of excellence in research,
scholarship, and education by publishing worldwide in
Oxford New York

Auckland Bangkok Buenos Aires Cape Town Chennai
Dar es Salaam Delhi Hong Kong Istanbul Karachi Kolkata
Kuala Lumpur Madrid Melbourne Mexico City Mumbai Nairobi
São Paulo Shanghai Taipei Tokyo Toronto

Oxford is a registered trade mark of Oxford University Press in the UK
and in certain other countries

Published in the United States
by Oxford University Press Inc., New York

British Library Cataloguing in Publication Data
Data available

Library of Congress Cataloging in Publication Data
Data available
ISBN 0-19-926627-1

1 3 5 7 9 10 8 6 4 2

THE AUTHOR

Adrian Palmer is Professor of Services Marketing at the University of Gloucestershire, Cheltenham, UK.

ACKNOWLEDGEMENTS

The following have contributed material to chapters in this book:

Tony Conway, University of Salford: Chapter 7—Developing the Product

Nick Ellis, University of Leicester: Chapter 9—Distribution

Richard Mayer, University of Derby: Chapter 10—Introduction to Promotion Planning

Countless additional colleagues, reviewers and organizations, too numerous to mention here, helped to bring this book to fruition and their assistance is greatly acknowledged. Many authors and organizations kindly granted permission to reproduce copyright material and this is specifically acknowledged throughout the book. The efforts of Angela Parks in co-ordinating much of this material are particularly acknowledged.

Preface

Marketing is an exciting subject to study. Markets are the basis for the wealth of western economies, and marketers help make markets become more efficient and effective. It is marketers who have been a driving force in making an ever-wider range of goods and services available to buyers, seeking to acquire a better understanding of buyers' needs and trying to deliver better products at lower prices than competitors.

This book provides an introduction to the principles of marketing, beginning with the underlying theoretical bases which are often borrowed from the disciplines of economics, sociology, and psychology. Practical application of theory is provided through case studies and vignettes. These practical applications highlight some of the challenges of established frameworks for the study of marketing, and readers are encouraged to formulate alternative frameworks. The book tries not to present prescriptive solutions to marketing problems, but encourages debate about causes and effects. Underlying much of the discussion in the text is the interplay between marketing as a science and marketing as a creative art.

The book has necessarily been divided into a number of chapters in order to provide some form of structure. In the real world, marketing cannot be neatly compartmentalized in this way. With a holistic vision, it will be seen that any change in one aspect of marketing is likely to have consequences in other aspects. In an attempt to emphasize these linkages, each chapter closes with a summary of how it relates to other chapters. Vignettes and case studies provide integrative perspectives.

To begin, definitions of marketing are discussed and essential characteristics identified. Marketing takes place within a complex environment of social, economic, political, and technological forces and Chapter 2 examines the continual interplay between marketing managers and their marketing environment. Chapter 3 focuses on a crucial aspect of marketing—understanding the complex factors that lead to buying decisions. Our understanding of buying processes and other marketing phenomena calls for appropriate information gathering, analysis, and dissemination (Chapter 4). Knowledge of buyer behaviour, backed by good-quality research, leads to the concept of segmentation and targeting (Chapter 5), from which companies seek to develop a sustainable competitive advantage (Chapter 6). The following chapters look at the strategic and tactical decisions that marketing managers make, classified under the marketing mix headings of Product (Chapter 7), Price (Chapter 8), Place (Chapter 9), and Promotion (Chapters 10 and 11). The final chapters integrate the previous ones and provide an overview of the marketing management process (Chapter 12), the marketing of services (Chapter 13), and the challenges presented by global marketing (Chapter 14).

Current developments in the internet are reflected in vignettes and case studies in each chapter. The growing recognition of the social responsibilities of marketing is stressed throughout.

This book is published at a time of great debate in marketing. Discussion abounds about the nature of marketing knowledge and theory. New ideas and even claims of shifts in marketing paradigms appear regularly. The book seeks to develop a well-founded and balanced view of marketing and makes no apology for raising as many questions as it answers. Marketing is more about a way of thinking than a series of prescriptive rules.

The book is supported by a companion website (**www.oup.com/uk/booksites/busecon**), where you will find supplementary reading lists and web links relevant to each chapter. Additional case studies and questions are provided for each chapter. Your knowledge can be tested with a series of multiple-choice questions. For tutors, Power-Point slides and lecture plans are linked to each chapter. An additional multiple-choice testbank of questions is provided.

Guided tour

CHAPTER OBJECTIVES

Identify the abilities and skills the reader should demonstrate after reading the chapter

BOXED VIGNETTES
highlighting up-to-date issues

CASE STUDY REVIEW QUESTIONS
are designed to help you apply your understanding of the concepts and develop your knowledge

CASE STUDIES

Each chapter ends with a case study which will cover the themes that have been raised in the chapter and help you to analyse and reflect upon them

CHAPTER REVIEW QUESTIONS
can be used for assessing your under-standing or for dis-cussing in small groups

REFERENCES

indicate sources used and can be used to help explain the subject further

USEFUL WEB LINKS

Guide the student in their further research

The book is supported by a companion website. Here, students will find supplementary reading lists and web links relevant to each chapter which can be clicked through. For each chapter, additional case studies and multiple-choice questions are provided. Lecturers will find lecture notes and PowerPoint slides for each chapter. They will also have access to a testbank of 400 multiple-choice questions.

www.oup.com/uk/booksites/busecon

Contents

PART 2 Understanding customers

PART 3 **Developing the marketing mix**

PART 4   Bringing it together

PART 1

Marketing: the fundamentals

What is marketing?

CHAPTER OBJECTIVES

There is much misunderstanding about what marketing is. Many people equate it with promotion, or 'trying to sell things that people don't really want'. With higher levels of business education, that misperception is changing. This chapter sets out the foundations of marketing and distinguishes between marketing as a fundamental philosophy and marketing as a set of techniques. While the techniques have now been widely adopted, many organizations still have a long way to go in developing a true customer focus, which is at the heart of the marketing philosophy. This chapter discusses the relationship of marketing to other organization functions and reviews current debate about the nature of marketing. It is essentially a foundation chapter, and many themes discussed will be returned to in more detail in later chapters.

Introduction

Marketing is essentially about marshalling the resources of an organization to meet the changing needs of customers on whom the organization depends. As a verb, market*ing* is all about how an organization addresses its markets.

There are many definitions of marketing which generally revolve around the primacy of customers as part of an exchange process. Customers' needs are the starting point for marketing activity. Marketing managers try to identify these needs and develop products that will satisfy customers' needs through an exchange process. The Chartered Institute of Marketing provides a typical definition of marketing:

Marketing is 'The management process which identifies, anticipates and supplies customer requirements efficiently and profitably'.

While customers may drive the activities of a marketing-oriented organization, the organization will be able to continue serving its customers only if it meets its own objectives. Most private sector organizations operate with some kind of profit-related objectives, and if an adequate level of profits cannot be earned from a particular group of customers, a firm will not normally wish to meet the needs of that group. Where an organization is able to meet its customers' needs effectively and efficiently, its ability to gain an advantage over its competitors will be increased (for example by allowing it to sell a higher volume and/or at a higher price than its competitors). It is consequently also more likely to be able to meet its profit objectives.

Even in fully marketing-oriented organizations, it is not just customers who are crucial to the continuing success of the firm. The availability of finance and labour inputs may be quite critical, and in times of shortage of either one of these an organization must adapt its production processes if it is to continue meeting customers' needs. In addition, a whole range of internal and external pressures (such as government legislation and the emergence of new technologies) can affect its ability to profitably meet customers' needs. Organizations must adapt to a changing marketing environment if they are to survive and prosper. In Chapter 2 we will look more closely at these pressures on businesses.

■ Marketing as a philosophy and as a set of techniques

As a **business philosophy**, marketing puts customers at the centre of an organization's considerations. This is reflected in basic values, such as the requirement to understand and respond to customer needs and the necessity to search constantly for new market opportunities. In a truly marketing-oriented organization, these values are instilled in all employees and should influence their behaviour without any need for prompting. For a fast food restaurant, for example, the training of serving staff would emphasize those items—such as the speed of service and friendliness of staff—that research has found to be most valued by existing and potential customers. The personnel manager would have a selection policy that recruited staff who could fulfil the needs of customers rather than simply minimizing the wage bill. The accountant would investigate the effects on customers before deciding to save money by cutting stockholding levels. It is not sufficient for an organization to simply appoint a marketing manager or set up a marketing department—viewed as a philosophy, marketing is an attitude that applies to *everybody* who works for the organization.

To many people, marketing is simply associated with a set of **techniques**. For example, market research is seen as a technique for finding out about customers' needs, and advertising is thought to be a technique for communicating the benefits of a product offer to potential customers. However, these techniques can be of little value if they are undertaken by an organization that has not fully taken on board the *philosophy* of marketing. The techniques of marketing also include pricing, the design of channels of distribution, and new product development. Although many of the chapters of this book are arranged around specific techniques, it must never be forgotten that all of these techniques are interrelated and can be effective only if they are unified by a shared focus on customers.

MARKETING in ACTION

Are they really marketing oriented?

Companies that have wholly embraced the marketing philosophy put customers at the centre of everything they do, so that being 'marketing oriented' becomes a state of mind for *all of their employees*. They should all be aware that if they don't put customers first somebody else will, and will win their profitable business. Here are some tell-tale signs of a company that may claim to be marketing oriented but where, in fact, not all of its employees have taken on board a genuine marketing orientation.

- In the car park, the prime parking spots are reserved for directors and senior staff rather than customers.
- Opening hours are geared towards meeting the social needs of staff rather than the purchasing preferences of customers.
- Management's attitudes towards lax staff is conditioned more by the need to keep internal peace than by the need to provide a high standard of service to customers.
- When confronted with a problem from a customer, an employee will refer the customer on to another employee without trying to resolve the matter themselves ('it's not my job').
- The company listens to customers' comments and complaints, but has poorly defined procedures for acting on them.
- Advertising is based on what senior staff want to say, rather than a sound analysis of what prospective customers want to hear.
- Goods and services are distributed through channels that are easy for the company to set up, rather than on the basis of what customers prefer.

Can you think of any more tell-tale signs? Can you identify companies that exhibit the characteristics described above? Why do you think the company can behave in such a way? Are there insufficient competitive pressures facing the company to warrant change? What, if anything, would you do to bring about change in the company?

Of course, the principles of marketing are not new. Some of the elements of marketing orientation can be traced as far back as ancient Greece, the Phoenicians, and the Venetian traders. The bartering that still takes place in many eastern kasbahs is a form of marketing. In modern times, marketing orientation developed in the more affluent countries, especially for products where supply was outstripping demand and suppliers therefore faced high levels of competition for custom. Marketing first became an

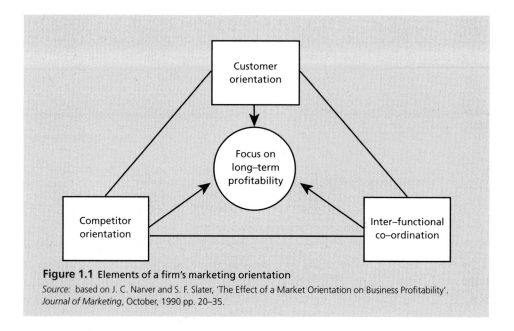

Figure 1.1 Elements of a firm's marketing orientation
Source: based on J. C. Narver and S. F. Slater, 'The Effect of a Market Orientation on Business Profitability'. *Journal of Marketing*, October, 1990 pp. 20–35.

important discipline in the United States in the 1930s and has since become dominant around the world. In a competitive business environment, an organization will survive in the long term only if it focuses on the needs of clearly defined groups in society and produces goods and services that satisfy their requirements efficiently and effectively. The emphasis is on the customer wanting to buy, rather than on the producer needing to sell.

There have been many attempts to define just what is meant by marketing orientation. (A good review has been provided by Lafferty and Hult [10].) Among empirical attempts to measure marketing orientation, a study by Narver and Slater [13] identified three important components (Figure 1.1):

- **Customer orientation**: An organization must have a thorough understanding of its target buyers, so that it can create a product of superior value for them. Remember that value can be defined only by customers themselves, and can be created by increasing the benefits to the buyer in relation to the buyer's costs or by decreasing the buyer's costs in relation to the buyer's benefits. A customer orientation requires that a company understand not only the present value to the customer, but also how this is likely to evolve over time.

- **Competitor orientation**: As well as focusing on its customers, a firm should look at how well its competitors are able to satisfy buyers' needs. It should understand the short-term strengths and weaknesses and long-term capabilities and strategies of current and potential competitors.

- **Interfunctional co-ordination**: It is futile for marketing managers to develop marketing plans that are not acted upon by people who are capable of delivering promises made to customers. Many individuals within an organization have a responsibility for creating value—not just marketing staff—and a marketing orientation requires that the organization draw upon and integrate its human and physical resources effectively and adapt them to meet customers' needs.

Foundations for success in business

So far, marketing has been presented as an indispensable approach to doing business. In fact, marketing is not appropriate to all firms at all times and in all places. Essentially, marketing assumes greatest importance where the main factor constraining a firm's survival and growth is the shortage of customers for its products. If a firm can be assured of selling all that it produces, it may consider marketing to be the least of its worries. There are other factors that may be critical for success to some companies:

- Where the raw materials and components that a company requires are scarce but demand for its finished products is very strong, a company may consider that obtaining inputs to its production processes is its top priority. During the late 1990s, the shortage of organic vegetables, rather than a shortage of customers, posed the biggest

Figure 1.2 During 2003, mobile phones that could be used as a camera to send pictures were a hot new product which helped to reinvigorate the mobile phone market. This market had become saturated and mobile phones had become a commodity-type product. The new-type phones allowed companies to add features that consumers valued. But how long would it be before *these* phones became standard and customers were no longer willing to pay a premium price for them? What would be the next features and benefits that customers will value as the technology of mobile phones develops?

challenge to companies seeking to develop the market for organic products (see 'Marketing in Action' later in this chapter).

- For firms requiring high levels of skill among their employees, being able to recruit and retain the right personnel can be critical to business success. Firms in sectors as diverse as computer programming, direct marketing, specialist craft industries, and electrical engineering have had market-led growth held back by difficulties in filling key positions.

- Where a company is given a licence by government agencies to provide a monopoly service, its actions may be motivated more by the desire to keep the regulatory agency satisfied than to keep its customers happy.

Modern marketing emerged in the 1930s at a time when the volume of goods supplied to markets was increasing faster than consumers' demand for them. Instead of taking markets as a given element of their business plans, firms had to actively address the needs of their markets—if they didn't, the market would slip into their competitors' hands.

Figure 1.3 The fast-moving consumer goods (FMCG) sectors were the first to adopt modern marketing. The soap powder, toothpaste, and shampoo markets have become fiercely competitive and great efforts have been made by the manufacturers to develop differentiated versions of a fairly standard product in order to meet the needs of small groups of consumers more effectively than their competitors. Next time you are in a shop choosing toothpaste, look at all of the different product formulations, packaging design, and price offers that companies have deployed to try to get you to buy their product rather than the competitors'. It is often said that experience in the tough world of an FMCG company's marketing department is the best apprenticeship that a new marketer can serve. While FMCG sectors were early adopters of marketing, many more sectors have followed their example (Photograph: Angela Parks)

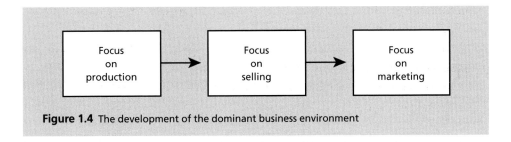

Figure 1.4 The development of the dominant business environment

It is common to talk about the production-oriented firm, where production and not marketing is the focal point for business planning. However, when markets became more competitive, the first reaction of many companies was to take on board not the full philosophy of marketing, but only the selling function. Eventually, firms have come to realize that, instead of trying to sell products that buyers do not really want, it would be better to take on board the full philosophy of marketing, which puts customers' needs at the centre of all business planning.

A production or a sales orientation may be appropriate to firms at certain stages in the evolution of markets. Where the dominant business environment is based on the need for good production planning above all else, the company that does this best will achieve the greatest overall business success. Likewise, in competitive markets, the company that achieves the greatest business success is likely to be one that has the most effective marketing.

Because they are business environments that still occur in some markets in some places, production and selling orientations are described below. There has, however, been an almost inevitable tendency for such business environments to progress to a full marketing orientation. Firms that have identified such trends and adapted have tended to survive, while those set in their traditional ways of doing business have fallen behind.

Production orientation

Marketing as a business discipline has much less significance where goods or services are scarce and considerable unsatisfied demand exists. If an organization is operating in a stable environment in which it can sell all that it can produce, why bother spending time and money trying to understand precisely what benefit a customer seeks from buying the product? If the market is stable, why take time trying to anticipate future requirements? Furthermore, if a company has significant monopoly power, it may have little interest in being more efficient in meeting customer requirements. The former state monopolies of eastern Europe are frequently cited as examples of organizations that produced what they imagined consumers wanted, rather than what they actually

wanted. Planning for full utilization of capital equipment was often seen as more important than ensuring that the equipment was used to provide goods and services that
people actually wanted. Production-oriented firms generally aim for efficiency in production rather than effectiveness in meeting customers' needs.

In the developed countries of America and Europe, production orientation was quite
pervasive until the 1930s; up to then, a general shortage of goods relative to the
demand for them, and a lack of competition, resulted in a sellers' market. In many
goods markets, however, the world depression of the 1920s and 1930s had the effect of
tilting the balance of supply and demand more in favour of buyers, resulting in sellers'
having to address more seriously the needs of increasingly selective customers. In most
countries markets for services have tended to retain a production orientation longer
than most goods markets, reflecting the fact that many key services, such as postal services, telecommunications, electricity, gas and water supply, have been dominated by
state or private monopolies which gave consumers very little choice of supplier—if consumers did not like the service they received from their water supplier, they could not
switch their business to another water company. Management in such circumstances
had greater freedom to satisfy its own interests than those of the consumer, and could
increase profits more effectively by keeping production costs down rather than applying effort and possibly taking greater risk through developing new services based on
consumers' needs.

During periods of shortages, production orientation sometimes returns to an industry sector. The shortage might come about through supply limitations caused by strikes
or bad weather, or it could be the result of a sudden increase in demand relative to
supply. For example, during a bus or train drivers' strike, taxi operators may realize that
there is a temporary massive excess of demand relative to supply and so may be tempted
to lower their standards of service to casual customers (for example by responding
to requests much more slowly and doing so in a less friendly manner than regular
customers would have come to expect). Sometimes shortages may show little sign of
abating. During the boom in property prices that occurred in the UK during 2000–3, the
services of builders were in short supply, especially in South-east England. Stories
abounded of builders 'selecting' customers and delaying the completion of jobs because
they knew that customers had very little choice.

Selling orientation

Faced with an increasingly competitive market, the natural reaction of many organizations has been to shout louder in order to attract customers to buy its products. Product
policy was driven by the desire to make those products that the company thought it was
good at producing, rather than seriously asking what benefits customers sought from
buying its products. In order to increase sales, the focal point of the business moved
away from the production manager to the sales manager, who set about increasing

MARKETING in ACTION

Demand boomed for organics, but where were the vegetables?

When a company faces acute problems of supply, it may simply not be realistic for the company to be customer-led. The UK market for organic vegetables during the late 1990s illustrates this point. A combination of rising incomes, greater awareness of health issues, and a stream of food safety scares led to a rapid growth in demand for organic produce throughout Europe (see Chomka [4]). But how could farmers grow organically on land that had been saturated by decades of artificial fertilizers? The Soil Association, which operates an accreditation scheme for organic produce, required that farmland should be free of artificial fertilizer for at least five years before any crops grown on it could be described as organic. So, despite the rapid growth in demand and the price premiums that customers were prepared to pay, retailers found it difficult to satisfy demand. Furthermore, with a difficult and intermittent supply, could retailers risk their brand names by being seen as unreliable suppliers of second-rate produce? Marks & Spencer launched a range of organic vegetables in 1997, only to temporarily withdraw them soon afterwards, blaming the difficulty in obtaining regular and reliable supplies. In the short term, it was suppliers and not customers who guided the retailer's policy on organic produce. However, by 2002 previous initiatives to grow more organic food were finally coming on stream, resulting in a glut of produce which depressed the prices that farmers received. It was now a buyers' market. One retailer, Iceland, took advantage of the glut by announcing its plans to sell only organic vegetables in its stores.

effective demand by the use of various sales techniques. Advertising, sales promotion, and personal selling were used to emphasize product differentiation and branding.

A sales orientation was a move away from a strict product orientation, but it still did not focus on satisfying customer needs. Little effort was made to research customer needs or to devise new product offerings that were customer-led rather than production-led.

A sales orientation has been characteristic of a number of business sectors. UK package holiday companies have often grown through heavy advertising of their competitive price advantage, supported by aggressive sales promotion techniques, such as subsidized insurance and free child places. There are signs that this sales-led approach is now being replaced by a greater analysis of the diverse needs that customers seek to satisfy when buying a package holiday, such as the quality of airport check-in facilities, reliable departures, and assurance about the standards of the booked hotel.

If a company were accurately identifying consumer needs and offering a product that satisfied these needs, then consumers would want to buy the product, and the company would not have to rely on intensive sales techniques. In the words of Peter Drucker [5],

The aim of marketing is to make selling superfluous. The aim of marketing is to know and understand the customer so well that the product or service fits him and sells itself. Ideally, marketing should result in a customer who is ready to buy. All that should be needed is to make the product or service available . . .

MARKETING and the INTERNET

New marketing, or old ideas?

In the late 1990s it became fashionable to talk about a 'new marketing'. For its proclaimers, the environment of business organizations was to be changed for ever in a brave new world in which 'new' Britain was ruled by 'new' Labour, inhabited by 'new' man, who worked in the 'new' economy and learnt about the world through 'new' media. Electronic commerce would allow for almost infinite communication possibilities, breaking down international trade and cultural barriers in the process. Monopolies would be broken by the powerful forces of global competition facilitated by the Internet, and our neighbours would become not the people who lived next door, but anybody, anywhere in cyberspace who shared our interests and life-style. The prophets of doom for marketing were out in force, with 'Postmodernists' arguing that chaos was the order of the day and that the traditional rules of marketing could no longer be applied to increasingly individualistic consumers. As the world entered the new millennium, it seemed that marketing would never be the same again—or at least this is what many people thought.

Of course, many 'big ideas' have a habit of imploding, and we need to ask whether any of the promises of the 'new marketing' have been delivered, or are ever likely to be. The idea that the 'new economy' had banished the economic cycle of prosperity and recession appeared to be dubious as the United States economy entered recession in 2001 after a prolonged period of expansion. Many questioned the myth of 'new man' as something that was more talked about in glossy magazines than experienced in everyday life.

Many of the 'new' world phenomena that helped to define the new marketing soon began to lose their sparkle, leaving observers to wonder whether there really was anything new. It soon became recognized that the 'new' economy was very dependent upon the 'old' economy. Electronic communication may be fine in theory as a means of improving global competition, but somebody still has to manufacture goods and deliver them, invariably using 'old economy' methods. Many commentators were excited by the prospects of new media advertising, and justified this by pointing to Procter and Gamble's decision to direct 80% of its promotion budget to new media. But old media has a habit of fighting back hard, as witnessed by the huge amount of advertising by the new media owners themselves in traditional newspapers and television channels.

Practitioners of marketing make excessive use of the word 'new', to describe anything from a 'new and improved' breakfast cereal to a new marketing paradigm. However, this example serves to remind us that many of the underlying principles of marketing are quite timeless. We really need to distinguish between genuinely new marketing ideas—which are quite rare—and old ideas that have been applied to a new marketing environment.

■ What organizations undertake marketing?

Marketing developed in competitive fast-moving goods sectors, with private sector services following in their footsteps. More recently, marketing has been adopted by various public sector and not-for-profit organizations, reflecting the increasingly competitive environments in which these now operate. Operationalizing marketing within these organizations poses a number of challenges (see Sargeant, Foreman, and Liao [14]). If an organization has a market that it needs to win over, then marketing has a role. But without markets, can marketing ever be a reality? Many organizations claim to have introduced marketing when in fact their customers are captive, with no market-place within which they can choose competing goods or services. What passes for marketing may be little more than a laudable attempt to bring best practice to their operations in selected areas, for example in providing customer care programmes for front-line staff. But if customers have to come to the company anyway (as they do in the case of many local authority services), is this really marketing?

Within the public/not-for-profit sectors, financial objectives are often qualified by non-financial social objectives. An organization's desire to meet individual customers' needs must be further constrained by its requirement to meet these wider social objectives. In this way, a leisure centre may set an objective of providing a range of keep-fit programmes for disadvantaged members of the local community, knowing that it could have earned more money by opening its facilities to the larger group of full fee paying visitors. Nevertheless, marketing can be employed to achieve a high takeup rate among this group, persuading them to spend their time and money at the leisure centre rather than on other leisure activities.

In recent years, the principles of marketing have been applied to organizations that essentially promote ideas, for example charities, political parties, and religious groups. Some of the principles of marketing may be evident in the way that the UK Labour Party 'rebranded' itself as New Labour after careful research of its audiences. This was backed up with a very effective advertising campaign, based on many of the principles of segmentation and targeting, which helped it to win the 1997 and 2001 General Elections. However, some purists would argue that, in its application to social and political causes, marketing is inappropriate because of the absence of markets and exchanges as conventionally understood by marketers.

◼ Key marketing concepts

In this section, the philosophy of marketing will be developed a little further by defining a number of key concepts which go to the heart of the philosophy. The concepts of customers, needs, value, exchange, and markets will be briefly introduced, but returned to in following chapters.

Customers

Customers provide payment to an organization in return for the delivery of goods and services and therefore form a focal point for an organization's marketing activity. Customers can be described by many terms, including client, passenger, subscriber, reader, guest, and student. The terminology can imply something about the relationship be-tween a company and its customers, so the term 'patient' implies a caring relationship, 'passenger' implies an ongoing responsibility for the safety of the customer, and 'client' implies that the relationship is governed by a code of ethics (formal or informal).

The customer is generally understood to be the person who makes the decision to purchase a product, and/or who pays for it. In fact, products are often bought by one person for consumption by another, therefore the customer and consumer need not be the same person. For example, colleges must market themselves not only to prospective students, but also to their parents, careers counsellors, local employers, and govern-ment funding agencies. In these circumstances it can be difficult to identify who an organization's marketing effort should be focused upon. The role of influencers in the decision process is discussed further in Chapter 3.

For many public services, it is society as a whole, and not just the immediate cus-tomer, that benefits from an individual's consumption. In the case of health services, society can benefit from having a fit and healthy population in which the risk of con-tracting a contagious disease is minimized.

Different customers within a market have different needs which they seek to satisfy. To be fully marketing oriented, a company would have to adapt its offering to meet the needs of each individual. In fact, very few firms can justify aiming to meet the needs of each specific individual; instead, they target their product at a clearly defined group in society and position their product so that it meets the needs of that group. These sub-groups are often referred to as 'segments' and are explored in Chapter 3.

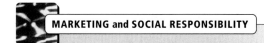

MARKETING and SOCIAL RESPONSIBILITY

When does a student become a customer?

As a hospital *patient*, would you cringe at being referred to as a 'customer'? Or what about the transformation of rail users from 'passengers' to 'customers'? Some universities now refer to their paying students as 'customers'. The use of the word 'customer' may sharpen minds within an organization, making everybody aware that they cannot take users for granted. 'Passenger', 'patient', and 'student' are relatively passive terms, but 'customer' provides a reminder that custom can be quite transient. Do terms used by professionals, such as 'patient' and 'student', imply a professional code of ethics which puts some groups of consumers in a very special, trusting relationship with their supplier? Is it realistic to describe as 'customers' the users of some public services (such as the police and fire services) when there is no alternative supplier they could customize? Does the use of the generic title of 'customer' undermine this special relationship? Could the use of the term 'customer' even be a double-edged sword, by raising consumers' expectations about standards of service to levels that may be undeliverable? Can being a patient in an NHS hospital ever be likened to being a customer of Sainsbury's supermarket?

Needs

Consumers are motivated by their desire to satisfy complex needs, and these should be the starting point for all marketing activity. We no longer live in a society in which the main motivation of individuals is to satisfy the basic needs for food and drink. Maslow [11] recognized that, once individuals have satisfied basic physiological needs, they may be motivated by higher-order social and self-fulfilment needs. Needs as motivators are explored further in Chapter 3.

'Need' refers to something that is deep-rooted in an individual's personality. How individuals go about satisfying that need will be conditioned by the cultural values of the society which they belong to. So in some cultures the need for self-fulfilment may be satisfied by a religious penance, while other societies may seek it through a development of their creative talents.

It is useful to make a distinction between needs and wants. Wants are culturally conditioned by the society in which an individual lives. Wants subsequently become effective demand for a product where there is both a willingness and an ability to pay for the product.

Marketers are continually seeking to learn more about underlying needs which may eventually manifest themselves as demand in the form of people actually being willing to pay money for its products.

It must not be forgotten that commercial buyers of goods and services also have complex needs which they seek to satisfy when buying on behalf of their organizations.

Nature of need	Likely sources of need satisfaction in primitive societies	Likely sources of need satisfaction in western Europe
Status	Ownership of animals Multiple wives	Make and model of car Type and location of house
Excitement	Hunting Inter-tribe rivalry	Fast car Adventure holiday
Identification with group	Body painting Adopting rituals of the group	Wearing branded clothing Patronizing 'cool' nightclubs and bars

Figure 1.5 Some basic human needs and how people in different societies may go about satisfying them

Figure 1.6 Traditional street markets have been experiencing a revival in the UK. Although market traders may not use many of the terms used in books on marketing theory, they are nevertheless very adept marketers. Traders learn very quickly which product lines are selling quickly and the effects of price changes on sales levels, among other things. They must adapt quickly, or risk business going to another trader in the same market who is more in tune with customers' needs, or to another trader outside of the market. Market traders do no have layers of bureaucratic control which may slow up a decision and individual traders cannot easily shelter in a bureaucratic structure where blame can be passed around without the fundamental issue of responding to customers' needs being addressed. It is not surprising that market traders who have survived and prospered in this environment have gone on to establish and run successful enterprises. Many marketers from large organizations could benefit by taking a walk through their local market and reconnecting with the fundamental principles of marketing (Reproduced with permission of National Market Traders Federation)

Greater complexity occurs where the economic needs of the organization may not be entirely the same as the personal needs of individuals within the organization.

Value

For customers, value is represented by the ratio of perceived benefits to price paid. Customers will evaluate benefits according to the extent to which a product allows their needs to be satisfied. Customers also evaluate how well a product's benefits add to their own well-being as compared with the benefits provided by competitors' offerings:

Figure 1.7 Value can be a very personal issue, and one person's highly prized object may be regarded by somebody else as their rubbish. During 2003 denim jeans with a slightly worn look became very fashionable, and many buyers were ready to pay a premium price for a pair of jeans that looked as if they had been previously worn. To others, however, the idea of prematurely ageing clothes may sound like a sacrilege—for them, prematurely aged jeans should have a lower rather than a higher value. Value is essentially about personal judgements

$$\text{Customer perceived value} = \frac{\text{Benefits deriving from a product}}{\text{Cost of acquiring the product}}$$

Consumers often place a value on a product offer that is quite different from the value presumed by the supplier. Business organizations succeed by adding value at a faster rate than they add to their own production costs. Value can be added by better specifying a product offer in accordance with customers' expectations, for example by providing the reassurance of effective after-sales service.

Estimating customers' assessment of value is not easy for marketers. Chapter 8 deals with theoretical and practical approaches to pricing which aim to set prices at a level that meets the needs of buyer and seller. Segmentation is crucial to this exercise, as some groups of buyers are likely to place significantly higher values on the firm's goods than others (Chapter 3). If the price of a good is set too high, no sale may take place, or at least only a one-off sale which may be regarded by the buyer as a 'rip-off'. If the price is set too low, the supplier may achieve high levels of sales, but fail to make any profit because the price is too low to cover its costs. Firms need to understand not just what constitutes value today, but how customers' perceptions of value will change over time.

Exchange

Societies have different ways in which they arrange for goods and services to be acquired. In some less developed societies hunting for food, or begging, may be a norm. In centrally planned economies goods and services may be allocated to individuals and firms by central government planners. In modern market-based economies, goods and services are acquired on the basis of exchange. Exchange implies that one party makes some sacrifice to another party in return for receiving something it values; the other party similarly makes a sacrifice and receives something that *it* values. Of course, the sacrifices and valuations of goods received and given up are essentially based on personal opinion and preferences, so there is no objective way of defining what is a 'fair' exchange, other than observing that both parties are happy with the outcomes. In market-based economies there is a presumption that each party can decide whether or

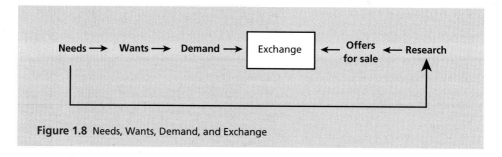

Figure 1.8 Needs, Wants, Demand, and Exchange

not to enter into an exchange with the other. Each party is also free to choose between a number of alternative potential partners. Exchange usually takes the form of a product being exchanged for money, although the bartering of goods and services is still common in some trading systems.

Can the concept of exchange be generalized to cover the provision of public services? Some have argued that the payment of taxes to the government in return for the provision of public services is a form of social marketing exchange. Within marketing frameworks, the problem with this approach to exchange is that it can be difficult to identify what sovereignty consumers of government services have in determining which exchanges they should engage in.

A single exchange should not be seen in isolation from the preceding and expected subsequent exchanges between parties. Marketers are increasingly focusing on analysing ongoing exchange relationships, rather than one-off and isolated exchanges. (We will come back to this again in Chapter 3.)

Markets

The term 'market' has traditionally been used to describe a place where buyers and sellers gather to exchange goods and services (for example a fruit and vegetable market or a stock market). Economists define a market in terms of a more abstract concept of interaction between buyers and sellers, so that the 'UK cheese market' is defined in terms of all buyers and sellers of cheese in the UK. Markets are defined with reference to space and time, so marketers may talk about sales of a particular type of cheese in the northwest region for a specified period of time. Various measures of the market are commonly used, including sales volumes, sales values, growth rate, and level of competitiveness.

■ The marketing mix

Central to marketing management is the concept of the marketing mix (Figure 1.9). In this section the elements of the marketing mix are briefly introduced, but they are returned to in greater detail in following chapters. The marketing mix is not a theory of management that has been derived from scientific analysis, but a conceptual frame-

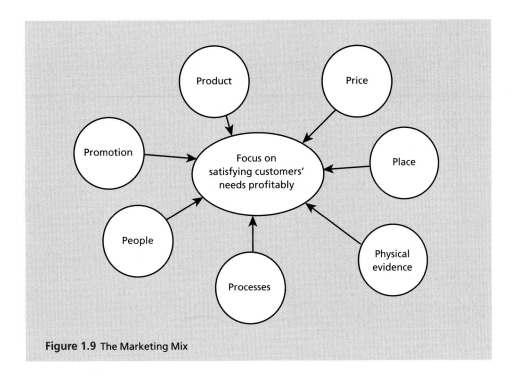

Figure 1.9 The Marketing Mix

work which highlights the principal decisions that marketing managers make in configuring their offerings to suit customers' needs. The tools can be used to develop both long-term strategies and short-term tactical programmes.

A marketing manager can be seen as somebody who mixes a set of ingredients to achieve a desired outcome in much the same way as a cook mixes ingredients for a cake. At the end of the day, two cooks can meet a common objective of baking an edible cake, but using different blends of ingredients to achieve their objective. Marketing managers are essentially mixers of ingredients, and, as with the cooks, two marketers may each use broadly similar ingredients, but fashion them in different ways to end up with quite distinctive product offers. The nation's changing tastes result in bakers producing new types of cake, and so too the changing marketing environment results in marketing managers producing new goods and services to offer to their markets. The mixing of ingredients in both cases is a combination of a science—learning by a logical process from what has proved effective in the past—and an art form, in that both the cook and marketing manager frequently come across new situations where there is no direct experience to draw upon, and where a creative decision must therefore be made.

The concept of the marketing mix was first given prominence by Borden [1], who described the marketing manager as

a mixer of ingredients, one who is constantly engaged in fashioning creatively a mix of marketing procedures and policies in his efforts to produce a profitable enterprise.

There has been debate about which tools should be included in the marketing mix. The traditional marketing mix has comprised the four elements of Product, Price, Promotion, and Place. A number of people have additionally suggested adding People, Process, and Physical Evidence decisions, which can be important aspects of marketing planning in services industries. There is overlap between each of these headings, and their precise definition is not particularly important. What matters is that marketing managers can identify the actions they can take that will produce a favourable response from customers. The marketing mix has merely become a convenient framework for analysing these decisions. A brief synopsis of each of the mix elements is given below, and each is returned to for a fuller discussion in the following chapters.

Products

Products are the means by which organizations satisfy consumers' needs. A product in this sense is anything that an organization offers to potential customers which might satisfy a need, whether tangible or intangible. After initial hesitation, most marketing managers are now happy to talk about an intangible service as a product.

The elements of the product mix that the marketer can control include quality levels, styling, special design features, durability, packaging, range of sizes or options, warranties, after-sales service, and the brand image. Trade-offs are involved between these elements. For example, one firm may invest in quality control and high-grade materials to provide a durable, top-quality product requiring a low level of after-sales service, while another company might offer lower quality but would ensure that a much more effective after-sales service did not make their customers any worse off than if they had bought the higher-quality product. Brands are used by companies to help differentiate their product from those of their competitors. A brand is a name, term, symbol, or combination of these intended to differentiate the goods of one seller from all other sellers (see Chapter 6).

The range of products offered by firms needs to adapt to changes in the marketing environment. As an example, cosmetics companies have responded to changes in male attitudes by launching new ranges of cosmetics targeted at men. (New product development is discussed in Chapter 7.)

Pricing

Pricing is a critical element of most companies' marketing mix, as it determines the revenue that will be generated. By contrast, the other mix elements are concerned essentially with items of expenditure. If the selling price of a product is set too high, a company may not achieve its sales volume targets. If it is set too low, volume targets may be achieved, but no profit earned. Setting prices is a difficult part of the marketing mix. In theory, prices are determined by the interaction of market forces, and the bases of such price determination is explored further in Chapter 8. In practice, marketers set prices for individual products on the basis of what they cost to produce, what the competition is charging, and what customers are prepared to pay. Marketing managers in many public utilities must additionally contend with interventions by government regulatory agencies.

Price decisions also involve deciding on the relationship between prices charged for different products within a firm's range (e.g., should the core product be sold at a low price in order to encourage sales of highly profitable optional extras?) and deciding a pricing strategy over time (should a new product be launched as a prestige product, and its price gradually lowered as it becomes more commonplace?)

Place

Decisions concerning place really comprise two related areas of decisions. Companies usually make their goods and services in places that are convenient for production, but customers prefer to buy them where the purchase process and/or consumption is easiest. So place decisions involve determining how easy a company wants to make it for customers to gain access to its goods and services. In the first place, this involves deciding which intermediaries to use in the process of transferring the product from the manufacturer to final consumer (usually referred to as designing a 'channel of distribution'). Secondly, it involves deciding how physically to move and handle the product as it is transported from manufacturer to final consumer (often referred to as 'logistics' or 'physical distribution management'). Place decisions are considered in more detail in Chapter 9.

Promotion

Promotion is used by companies to communicate the benefits of their products to their target markets. Promotional tools include advertising, personal selling, public relations, sales promotion, sponsorship, and—increasingly—direct marketing methods. Just as product ranges need to be kept up to date to reflect changing customer needs, so too promotional methods need to be responsive to changes in a firm's operating environment. Promotion decisions to be taken include: what message to use? which media? what timing for an advertising campaign? how much to spend? how to evaluate this expenditure? Promotional decisions are considered in more detail in Chapters 10 and 11.

People

People decisions are particularly important to the marketing of services. In the services sector, in particular, people planning can be very important where staff have a high level of contact with customers. Marketing effectiveness is likely to be critically affected by the actions of front-line employees who interact with customers. While a car manufacturer's employees may be unseen by its customers, a restaurant's waiters can make or break the benefits that visitors to the restaurant perceive. People decisions call for close involvement between marketing and human resource management functions to answer such questions as: what are the pre-requisite skills for front-line employees? how should staff be rewarded and motivated? The particular needs of services industries are discussed in Chapter 13.

Process

Process decisions are again of most importance to marketers in the services sector. The process of production is usually of little concern to the consumer of manufactured goods, but it is often of critical concern to the consumer of 'high contact' services. A customer of a restaurant is deeply affected by the manner in which staff members serve them. For busy customers, the speed and friendliness with which a restaurant processes its customers may be just as important as the meal itself. Marketers must work closely with operations managers to design customer handling processes that are both cost-efficient and effective in satisfying customers' needs.

Physical evidence

Physical evidence is important in guiding buyers of intangible services through the choices available to them. This evidence can take a number of forms. At its simplest, a brochure can describe and give pictures of important elements of the service product—a holiday brochure gives pictorial evidence of hotels and resorts for this purpose. The appearance of staff can give evidence about the nature of a service—a tidily dressed ticket clerk for an airline gives some evidence that the airline operation as a whole is run with care and attention. A clean, bright environment used in a service outlet can help reassure potential customers at the point where they make a service purchase decision. For this reason, fast food and photo processing outlets often use red and yellow colour schemes to convey an image of speedy service.

Interdependency of the marketing mix

The definition of the elements of the marketing mix is largely intuitive and semantic. The list of mix elements has a lot of everyday practical value, because it provides headings around which management thoughts and actions can be focused. However, dividing management responses into apparently disconnected areas of activity may lead to the interaction between elements being overlooked. Promotion mix decisions, for example, cannot be considered in isolation from decisions about product characteristics or pricing. Within conventional definitions of the marketing mix, important customer-focused issues such as quality of service can become lost. A growing body of opinion is therefore suggesting that a more holistic approach should be taken by marketing managers in responding to their customers' needs. This view sees the marketing mix as a production-led approach to marketing in which the agenda for action is set by the seller and not by the customer. An alternative relationship marketing approach starts by asking what customers need from a company and then proceeds to develop a response that integrates all the functions of a business in a manner that evolves in response to customers' changing needs. Although the chapters of this book roughly follow the elements of the marketing mix, the interlinkages between the mix elements must never be forgotten.

Marketing management

Successful marketing does not generally come about by accident: it needs to be managed effectively. (Although there are nevertheless many cases of successful marketing that occurred more by good luck than by judgement!) Three fundamental aspects of marketing management can be identified: processes, structures, and outcomes.

The marketing management process

Some companies, as they emerge from a production orientation, may think that they need only 'do some marketing' when trading conditions get tough. In fact, for well-managed businesses, marketing is an ongoing process that has no beginning or end (Figure 1.10). It is usual to identify four principal stages of the marketing management process, which involves asking the following questions:

- **Analysis**: Where are we now? How does the company's market share compare with that of its competitors? What are the strengths and weaknesses of the company and its products? What opportunities and threats does it face in its marketing environment?

- **Planning**: Where do we want to be? What is the mission of the business? What objectives should be set for the next year? What strategy will be adopted in order to achieve those objectives (e.g. should the company go for a high price/low volume strategy, or a low price/high volume one)?

- **Implementation**: How are we going to put into effect the strategy that will lead us to our objectives?

- **Control**: Did we achieve our objectives? If not, why not? How can deficiencies be rectified? (In other words, go back to the beginning of the process and conduct further analysis.)

Marketing management structures

Internally, the structure and politics of an organization affect the manner in which it can respond to changing customer needs. An organization that gives all marketing

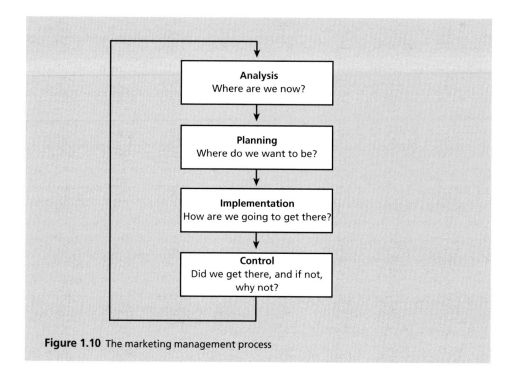

Figure 1.10 The marketing management process

responsibilities to just a narrow group of people may in fact create tensions within the organization that make it less effective at responding to change, compared with an organization where the philosophy and practice of marketing are shared more widely. Marketing plans cannot be developed and implemented without a sound understanding of marketing managers' relationship to other members of their organization. There has been extensive research into the internal barriers that prevent companies developing a marketing orientation (e.g. Harris [9]; Morgan [12]).

There are two aspects of management structures that particularly affect the role of marketers: the internal structure and processes of the marketing department itself (where one actually exists), and the relationship of the marketing functions to other business functions, which affects the marketing effectiveness of an organization. Issues of marketing management structures and processes are explored in Chapter 12.

Outcomes of the marketing management process

Ultimately, the aim of good marketing management is to allow a company to survive and produce an acceptable level of profits. Leading up to this, a tangible outcome of the management process is the marketing plan. A plan should be distinguished from the process of planning: a plan is a statement fixed at one point in time, while planning refers to an ongoing process, of which the plan is just one outcome.

Companies typically produce a strategic marketing plan for a five-year period. Over this time period, projections can be subject to a lot of speculative estimation. Nevertheless, a five-year strategic plan can be vital to give a sense of direction to a company's marketing effort. Over the shorter term, companies usually produce an annual plan which gives more details of how the strategy will be implemented over the forthcoming 12-month period. Sometimes, where a marketing plan is based on a set of assumptions that are highly speculative, a company may choose to develop an additional contingency plan to use, should the assumptions on which the original plan was based turn out to be invalid.

There is continuing debate about the extent to which marketing plans should be flexible. If they are too flexible, they lose value in being able to act as a blueprint for all individuals in an organization to plan by. If the marketing department changes its sales targets halfway through the plan period, this might cause havoc in the production department, which had geared up to meet the original budgeted level of sales. On the other hand, fixed plans may become an irrelevance when the company's marketing environment has changed significantly.

■ Marketing and its relationship to other business functions

Companies have learned that their marketing departments cannot exist in isolation from the other functional departments of their organization. The importance attached to an organization's marketing activities is influenced by the nature of the environment in which the organization operates. In a production-oriented firm, a marketing department has little role to play, other than merely processing orders.

In a truly marketing-oriented company, marketing responsibilities cannot be confined to something called a marketing department. In the words of Drucker [5],

Marketing is so basic that it cannot be considered to be a separate function. It is the whole business seen from the point of view of its final result, that is, from the customer's point of view.

In marketing-oriented organizations, the customer should be the concern not just of the marketing department, but also all of the production and administrative personnel whose actions may directly or indirectly create value in the mind of customers. In a typical company, the activities of a number of functional departments can affect customer value:

• The selection, training, motivation, and control of staff by personnel managers cannot be considered in isolation from marketing objectives and strategies. Possible conflict between the personnel and marketing functions may arise where, for example, marketing demands highly trained and motivated front-line staff, but the personnel function pursues a policy that places cost reduction and uniform pay rates above all else.

- A marketing manager may seek to respond as closely as possible to customers' needs, only to find opposition from production managers who argue that a product of the required standard cannot be achieved. Production managers tend to prefer long production runs of standardized products, but marketers increasingly try to satisfy market niches with specially adapted products.

- At a strategic and operational level, finance managers' actions in respect of the level of credit offered to customers, or towards stockholdings, can significantly affect the quality of service and the volume of customers with which the marketing department is able to do business.

Marketing orientation requires all of these departments to 'think customer' and to work together to satisfy customer needs and expectations. In practice, this can be very difficult to achieve, as witnessed by the many instances where it may appear that 'the left hand of the organization doesn't know what the right hand is doing'. A number of initiatives have sought to organize the activities of a company around processes that create value as perceived by customers (see Chapter 12). However, there is a danger that, as groups work more collectively, individual responsibilities and accountabilities can diminish.

■ Marketing and social responsibility

Traditional definitions of marketing have stressed the supremacy of customers, but this is increasingly being challenged by the requirement to satisfy the needs of a wider range of stakeholders in society. There have been many recent cases where companies have neglected the interests of this wider group with disastrous consequences, and we will look at some of these in the next chapter. Scenes of protesters outside a company's premises and newspaper coverage of anti-social behaviour by firms can take away from the company something that its marketing department had spent years developing— its image. The opposite can be true where companies go out of their way to be good citizens.

There are segments within most markets that place high priority on ensuring that the companies they buy from are 'good citizens'. Examples can be found among consumers who prefer to pay a few pennies extra for timber from ecologically managed forests, or avoid buying from companies who test their products on animals.

Wider issues are raised about the effects of marketing practices on the values of a society. It has been argued by some that, by promoting greater consumption, marketing is responsible for creating a greater feeling of isolation among those members of society who cannot afford to join the consumer society where an individual's status is judged by what they own, rather than by their contribution to family and community life. Much advertising has been criticized as being socially harmful, e.g. for high-fat 'junk' food and alcohol, which may appeal against an individual's better judgement, bring bad health to millions, and raise the costs of health care for sufferers.

Determining the social responsibilities of organizations is a controversial subject and is discussed further in Chapter 2.

Is marketing a science or an art?

Is marketing based on a scientific method of inquiry, or is it essentially about an artistic process of creativity?

Studies of marketing using the scientific frameworks of the natural sciences have found favour with followers of the positivist approach. This holds that, from observations of the real world, it is possible to deduce models that are of general applicability. On this basis, models have been developed to predict consumer behaviour, the profitability of retail locations, and price–volume relationships, among many other phenomena.

The great merit of the scientific approach is its claim to great objectivity, in that patterns and trends can be identified with greater confidence than if they were based on casual observation. Many marketers have appreciated the value of this scientific approach. Most major retailers rely heavily on models of retail location before deciding where to locate their next outlet. Armed with trading statistics from their existing network of stores and background information about their locations (e.g. the number of people living within 20 minutes' driving time, passing vehicle traffic per day, proximity

MARKETING and SOCIAL RESPONSIBILITY

Sponsor a cop?

'Handcuffs courtesy of Yale' could be the future as British police forces recruit marketing officers and embrace the practices of sponsorship. Since 1994, British police forces have been able to raise up to 1% of their overall budget through sponsorship. Proposals so far have included police vehicles sponsored by car manufacturers and insurance companies sponsoring anti-burglary and crime prevention crack-downs. But the head of public relations for West Yorkshire Police conceded that this would not mean police officers walking around with McDonald's logos on their uniforms. Nevertheless, the sponsoring of vital public services does raise ethical issues. What would happen if a sponsor itself were being investigated of a suspected crime? Are there some essential public services that should be driven solely by social policy needs and not by market forces?

to competitors, etc.), a regression model can be developed which shows the significance of each specified factor in explaining sales success.

To many people, marketing has no credibility if it does not adopt a rigorous, scientific method of inquiry. In the USA the Marketing Sciences Institute in 1998 made 'marketing metrics' its research priority. In the UK the Chartered Institute of Marketing has launched a similar initiative. This method of inquiry implies that research should be carried out in a systematic manner and results should be replicable. So a model of buyer behaviour should be able repeatedly to predict consumers' actions correctly, based on a sound collection of data and analysis. In the scientific approach, data are assessed using tests of significance and models are accepted or rejected accordingly.

To counter this view, it has been argued that marketing cannot possibly copy the natural sciences in its methodologies. Positivist approaches have been accused of seeking meaning from quantitative data in a very subjective manner which is at variance with scientific principles (Brown [2]). Experimental research in the natural sciences generally involves closed systems in which the researcher can hold all extraneous variables constant, thereby isolating the effects of changes in a variable that is of interest. For social sciences, experimental frameworks generally consist of complex social systems over which the researcher has no control. So a researcher investigating the effects of a price change in a product on demand from customers cannot realistically hold constant all factors other than price. Indeed, it may be difficult to identify just what the 'other factors' are that should be controlled for in an experiment, but they may typically include the price of competitors' products, consumer confidence levels, the effects of media reports about that product category, and changes in consumer fashions and tastes, to name some of the more obvious. Contrast this with a physicist's laboratory experiment, where heat, light, humidity, pressure, and most other extraneous variables can be controlled, and the limitations of the scientific methodology in the social sciences become apparent. Marketers are essentially dealing with 'open' systems, in contrast to the 'closed' systems that are more typical of the natural sciences.

Post-positivists place greater emphasis on exploring in depth the meaning of individual case studies than on seeking objectivity and replicability through large sample sizes. Many would argue that such *inductive* approaches are much more customer-focused, in that they allow marketers to see the world from consumers' overall perspective, rather than through the mediating device of a series of isolated indicators. Post-positivist approaches to marketing hold that the 'real' truth will never emerge in a research framework that is constrained by the need to operationalize variables in a watertight manner. In real-life marketing, the world cannot be divided into clearly defined variables that are capable of objective measurement. Constructs such as consumers' attitudes and motivation may be very difficult to measure and model objectively. Furthermore, it is often the interaction between various phenomena that is of interest to researchers, and it can be very difficult to develop models that correspond to respondents' holistic perceptions of the world.

There is another argument against the scientific approach to marketing, which sees the process as essentially backward looking. The scientific approach is good at making sense of historic trends, but less good at predicting what will happen following periods of turbulent change. During the early 1990s, for example, models based on the scientific approach failed to predict accurately the change in UK consumer spending following changes in household income, taxation levels, and interest rates. These had traditionally been associated with changes in consumer spending. A more in-depth analysis of consumers' attitudes suggested that feelings of greater insecurity (brought about by the casualization of many jobs) and the memory of a recent fall in house prices had served as a warning to consumers, which rendered many previously developed models of consumer spending obsolete.

Creativity combined with a scientific approach can be essential for innovation. The scientific approach to marketing planning has a tendency to minimize risks, yet many major business successes have been based on entrepreneurs using their own judgement, in preference to that of their professional advisers. Consider the following cases.

- In the run-up to London's Millennium celebrations, the Millennium Dome was the outcome of a fairly bureaucratic process of planning. The forecasts turned out to be far too optimistic. By contrast, the London Eye was a great success, despite relying on largely intuitive estimates of likely demand.

- Demand for SMS text messaging services was greatly underestimated, partly reflecting a technological basis for forecasting, rather than a deeper understanding of individuals' life-styles.

- A scientific analysis of the transatlantic airline market in the 1980s would have concluded that the market was saturated and there was no opportunity for a new British operator. This did not stop the entrepreneur Richard Branson from launching his own airline and, by using his own creative style, developing a distinctive and profitable service within the crowded market.

Marketing has to be seen as a combination of art and science. Treating it excessively as an art can lead to decisions that are not sufficiently rigorous. Emphasizing the scientific approach can lead a company to lose sight of the holistic perceptions of its customers. Successful firms seek to use scientific and creative approaches in a complementary manner.

■ Marketing as an academic discipline

It is only since the 1970s that marketing has featured significantly on university syllabuses. To some of the more traditional academic institutions, marketing has been seen as essentially a topic of application rather than a discipline in its own right.

Marketing has borrowed heavily from other discipline areas. Its roots can be traced back to industrial economics, but in the process of growth it has drawn on the following discipline areas.

- Psychology has been central to many studies of buyer behaviour. Psychological theory in the fields of human motivation and perception has found ready application by marketers (e.g. Maslow [11]).

- Because of the importance of peer group pressures on many consumer and commercial purchases, a body of knowledge developed by sociologists has been used by marketers. As an example, social psychologists have contributed an understanding of the processes by which interpersonal trust develops, which has been applied to the study of long-term buyer–seller relationships (e.g. Dwyer, Schurr, and Oh [6]).

- In its claim to be a science, marketers are constantly borrowing statistical techniques. Large-scale empirical research into buyer behaviour, product design preferences, and pricing effectiveness draws heavily upon previously developed statistical techniques which have conceptual and empirical validity.

- The law represents an embodiment of a society's values, and legal frameworks are becoming increasingly important to the study of marketing.

- Finally, economics remains an important discipline area on which marketing draws. As an example, marketers' pricing strategy has to be based on an understanding of the underlying theory of price determination in different market conditions.

Of course, as marketing has developed, the flow of theory has become more two-way. As well as borrowing from other discipline areas, marketers have developed theory and techniques that have been adopted by other discipline areas. (For example, marketers contributed significantly to the development of conjoint analysis in the study of consumer preferences, and this statistical methodology has now found widespread application elsewhere.) In universities the subject has benefited from multi-disciplinary teams being brought together to develop new techniques that are appropriate to marketing. Unfortunately, the structure of many universities still has a tendency to inhibit research between discipline areas that are based in different faculties.

What makes a good marketer?

Finally, what characteristics make for a good marketer? Are good marketers born or bred? To answer this question, it is necessary to have a clear understanding of just what marketing is about. The ability to identify, anticipate, and respond to customer needs puts a lot of onus on skills of observation and analysis. Outdated ideas that marketing is all about selling harder by shouting more loudly were probably never appropriate to even the most aggressive sales personnel, for whom listening to customers' needs has always been crucial to developing a winning sales pitch. The great emphasis on listening skills is one explanation of the growing number of females who have made successful careers in marketing. Numerous studies have found that women have much stronger traits of empathy and listening ability than males.

Of course, marketing as a business function is very broad, and particular branches demand quite specific skills. Within the advertising sector, creativity is essential for successful copywriters, whereas a market analyst would be better equipped with patience and a rigorous methodical approach.

Can marketers be trained? There is a feeling among some employers that a little marketing knowledge by incoming employees may be quite dangerous. This idea holds that it may be better to take on staff who have an ability to think critically, communicate effectively, and show creativity. These abilities may have been developed in non-marketing environments, but the skills are easily transferable. Many engineers and biologists, to name but two science-based disciplines, have gone on to become very successful marketers, because of their ability to approach any new problem with clear, critical thinking combined with creativity.

This book seeks to cut through much of the jargon and mystique that has grown up around marketing and points out that many models are essentially based on straightforward critical analysis. By this argument, segmentation can be seen either as a specialist marketing technique or, more generally, as a logical process of breaking down a large problem (how to serve a market) into a series of smaller problems (how to serve different parts of that market). This book aims to develop a critical awareness of marketing theories and concepts, and to illustrate these with contemporary examples.

Recently, discussion about whether marketing is a free-standing discipline in its own right has added fuel to the debate about marketing education. Today, a rising number of new graduates are entering employment with at least some exposure to the principles of marketing. From being a specialist subject, marketing has now become mainstream. Michael Thomas eloquently summed up the state of marketing in the mid-1990s when he told the Chartered Institute of Marketing's Annual Conference that 'the ownership of the ideological resource, known as marketing knowledge, now extends beyond our specialism and threatens to dissolve its distinctiveness'.

■ Chapter summary and linkages to other chapters

This chapter has introduced the basic principles of marketing which act as building blocks for more detailed discussion in the following chapters. Having read this chapter, you should be aware of the wide definition of marketing as a philosophy and a set of practices. Although subsequent chapters analyse marketing practices under a number of headings, it should never be forgotten that all elements of the marketing mix should support each other. Customers take a holistic view of a company and its product. Product decisions (Chapter 7), price decisions (Chapter 8), place decisions (Chapter 9), and promotions decisions (Chapters 10 and 11) must focus on meeting targeted customer segments (Chapter 5) effectively and efficiently in the face of competitors' products (Chapter 6).

KEY PRINCIPLES OF MARKETING

- Marketing is essentially about organizations meeting customers needs as a means of achieving the organizations' own objectives.
- Marketing is both a philosophy and a set of techniques. Marketing techniques have less value if an organization has not embraced the philosophy of marketing.
- The principles of marketing are not new, but a continually changing marketing environment demands new ways of applying the basic principles.
- Marketing can be adopted by both profit-seeking and not-for-profit organizations.
- Marketing operates in an environment in which stakeholders have rising expectations for the ethical standards of marketers.

CASE STUDY

Can the Body Shop survive without marketing?

The Body Shop may have grown rapidly during the 1970s and 1980s, but its founder has publicly dismissed the role of marketing. Anita Roddick ridiculed marketers for putting the interests of shareholders before the needs of society. She had a similarly low opinion of the financial community, which she referred to as 'merchant wankers'. While things were going well, nobody seemed to mind. Maybe Roddick had found a new way of doing business, and if she had the results to prove it, who needed marketers? But how could even such an icon as Anita Roddick manage indefinitely without consulting the fundamental principles of marketing? By the end of the 1990s, the Body Shop was suffering bad times and the sceptics among the marketing and financial communities were quick to round on the folly of its founder's apparently idiosyncratic ways.

From a high of 370p in 1992, the Body Shop's share price fell to just 65p at the start of 2003, despite the FTSE 100 index rising over that period. Profits remained similarly depressed, with performance in the continental European, North American, and Far Eastern markets stagnant.

Roddick has been the dynamo behind the Body Shop. From a small single outlet, she inspired the growth of the chain to some 1,500 familiar green-fronted shops in 46 countries around the world. Yet until the late 1990s she boasted that the Body Shop had never used, or needed, marketing. Much of the company's success has been tied up with its campaigning approach to the pursuit of social and environmental issues. But while Roddick campaigned for everything from battered wives and Siberian tigers to the poverty-stricken mining communities of southern Appalachia, the company was facing major problems in its key markets.

Part of the problem of the Body Shop was its failure fully to understand the dynamics of its marketplace. Positioning on the basis of good causes may have been enough to launch the company into the public's mind in the 1970s, but how could this position be sustained? Other companies soon launched similar initiatives; for example, the Boots company matched one of the Body Shop's earliest claims that it did not test its products on animals. Even the very feel of a Body Shop store—including its decor, staff, and product displays—had been copied by competitors. How could the company stay ahead in terms of maintaining its distinctive positioning? Its causes seemed to become increasingly remote from the real concerns of shoppers. While most UK shoppers may have been swayed by a company's unique claim to protect animals, how many would be moved by its support for Appalachian miners? If there was a Boots or a Superdrug store next door, why should a buyer pay a premium price to buy from the Body Shop? The Body Shop may have pioneered a very clever retailing formula over twenty years earlier, but, just as the concept had been successfully copied by others, other companies had made enormous strides in terms of their social and environmental awareness.

Part of the company's problems has been blamed on the inability of Roddick to delegate. She is reported to have spent half of her time globetrotting in support of her good causes, but has had a problem in delegating marketing strategy and implementation. Numerous strong managers who have been brought in to try to implement professional management practices have apparently given up in bewilderment at the lack of discretion that they have been given, and then left.

The Body Shop's experience in America has typified Roddick's pioneering style which frequently ignores sound marketing analysis. She sought a new way of doing business in America, but in doing so dismissed the experience of older and more sophisticated retailers—such as Marks & Spencer and the Sock Shop, which came unstuck in what is a very difficult market. The Body Shop decided to enter the US markets in 1988 not through a safe option such as a joint venture or a franchising agreement, but instead by setting up its own operation from scratch—fine, according to Roddick's principles of changing the rulebook and cutting out the greedy American business community, but dangerously risky. Her store format was based on the British town centre model, despite the fact that Americans spend most of their money in out-of-town malls. In 1996 the US operations lost £3.4 million.

Roddick's critics claim that she has a naive view of herself, her company, and business generally. She has consistently argued that profits and principles don't mix, despite the fact that many of her financially successfully competitors have been involved in major social initiatives.

The rift between Roddick's and others' view of the world was exemplified in the results of an innovative independent social audit commissioned by the Body Shop in 1996. The company was prompted to commission the report following media criticism that its social and environmental credentials might not actually be as good as the company claimed. The results highlighted short-comings in virtually every one of the company's stakeholder relationships. The company scored well in areas such as promoting human and civil rights, pollution control, product information, wages and benefits, women's opportunities, and energy conservation; but it scored badly on corporate governance, relationships with shareholders, responsiveness to customer and franchises complaints, accuracy of promotional claims, communication, and reaction to criticism.

Critics claim that, had Roddick not dismissed the need for marketing for so long, the Body Shop could have avoided future problems. But by 2000 it was paying the price for not having devoted sufficient resources to new product development, to innovation, to refreshing its ranges, and to moving the business forward. It seems that heroes can change the rulebook when the tide is flowing with them; but adopting the disciplines of marketing allows companies to anticipate and react when the tide begins to turn against them.

Case study review questions

1. In what ways could Anita Roddick have maintained her identification with social and environmental causes as a unique positioning feature?

2. To what extent are the pursuits of profit and meeting the needs of wider groups of stakeholders incompatible? What companies, if any, have managed to sustainably reconcile these two aims?

3. What are the basic lessons in marketing that the Body Shop might have taken on board in its early years in order to improve its chances of long-term success?

▣ CHAPTER REVIEW QUESTIONS

1. Discuss how a car wash business might operate if management embraced a production orientation? A sales orientation? A marketing orientation? A societal marketing orientation?

2. Of what relevance is marketing to the public sector?

3. Of what value is the concept of an expanded marketing mix (as opposed to the traditional '4Ps')?

4. Why is it important for companies to segment their markets? Should providers of public services (e.g. city police forces) segment their markets?

5. Analyse the nature of the needs which may be satisfied by a household mortgage.

6. What is the difference between selling and marketing?

REFERENCES

[1] Borden, N. H. (1965), 'The Concept of the Marketing Mix'. In G. Schwartz (ed.), *Science in Marketing*. New York: John Wiley, pp. 386–97.

[2] Brown, S. (1995), *Postmodern Marketing*. London: Routledge.

[3] Brown, S. (1998), 'Romancing the Market: sex, shopping and subjective personal introspection'. *Journal of Marketing Management*, 14: 783–98.

[4] Chomka, S. (2002), 'Organic Market Figures Could Help Processors'. *Food Manufacture*, 77(9): 7–9.

[5] Drucker, P. F. (1973), *Management: tasks, responsibilities and practices*. New York: Harper & Row.

[6] Dwyer, F. R., Schurr, P. H., and Oh, S. (1987), 'Developing Buyer and Seller Relationships'. *Journal of Marketing*, 51(April): 11–27.

[7] Gronroos, C. (1994), 'From Marketing Mix to Relationship Marketing'. *Management Decision*, 32(1): 4–20.

[8] Gummesson, E. (1993), 'Relationship Marketing: a new way of doing business'. *European Business Report*, 30(Autumn): 52–6.

[9] Harris, L. C. (2002), 'Developing Market Orientation: an exploration of differences in management approaches'. *Journal of Marketing Management*, 18: 603–32.

[10] Lafferty, B. A. and Hult, G. T. M. (2001), 'A synthesis of Contemporary Market Orientation Perspectives'. *European Journal of Marketing*, 35: 92–109.

[11] Maslow, A. (1943), 'A Theory of Human Motivation'. *Psychological Review*, 50(July): 370–96.

[12] Morgan, N. A. (2002), 'Antecedents and Consequences of Market Orientation in Chartered Surveying Firms'. *Construction Management & Economics*, 20: 331–41.

[13] Narver, J. C. and Slater, S. F. (1990), 'The Effect of a Market Orientation on Business Profitability'. *Journal of Marketing*, October: 20–35.

[14] Sargeant, A., Foreman, S., and Liao, M.-N. (2002), 'Operationalizing the Marketing Concept in the Nonprofit Sector'. *Journal of Nonprofit & Public Sector Marketing*, 10(2): 41–64.

SUGGESTED FURTHER READING

This chapter has taken a very broad overview of marketing and sets the scene for the subsequent chapters. Further reading that relates to issues raised in this introductory chapter will be listed in chapters where introductory topics are returned to for a fuller discussion.

To review the debate about the nature of marketing, the following are significant contributors to the debate:

Brown, S. (1996), 'Art or Science? Fifty years of marketing debate'. *Journal of Marketing Management*, 12: 243–67.

Gronroos, C. (1989), 'Defining Marketing: a market-oriented approach'. *European Journal of Marketing*, 23(1): 52–60.

Houston, F. S. (1986), 'The Marketing Concept: what it is and what it is not'. *Journal of Marketing*, 50(April): 81–7.

Kohli, A. K. and Jaworski, B. J. (1990), 'Market Orientation: the construct, research propositions and management implications'. *Journal of Marketing*, 54(April): 1–18.

Lafferty, B. A. and Hult, G. T. M. (2001), 'A synthesis of Contemporary Market Orientation Perspectives'. *European Journal of Marketing*, 35: 92–109.

Further suggestions for reading on the topics covered by this chapter are given in the companion website:

    www.oup.com/uk/booksites/busecon

USEFUL WEB LINKS

Visit the companion website to this book, with lots of interesting additional material and links for each chapter:

    www.oup.com/uk/booksites/busecon

Chartered Institute of Marketing

    www.cim.co.uk

American Marketing Association

    www.ama.org

Marketing Magazine Online

    www.marketing.haynet.com

Marketing Week online

    www.marketing-week.co.uk

Biz/ed: A student and lecturers' resource site containing items relating to marketing within organizations

    www.bized.ac.uk

KEY TERMS

- **Competitor orientation**
- **Customer orientation**
- **Customers**
- **Demand**
- **Exchange**
- **Inter-functional co-ordination**
- **Marketing management**
- **Marketing mix**
- **Marketing orientation**
- **Markets**
- **Needs**
- **Not-for-profit organization**
- **Place**
- **Positivism**
- **Pricing**

- **Production orientation**
- **Products**
- **Promotion**
- **Scientific method**
- **Selling orientation**
- **Social responsibility**
- **Value**
- **Wants**

2

The marketing environment

CHAPTER OBJECTIVES

In the previous chapter we established that marketing is essentially about firms identifying customers' needs and responding to those changing needs with appropriate product offers. In this chapter we will explore how customers' needs are a product of an organization's marketing environment. The marketing environment can be defined as everything that surrounds an organization's marketing function and can impinge on it. Macro-environmental factors, such as a change in the birth rate, may seem inconsequential now, but could quickly have a direct effect on a firm's micro-environment, expressed through demand for its products. This chapter explores the relationships between the different elements of a firm's environment and the ways in which it can respond effectively to environmental change.

The marketing environment of organizations includes stakeholders. Although these may not themselves be customers, addressing their needs can be crucial. While the adoption of marketing can undoubtedly bring benefits to society, some aspects of marketing may be questionable on ethical grounds. This chapter will explore the social responsibilities of organizations and the nature of their responsibilities to society. Ethics is a complex concept to define, and an attempt is made to understand ethical behaviour in a marketing context.

Introduction

In the previous chapter, marketing orientation was defined in terms of a firm's need to begin its business planning by looking outwardly at what its customers require, rather than inwardly at what it would prefer to produce. The firm must be aware of what is going on in its broader marketing environment and appreciate how change in this environment can lead to changing patterns of demand for its products.

An environment can be defined as everything that surrounds and impinges on a system. Systems of many kinds have environments they interact with. A central heating system operates in an environment where a key environmental factor will be the outside temperature. A good system will react to environmental change, for example by using a thermostat to increase the output of the system in response to a fall in the temperature of the external environment. The human body comprises numerous systems which constantly react to changes in the body's environment; for example, the body perspires in response to an increase in external temperature.

Marketing can be seen as a system that must respond to environmental change. Just as the human body may die if it fails to adjust to environmental change (for example by not compensating for very low temperatures), businesses may fail if they do not adapt to external changes such as new sources of competition or changes in stakeholders' expectations of companies.

An organization's marketing environment is defined here as

the individuals, organizations, and forces external to the marketing management function of an organization that impinge on the marketing management's ability to develop and maintain successful exchanges with its customers.

Naturally, some elements in a firm's marketing environment are more direct and immediate in their effects than others. Sometimes parts of the marketing environment may seem quite nebulous and difficult to assess in terms of their likely impact on a company. It is therefore usual to talk about a number of different levels of the marketing environment.

- The **micro-environment** describes those elements that impinge directly on a company. The micro-environment of an organization includes customers, suppliers, and distributors. It may deal directly with some of these, while there is currently no direct contact with others, but they could nevertheless influence its policies. Similarly, an organization's competitors could have a direct effect on its market position and form part of its micro-environment.

- The **macro-environment** describes things that are beyond the immediate environment but can nevertheless affect an organization. A business may have no direct relationships with legislators as it does with suppliers, yet legislators' actions in passing new laws may have profound effects on the markets it seeks to serve, as well as affecting its production costs. The macro-environmental factors cover a wide range of nebulous phenomena—they represent general forces and pressures rather than institutions, to which the organization relates directly.

- As well as looking to the outside world, marketing managers must also take account of factors within other functions of their own firm. This is often referred to as an organization's *internal marketing environment*.

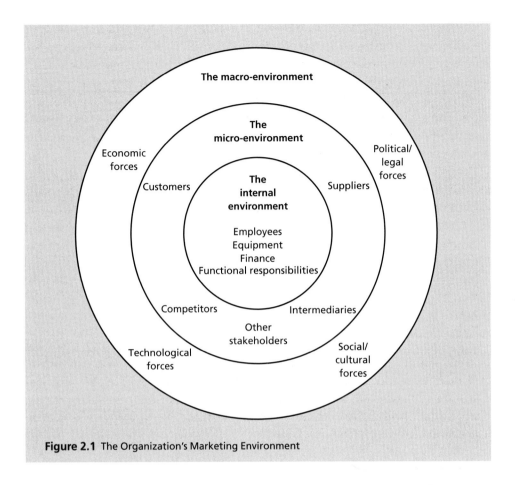

Figure 2.1 The Organization's Marketing Environment

The elements within each of these parts of an organization's environment are described in more detail below and illustrated schematically in Figure 2.1.

The micro-environment

The micro-environment of an organization can best be understood as comprising all those other organizations and individuals that, directly or indirectly, affect the activities of the organization.

The following key groups can be identified.

Customers

These are a crucial part of an organization's micro-environment. For a commercial organization, no customers means no business. An organization should be concerned about the changing requirements of its customers and should keep in touch with these changing needs by using an appropriate information gathering system. Chapter 4 will return to the subject of collecting, analysing, and disseminating information. In an ideal world, an organization should know its customers so well that it is able to predict what they will require next, rather than wait until it is possibly too late and then follow. Most of this book is devoted to studying the interface between a company and its customers, for example in terms of customers' responses to promotional messages and prices.

There is sometimes a strong argument that the customer is *not* always right in the goods and services they choose to buy from a company, and that organizations should act in a socially responsible manner by not exploiting customers. Taking a long-term and broad perspective, companies should have a duty to provide goods and services that satisfy these longer-term and broader needs rather than immediately felt needs. There have been many examples where the long-term interests of customers have been ignored by companies, either deliberately or inadvertently. Regulatory authorities have recognized the wider interests of customers, for example by requiring pensions companies to provide compensation to customers who were sold a pension policy that was inappropriate to their long-term needs.

There are many more examples of situations where customers' long-term interests have been neglected by companies, including:

- In 2002 the Consumers' Association launched a campaign against financial services companies which it claimed had mis-sold endowment policies to individuals. Salespeople may have been tempted by a high level of commission to sell a policy that the customer did not understand and was clearly not in their best interest (for example, a policy that would pay out only some time after the customer's mortgage was due to be paid off).

- Manufacturers of milk for babies should make mothers aware of the significant long-term health benefits to children of using breast milk rather than manufactured milk products.

- Car manufacturers often add expensive music systems to cars as standard, but relegate vital safety equipment to the status of 'optional extra'.

In each of these cases most people might agree that, objectively, buyers are being persuaded to make a choice against their own long-term self-interest. But on what moral grounds, can society say that consumers' choices in these situations are wrong? According to some individuals' sense of priorities, an expensive in-car music system may indeed be considered to offer a higher level of personal benefit than an airbag.

Competitors

You will recall from Chapter 1 that a competitor orientation is one of the defining characteristics of a marketing orientation. In highly competitive markets, keeping an eye on competitors and trying to understand their likely next moves can be crucial. Think of the manoeuvring and out-manoeuvring that appears to take place between competitors in such highly competitive sectors as soft drinks, budget airlines, and mobile phones. But who are a company's competitors? *Direct* competitors are generally similar in form and satisfy customers' needs in a similar way. *Indirect* competitors may appear different in form, but satisfy a fundamentally similar need. It is the indirect competitors that are most difficult to identify and to understand. What is a competitor for a cinema? Is it another cinema? A home rental movie? Or some completely different form of leisure activity which satisfies a similar underlying need for entertainment.

Because of the importance of competitors to a firm's marketing environment, in Chapter 6 we will have a more detailed analysis of competitors and how a company can position itself against these in order to gain a sustainable competitive advantage.

Intermediaries

Companies must not ignore the wholesalers, retailers, and agents who may be crucial interfaces between themselves and their final consumers. Large-scale manufacturing firms usually find it difficult to deal with each one of their final consumers individually, so they choose instead to sell their products through intermediaries. In some business sectors access to effective intermediaries can be crucial for marketing success. For example, food manufactures who do not get shelf space in the major supermarkets may find it difficult to achieve large-volume sales.

Channels of distribution comprise all those people and organizations involved in the process of transferring title to a product from the producer to the consumer. Sometimes products will be transferred directly from producer to final consumer—a factory selling specialized kitchen units directly to the public would fit into this category. Alternatively, the producer may sell its output through retailers; or, if these are considered too numerous for the manufacturer to handle, it could deal with a wholesaler who in turn would sell to the retailer. More than one wholesaler could be involved in the process.

Because of the importance of intermediaries in making a firm's goods and services accessible to its buyers, Chapter 9 of this book is devoted to understanding how they are selected, motivated, rewarded, and controlled. In addition, the chapter reviews physical distribution management and the decisions that firms make in physically moving goods from where they are produced to where customers wish to buy them.

Intermediaries may need reassurance about the company's capabilities as a supplier that is capable of working with them to supply goods and services in a reliable and ethical manner. Many companies have suffered because they have failed to take adequate account of the needs of their intermediaries. (For example, Body Shop and McDonald's have faced protests from their franchisees, which felt threatened by a marketing strategy that was perceived as being against their own interests.)

Suppliers

These provide an organization with goods and services that are transformed by the organization into value-added products for customers. For companies operating in highly competitive markets where differentiation between products is minimal, obtaining supplies at the best possible price may be vital in order to be able to pass on cost savings in the form of lower prices charged to customers. Where reliability of delivery to customers is crucial, unreliable suppliers may thwart a manufacturer's marketing efforts.

In business-to-business marketing, one company's supplier is likely to be another company's customer, and it is important to understand how suppliers, manufacturers, and intermediaries work together to create value. The idea of a value chain is introduced later in this chapter. Buyers and sellers are increasingly co-operating in their dealings with each other, rather than bargaining each transaction in a confrontational manner. (Buyer–seller relationships are discussed further in Chapter 3.)

There is an argument that companies should behave in a socially responsible way to their suppliers. Does a company favour local companies rather than possibly lower priced overseas producers? (For example, Marks & Spencer prided itself on sourcing nearly all of its supplies through long-standing supply arrangements with a number of UK manufacturers, so many suppliers felt let down when it started placing a high proportion of its orders with lower cost overseas producers.) Does it divide its orders between a large number of small suppliers, or place the bulk of its custom with a small handful of preferred suppliers? Does it favour new businesses, or businesses representing minority interests, when it places its orders?

Taking into account the needs of suppliers entails a combination of shrewd business sense and good ethical practice.

Government

The demands of government agencies often take precedence over the needs of a company's customers. Government has a number of roles to play as stakeholder in commercial organizations:

- Commercial organizations provide governments with taxation revenue, so a healthy business sector is in the interests of government.
- Government is increasingly expecting business organizations to take over many responsibilities from the public sector, for example with regard to the payment of sickness and maternity benefits to employees.
- It is through business organizations that governments achieve many of their economic and social objectives, for example with respect to regional economic development and skills training.

As a regulator that impacts on many aspects of business activity, companies often go to great lengths in seeking favourable responses from such agencies. In the case of many UK private-sector utility providers, promotional effort is often aimed more at regulatory bodies than at final consumers. In the case of the water industry, promoting greater use of water to final consumers is unlikely to have a significant impact on a water utility company, but influencing the disposition of the Office of Water Regulation, which sets price limits and service standards, can have a major impact.

The financial community

This includes financial institutions that have supported, are currently supporting, or may support the organization in the future. Shareholders, both private and institutional, form an important element of this community and must be reassured that the organization is going to achieve its stated objectives. Many market expansion plans have failed because the company did not adequately consider the needs and expectations of potential investors.

Local communities

Market-led companies often try to be seen as a 'good neighbours' in their local communities. Such companies can enhance their image through charitable contributions, sponsorship of local events, and support of the local environment. Again, this may be interpreted either as part of a firm's genuine concern for its local community, or as a more cynical and pragmatic attempt to buy favour where its own interests are at stake. If a fast food restaurant installs improved filters on its extractor fans, is it doing this genuinely to improve the lives of local residents, or merely to forestall prohibitive action taken by the local authority?

Pressure groups

Members of pressure groups may have never been customers of a certain company and may never likely be. Yet a pressure group can detract seriously from the image of a company that its marketing department has worked hard to develop.

Pressure groups can be divided into those that are permanently fighting for a general cause, and those that are set up to achieve a specific objective and are dissolved when this objective is met. Pressure groups can also be classified according to their functions; for example, sectional groups exist to promote the common interests of their members over a wide range of issues (e.g. trades unions and employers associations), while promotional groups fight for specific causes (e.g., the Countryside Alliance campaigns for a range of countryside issues).

Pressure groups can influence the activities of businesses in a number of ways:

- Propaganda is used to create awareness of the group and its cause (e.g. through press releases to the media).

- The pressure group can seek to represent the views of the group directly to businesses on a one-to-one basis. (Many environmental pressure groups seek to advance their cause by 'educating' companies that may be ignorant of the pressure group's concerns.)

- Increasingly, pressure groups have resorted to direct action against companies, which can range from boycotts to physical attacks on a company's property.

Campaigners for animal rights, or those opposed to the use of genetically modified crops, have on occasions given up on trying to change the law and instead have sought to disrupt the activities of organizations giving rise to their concerns. Organizations targeted in this way may initially put on a brave face when confronted with such activities by dismissing them as inconsequential, but often the result is to change the organization's behaviour, especially where the prospect of large profits is uncertain. Action by animal rights protestors contributed to the near collapse of Huntingdon Life Sciences (an animal testing laboratory), and many farmers have been discouraged from taking part in GM crops trials by the prospects of direct action against their farms.

It should not be forgotten that businesses themselves are often active members of pressure groups, which they may join as a means of influencing government legislation that will affect their industry sector. The British Road Federation and the Tobacco Advisory Council are two examples of high-profile industry-led pressure groups.

Pressure groups themselves are increasingly crossing national boundaries to reflect the influence of international governmental institutions such as the EU and the increasing influence of multinational business organizations. Friends of the Earth and Greenpeace are examples of multinational pressure groups.

Value chains

The concept of a value chain is explored more fully in Chapter 9 in the context of channels of distribution. Here it is introduced to help understand the complex marketing relationships that can exist between a company and its customers, suppliers, and intermediaries.

Most products bought by private consumers represent the culmination of a long process of value creation. The company selling the finished product probably bought many of its components from an outside supplier, which in turn bought raw materials from another outside supplier. This is the basis of a value chain in which basic raw materials progressively have value added to them by members of the value chain. Value adding can come in the form of adding further components, changing the form of a product, or adding ancillary services to the product offer.

Figure 2.2 Pressure groups have claimed that Esso (Exxon Mobil) has been doing more than any other company to keep the USA hooked on oil. By opposing government policies that would reduce the USA's need for oil, the company has been accused of putting its shareholders' interests before the interests of ecological sustainability. A pressure group (**www.stopesso.com**) has sought to change the behaviour of Esso through boycotts and demonstrations, among other things. In 2003 the Stop Esso campaign reached new heights when Greenpeace activists abseiled on to the roof of the company's UK headquarters in Surrey, shutting it down in protest against the firm's environmental policies. About 100 Esso garages were closed for a few hours as activists dressed as tigers chained themselves to the pumps. Other oil companies have taken the hint and responded with initiatives such as support for research on hydrogen fuel cells. How much pressure would it take before Esso found the bad publicity and boycotts eating into its profits? Or should it stick to its principles and offer its customers what a majority appear to want most—the cheapest possible oil to support their chosen lifestyles?

Reproduced with permission of Stop Esso campaign.

Value chain member	Functions performed
Grower	produces a basic commodity product—coffee beans
Merchant	adds value to the coffee beans by checking, grading, and making beans available to coffee manufacturers
Coffee manufacturer	by processing the coffee beans, adding other ingredients and packaging, turns beans into jars of instant coffee; through promotion, creates a brand image
Wholesaler	buys bulk stocks of jars of coffee and stores in warehouses close to customers
Retailer	provides a facility for customers to buy coffee at a place and a time that is convenient to them, rather than from the manufacturer
Coffee shop	adds further value by providing a ready-made cup of coffee in pleasant surroundings

Figure 2.3 A value chain for coffee

Consider the example shown in Figure 2.3 of a value chain for instant coffee. The value of the raw beans contained in a jar of instant coffee may be no more than a few pence, but the final product may be sold for over £2. Customers are happy to pay this amount because a basic product that they place little value on has been transformed into something that they perceive as highly valuable. Some consumers would be happy to pay a higher price to buy their coffee ready prepared for consumption in a coffee shop rather than make it themselves at home. In the case of some trendy coffee shops such as Starbucks, customers may be prepared to pay quite a hefty premium for the atmosphere in which the coffee is served—over £2 for a smartly presented cappuccino or a 'skinny latte' is not uncommon, even though the cost of the beans used in the coffee may be no more than a few pence. Value can be defined only in terms of customers' perceptions, so much of the transformation process described above may be considered by some people to have no value. Some coffee drinkers may consider that processing the coffee to make it into instant granules destroys much of the taste that can be obtained from raw beans. For such people, the most important point in the value creating process probably derives from the growing and selection of the coffee beans.

Who should be in the value chain? The coffee manufacturer might decide that it can add value at the preceding and subsequent stages better than other people are capable of doing. It may, for example, decide to operate its own farms to produce beans under its own control, or sell its coffee direct to customers. The crucial question to be asked is whether the company can add value better than other suppliers and intermediaries could. In a value chain, it is only value in the eyes of customers that matters. If high value is attached to having coffee easily available, then distributing it through a limited number of company-owned shops would not add much value to the product.

The Internet has led to the development of a modified form of 'virtual value chain' to try and explain how information-based industries operate a value chain that is distinct from traditional models based on raw materials, production, and distribution (Rayport and Sviokla [12]). While the traditional value chain may be applicable to industries involved in the movement of goods through a tangible, physical marketplace, other information-based industries (such as financial services) operate in a market 'space'. It has been argued that for these companies the value chain consists of content, infrastructure, and context. The content is what is being offered, the infrastructure is what exists to enable transactions to take place, and the context is how the goods are offered.

Relationships between members of an organization's micro-environment

The discussion of value chains emphasizes the point that marketing effectiveness for a firm can be highly dependent upon its relationships with other members of its micro-environment. The individuals and organizations that make up a firm's micro-environment are often described as its *environmental set*. An example of an environmental set for a furniture manufacturer is shown in Figure 2.4.

An organization needs to be constantly alert to changes in the relationships between members of its environmental set. Consider the following recent changes in firms' environmental sets:

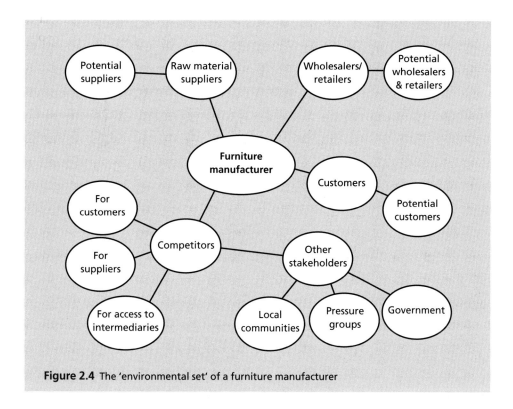

Figure 2.4 The 'environmental set' of a furniture manufacturer

- There have been changes in the balance of power between set members (for example between retailers, wholesalers, and manufacturers).
- New groups of potential customers may emerge (for example, elderly people have emerged as new groups of customers for fast food restaurants), while other groups decline.
- New pressure groups are formed in response to emerging issues of widespread social concern.
- Fringe pressure groups have a tendency to become mainstream groups in response to changes in social attitudes.

In the UK in recent years there has been some significant redistribution in the power of manufacturers relative to retailers. The growing strength of retailers in many sectors has given them significantly increased bargaining power in their dealings with manufacturers whose goods they sell. By building up their own strong brands, large retailers are increasingly able to exert pressure on manufacturers in terms of product specification, price, and the level of promotional support to be given to the retailer. It has been estimated that in Britain the four largest grocery retailers may account for over half of the sales of a typical manufacturer of fast-moving consumer goods. The dependency is not reciprocated, with very few retailers relying on one single manufacturer for more than a small percentage of their supplies.

Increasingly, firms are changing the way they do business, away from one-off transactions that are individually negotiated, towards ongoing co-operative relationships. The process of turning casual, one-off transactions between buyers and sellers has often been described as 'relationship marketing'. There is nothing new in the way firms have sought to develop ongoing relationships with their customers, as close relationships between small-scale businesses and their customers have been characteristic of economies in an early stage of their economic development. Many companies now put a lot of effort into developing ongoing relationships with their private and commercial customers. Chapter 3 provides further discussion of reasons for firms to seek closer relationships with their customers, and the methods adopted to achieve this.

Communication within the micro-environment

Communications bring together elements within a firm's environmental set. With no communication, there is no possibility for trading to take place. Although we talk today about a communications 'revolution', marketers of previous centuries have faced the challenge of rapid developments in communication. Consider the following historic developments in communications and their impacts on marketing.

- The development of canals and railways during the industrialization of nineteenth-century England allowed manufacturers to communicate with customers who had previously been impossible or very expensive to reach. Manufacturers used improved communications to exploit emerging mass production techniques, which allowed them to compete in distant markets with relatively low-price mass-produced goods.

- The development of steamships allowed companies to communicate with distant parts of the world, opening up new markets for their finished products and allowing new sources of supply of raw materials. British manufacturers of consumer goods exploited new markets in parts of the Empire served by the new shipping lines.

- The absence of a reliable postal and telephone system has often been cited as a reason for the failure of businesses to grow in less developed parts of the world where these facilities are lacking.

Today, the internet has emerged as a versatile tool in an organization's relationship with its marketing environment, combining a communication function with a distribution function. The ability of companies to rapidly exchange information with their suppliers and intermediaries has allowed for the development of increasingly efficient supply chains, initially using Electronic Data Interface (EDI) systems, but increasingly using internet, intranet, and extranet-based systems. Without efficient communication systems, attempts to introduce just-in-time production systems and rapid customer response are likely to be impeded.

The internet plays an increasingly significant role in allowing companies to communicate with their final consumers via e-mail and SMS text messaging. Some companies have used the internet to cut out intermediaries altogether through a process of 'disintermediation', although in reality the internet has allowed a new generation of 'information intermediary' (e.g. Expedia.com and esure.com) to appear in large numbers. As a promotional medium, the great strength of the internet is to target promotional messages that are directly relevant to the user; so, for example, a train operator's website may give information relating to a specific journey that the user was enquiring about. Websites are increasingly being enabled to allow immediate fulfilment of a request, such as confirmation of a hotel booking or reservation of a plane ticket. The internet has narrowed the gap between a potential buyer's receiving a message and being able to act upon it. The prospect of m-mail to individuals' mobile phones raises the prospect of a huge amount of low-cost messages being targeted at individuals, and senders of messages must ensure that their messages stand out from competitors and have immediate relevance to the recipient.

The macro-environment

While the micro-environment comprises identifiable individuals and organizations with whom a company interacts (directly and indirectly), the macro-environment is more nebulous. It comprises general trends and forces which may not immediately affect the relationships that a company has with its customers, suppliers, and intermediaries, but sooner or later, as this environment changes, will alter the nature of such micro-level relationships. As an example, change in the population structure of a country does not immediately affect the way in which a company does business with its customers, but over time it may affect the numbers of young or elderly people with whom it is aiming to do business.

Most analyses of the macro-environment divide the environment into a number of subject areas. The subject headings that are most commonly used are described below. It must, however, be remembered that the division of the macro-environment into subject areas does not result in water-tight compartments. The macro-environment is complex and interdependent.

The macroeconomic environment

An analysis of many companies' financial results will often indicate that business people attribute their current financial success or failure to the state of the economy. For example, in 2002 the house builder Taylor Woodrow reported increased profits, which it attributed to a buoyant housing market, based on a high level of consumer confidence within the economy. Ten years earlier, a weak economy and falling house prices had led to big losses for many house builders, and some went out of business.

Economic growth and the distribution of income

Few business people can afford to ignore the state of the economy, because it affects the willingness and ability of customers to buy their products. Marketers therefore keep their eyes on numerous aggregate indicators of the economy, such as Gross Domestic Product (GDP), inflation rates, and savings ratios. However, while aggregate changes in spending power may indicate a likely increase for goods and services in general, the actual distribution of spending power among the population will influence the pattern of demand for specific products. In addition to measurable economic prosperity, the level of perceived wealth and confidence in the future can be an important determinant of demand for some high-value services. If consumers' confidence is low, a high proportion of income tends to be saved. If confidence is high, consumers are more likely to borrow, so that their expenditure is greater than their income (Figure 2.5).

The effects of government policy objectives on the distribution of income can have profound implications for marketers. During most of the post-war years, the tendency has been for income to be redistributed from richer to less well-off groups. Higher rate taxation and the payment of welfare benefits have been instrumental in achieving this. During the late 1980s, this trend was reversed by a number of measures introduced by the Conservative government. Since 1997, the trend towards redistribution has been restored.

Multiplier and accelerator effects

Through models of national economies, firms try to understand how increases in expenditure (whether by government, households, or firms) will affect their specific sector. The multiplier effect of increases in government spending (or cuts in taxation) can be compared to the effects of throwing a stone into a pond of water. The initial spending boost will have an initial impact on households and businesses directly affected by the additional spending, but through a ripple effect will also be indirectly felt by households and firms throughout the economy.

A small increase in consumer demand can lead, through an accelerator effect, to a sudden large increase in demand for plant and machinery as manufacturers seek to increase their capacity with which to meet this demand. Demand for industrial capital goods therefore tends to be more cyclical than for consumer goods, so when consumer demand falls by a small amount, demand for plant and machinery falls by a correspondingly larger amount, and vice versa.

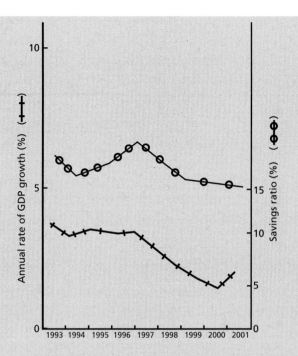

Figure 2.5 Two key macroeconomic indicators that marketers pay attention to are the annual rate of growth in GDP and the savings ratio. The first shows how rapidly the national economy is expanding, and therefore the capacity of the economy to purchase more products. However, what is just as important to marketers is whether this economic wealth is saved or spent. If consumers' confidence is low, a high proportion of income tends to be saved. If confidence is high, consumers are more likely to borrow, so that their expenditure is greater than their income. The high levels of consumer confidence in the UK during 2002 saw record levels of mortgage borrowing, resulting in a house price boom and strong demand for many house-related items such as conservatories and furnishings

Source: based on Annual Abstract of Statistics.

Business cycles

Companies are particularly interested in understanding business cycles and in predicting the cycle as it affects their sector. If the economy is at the bottom of an economic recession, this may be the ideal time for firms to begin investing in new production capacity, ahead of the eventual upturn in demand. In the past, firms have often invested in new capacity only after overseas competitors have built up market share, and possibly created some long-term customer loyalty too. Adding new production capacity during a period of recession is also likely to be much cheaper than waiting until an upturn in the economy puts upward pressure on its input prices. During periods of economic boom, firms should look ahead to the inevitable downturn that follows. A problem of excess capacity and stocks can result when a firm fails to spot the downturn at the top of the business cycle. Analysing turning points in the business cycle has therefore

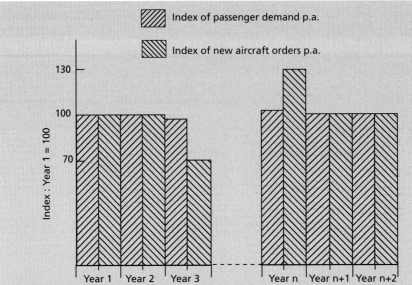

Figure 2.6 The accelerator effect can lead to volatility in demand for companies supplying capital equipment, as customers will rapidly change their orders for equipment in response to just a small change in final consumer demand. This can be illustrated by reference to the demand for new aircraft following a change in demand from passengers. In this simplified example, an airline operates a fleet of 100 aircraft and during periods of stable passenger demand buys 10 new aircraft each year and retires 10 older aircraft, retaining a stable fleet size of 100 aircraft. Then, some extraneous factor (e.g. a decline in the world economy) may cause the airline's passenger demand to fall by 3 per cent per year. The airline responds to this by reducing its capacity by 3 per cent to 97 aircraft (assuming that it can reschedule its aircraft so that it is able to accommodate all of its remaining passengers). The easiest way to achieve this is by reducing its annual order for aircraft from 10 to 7. If it continued to retire its 10 oldest aircraft, this would have the effect of reducing its fleet size to 97, in line with the new level of customer demand. What is of importance here is that, while consumer demand has gone down by just 3 per cent, the demand facing the aircraft manufacturer has gone down by 30 per cent (from 10 aircraft a year to 7). If passenger demand settles down at its new level, the airline will have no need to cut its fleet any further, so will revert to buying 10 new aircraft a year and selling 10 old ones. If passenger demand picks up once more, the airline may seek to increase its capacity by ordering not 10 aircraft but, say, 13

become crucial to marketers. To miss an upturn at the bottom of the recession can lead to missed opportunities when the recovery comes to fruition. On the other hand, reacting to a false signal can leave a firm with expensive excess stocks and capacity on its hands.

It is extremely difficult to identify a turning point at the time when it is happening. Following the UK economic recession of the early 1990s, there were many false predictions of an upturn. When the predicted revival in domestic consumer expenditure failed to transpire, marketers in product fields as diverse as cars, fashion clothing, and electrical goods were forced to sell off surplus stocks at low prices.

Marketers try to react to turning points as closely as possible. Many subscribe to the services of firms that use complex models of the economy to make predictions about the future performance of their sector. Companies can be guided by key lead indicators which have historically been a precursor of change in activity levels for their business sector. For a company manufacturing process plant equipment, the level of attendance at major trade exhibitions could indicate the number of buyers that are at the initial stages in the buying process for new equipment. An alternative to trying to predict the economic performance of their sector a long way ahead is to manage operations so that a firm can respond almost immediately to changes in its macroeconomic environment. The use of short-term contracts of employment and outsourcing of component manufacture can help a company to downsize rapidly at minimum cost when it enters a recession, and to expand production when a recovery occurs. This approach is particularly important when an organization needs to respond to an unforeseen shock to the macroeconomic environment, as occurred following the terrorist attacks of 11 September 2001.

Market competitiveness

An analysis of the macroeconomic environment will also indicate the current and expected future level of competitor activity. An over-supply of products in a market sector (whether actual or predicted) results in a downward pressure on prices and profitability. Markets are dynamic, and what may appear an attractive market today may soon deteriorate as the market matures. Market dynamics are discussed further in Chapter 6.

The political environment

The political environment can be one of the less predictable elements in an organization's marketing environment. Marketers need to monitor the changing political environment because political change can profoundly affect a firm's marketing. Consider the following effects of politicians on marketing.

- At the most general level, the stability of the political system affects the attractiveness of a particular national market. While western Europe is generally politically stable, the instability of many governments in less developed countries has led a number of companies to question the wisdom of marketing in those countries.

- Governments pass legislation that directly and indirectly affects firms' marketing opportunities. There are many examples of the direct effects on marketers, for example laws giving consumers rights against the seller of faulty goods. At other times the effects of legislative changes are less direct, as where legislation outlawing anti-competitive practices changes the nature of competition between firms within a market.

- Governments are responsible for protecting the public interest at large, imposing further constraints on the activities of firms (for example controls on pollution, which may make a manufacturing firm uncompetitive in international markets on account of its increased costs).

- The macroeconomic environment is very much influenced by the actions of politicians. Government is responsible for formulating policies that can influence the rate of growth in the economy and hence the total amount of spending power. It is also a political decision as to how this spending power should be distributed between different groups of consumers and between the public and private sectors.

- Government policies can influence the dominant social and cultural values of a country, although there can be argument about which is the cause and which is the effect. (For example, did the UK government's drive for economic expansion and individual responsibility during the late 1980s change public attitudes away from good citizenship and towards those of 'greed is good'?)

- Increasingly, the political environment affecting marketers includes supra-national organizations, which can directly or indirectly affect companies. These include trading blocs (e.g. the EU, ASEAN, and NAFTA) and the influence of worldwide intergovernmental organizations whose members seek to implement agreed policy (e.g. the World Trade Organization).

The social and cultural environment

It is crucial for marketers to fully appreciate the cultural values of a society, especially where an organization is seeking to do business in a country that is quite different to its own. Attitudes to specific products change through time and at any one time can differ between groups in society.

Even in home markets, business organizations should understand the processes of gradual cultural change and be prepared to satisfy the changing needs of consumers. Consider the following examples of contemporary cultural change in western Europe and the possible responses of marketers.

- Leisure is becoming a bigger part of many people's lives, and marketers have responded with a wide range of leisure related goods and services.

- Attitudes towards the work/life balance are changing. The nature of work relationships can affect companies profits; for example, the dotcom bubble and dress-down Friday had a calamitous impact on the formal clothing retailer Moss Bros' fortunes as consumers' attitudes to work changed (Doward [3]).

- The role of women in society is changing as men and women increasingly share expectations in terms of employment and household responsibilities. This is reflected in the observation that women made up 47% of the UK paid workforce in 1997, compared with 37% in 1971. Examples of marketing responses include cars designed to meet the aspirational needs of career women and ready prepared meals, which relieve working women of their traditional role in preparing household meals.

MARKETING in ACTION

EU legislators influence the UK, so UK marketers must try and influence the EU

If there is one topic of political conversation that divides people throughout Europe, it is the quest for ever closer European integration. The EU was founded by the Treaty of Rome, signed in 1957 by the original six members of the European Coal and Steel Community: France, West Germany, Italy, Belgium, the Netherlands, and Luxembourg. Britain joined in 1972, together with Ireland and Denmark; Greece joined in 1981, Spain and Portugal in 1986, and Austria, Finland, and Sweden in 1995. In 2002 the Treaty of Copenhagen confirmed accession procedures for 10 further countries—Latvia, Lithuania, Estonia, Poland, Hungary, Slovakia, Czech Republic, Slovenia, Cyprus, and Malta—to join the EU in 2004. The combined population of the 15 EU countries in 2002 was 729 million, with the 10 new countries accounting for a further 80 million (EU Office of Statistics 2003 [7]).

Economic and political integration of the EU are difficult to separate, and, whether they like it or not, marketers throughout Europe are increasingly having to look not just to their own domestic political environment, but also to the EU government, comprising the Commission, the Council of Ministers, Parliament, and the Court of Justice. The Single European Act which came into effect in 1993 switched a lot of the decision making that affects marketers away from domestic governments to the EU. Directives made by the EU affecting issues such as product design and advertising require member states to implement through their domestic legislation. If new legislation looks threatening, it has become futile to lobby the domestic government, as it will have been the EU that inspired the legislation.

The role of the EU in marketers' political environment was demonstrated during 2002 when the EU passed two Directives, which would place all herbal medicines and vitamin and mineral supplements on the same regulatory basis as medicines. More than 300 widely used 'natural remedies' would be banned altogether, and the cost of licensing each product—estimated at up £2,000 per product—would be beyond the means of many of the small producers who dominated the market for natural remedies. The big pharmaceutical companies had been lobbying the EU hard to get such a change, citing 'adverse reactions' from many herbal remedies and vitamin supplements such as vitamin B6. Of course, they knew that driving thousands of small herbal producers out of business would draw customers to the pharmaceutical companies' mass-produced products. The natural remedies producers were much more fragmented than the large pharmaceutical companies and were slow to get their lobbying together. In November 2002, the sector presented to the UK government a petition protesting about the proposed changes. It contained over one million signatures, including those of Sir Paul McCartney and Sir Elton John, but it was too late, because the Directives had already been passed by the EU and hence there was little discretion left for the UK government. The lobbyists of the pharmaceutical industry seemed to have outsmarted the lobbyists of the natural remedies firms and understood where and when to apply pressure.

The EU is accounting for an increasing proportion of the legislation that affects marketers, and with the advent of the single European currency its influence on the macroeconomic environment has increased. But are marketers simply opportunistic in their support for greater integration of member states? As an example, brewers have in the past condemned the European Commission's plans for tighter control over the labelling of beer, claiming their national beer is unique, but this has not prevented them also campaigning for a harmonization of taxes where the tax paid in their own country is higher than the EU average.

Figure 2.7 Busy life-styles have opened new opportunities for marketers. The increasing number of money rich, time poor households has been targeted by suppliers of services ranging from home shopping to domestic cleaning personal coaching. Busy life-styles have contributed to an increase in the number of parents seeking kindergartens for their young children. A desire for mothers to return to their career as soon as possible after the birth of their child and a decline in the geographically close extended family have led to an increase in private child care services (Reproduced with permission of Bushbabies Kindergarten)

- Greater life expectancy is leading to an ageing of the population and a shift to an increasingly 'elderly' culture. This is reflected in product design which is increasingly emphasizing durability rather than fashionability.
- The growing concern among many groups in society with the environment is reflected in a variety of 'green' consumer products.

Figure 2.8 The launch of culturally distinctive products such as Mecca cola challenges marketing plans which are based on assumptions of cultural convergence. Rival Coca Cola has spent many years becoming a market leader in many of the markets that it serves. In some developing countries, Coke has acquired iconic significance as a representation of a western life-style. However, in 2002 the rival Mecca Cola launched its slogan 'No more drinking stupid—drink with commitment!', and challenged some of the cultural values that underlie Coke's success. Mecca Cola promises to put back profits into the communities that it serves

Some indication of the minutiae of changing life-styles and their implications for marketing was revealed in a report, *Complicated Lives II: The Price of Complexity* [06], commissioned by Abbey National from the Future Foundation. The report brought together quantitative and qualitative research with extensive analysis of a range of trends affecting families and their finances. The findings show that, between 1961 and 2001,

- the average time women spent in a week doing cleaning and laundry fell from 12 hours and 40 minutes to 6 hours and 18 minutes;
- the average time that parents spent helping their children with homework had increased from 1 minute a day to 15 minutes a day;
- time spent caring for children increased from 30 minutes a day to 75 minutes a day;
- the average amount of time spent entertaining went up from 25 minutes to 55 minutes;
- time spent cooking has decreased for women, down from more than 1 hour and 40 minutes to just over an hour (73 minutes) per day. At the same time, men marginally increased their time in the kitchen, from 26 to 27 minutes per day.

There has been much discussion recently about the concept of 'cultural convergence', referring to an apparent decline in differences between cultures. It has been argued that basic human needs are universal in nature and, in principle, capable of satisfaction with universally similar solutions. Many companies have sought to develop one core product for a global market, and there is some evidence of firms achieving this (for example Coca Cola, McDonald's). The desire of a subculture in one country to imitate the values of those in another culture has also contributed to cultural convergence. This is nothing new. During the Second World War many people in western Europe sought to follow the American life-style, and nylon stockings from the USA became highly sought-after cultural icons by some groups. The same process is at work today in many developing countries, where some groups are seeking to identify with western cultural values through the purchases they make.

Critics of the trend towards cultural convergence point to a growing need for cultural identity which has been expressed, for example, in the rejection by some Muslim fundamentalist groups of the values of western society. This poses new challenges for western companies that seek overseas expansion. How can Coca Cola be sure that its brand name and product offer will be the object of aspiration for the dominant groups in a country, rather than a hated symbol of an alien system of capitalism?

In western countries, new challenges and opportunities for marketing are posed by the diverse cultural traditions of ethnic minorities. A report on *Marketing to Ethnic Minorities* [11], published by Interfocus in 2001, identified a number of issues, such as differing household structures and value systems.

The demographic environment

Demography is the study of populations in terms of their size and characteristics. Among the topics of interest to demographers are the age structure of a country, the geographic distribution of its population, the balance between males and females, and the likely future size of the population and its characteristics. Changes in the size and age structure of the population are critical to many firms' marketing. Although the total population of most western countries is stable, their composition is changing. Most countries are experiencing an increase in the proportion of elderly people, and companies who have monitored this trend have responded with the development of residential homes, cruise holidays, and financial portfolio management services aimed at meeting this group's needs. At the other end of the age spectrum, the birth rate of most countries is cyclical, resulting in a cyclical pattern of demand for age-related products such as baby products, fashion clothing, and family cars (Figure 2.9).

Consider the following changes in the structure of the UK population and their effects on marketers.

1. There has been a trend for women to have fewer children. (The average number of children for each woman born in 1930 was 2.35, it was 2.2 for those born in 1945 and it is projected to be 1.74 for those born in 1970.) There has also been a tendency for women to have children later in life. (The average age at which women in the UK have their first child has increased from 24 years in 1945 to 28 in 1994.) In addition, there has been an increase in the number of women having no children. (According to the Office of Population Census and Surveys, this has risen from 10% of women born in 1950 to a projected 20% of women born in the early 1960s.) Fewer children has resulted in parents spending more per child (more designer clothes for children rather than budget clothes) and has allowed women to stay at work longer (increasing household incomes and encouraging the purchase of labour-saving products).

2. Alongside a declining number of children has been a decline in the average household size (from an average of 3.1 people in 1961 to 2.3 in 1997). There has been a particular fall in the number of large households with five or more people (down from 9% of all households in 1961 to less than 5% in 2002) and a significant increase in the number of one-person households (up from 11% to 27% over the same period). Statistics from the Halifax, Britain's largest mortgage lender, shows that

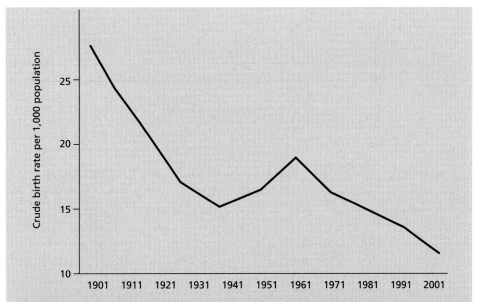

Figure 2.9 The UK birth rate fluctuated greatly during the past century. As one 'baby boom' generation grew up, they had children which contributed to a further baby boom. This figure shows how the number of births per 1,000 has fluctuated over time. For some companies, these changes can have a major effect on consumer demand. Inevitably, it is the specialist children's shops such as Mothercare that are first to feel the effects of a rise or fall in birth numbers, but eventually all companies who target specific age groups will experience a change in the number of buyers available to purchase their goods and services

more than 40% of all homebuyers in 2001 were single, compared with only 25% in 1983, with the largest rise evident in the percentage of single women buying their own home—up from 8% of all buyers in 1983 to 17% in 2001 (*The Guardian* [7]).

The growth in small or one-person households has had numerous marketing implications, ranging from an increased demand for smaller units of housing to the types and size of groceries purchased. A single person buying for him or herself is likely to use different types of retail outlets compared with the household buying as a unit.

3. The ethnic composition of the UK population has become increasingly diverse. The Office for National Statistics has estimated that almost 60% of the 4.3 million population increase expected to occur between 2000 and 2025 will be accounted for by inward migration. Ethnic diversity has created new opportunities to cater for ethnic preferences in fields as diverse as food, travel, and music.

4. Marketers also need to monitor the changing geographical distribution of the population (between different regions of the country and between urban and rural areas). The current drift towards rural and suburban areas has resulted in higher car ownership levels and a preference for using out-of-town shopping centres.

Figure 2.10 **Statistics show a steady increase in the number of elderly people in the population.** Stannah Stairlifts has identified an opportunity to serve the growing market of very old people who wish to continue living at home and for whom a stair lift allows a more independent lifestyle
Reproduced with permission of Stannah Stairlifts Ltd.

 **MARKETING in ACTION**

McDonald's recognizes new family values

Statistics have continued to chart the decline of the stereotypical nuclear family of two parents and 2.4 children. However, advertisers have continued to portray this ideal type family in their advertising, despite the fact that fewer people can relate directly to it. The fast food restaurant McDonald's recognized this trend with an advertising campaign that portrayed a boy arranging for a meeting between his separated parents in a branch of McDonald's. Behind the departure from the happy-families norm in fast food marketing is the realization that the number of families in the UK with single parents has risen from 8% in 1971 to nearly one quarter in 2002. McDonald's claimed that it could not credibly position itself as a family restaurant and show only pictures of mum and dad and two kids without the risk of alienating parents and children from different households. But could McDonald's incur the wrath of critics who might accuse the company of actually contributing to family breakdown? With an eye on such worries, McDonald's advertisements left the impression that the couple were going to get together again.

The technological environment

The pace of technological change is becoming increasingly rapid, and marketers need to understand how technological developments might affect them in four related business areas:

- New technologies can allow new goods and services to be offered to consumers—internet banking, mobile telecommunications, and new anti-cancer drugs for example.

- New technology can allow existing products to be made more cheaply, thereby widening the market for such goods by enabling prices to be lowered. In this way, more efficient aircraft have allowed new markets for air travel to develop.

- Technological developments have allowed new methods of distributing goods and services. (For example, amazon.com used the internet to offer book buyers a new way of browsing and buying books.)

- New opportunities for companies to communicate with their target customers have emerged, with many financial services companies using computer databases to target potential customers and to maintain a dialogue with established customers. The internet has opened up new distribution opportunities for many services-based companies. The development of mobile internet services offers new possibilities for targeting buyers at times and places of high readiness to buy.

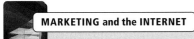

MARKETING and the INTERNET

The internet and the law of unintended consequences

The development of the internet has had profound impacts on the marketing activities of some business sectors. As an example, the budget airline sector has capitalized on the ability of the internet to cut out intermediaries and reduce the airlines' costs. The low-cost carrier EasyJet now claims that over 90% of its bookings are made online, helping it to become the largest low-cost carrier in Europe.

However, while many observers correctly predicted that travel and financial services would rapidly embrace the internet, some other predictions have proved wide of the mark, suggesting that there is a very complex interaction between the technological, social, and economic environments. Consider the following predictions, which were made in 2000 when 'dotcom' mania was at its height.

- Predictions were made that commuting would lessen as more people would work from home, using the internet to communicate with their work colleagues. Traffic congestion would disappear and commuter rail services would lose customers. In fact, technology has allowed many people to choose a pleasant residential environment and to live much further away from their work, because they now have to travel to the office only on a couple of days each week rather than every day. Overall, however, the travelling distances of many people in this situation have actually increased, resulting in more rather than less total commuting.

- Conferences were predicted to disappear in favour of video conferencing. Why bother travelling to a meeting or conference when you could meet 'virtually' from the comfort of your desk, and at lower cost? However, face-to-face conferences have continued to prosper. The technology that enables many people to work in isolation may have indirectly contributed to a desire to counter this with more face-to-face meetings with a greater social content.

- High Street shops were being written off in 2000, when quite extraordinarily the pure internet company lastminute.com had a market capitalization value far in excess of the 110-outlet Debenhams store. But the convenience of shopping in the High Street or at out-of-town shopping centres and the problems of arranging home delivery of internet suppliers were underestimated by advocates of internet-based shopping.

We seem to have an inherent tendency to overstate the short-term effects of technological change, but to understate the long-term effects on our behaviour. With the development of new technologies enabling high-speed mobile internet services, further predictions were being made in 2003. Would we really want to download full-length feature films to watch on our mobile phones? Would we really want to surf the net while travelling on a train? Would there be unforeseen 'killer applications' such as SMS text messaging which was almost left out of the specification of first-generation mobile phones, because no useful role for it was foreseen? Perhaps the long-term effects of the internet may be more subtle, by contributing to individuals' sense of connectedness with narrowly selected commercial and social groups, no matter where they may be located, while reducing the sense of community, with diverse groups of people living together in close proximity.

The unforeseen consequences of the internet emphasize how difficult it can be to understand the consequences for the marketer of a changing marketing environment. These examples demonstrate the importance of understanding the linkages between different elements of the marketing environment, so developments in the technological environment can be sensibly understood only in conjunction with changes in the social environment.

The ecological environment

Issues affecting our natural ecology have captured the public imagination in recent years. The destruction of tropical rain forests and the depletion of the ozone layer leading to global warming have serious implications for our quality of life—not necessarily today, but for future generations. Marketing is often seen as being in conflict with the need to protect the natural ecology. It is very easy for critics of marketing to point to cases where greed and mismanagement have created long-lasting or permanent ecological damage. Have rain forests been destroyed partly by our greed for more hardwood furniture? More locally, is our impatience for getting to our destination quickly the reason why many natural habitats have been lost to new road developments?

There is argument about whether ecological problems are *actually* getting worse, or whether our perceptions and expectations are changing. Charles Dickens' description of Victorian London painted a grim picture of heavy manufacturing industry causing widespread pollution and using up natural resources in a manner that today would be considered quite profligate. Any comparison with industry today would probably give the impression that environmental issues are lessening in their importance. Supporters of this view will point to the relatively clean air that we enjoy today, compared with the smogs that used to descend on industrial areas, often for very lengthy periods. When salmon were caught in the River Thames in the 1990s for the first recorded time in over fifty years, it would have been easy to gain the impression that the ecological environment was improving. Set against this is the worry that the actions that we are taking today could be storing up major ecological problems for the future. A lot of ecological change—such as the depletion of the ozone layer over Antarctica—is happening at a much faster rate than previously and there is no certainty about the magnitude of the consequences.

A market-led company cannot ignore threats to the natural ecology. Commercial organizations' concern with the ecological environment has resulted from two principal factors:

1. There has been growing pressure on natural resources, including those that, directly or indirectly, are used in firms' production processes. This is evidenced by the extinction of species of animals and the depletion of hardwood timber resources. As a result of overuse of natural resources, many industry sectors, such as North Sea fishing, have faced severe constraints on their production possibilities.

2. The general public has become increasingly aware of ecological issues, and, more importantly, some segments have shown a greater willingness and ability to spend money to alleviate the problems associated with ecologically harmful practices (see Laroche, Bergeron, and Barbaro-Forleo [10]).

At a macro-environmental level, support for the ecological environment has sometimes been seen as a 'luxury' which societies cannot afford as they struggle to satisfy the essentials of life. As these necessities are satisfied, individuals, and society collectively, can move on to satisfy higher-order needs to protect what are seen as aesthetic benefits such as fresh air and a rich flora and fauna. The idea of environmentalism being a luxury is supported by the observation that countries with the strongest environmental movements, such as the USA and Germany, tend also to be the richest economically. And when consumers do take into account environmental concerns, they tend to focus on immediate threats, rather than longer-term issues. In one survey, Gallup found that, while 68% of respondents mentioned pollution of drinking water as a great concern, acid rain (mentioned by 29%) and global warming (34%) generated less concern (Murray [11]). Many poorer countries tolerate poor environmental conditions in order to gain a competitive cost advantage over their more regulated western competitors.

Is marketing's pursuit of greater consumption fundamentally opposed to ecological interests? Taken to its logical extreme, consumption of the vast majority of goods and services can result in some form of ecological harm. For example, the most ecologically friendly means of transport is to avoid the need for transport in the first place; the most ecologically friendly holiday is to stay at home. Individuals with a true concern for preserving their ecological environment would choose to reduce their consumption of goods and services in total. At the moment such attitudes are held by only a small minority in western societies, but the development of a widespread anti-consumption mentality would have major implications for marketers.

◼ Monitoring and responding to environmental change

It was stated earlier that the relationship between a firm and its business environment is crucial to marketing success. There are many examples of firms that have neglected this relationships and eventually withered and died. To avoid this fate, a firm must:

- understand what is going on in its business environment, and
- respond and adapt to environmental change.

As organizations become larger and national economies more complex, the task of understanding the marketing environment becomes more formidable. Information about a firm's environment becomes crucial to environmental analysis and response.

Information about the current state of the environment is used as a starting point for planning future marketing strategy, based on assumptions about how the environment will change. Information is also vital to monitor the implementation of an organization's marketing plans and to note the cause of any deviation from plan. Information therefore has both a planning function and a control function.

Information collection, processing, transmission, and storage technologies are continually improving, as witnessed by the development of Electronic Point of Sale (EPOS) systems. These have enabled organizations to greatly enhance the quality of the information they have about their operating environment. However, information is becoming more accessible not just to one particular organization, but also to its competitors. Attention is therefore moving away from how information is collected, to who is best able to make use of the information.

Large organizations operating in complex and turbulent environments often use information to build models of their environment, or at least sub-components of it. Some of these can be quite general, as in the case of the models of the national economy which many large companies have developed. From a general model of the economy, a firm can predict how a specific item of government policy (for example, increasing the rate of value added tax on luxury goods) will impact directly and indirectly on sales of its own products.

The crucial role of information in marketing analysis and planning will be returned to in Chapter 4.

SWOT analysis

SWOT is an acronym for Strengths, Weaknesses, Opportunities, and Threats. SWOT analysis is a useful framework for assessing an organization and its marketing environment, summarizing the main environmental issues in the form of opportunities and threats facing an organization. These external factors are listed alongside the organization's internal strengths and weaknesses. An opportunity in an organization's external environment can be exploited only if it has the internal strengths to do so. If, on the other hand, the organization is not capable of exploiting these because of internal weaknesses, then they should perhaps be left alone. For this reason, the terms 'opportunities' and 'threats' should not be viewed as 'absolutes', but assessed in the context of an organization's resources and the feasibility of exploiting them.

The principles of a SWOT analysis are illustrated in Figure 2.11 by examining how an established manufacturer of ready prepared chicken products might view its strengths and weaknesses in terms of the opportunities and threats that it faces in its environment.

Marketing opportunities can come in many forms, and each should be assessed for its attractiveness and success probability. Attractiveness can be assessed in terms of potential market size, growth rates, profit margins, competitiveness, and distribution channels. Other factors may be technological requirements, the extent of government restrictions, availability of government grants, ecological concerns, and energy requirements. Measures of attractiveness must be qualified by the probability of success, which depends on the company's strengths and competitive advantage. Probability of success is likely to be influenced by, among other things, the firm's access to cash, lines of credit or capital to finance new developments, technological and production expertise, marketing skills, distribution channels, and managerial competence. A simple matrix can be constructed to show the relationship between attractiveness and success probability. We will return to this in Chapter 5.

An environmental threat is a challenge posed by an unfavourable trend or development in a company's environment that would lead, in the absence of action by the company, to the erosion of the company's market position. In this case the threats should be assessed according to their seriousness and the probability of occurrence. A threat matrix can then be constructed.

In order for an environmental analysis to have a useful input to the marketing planning process, a wide range of information and opinions needs to be summarized in a meaningful way. The information collated from a detailed environmental analysis can be simplified in the form of an Environmental Threat and Opportunity Profile (ETOP). This provides a summary of the environmental factors that are most critical to the or-

Strengths	Weaknesses
Established and widely recognized brand name Good distribution network Strong financial base	Only has a narrow product range Shortage of production staff
Opportunities	**Threats**
Growing demand for chicken products Rising income will result in increased demand for ready prepared meals	Possibility of health scares Intense competition from supermarkets' own label products Tighter safety standards may increase costs

Figure 2.11 SWOT analysis for a hypothetical established UK manufacturer of ready prepared chicken meals

ganization (Figure 2.12) and can be useful in stimulating debate among senior management about the future of the business. Some analysts suggest trying to weight these factors according to their importance, and then rating them for their impact on the organization.

◼ The internal environment

Finally, we must remember that marketers do not operate in a vacuum within their organizations. Internally, the structure and politics of an organization affect the manner in which it responds to environmental change. We are all familiar with lumbering giants of companies who, like a super-tanker, have ploughed ahead on a seemingly predetermined course and had difficulty in changing direction. During the late 1990s such well-respected companies as Sainsbury and Marks & Spencer were accused of having

Factor	Major opportunity	Minor opportunity	Neutral	Minor threat	Major threat	Probability of occurrence
Political						
New transport policy sees introduction of tax on use of cars in town centres					✓	0.1
Economic						
Tax on petrol increases by 5p				✓		0.4
Household spending falls for two quarters in succession					✓	0.2
VAT on new cars reduced	✓					0.1
Market						
Overseas competitors enter market more aggressively				✓		0.3

Figure 2.12 An Environmental Threat and Opportunity Profile, applied to a car manufacturer

internal structures and processes that were too rigid to cope with a changing external environment. Simply having a strong marketing department does not guarantee that a firm will be best able to adapt to change. Such companies may in fact create internal tensions, which make them less effective at responding to changing consumer needs than where marketing responsibilities in their widest sense are spread throughout the organization.

Two aspects to a marketing manager's internal environment are of importance here: the internal structure and processes of the marketing department itself (where one actually exists), and the relationship of the marketing function to other business functions.

Marketing departments allocate responsibilities to individual managers on a number of bases, the most common being functions performed, products managed, customer segments, and geographical areas; but in practice, most marketing departments show more than one approach to structure. Chapter 12 will review some of the advantages and disadvantages of each of these approaches.

Figure 2.13 **Labour intensive service industries have long realized that recruiting, training and motivating the right staff is an important basis for delivering value to customers.** In conditions of full employment, companies must sell themselves as a good employer so that they can recruit the people who will ultimately deliver marketers' promises to customers. The Sunday Times conducts an annual survey of Britain's best companies to work for, and the shoe repair and key cutting chain Timpson has scored highly for a number of years. Employee benefits include at least 16 weeks' maternity leave on full pay (compared to statutory minimum of six weeks at 90% pay) and/or at least four weeks' leave above the statutory minimum of 40 weeks. One sign of the company's success is a low level of staff turnover—at least 40% of its staff have worked at the company for more than five years. Managers are given considerable discretion in how they run their branch, for example the prices that they charge. Customers have come to trust the chain and rewarded it with sustainable long-term profits (Reproduced with permission of Timpsons)

In a genuinely marketing-oriented organization, marketing activities cannot be confined to something called a marketing department. As Drucker [6] noted, marketing is so basic that it cannot be considered a separate function: it has to be the whole business seen from the customer's point of view. In marketing-oriented organizations, customers should be the concern not simply of the marketing department, but also of all those operational and administrative personnel whose actions may directly or indirectly affect customers' perceptions of quality and value. Some of the most successful companies are those that have successfully integrated marketing into all functional areas of the organization.

An important element of an organization's internal environment is its dominant 'culture'. Culture in this sense refers to a set of values that are shared by all members of the organization. Some organizations, for example, have a culture that stresses that 'the customer is always right', while others have a bureaucratic culture that stresses the need to conduct business in an administratively 'correct' way. Numerous comparative studies into the performance of European, American, and Japanese-managed organizations have identified the concept of culture as a possible explanation for differences in competitive effectiveness.

It can be very difficult to change cultural attitudes within an organization, and the process of change can be painful for many. Some organizations appear to have successfully managed the transition from a production-oriented culture to one focused on customers (for example many former state-owned bus companies). In many cases, however, this change has been slow, leading to competitive disadvantage where culture does not keep up with changes in the external environment. As an example, UK clearing banks have continued to be dominated by a culture based on prudence and caution whereas in some product areas such as home insurance a more aggressive approach to marketing management is called for.

It used to be thought that customers were not concerned about how their goods were made, just so long as the final product lived up to their expectations. There has been a trend for increasingly large segments of the population to take into account the ethics of a firm's employment practices when evaluating alternative products. If all other things are equal, a firm that has a reputation for ruthlessly exploiting its employees, or not recognizing the legitimate rights of trade unions, may be denigrated in the minds of many buyers. For this reason some companies, such as Marks & Spencer, have gone to great lengths to challenge allegations made about poor employment practices of their overseas suppliers.

Firms often go way beyond satisfying the basic legal requirements of employees. For some businesses, getting an adequate supply of competent workers is the main constraint on growth, and it would be in their interest to promote good employment practices. This is true of many high-tech industries. In order to encourage staff retention, in particular of women returning after having children, companies have offered attractive packages of benefits, such as working hours that fit around school holidays, and have sponsored various events in order to promote a caring image.

Can going beyond the legal requirement for employees ever be considered altruistic rather than just good business practice? Quaker companies such as Cadburys have a historic tradition of paternalism towards their staff. But might such altruism result in a payback in terms of better motivated staff?

The flexible organization

The management of change is becoming increasingly important to organizations, driven by the increasing speed with which the external environment is changing. Flexibility can be called for on a day-to-day basis and long-term. Chapter 9 will return to issues of supply chain management which allow companies to respond very quickly to changing customer demand. Flexibility is also required at a more strategic level.

Flexibility within an organization's workforce can be achieved by segmenting it into *core* and *peripheral* components (Figure 2.14). Many organizations have given their core workers greater job security, with defined career opportunities. In return for this relative job security, core workers may have to accept what Atkinson [1] termed 'functional

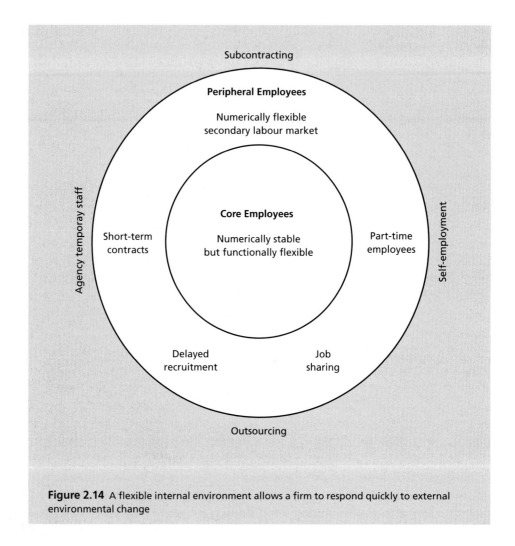

Figure 2.14 A flexible internal environment allows a firm to respond quickly to external environmental change

flexibility' by becoming responsible for a variety of jobs, as and when required. During their career with a company, such employees may undertake a variety of roles. In contrast to this group, peripheral employees have less job security and relatively limited career opportunities. They are 'numerically flexible', and often are employed on short-term contracts or treated as self-employed sub-contractors. It is not just operational staff whose jobs have been casualized in this way. Increasingly, many management jobs are being 'outsourced', and undertaken by consultants who are taken on as and when required. There is, however, debate about whether excessive use of short-term, flexible labour increases the effectiveness of an organization. Many have pointed to a possible downside in the form of reduced commitment of employees to the firm, which can ultimately damage the company's dealings with its customers.

Figure 2.15 In market sectors which are dominated by basically similar product offers, an ethical positioning may give a business a competitive advantage in the eyes of some customer segments. Many people would regard the major coffee shop chains as being essentially similar in what they offer, and many customers may question the disparity between the seemingly high price charged to consumers for a cup of coffee and the low price that third world producers receive for raw coffee beans. Starbucks has developed a loyal following of customers for whom the atmosphere of its stores warrants a premium price. However, the company is conscious of critics who point to low prices paid to producers, and addresses this by offering 'Fairtrade' certified coffee. Fairtrade seeks to improve the lives of coffee growers by ensuring that they receive a fair price for their harvest. For many western consumers, this ethical positioning is a basis for differentiating Starbucks from other coffee shops (Reproduced with permission of Starbucks Coffee Company)

STARBUCKS AND FAIRTRADE

Supporting a better life for coffee farmers

Organizations differ in the speed with which they are able to exploit new opportunities as they appear in their environment, partly reflecting the flexibility of their employment practices. Being the fastest company in a market to adapt can pay good dividends, so recent years have seen attempts by firms to increase their flexibility. This can be seen in the way that companies have moved personnel from areas in decline to those for which there is a prospect of future growth. For example, the major UK banks have moved staff away from basic banking activities—which face mature markets and challenges from new technology—towards broader financial services, which have been seen as more promising growth areas.

Marketing ethics

'The customer is king' is a traditional marketing maxim, and according to this, everything that a company does should be geared towards satisfying the needs of its customers. But should commercial organizations also have responsibilities to the public at large? The question is becoming increasingly important, as marketers have never before been subjected to such a critical gaze from those who are quick to identify the harmful side effects of market-led growth.

There are philosophical and pragmatic reasons why marketers should act in a socially responsible manner. Models of a responsible society would have marketers doing their bit to contribute towards a just and fair society, alongside the contributions of other institutions such as the family and the church (see Crane and Desmond [2]). More pragmatically, marketers need to take account of society's values, because if they don't they may end up isolated from the values of the customers they seek to attract. In increasingly discriminating markets, buyers may opt for the more socially responsible company. Acting in an anti-social way may have a long-term cost for a company and ultimately will not serve the needs of those customers who prefer to deal with a socially acceptable company.

Ethics is essentially about the definition of what is right and wrong. However, a difficulty occurs in trying to agree just what is right and wrong. No two people have precisely the same opinions, so some critics would argue that ethical considerations are of little interest to business. It can also be difficult to distinguish between ethics and legality; for example it may not yet be strictly illegal to exploit the gullibility of children in advertisements, but it may nevertheless be unethical.

Culture has a great effect in defining ethics, and what is considered unethical in one society may be considered perfectly acceptable in another. In western societies, ethical considerations confront marketers on many occasions. For example:

- A company marketing food supplements may stress the benefits of the product and provide information that is technically correct, but omits to provide vital information about side-effects associated with using the product. Should a marketing manager be required to spell out the possible problems of using its products, as well as the benefits?

- A dentist is short of money and diagnoses spurious problems which call for unnecessary dental treatment. How does he reconcile his need to maximize his earnings with the need to provide what is best for his patient?

- In order to secure a major new construction contract, a salesperson must entertain the client's buying manager with a weekend all-expenses paid holiday. Should this be considered ethical business practice in Britain? In Nigeria?

It is often suggested that society is becoming increasingly concerned about the ethical values adopted by its commercial organizations. With expanding media availability and an increasingly intelligent audience, it is becoming easier to expose examples of unethical business practice. Moreover, many television audiences appear to enjoy watching programmes that reveal alleged unethical practices of household-name companies. To give one example, the media has on many occasions focused attention on alleged exploitative employment practices of suppliers used by some of the biggest brand names in sportswear.

Firms are responding to increasing levels of ethical awareness by trying to put their own house in order. The following are some examples of how firms have gone about the task.

- Many companies have identified segments of their market that are prepared to pay a premium price in order to buy a product that has been produced in an ethical manner, or from a company that has adopted ethical practices. Many personal investors are concerned not just about the return that they will get, but the way in which that return will be achieved. This explains the increasing popularity of ethical investment funds that avoid investing in companies that are considered to be of a socially dubious nature. In the food sector, many consumers would consider the treatment of cattle grown for meat to be inhuman and unethical and would be happy to buy from a supplier who they knew acted ethically in the manner in which the cattle were raised and slaughtered.

- Greater attention to training can make clear to staff just what is expected of them, for example that it is unethical (and in the long-term commercially damaging) for a pensions company's sales personnel to try and sell to a person a policy that doesn't really suit their needs. Training may emphasize the need to spend a lot of time finding out just what the true needs of the customer are.

- More effective control and reward systems can help to reduce unethical practices within an organization. For example, sales personnel employed by a financial services company on a commission-only basis are more likely to try to sell a policy to a customer regardless of the customer's needs than a salaried employee who can take a longer-term view of the relationship between the company and its clients.

There are many documented cases to show that acting ethically need not conflict with a company's profit objectives, and indeed can add to profitability. For example, good safety standards and employment policies can improve productivity. In the UK, the DIY retailer B&Q has reduced discrimination against older workers by employing predominantly older people in some of its stores. It is claimed that these stores have become the firm's most profitable.

Corporate governance

The media have been taking a great interest in major companies whose internal style of governance appears to be inconsistent with their role as trusted market-led organizations. Recent examples of poor corporate governance have included numerous cases of so called 'fat cat' directors paying themselves large salary increases while worsening the employment conditions of their lower paid employees.

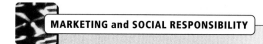

MARKETING and SOCIAL RESPONSIBILITY

Investing in a better environment?

The 1990s saw a growth in investment funds that claimed to invest only in businesses that are run ethically. Many investors preferred to know that their investment was benefiting not just themselves, but society as a whole. It was also claimed that a good ethical investment fund need perform no worse than one run without explicit ethical considerations. By 2000 there were over 30 ethical investment funds in the UK.

But how can you define ethical investment? Ethics is very much about statements of what is right and wrong, and these vary among individuals and among cultures, and they change through time. Can an investment trust ever be said to represent the views of a society as a whole? A report by the Social Affairs Unit was scornful of the whole concept of ethical investment, because ethics is about judgements on what people do with products. It cited the example of the refusal of ethical investment funds to invest in the nuclear industry, which implied that the industry was totally bad, despite the valuable role that nuclear radiation plays in medicine. Similarly, it is very much an individual judgement whether nuclear electricity generation is good or bad.

Many other financial services that appeal to individuals' sense of ethics and desire for wider social benefits may be questioned. Many credit cards, for example, make a donation to a specified charity for each pound that a customer spends via their credit card. However, such cards invariably charge customers higher than average annual fees and interest charges, and a report by the Consumers Association calculated that charities would be even better off if customers had taken out the cheapest credit card available to them and paid the resulting savings directly to a good cause.

In view of the subjectivity of definitions, should marketers even try to understand what is ethical and what is not? Is ethical marketing best understood as providing peace of mind to consumers, regardless of the technical merits of an argument?

In the UK, a number of attempts to develop blueprints for corporate governance have been developed (e.g. the 2003 Higgs report on the role of non-executive directors). 'Good practice' in corporate governance is increasingly being defined in terms of:

- having in place internal control systems which prevent the type of abuse of directors' power that occurred in the former Maxwell group of companies, where an unchecked director was allowed to manipulate pensioners' funds for his own personal use;

- having an appropriate structure for the board of directors which combines full-time executive directors with non-executive directors brought in from outside;

- striking a balance when remunerating senior directors and employees between the reassurance of a long-term salary and performance for results;

- recognizing employees as increasingly important stakeholders in organizations, for example through initiatives such as 'Investors in People', to promote the training and development of an organization's workforce.

Good corporate governance is culturally conditioned, and what may constitute bad governance in one culture may be accepted as normal in others, reflecting economic, political, social, and legal traditions in each country. Despite convergence, however, differences still occur, for example in attitudes towards the disclosure of directors' salaries.

■ Chapter summary and linkages to other chapters

The marketing environment comprises the individuals, organizations, and forces that impinge on the activities of marketers. Some of the effects are direct and relatively immediate (the micro-environment), while others are essentially forces for change in the future (the macro-environment). Marketers must also understand the internal structures and processes of their organization, as these can affect the development and implementation of marketing plans (the internal environment).

Marketers have developed methodologies for capturing information about the marketing environment and these will be developed in Chapter 4. Following analysis of their environment, marketers seek to develop a competitive position within that environment (Chapter 6). Increasingly, marketers are seeing the marketing environment in terms of not just the local market, but also the international environment (Chapter 14).

This chapter has stressed that marketers should understand the needs not just of their customers, but of a much broader range of stakeholders. Although social responsibility by firms can achieve long-term paybacks, there can still be doubt about what is the most responsible course of action.

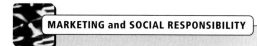

MARKETING and SOCIAL RESPONSIBILITY

Anti-capitalism, or victims of multinational brands?

Over recent years, we have witnessed scenes of young radical anti-capitalists smashing branches of McDonald's during protests against the World Trade Organization in particular, and global capitalism in general. Should such actions be enough to frighten the life out of marketing managers in our largest companies? While the radical anti-capitalist movement may have attracted high-profile support from such youth icons as Radiohead, how general is this apparent threat to the marketing activities of multinational companies?

Research by the Future Foundation appears to challenge the idea that young people are becoming more hostile towards global brands. According to a 2001 study by the organization, 16 to 24-year-olds have more positive feelings towards multinationals than older groups, with the original protest generation—those who came of age in the 1960s—least likely of all to trust multinationals.

In the wake of recent violent protests surrounding the World Trade Organization's Seattle and Prague meetings, research revealed that younger generations are less inclined towards direct action than their parents and grandparents. Nearly half of all 16 to 34-year-olds claimed they would not demonstrate if a multinational company had done something wrong. Further confounding the myth of young people wanting to change the world was the statistic that fewer than one in 20 strongly agreed that they 'would not buy the products of a large multinational company that had done something wrong'. A third of teens and twenty-somethings also agreed with preserving the power of multinational companies, and a further one in 10 believed that multinationals are 'ultimately for the good of consumers' and should be encouraged to grow. By contrast, two-thirds of their grandparents—those aged 55 and above—claimed they would boycott goods to punish companies they considered guilty of corporate crimes. Even the thorny issue of genetic engineering failed to provoke a strong response from young people, with only four in 10 mistrusting the claims of the multinationals, compared with six in 10 of their parents and grandparents.

Does this research indicate the ultimate supremacy for the superbrand, where the golden arches of McDonald's and the Nike logo are symbols of its global sovereignty? Traditionally, the younger generations have been in the vanguard of any protest movement, so why should they appear to be less willing than their parents and grandparents to challenge authority? Are our images of young people and their attitudes towards global capitalism unduly influenced by television coverage of what amounts to a small minority of protesters?

KEY PRINCIPLES OF MARKETING

- Marketing takes place within a broad system of economic, social, political, and technological relationships.
- Value is created through interaction with other individuals and organizations that make up the marketing environment.

- The marketing environment cannot be neatly divided into distinct areas. A good marketer seeks to understand the complex linkages between different parts of the marketing environment.
- Micro-environment influences may demand urgent attention, but macro-environment influences can have a more profound long-term effect on an organization's marketing.

CASE STUDY

Smoking may be bad, but tobacco companies' profits have never looked so good

Next to the arms industry, the tobacco industry must be one of the most politically incorrect business sectors. Yet during the late 1990s tobacco companies in the UK appeared to be very popular with the Stock Market, outperforming the FTSE all-share index by 36% during 1998, and continuing to hold their ground in the falling stock market conditions from 2001. This was despite an EU directive which finally put an end to all tobacco advertising in the UK from March 2003.

Tobacco companies now place less emphasis on fighting the health lobby, and no longer pretend that tobacco is anything other than harmful. But, fortunately for the tobacco firms, nicotine is an addictive drug. Although cigarette consumption has declined in most developed countries, one person in four still smokes. Moreover, among some groups, especially young women, the rate of smoking has shown some increase in recent years. Tobacco companies also benefit from periods of economic recession. While job cuts may be bad news for most consumer goods and services companies, it has historically also been linked to an increase in smoking.

The tobacco companies have survived many years of attempts to control tobacco sales throughout Europe, but the EU directive banning all tobacco advertising made it increasingly difficult for tobacco companies to get new brands established. The big three UK companies—BAT, Gallagher, and Imperial Tobacco—considered strengthening their brands with joint ventures. BAT linked up with the Ministry of Sound nightclub to push its Lucky Strike brand, while Gallagher tried to promote the Benson and Hedges name through a branded coffee. One industry expert expected to see an army of cigarette girls pushing cigarettes in pubs and corner shops, thereby trying to get round controls on advertising.

While promoting cigarettes in Europe has been getting more difficult, tobacco companies have been keen to exploit overseas markets where measures to protect the public are less stringent. The companies have pushed their products in the countries of eastern Europe, hoping to capitalize on the hunger for western brands. Gallagher has a plant in Kazakhstan and has heavily promoted its Sovereign brand in the former Soviet Union. The biggest opportunities for western tobacco companies, however, are in China, which is the world's biggest market in terms of volume. The Chinese smoke 1.7 trillion cigarettes a year, making the British market of just 77 billion look quite small. State-owned brands such as Pagoda dominate the market with an estimated 98% market share. With import duties of 240%, most foreign cigarettes enter the Chinese market through unauthorized channels, including those smuggled by the Chinese army. Greater trade liberalization will inevitably give freer access to the Chinese market for western tobacco companies. These will undoubtedly pay significant levels of taxes to the authorities, so a financially strained government may be unwilling to reduce tobacco consumption too much, especially when smoking is so pervasive through the population.

Case study review questions

1. How effective is the EU ban on tobacco advertising likely to be for reducing smoking? What measures could governments take to bring about a significant reduction in smoking?

2. What factors could explain a booming share price for tobacco companies at the same time as Europeans' attitudes towards smoking are becoming more hostile?

3. How would you defend a western tobacco company in its attempts to develop the Chinese market for cigarettes?

CHAPTER REVIEW QUESTIONS

1. Explain briefly what you understand by the 'marketing environment' of a business.

2. 'Suppliers and intermediaries are important stakeholders in the micro-environment of the business.' Explain the evolving role and functions of these stakeholders in today's marketing-orientated business.

3. Using a company of your choice, produce and justify an environmental set.

4. Giving examples, explain what is meant by the term 'pressure groups'. Provide a resume of the tactics you would advise a high profile company to use in managing relations with these groups.

5. For what reasons might a fast food restaurant company choose to adopt ecologically sound practices?

6. Is it possible to define an ethical code of conduct which is applicable in all countries? How should a multinational company attempt to define a global ethical code of conduct?

REFERENCES

[1] Atkinson, J. (1984), 'Manpower Strategies for Flexible Organizations'. *Personnel Management*, August: 77–93.

[2] Crane, A. and Desmond, J. (2002), 'Societal Marketing and Morality'. *European Journal of Marketing*, 36: 548–69.

[3] Doward, D. (2002), 'Turnaround Job is Made to Measure for Moss Bros Boss'. *The Observer*, 15 December: 18.

[4] Drucker, P. F. (1973), *Management: tasks, responsibilities and practices*. New York: Harper & Row.

[5] *Eurostat Yearbook 2003*, Luxembourg, Eurostat.

[6] The Future Foundation (2002), *Complicated Lives II: The Price of Complexity.* London: EU Office of Statistics. The Future Foundation.

[7] *The Guardian* (2002), 'Halifax Warns on Rise in Single Homebuyers: demographic shift adds to supply concerns'. 22 August: 27.

[8] Higgs, D. (2003), 'Review of the Role and Effectiveness of Non-executive Directors', London, DTI.

[9] Interfocus Marketing (2001), Marketing to Ethnic Minorities. Londo, Interfocus Marketing.

[10] Laroche, M., Bergeron, J., and Barbaro-Forleo, G. (2001), 'Targeting Consumers Who are Willing to Pay More for Environmentally Friendly Products'. *Journal of Consumer Marketing*, 18: 503–20.

[11] Murray, S. (2001), 'Green Products: consumers count cost over ecology'. *Financial Times*, 5 November: 4.

[12] Rayport, J. F. and Sviokla, J. J. (1995), 'Exploiting the Virtual Value Chain'. *Harvard Business Review*, November–December: 75–85.

SUGGESTED FURTHER READING

A wide-ranging review of organizations' environment is given in the following:

Palmer, A. and Hartley, B. (2002), *The Business Environment*, Maidenhead, Berks: McGraw-Hill.

Marketing's changing role within commercial organizations is discussed in the following:

Achrol, R. (1991), 'Evolution of the Marketing Organization: new forms for turbulent environments'. *Journal of Marketing*, October: 77–93.

Gummesson E. (1991), 'Marketing Orientation Revisited: the crucial role of the part-time marketer'. *European Journal of Marketing*, 25(2): 60–75.

Piercy, N. (2003), *Market-Led Strategic Change: transforming the process of going to market.* Oxford: Butterworth–Heinemann.

The following references provide further discussion of marketing relationships between a company and its suppliers and customers:

Christopher, M., Payne, A., and Ballantyne, D. (2002), *Relationship Marketing: creating shareholder value.* Oxford: Butterworth Heinemann.

Gummesson, E. (2001), *Total Relationship Marketing: rethinking marketing management.* Oxford: Butterworth Heinemann.

Varey, R. J. (2002), *Relationship Marketing: dialogue and networks in the e-commerce era.* Chichester: John Wiley.

The difficulties of understanding and assessing the impacts of change in the economic environment on a firm's marketing activities are discussed in the following:

Cleaver, T. (2002), *Understanding the World Economy.* London: Routledge.

Griffiths, A. and Wall, S. (eds.) (2001), *Applied Economics: an introductory course*, 9th edn. Hemel Hempstead (UK): Prentice-Hall.

Organizational culture has been referred to in this chapter as having a major impact on an organization's marketing effectiveness, and the following references explore internal and external dimensions of culture:

Ahmed, P. K. and Rafiq, M. (2002), *Internal Marketing: tools and concepts for customer focused management*. Oxford: Butterworth Heinemann.

Cray, D. and Mallory, G. (1998), *Making Sense of Managing Culture*. London: International Thomson Business Press.

Hofstede, G. (1997), *Culture and Organizations*. Maidenhead, Berks: McGraw-Hill.

For a general review of 'environmentalism', and its effects on business, the following references provide a useful overview of the issues involved:

Freeman, E., Dodd, R., and Pierce, J. (2000), *Environmentalism and the New Logic of Business*. New York: Oxford University Press.

Prakash, A. (2000), *Greening the Firm: the politics of corporate environmentalism*. Cambridge: Cambridge University Press.

For a discussion of business ethics and good corporate governance, the following references are useful:

Monks, R. and Minow, N. (eds.) (2001), *Corporate Governance*. Oxford: Blackwell.

Schlegelmilch, B. B. (1998*), Marketing Ethics: an international perspective*. London: International Thomson Business Press.

Velasquez, M. G. (2001), *Business Ethics: concepts and cases*. Englewood Cliffs, NJ: Prentice-Hall.

USEFUL WEB LINKS

Visit the companion website to this book, with lots of interesting material and links for each chapter:

www.oup.com/uk/booksites/busecon

UK Open Government home page

www.open.gov.uk

EU home page:

europa.eu.int

Biz/ed: a student and lecturers' resource site containing items relating to marketing within organizations

www.bized.ac.uk

Greenpeace International

www.greenpeace.org

Corporate Governance Institute, Blueprint for Good Governance

www.pli.edu/chb/Corporate_Gover.html

KEYWORDS

- **Accelerator effect**
- **Birth rate**

- Business cycle
- Competitors
- Corporate governance
- Cultural convergence
- Demography
- Disintermediation
- Ecological environment
- Economic growth
- Ethics
- Flexible organization
- Gross Domestic Product (GDP)
- Intermediaries
- Internal environment
- Internet
- Macro-environment
- Marketing environment
- Micro-environment
- Multiplier effect
- Pressure groups
- Relationship marketing
- Shareholders
- Stakeholders
- System
- SWOT analysis
- Value chain
- Virtual organization

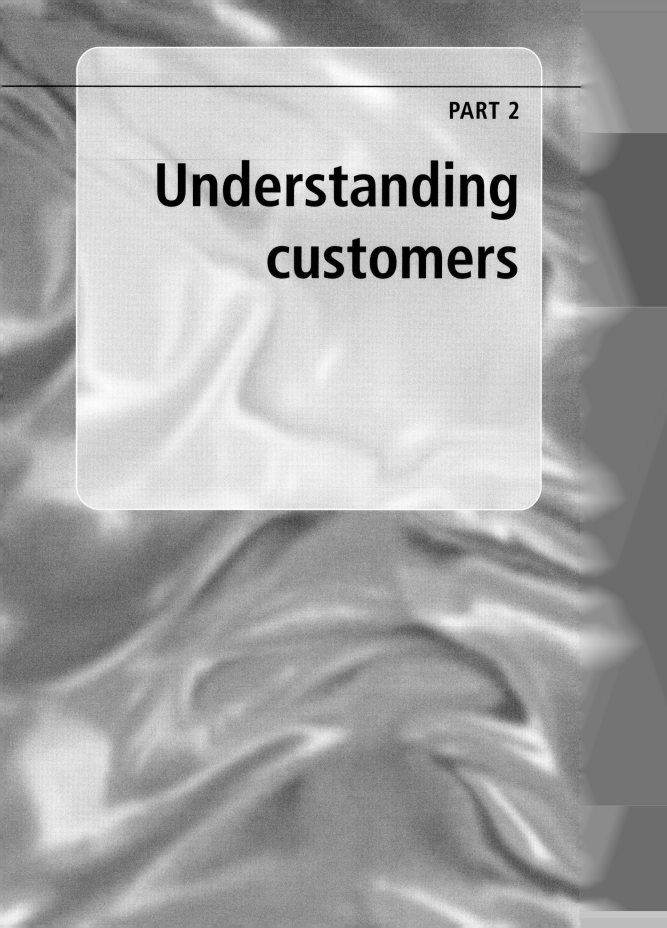

PART 2

Understanding customers

Buyer behaviour and relationship development

CHAPTER OBJECTIVES

Faced with competing products, it is important for companies to understand how buyers go about choosing between the alternatives. A thorough understanding of buyer behaviour should be reflected in product design, pricing, promotion, and distribution, all of which should satisfy the needs of individuals' buying processes. This chapter explores basic theories of buyer behaviour. Distinctions between personal and organizational buyer behaviour are noted, especially in the composition of the decision-making unit. Companies generally seek to influence buyer behaviour so that the company becomes customers' first choice of supplier. This chapter reviews methods by which companies seek to turn one-off casual buying behaviour into ongoing buyer–seller relationships.

Introduction

A company may think that it has developed the perfect product, one that customers will be queuing up to buy. But despite putting possibly years into new product development, it could find its efforts wasted as buyers reject its product in the few minutes, or sometimes even seconds, that it might take them to choose between competing products. The company may have failed to understand the complex processes by which buyers make purchasing decisions. It may, for example have underestimated the role played by key influencers in the decision process and aimed its marketing effort at those individuals who really don't count for a lot in the final decision. It may have spent the bulk of its promotional effort at a time when buyers were not at a receptive stage in the buying process.

Companies undertake marketing activities in order to elicit some kind of response from buyers. The ultimate aim of that activity is to get customers to buy their products, and to come back again. Most of this book breaks marketing activities down into distinct areas of decisions that have to be made by marketing managers, for example pricing decisions and promotion decisions. However, while companies may break their planning down into small manageable chunks, customers make an assessment based on a holistic view of the total product offer. How customers perceive the whole offer and react to it may be quite different from what the company had expected when it was developing its marketing plan. In the case of sales to commercial buyers, the task of understanding who is involved in the buying process and what procedures are adopted becomes even more complex. Faced with a sometimes bewildering array of choices, buyers seek to simplify the choice process, for example by sticking with brand names they are familiar with.

In short, buying processes can be complex, involving many people over a sometimes lengthy period of time. Making false assumptions about these processes can result in an otherwise good product not being bought.

This chapter will explore a number of dimensions in the complexity of buying behaviour:

- What factors motivate an individual to seek out a purchase?

- What sources of information are used in evaluating competing products?

- What is the relative importance attached by decision makers to each of the elements of the product offer?

- What is the set of competing products from which consumers make their final choice?

- Who is involved in making the purchase decision?

- How long the does the process of making a decision take?

- How can a seller affect buyers' subsequent behaviour so that it becomes the preferred supplier, tied by a formal or informal relationship?

Buying situations

Of course, buying processes vary between products and between individuals. For the purpose of studying buying behaviour, a number of categories of buying situations can be identified.

- **Routine rebuy**: The buyer makes a purchase decision in these situations almost instinctively, without giving the process any thought. It is like routinely buying the same daily newspaper.

- **Modified rebuy**: The buyer may be familiar with a class of product, but this time want something a little different. For example, she may often buy a tin of paint, but on this occasion she needs paint specifically for a job in hand which may be novel to her (such as covering external masonry), so she is likely to engage in limited search processes to identify and evaluate alternatives.

- **Completely novel**: The buyer has no previous experience of buying this type of product, so the search process is likely to be longer, with a greater range of information sources being consulted.

In addition, the sophistication of the buying process is influenced by the level of **involvement** that a buyer has in the product being purchased.

- With high-involvement products, buyers have a close relationship with the product. The manner in which the product is used has the capacity to deeply affect their happiness and they cannot easily ignore the product. Items of clothing and many personal medical services fall into this category.

- Low-involvement products have less consequence for individuals' psychological well-being. If a mistake is made in choosing an unsuitable product, they will not worry about it unduly. They can normally live with the consequences of making a mistake in their washing powder purchase, but a mistake in their choice of outer clothing may affect their self-image.

Involvement is closely associated with risk. High-involvement purchase decisions are seen as being more risky in terms of their outcomes, so buyers are likely to spend more time and effort in trying to avoid a bad purchase for such products.

Further variety in the buying process is evident from the major differences that can occur between private individuals and organizations in the way they make purchase decisions. These differences are considered later in this chapter.

■ The buying process

The basic processes involved in purchase decisions are illustrated in Figure 3.1. Simple models of buyer behaviour usually see an underlying need triggering a search for need-satisfying solutions. When possible solutions have been identified, these are evaluated according to some criteria. The final purchase decision is often a result of the interaction between the final decision maker and a range of influencers. Eventually, after purchase and consumption, the consumer will develop feelings about the purchase that will influence future purchase decisions. In reality, however, purchase decision processes can be complex iterative processes involving large numbers of influencers and a variety of decision criteria. It is often unrealistic to see the stages of the buying process as being completely separate; for example, evaluation often takes place while the search for information is still ongoing.

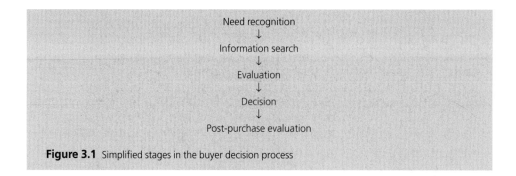

Figure 3.1 Simplified stages in the buyer decision process

Needs as buying process initiators

A need for something triggers the buying process. Needs provide a motive for an individual's action and can be very complex. Because they are a deep-seated initiator of buying behaviour, marketers are very keen to understand how needs are formed and manifested.

A need can be defined as a perceived state of deprivation, which motivates an individual to take actions to eliminate that sense of deprivation. A *need* is deep-rooted in an individual's personality. How the individual seeks to satisfy a need will be conditioned by the society of which he is a member. As an example, the need for status may be fairly universal, but its expression differs between cultures. In many less developed economies the need for status may be acquired by owning large numbers of cattle. In western countries the need is more likely to be satisfied by ownership of a particular brand of car. These manifestations of needs are sometimes referred to as *wants*. Wants are the culturally influenced manifestation of a deep-seated need. Of course, we can all want many products, but not buy or be able to buy them. Marketers are ultimately interested in *demand*, which can be defined as a willingness and ability to buy a product that satisfies a need.

An individual's needs are influenced by a wide range of psychological and sociological factors. We can begin our understanding of needs by focusing on those psychological factors that are inherent to an individual.

Physiological and psychological bases of needs

Genetic makeup clearly has some effect on buying behaviour. For example, physiological factors can influence an individual's appetite for food. Some people are said to be more 'impulsive' shoppers than others, and researchers have attributed part of the explanation for this behaviour to genetics. Differences have also been noted in the needs of male and female buyers and the way they approach purchasing decisions. Of course, there is continuing debate about whether, and to what extent, such behaviours are inherent in our nature, or are the result of nurture through a socialization process. Either

Figure 3.2 The market for sun protection products has become increasingly complex, as consumers' needs have changed. Marketers have recognized that the cheap bottle of sun oil from a pharmacy or supermarket is not going to satisfy the needs of increasingly discerning buyers who seek a sun oil that is suitable for their particular skin type. In addition, the desire for a natural tan has been supplemented with a growing awareness of the need to avoid the dangers of skin cancer. The Calypso brand has been progressively extended and developed to cater for these increasingly complex needs (Reproduced with permission of Linco CARE Limited)

way, it is important for marketers to recognize differences between individuals in what motivates them to buy.

It is wrong to equate needs solely with physiological drivers. We no longer live in a society in which the main motivation of individuals is to satisfy the basic needs for food and drink.

Maslow [10] recognized that, once individuals have satisfied these basic physiological needs, they may seek to satisfy social needs—for example, the need to have meaningful

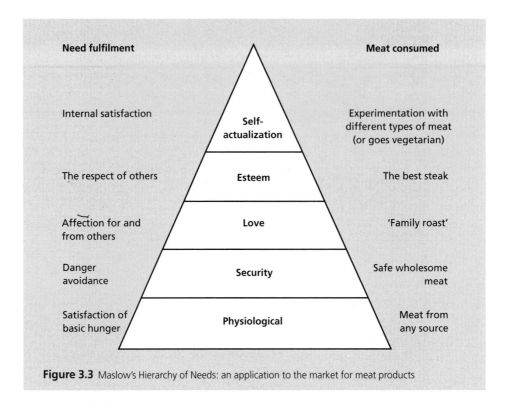

Need fulfilment   **Meat consumed**

Internal satisfaction   Self-actualization   Experimentation with different types of meat (or goes vegetarian)

The respect of others   Esteem   The best steak

Affection for and from others   Love   'Family roast'

Danger avoidance   Security   Safe wholesome meat

Satisfaction of basic hunger   Physiological   Meat from any source

Figure 3.3 Maslow's Hierarchy of Needs: an application to the market for meat products

interaction with peers (see Figure 3.3). More complex still, western cultures see increasing numbers of people seeking to satisfy essentially internal needs for self-satisfaction. Products therefore satisfy increasingly complex needs. Food is no longer seen as a basic necessity to be purchased and cooked for self-consumption. With growing prosperity, people have sought to satisfy social needs by eating out with friends or family. Satisfaction of such social needs may be supplemented with a higher-order need to experience different types of meals. The great growth in eating out that occurred during the 1970s and 1980s has been followed by a growing diversity of restaurants that cater for people's need for variety and curiosity—hence the emergence in most larger European towns of Balti, Creole, and Far Eastern restaurants.

Maslow's hierarchy of needs is no more than a conceptual model, and it is difficult actually to measure where an individual is positioned on the hierarchy of needs. Furthermore, it is essentially based on western values of motivation, and there is a lot of evidence of cultural influences on needs (e.g. Jai-Ok *et al.* [9]). How, for example, would you explain religious sacrifice and penance, which are important motivators for many non-western consumers?

Maslow has presented one model of motivation which marketers have adopted widely as a conceptual framework. There are other frameworks for understanding the psychological bases for human motivation.

- **Freudian analysis** sees human behaviour as directed by a repression of feelings from early childhood. What comes naturally to a young child is often considered socially unacceptable, so such behaviour is socialized out before the child reaches adulthood. Behaviour is the outcome of the interaction between the id (the primitive unconscious basis of the psyche dominated by primary urges) and the ego (conscious perceptions that act as an inhibiting agency).

- **Stimulus–response models of motivation** have been widely used by marketers to understand needs. Analogies have been drawn between Pavlov's dog (who came to associate the sound of a bell with food) and everyday marketing situations. The existence of cues in the environment, such as advertising, can help trigger the buying process, even though the initial cue has no direct connection with the need an individual is seeking to satisfy. In this way, the sight of a well-known celebrity endorser can trigger the process of seeking out a brand of food that she endorses.

MARKETING in ACTION

Is Freud fit for marketing?

Freudian analyses of human motivation based on repression have sometimes achieved notoriety for their explanations of human behaviour. Is smoking really a substitute for the repressed desire of a child to suck its thumb? Think about the two following cases of supposedly repressed feelings, their explanation, and possible opportunities for marketers:

1. Children inherently dislike order and prefer creative chaos: it is only adults that teach children to be tidy and to structure their lives. Possible marketing opportunity—toys and novelties for adults that recreate a sense of chaos, such as 'silly string', party poppers, and some modern art.

2. Children like to be cared for by a mother figure. As adults we take on board such responsibilities, but we would sometimes be happy to go back to a simple dependent child–mother relationship. Possible marketing opportunity—a wide range of personal services aimed to pamper adults as if they were children again, including hairdressing, beauty salons, and health farms. Who else can exploit this desire to be a pampered, dependent child? Restaurants? Airlines?

Is an analysis of repression of any use to marketers in trying to understand human motivation? Or is it a highly speculative approach that may be intuitively appealing, but is only one of a number of possible explanations of the observed behaviour?

Sociological influences on needs

You will recall that needs were defined earlier as being inherent in an individual. However, the manifestation of these needs is influenced by the society in which an individual lives, and there is a lot of research evidence of how these social influences work (see e.g. Butcher, Sparks, and O'Callaghan [3]). A number of levels of influence can be identified:

- The family influences a child's perception of the world, and this influence lasts into adulthood. Examples of this effect on buying processes can be found in adults' selection of a particular brand of breakfast cereal because it is the one that they were brought up with.

- Individuals are surrounded by peer groups (or reference groups) which act as a guide for behaviour. Peer groups can be primary and direct in their influence (e.g. colleagues at work and school), or they can be secondary and indirect (for example the guidance to behaviour provided by pop stars or media figures).

- Individuals can identify with a social class, and the values of this class can influence behaviour. As an example, individuals who identify with the 'working class' may feel alienated by an up-market retail outlet such as the Gap compared with the traditional values epitomized in Woolworths.

- Culture in its widest sense influences our buying behaviour. Concepts such as self-centredness, the desire for immediate results, and deference to suppliers can differ significantly between cultures (see Hofstede [7]).

Situational factors influencing needs

In addition to our inherent physiological and psychological makeup, our needs are influenced by the situation in which we currently find ourselves. The subjects of age and socio-economic status can have profound effects on buying behaviour, as we will see in Chapter 5 when we look at market segmentation. In addition, the stage that an individual has reached in the 'family life-cycle' has a significant influence on needs. There have been numerous descriptions of the typical family life-cycle. One of the earliest—and still widely cited—classifications was developed by Wells and Gubar [16], who identified a number of stages, each associated with distinctive sets of needs:

1. Bachelor stage: young, single people not living at home
2. Newly married couples: young, no children
3. Full nest 1: youngest child under 6
4. Full nest 2: youngest child over 6
5. Full nest 3: older married couples with dependent children
6. Empty nest 1: older married couples, no children living at home
7. Empty nest 2: older married couples, retired, no children living at home
8. Solitary survivor: still working
9. Solitary survivor 2: retired

Figure 3.4 The shoemaker Clarks has a long tradition of making comfortable, rugged shoes which have created high levels of customer loyalty. However, among many younger people the company's shoes have been regarded as something their parents might wear, but as not having the street credibility of shoes bearing the brand name of competitors' such as Timberland. Clarks has set about the task of winning social approval for its shoes among younger segments' peer groups, something that is communicated in this advertisement

Reproduced with permission of C & J Clark International Limited.

More recent refinements of family life-cycle stages have sought to take account of their increasing complexity, brought about by the breakdown of the traditional nuclear family and the emergence of deviations from the norm such as single-parent families, extended cohabitation before marriage, and groups of young people sharing a house before they can afford their own. However, all family life-cycle models make the same important point: an individual's needs are likely to change as he or she goes through life. An individual moving from a bachelor stage to one with dependent children will face a reordering of priorities, reflecting a different set of needs. This will also most likely be matched by a reduction in discretionary expenditure.

Information search

Once a need has triggered a search for need-satisfying solutions, the search for information will begin. But where do buyers look for information when making purchases? In the case of the routine repurchase of a familiar product, probably very little information is sought about the product. But where there is a greater element of uncertainty, buyers will seek out information about the alternative ways in which they can satisfy their needs, especially where a high level of risk is involved. The following information sources are likely to be used.

- Personal experience will be a starting point, so, if a buyer has already used a company's products, the suitability of the proposed purchase may be assessed in the light of the previous purchases.
- Word-of-mouth recommendation from friends is important for many categories of goods and services where an individual may have had no previous need to make a purchase. When looking for a plumber or a solicitor, for example, many people will seek the advice of friends. Increasingly, buyers are looking to the internet to gather recommendations, through web sites, chat rooms, bulletin boards, and e-mail requests to friends.
- Rather than referring to people we know, we may use various other reference groups to guide us. What type of sports shoes are sports heroes wearing at the moment? What kind of drink is considered to be fashionable with our age group?
- Newspaper editorial content and directories such as those published by the Consumers' Association may be consulted as a relatively objective source of information. Internet guides such as Goldfish (**www.goldfish.co.uk**) may be consulted.
- Advertising and promotion in all of its forms is taken on board, sometimes being specifically sought and at other times just being casually noticed.

The greater the perceived risk of a purchase, the longer and more widespread is the search for information. Of course, individuals differ in the extent to which they are prepared to collect information methodically—some may make a purchase more impulsively than other, more calculating, individuals.

Perception

We may consciously seek out information, but may nevertheless fail to process the information that is presented to us. There are three key perceptual processes that can get

Figure 3.5 In the UK domestic gas and electricity supply market, consumers are faced with a sometimes bewildering and confusing choice of suppliers, all offering a basic commodity product, which by law cannot be differentiated. Evaluation is made more difficult because the different companies choose different bases for pricing, with many companies offering several different price plans. Some give introductory discounts, some give low user discounts and many give discounts for payment by direct debit. The website www.buy.co.uk has become a popular choice for many consumers seeking comparative information on a novel purchase. This calculator for gas and electricity guides consumers through all the choices available and identifies which supplier and price plan is best for them. It is claimed that an average family who switches suppliers on buy.co.uk or uSwitch.com saves £140 on their annual energy bills (Reproduced with permission of buy.co.uk)

in the way between the presentation of information and the using of that information for evaluation:

1. We may fail to perceive the information because it fails to attract our attention (**selective attention**).

2. We may perceive the information, but then distort its content (**selective distortion**).

3. We may perceive the information, but then forget it very quickly *(***selective retention***)*.

There is evidence that each sense receptor requires some minimum level of energy (or 'absolute threshold') to excite it before perception is organized. As well as the absolute threshold, there is a 'differential threshold', which is the smallest amount by which two stimuli must be different in order to be perceived as different. These thresholds are known to fluctuate, and individuals have many different perceptions that are influenced by their education, upbringing, experience, and many other factors.

We will return to the subject of perception in Chapter 10 when we look at communication processes within the context of the promotional mix.

Evaluation

In the process of gathering information, the total range of products available in the marketplace is gradually filtered down to a manageable number for evaluation (Figure 3.6). Choice is made from a select set of possibilities, and these choice sets can be classified according to their selectivity:

- The **total set** comprises all products that are capable of satisfying a given need.

- The **awareness set** comprises all of those products that the consumer is aware of. (The 'unaware set' is the opposite of the awareness set.)

- The **consideration set** includes those items within the awareness set that the consumer considers buying.

- The **choice set** is the group of products from which a final decision is ultimately made.

- Along the way to defining the choice set, some products will have been rejected as they are perceived to be unavailable, unaffordable, unsuitable, etc. These comprise the **infeasible set**.

Research should seek to establish the choice set against which a company's product is being compared, and on this basis the marketing programme can be adapted in order to achieve competitive advantage against other members of the choice set.

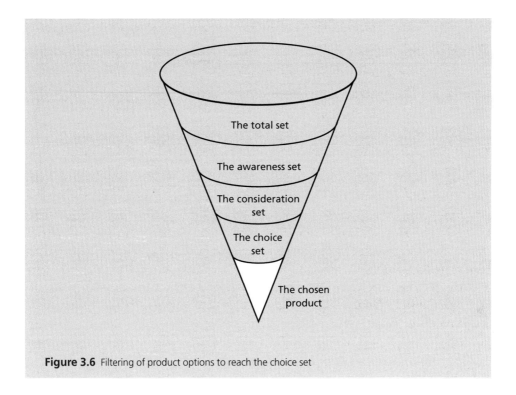

Figure 3.6 Filtering of product options to reach the choice set

A private buyer seeking to buy a low-value, low-involvement product such as an electric kettle may have narrowed down the choice set to four kettles. Analysts of buyer
behaviour have developed a number of frameworks for trying to understand how a
consumer chooses between these competing alternatives. In one such framework the
consumer uses a sense of intuition as to which seems best. Such non-systematic methods of evaluation may be quite appropriate where the product in question involves low
levels of cost, risk, and involvement.

Even apparently intuitive bases of evaluation can be reduced to a series of rules,
implying some systematic foundation. One framework is a multiple-attribute choice
matrix which holds that consumers refer to a number of component attributes of a
product to evaluate its overall suitability. Figure 3.7 shows a typical matrix in which
four competing electric kettles are compared in terms of five important attributes. In
this matrix, the four short-listed kettles in the choice set are shown by the column
headings A, B, C, and D. The left-hand column lists five attributes which research
has suggested buyers use to make their purchase decision (price, reputation of the
brand name, colour, styling, capacity). The second column shows the importance the

	Importance weights (out of 10)	Scores for each attribute for each kertle (0 = poor, 10 = excellent)			
		A	B	C	D
Price	10	10	7	8	10
Brand name	9	10	9	8	8
Colour	8	10	10	9	9
Styling	7	10	10	10	5
Capacity	6	4	10	10	4
Overall rating		44	46	45	36
Weighted rating		36.4	36.1	35.4	30.3

Overall rating = the sum total of scores for all attributes;

Weighted rating = the sum total of scores for all attributes, in which each attribute has been multiplied by its importance weight. (The importance weight is expressed as a percentage of the maximum score of 10 points.)

Figure 3.7 A hypothetical choice set for kettles: a multiple attribute matrix

consumer attaches to each attribute of the service (with maximum importance being given a score of 10 and a completely unimportant attribute a score of zero). The following four columns show how each kettle scores against each of the five evaluation attributes.

If it is assumed that a consumer evaluates each product without weighting each attribute, kettle B will be preferred, as it has the highest overall rating. However, it is more realistic to expect that some attributes will be weighted as being more important than others; therefore the alternative *linear compensatory* approach is based on consumers creating weighted scores for each product. The importance of each attribute is multiplied by the score for each attribute, so in this case kettle A is preferred, as the attributes of A that consumers rank most highly are also those that are considered to be the most important.

A third approach to evaluation is sometimes described as a *lexicographic approach*. This involves the buyer in starting his evaluation by looking at the most important attribute and ruling out those products that do not meet a minimum standard; evaluation is then based on the second most important attribute, with products being eliminated that do not meet this standard. The process continues until only one option is left. In Figure 3.7 price is given as the most important attribute, so the initial evaluation may have reduced the choice set to A and D (which score highest on price). In the second round, brand name becomes the most important decision criterion; only A and D remain in the choice set, and as A has the highest score for brand name, it will be chosen in preference to A.

Decision

It is important to understand who is actually responsible for making a purchase decision. Both private and organizational purchases usually involve large numbers of people; for example, household purchases may involve joint decision making between a husband and wife, with other family members acting as influencers. The subject of 'The Decision-Making Unit' is considered later in this chapter.

The outcome of the evaluation process may be a decision to do any of the following:

1. buy now;
2. do not buy at all;
3. defer the process;
4. start the process again.

Even when a positive decision to buy a product (e.g. the electric kettle used in the example above) is made, further decisions have to be taken to put the main decision into effect; for example:

- When will the product be bought?
- From which retailer?
- How many will be bought?
- Will any optional accessories be bought?
- How will the purchase be paid for (e.g. cash or credit card)?

Post-purchase evaluation

Wise marketers realize that purchasing activity doesn't end when a sale has been made. The buyer takes the product away and continues to develop feelings about it that will influence his decision next time he needs to make a purchase in that product category. The buyer will also be likely to tell his friends about the purchase, making either favourable or unfavourable comments. Many companies regard satisfied customers as their best form of promotion.

Cognitive dissonance

Buyers approach a purchase with a set of expectations about the performance of the product they are purchasing. A company's advertising and sales messages often serve to heighten expectations about the product's performance. Of course, these expectations are often not met. Maybe the product didn't perform adequately, or the buyer's expectations were simply unrealistically high. In either case, the result is to create what is

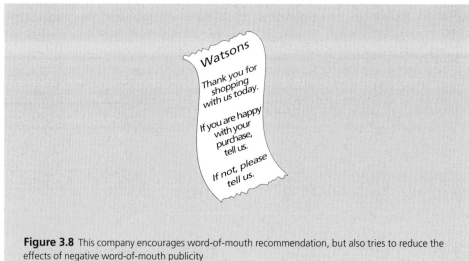

Figure 3.8 This company encourages word-of-mouth recommendation, but also tries to reduce the effects of negative word-of-mouth publicity

often referred to as *cognitive dissonance*, in which our expectations are out of line with the reality around us. We can handle dissonance in a number of ways.

- We can often simply return the goods and make a fresh purchase decision. The failed decision becomes part of a learning experience.

- Sometimes it is not possible to return the product. In the case of services that have already been consumed, this option is generally impossible. We may, alternatively, go about complaining and telling our friends about the bad product. Estimates vary, but it is reckoned that on average a dissatisfied customer tells between five and ten people about his or her bad purchase.

- We can try and reduce dissonance by internal psychological processes. We may convince ourselves that we didn't really make a bad decision, but our expectations were simply too high. We may clutch at minor features of the product that we like, to offset the major features that we dislike. We do not like to think that we made a mistake, so we may try to convince ourselves that we were right in our choice.

Companies often devote part of their promotional budget to reminding customers that they made the right choice in their purchase. Many companies write a short letter to recent customers, providing further reassurance to waverers that they have made the best choice. A convinced happy customer will be more likely to recommend a product to friends and to return to the same supplier next time.

MARKETING and the INTERNET

From word of mouth to word of mouse

Word-of-mouth recommendation can be an important way of influencing buyers' choices, but it has traditionally been a fairly slow means of spreading recommendation about a product. Now, the internet has allowed the whole process to be speeded up and has widened its impact. From word of mouth, companies now talk about 'word of mouse', leading to 'viral marketing', in which a purchase recommendation can spread very quickly as one person passes on a message to half a dozen friends, each of whom in turn passes on the message to another half dozen friends. Chat rooms and websites devoted to customer complaints and comments (e.g. **www.complaints.com; www.dooyou.com**) allow happy or complaining customers to spread their message very quickly. Some companies have attracted unauthorized websites devoted to criticism of the company (e.g. the McSpotlight site **www.mcspotlight.org**, which carries information critical of McDonald's Restaurants, and the Boycott Shell site **www.essential.org/action/shell**). News now crosses geographical frontiers more quickly than a blink of the eye, and corporate reputations can be savaged as disgruntled customers and shareholders swap comments on the World Wide Web.

Specialist agencies try to manage this growing word of mouse. One consultancy, Edelman, monitors the internet and claims to routinely check 33,000 user groups and bulletin boards. From what it finds, it often prepares web pages for its clients in anticipation of crises, which are then 'hidden' on the website, ready to be activated if needed. Businesses have had to face up to the new realities of the internet, and response times need to be immediate.

However, even though technology may have advanced, old questions remain, especially: Why did a company allow itself to get into the position of exposing itself to criticism? Could this not have been foreseen? If there is little for people to spread bad stories about, the dissident websites would probably lose much of their support.

The decision-making unit (DMU)

In practice, few purchase decisions are made by an individual without reference to others. Usually other people are involved in some sort of role and have a bearing on the final purchase decision. It is important to recognize who the key players in this process are, in order that a product can be configured to meet these people's needs, and that promotional messages can be adapted and directed to the key individuals involved in the purchase decision. A number of roles can be identified among people involved in the decision process (Figure 3.9).

Influencers

These are people or groups of people whom the decision maker refers to in the process of making a decision. You will recall that reference groups can be primary in the form

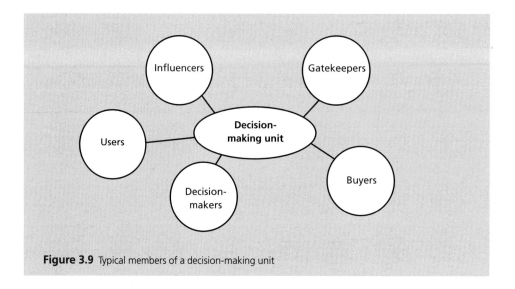

Figure 3.9 Typical members of a decision-making unit

of friends, acquaintances, and work colleagues, or secondary in the form of remote personalities with whom there is no two-way interaction. Where research indicates that the primary reference group exerts a major influence on purchase decisions, this could indicate the need to take measures that will facilitate word-of-mouth communication—e.g. giving established customers rewards in return for the introduction of new customers. An analysis of secondary reference groups used by consumers in the decision process can help in a number of ways. It will indicate possible personalities to be approached who may be used to endorse a product in the company's advertising. It will also indicate which opinion leaders an organization should target as part of its communication programme in order to achieve the maximum 'trickle-down' effect. The media can be included within this secondary reference group—what a newspaper writes in its columns can have an important influence on purchase decisions.

Gatekeepers

These are most commonly found among commercial buyers. Their main effect is to act as a filter on the range of products that enter the decision choice set. Gatekeepers can take a number of forms—for example, a buying manager's personal assistant barring calls from sales representatives has the effect of screening out a number of possible choices. In many organizations it can be difficult to establish just who is acting as a gatekeeper; identifying a marketing strategy that gains acceptance by the gatekeeper, or bypasses him completely, is therefore made difficult. In larger organizations, and the public sector in particular, a select list of suppliers who are invited to submit tenders for work may exist—and if it is not on this list a supplier will be unable to enter the decision set.

Although gatekeepers are most commonly associated with purchases made by organizations, they can also be found in consumer purchase processes. In the case of many household goods and services, such as buying wallpaper or booking an overseas holiday, an early part of the decision process may be the collection of samples or brochures. While the final decision may be the subject of joint discussion and action, the initial stage of collecting the items for the decision set is more likely to be left to one person. In this way, one member of a family may pick up holiday brochures or samples of wallpaper, thereby acting as a gatekeeper and restricting the subsequent choice to the products of those companies whose brochures or samples were originally collected.

Buyers

In some cases, ordering a product may be reduced to a routine task and delegated to an individual. In the case of industrial goods and services, low-budget items that are not novel may be left to the discretion of a buyer. In this way, office stationery may be contracted by a buying clerk within the organization without immediate reference to anybody else. In the case of modified rebuys, or novel purchases, the decision-making unit is likely to be larger.

Users

The user of a product may not be the person responsible for making the actual purchase decision. This is typical of many items of clothing bought within household units. For example, it has been estimated that in the UK over half of all men's socks are bought by women. Parents buy products for their children, with varying levels of influence (or 'pester power') from the children who will be the actual users of the product. In the case of organizational purchases, there is often a separation between users and buyers and research should be undertaken to reveal the extent to which users are important contributors to the decision process. In the case of the business air travel market, it is important to understand the degree of pressure that individual travellers can exert on their choice of airline, as opposed to the influence of a company buyer (who might have arranged a long-term contract with one particular airline), a gatekeeper (who may discard promotional material relating to new airline services), or other influencers within the organization. (For example, cost centre managers might be more concerned with the cost of using a product, in contrast to the user's overriding concerning with its quality.)

Decision maker

This is the person (or groups of individuals) who makes the final decision to purchase, whether he executes the purchase himself or instructs others to do so. With many

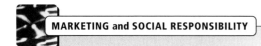

MARKETING and SOCIAL RESPONSIBILITY

Pester power pays

What role do children play in the purchase of the goods that they ultimately consume? There has been considerable debate about the extent of 'pester power', whereby parents give in to the demands of children. Increasingly, advertisers are aiming their promotional messages over the heads of adults and straight at children. The ethics of doing this have been questioned by many, and some countries, such as Sweden and Greece, have imposed restrictions on television advertising of children's products. A report published by the UK children's research company Childwise (*Childwise Monitor Report: Tracking Trends from 1994 to 2000*) showed how children's awareness of brands had continued to grow during the period covered. The report indicated that 50% of children aged 5–6 could name a brand of crisps or snack, and this rose to 83% for children aged 9–10. There was speculation about how children came to learn about these brands, with some pointing the finger at television advertising, especially during the breaks in children's programmes, while others who have studied children's behaviour claimed that children pick up 'cool' brands from their peer group. Despite a denial of its effects on children, many marketers of products consumed by children are quietly concerned by any moves towards EU integration of legislation on advertising to children. However, even with advertising restrictions, companies have managed to get through to children in more subtle ways, for example by sponsoring educational materials used in schools and paying celebrities to endorse their products. When it comes to such items as confectionery and toys, just what influence do children exert on the purchase decision? And when football clubs deliberately change their strip every season, is it unethical for the clubs to expect fanatical children to pester their parents to buy a new one so that they can keep up with their peer group?

family-based consumer products, it can be difficult to identify just who within the family carries most weight in making the final decision. Research into family purchases has suggested that, in the case of package holidays and furniture, women dominate in making the final decision, whereas in the case of financial services it is men who dominate. An analysis of how a decision is made can realistically be achieved only by means of qualitative in-depth research. In the case of decisions made by organizational buyers, the task of identifying the individuals responsible for making a final decision—and their level within the organizational hierarchy—becomes even more difficult.

Models of buyer decision-making

The buying process has now been portrayed as a highly complex one, in which a variety of personal and environmental factors influence the decisions we make. We can process a lot of information with outcomes that can sometimes be seen as

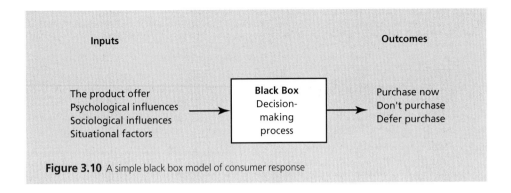

Figure 3.10 A simple black box model of consumer response

quite irrational. So how do we arrive at a decision to purchase one product rather than another?

A simple starting point is to take a 'black box' model of consumer response (Figure 3.10). The inputs to the decision process are the range of psychological, sociological, economic, and situational factors. The outcome is the decision (e.g. whether or not to purchase; whether to purchase now or to defer; where to buy from; how many; etc.). In between is the 'black box', comprising our decision-making processes. The black box determines how we translate complex information into decisions. As individuals, we differ in the way that our processing occurs.

Of course, a black box is a simple representation of the input–decision–outcome process. In itself, it does not explain how a decision is actually made. For this, a number of models of buyer behaviour have been developed. If a model is to have value to marketing managers, it should be capable of use as a predictive tool, given a set of conditions on which the model is based. For this reason, a number of researchers have sought to develop models that explain how buying decisions are made in specified situations, and from this to predict the likely consequences of changes to marketing strategy. Modelling buyer decision processes poses many problems. At one extreme, simple models may help in very general terms in developing marketing strategies, but are too general to be of use in any specific situation. At the other extreme, models of buyer behaviour based on narrowly defined sectors may lose much of their explanatory and predictive power if applied to another sector where assumptions on which the original model was based no longer apply. In any event, most models of buyer behaviour provide normative rather than strictly quantitative explanations of buyer behaviour, and there can be no guarantee that the assumptions on which the model was originally based continue to be valid.

One widely used model that has been widely applied and subsequently developed is that developed by Howard and Sheth [8]. The principles of their model are shown in Figure 3.11.

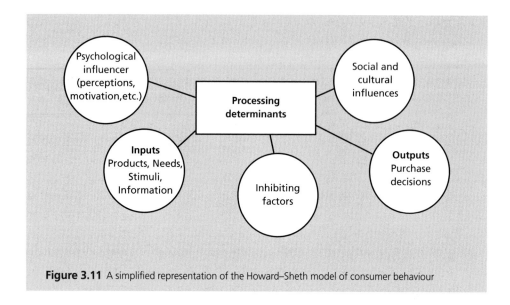

Figure 3.11 A simplified representation of the Howard–Sheth model of consumer behaviour

The framework incorporates a number of elements:

- **Inputs**: This element comprises information about the range of competing products that may satisfy a consumer's need. Information may be obtained from personal or published sources.

- **Behavioural determinants**: Individuals bring to the purchase decision a predisposition to act in a particular way. This predisposition is influenced by the culture that they live in and family and personality factors, among others.

- **Perceptual reaction**: Inputs are likely to be interpreted in different ways by different individuals, based on their unique personality makeup and conditioning which is a result of previous purchase experiences. While one person might readily accept the advertising messages of a bank, another might have been disappointed by that bank in the past, or by banks' advertising in general; she is therefore less likely to perceive such inputs as credible.

- **Processing determinants**: This part of the model focuses attention on the way in which a decision is made. Important determinants include the motivation of the individual to satisfy a particular need, the individual's past experience of a particular product or organization, and the weight attached to each of the factors used in the evaluation. For some consumers for some products, critical product requirements may exist which must be present if a product is to be included in the decision set. At other times, consumers attach weights to each of its attributes and select the product with the highest weighted 'score' (see Figure 3.7).

- **Inhibitors**: A number of factors might prevent an individual from making a decision to purchase a particular product, such as the ease of access to the product, its price, and the terms and conditions for delivery.

- **Outputs**: The outcome of the decision process may either be to go ahead and purchase, or alternatively, not to buy or to defer a decision to a later date.

More specific models of buyer behaviour have been developed as a result of research into specific sectors. Many of these have sought to rank in order of importance the factors that contribute towards the purchase decision, and to identify critical factors, the absence of which will exclude a possibility from a decision set. As an example, research into restaurant choice decisions by Auty [1] identified five key factors, ranking food quality as the most important, then image and atmosphere. However, it was also noted that the importance attached to each of these factors differed according to the purpose of the visit to the restaurant; the factors influencing a choice of restaurant for a celebration were quite different from those used for a general social occasion.

Personal and organizational buyer behaviour compared

At the beginning of this chapter it was noted that buying processes are likely to differ for situations where it is an organization rather than an individual making a purchase. Instead of being seen as completely different processes, all personal and organizational buying processes can be placed along a continuum (Wilson [17]). However, there are a number of features which characterize organizational buying processes.

- Two sets of needs are being met when an organization buys a product: the formal needs of the organization, and the personal needs of the individuals who make up the organization. The former might be thought of as being the more 'rational'. However, individuals within the organization seek to satisfy needs that are influenced by their own perceptual and behavioural environment, very much in the same way as would be the case with private consumer purchases.

- More people are typically involved in organizational purchases. High-value purchases may require evaluation and approval at a number of levels of an organization's management hierarchy. Research might indicate, for particular organizations or types of organization, the level at which a final decision is normally made. The analysis of the decision-making unit might also reveal a wider range of influencers present in the decision-making process.

- Organizational purchases are more likely to be made according to formalized routines. At its simplest, this may involve delegating to a junior buyer the task of making

Figure 3.12 If a domestic telephone breaks down, it may cause no more than annoyance and inconvenience to the owner. However, for business users, the consequences of a failure can be much more serious, possibly leading to lost sales, delayed orders and missed production. Few members of the organizational decision making unit would want to carry the blame for selecting a phone provider which subsequently lets the company down. For business customers, telephone providers must appeal to all members of the decision-making unit by stressing that its services are reliable and have benefits in use which will be good value to the company. BT, the largest provider in the UK telecoms market, offers numerous packages for its domestic market. However, this advertisement aimed at the business sector stresses a particular concern of business user—the need to get a faulty phone repaired quickly so that business is not interrupted (Reproduced with permission of British Telecom PLC)

repeat orders for goods and services that have previously been evaluated. At the other extreme, many high-value purchases may be made only after a formal process of bidding and evaluation has been undertaken.

- The elements of the product offer that are considered critical in the evaluation process are likely to differ. For many products, the emphasis placed on price by many personal buyers is replaced by reliability and performance characteristics by the organizational buyer. In many cases, poor performance of a product can have direct financial consequences for an organization—a low-price but unreliable computer might merely cause annoyance and frustration to a private buyer, but might lead to lost production output or lost sales for an organizational buyer.

- The greater number of people involved in organizational buying also often results in the whole process taking longer. A desire to minimize risk is inherent in many formal organizational motives and informally present in the motives of individuals within organizations. This often results in lengthy feasibility studies being undertaken. In some new markets, especially overseas markets, trust in suppliers might be an important factor for purchasers when evaluating competing suppliers, and it may take time to build up a trusting relationship before any purchase commitment is secured.

Developing ongoing relationships with buyers

It was noted earlier that the buying process generally does not end when a purchase is completed. For many products, the purchase and subsequent use of the product provides input to the next purchase decision. Companies have recognized that it can be profitable to cultivate long-term customers; hence the emergence of 'relationship marketing' as an alternative to a one-off transaction-based approach to marketing. Mar-

1. **Before the development of relationship marketing**
   - Assume that the bank has 500,000 customers and loses 10% of these each year, for one reason or another.
   - This implies that the average length of relationship between the company and its customers is 10 years.
   - It costs £100 to recruit a new customer (in advertising, incentives, and processing costs). In order to replace its lapsed customers, it spends £5,000,000 a year (50,000 lapsed customers to replace × £100) on advertising and customer recruitment.
   - The company makes an average profit of £50 per year from each of its customers.

2. **After the introduction of a relationship marketing programme**
   - A customer care programme is introduced which costs £20 per customer. (This may include the cost of sending a magazine to all customers, setting up an improved customer service centre, offering rewards for loyalty, etc.)
   - The customer defection rate falls from 10% to 5% per year.
   - The average relationship duration is therefore extended from 10 to 20 years.

3. **Financial effects on the company**
   - Each new customer now represents a profit potential of 20 years × £50 per year = £1,000, rather than 10 years × £50 = £500, a gain of £500.
   - The net effect, after taking into account the additional expenditure of £20 per year per customer for a customer care programme, is to increase the lifetime profitability of each new customer by £100 (previously 10 years × £50 per year profit = £500 lifetime value; now 20 years × (£50 per year profit − £20 per year customer care programme) = £600.
   - If the company were content to maintain a stable volume of business, it could cut by half the number of new customers it needs to recruit each year, from 50,000 to 25,000. At a recruitment cost of £100 per new customer, this saves the company £2,500,000 per year.

In summary, on the basis of these very simplistic assumptions, revenues (in terms of customer lifetime value) have been increased and costs (recruitment of new customers) have fallen.

Figure 3.13 An illustrative example of the financial effects of developing customer retention strategies for a bank

keting managers have seen the potential advantages of reducing levels of customer 'churn' by improving the retention rates of profitable customers. Within the academic community, although some have viewed relationship marketing merely as an applied topic of marketing with an insubstantial theory base, others have argued that relational exchange represents a paradigm shift in marketing thought (e.g. Gronroos [6]; Morgan and Hunt [11]).

There have been many attempts to demonstrate the benefits to a company of retaining its existing customers rather than continually seeking new customers to replace lapsed ones (e.g. Reichheld and Sasser [14]). The benefits can be demonstrated by reference to the example shown in Figure 3.13, which shows the effects on a bank's profits of reducing its customer defection rate. Of course, this simple example is based on many assumptions, for example that all customers are of equal profit potential. Nevertheless, it powerfully illustrates the potential financial benefits to a company resulting from successfully developing a relationship marketing strategy.

 **MARKETING in ACTION**

A £20 meal or a lifelong relationship?

What is the lifetime value of a restaurant customer? First-time customers may be spending only £20 on this occasion, but if they like what they get, how much are they likely to spend in the future? A typical diner eating out just once a month could be worth £2,000 in five years. If customers are happy, they are likely to tell their friends—if they're not, they are likely to tell even more of their friends. It follows that customers should be seen as investments, to be carefully nurtured over time. When things go wrong (for example through overbooking) it would probably be to the restaurant's advantage to spend heavily on putting things right for the customer (e.g. by offering money off a future meal). Judged on the basis of the current transaction, the restaurant may make a loss, but it will have protected its investment in a future income stream.

Like all investments, some are worth more than others. How should a company decide which customers are worth investing in? And what level of investment can be justified in terms of the speculative future income that could result from the relationship?

Reasons for the development of ongoing customer relationships

Relational exchange is not a new concept; it has been observed, for example, in the pattern of exchanges between textile manufacturers and intermediaries in Victorian England (Clegg [4]). Also, while relationships may have been rediscovered in the west, they have remained a fundamental part of exchange in many eastern cultures (Ohame [13]).

In recent times, organizations' growing interest in developing closer relationships with their private and corporate customers has come about for two principal reasons.

1. In increasingly competitive markets, good product quality alone may be insufficient for a company to gain competitive advantage. Superior ongoing relationships with customers supplement a firm's competitive advantage. This is evident in the car market, where the focal point of marketing has shifted from a preoccupation with better design, to better service and now to better relationships. Today, many private buyers of cars choose a car that comes with the best support package, keeping the car financed, maintained, insured, and replaced at the end of a specified period (Figure 3.14). For many, the three-yearly purchase of a car has been turned into an ongoing relationship with a car company to supply all the services that make a car available to the consumer.

2. The emergence of powerful, user-friendly databases has enabled large companies to know much more about their customers as individuals, recreating in a computer what the small business owner knew in his or her head. Many of the current developments in relationship marketing would have been unthinkable without modern information technology capabilities.

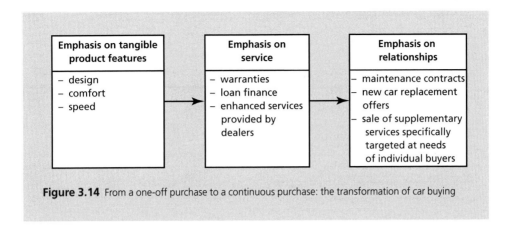

Figure 3.14 From a one-off purchase to a continuous purchase: the transformation of car buying

Traditional transaction-oriented marketing	Relationship marketing
Focus on a single sale	Focus on customer retention
Short-term orientation	Long-term orientation
Sales to anonymous buyers	Tracking of named buyers
Salesperson is the main interface between buyer and seller	Multiple levels of relationships between buyer and seller
Limited customer commitment	High customer commitment
Quality is the responsibility of production department	Quality is the responsibility of all

Figure 3.15 The components of transactional and relational exchange compared

The main differences between traditional one-off transaction-based exchanges and relationship-based exchanges are summarized in Figure 3.15.

The extent to which the development of ongoing relationships with customers represents a desirable marketing strategy is dependent upon three main factors:

1. **The characteristics of the product:** Where products are complex and involve a high degree of uncertainty on the part of buyers, the likelihood of customers seeking a relationship is increased. Relationships are often a necessity where the stream

of product benefits is produced and consumed over a period of time—a programme of medical treatment, for example. For some products, a relationship may allow preferential treatment or semi-automatic responses to requests for service, thereby reducing transaction costs associated with multiple service ordering. It has also been suggested that both suppliers and customers seek the security of relationships where the market environment is turbulent.

2. **The characteristics of customers:** Some customers may be happy to shop around each time they approach a purchase, while others may value the perceived security of an ongoing relationship with a supplier they have come to trust. Some buyers may value social aspects of an ongoing relationship and judge a transaction not just by its economic outcomes. Research has also suggested that the importance attributed to components of a relationship differ between groups, for example in the way that women place more emphasis on trust and commitment in their relationships than men (Shemwell, Cronin, and Bullard [15]).

3. **The characteristics of suppliers:** By developing relationships with their customers, suppliers add to the differentiation of their products and give customers a reason to remain loyal. The extent to which organizations are relationship rather than product oriented can be related to their structure, processes, and core values. Organizations differ in the extent to which they are able, or willing, to calculate the lifetime value of a customer.

What is relationship marketing?

The term 'relationship marketing' has become extensively used and covers a wide range of activities used by firms to encourage repeat purchasing behaviour. Building on Berry's conceptualization of three levels of relationship marketing (Berry [2]), three broad approaches to relationship marketing can be identified.

1. At a *tactical* level, relationships are developed using sales promotion tools. Developments in information technology have spawned many short-term loyalty schemes which aim to predispose a buyer to stick with a chosen supplier. However, the implementation of such schemes has often been opportunistic, leading buyers to become loyal to the incentive rather than emotionally attached to the company and its products.

2. At a more *strategic* level, relationship marketing has been seen as a process by which suppliers seek to 'tie in' customers through legal, economic, technological, geographical, and time bonds. If a customer has taken out a one-year maintenance contract on his central heating system, he will become tied to using the maintenance company's services. In many situations, this greatly helps the buyer, because it reduces the financial and psychological costs of searching for a supplier every time he

Figure 3.16 WHSmith is one of many UK retailers that offers its customers a loyalty programme.
An important aim of many loyalty programmes is to gain a greater share of a customer's total expenditure. Here, the prospect of a special event for members is promoted as a benefit of membership. Because many loyalty programmes involve a dialogue between a company and its programme members, the company can gather a lot of information about customers who would otherwise have been quite anonymous. This allows the company to learn more about the demographics and lifestyle of its customers, as well as allowing targeting of specific offers Reproduced with permission of WHSmith.

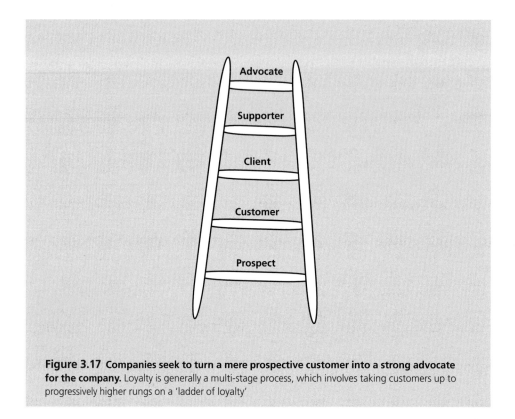

Figure 3.17 Companies seek to turn a mere prospective customer into a strong advocate for the company. Loyalty is generally a multi-stage process, which involves taking customers up to progressively higher rungs on a 'ladder of loyalty'

needs to make a purchase. However, it has been pointed out that such bonds may lead to customer *detention* rather than *retention* (Dick and Basu [5]) and that a company that has not achieved a more deep-seated emotional relationship with its customers may be unable to sustain those relationships if the legal or technological environment changes.

3. At a more *philosophical* level, relationship marketing goes to the heart of the marketing philosophy. Traditional definitions of marketing focus on the primacy of customer needs and relationship marketing as a philosophy refocuses marketing strategy away from products and their life-cycles towards customer relationships and their life-cycles. Conceptualizations of marketing as being the integration of a customer orientation, competitor orientation, and inter-functional co-ordination (Narver and Slater [12]) stress the key features of a relationship marketing philosophy: using all employees of an organization to profitably meet the lifetime needs of targeted customers better than competitors.

Companies seek to move buyers up what has often been described as a 'ladder of loyalty' to the point where they become enthusiastic advocates for a firm's products (Figure 3.17). As customers move up this ladder, the relationship they have with a company changes from one based on convenience or necessity to one that is emotionally valued by the buyer.

However, considerable double-speak is often present in attempts by firms to develop customer relationships. In the service sector, many organizations are simplifying and 'industrializing' their processes, usually in an attempt to improve their operational efficiency and consistency of performance. Such companies may talk about relationship development with customers, based on dialogue that is driven by information technology. But such relationships can be qualitatively quite different from those based on social bonds founded on emotional commitment and trust. While UK clearing banks have become vigorous in their development of customer databases and named personal banking advisers, many customers may feel that the relationship with their bank today is qualitatively worse than when a branch manager was able to enter into a more holistic dialogue with them. Many unhappy customers do not switch banks, however, because the perceived financial and psychological costs are too great.

Managers of firms seeking to develop relationships with their customers should avoid the arrogant belief that customers seek such relationships. Surveys have indicated that many categories of buyers are becoming increasingly confident in venturing outside of a business relationship and increasingly reluctant to enter into an ongoing relationship. Relationship marketing strategies may fail where buyers' perceptions are of reduced choice and freedom to act opportunistically rather than the added value to be derived from a relationship. Added value must be defined by sellers in terms of buyers' needs, rather than focusing on customers as captives who can be cross-sold other products from a firm's portfolio.

Methods used to develop ongoing relationships with customers

Why should buyers wish to go back repeatedly to the same supplier? Below we consider some of the methods used by companies to create ongoing relationships with customers.

Customer satisfaction

In a competitive marketplace, customer satisfaction can be the most important reason for customers deciding to make a repeat purchase, and telling their friends about their satisfaction. To achieve high levels of satisfaction requires the effort of all functions within an organization. Relationship development cannot simply be left to a relationship manager. There are many notable cases of companies that have not developed any explicit relationship marketing programme, but nevertheless achieve very high levels of recommendation by their customers. Consider for example the chocolate retailer

Thorntons, which has developed strong loyalty from customers who return to its shops for indulgence and gift purchases of chocolate, despite having no formally stated relationship marketing programme.

Of course, many companies enjoy high levels of repeat business without providing high levels of customer satisfaction. Many train passengers may complain about the price and reliability of their train service, but they return because they have no realistic alternative.

Even companies that have an apparently poor standard of service can achieve high levels of repeat business in a competitive market by charging low prices. Retail chains such as Aldi and Lidl have developed strong loyalty from price-sensitive customers who consider that the total service offer (access to the store, range of products, cleanliness, friendliness, etc.) are acceptable in return for the price they have paid. The danger here is that competitors may enter the market with similarly low prices, but offering higher levels of service. Would customers still remain loyal?

Trust

The top of the loyalty ladder is more likely to be reached by a customer who trusts a company. Trust is a complex multi-faceted concept which has been extensively re-searched by marketers. Some retailers, such as Boots and John Lewis, consistently score highly in surveys of customers' trust in firms, and these companies generally tend to have high levels of customer loyalty. However, merely being trusted doesn't guarantee profitability for a firm—the rest of its operational and financial strategies must also be right.

Adding value to a relationship

A relationship, to be sustainable, must add value in the eyes of customers. This value can come about in a number of ways, including:

- making the reordering of goods and services easier (for example, many hotels record guests' details and preferences so that they do not have to be re-entered each time the guest checks in);

- offering privileges to customers who wish to enter into some type of formal relation-ship. As an example, many retailers hold special preview events for loyalty card hold-ers, and send a free copy of the store's magazine. Loyalty cards allow companies to gather a lot of valuable data about their customers' buying behaviour. Customers will generally participate in a loyalty card programme only if they believe that they will gain something of value out of it. Many companies have been imaginative in creat-ing value in the buyer's mind, beyond basic cash rebate schemes;

- developing an ability to jointly solve problems. For example, a car repair garage may endeavour to identify exactly what the problem is that a customer wants put right, rather than leaving it to the customer to specify the work that she wants carried out. Such joint problem solving requires a considerable level of trust to have been developed between the parties. In some cases, professional codes of conduct govern the delegation of problem-solving responsibilities.

Creating barriers to exit

Companies can bring about repeat buying by trying to make it difficult for customers to defect to a competitor. Customers can unwittingly walk into traps where they become dependent upon a supplier for continuing support. Suppliers of industrial machinery create ongoing relationships whereby they are the sole supplier of the spare parts or consumable items that the purchaser must buy in order to continue using their equipment. Many companies negotiate exclusive supply agreements with a supplier in return for a promise of preferential treatment. In both cases, the customer becomes dependent in the short term. However, such ties can usually be broken eventually (for example when the machinery is replaced, or when an exclusive supply contract comes up for renewal), and it is at that point that the true loyalty of a customer is put to the test.

Problems of creating ongoing relationships with buyers

There are many situations in which buyers are not responsive to firms' efforts to create ongoing relationships. Many companies serve market segments where customers have no underlying need to make further purchases of a category of product that the company is able to supply. In the extreme case, a small-scale company may appeal to the curiosity of buyers, for whom a second-time purchase will have little of its original value—curiosity. This phenomenon is present in many tourism-related businesses in destinations of symbolic rather than aesthetic quality. (For example, many people make a religious pilgrimage once in their lifetime with little incentive to return again.) In the case of supplies to governmental organizations (and often to larger private-sector organizations), rules for tendering of new purchases may nullify sellers' attempts to develop continuing and uninterrupted relationships. Where relationships between commercial buyers and sellers are deemed to be against the public interest (for example where they make it difficult for new entrants to enter a market), regulatory agencies may order them to be reduced in scope. (For example, soft drinks companies' exclusive supply agreements with retail customers have in some circumstances been held to be against the public interest.) Finally, attempts to create ongoing relationships by firms can be costly and may put a firm at a competitive disadvantage in markets where price is the most important decision factor.

MARKETING in ACTION

Spurious loyalty?

Just because customers repeatedly come back to a company does not necessarily mean that they have a loyal relationship to the company. This point was made, tongue-in-cheek, during a war of words between British Airways and Virgin Atlantic Airways. The latter had objected to BA's use of the advertising slogan 'The World's Favourite Airline'. Statistically, it was true at the time that more passengers travelled internationally with British Airways than with any other airline, but surveys of airline users had consistently put Virgin ahead of BA in terms of perceived quality of service. Virgin's Richard Branson claimed that on BA's logic the M25, London's notorious orbital motorway, could be described as the world's favourite motorway. Despite coming back to the motorway day after day, few motorists could claim to be loyal to it—they simply had no other choice.

The spat between BA and Virgin serves to underline the point that customer loyalty is about more than mere repetitious buying. True loyalty involves customers becoming enthusiastic advocates of a company.

Chapter summary and linkages to other chapters

A sound understanding of buying processes is essential for the development of an appropriate marketing mix. A purchase decision is influenced by a wide range of personal, social, economic, and situational factors, and varies between different types of product and different individuals. The outcome of the decision-making process may be to buy now, to not buy, or to defer a decision. Few buying decisions are made without reference to others, so it is important to identify the members of the decision-making unit. This is particularly true in the case of organizational purchases, where it is important to know what product features and promotional messages motivate different individuals.

Study of buyer behaviour is increasingly extending beyond the initial purchase by attempting to understand how buyers can be turned into loyal repeat customers. Relationship marketing is becoming an important part of many companies' marketing plans as they realize that it can be more profitable to take care to retain the customers they currently have, than to search expensively for new customers to replace lapsed ones.

In the first two chapters we noted in general terms that marketing is essentially about satisfying customers' needs profitably. This chapter has focused more specifically on buyers' evaluation of sellers' attempts to satisfy their needs. In subsequent chapters we will explore how companies undertake research into needs and buying processes (Chapter 4) and subsequently will group together buyers that have essentially similar needs (Chapter 5). Companies then develop a distinctive marketing mix which will give them a competitive advantage in satisfying the needs of the customers they are targeting (Chapters 6–11).

⬚ KEY PRINCIPLES OF MARKETING

- Buying is a process with a number of overlapping stages and a feedback loop from post-consumption to the start of the next buying cycle,
- The effort that buyers put into the buying process is influenced by their level of involvement with the product.
- We rarely make decisions entirely on our own. Marketers need to be aware of the broader decision-making unit of people who may knowingly or unknowingly influence a purchase decision.
- Models of buyer behaviour attempt to portray the buying process. Because of the situational nature of buying decisions, general models cannot hope to give any more than a general indication of these processes.
- It is generally more profitable for companies to retain existing customers than to replace lapsed customers with new ones.

CASE STUDY

Research company tries to show that you can only understand consumer behaviour by living with their behaviour

How can any marketer get inside *your* mind to understand how *you* actually make purchase decisions? Structured questionnaire surveys may have a role for collecting large-scale factual data, but they have major weaknesses when it comes to understanding individuals' attitudes. Qualitative approaches such as those using focus groups can get closer to the truth, but participants often still find themselves inhibited from telling the full story. Many marketing managers, especially those without large research budgets, inevitably end up relying on their own personal experiences to understand how consumers behave. This may be easy for target markets that are in the 20–40 age range (the age of typical marketers), but how do you get inside the mind of teenagers, or elderly people?

Ethnographic approaches are becoming increasingly popular among marketers as a means of getting closer to the truth about consumer behaviour. Ethnographic research is nothing new, having been used by anthropologists in their study of the rituals of tribal people. Marketers have been relatively recent converts to the techniques of ethnography. The advertising agency BMP DDB has taken on board the techniques of ethnography in its 'Project Keyhole' in a manner that is reminiscent of anthropologists' practice of living with tribes in order to understand them. Its consumer researchers live with a family for several days in order to record their every move. The project is designed to meet the needs of client companies who are looking for more than the data gathered using traditional quantitative and qualitative research techniques.

Participants record their views and actions on a digital video camera, in the presence of a researcher who stays with them from 8 am until 10 pm for a few days. A normal project would last four or five days and the client may be invited along for part of the time. Participants are paid £100 for their troubles. What did they do with the direct mail when it came through the letter box? Did they use the coupon offer it contained? Who drinks the fresh orange juice in the house? How long do they spend cooking dinner? How do they actually cook the ready-prepared meals they bought earlier? Does the family eat together? These are examples of the vital information that sponsoring companies hope to get hold of in order to position their products more effectively.

According to the advertising agency, the advantage of this method over conventional research is that it picks up inconsistencies between what people say they do and what they actually do. Following them throughout the day allows the researcher to see why a person's habits might change according to random factors such as their mood, the time of day, or the weather. Crucially it reveals the quirks in our behaviour that marketers are desperate to gain an insight into. For example, a person's store-card data might tell you that they buy bread and margarine, but it doesn't tell whether they eat the bread fresh, or toast it first before putting margarine on it.

In 1998, the magazine *Marketing* put this novel research method to the test with a guinea-pig family called the Joneses. It then compared the results of this approach with more traditional methods of profiling customers. In short, established systems such as CACI, Claritas, and Experian might say one thing about the buying behaviour of a family, using life-style and electoral roll data, but did they bear any relation to reality?

The information that the researcher gathered in a short space of time told a lot about the Joneses. By contrast, the database information about the Joneses, although detailed and often accurate, could not capture the quirks and details that make up the personality of the family. For example, it transpired that the Joneses had a keener than average eye on value for money. Although information on them from the four database companies correctly suggested that they enjoy luxuries like good food and foreign holidays, it didn't say anything about the real-life factors that influence their purchasing decisions. The most noticeable of these was that, although they like good food, Mrs Jones mixed her shopping between the supermarket and a local discount store selling cut-price brands. This meant that she bought at Tesco or Sainsbury's only what she could not get cheaper elsewhere. She showed the researcher a can of branded plum tomatoes that she'd got for 10p at the discount store as an example, explaining that it would have cost 26p in the supermarket. Mrs Jones prided herself on being able to hunt down bargains like this and occasionally rewarded herself by buying 'something luxurious', such as smoked salmon from Marks & Spencer. The freezer had an important role to play as it allowed Mrs Jones to buy things she saw on special offer even if she didn't need them immediately.

Mrs Jones's eye for an offer made her a keen scrutinizer of direct mail. She checked mailings for 'catches' in the small print and for any special offers. She collected mailers worth chasing up on a clip on the fridge door, along with vouchers collected from magazines. Mrs Jones's financial *nous* meant that she managed the family's money.

Not surprisingly, these details did not come out in database information. Of the commercial databases, CACI's People UK and Lifecycle UK databases seemed to be most at variance with the reality of the Joneses' life. They got their ages wrong, incorrectly surmised that they took business flights, and incorrectly attributed Mr Jones with being computer-literate. Nobody in the household read the *Financial Times* or the *Independent* as predicted—they read the *Daily Mail* instead. Some of the other points made by CACI were correct, but were felt to be very generalized and could apply to anybody.

Claritas seemed to be much closer to reality. The Joneses' predicted jobs were about right and the database was correct in stating that they had credit and store cards. They managed to say that the Joneses liked antiques, perhaps learnt as a result of their occasionally buying *Homes and Antiques* magazine. They similarly were correct in stating that they like gardening, DIY, foreign travel, and eating out. The database had predicted that the family would be most likely to own a Ford or Renault car: in fact, Mrs Jones owned a Ford, while Mr Jones had a company Renault.

(Based on 'Keeping up with the Joneses', *Marketing*, 19 November 1998, pp. 28–9)

Case study review questions

1. Why is it important to study the composition of the decision-making unit? To what extent do you think this research approach will give a complete understanding of how family units make purchases?

2. What new possibilities, if any, for market segmentation are opened up by this approach to the study of buyer behaviour?

3. Critically assess the scope for expanding this type of research as a means of learning more about buyer behaviour.

CHAPTER REVIEW QUESTIONS

1. Is it realistic to represent the buying process as a simple linear process? What factors might complicate such apparently smooth progress?

2. Reflect on the last time that you went for a night out with a group of friends to a bar/restaurant or nightclub. Analyse the decision processes, information sources, and evaluation criteria that you used in arriving at a decision as to where to go and what to order.

3. How can firms encourage positive post-purchase feelings? With reference to an example, assess whether a company is doing enough in this respect. What improvements could it make?

4. Summarize the main ways in which buying processes for airline travel typically differ between private buyers and business buyers? How might airlines adapt their product offer to take account of these differences?

5. What criteria might a company use to assess whether a prospective customer is likely to be worth developing a relationship with?

6. Critically assess methods used by banks to develop ongoing relationships with their personal customers.

REFERENCES

[1] Auty, S. (1992), 'Consumer Choice and Segmentation in the Restaurant Industry'. *Services Industries Journal*, 12: 324–39.

[2] Berry, L. L. (1995), 'Relationship Marketing of Services: growing interest, emerging perspectives'. *Journal of the Academy of Marketing Science*, 23: 236–45.

[3] Butcher, K., Sparks, B., and O'Callaghan, F. (2002), 'Effect of Social Influence on Repurchase Intentions'. *Journal of Services Marketing*, 16: 503–12.

[4] Clegg, P. (1956), *A Social and Economic History of Britain 1760–1955*. London: Harrap.

[5] Dick, A. S. and Basu, K. (1994), 'Customer Loyalty: toward an integrated conceptual framework'. *JAMS*, 22(2): 99–113.

[6] Gronroos, C. (1994), 'From Marketing Mix to Relationship Marketing'. *Management Decision*, 32(1): 4–20.

[7] Hofstede, G. (1991), *Culture and Organizations*. Maidenhead, Berks: McGraw-Hill.

[8] Howard, J. A. and Sheth, J. N. (1969), *The Theory of Buyer Behaviour*. New York: John Wiley.

[9] Jai-Ok, K., Forsythe, S., Qingliang, G., and Sook, J. M. (2002), 'Cross-cultural Values, Needs and Purchase Behavior'. *Journal of Consumer Marketing*, 19: 481–502.

[10] Maslow, A. (1943), 'A Theory of Human Motivation'. *Psychological Review*, 50: 370–96.

[11] Morgan, R. M. and Hunt, S. D. (1994), 'The Commitment–Trust Theory of Relationship Marketing'. *Journal of Marketing*, 58(July): 20–38.

[12] Narver, J. and Slater, S. (1994), 'Marketing Orientation, Customer Value and Superior Performance'. *Business Horizons*, 37(2): 22–9.

[13] Ohame, K. (1989), 'The Global Logic of Strategic Alliances'. *Harvard Business Review*, 67: 143–54.

[14] Reichheld, F. F. and Sasser, W. E. (1990), 'Zero Defections'. *Harvard Business Review*, 68(5): 105–11.

[15] Shemwell, D., Cronin, J., and Bullard, W. (1994), 'Relationship Exchanges in Services: an empirical Investigation of ongoing customer service–provider relationships'. *International Journal of Service Industry Management*, 5(3): 57–68.

[16] Wells, W. D. and Gubar, G. (1966), 'Life Cycle Concepts in Marketing Research'. *Journal of Marketing Research*, 3: 355–63.

[17] Wilson, D. F. (2000), 'Why Divide Consumer and Organizational Buyer Behaviour?' *European Journal of Marketing*, 34: 780–6.

SUGGESTED FURTHER READING

There are numerous textbooks that provide a good overview of buyer behaviour, including the following:

Blackwell, R. D., Miniard, P. W., and Engel, J. F. (2000), *Consumer Behaviour*, 9th edn. London: Thomson Learning.

Foxall, G., Goldsmith, R. E., and Brown, S. (1998), *Consumer Psychology for Marketing*. London: International Thomson Publishing.

Solomon, M., Bamossy, G., and Askegaard, S. (2001), *Consumer Behaviour: a European perspective*, 2nd edn. Englewood Cliffs, NJ: Prentice-Hall.

For an introduction to the general principles of relationship marketing and its role in turning buyers into regular customers, the following are useful:

Newell, F. (2000), *Loyalty.com: customer relationship management in the new era of internet marketing*. New York: McGraw-Hill.

Sheth, J. N. and Parvatiyar, A. (2000), *Handbook of Relationship Marketing*. Beverly Hills, CAl.: Sage.

Varey, R. J. (2002), *Relationship Marketing: dialogue and networks in the e-commerce era*. Chichester: John Wiley.

🔲 USEFUL WEBLINKS

Visit the companion website to this book, with lots of interesting additional material and links for each chapter:

www.oup.com/uk/booksites/busecon

The Association for the Advancement of Relationship Marketing provides a forum for the advancement and understanding of the disciplines of relationship marketing:

www.aarm.org/theory

🔲 KEYWORDS

- **Black box model of buyer behaviour**
- **Buying process**
- **Cognitive dissonance**
- **Decision-making unit (DMU)**
- **Family life-cycle**
- **Gatekeepers**
- **Hierarchy of needs**
- **Influencers**
- **Involvement**
- **Ladder of loyalty**
- **Models of buyer behaviour**
- **Need**
- **Peer groups**
- **Perception**

- 'Pester power'
- Reference groups
- Stimulus–response models
- Word-of-mouth

4

Marketing research

CHAPTER OBJECTIVES

So far in this book, we have spoken in general terms of marketing being essentially about providing what the customer wants. But how do we know what the customer *actually* wants? How can we find out how buyers *actually* go about the buying process? How can we tell whether a company has succeeded in providing the goods and service that a buyer seeks? And how does a company gather, analyse, and disseminate information about its marketing environment, which we looked at in general terms in the previous chapter?

This chapter explores information as a valuable asset which can help marketers improve their knowledge of customers and their ability to meet customers' needs profitably. Marketing research is essentially about keeping in touch with a company's customers and its broader marketing environment, and this chapter reviews the main methodological approaches. Sources of data are discussed in terms of their timeliness and relevance. It is important that a company knows about its markets not just as they are now, but as they are likely to be in the future; therefore, demand forecasting and knowledge management become crucial.

■ Introduction

Most definitions of marketing focus on a firm satisfying its customers' needs. But how does a firm know just what those needs are? And how can it try and predict what those needs will be in a year's time, or five years' time? A small business owner in a stable business environment may be able to manage by just listening to her customers and forming an intuitive opinion about customers' needs and how they are likely to slowly change in the future. But how can such an informal approach work in today's turbulent business environments, where the senior managers of very large businesses probably have very little contact with their customers?

Marketing research is essentially about the managers of a business *keeping in touch* with their markets. The small business owner may have been able to do marketing research quite intuitively and adapt her product offer accordingly. Larger organizations operating in competitive and changing environments need more formal methods of collecting, analysing, and disseminating information about their markets. It is frequently said that information is a source of a firm's competitive advantage, and there are many examples of firms that have used a detailed knowledge of their customers' needs to develop better product offers which have given the firm a competitive advantage. Interestingly, a recent trend has been for market researchers to rename themselves as 'Customer Insight Departments'. This is a recognition that marketers value insights above *everything* else—above being objective, above classic methodology, even above validity and reliability.

The range of techniques used by companies to collect information and turn it into actionable knowledge is increasing constantly. Indeed, companies often find themselves with more information than they can sensibly use. The great advances in Electronic Point of Sale (EPOS) technology, for example, have given retailers a wealth of new data which not all companies have managed to make full use of. As new techniques for data collection appear, it is important to maintain a balance between techniques so that a good overall picture is obtained. Reliance on just one technique may save costs in the short term, but only at the long-term cost of not having a good holistic view of market characteristics.

■ Market research *v.* marketing research

The terms 'market research' and 'marketing research' are often used interchangeably. This is incorrect, and the distinctive characteristics of each should be noted.

- **Market research** is about determining the characteristics of a *market*, for example in terms of its size, requirements, growth rate, market segments, and competitor positioning.
- **Marketing research** is broader and is about researching the whole of a company's marketing activities. In most organizations, such research would probably include monitoring the effectiveness of its advertising, intermediaries, and pricing position.

This chapter focuses on how a company goes about assessing its customers' needs. Of course, research into areas such as customers' perceptions of advertising messages is closely related to an understanding of their needs and expectations, so it is unwise to see the two aspects of research as completely separate.

Market research should be seen as just one component of a firm's information gathering procedures. It is usual to talk about integrating market research within a company-wide marketing information system, which itself is part of a wider corporate

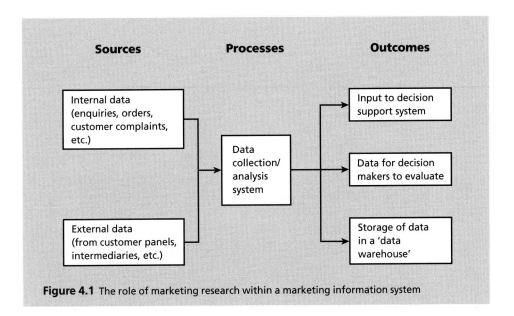

Figure 4.1 The role of marketing research within a marketing information system

management information system. From this, knowledge is created, and there is a lot of interest in how this knowledge can be shared to create a 'learning organization'.

In Figure 4.1, an attempt has been made to put market research in the context of a broader marketing information system.

Major uses of marketing research

As markets become more competitive, marketing research is being called upon to perform an ever-increasing range of tasks. Some of the more important specific marketing research activities are listed below.

- **Research into customer needs and expectations**: Research is undertaken to learn what underlying needs individuals seek to satisfy when they buy goods and services. Identifying needs that are currently unmet by existing products spurs new product development. Needs should be distinguished from expectations, and a variety of qualitative techniques are used to study the often complex sets of expectations that customers have with respect to a purchase. For example, when buying a personal computer, what are customers' expectations with respect to reliability, after-sales support, design, etc.?

- **Customer surveys**: These are a means of keeping in touch with customers, either on an ad hoc basis or as part of a regular programme of survey research. A variety of survey methods are available (discussed later). Surveys can have the dual function of provid-

Figure 4.2 It is easy for marketers to make sweeping generalisations about their target market and detailed research is often required in order to understand the minutiae of buyers' life-styles. Even the same person can take on quite a different life-style at different times of the day or week. Is the young male who drinks heavily with his mates on a Friday night likely to continue this drinking habit at home during the week? Is the goal-orientated career woman always driven by a desire to succeed in the fast lane? This ad for Black Tower reminds us of the need for marketers to get a complete insight into the lives of the target market and to identify apparent inconsistencies, which can represent market opportunities (Reproduced with permission of Reh Kendermann)

ing a company with valuable information and providing a public relations tool, allowing customers to feel that they have made their feelings known to the company.

- **Customer panels**: These are often used to assess the effectiveness of a company's marketing strategy, for example whether its advertising has been remembered by the target audience, or whether a price reduction was large enough to bring about trial of a new product. Customer panels are also used to provide valuable information about proposed new product launches.

- **Similar industry studies**: By researching other companies, including competitors and companies in completely unrelated business sectors, marketing managers can learn a lot about how to improve their own marketing effectiveness. Through a process sometimes referred to as 'benchmarking', an organization can set itself targets based on best practice in its own, or a related, industry.

- **Key client studies**: Where a company derives the majority of its income from just a small number of customers, it may make special efforts to ensure that these customers are totally satisfied with its standards of service and prices. The loss of their business as a result of shortcomings of which it is unaware could otherwise be catastrophic. In some cases, the relationship with key customers may be of such mutual importance that each partner may spend considerable time jointly researching shared problems (for example, airport operators sharing with airlines the task of researching customers' perceptions of the airport's handling procedures).

- **Research into intermediaries**: Agents, dealers, and other intermediaries are close to consumers and therefore form a valuable means for gathering information about consumers' needs and expectations. In addition, intermediaries are themselves customers of manufacturers and service principals. It follows that the latter should be very interested in how they are perceived by their intermediaries, for example in relation to reliability, delivery times, and after-sales service.

- **Employee research**: For many services organizations, front-line employees are close to customers and are valuable sources of information about customers' needs. Research can also focus on employees as 'customers' of an organization, for example by measuring their attitudes towards the company. Employee suggestion schemes can form an important part of research into employees' attitudes.

- **Environmental scanning**: We saw in Chapter 2 that a company's marketing environment can be highly complex and that it is crucial to understand how even quite nebulous changes today may affect the marketing activities of a company in the future. Environmental scanning is about gathering information on trends in the environment and disseminating this information to individuals who may be able to act on it.

◾ The marketing research process

The small business owner may have been able to get by with a fairly intuitive system of market research in the past. Larger organizations operating in complex environments need to adopt a more structured approach to their market research activities. To be useful, keeping in touch with customers' needs should be carried out objectively accurately and should use a variety of methods. Casual, unstructured research may at best be wasteful, and at worst misleading. Data collected should be as up-to-date and relevant to a problem as time and cost constraints allow.

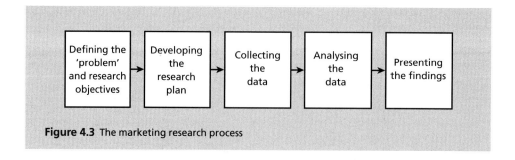

Figure 4.3 The marketing research process

The stages of the marketing research process can be described in a simple, linear format. A model of this process, which begins with the definition of the research problem and ends with the presentation of the findings, is shown in Figure 4.3. The process follows the basic pattern of inquiry that is adopted for other forms of scientific or academic research.

The trigger for research can usually be related to a gap in the market information that is currently available to a firm. For example, a company may have comprehensive information on the current market for its products, but lack information on new market opportunities for which its product range could be adapted.

Very often, marketing research activity fails because the 'problem' to be researched has been inadequately thought through and expressed as a research brief. For example, a company may be facing declining sales of a product and may then commission research to investigate customers' liking of the product's features relative to competitors' products. However, the real problem may be to understand the macroeconomic environment, which may explain why sales of that category of product are declining.

The marketing research process operates at a number of levels.

- At the simplest level, a researcher may simply be required to provide a normative description of market characteristics (for example defining the attributes that buyers evaluate when choosing between competing personal computer brands, or describing the buying behaviour of families buying a personal computer for the first time).

- The research task may additionally call for the measurement of market characteristics, for example by measuring the size of the UK personal computer market and the market shares of the main suppliers.

- A more thorough investigation would require an analysis of data, both quantitative and qualitative (e.g. an analysis of personal computer buying behaviour according to the age, income, or life-style of different segments of the population).

- With further analysis, a predictive model for targeting may be sought (e.g. a model to predict the level of computer sales based on individuals' occupation, family structure, and postcode).

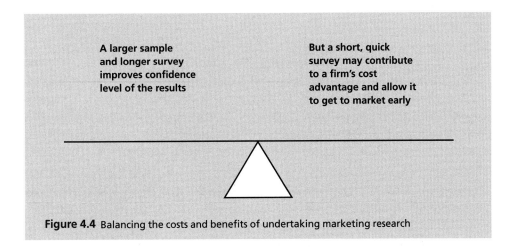

A larger sample
and longer survey
improves confidence
level of the results

But a short, quick
survey may contribute
to a firm's cost
advantage and allow it
to get to market early

Figure 4.4 Balancing the costs and benefits of undertaking marketing research

Once the objectives of a research exercise have been defined, plans can be developed to collect relevant data. Data collection methods are considered below. A time plan is essential to ensure that decision makers can have the most up-to-date information on market characteristics as they are at present, rather than as they were some time ago. In rapidly changing markets, timeliness can be crucial. The outcome of market research should be actionable by those who receive it.

How extensive should a firm's marketing research processes be? The amount of time and expense incurred in undertaking research must be compared with the benefits that will result from it in terms of making a better informed decision. Very often, the issue is how harmful a badly informed decision could be to a firm. Where the capital costs involved in developing a new product are low, and the market is changing rapidly, it may make sense to do very little research and go straight to the market with a new product. This is true of many fashion designers, who can run up sample items and see how well they sell. If they sell well, follow-up production can be put in hand rapidly; if they fail to sell, they can be consigned to a bargain clearance store. Little will have been lost, whereas had the designer taken time to carry out lengthy market research, he could have got his designs to the market just as the current fashion was changing again, rendering his research historic and obsolete. Contrast this to the marketing research needed for a much more risky major infrastructure investment such as an airport, which will have a high capital cost and a long life-span. The research process here will typically last several years and take many forms (Figure 4.4).

■ Primary *v.* secondary research

A further question is whether to use primary data collection techniques, secondary research, or a combination of the two. Data sources are traditionally divided into two categories according to the methods by which they were collected. Secondary research is often referred to as desk research, while primary research is often called field research.

MARKETING in ACTION

Paralysis by analysis?

Is marketing an art or a science? This age-old debate has been given new impetus in recent times by developments in information technology which allow marketing managers to make supposedly scientific decisions, rather than relying on gut instinct. But when all marketing managers have access to the same data analysis packages, might this not result in a series of 'me-too' decisions being made? A survey carried out in 1997 by Taylor Nelson found that 59% of 105 marketers who were interviewed believed that marketing is more of an art than a science. Many marketing managers seemed to be sheltering behind their piles of numbers and used research merely as a justification for their earlier decisions.

Another picture was painted by research commissioned for the decision support software specialist Business Objectives into the way managers use information to make decisions. Of 100 senior managers from the Times Top 1000 companies, more than three-quarters claimed to rely mainly on gut instinct rather than hard facts when making decisions; 60% of managers claimed not to receive the right quality or quantity of information to make a decision, even though almost all of them had access to a personal computer. More worryingly, a majority of sales and marketing managers surveyed claimed that they relied on other people for information that they are dubious about, or that is out-of-date. The picture emerged of an information underclass that relies on instinctive decision-making processes.

Many of the great marketing developments of recent times have come about from individuals taking inspired decisions which might have seemed irrational when assessed by scientific processes. It must be remembered that information cannot in itself give answers. Indeed, too much information can lead to a 'paralysis by analysis'. In a turbulent marketing environment, it is the quality of the interpretation of data that gives a firm a competitive advantage.

These reported studies seem to be consistent with Smith and Dexter's observation that 'All knowledge starts with prejudice', in which information gathering is punctuated by a constant 'shuttling between the initial pet theory and the available evidence', as a fit between the two is sought [7]. Together, the reported research leaves unanswered the question of whether managers should be criticized for their failure to use hard information, or applauded for being bold and creative in their decision making.

Most organizations approach a research exercise by examining the available sources of secondary data. Secondary data refers to information which in some sense is second-hand to the current research project. Data can be second-hand because they have already been collected internally by the organization, although for a different primary purpose. Alternatively, the information may be acquired second-hand from external sources.

Internal information, on products, costs, sales, etc., may be accessed through an organization's marketing information system. Where such a system does not exist formally, the information may still be available in relevant departmental records, though it would probably need to be reworked into a format that market researchers

can use. It was mentioned earlier that many firms amass data that they have no immediate means of analysing, so the process of digging deep into piles of old data, whether
in manual or electronic format, is not unusual.

Secondary, or desk, research can be a useful starting point for a research exercise. If
somebody else has collected data or published a report in a closely related area, it is
often much cheaper to buy that report rather than start to collect data afresh. Reports
by organizations such as the Economist Intelligence Unit (EIU) may at first sight seem
to be very expensive, but when set against the cost of undertaking the research from
scratch the cost begins to look relatively good value.

Secondary research can be carried out internally by a company's own employees,
although some specialist knowledge is required in knowing which sources of information are likely to be useful. Undertaking unnecessary primary research when similar information is available through secondary sources is an expensive and time-consuming
exercise.

Primary, or 'field', research is concerned with generating new information direct from
the target population. The phrase 'keeping in touch' was highlighted earlier, and marketing researchers spend most of their time designing and implementing such studies,
either on a one-off or a continuous monitoring basis. Primary research tends to be
much more expensive to conduct than secondary research, but the results are invariably more up-to-date and specific to a company's research objectives. Many marketing
research agencies and consultancies commission their own primary research and sell
the results to clients. Of course, by the time that they are published they have all the
limitations of secondary research.

The range of primary research techniques is constantly increasing, and some of the
important ones are discussed later in this chapter.

MARKETING and the INTERNET

A 'Wild West' for data?

The internet has spawned a new generation of researchers who seem to have boundless
amounts of data. But how valuable are these data?

One of the big advantages of doing business through the internet is that all
transactions are recorded in a form that is immediately available for analysis. No more
transcribing the newspaper enquiry coupon into a database, or recording the essence of
a customer's telephone call in a series of codes to be saved in a database. In both cases,
creating a database can be time-consuming, costly, and subject to human transcription
error—better to let the customer himself enter the data. Where a prospective customer
approaches a company's website with an enquiry, the fact can automatically be recorded.
Fairly simple software will allow a company to record how the visitor got to its site, how
long she spent at each page, the results of the visit (e.g. a request for further
information; quotation request, purchase order), and where she went to after leaving the

site. More sophisticated data are provided by companies, such as doubleclick.com, which inserts 'cookies'—often unknowingly—into users' PCs which are then used to send back to the company information about all of the sites that the user has visited. This can be very valuable information that third-party companies buy to improve their targeting. Of course, collecting information through use of such 'spyware' raises ethical questions.

Faced with such a huge amount of research data, just how valuable is it all to marketers? Inevitably, there are some gems amidst a mass of debris. The ability to measure response rates to different page designs and/or different links to a company's site can sharpen marketers' analytic skills and improve their accountability for their actions. It is no longer good enough to just have a hunch that a website is effective when there is copious information to measure its performance.

How useful are the statistics that marketers routinely collect from the web? Simple records of visitors to a website are prone to many errors, including the problem of identifying 'unique' visitors from those who might repeatedly enter and leave a site in quick succession. Many apparent visits are actually hits recorded by 'spiders'—search engines that routinely seek out websites for indexing. A bigger problem of internet data is the difficulty that often prevents internet-based databases being integrated with existing records of consumers' behaviour, life-styles, and attitudes. With concerns over internet security remaining high, individuals may be reluctant to divulge personal information through the internet which would allow a company to build up a full picture. Unfortunately, the people with the greatest concerns about privacy are often in those very groups that many companies are most interested in learning more about (see Graeff and Harmon [4]).

In its early days of development, the internet was described as the new 'Wild West', where rules were few and far between and anything went. Unfortunately, this description can also be applied to many of the statistics circulating about website usage, with potential advertisers unsure about the true value of advertising on a particular site. More recently, the development of audit schemes (e.g. VeriSign) have helped to provide some reassurance to users about the validity of web statistics.

The development of the internet as a marketing research tool has not always been helped by the sometimes confused communications between marketing and IT departments within a company, highlighted in a report published by the Chartered Institute of Marketing in 2000. IT systems often fail to meet marketers' expectations, because needs have not been defined accurately. As in other aspects of marketing, getting the inter-functional dynamics of a company right can be crucial in the quest for competitive advantage, and may explain the success of, among others, Direct Line Insurance and First Direct.

■ Secondary research information sources

A good starting point for secondary research is to examine what a company already has available in-house. Typically, a lot of information is generated internally within organizations; for example, sales invoices may form the basis of a market segmentation exercise. To make the task of desk research as easy as possible, routinely collected

- Government departments and official publications—e.g. *General Household Survey*, *Social Trends*, *Transport Statistics*
- National media—e.g. *Financial Times* country surveys
- Professional and trade associations—e.g. Association of British Travel Agents, British Roads Federation
- Trade, technical, and professional media—e.g. *Travel Trade Gazette*, *Marketing Week*
- Local chambers of trade and commerce
- Yearbooks and directories, e.g. Dataquest
- Companies' Annual Reports and Accounts
- Subscription services, providing periodic sector reports on market intelligence and financial analyses, such as Keynote, Mintel, etc.
- Subscription electronic databases, e.g. Forrester Research, Gartner, Mintel Online

Figure 4.5 Examples of secondary data used in marketing research

information should be analysed and stored in a way that facilitates future use. Of course, a balance needs to be struck between having data readily available, and spending money on the collection and storage of data that may subsequently (but not necessarily) be used.

The range of external sources of secondary data is constantly increasing, both in document and in electronic format. These sources include government statistics, trade associations, and specialist research reports. A good starting point for a review of these is still the business section of a good library. Some examples of secondary data sources are shown in Figure 4.5.

In many cases, other organizations, possibly even competitors, will have conducted similar studies to the one that is proposed. These may be available to purchase (or may be publicly available, as in the case of companies' annual reports, which often contain useful market information). There is also a dark world of espionage, where companies seek to gather information from competitors. Numerous catalogues exist which list sources of external secondary market research data (e.g. MarketSearch, a directory of 20,000 market research studies on worldwide markets, accessible through **www.shef.ac.uk/library/cdfiles/mksearch.html**).

Primary research methods

Primary, or field, research is becoming increasingly sophisticated, and this chapter can give only a brief overview of the range of techniques available. There are now many texts that go into market research methods in great detail. We will begin by looking at methodological issues concerning primary research. Later, we will look at how data collected using these methods can be analysed to give a company new insights.

Sampling procedures

Primary research involves looking directly at the phenomena or individuals that we are interested in, and recording the characteristics about them that we are particularly interested in. In most circumstances, it would be impractical to measure details of everybody who makes up the 'population'. (For example, if we were interested in the preferences of intensive mobile phone users in the UK, it would not be practical to talk to every single intensive user in the country.) As an alternative, primary research usually uses just a *sample* of the population that we are interested in. From this small sample, we can extrapolate to infer characteristics of the population as a whole. Any inference made about the population is limited by the extent to which the sample is truly representative of the population as a whole.

Sampling is essentially concerned with quantitative techniques, and there are a number of widely used techniques for sampling:

- A random sample implies that everyone within the target population has an equal chance of being selected for inclusion in the sample. For a completely random sample of all adult members of the population, the Electoral Register is frequently used and a proportion of names selected at random. (However, from 2002, UK residents have been able to 'opt out' of the part of the electoral register that is made available to commercial organizations.) A variant on this approach is stratified random sampling, in which the population is divided into a number of sub-groups and a random sample obtained from each sub-group. The proportion sampled from each sub-group can be varied according to the researcher's interest.

- Rather than picking specific individuals to be included in the sample, the researcher can specify the characteristics of each sub-group and the number required from each such group. The interviewer is then free to include in her *quota* sample individuals who meet the specification. This method of sampling is only as good as the specification of the quota's characteristics. If data collectors are given too much freedom to choose their sample, it can best be described as a *convenience* sample and is likely to be biased in terms of respondents' characteristics. (The researcher may consciously or unconsciously recruit respondents who are easiest to find, rather than those whom it is most valuable to learn about.) A biased sample may limit the generalizability of the research results to the population as a whole.

- Many survey techniques are effectively *self-selecting* in their sampling procedure. Where questionnaires are made widely available to the public, the researcher has little control over who will actually return a questionnaire. There is evidence that responses can be dominated by vociferous minorities of individuals who hold extreme views, which may not be typical of the views of the large group of 'average' customers. There is also evidence that retired people and housewives with more time to spare are more likely to volunteer to complete a survey, even though a research exercise may be more interested in the views of busy working people.

Data collection methods

The range of field research techniques is constantly increasing. Two main approaches to collecting primary data can be identified: by observation of the individuals who the researcher is interested in, or by interaction with them through a survey.

Observation techniques

Observational techniques are limited to descriptions of behaviour, and cannot explore the reasons that might explain such behaviour. However, they do claim to be highly objective and free of bias from respondents.

The following are some examples of observation techniques.

- When a retailer is assessing the attractiveness of a proposed new store location, it may undertake observational research into pedestrian or vehicle flows past a proposed site.

- Many firms routinely monitor their competitors' marketing programmes, for example by collecting their brochures or by observing prices and products on offer in retail outlets.

- The use of 'mystery shoppers' is becoming increasingly common among services companies who use them to check on standards of service delivery. Typical uses have been to assess the efficiency and friendliness of restaurant waiting staff, the attention received from staff in a car showroom, and whether a travel agent is recommending a sponsoring tour operator's products.

- Experimental laboratory research may observe how consumers interact with a product, for example by observing how, and in what order, an individual reads an advertisement.

- The internet has created new opportunities for observing how individuals move around a company's web site. Which hyperlinks were most productive in bringing visitors to the company's site? Which combination of pages did they visit? In what order were they visited? How long did they spend on each page? Companies often use alternative page designs which are randomly allocated to visitors, then the results (an order, further enquiry, etc.) compared. A number of specialist information intermediaries have emerged to carry out mass observation of web site users (using 'cookies') and sell the data back to companies. From this, a company can assess overall viewing patterns of an individual, which can be valuable information for web site developers, and for companies who can then target customers more accurately.

Observational techniques may be good at describing phenomena, but they do not in themselves provide explanations. For this, other techniques need to be used. Observational techniques can raise ethical questions, where those being observed are not aware that they are being studied. Many people may be unhappy at the thought that CCTV footage of them walking round a store is being used in a study of flow around the store. The use of unseen 'cookies' to observe internet usage has been challenged by many on ethical and legal grounds.

MARKETING and SOCIAL RESPONSIBILITY

Snooping or learning?

Finding out about how people actually live their lives can be a daunting task, because there are so many barriers that get in the way between what people actually do, what they say they do, and what researchers subsequently interpret that they do. Where researchers are far removed from the subjects they are interested in, a very false picture of consumer behaviour can be the basis for marketing decisions. Observing behaviour is not new to marketers, who have often preferred to know about the reality of what people actually do than about individuals' expressed attitudes, which may never be manifested in actual purchasing behaviour.

In a nation that has been gripped by voyeuristic 'reality' television programmes such as 'Big Brother', it is not surprising that marketers too should try to gain a better insight into behaviour that might previously have been considered private. How far should marketers legitimately be able to go in their pursuit of these better insights? And at what point does it become intrusive?

'Mystery customers' have been around for some time now, and are widely used to monitor the performance of front-line service personnel. To some, they are spies, but marketers insist that they are assessors, helping to raise standards for all. In fact, mystery shoppers are generally highly trained, professional assessors. Rather than being seen as sneaky spies, companies should seek to involve staff in the whole 'mystery shopper' process. Not only will staff provide useful insights to the service, but they will be able to feel a sense of involvement in the programme.

In recent years, researchers have paid increasing attention to the use of ethnography in the study of consumer behaviour. This involves studying the rituals of consumers at first hand. In the previous chapter, the case study described one company that was using an ethnographic approach consensually with a household to study how the family as a whole chose to purchase and use products. But what if consumers are observed in a non-consensual manner? In one widely reported study, ethnographic researchers travelled on London's number 73 bus to observe how passengers used their mobile phones and revealed a variety of behaviours that were not moderated by respondents' need to conform.

More recently, marketers have used technology to probe individuals' behaviour, but critics have argued that such 'Big Brother' techniques may be exploiting consumers without their agreement. It was noted earlier that many people may be unaware that 'cookies' lodged in their computer are spying on them. Close-circuit television (CCTV) has been used by researchers to study how people move around a supermarket and the processes they use in searching for products. Would you be happy in the knowledge that all of your indecisions, strained facial expressions, and bad tempers were being recorded to be replayed over and over again by researchers?

Survey-based research methods

A survey questionnaire involves some form of interaction with the subject being studied and would normally seek some attitudinal, personal, or historical information about the respondent. Questions in a survey can be asked face-to-face, by telephone, or distributed for self-completion.

- *Face-to-face interviewing* is a traditional method of carrying out surveys. It can achieve high rates of response and can be free of the self-selection bias commonly associated with self-completion surveys. Bias can however occur where respondents give an answer that they believe the interviewer expects them to give, rather than one they truly believe. Face-to face interviewing, whether carried out house-to-house (which is the best approach for sampling purposes), in the street, or in hired locations, is labour-intensive. The cost and difficulty of obtaining good-quality, trained staff to undertake survey research, often at unsociable times of the day, has led researchers to search for lower-cost alternatives. There have been innovations with electronic questionnaires, especially on the internet, although sampling and the reliability of answers remain a problem.

- Another alternative to face-to-face interviewing is the *telephone survey*. While considerably cheaper than face-to-face interviews, the refusal rate for telephone surveys can be up to three times higher than for personal interviews, and response rates appear to be falling rapidly (Tuckel and O'Neill [8]). The increased use of computer-assisted information collection for telephone (CATI) and personal interviews (CAPI) has speeded up the whole survey process dramatically, with responses being processed as they are received. Immediately prior to the 2001 UK General Election, these systems were used in the next-day publication of survey results from total sample sizes extending into thousands.

- In the case of *self-completion surveys*, respondents obviously self-select, so no matter how carefully the original sample to be contacted is chosen, the possibility of bias is highest. Furthermore, the response rate may be lower than 10%, particularly where a postal survey is used.

Figure 4.6 The UK supermarket operator ASDA (part of Wal Mart), appreciates the value of feedback from customers. Like many well-run companies, ASDA provides comment cards and a freephone telephone number that customers can use to pass on their suggestions, complaints and praise about the company's operations. ASDA recognizes the value of this customer insight and goes one step further by making a donation to charity for each call that it receives on its freephone number. It also completes the process of information exchange by displaying in its stores a list of suggestions that customers have made, and actions that the company has taken in response to them (Reproduced with permission of Asda)

- In *qualitative research*, the open-ended nature of the questions and the need to establish the confidence of respondents preclude the use of telephone and self-completion interviews. Face-to-face depth interviews are used, particularly in business-to-business research, where confidentiality is especially important and the scheduling difficulties and cost of getting a group of busy buyers together in one place can be a major problem; for this reason, it is usually most convenient for respondents to be interviewed at their place of work.

- In consumer markets, *focus group discussions* are frequently used. Groups normally consist of about eight people, plus a trained moderator who leads the discussion. Respondents are recruited by interviewers, who use recruitment questionnaires to ensure that those invited to attend reflect the demography of the target market, and to filter out unsuitable respondents. Focus groups do not claim to be statistically representative of the population that they come from, but nevertheless there would be little value in recruiting a group that was not typical of the target population as a whole. In national markets, groups are arranged at central points throughout the country, the number of groups in each region reflecting the regional breakdown of the target population.

Quantitative *v.* qualitative research

It was noted earlier that research techniques need to be varied and appropriate to the problem being studied. One important decision that needs to be made when developing a survey-based research plan is whether to conduct a qualitative or quantitative survey, or a combination of the two. Although quantitative and qualitative research are often seen as opposite ends of a research techniques spectrum, their methods overlap. Market researchers need to feel comfortable 'operating in all slices of the information map' (Smith and Dexter [7]), incorporating harder, more scientific, objective data with softer, anecdotal, qualitative data.

Quantitative research

This is used to measure consumers' attitudes and behaviour where the nature of the research has been defined and described. Quantitative research is designed to gather information from statistically representative samples of the target population. The sample size is related to the size of the total population being studied, the variability within it, and the degree of statistical reliability required, balanced against time and cost constraints. In order to achieve margins of error small enough to make the final measurements useful, however, quantitative research, as its name implies, is usually conducted among several hundred, sometimes thousands, of respondents. For this reason, information is generally obtained using standardized structured questionnaires.

Unfortunately, many phenomena that marketers are interested in cannot be easily measured using single, simple indicators. In these cases, composite sets of scales are used and factor analysis is carried out to try and identify distinctive dimensions of a phenomenon. For example, marketers are often interested in whether customers trust a brand, but a lot of research evidence has suggested that trust is a complex phenomenon; hence it is not uncommon in quantitative studies to use 30 or more questions in a survey of trust. Perhaps the best known multiple item measure used by marketers is the SERVQUAL methodology for measuring service quality. A company may wish to learn more about customers' perceptions of its service and to match these with what they have expected. The methodology uses 22 questions to probe a respondent's attitudes about service quality. Previous research has shown that these 22 questions are reliable indicators of five distinct dimensions of service quality: reliability, attentiveness, tangibles, empathy, and responsiveness. The survey instrument has been widely used in the services sector to compare customers' perceptions of service quality between different branches, and to plot changes in performance over time.

The marketer has available a wide range of quantitative techniques with which to collect and analyse data. The following is a brief summary of the techniques most commonly used by marketers. Further details can be found in any good research methods book. And see suggested Further Reading at the end of this chapter.

Correlation analysis

Marketers are often interested in the extent to which two phenomena are associated with each other, for example whether change in household income is associated with the amount that a household spends on eating out. A correlation coefficient of 1 would indicate perfect association between the two variables and 0 would indicate no association at all. A correlation does not imply causation, and, as with all quantitative techniques, care needs to be taken in interpreting a correlation coefficient. Researchers have, for example, found significant correlations between firms' advertising expenditure on a product and sales revenue for it. However, this correlation could imply either that advertising expenditure leads to increased sales, or that firms increase their advertising expenditure in response to increasing sales revenue, because advertising is now more affordable. Each of these hypotheses is plausible, and the observed correlation must be interpreted in the context of theoretical foundations and previous evidence. In the light of theory, it may be concluded that the most relevant correlation is between sales in one period and advertising revenue in the preceding period.

MARKETING in ACTION

Mining for gold—or have garbage data been dug up?
Companies are able to capture ever-increasing amounts of information through electronically stored till receipts, order forms, registration cards, etc., from which almost endless correlation coefficients may be calculated. In recent times, researchers' analyses

have shown correlations between an individual's height and his annual expenditure on clothing; shoe size and usage of gyms; and purchases of milk and purchases of paint. Some of these might at first sound quite spurious, and the researcher's task is to probe more deeply to establish whether there really is any direct causative relationship between the two variables, or whether there is some other intervening factor that may explain the observed correlation. Of course, sometimes the correlation is of little more than amusement value, and often it is used by research sponsors for its PR value. Would gym operators ever really want to target customers with large or small feet?

The retailer Tesco has gathered a large database using till receipt analysis, loyalty card data, and other bought-in data, giving previously unimaginable opportunities for data mining. One discovery that is reported to have intrigued the company's analysts was the apparent correlation between sales of beer and sales of nappies. The two products were not in any way complementary to each other, so why should their sales appear to be associated? Was this just another spurious correlation, to be binned along with such gems of information as the correlation between shoe size and gym usage? The company didn't give up, and refined its analysis to study the correlation for different categories of store and by different times of day. Where it also had details of customers' demographic characteristics (gathered through its Club Card loyalty programme) it was able to probe for further insights. The company was edging towards a better understanding of why the sales of these two products should be closely correlated, but it took further qualitative analysis techniques to provide a fuller explanation. It appeared that men were offering to run a household errand to the shops to buy babies' nappies. This was an excuse to leave the family home in order to buy more beer for their own consumption. The company learnt from this exercise, and subsequently positioned the two products closer together in selected stores.

But should it take data-mining to reveal these insights into consumer behaviour? The traditional Irish pub spotted this link long ago, with pubs doubling up as the local post office, bookseller, or grocer, giving the Irish drinker plenty of good reasons for visiting it.

Regression analysis

Regression models are used to build a model of causes (independent variables), which lead to an effect (the dependent variable). Companies would use a historical database to test models that are assessed for the amount of variance in the dataset that they explain. A regression analysis would comprise one dependent variable, a constant, and any number of independent variables. The significance of each of these independent variables is calculated, allowing a company to understand which of them are having a significant effect on the dependent variable.

A typical application of regression modelling is retailers' use of it to predict sales at possible new sales locations. A regression model will be able to discover, on the basis of performance of the company's other sites, the relative contribution to sales that will be made by such factors as passing pedestrian traffic, passing vehicle traffic, proximity to a major attractor, and the number/proximity of competitors. Regression analysis is only as good as the data and context on which the initial model was calibrated. The model may not be relevant if it is applied outside the context of the original dataset (e.g. a UK based model applied to US retailing), and environmental factors may change the validity of the model over time.

Analysis of variance

Analysis of variance, or 'ANOVA', is used to test hypotheses about differences between two or more means. It is widely used in experimental frameworks where the researcher wishes to examine the effects of two or more 'treatments' on customers. A store interested in the effects of background music on the daily value of sales may develop an experiment in which shoppers are treated to one of three types of background music: (1) slow, soft music; (2) strident, loud music; or (3) no music. Analysis of variance can be used to test whether there is any significant difference between sales values associated with different types of music.

ANOVA designs can be used to test for differences within subject variables and between subject variables.

Conjoint analysis

This is a versatile marketing research technique that can provide valuable information for market segmentation, new product development, forecasting, and pricing decisions. Conjoint analysis can analyse the real-life trade-offs that shoppers make when evaluating a range of features or attributes that are present in a range of products. Once data are collected about consumers' preferences for particular attributes and features, the researcher can conduct a number of 'choice simulations' to estimate market share for products with different attributes/features. This can improve the researcher's ability to predict which formulation of a product will be successful before a product is launched on the market. A limitation of this technique is that consumers' evaluation of individual attributes of a product may be quite meaningless on their own, and it is the creative combining of attributes that determines their final choice.

Cluster analysis

Segmentation exercises involve trying to allocate individuals within a survey/population sample into distinctive groups, so that differences within the groups are minimized relative to the differences between the groups. Cluster analysis is frequently used in segmentation studies, but does not provide the marketer with a unique solution, as the process of clustering involves subjective decisions about the grouping of data.

Neural network analysis

This technique splits a dataset into a training set and a testing set. It essentially combines the features of regression modelling with an analysis of variance to give a 'best fit' model of dependent and independent variables.

Limitations to quantitative techniques

Quantitative surveys may give the appearance of a rigorous, scientific approach, and many marketers may delude themselves (and others) into thinking that you 'can't argue with the figures'. However, quantitative analysis techniques can suffer from a number of weaknesses.

Sampling error

Many quantitative studies fail because the sample is not truly representative of the population about which inferences are being made. A growing problem is non-response bias, which occurs when people who don't respond to a survey hold significantly different views from those who do respond, resulting in a biased estimate of population characteristics. A company will never know for sure what the views of non-respondents are, and how these differ from respondents, but there is some research evidence that, in the case of service quality surveys, responses are likely to be biased in favour of those who are either very happy or very unhappy with service levels, leaving the bulk of average customers under-represented. There are some methods to try and overcome this bias (e.g. comparing early respondents with late respondents), but the problem of non-response bias is a big one. (Typically, less than 5% of targeted individuals reply to a mail survey.) Concerns over data privacy, among other things, are exacerbating the problem.

Measurement error

This occurs where there is a difference between the true value of the information being sought and the information that is actually obtained by the measurement process. There are many sources of measurement error, the most common being using measurement variables that are inappropriate to the research problem; interviewer bias (which often occurs in face-to-face surveys where the respondent may give a 'polite' or 'expected' response, rather than the truth); problems with the research instrument (e.g. loaded questions used in a questionnaire); and processing errors (e.g. incorrect coding and data entry).

Significance level

Sample surveys can give only an estimate of population characteristics, and this estimate is subject to a margin of error. In general, as the size of the sample relative to the population increases, the confidence with which population parameters can be predicted increases. Also, greater confidence in predicting population parameters occurs where the amount of variability within the population is low. Before accepting an estimate of population characteristics, it is important to note the confidence interval of these predictions.

Inappropriate tests

Estimates of population may be invalidated because of the use of inappropriate statistical tests. Many of the tests described above are based on an assumption that data are normally distributed. If they are not, the test is invalidated.

Inappropriate interpretation

The interpretation of results can be highly subjective. This can derive from the validity of the measures being used—do they really measure the phenomena that they purport to (e.g. does SERVQUAL truly measure service quality as it applies in a specific industry sector)? Often a variety of significance tests are available to the researcher and a test may be chosen that is the most significant, but not the most valid. Finally, all inferences are subject to interpretation of meaning; for example, at what point does an observed fall in sales become a long-term trend rather than a temporary blip?

It should always be remembered that there are many 'noise' factors getting in the way of what is reported and the true state of the phenomenon that is being researched. Survey knowledge is a representation (researcher's interpretation) of a representation (data analysis) of a representation (survey instrument) of a representation (sample) of a representation (respondents' views of what really is going on) (Brown [1]).

Qualitative research

Qualitative techniques essentially seek to recreate the listening ear and interpretative mind that so many entrepreneurs use so well. In today's large corporation, key decision-makers are likely to be some way removed from everyday transactions with customers, so they employ qualitative researchers to be their listening ears for them.

Qualitative marketing research involves the exploration and interpretation of the perceptions and behaviour of small samples of individuals, and the study of the motivators behind observed actions. It can be highly focused, exploring in depth, for example, the attitudes that buyers have towards particular brand names. The techniques used to encourage respondents to speak and behave honestly and un-selfconsciously are derived from the social sciences, in particular psychology.

During the early stages of the research process, definitions and descriptions may be needed, and it is here that qualitative research is at its most useful. It can define the parameters for future studies, and identify key criteria among consumers that can subsequently be measured using quantitative research. For example, if a supermarket observed that its older customers were unwilling to register for its loyalty card programme, it might conduct some qualitative research among its older customers in order to develop greater understanding about why this particular group was reluctant to subscribe. (Perhaps it might uncover an underlying scepticism towards the idea of deferring rewards to the future; or there may be greater concerns over privacy; or perhaps a loyalty card may even subliminally bring back memories of wartime ration cards.)

Probably the most widely used qualitative approach in marketing research is the focus group. This entails inviting a group of individuals to discuss an issue that a company is interested in learning more about. Participants are invited to contribute to an understanding of an issue on the basis of their ability, rather than on the basis of being a statistically significant representation of the population being studied. A trained moderator will guide the discussion, but she needs to be careful not to put too many ideas into the minds of participants, which might stifle their originality of thought. There are numerous approaches to managing a focus group which have the aim of reducing the bias caused by the intervention of the moderator and stimulating contribution from the invited members. Some researchers have had success by recording conversations between friends which tend to be relatively uninhibited.

An alternative to the focus group is to use a one-to-one discussion format, which is especially useful for studying the behaviour and attitudes of employees of organizations, and also where confidentiality is an important concern of participants. Although one-to-one discussions may reduce problems of confidentiality, this approach does not allow the researcher to study peer group interaction, which may be important when studying attitudes to items of ostentatious consumption.

In seeking to discover hidden meanings of phenomena, qualitative researchers use a number of techniques that are not available to the quantitative researcher. Projective techniques, including word association (often used in connection with research into proposed brand names), sentence completion, and interpreting a story board, are commonly used, but can demand skill in their interpretation.

It is very difficult to assess the validity of qualitative research techniques, and the tests for significance that are available for most quantitative techniques are largely lacking for qualitative techniques. So how can a client company that has commissioned qualitative research assess whether the findings are credible? Consider the following possibilities:

- Market research demands co-operation and trust between the client commissioning a study and the company carrying it out. The reputation that a market research agency has built for itself is particularly important where qualitative research is involved.

- Increasingly, qualitative research techniques are utilizing quantitative techniques in order to enhance their credibility (or at least the appearance of credibility). There are now a number of computer programs (e.g. NUD*IST and NVivo) which essentially analyse the content of discussions and count key words, phrases, and contexts.

Qualitative research has been a major growth activity in marketing over the past couple of decades.

Who carries out marketing research?

Marketing researchers fall into two groups.

1. There are those employed by manufacturers and services companies (often referred to as 'client' companies) who collect internal data and commission research from outside organizations when needed.

2. A large industry of market research firms is available to carry out the research that client companies are unable or unwilling to carry out themselves. (Among the larger companies in this category are BMRB, MORI, and Taylor Nelson Sofres.) Staff employed by these companies can achieve a high level of expertise in particular research techniques or particular product areas. (For example, Verdict Research has achieved particular skills in the field of retailing.) Some of these companies undertake 'omnibus' surveys on behalf of a number of clients simultaneously, thereby reducing the costs to each client.

The research process shown in Figure 4.3 allows for the expertise of both groups to be used at different stages. Client company researchers initially define a research problem, after internal discussion with marketing and other management. This is usually communicated to potential suppliers in the form of a research brief. The objectives of the study are determined by matching management information needs with what can realistically be obtained from the marketplace, particularly in the light of time and budgetary constraints, and these may well be defined after initial discussions with possible suppliers.

Specialist market research suppliers tend to dominate at the stage of data collection, for two main reasons. First, very few client companies, however large or diverse their product range, can generate sufficient research to warrant employing full-time specialist interviewers throughout the country. Much research is seasonal or one-off, and it would be more expensive for a company to retain research capacity that is required only intermittently, than to buy it in as and when required. The second reason is that respondents are more likely to give honest answers to third parties than when replying directly to representatives of the organization being discussed. Data collectors are also less likely to be biased when they are working for a company that is independent of their own employer. However, commercial market research companies have sometimes been accused of focusing more on techniques than on identifying really useful information to a company (Savage [6]).

Relationships between client companies and their suppliers can involve high levels of trust and co-operation, and many relationships between the two are very long-standing. Before deciding on the final plan, however, it is usual for client companies to approach several possible suppliers and ask for their suggestions in the form of a research proposal. The extent of involvement of the client company in the research process is largely dependent upon the size and expertise of its research department.

Marketing intelligence

Market research has so far been described in terms of establishing customers' characteristics and preferences in a structured manner. Another approach is to gather relatively unstructured information about the environment in a format that is often referred to as 'marketing intelligence'. Business owners have developed over a long time the art of 'keeping their ear close to the ground' through informal networks of contacts. With the growing sophistication of the business environment, these informal methods of gathering intelligence often need to be supplemented. In contrast to market research, intelligence gathering concentrates on picking up relatively intangible ideas and trends, especially about competitors' developments.

Carson *et al.* [2] describe how marketing managers use networks, often haphazardly and informally, to gather information. They note that for many small business owners, 'research' is inseparable from daily business. According to their study, research by networking is 'informal, often discreet, interactive, interchangeable, integrated, habitual, reactive, individualistic, and highly focused on the enterprise' ([2], p. 56).

Marketing managers can gather this intelligence from a number of sources, including the following.

- By regularly scanning newspapers, especially trade newspapers, a company can learn about competitors' planned new product launches.

- There are now many specialized media cutting services which will regularly review published material and alert a company to items that fall within pre-determined criteria.

- Employees are a valuable source of marketing intelligence, especially in services organizations where they are in regular contact with customers. Sales personnel can act as the ears as well as the mouth for an organization. Staff suggestion schemes and quality circles are often used to gain market intelligence, in addition to informal methods of listening to front-line employees.

- Similarly, intermediaries are close to customers, and their observations are often encouraged through seminars, consultation meetings, and informal communication methods.

- When a firm feels that it doesn't have the resources to undertake any of the above, it may retain consultants to provide regular briefings.

Market intelligence is a valuable contributor to the development of corporate knowledge, which is considered next.

◼ Knowledge management

Knowledge is one of the greatest assets of most commercial organizations, and its contribution to sustainable competitive advantage has been noted by many. Information represents a bridge between the organization and its environment and is the means by which a picture of the changing environment is built up within the organization. Marketing management is responsible for turning information-based knowledge into specific marketing plans.

In 1991, Ikujiro Nonaka began an article in the *Harvard Business Review* with a simple statement: 'In an economy where the only certainty is uncertainty, the one sure source of lasting competitive advantage is knowledge' (Nonaka [4]). A firm's knowledge base is likely to include, among other things, an understanding of the precise needs of customers; how those needs are likely to change over time; how those needs are satisfied in terms of efficient and effective production systems, and an understanding of competitors' activities. We are probably all familiar with companies in which knowledge seems to be very poor—the hotel reservation that is mixed up, the delivery that does not happen as specified, or junk mail which is of no interest at all. On the other hand, customers may revel in a company that delivers the right service at the right time and clearly demonstrates that it is knowledgeable about all aspects of the transaction. The small business owner may have been able to achieve all of this in his head, but in large organizations the task of managing knowledge becomes much more complex. Where it is done well, it can be a significant contributor to a firm's sustainable competitive advantage.

We need to distinguish between the terms 'knowledge' and 'information'. Even though in some senses they may be used interchangeably, many writers have suggested that the two concepts are quite distinct. Knowledge is a much more all-encompassing term, incorporating the concept of beliefs that are based on information.

Knowledge also depends on the commitment and understanding of the individual holding these beliefs, which are affected by interaction and the development of judgement, behaviour, and attitude. Knowledge has meaning only in the context of a process or capacity to act. Drucker noted that 'There is no such thing as knowledge management, there are only knowledgeable people. Information only becomes knowledge in the hands of someone who knows what to do with it' (Drucker [3]). Knowledge, then, is evidenced by its association with actions, and its source can be found in a combination of information, social interaction, and contextual situations which affect the knowledge accumulation process at an individual level.

We need to distinguish between knowledge at the level of the individual, and knowledge at the level of the organization. Organizational knowledge comprises shared understandings; it is created within the company by means of information and social interaction, and provides potential for development. It is this form of knowledge that is at the heart of knowledge management. One outcome of a knowledge-based organization has often been referred to as the 'learning organization', in which the challenge is to learn at the corporate level from what is known by individuals who make up the organization.

Two different types of knowledge can be identified.

1. Knowledge that is easily definable and is accessible is often referred to as 'explicit' knowledge. This type of knowledge can be readily quantified and passed between individuals in the form of words and numbers. Because it is easily communicated, it is relatively easy to manage. Knowledge management is concerned with ensuring that the explicit knowledge of individuals becomes a part of the organizational knowledge base and that it is used efficiently and contributes where necessary to changes in work practices, processes, and products.

2. The second type of knowledge comprises the accumulated knowledge of individuals, which is not explicit, but can still be important to the successful operation of an organization. This type of knowledge, often known as 'tacit' knowledge, is not easy to see or express; it is highly personal and is rooted in an individual's experiences, attitudes, values, and behaviour patterns. Tacit knowledge can be much more difficult to formalize and disseminate within an organization. If tacit knowledge can be captured, mobilized, and turned into explicit knowledge, it will then be accessible to others in the organization and will enable the organization to progress, rather than require individuals within it continually to have to relearn from the same point. The owner of a small business could have all of this information readily available to him in his head. The challenge taken on by many large corporations is to emulate the knowledge management of the small business owner.

MARKETING in ACTION

Management by walking about

Information is often described as management's window on the world. But what happens if management works in a large corporate head office, far removed from customers and day-to-day operations? It is sadly all too familiar for senior management to become cut off from the operations that they manage. A recent BBC television series, 'Back to the Floor', invited chief executives to spend a few days changing their role to that of a front line employee. For some of the participants this was unfamiliar territory, which hadn't been witnessed at first hand for some time (if ever). The gulf between what these key decision-makers thought was happening and what was actually happening was sometimes quite marked. In one case, the chief executive of the grocery retailer Sainsbury's seemed to be oblivious of customers' annoyance with shopping trolley design and availability, and in another the chief executive of Pickford's Removals couldn't understand why the company was so inflexible when minor changes in customers' requirements occurred. Of course, the managers of small businesses do not generally have such problems, as they are in regular contact with their customers and do not need structured information management systems to give them a window on the world. Their success in keeping in touch with customers has led many larger businesses to emulate some of their practices. 'Management by Walking About' has become a popular way in which senior executives try to gain knowledge about their marketing environment which is not immediately apparent from structured reporting systems. Archie Norman, when head of the retailer Asda, is reported to have introduced a number of innovations learnt during his regular visits to the company's shop-floors. Some companies have adopted a formal system of role exchanges where senior executives spend a period at the sharp end of their business.

If you are studying at a university, do you believe that the vice chancellor really has a good understanding of the day-to-day issues that are of greatest concern to students? Some vice chancellors have taken the bold step of trying to live student life for a day or a week. What benefits can you see in this approach? Are there any possible problems in this approach?

The transition from individuals' information to corporate knowledge requires a sharing of knowledge by all concerned. This raises problems in which employees perceive that knowledge is a powerful asset which they can use in their negotiations with senior management or other functional departments. A knowledge management programme is needed to break down a *laissez-faire* attitude, and typically would include the following elements:

- a strong knowledge-sharing culture, which can emerge only over time with the development of trust;

- measures to monitor that sharing, which may be reflected in individuals' performance reviews;

- technology to facilitate knowledge transfer, which should be as user-friendly as possible;

- established practices for the capture and sharing of knowledge—without clearly defined procedures, the technology is of only limited value;

- leadership and senior management commitment to sharing information—if senior management doesn't share information, why should anybody else bother?

It must be remembered that marketing information cannot in itself produce decisions: it merely provides data which must be interpreted by marketing managers. Also, as information collection, processing, transmission, and storage technologies improve, information is becoming more accessible not just to one particular organization, but also to its competitors. Competitive advantage is more likely to go to those companies that are best able to make use of the available information.

■ Demand forecasting

It should never be forgotten that a key task of marketing management in general, and of marketing research in particular, is to gather a better picture of the future so that a company can be prepared for it more efficiently and effectively than its competitors. Demand forecasting can involve predicting general changes in the marketing environment, which were discussed in Chapter 2. This in itself can be very difficult; for example, economists frequently disagree in their forecasts of economic growth during the year ahead. When it comes to predicting macro-environmental change, larger companies often retain expert consultants, such as the Future Foundation (**www. futurefoundation.net**), who employ economists, sociologists, and psychologists, among others, to try to build a picture of the world as it will evolve. Such macro-level forecasts can inform more detailed forecasts about market size, growth rates, market share, etc.

There have been many cases of spectacular failures to forecast demand accurately, of which the following are a few examples:

- When the Prudential Assurance company launched its new Egg credit card, it experienced an unexpectedly high level of take-up, resulting in delays and frustration for potential customers.

- Many people in the industry expected the launch of 'Freeview' digital television services in 2002 to be a flop, following the previous low levels of takeup of ITV digital services. In fact, Freeview quickly became very popular, with reports of shortages of set-top adapter boxes.

- Each Christmas seems to witness another new toy which has become an unexpected success with children, leading to shortages, while other new toys fail to sell and end up being discounted in the January sales.

Figure 4.7 London's Millennium Dome, open to the public for just one year in 2000, proved to be a disappointment in terms of visitor numbers. Against forecasts of 12 million paying visitors, only about half this figure actually visited. Forecasts were made difficult because of the absence of comparable previous projects which might have given some idea of the likely take-up. Many uncertainties remained during the forecasting process, including the effects of competing millennium attractions, the impact of press reviews, the state of the national economy, and the capacity of the local transport infrastructure

A forecast of likely demand is a crucial input to a firm's strategic and operational planning processes. In the case of the Egg credit card, the forecast of new customer applications was used as an input to the firm's human resource plan, so when the marketing demand forecast proved to be wrong, the human resource plan—which had recruited to cater for a lower level of forecast demand—also proved wrong.

The amount of effort that a firm puts into refining its demand forecasting techniques calls for a balancing of the cost of undertaking a detailed study against the cost of making an inaccurate forecast. Where capital costs are low, it may make sense to go straight to the market with a product to see what happens. It was noted earlier that this is common in the fashion clothing industry. At other times, a more analytic approach to demand forecasting is required (refer back to Figure 4.3).

A number of approaches to demand forecasting are available. Qualitative and quantitative techniques may be used as appropriate. In looking at the future, facts are hard to come by. What matters is that senior management is in a position to make better informed judgements about the future in order to aid strategic marketing planning.

Demand forecasting uses many of the analytic techniques described earlier in this chapter. A starting point for demand forecasting is an examination of historical trends. At its simplest, a firm identifies a historic and consistent long-term change in demand for a product over time and seeks to explain this in terms of change in some underlying variables, such as household income levels or price levels. Correlation and regression techniques can be used to assess the significance of historical relationships between variables. However, a simple extrapolation of past trends has a number of weaknesses. One variable, or even a small number of variables, is seldom adequate to predict future demand for a product, yet it can be difficult to identify the full set of variables that have an influence. New variables may emerge over time. There can be no certainty that the trends identified from historic data are likely to continue in the future, and the data are of diminishing value as the length of time that they are used to forecast increases.

Models have become increasingly sophisticated in their ability to forecast consumer demand. This can be explained partly by a growing amount of readily available data which can be used to build and validate a model. Reliability is improved by increasing the volume of data on which a model is based and the number of variables that are used for prediction.

Inevitably, models, no matter how sophisticated, need interpretation. This is where the creative side of marketing management is called for, especially in combining market intelligence with harder economic approaches. In interpreting quantitative demand forecasts, management must use its judgement, based on a holistic overview of the market situation.

> Marketing information can be misused by marketers, just like a drunk misuses a lamppost. Both statistics and lampposts can give support, but may provide very little illumination.

■ Chapter summary and key linkages to other chapters

Understanding customers is critical to business success, and this chapter has discussed some of the approaches to market research. Marketing management is a combination of a science and an art, and this is reflected in approaches to gathering and analysing marketing information. The chapter has built on our review of the marketing environment (Chapter 2) and buyer behaviour (Chapter 3), which marketers must try to understand and predict into the future. Appropriate research methods are necessary for conducting segmentation exercises, to be discussed in Chapter 5. In the following chapters we will look at how research is used to inform decisions about a company's product development, pricing, distribution, and promotion activities.

⬛ KEY PRINCIPLES OF MARKETING

- The ultimate aim of a company's research activity is essentially to gain a better understanding of its likely future marketing environment.
- Information is a source of a company's competitive advantage.
- Information on its own does not make decisions—management must use its judgement to interpret information.
- Learning organizations develop knowledge at a corporate level in order to provide a more efficient and effective response to environmental change.
- Research techniques need to be appropriate to the task in hand.
- Qualitative techniques provide for depth of understanding, while quantitative techniques provide for broad representation. The two techniques overlap.

CASE STUDY

Market research companies run out of information

A ready supply of information about customers, actual and potential, is vital to marketing managers. Consumers have become increasingly fragmented and sophisticated in their buying habits, while the growth in size of business units calls for information that can be easily analysed and acted upon. Gone are the days when most market research could be done simply by the owner/manager of a business listening to his customers.

Specialist data collection companies have come to play an important role in the task of collecting information about buyers. Organizations such as Experian, CACI, and Claritas have developed a role in providing socio-economic and life-style data which are sold on to client companies to make their targeting more effective. With the growth in direct marketing, it is important to many clients to have specific information about each individual customer, rather than a general aggregate for the whole market. This applies to information about new prospects, as well as new and additional information from people already on their databases, which is important because people's circumstances change. In contrast to client firms' need for this information, consumers by the end of the 1990s were showing increasing resistance to providing information for commercial purposes.

The market research industry has been concerned for a number of years about falling response rates to quantitative surveys. A Market Research Society report of 1997 pointed out that the public rarely distinguishes between anonymous research, database building, or telephone calls that start off asking for information but end up with a hard sell. A report prepared in 1998 by the Future Foundation found that only 50% of consumers were happy to provide personal information to firms with which they deal, down from over 60% in 1995. A core of people appear to be not interested in taking part in data collection exercises at all, and won't fill in questionnaires. The 2001 UK Census of Population—a foundation for many research exercises—appears to have fallen short of its claim to be a universal survey of the entire UK population, with reports of up to 2 million 'missing' people. For marketers, this is a worrying development. If the public does not offer information about their needs, wants, attitudes, and behaviour, it makes the life of the marketer more difficult.

There are a number of factors that may explain this trend. The first is that many more companies are now seeking to obtain information from buyers. Globally, ESOMAR's monitoring of the industry shows that the total market for market research worldwide in 2001 was US$15,890 million, with the USA accounting for 39% of this total, and the EU 37%. The Market Research Society estimated that in 2000 the size of the UK market research industry was £955 million, with one of the biggest growth areas being opinion research about social or moral issues. In addition, direct marketing companies have been building marketing databases of their own customers. Saturation appeared to be setting in. The result is that we can hardly visit a restaurant, buy a new item of electrical equipment, or take an aeroplane journey without being invited to give our comments. Sometimes we are approached unsolicited for our views, whether in the street or by telephone. Information is a key element of a firms' competitive advantage, so they are putting more and more effort into collecting information about customers.

Secondly, consumers are becoming increasingly aware that information which only they can reveal about themselves has commercial value. Research from the Future Foundation suggested that the majority of people were happy to provide personal details if the result was better products or services. However, the public's experience of how well such information is used often falls short of their expectations in terms of how it benefits them personally.

But with so much information-gathering going on, is there a danger of 'survey fatigue' setting in? Just how many times can a company ask customers questions about what they think of it before the whole process of carrying out a survey becomes an irritation in itself? Do customers think that their comments will ever be taken notice of by management? Careful organization of surveys can improve response rates. Stopping people when they are in a hurry to catch a train will not make an interviewer popular, but approaching them when they are captive with nothing else to do (e.g. waiting for baggage at an airport following a flight) may be more successful.

Developing some form of meaningful relationship with a recipient prior to receiving a questionnaire seems to be important. At its simplest level, an individual would receive a very simple first form. If this is completed and returned, it is followed a couple of months later with a reward pack of money-off vouchers and samples, plus a second, more detailed, questionnaire. As an example, research by Air Miles concluded that the company gets much better, more robust data if it saves detailed questions until members have had some experience of its services, rather than asking detailed questions of new recruits. And drinks retailer Bottoms Up was able to persuade 10,000 members of its loyalty programme, the Imbibers' Club, to agree to telephone interviews on their drinking habits, something that would be very difficult to do out of the blue.

A more sophisticated approach is used by Consodata, which has a contract to collect, manage, and analyse household data for the 'Jigsaw' Consumer Needs Consortium (Kimberly-Clark, Unilever, and Cadbury Schweppes). The chosen vehicle is a magazine with special offers, which over time is tailored to the individual needs of respondents as more is learned about them. As an incentive, everybody gets a reward, instead of being offered a minuscule chance of winning a jackpot. Industry sources suggested that the response rate to the first issue of the Jigsaw consortium's magazine was 30–35%, in line with the results sometimes claimed for similar data-collecting surveys undertaken via customer magazines. Again, the point is clear that consumers are freer with their information when dealing with organizations they already know and trust.

Bigger bribes to encourage people to provide data are part of the researcher's armoury. This ploy has reached new heights in the USA with reports of home shopping companies offering free computers and internet access in return for household data and the acceptance of advertising on their screen. But large bribes can lead to another problem, of samples being biased towards a new breed of professional market research respondent. There have been reports that focus groups are increasingly being dominated by a small circle of individuals who can make a reasonable living off the fee paid to participants. For the research companies, such people may be readily available and need less training and instruction than a novice. But is the information that they yield of any great value?

(Adapted from 'Data firm react to survey fatigue', *Marketing*, 29 April 1999, pp. 29–30)

Case study review questions

1. Suggest additional methods that companies can use to improve the effectiveness of their consumer data collection. What examples have you encountered?

2. Discus the limitations of statistically based consumer databases of the type discussed here. Do qualitative approaches based on small groups offer any advantages?

3. What effects do you expect the development of interactive electronic media to have on the collection of marketing research information from consumers?

CHAPTER REVIEW QUESTIONS

1. In what ways does information contribute to a firm's competitive advantage? Can a company ever have too much information?

2. What factors should influence the amount of time and money that a firm commits to the collection, analysis, and dissemination of marketing information?

3. Why is it important for large organizations to have a structured approach to marketing research?

4. Identify the most likely marketing research objectives for a hotel chain.

5. The view is often expressed that quantitative survey techniques fail to tell the whole truth about customers' perceptions of a company's products. To what extent is this true, and how can companies address this issue?

6. Compare and contrast the roles of market research and marketing intelligence. Is there a clear distinction in aims and methodologies, or are they part of a continuum?

REFERENCES

[1] Brown, S. (1998), *Postmodern Marketing*, 2. London: International Thomson Publishing.

[2] Carson, D., Gilmore, A., Perry, C., and Gronhaug, K. (2001), *Qualitative Marketing Research*. London: Sage.

[3] Drucker, P. (1999), *The Frontier of Management: where tomorrow's decisions are being shaped today.* New York: Truman Talley.

[4] Graeff, T. R. and Harmon, S. (2002), 'Collecting and Using Personal Data: consumers' awareness and concerns. *Journal of Consumer Marketing*, 19: 302–16.

[5] Nonaka, I. (1991), 'The Knowledge Creating Company'. *Harvard Business Review*, 69 (Nov–Dec): 96–104.

[6] Savage, M. (2001), 'A View from the Board Room'. *Research*, August: 16–18.

[7] Smith, D. and Dexter, A. (2001), 'Whenever I Hear the Word Paradigm I Reach for my Gun: how to stop talking and start walking'. *International Journal of Market Research*, 43: 321–40.

[8] Tuckel, P. and O'Neill, H. (2002), 'The Vanishing Respondent in Telephone Surveys'. *Journal of Advertising Research*, 42(5): 26–48.

SUGGESTED FURTHER READING

The market research process in general is described in more detail in a number of books. The following texts provide useful coverage of the principles introduced in this chapter:

Churchill, G. A. (2001), *Marketing Research: methodological foundations*. London: International Thomson Publishing.

Malhotra, N. and Birks, D. (2000), *Marketing Research*, European edn. Hemel Hempstead: Prentice-Hall International.

Wright, L. T. and Crimp, M. (2000), *Marketing Research*, 5th edn. Hemel Hempstead: Prentice-Hall.

For a more detailed discussion of some of the research methods mentioned in this chapter, the following provide an accessible insight which is of relevance to marketing students:

Gummesson, E. (1999), *Qualitative Methods in Management Research*. London: Sage.

Oakshott, L. (2001), *Essential Quantitative Methods for Business, Management and Finance*. Basingstoke: Palgrave Macmillan.

Saunders, M. N. K., Lewis, P., and Thornhill, A. (2002), *Research Methods for Business Students*. Hemel-Hempstead: Prentice-Hall.

The following regularly updated UK government statistics are frequently used as a basis for marketing research:

Basic Statistics of the European Community

Economic Trends: a monthly compendium of economic data which gives convenient access from one source to a range of economic indicators

Family Expenditure Survey: a sample survey of consumer spending habits, providing a snapshot of household spending; published annually

Population Trends: statistics on population, including population change, births and deaths, life expectancy, and migration

Regional Trends: a comprehensive source of statistics about the regions of the UK allowing regional comparisons

Social Trends: statistics combined with text, tables, and charts which present a narrative of life and lifestyles in the UK; published annually

UK National Accounts (the Blue Book): the principal annual publication for National Account statistics, covering value added by industry, the personal sector, companies, public corporations, central and local government; published annually

The subject of turning research information into corporate knowledge is addressed in the following:

Davenport, T. H. and Prusak, L. (2000), *Working Knowledge: how organizations manage what they know*. Cambridge, Mass.: Harvard Business School Press.

Gamble, P. and Blackwell, J. (2001), *Knowledge Management: a state of the art guide*. London: Kogan Page.

Pfeffer, J. and Sutton, R. (2000), *Knowing–Doing Gap: how smart companies turn knowledge into action*. Cambridge, Mass.: Harvard Business School Press.

USEFUL WEB LINKS

Visit the companion website to this book, with lots of interesting additional material and links for each chapter:

www.oup.com/uk/booksites/busecon

Office for National Statistics

www.ons.gov.uk

The Market Research Society

www.marketresearch.org.uk

The World Association of Opinion and Marketing Research Professionals

www.esomar.nl

Decision Analyst, Inc., provides a website which offers organized, indexed, and annotated links to sources of free economic and marketing research data available on the web

www.SecondaryData.com

KEYWORDS

- **Analysis of variance**
- **Cluster analysis**
- **Conjoint analysis**
- **Correlation analysis**
- **Customer panels**
- **Desk research**

- **Environmental scanning**
- **Explicit knowledge**
- **Field research**
- **Focus group**
- **Key clients**
- **Knowledge**
- **Management By Walking About**
- **Market research**
- **Marketing intelligence**
- **Marketing research**
- **Models**
- **Mystery shoppers**
- **Neural network analysis**
- **Omnibus surveys**
- **Primary research**
- **Qualitative research**
- **Quantitative research**
- **Regression analysis**
- **Sampling**
- **Secondary research**
- **SERVQUAL**
- **Tacit knowledge**

Segmentation positioning and targeting

CHAPTER OBJECTIVES

Customers are becoming increasingly diverse in their needs and aspirations, and less inclined to accept an 'average' product. Some of the bases for identifying different types of customer are familiar and readily observable, such as age, gender, and geographical location. Others, such as attitudes and life-style, may be more difficult to identify, but can be crucial for understanding consumers' buying processes. The purpose of segmentation is to identify groups of buyers who respond in a similar way to any given marketing stimuli. This chapter explores the bases for market segmentation and how these are used by companies to target selected groups. To be effective, a company's products must be positioned relative to competitors' products in such a way that targeted segments find them the most attractive for satisfying their needs.

Why segment markets?

From Chapter 1 you will recall that a focus on meeting customers' needs is a defining characteristic of marketing. Organizations that make presumptions about customers' needs, or produce goods and services that are chosen for their convenience in production, are probably not practising the marketing concept. A true marketing orientation requires companies to focus on meeting the needs of individual customers. In a simple world where consumers all have broadly similar needs and expectations, a company could probably justify developing a marketing programme that meets the needs of the 'average' customer. In the early days of motoring, Henry Ford successfully sold as many standard, black Model T Fords as he was able to produce. In the modern world of marketing, few companies can have the luxury of producing just one product to satisfy a very large market. Some still can—for example, water supply utility companies generally produce a single standard of water for all of their customers—but this is the exception rather than the rule. Most companies face markets that are becoming increasingly fragmented in terms of the needs customers seek to satisfy. So, while Henry Ford's customers may have been quite happy to have a plain black car, today's car buyers seek to satisfy a much wider range of needs. The 'average' customer that Henry Ford appealed to is becoming increasingly a myth.

Segmentation, then, is essentially about identifying groups of buyers within a marketplace who have needs that are distinctive in the way they deviate from the 'average' consumer (Figure 5.1). Some consumers may treat satisfaction of one particular need as a high priority, whereas others may regard this need as quite trivial. We saw in Chapter 3 how an understanding of needs is crucial to the study of buyer behaviour. We will pick up the question of needs again by considering the buying behaviour for cars. Buyers no longer select a car solely on the basis of a car's ability to satisfy a need to get them from A to B: in addition, they may seek to satisfy any of the following needs from a car purchase:

- to give them status in the eyes of their peer group;
- to provide safety and security for themselves and their families;
- to project a particular image of themselves;
- to provide a cost-effective means of transport;
- to be seen making a gesture towards the environment by buying a 'green' car;
- if it is a company car, to save company car tax.

There are many more possible factors that might influence an individual's choice of car. The important point here is that the market is composed of buyers who approach their decisions to buy a car in very different ways. Therefore, the features that each looks for in the product offer may differ quite markedly from the market average. It follows that, with a wide dispersion of market needs, a marketing plan based on satisfying the needs of the average buyer will be unlikely to succeed in a competitive marketplace. If another company can better satisfy the needs of small specialist groups, then the company that seeks to serve them with just an 'average' product offer will lose business from this group.

We will define the process of market segmentation as

the identification of sub-sets of buyers within a market who share similar needs and who have similar buying processes.

In an ideal world, each individual buyer would be considered to have a unique set of needs which she seeks to satisfy, and firms would tailor their product offering to each of their customers. In the case of some expensive items of capital equipment bought by firms, this indeed does happen. (For example, there are very few buyers of large power

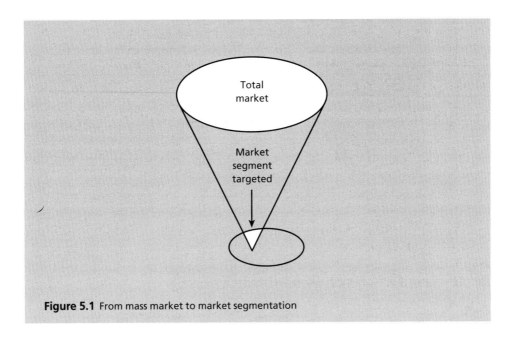

Figure 5.1 From mass market to market segmentation

stations in the UK, so firms can justifiably treat each customer as a segment of one.) In the case of products that are relatively low in value and high in sales volume, it would be practically impossible for firms to cater to each individual's needs, although there is evidence that developments in technology are allowing for a much greater degree of customization than has previously been the case. (We will return to this in Chapter 11 when we discuss direct marketing.)

Segmentation should not be regarded as a technique that is unique to marketing. In fact, wise marketers are simply following a critical approach to decision making which is shared by many other professions and disciplines. The critical approach revolves around breaking a large problem down into a number of smaller problems and resolving those smaller problems in the most appropriate way. In this case, the 'problem' for the marketer is how to get the market to buy its products. The problem can be broken down into the sub-problems of how to get particular sub-groups within those markets to buy its products. The solution to each of these problems might be quite different. Analogies can be drawn with many other problems of decision making. An engineer designing a bridge breaks the bridge down into component parts when specifying materials to be used. The needs of the different parts of the structure would probably call for quite different strengths of material. Just as the marketer would not use one product to satisfy the needs of the entire market, the engineer would not use just one gauge of metal to build the entire bridge structure. Both the marketer and the engineer have used critical thinking to break a large problem down into smaller problems (Figure 5.2).

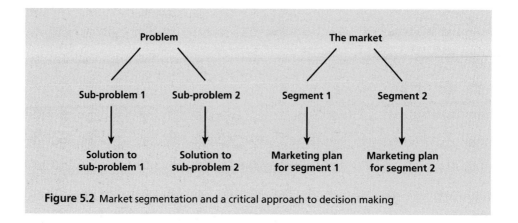

Figure 5.2 Market segmentation and a critical approach to decision making

■ Criteria for effective segmentation

Market segmentation should be regarded as the product of critical thinking rather than as some pre-determined set of procedures. There is no underlying theory to the process of market segmentation. It follows that what is an appropriate basis for segmenting one market may not be appropriate to all markets.

Before we begin to look at the bases on which marketers can segment any given market, we need to be aware of the criteria by which the effectiveness of any segmentation basis can be assessed. We will consider here four important criteria: usefulness to a company's marketing planning; size of the resulting segments; their measurability; and their accessibility.

Is the basis of market segmentation useful to the company?

It is easy to develop bases for market segmentation while losing sight of the purpose of the exercise. Essentially, the exercise is worthwhile only if it allows a company profitably to penetrate a greater proportion of its market than would have been the case if the exercise had not been undertaken. Groups identified as homogeneous market segments must be just that: similar in terms of the needs and buying behaviour of the individuals they contain. Many companies fail in their segmentation exercises because their assumptions about homogeneity within a segment overlook some critical differences within the segment which leads to varied responses to a product offer that has been specifically targeted at the segment. For example, a segment for overseas package holidays defined as 'affluent, married working women' may overlook the fact that women within this segment have very divergent views on the features they seek from a holiday, depending on the age and structure of their families. The buying behaviour of those affluent, married, working women who seek to take their children away with them is quite likely to be significantly different from those who seek to travel by themselves or just with their partners. To be more effective, market segmentation must recognize the diversity of needs within this group.

Are the segments of an economic size?

Any basis for segmentation should yield segments that are of a size that a company can profitably exploit. Companies face a dilemma here, because as segments get smaller they get closer to achieving the marketing philosophy of satisfying each customer's needs as though each one were the centre of all the company's attention. The problem for the company is that smaller segments may be uneconomic to provide for. What is a reasonable size of segment varies from one market to another, and is constantly changing over time. In the financial services industry, it is possible to develop quite specific products to target very small segments of a market. For example, it would involve relatively little effort by an insurance company to develop motor insurance policies that specifically meet the needs of people driving 'classic' vintage cars, further sub-divided into those who live in the North of England, and further sub-divided into those aged over 50 years. In principle, there are few operational reasons why an insurance broker should not focus on a segment that small. At the other extreme, a company manufacturing paint for the private household market might find it difficult to offer a range as customer-focused as this. For example, a paint manufacturer might wish to produce variants of paints for the following identified segments:

- users who are averse to painting (for this group, the manufacturer might develop a product that is non-spill and delicately perfumed);
- the 'professional' home decorator segment who seeks perfection through multi-coat application;
- the time-constrained perfectionist who seeks a one-coat paint with durable finish;
- the adventurous, who seek special-effect patterns from their paint (e.g. mottled effects).

To produce each new variant of paint, the manufacturer would probably have to stop its production lines to prepare for the next specialized product. Worse still, it would have to persuade its wholesalers and retailers to stock each such variant. When each colour variant is multiplied by the number of segment-specific formulations, it is clear that the stockholding problems for retailers and wholesalers would be immense.

Manufacturers are becoming increasingly able to offer specialized goods to meet the needs of small market segments. Service industries have had this flexibility for some time, and are now exploiting it to the full with the use of information technology. Within the manufacturing sector, flexible manufacturing systems are allowing smaller production runs to be achieved economically. For Henry Ford, producing even a slight

Figure 5.3 The marketing environment has tended to allow firms to target increasingly small market segments. Flexible manufacturing systems, interactive communication via the internet and more flexible stock handling methods have contributed to this. In the consumer market for paint, which is dominated in the UK by two large manufacturers and a handful of major retail outlets, a market exists for specialist organic paints. Ecos Organic Paints offers a range of environmentally friendly paints targeted at niche markets of paint buyers who may be concerned about allergies or environmental damage. Using flexible manufacturing and stock handling systems, the company is able to offer next day delivery of a wide range of paints (Reproduced with permission of Ecos Organic Paints)

variant of his original car would have meant stopping the production line and re-tooling for a new model. Today, car assembly lines employ computerized design and manufacturing systems, which, combined with interchangeability of components, allow many different models to come off the same production line.

Can the market segments be measured?

Ideally, companies should be able to know the precise size of all market segments that it has identified. This is important in order that segments can be compared and their profit potentials assessed. Unfortunately, data are often not available to quantify market segments. Marketers therefore face a further dilemma in defining market segments. Should they go for segments that they believe exist but cannot measure, or should they define segments only on the basis of what can accurately be measured, but which may have little bearing on the homogeneity of consumers' needs and buying processes? As an example, the UK Population Census gives a lot of valuable information which is frequently used as a basis for identifying market segments (for example the age profile of an area, number of people per household, etc.). However, marketers are often interested in a more subjective assessment of individuals, such as their attitudes and life-styles. Unfortunately, there is very little published information on these more subjective aspects of market segments. While we know quite accurately the size of the segment of people aged over 60 and living alone in a particular area, there is very little readily available information about how many people living in that area can be described as 'environmentally aware' or 'liberal in attitudes' or any other measure of attitudes or life-style. Inevitably, marketing managers must make a trade-off between the need for information that is objective and reliable on the one hand and subjective and creative on the other.

Fortunately for marketers, the sources of information available that can be used to segment markets are constantly increasing. In addition to traditional government statistical sources, many private-sector organizations (for example Mintel, Keynote, and the Henley Centre) frequently commission and publish research that is based on surveys of samples of the population.

Are the segments accessible to the company?

There is little point in going to a lot of effort in defining segments of a market when those segments are not accessible to the company, or ever likely to be. Inaccessibility can come about for a number of reasons.

- The company may be prohibited by law from entering certain markets. (For example, many overseas governments restrict the rights of foreign companies to serve their domestic market.)

- Some buyers in a market may be tied to suppliers by long-term supply contracts. In the case of subsidiaries of large corporations, the holding company may require its subsidiaries to obtain its purchases from within the group.

- Although it may be possible, the cost of gaining access to a market segment may be prohibitive. A manufacturer of building materials in the UK may in theory be able to supply a segment of small building contractors in southern Italy, but the cost of transporting its bulky goods over the distances involved may make the segment effectively inaccessible.

Although a segment may be inaccessible to a company now, this may not always continue to be the case. Changes in legislation may make possible something that was previously illegal for a company. Policies of large companies towards the contracting out of supplies may present new opportunities. Even segments that seemed inaccessible because of high transport costs may become accessible through the development of a joint venture company.

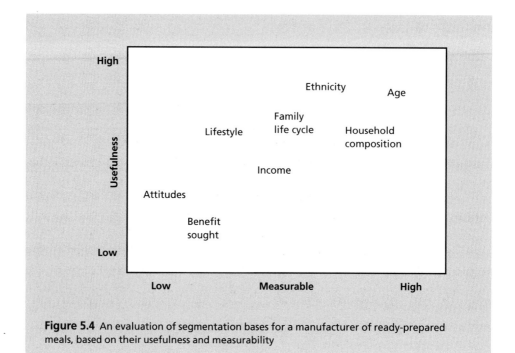

Figure 5.4 An evaluation of segmentation bases for a manufacturer of ready-prepared meals, based on their usefulness and measurability

Bases for market segmentation

A basis for segmenting a market should satisfy the criteria described above. It was noted that companies often need to make trade-offs in arriving at a basis for market segmentation that meets these criteria. It follows therefore that firms seldom use one basis for market segmentation alone. In Figure 5.4 a number of segmentation bases are plotted in terms of their measurability and usefulness to a typical manufacturer of ready-prepared meals. (Segmentation here is defined in terms of final consumers, although, as Chapter 9 will discuss, segmentation can also be applied to different types of intermediary who will handle the product.)

Markets can be segmented using a variety of philosophical approaches. In terms of operationalizing these approaches, demographic approaches, socio-economic approaches, and psychographic approaches are commonly used. Overlap often occurs between these approaches to segmentation.

Demographic bases for segmentation

Demography is the study of population characteristics, and demographers have used a number of key indicators in their studies of populations. Most methods of segmenting consumer markets make some use of demographic characteristics. In this section we will consider a number of demographic-related bases for segmenting markets: age, the stage in the family life-cycle, gender, and household composition.

Age

Age is probably one of the most widely used bases for market segmentation. It satisfies many of the criteria for effective segmentation discussed above. It is useful to companies because demand for many products appears to be age related. There are many obvious examples; for example, music buying peaks among the 18–25 year age group, and the purchase of cruise holidays increases after the age of 50. There are also more subtle age related patterns of demand within particular categories of product. Within the UK retail sector, for example, many chains are associated with particular age groups. So, while the Arcadia clothing chain's Top Shop brand attracts a mainly young 18–30 year age segment, its Principles brand is more attractive to the 21–40 year segment and its Hawkshead brand appeals more to a 35+ year segment. The usefulness of age can be partly explained by the observation that people's tastes change as they grow older. Some of this may be related to their stage in the family life-cycle, which is age related, as well as to changes in disposable income (see below).

Age segmentation meets another important criterion in that it is generally easy to measure the size of segments. Population censuses record respondents' ages, while many privately collected sources of information (such as company sponsored questionnaires) frequently ask for such information. A company can therefore be reasonably confident about how many people belong to a particular age segment within a specific area. This information might be vital to a retail chain seeking the best areas in which to locate new branches, given that demand for its format of stores is very age specific.

Of course, age alone is not usually a good basis for market segmentation. Within any age segment, individuals can be observed who exhibit quite different buying behaviour. However, differences often relate to the preference for specific brands rather than the consumption of a particular product. For example, while consumption of whisky is related to age, considerable diversity exists within age segments in brand preferences.

A further reservation on the use of age as a segmentation variable is that there may be little correlation between an individual's actual biological age and his perceived age. This can be seen at one extreme in 'wannabe' teenagers who seek to act out the life-style of their older peers, and at the other extreme by the 'young at heart' who believe themselves to be ten or twenty years younger than they actually are. There has been interesting research into the increasing desire of older people to perpetuate their youth and the effects on marketing of differences between actual age and self-ascribed age. It could be argued that the most important determinant of a person's buying behaviour is the age that he thinks he is, rather than his actual age. Many companies have exploited this opportunity; for example, tour operators offer activity cruises targeted at retired people (Precision Marketing [7]). However, while information on biological age is often readily

Stage in family life cycle	Possible main emphasis of food buying
Dependent child	Main food purchased is for snacks. Attracted by the novelty and packaging of food.
Young independent adult	Eating out, possibly at fast food outlets. Minimum effort put into preparing food at home—home-consumed food is often from simple ready-made meals.
Adult, married, no children	Quite likely to eat out at restaurants. Willing to experiment in home cooking, although may still buy ready-made meals for home consumption.
Adult, married, dependent children	Eating out is reduced and cooking at home concentrates on meeting the needs of the whole family. Budgeting becomes tighter and economy replaces variety as a driving force behind food purchases.
Adult, married, independent children	Greater time and money now available for eating out and being adventurous with home-prepared food. Can afford ready-made meals, but prefers to prepare own food.
Sole survivor	Average size of food purchase declines. Emphasis on food items that are easy to prepare.

Figure 5.5 Effects of stage in family life-cycle on an individual's food buying behaviour

available, data relating to perceived age can generally be established only by sample survey approaches.

Family life-cycle

Individuals typically go through a number of family roles, beginning with that of a dependent child and proceeding through a young single adult, a married adult with dependent children, a married adult with independent children, and finally a sole survivor. At each stage of development, an individual's buying preferences are likely to change—and, just as importantly, their ability to pay for those purchases will change too. There are many obvious marketing opportunities associated with specific stages in the life-cycle. For example, a young adult with no financial responsibilities is a prime target for many leisure related items such as music, while an individual with a young dependent family is an important target for firms selling childcare products. Figure 5.5 illustrates some of the changes in food buying habits which may arise as an individual progresses through the family life-cycle.

Marketers are often particularly interested in 'trigger' points in people's lives. These are events that suddenly change a person's behaviour, and they are frequently family related. Setting up home together, the birth of a first child, and the death of a partner are examples of events that can profoundly affect what an individual buys and how she buys it.

Figure 5.6 Market segments are often defined in terms of individuals who are at transition points in their lives. Life-cycle Marketing Limited publishes the pregnancy guide 'Emma's Diary' and an interactive website (http://www.emmasdiary.co.uk) which guide parents-to-be through the various stages of pregnancy and childbirth. By registering with the company, individuals receive further information and offers appropriate to their needs at the different stages of their pregnancy. The company has built up a valuable database of customers who have come to trust the advice given by Emma's Diary. Advertisers in its book and website realize that the birth of a child, especially the first one, is a significant trigger to new patterns of expenditure. Targeted individuals are likely to be highly receptive to the firms' messages (Reproduced with permission of Life-cycle Marketing Ltd)

Of course, the family life-cycle shown in Figure 5.5 is an ideal type, and most western countries are seeing increasing deviation from it. Later marriage, a rising divorce rate, and more single-parent families have created family units that do not fit into this ideal. Marketers have responded to such change, for example by offering domestic support services aimed at busy, affluent single-parent families.

Gender

It is quite evident that gender differences account for many variations in consumer buying behaviour. At first sight it might seem obvious that companies providing a wide range of goods and services will have developed product offers that are particularly targeted at males or females. So there are men's clothes and women's clothes; magazines aimed at women and those aimed at men; and cosmetics emphasizing their appeal to one gender or the other. Gender is a very commonly used basis for segmenting markets. Not only does it often correspond to crucial differences in buying behaviour, but it is also an easy one to measure. Firms can have a reasonably good idea of the gender-specific market in any given area.

We do however need to be careful how we use gender as a basis for market segmentation. In the first place, it has to be remembered that one of the criteria for effective segmentation is that it should identify homogeneity in *buying* behaviour. There is a lot of evidence that for many products a person of one gender may buy a product that is intended for use by someone of the other gender. It has been estimated, for example, that in the UK over half of all men's' underwear is purchased by women, with men having a relatively minor part in the buying process. A segment of men's underwear buyers that should be of interest to manufacturers is therefore women. The way women buy underwear, the retailers that they buy from, and the features that they look for are likely to be quite different from these processes of men. It follows therefore that the female buyer segment represents an important segment for manufacturers of men's underwear.

A further reservation to the use of gender as a segmentation basis is its frequent confusion with a classification based on sex. Sex is essentially a biological description, which in itself explains many of the observed differences in products sought by men and women (e.g. the use of bras and tampons). Gender is essentially a social construct and is influenced by social conditioning. Western societies have seen a convergence in many male and female values, although there remains argument about just how far this has gone. Concepts such as aggressiveness, competitiveness, and sensation seeking, which have traditionally been associated with male values, are increasingly being seen in females (e.g. heavy drinking 'ladettes'). Similarly, some observers have suggested that 'new men' are taking on traditional female traits of caring, nurturing, and reconciling. Many marketers have therefore moved on from segmentation based on a dichotomous male/female sex classification to a segmentation basis which recognizes a wide range of gender orientations. For example, the life-style and buying behaviour of career women is likely to be quite different from that of housewives.

A further issue in gender based segmentation is the emergence of segments of gay or lesbian people, whose buying behaviour may not fit neatly within dichotomous segments of male/female. Many companies have developed marketing programmes that are aimed at these groups, often seeking through promotional messages to promote accommodating and positive images of them. Manipulating gender images to accommodate different groups can create its own problems if not done carefully. If a company seeks to associate a product targeted at men with the values held by gay groups, it may alienate men with more traditional male values.

Ethnic group

The United Kingdom, like many other western countries, has become much more diverse in the ethnic backgrounds of its population. Despite years of integration, there is evidence that many ethnic groups retain distinctive preferences in their purchases which distinguishes them from the native community (Interfocus [5]). For example, many Chinese migrants who have settled in the UK continue to buy authentic eastern style food, providing a marketing opportunity for many small retailers which has not been fully exploited by the larger supermarkets. Ethnic groups remain important segments for travel related services—for visiting friends and relatives, and for pilgrimages.

As in the case of gender, segmentation purely on the basis of biological origins may not be as useful as an individual's self-ascribed ethnic background. While some members of an ethnic group may wish to associate themselves primarily with the values and life-style of their host community, others may be proud of their background and make purchases that reinforce their ethnicity. This may lead, among other things, to such groups being accessible to a consumer goods manufacturer only if that firm distributes through the ethnically owned businesses to which this group may be loyal.

MARKETING and SOCIAL RESPONSIBILITY

Segmentation or discrimination?
Segmentation and targeting are central to the marketers' task of meeting consumers' needs at a profit to their organization. But to other social commentators, the practices of segmentation and targeting may appear to be more like discrimination, with all the connotations of social divisiveness that have been associated with various forms of social discrimination. Admittedly, marketers seldom find themselves practising the kind of discrimination that typified South Africa during its years of apartheid, but there can be a thin line between the desirable aims of segmentation and the undesirable consequences of discrimination.

Legislation in most western countries is gradually squeezing out the opportunities for marketers blatantly to sell their goods and services to one group but not to another. The days when the owner of a bar could admit customers on the basis of their colour are now long gone. Nightclubs in the UK that once advertised different prices for men and women would now most likely find themselves breaking the Sex Discrimination Act. However, marketers have found more subtle ways of pursuing their segmentation and targeting strategies. A bar may subtly make its atmosphere more conducive to one ethnic group and less attractive to others; nighclubs have learnt that discriminating on the basis of gender may be illegal, but a differential pricing policy based on whether a customer is wearing trousers or a skirt may come close to achieving the nightclub's objectives legally.

Despite a growing volume of legislation in developed countries to protect clearly identifiable groups based on sex, race, disability, and, increasingly, age, many people remain concerned that the processes of segmentation and targeting are leaving pockets of individuals who are denied access to many basic services. This is seen in the way that banks in most western countries have targeted relatively affluent individuals with a steady source of income. In the UK a sizeable group of people find it difficult to borrow money from the mainstream banks, or even to open a basic bank account. Without a bank account, many life opportunities are closed to individuals. In the United States, banks have been suspected of 'redlining' certain areas of towns, from which the banks will not take new customers. Many states have responded with legislation making such geographically generalized basis for selection illegal. In the UK, geodemographics remains an important basis for banks' segmentation and targeting, but, although there is no legislation to prevent geodemographic targeting, the government has shown its impatience with banks' reluctance to target poorer groups, even with basic bank accounts. One initiative in response to this apparent problem was the creation of a 'Universal Bank', based on collaboration between the main banks and local post offices, making a basic bank account facility available to poorer people with a bad credit history.

When does segmentation become discrimination? To what extent should commercial organizations be expected to do business with individuals who, on a narrow commercial basis, are unlikely to be profitable? How far will companies' shrewd analysis of their social and political environment—and a visible response to problems of emerging discrimination—allow these issues to be resolved? Or will it take further government legislation to protect the interests of disadvantaged groups who may be further marginalized in society by commercial firms' segmentation and targeting policies?

Household composition

A wide range of goods and services are bought by households as an economic unit. The weekly household shopping, the annual holiday, and the family car are typically purchased to meet the needs of the economic unit as a whole rather than of individuals within it. Households differ in their size and composition, and these differences are associated with diverse buying behaviour. Segmenting markets on the basis of the size of the household buying unit therefore makes a lot of sense for many products. Furthermore, there is a lot of readily available information about household structure from the national census and other sources.

One indicator of household structure is the number of people that the household comprises. In the UK, as in most western countries, the average size of household units has declined as extended families have given way to nuclear families. More recently, there has been growth in the number of single-person households, which now account for over 10% of all households. The buying needs of single-person household can differ quite markedly from those of a family unit; for example, it is more likely to seek smaller pack sizes and products which satisfy the needs of the individual buyer rather than the whole household. As with all bases of segmentation, it is important to avoid over-generalization, as the single-person household comprising a retired state pensioner is likely to behave very differently from that of a young, professional single person.

A second indicator of household structure is the composition of individuals' roles within it. This is much more difficult to measure than size alone, but can be very useful because it is associated with quite distinctive buying patterns. In recent years, most western countries have seen a growth in the numbers of households that are composed of something other than the ideal type family of husband, wife, and two children. A rising divorce rate has meant that there is a growing segment of consumers who live in single-parent households, and who are often (but not always) poorer than a two-parent family in terms of money and time. Some travel companies have specifically targeted this segment to fill capacity at quiet times of the year.

Other types of household that may present opportunities to particular companies include those comprising groups of friends sharing, an elderly parent living with grown-up children, and people living in institutionalized homes.

Socio-economic bases for segmentation

It has been traditional to talk about class differences in the way that goods and services are purchased. We saw in Chapter 3 that an individual's perception of her class may be an important influence on her buying behaviour. However, marketers find the concept of social class too value-laden and imprecise to be of much practical use. Instead, more measurable indicators of social class are generally used, in particular occupation and income.

Occupation

Since 1921, government statisticians in the UK have divided the population into six classes, based simply on occupation. This has resulted in the following familiar classification system:

Class category	Occupation
A	Higher managerial, administrative, or professional
B	Intermediate managerial, administrative, or professional
C1	Supervisory or clerical, and junior managerial, administrative, or professional
C2	Skilled manual
D	Semi-skilled and unskilled manual
E	State pensioners or widows (no other earners), casual or lower grade workers, or long-term unemployed

These segment labels have been widely used. For example, some newspapers have traditionally stressed the number of A/B readers they have. However, it became increasingly clear that six classifications could not fully explain the impact of class on buying behaviour. In a 1998 report by Rose and O'Reilly [8], the Government accepted the shortcomings of traditional classifications and the report's main recommendations for a new classification, to be called National Statistics Socio-economic Classification (NS-SEC) and implemented from the 2001 Census. The uncertainty of work and the demise of a job for life had undermined the old classification system, so the new system is intended to take account of such things as the size of individuals' employing firms and their pension rights, effectively reflecting an individual's status in the purchasing marketplace.

Despite the improvements noted above, segmentation based on occupation remains fairly crude compared with the advances achieved using geodemographic methods (discussed below). Perhaps surprisingly, many marketers still refer to the old A/B/C1/C2/D/E basis of classification, perhaps because of its simplicity and a shared general understanding about the type of person contained in each of these groups.

Income

Many studies have shown that, as individuals' incomes increase, their expenditure on certain categories of product increases. For example, Mintel, in a study of the leisure industry, found a strong correlation between income and expenditure on a range of leisure activities.

There are three commonly used approaches to measuring income:

1. *Total income before taxation*: This is gross income, which is widely quoted and understood by most people.

2. *Disposable income*: This refers to the income that individuals have available to spend after taxation. It follows that, as taxes rise, disposable income falls.

3. *Discretionary income*: This is a measure of disposable income less expenditure on the necessities of life, such as mortgage payments. Discretionary income can be

significantly affected by sudden changes in the cost of mortgages and other items of expenditure, such as travel-to-work costs, which form a large component of household budgets.

All of these can be measured at the unit of the individual, or of the whole household.

Marketers are most often interested in consumers' discretionary incomes. A casual analysis of advertisements on television will show that most are aiming to gain an increased share of discretionary income—on an overseas holiday, a new mobile phone, or a takeaway meal, for example.

Despite its apparent correlation with buying behaviour, the use of income as a segmentation variable has some limitations. Obtaining data on individuals' incomes can be much more difficult than for occupation, and people are often reluctant to give this information when asked. Surveys that attempt to gather this information can be subject to mis-reporting by individuals. Even within segments of similar discretionary income, differences in actual spending levels arise, accounted for by differences in spending/ saving ratios.

Psychographic bases for segmentation

So far, most of the bases for segmentation have been reasonably measurable. However, they are often criticized for missing the unique personality factors that distinguish one person from another, and many studies have suggested that psychographic segmentation has better predictive power than demographic bases (e.g. Lin [6]). Under the heading of psychographic factors, we will consider the effects of life-style, attitudes, values, benefits sought, and loyalty.

Life-styles

People of a similar age and socio-economic status can nevertheless lead quite different life-styles, and firms have been quick to adapt their products to meet the needs of these life-styles. Many companies in the tourism sector, for example, have been observed to base their segmentation and targeting on life-style factors (e.g. Gonzalez and Bello [3]). It is very difficult to accurately describe a life-style and even more difficult to have any realistic measure of the size of segments of different life-style groups. Nevertheless, as societies fragment into ever smaller groups of shared interests and activities, companies have recognized the need to develop ideal types of life-style segments. The depth of research that underlies these approaches to segmentation can be questionable, with many segments being held up as ideal-type segments on only a weak empirically derived basis. Thus, segments described by terms such as 'Yuppies' and 'Dinkies' have come to acquire a meaning among marketers, if only as unquantified ideal-types of the segment being targeted. Many life-style segmentation methods have been developed for specific sectors. In one study of grocery retailing in the UK, the Henley Centre for Forecasting identified segments of shoppers using a multi-variable approach which took account of demographic factors such as age, sex, and income as well as life-style, personality, and finally attitude to the shopping experience. As with so many of these studies, the resultant new breeds of shopper were given glib titles:

- The *Harried Hurrier* was typically burdened with squabbling children and crippled by a severe lack of time. Hurriers were averse to anything that eats into their precious minutes such as having too much choice, which makes them impatient.
- *Young-at-Hearts* spent less money than the Harried Hurriers; they tended to be middle-aged, but, in contrast to the first group, had time on their hands and liked to try new products.
- An important and growing species of grocery shopper was identified as the *Young, Affluent and Busy (or 'YABs')*; for these, money is not a major constraint in their quest for convenience and more interesting products, but they do have a low boredom threshold.
- The *Fastidious* were attracted by in-store hygiene and tidiness; these are expected to grow in importance.
- *Begrudgers* were mainly male and tended to shop only out of obligation to others.
- The *Perfect Wife and Mother* was concerned with the balanced diet; these appeared to be in numerical decline.
- To compensate for the decline in the Perfect Wife and Mother, the number of *Obsessive Fad-Followers* has been increasing; this group's choice of food tended to be dominated by brand image and current trends.

There have been many similar approaches to life-style segmentation. For example, Sony's Consumer Segment Marketing Division has a mission to 'develop an intimate understanding of Sony's end consumers . . . from cradle to grave', and divided its consumers into the following segments: Affluent; CE Alphas (early adopters); Zoomers (55+); SoHo (small office/home office); Young Professionals/DINKs (double income no kids, aged 25–34); Families (35–54); and Gen Y (under 25) (Elkin [2]). While such approaches may be very useful for defining possible target markets, they are difficult to measure because of the absence of data beyond sample surveys.

Attitudes

Life-styles are observable, even if it can be difficult to estimate how many of each life-style group exist in a particular population. Attitudes are much more difficult to identify and may be revealed only in subtle ways. More importantly for marketers, what is a

MARKETING in ACTION

What your sandwich says about you

What does an individual's choice of sandwich say about him? The retailer Tesco has undertaken research that has revealed how complex the market for ready-made sandwiches has become, with clear segments emerging of people who look for quite different types of sandwich. In an attempt to define and target its lunch customers more precisely, the company found that well-paid executives invariably insisted on 'designer' sandwiches made from ciabatta and focaccia with sun-dried tomatoes and costing about £2.50. Salespeople and middle ranking executives were more inclined to opt for meaty triple-deckers. Upwardly mobile women aged 25–40 chose low-calorie sandwiches costing around £1.49. Busy manual workers tended to grab a sandwich that looked affordable, simple, and quick to eat, such as the ploughman's sandwich that Tesco sold for £1.15. Tesco's research claimed that sandwiches have become an important statement made by individuals and need to be targeted appropriately. What do your snack meals say about you?

hidden attitude for an individual today may tomorrow become a behaviour that is manifested in purchase decisions to support a chosen life-style. Many people may possess an attitude towards an item but are afraid of being an early adopter of behaviour associated with that attitude. Among males, there may be a significant segment of the population that possesses an attitude that it should be acceptable for men to use cosmetics traditionally associated with women. They may, however, be reluctant to buy and use male cosmetics until they consider that it has become socially acceptable to do so. For this segment, the marketing programme should emphasize the need to gain gradual acceptability of the product among this group, for example by appealing to wives/girlfriends as key influencers on the decision to purchase.

Values

Sociologists have distinguished a higher level of individual distinctiveness in the form of values. Values are standards, rules, norms, goals, ideals, or underlying evaluative criteria which we use when making judgements. They are deep-seated and tend to be fairly enduring within an individual. Attitudes and life-styles are built on this higher-order structure of values. Individuals have been attributed with having a number of contrasting underlying values; for example, values of self-centredness alongside values of communality and sharing. Values can be even more difficult to measure than attitudes, and apparent inconsistencies may question the existence of a deep-seated value system. An individual may appear to have a value system based on caution when driving a car, but may nevertheless be quite reckless when investing in financial services.

Benefits sought

The same product may provide a variety of benefits to different people. A watch, for example, can be purchased by one segment primarily as an accurate timepiece, by another as a fashion item above all else, and by still others as items of ostentatious consumption. There will also be segments who buy a watch as a gift for someone. Each segment is likely to respond in different ways to variations in product design, packaging, pricing, and promotion. Inevitably, overlap between benefit categories exists and it is really possible to determine the size of each segment only on the basis of sample surveys.

Loyalty

In many markets, a segment can be found that shows considerable loyalty to one brand, while other segments will be prepared to switch between brands in response to products offering more benefits and/or lower prices. This may reflect differences in individuals' willingness to take on the risk of switching to a new supplier. For some people, loyalty may occur through inertia and a reluctance to take the perceived risk of changing supplier.

Geodemographic bases for segmentation

Marketers have traditionally used geographical areas as a basis for market segmentation. Very often, there have been very good geographical reasons why product preferences should vary between regions. The long, dark, cold winter nights of northern England and Scotland have led the inhabitants of these regions to take proportionately more winter sun holidays than their counterparts in the south of England, despite their having lower average levels of disposable income. Many companies have managed to adapt their product offer to meet the needs of different regional segments. National newspapers, for example, produce regional editions to satisfy readers' needs for local news coverage and advertisers' needs for a regional advertising facility.

More recently, geographical segmentation has been undertaken at a much more localized level, and linked to other differences in social, economic, and demographic characteristics. The resulting basis for segmentation is often referred to as *geodemographic*. The premise of geodemographic analysis is that where a person lives is closely associated with a number of indicators of his socio-economic status and lifestyle. This association has been derived from detailed investigations of multiple sources of information about people living in a particular neighbourhood. A very widely used system of geodemographic analysis is MOSAIC, provided by Experian Ltd (Figure 5.7).

Situational bases for segmentation

A further group of segmentation variables can be described as situational, because an individual may find herself grouped differently from one occasion to the next.

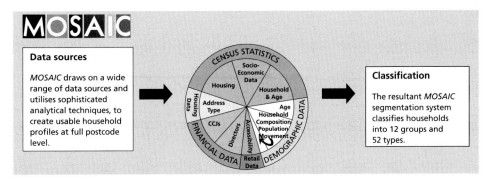

Figure 5.7 MOSAIC, a widely used method of geodemographic segmentation. From an individual postcode, MOSAIC can predict spending characteristics of the occupants of an address. It is widely used by firms for targeting direct mailshots and for identifying the best locations for proposed new retail outlets (Reproduced with permission of Experian Ltd)

Stage in buying process

For some high-value goods, it may take a considerable time for an individual to arrive at a purchase decision. It has been estimated that the average time private buyers take in deciding on a replacement for their current car is about one year. At each stage of the process, their needs will be quite different. A price incentive aimed at a buyer in the early stages of the search process may achieve no success, while for a buyer who has gone through the search and evaluation processes and is now ready to commit himself to a particular product, it may prove successful.

Occasion of use

We often buy a product at different times for quite different reasons. A meal in a restaurant taken during the lunch hour will probably have to satisfy quite different needs compared with a meal taken during the evening. At lunchtime the most important selection criteria may be speed and value for money, whereas in the evening they may be good service and a relaxing atmosphere.

Frequency of purchase

Infrequent buyers of a product may approach their purchase decision with caution and seek reassurance throughout the process. Their knowledge of prices and competing facilities available in the market may be low. At the other end of this segmentation spectrum, frequent buyers may have become much more price-sensitive, or more demanding in the features they expect from a category of product. A promotional programme that guides buyers through the stages of purchase will be less appropriate for this group.

Fuzzy logic in the bar

The days when all pubs in a town seemed to look alike are long gone, as pub operators segment their markets with increasingly refined detail. But how does a company handle the masses of information about customers' preferences and match these with specific pub locations? The brewery and leisure group Bass—until 2001 one of the UK's biggest pub operators—was an early adopter in the use of 'fuzzy logic' to match the sites of new pubs with its preferred segments of customers. A segmentation exercise was undertaken, and distinctive segments were given labels such as 'blue-collar hunters', 'premium wanderers', and 'pint and pensioners'. Blue-collar hunters, for example, were characterized by unskilled manual workers who spend most of their income in pubs with juke boxes and arcade games and prefer draft cider and ordinary lager.

The company used the outcome of its segmentation exercise as an input to a non-linear, pub profit optimization model. Each pub's cluster membership score was a significant indicator of pub profitability. This allowed the company to identify under- and over-performing pubs and to earmark the best opportunities for new pub openings or expansions. The company operated a number of pub formats, such as Vintage Inns, Harvester, and O'Neills, all targeted at different segments of pub customers.

The company developed a computerized mapping programme that helped it to identify the best location for any given format of pub. The programme uses a computer code called 'fuzzy logic' to come up with locations that match each pub format with the characteristics of a local neighbourhood. From this, a ranking of most desirable sites for new openings, expansions, or closure can be identified.

Such programmes can undoubtedly help management to make difficult decisions in a complex business environment. But can they sometimes reduce the scope for management intuition? Do they simply provide a bureaucratic source of justification for managers' decisions which may subsequently prove to be wrong?

Comprehensive approaches to segmentation

The preceding discussion has presented a seemingly bewildering array of segmentation variables, each of which has its strengths and weaknesses. In practice, a company uses a number of key variables which are most relevant to its product/market, and companies commonly segment consumers on the basis of multiple-category purchase data (Heilman and Bowman [4]). Geodemographic segmentation has become particularly popular because of the close correlation between where an individual lives and other indicators of income, occupation, and life-style. (Although there is some recent research evidence that demographics fails to provide a sound basis for segmentation of fast moving consumer goods markets in which competitive or substitutable brands have found to be chosen by the same kinds of people: Ehrenberg [1].) Companies are also likely to combine subjective approaches to segmentation with more traditional quantifiable techniques (Figure 5.8).

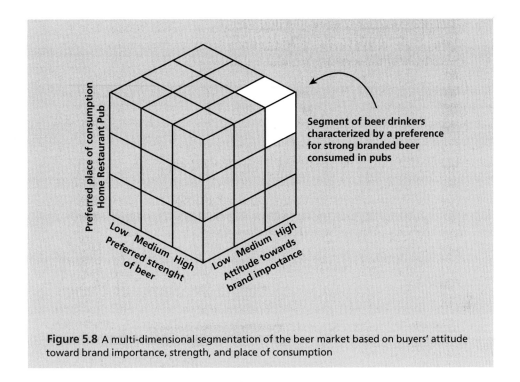

Figure 5.8 A multi-dimensional segmentation of the beer market based on buyers' attitude toward brand importance, strength, and place of consumption

🔲 Bases for segmenting business markets

The process of defining market segments for business buyers is similar in principle to that applied to consumer markets. Many of the bases described above, such as frequency of purchase and benefits sought, apply equally to private consumer purchases and business purchases. However, others, such as demographic and life-style bases, have little role to play, especially in segmenting very large corporate buyers. The following are additional bases for segmentation which are commonly used in business markets.

Size of firm

Within any industry sector, variations in corporate size are likely to be reflected in individual order sizes and the manner in which those orders are placed. In the printing industry, for example, very large printers obtain their inks direct from manufacturers, while smaller printers tend to rely on wholesale merchants. For a small intermediary, the latter may represent an important and accessible segment, whereas the former may be considered inaccessible.

Formality of buying processes

As organizations grow, they have a tendency to formalize their buying processes. Nevertheless, within any size category of firm, variation can be observed in the formality of buying process, in terms of the number of people involved in making a decision and the level of the management hierarchy at which approval is required. Large state-owned organizations have been noted for having slow and complicated ordering procedures. While many large private companies are similar, some have managed to delegate buying to a very local level, thereby speeding up and simplifying the process. It was noted in Chapter 3 that, in general, the more complex a firm's buying process, the greater the complexity of a seller's marketing that is called for. Instead of having to appeal to one individual with one set of needs, it must appeal to multiple influencers, who may each seek different benefits from a purchase.

Industry sector

An industry sector may be a large user of certain types of product but have little use for others. Within particular product categories, niche segments may appear in industries with quite specific needs. Many suppliers of industrial goods and services therefore target particular industry sectors or sub-sectors. In the case of information technology (IT) equipment, Fujitsu ICL has successfully targeted the special computing needs of the retail segment, while NCR has targeted the special needs of the banking segment.

■ Evaluating market segments

Defining market segments is a relatively passive task of analysis. While sound analysis is always important, the next stages involve critically evaluating the identified market segments and selecting one or more for targeting. In this section we consider the questions that a company should ask in deciding whether a segment is worth going after. In fact, a company is likely to avoid a dichotomous classification of 'develop/ignore' and prefer instead a ranking of segments ranging from 'very attractive opportunity' to 'let's ignore this one'.

Size of segment

In our criteria for effective segmentation, it was stated that to be useful a segment must be of a sufficient size that the company can serve it economically. What is an economic size varies between companies. A package holiday company selling low cost holidays to popular destination may be able to operate economically only with segments of several hundreds of thousands of customers. On the other hand, a small specialist holiday company with lower overhead costs may be able to justify serving much smaller segments of, say, a few thousand people who have distinctive needs. It was noted earlier that the size of market segments that can be economically served has tended to come down with the development of flexible production systems.

Growth prospects

Our definition of marketing (Chapter 1) spoke not only about identifying current customer demands, but also of anticipating what these will be in the future. Markets are seldom static, and what is an attractive segment today may not be so in the future. Many UK companies that, towards the end of the 1990s, targeted people working in the City of London with lavish restaurants and expensive designer apartments realized this when the financial services sector went into a significant decline from 2001 and spending by this group fell sharply. On the other hand, some segments that were once small have gone on to be very large before fragmenting into smaller sub-segments. In the UK the segment of adult ice cream consumers who sought sensual pleasures from consuming ice cream was small in the early 1980s, but grew significantly during the following decades. Suppliers of 'luxury' ice cream that had targeted this group saw their sales grow significantly faster than the ice cream industry average.

Profitability

The fact that a market segment is large does not necessarily mean that the segment can be served profitably. Many markets are characterized by a large segment which seeks low prices, and in which companies can make good profits only by stringent control of their costs, while a smaller segment is prepared to pay a premium for a product for which the cost of differentiation is less than the price premium charged.

Competition for the segment

Of course, the profitability of a segment is significantly affected by the level of competition for it. When a company is identifying potentially profitable segments to develop, the chances are that its competitors are doing exactly the same thing. The result is that an attractive segment soon becomes unattractive when large numbers of new entrants, all following the same logic, create intense competitive pressure. In evaluating a market segment, a company should consider not only how well *it* could develop the segment, but also how well its competitors could develop it. If its competitors in fact have more strengths with regard to this segment, the segment is likely to be less attractive to the company. Too many marketing plans fail because they make assumptions about a static market, when in fact markets are dynamic, with a changing composition of segments and of firms seeking to supply those segments.

Fit with company objectives

Many segments may appear large and profitable, but are then rejected because they would not sit easily within a company's broader marketing objectives and strategies. The following are some examples of market segments that might not 'fit' a company well.

- A manufacturer of high-value cars might be reluctant to serve a market segment that seeks more basic, low-value vehicles. What would happen to the image of BMW if it decided to develop the market segment for low-priced family hatchbacks using the BMW brand name?

- Will the image of a company be harmed by appearing to be too closely associated with a segment that is perceived by the public to be 'bad'? Many companies give priority to the preservation of their reputation, and being seen to supply products to a repressive government, for example, could cause unquantifiable damage to its long-term reputation.

MARKETING and the INTERNET

Targeting or spamming?

In the early days of the internet, the ability of firms to target millions of customers cheaply and quickly through e-mail appeared to open up new opportunities. Schedules of press and TV advertising, optimized to minimize the cost per target audience, would be a thing of the past when the whole world could be targeted with a cheap e-mail message. In reality, e-mail may be an efficient way of targeting a lot of potential buyers, but is it effective?

Many online sites grew rapidly by building databases through sometimes dubious means. Some websites, such as 4anything.com, used the lure of a free sweepstake to build up a database of names which was subsequently used for sending promotional messages on behalf of other companies. Of course, to be effective, targeting requires a much more thorough understanding of potential customers than is possible using crude database building techniques. As with junk mail, junk e-mail, or 'spam', quickly finds its way to the bin. Some computer owners have installed anti-spam software to try and reduce the extent of the nuisance caused by junk e-mail. In response, some companies have developed ingenious methods of getting round such anti-spam filters. They might just be lucky in achieving a sale that would not have been possible had their e-mail been blocked, but their approach still appears very crude, and similar to targeting in the early days of modern marketing.

How can the internet help segmentation and targeting for a company in a long-term and sustainable way? There are no surprises about the answer that traditional techniques work best. Targets are more likely to be responsive to a message where the message addresses a real need. Companies should amass information from multiple sources in order to build a profile of each potential target. The use of 'cookies' allows internet-based companies to understand quite a lot about a target from the websites the target has visited, but this seldom gives much insight into an individual's attitudes and life-style. Integrating online information with traditional data sources can greatly improve the effectiveness of targeting.

In an age of mass information, consumers' concerns over their privacy have become increasingly important. This is reflected in the ideas of 'permission marketing'. In his book of that title, Seth Godin, vice president of Yahoo, asserted that much of today's marketing is ineffective, as an overload of promotional messages is robbing people of one of their most precious assets—time. Godin has argued that the basis for marketing should be a relationship between company and customer that is based on consent and respects the customer's time. Seeking permission is key, and is more likely to result in an e-mail message being read.

For the future, new opportunities for targeting are arriving, with broadband internet access and the mobile internet through 'third-generation' mobile phones. The possibility of walking down the High Street and being bombarded with SMS messages from nearby shops may fill many people with horror. How can companies avoid the mistakes of spam e-mail? If permission marketing is the way forward, how can that permission be obtained?

Figure 5.9 Mercedes Benz identified a segment of car buyers who were seeking the benefits of a small city car that made a life-style statement about the individual. The company realized that targeting this segment with a small car might be inconsistent with the brand image that the company had built up in the market for larger luxury cars. It therefore decided to join a consortium to target this segment with the 'Smart' car

- Has the company a core competence in serving this segment? Would its funds and management effort be better applied to a project that better fits its competencies, leaving this segment to a competitor that may have a stronger base for developing it?

■ Selection of target markets

The time has now come for a company to select one or more market segments for further development. At this point, marketing becomes a blend of scientific analysis and creative thinking. The segmental analysis that we have just discussed cannot in itself produce answers: it can only guide decision making, which is influenced by a range of company and environment-specific factors, many of which cannot be easily quantified.

True entrepreneurs are able to understand their marketing environment and to use their knowledge of a market to identify target markets which will grow and give them a period of profitable sales before the market becomes saturated with competitors. The following are some examples of successful targeting by entrepreneurs:

- Alan Sugar, founder of Amstrad, who had experience of launching low-cost versions of household electrical items and who correctly forecast the demand for a low-cost desktop computer for use by private households and small businesses;
- Stelios Haji-Ioannou, founder of EasyJet, who understood the American airline market and sought to bring the benefits of low-cost domestic and European flights to the UK, where he had reasoned that there was a high level of suppressed demand from segments who were highly price-sensitive;
- Charles Dunstone, founder of the Carphone Warehouse, who foresaw the growth of privately owned mobile phones in the UK and of a segment that sought an impartial and independent retailer to guide them through the maze of competing networks and tariffs.

In each of these cases, success was a combination of good luck, good judgement, and good timing. Had there been a sudden rise in oil prices, or had its competitors responded more rapidly and vigorously, EasyJet might have been sunk at an early stage. If mobile phones had failed to become popular consumer items (perhaps because of high taxes, network charges, or concerns over health), the ambitious plans of Carphone Warehouse might have come to nothing. The history books are littered with entrepreneurs (and large corporations) who have failed to understand and predict the dynamics of market segments, resulting in a failure to sell a product to a selected target market. The C5 car is often cited as an example of an innovative product that just might have become a runaway success as a handy runabout or even a cult vehicle. It failed miserably, possibly because the entrepreneur behind the venture—Clive Sinclair—didn't have sufficient understanding of the market segment he was targeting. (Possibly its failure could also be put to bad luck, as initial press coverage portrayed the car as ridiculous and dangerous rather than as a smart cult icon.)

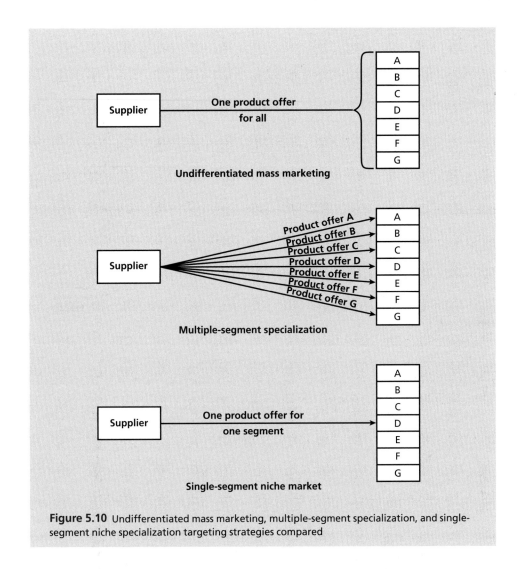

Figure 5.10 Undifferentiated mass marketing, multiple-segment specialization, and single-segment niche specialization targeting strategies compared

A fundamental issue for a company is how many segments to exploit and how to enter those segments. A number of targeting strategies can be identified—for example undifferentiated mass marketing, single segment specialization, and multiple segment specialization (Figure 5.10). While these are three ideal-type targeting strategies, companies frequently combine elements of all these approaches. The characteristics of each approach are described below.

Undifferentiated mass marketing

This doesn't really involve segmentation and targeting at all, as here a company seeks to satisfy the entire market with a single formulation of its product. It worked well for

Henry Ford, and cases can still be seen where companies serve the entire market with one product (for example electricity supply companies, which have traditionally offered one standard of service delivery to all of their domestic customers). Over time, however, consumers' needs tend to fragment into segments of different needs. Where markets are competitive, a company may no longer be able to ignore the special needs of small groups of its customers, because if it does its competitors may exploit the opportunities available. Very often, these groups with special needs represent the most profitable segments to serve. In the UK even the market for electricity has fragmented, spurred on by increasing competition which raises the expectations of consumers that their distinctive needs are capable of being met. Customers now have the choice of different pricing plans, bundling of electricity with other energy supplies, and a range of electrical appliance maintenance services to supplement the basic electricity supply.

Attempting to serve the entire market with one standard product offer is an extreme case of undifferentiated mass marketing. In its lesser form, companies seek to exploit as much of the market as possible without attempting to meet the needs of particular subgroups within it.

Single-segment specialization ('niche' marketing)

Many companies succeed by producing a specialized product aimed at a very focused segment of the market (or 'niche'). The Freeminer Brewery in Gloucestershire targets the small proportion of beer drinkers who can be described as real ale enthusiasts. By this strategy, the company gets to know the needs of its target segment extremely well and puts all of its efforts into satisfying their needs. This can give it strength over competitors whose efforts are spread more diffusely among a number of segments. It also avoids the problem of tarnishing a brand by associations with 'inferior' segments (Freeminer Brewery doesn't carry any of the bland, mass produced associations of the larger brewers.) By specializing on one particular segment and achieving a high level of success in it, a company might be able to achieve economies of scale that give it cost advantages over its competitors.

The danger of targeting a single market segment is that a company's fortunes rise or fall with those of its chosen target. UK hotels that had targeted premium-rate US business customers suffered badly after the terrorist attacks of 11 September 2001, when the number of business people travelling across the Atlantic declined sharply. The ability of a company to adapt its product to small market niches is not a guarantee of success. Many internet companies that offered a high level of personalization on their sites, e.g. Garden.com, have closed. The niche was probably too small to be satisfied economically.

Cars in any colour except black

Henry Ford would have been amazed at the lengths to which the car company he founded now goes in order to satisfy the needs of specific market segments. Car manufacturers have for some time recognized the differing needs of differing groups of buyers, for example:

- 'Boy racers' typically want plenty of features and external manifestations of the power and status of their car (e.g. 'GTI' badges and spoilers).

- Affluent elderly males put the emphasis on refinement of the interior, comfort, and reliability, but seek no vulgar manifestation of status.

- The family buying a 'runabout' car seeks low initial cost and subsequent low running costs; they are not too worried about comforts, but the car needs to be hard-wearing to stand up to rough treatment by dogs, children, etc.

- The professional career woman, although a difficult market to typify, often seeks a light and airy colour, reliability, and easy maintainance.

- Company car buyers look for an economical and reliable car which will have a high residual value after three years and will satisfy the status needs of employees.

A look through the brochure for a Ford model such as the 'Focus' indicates how far the company has been able to adapt its cars to meet the needs of each of these segments: the 'RS' has been aimed at the 'boy racers', the 'MP3' at the affluent young professional male, and the 'Ghia' at affluent elderly males; the 'CL' is a low-cost version produced as the family runabout; and Ford has produced a co-branded 'Elle' version of the car specifically targeted at professional career women. Finally, company car buyers find that the 'LX' model serves them well for reliable, cost-effective transport for employees.

The logistical problems of satisfying so many segments have been significant, with one basic car available in three basic body forms, with five different engines, 12 colour options, and the choice of automatic or manual transmission. After allowing for permutations that are not available, Ford promotes 72 versions of the Focus. Making these available on demand at each of its dealers has called for flexible manufacturing systems and a centralized stock management system. Can the company be accused of offering too much choice?

Multiple-segment specialization

A third ideal-type strategy is for a company to seek to serve multiple markets, but to differentiate its products in a way that meets the needs of each of the segments it seeks to serve. The aim here is to develop slightly differentiated products which add to customer value faster than they add to production costs. Car manufacturers have become quite skilful at adapting a basic car to meet the needs of different groups (see below). Many retailers have developed different brand formats to target different groups (for example the Arcadia group with its Top Shop, Principles, and Dorothy Perkins chains, among others).

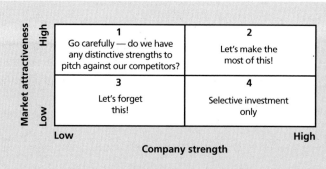

Figure 5.11 Market attractiveness-competitive position portfolio classification and strategies

Segment development plans

Most companies entering a new market realize that it would be unrealistic to use their limited financial and management resources to satisfy all possible segments from the outset. They therefore develop a strategy to 'roll out' their marketing plan from a central core segment through further segments. The roll-out plan can be defined geographically. (McDonald's restaurants did this in the UK, working out from the London-based market to provincial markets.) Very often, companies initially target high-value segments. Such segments may be prepared to pay a premium for the benefits of novelty, but soon the premium attached to this novelty wears off. The company meanwhile has established an 'upmarket' image for itself from which to appeal to aspiring segments of potential buyers. In the UK, mobile telephone companies have moved from segments of business users who are prepared to pay a premium for a mobile phone that will give them a competitive advantage, to more price-sensitive segments for whom a mobile telephone is a useful but not essential accessory.

Market attractiveness analysis

Of all the market segments that a company has identified, which ones should it target? A conceptually useful analytic tool is a grid comprising two dimensions: market attractiveness and competitive position (Figure 5.11). Market attractiveness includes such factors as the size of a market, its projected growth rate, and its earnings performance. Competitive position refers to a company's brand strength, its experience in a market, and the availability of financial, technical, and human resources to serve that market. In developing an index, weights must be attached to each of these components and a sometimes subjective assessment made of each component. Ownership of a strong brand may be an essential element of competitive advantage for a soft drinks firm and would therefore be given a relatively high weighting, although the task of assessing how strong a brand is remains very subjective.

For the purpose of analysis, each of the scales in Figure 5.11 is divided into two classifications, resulting in a matrix of four cells.

- **Box 1:** A market may appear attractive, but if a company has only a weak competitive position, it should think carefully before investing large amounts of cash. The market will appear attractive also to other companies, which may have a stronger competitive position.

- **Box 2:** A highly attractive market in which a company has a strong competitive position is the best position in the matrix, and in such a market the company should invest and build for future growth.

- **Box 3:** Unattractive markets for which a company does not have a strong competitive position should be avoided. However, a company may find that it has products in this box that were previously high performers, but whose market characteristics have changed. The best thing a company can do with the remaining products in this box is to refrain from new investment and to manage the products for the cash they generate.

- **Box 4:** Market attractiveness is low, but the company's competitive position is strong. The company should exploit its strengths by selectively investing in this market and building for future market growth.

As a basis for targeting, the grid focuses attention on finding strategies that match an organization's internal strengths and weaknesses with the opportunities and threats presented by its operating environment. The key to making this model useful in formulating marketing strategy is to measure the two dimensions of the grid not only as they are at the present time, but as they are likely to become in the future.

Developing a position within the target market

Having chosen a segment to target, a company must decide how to position itself in relation to the competitors for that segment. Positioning could be on the basis of the product's unique selling proposition, its price, design characteristics, method of distribution, or any other combination of factors that allow for differentiation. Within any market, position maps can be drawn to show the relative positions adopted by the principal competing products in respect of key customer evaluation criteria. In Figure 5.12, a position map has been drawn relating two important criteria used by customers in selecting a restaurant: speed of service, and the range of services provided by staff (e.g. whether the restaurant is self-service or waiter service). Position maps can use any criteria that are of relevance in influencing consumers' choices, and in reality they may be multi-dimensional rather than just two-dimensional, as in this example. Here, a number of UK restaurants have been plotted on this map in terms of two out of many possible relevant criteria.

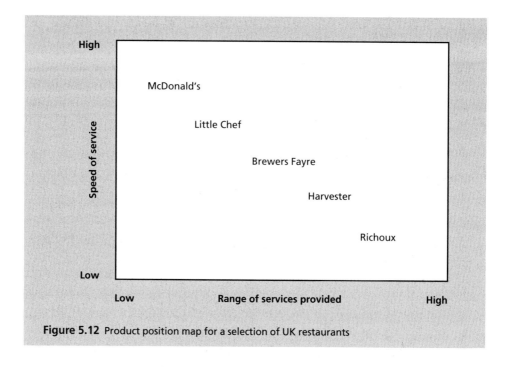

Figure 5.12 Product position map for a selection of UK restaurants

The fact that a position on a map is unoccupied does not necessarily mean that it is an unexplored opportunity waiting to be targeted. There is always the possibility that a product offering in that position will not satisfy the needs of a sufficiently large market segment. However, many gaps on product position maps have been identified and exploited successfully. In the UK there was for a long time a gap between low-price fast food restaurants offering little choice and higher priced gourmet restaurants offering a wide range of menu options. Restaurant chains such as Brewers Fayre and Harvester have since successfully exploited this mid-market position.

It must be emphasized that a product position map is essentially product-focused rather than customer-focused. By itself, it does not address the underlying needs of customers that a company seeks to satisfy. The process of adopting a product position is essentially about selecting specific target markets. In a market-oriented company, product features are developed only in response to the needs of clearly identifiable segments of consumers. We will return to the subject of competitive positioning and discuss it in more depth in Chapter 6.

◼ Chapter summary and linkages to other chapters

This chapter has emphasized the need for market-oriented companies to break markets down into segments comprising groups of people with similar needs and buying processes. Numerous bases for segmenting markets have been identified, but there is no unique 'right' way of segmenting a market. The best way is the one that allows a company most profitably to exploit the greatest possible share of a market. Segmentation alone does not produce a marketing plan. To this end, a company must evaluate the segment opportunities open to it and asses how well it will be able to exploit each of them. There are a number of approaches for entering a market, and companies often seek to exploit one segment at a time with products that are uniquely adapted to that segment.

The crucial importance of segmentation to the philosophy of marketing is reflected in the extensive linkages between this chapter and others. In Chapter 3 we saw how buying behaviour differs among individuals, and these differences form an important basis for segmentation. In Chapter 4 we explored methods by which companies can research the differences between individuals and thereby identify and evaluate segments. In the next chapter, we will pick up issues of competitive positioning which were introduced towards the end of this chapter. We will see how the development of brands facilitates the task of targeting and positioning. Subsequent chapters deal with the elements of the marketing mix that allow a company to develop products that are particularly suited to the needs of targeted segments.

▢ KEY PRINCIPLES OF MARKETING

- Segmentation is fundamental to marketing because of its emphasis on meeting the needs of identified groups of consumers.
- A trade-off must be made between the desire of individuals to be treated as a unique segment of one, and companies' desire to achieve segments that are large enough to achieve economic efficiencies.
- Segmentation exercises by themselves do not make decisions for management. Management must use creative thinking and a scientific analysis of segmentation data to decide which segments to target.
- Segments are rarely static in nature, and in deciding which segments to target, a company should focus on what each segment is likely to look like in the future.

CASE STUDY

Polaroid focuses its cameras on new market segments

The American based Polaroid company has become synonymous with instant photography, but this alone was insufficient to prevent a sharp decline in its fortunes. By the end of 1998 the company's stock market value had fallen to just one-third of what it was a year earlier. During 1998 alone, sales revenue dropped by 13% and profits by 18%. At the end of the 1990s the company was desperately trying to re-target its products at segments of the market that previously had not bought Polaroid products.

Polaroid was established in the 1940s by Edwin Lard, and from the start the company laid great stress on its research and development projects. But the company tended to be product-led rather than market-led, and carried out very little market research. Its emphasis on technical excellence caused it to lose out on opportunities that by Polaroid's standards might have been regarded as frivolous. It saw its traditional target market as private individuals and businesses needing high-quality instant photographs for serious purposes; for example, many professional photographers would take an instant picture with a Polaroid camera in order to judge the composition of a picture that they would later take with a standard camera.

Unfortunately, Polaroid's traditional target market had ceased to grow and was increasingly being challenged by new forms of electronic imaging which were beginning to be affordable for business users, although they were still prohibitive for most private buyers.

A new chief executive, Gary DiCamillo, took over in 1995 and set out to refocus the company. A key part of this task involved moving the company's positioning away from one of technical excellence to one of fun. The company reasoned that, if serious users of instant photography were becoming harder markets to target, segments of more casual users might be more promising.

The company's most promising new market segments was the under-17s, a far cry from its previous targeting strategy. For this segment, the company created a 'Barbie' instant camera which retailed for under $20 and in 1997 became one of the hottest Christmas toys, according to *USA Today*. In addition, the company created instant film that children could draw on, and developed a camera that turns photographic images into stickers. Children represented an ideal target market for Polaroid. Their impatience and need for instant gratification gave the firm's product big advantages over conventional photography, which required a typical wait of a week until a parent had been pestered into taking the film to be developed. Taking this theme further, the company developed a fun camera for adults which can be used as a toy and retailed for $18, whereby users could experiment with a range of abstract images when they took a picture.

While the 'fun' segment of the photography market was seen to have a lot of potential, there remained some opportunities for more professional market segments. One area of growth has been instant imaging for official identification documents. The increasing security consciousness of firms following the terrorist attacks of September 2001 and the desire of firms to issue staff with identify cards has helped to fuel this growth. The UK government's inclusion of a photograph on driving licences resulted in a new source of demand which Polaroid successfully won.

Further questions remain about the company's targeting strategy. The costs of developing its own electronic cameras was seen as too high and the competition was likely to be fierce from the major electronics companies. To gain a profitable market share among more serious users, the company would have to spend considerable amounts of money, something that wouldn't go well with its shareholders, given the company's recent financial performance. The emerging markets of eastern Europe represented hoped-for market segments, but with their economies floundering penetration of these markets has been difficult.

Case study review questions

1. How can Polaroid overcome an image problem that may result from serving both the 'professional' and 'fun' market segments?

2. Given the development of electronic imaging and Polaroid's limited resources to develop electronic cameras, suggest a targeting strategy that would be appropriate for Polaroid.

3. Suggest a framework by which Polaroid can assess the attractiveness of the under-17s market segment. Is this segment likely to be sustainable over the longer term? If not, what should the company do to develop this segment?

CHAPTER REVIEW QUESTIONS

1. 'Too much segmentation can be costly and can result in a paralysis by analysis.' Discuss the view that for many markets Henry Ford's approach of producing a limited range of products for the 'average' customer may be the most profitable option for a company.

2. It is common to talk about individuals belonging to social class A/B or C1, and newspapers often quote their readership figures in these terms. In reality, how useful is this as a basis for market segmentation?

3. Critically evaluate the likely future trend in segmentation techniques. Illustrate your answer with reference to a specific market sector.

4. Given the increasing fragmentation of society, and an apparent desire for greater individuality among consumers, are current scientific methods of analysis and segmentation a short-sighted over-simplification?

5. Discuss the criteria that might be used by a recently established small confectionery manufacturer in deciding which market segments to target.

6. For a market sector of your choice, analyse the positions adopted by companies in the market.

REFERENCES

[1] Ehrenberg, A. (2002), 'More on Modeling and Segmentation'. *Marketing Research*, 14(3): 42.

[2] Elkin, T. (2002), 'Sony Marketing Aims at Lifestyle Segments'. *Advertising Age*, 73(11): 3–4.

[3] Gonzalez, A. M. and Bello, L. (2002), 'The Construct "Lifestyle" in Market Segmentation: the behaviour of tourist consumers'. *European Journal of Marketing*, 36(1/2): 51–85.

[4] Heilman, C. M. and Bowman, D. (2002), 'Segmenting Consumers Using Multiple-Category Purchase Data'. *International Journal of Research in Marketing*, 19: 225–352.

[5] Interfocus (2001), *Marketing to Ethnic Minorities*. London: Interfocus.

[6] Lin, C.-F. (2002), 'Segmenting Customer Brand Preference: demographic or psychographic'. *Journal of Product & Brand Management*, 11: 249–70.

[7] Precision Marketing (2002), 'P&O Launches Push to Woo Over-40s "Cruising Virgins" '. *Precision Marketing*, 14(15): 3.

[8] Rose, D. and O'Reilly, K. (1998), *The ESRC Review of Government Social Classifications*. London: The Stationery Office.

SUGGESTED FURTHER READING

Segmentation, targeting and positioning are discussed in more detail in the following books. For additional articles on the subject, consult the companion website:
www.oup.com/uk/booksites/busecon

Dibb, S. and Simpkin, L. (1997), 'A Program for Implementing Market Segmentation'. *Journal of Business and Industrial Marketing*, 12(1): 51–64.

Hooley, G., Saunders, J. and Piercey, N. (1998), *Marketing Strategy and Competitive Positioning*, 2nd edn. Englewood Cliffs, NJ: Prentice-Hall.

McDonald, M. and Dunbar, I. (1998), *Market Segmentation*. Basingstoke: Palgrave Macmillan.

Ries, A., and Trout, J. (2001), *Positioning: the Battle for Your Mind: how to be seen and heard in the overcrowded marketplace*. New York: McGraw-Hill.

USEFUL WEBLINKS

Visit the companion website to this book, with lots of interesting additional material and links for each chapter:

www.oup.com/uk/booksites/busecon

For an example of geodemographic segmentation, visit **www.upmystreet.com**, type in a postcode, and see a description of the typical resident of that postcode.

The Data Laboratory consultancy provides case studies of segmentation applied to direct marketing:

www.datalab.co.uk/case_studies/segmentation.asp

KEY TERMS

- **Attitudes**
- **Differentiation**

- Discretionary income
- Disposable income
- Family life-cycle
- Geodemographics
- Household structure
- Life-style
- Mass market
- Niche marketing
- Permission marketing
- Positioning
- Position map
- Psychographic segmentation
- Segmentation
- Social class
- Socio-economic classification
- Targeting
- Trigger points
- Values

PART 3

Developing the marketing mix

6

Competitor analysis and the development of a brand

CHAPTER OBJECTIVES

This chapter marks a transition point in the book. In previous chapters we have been focusing on how companies can gain a better understanding of the external environment from which they earn their sales revenue. In the following chapters we will consider how companies try to develop the right products, and sell them through the right channels at the right price and with the right promotional messages. In this chapter we introduce concepts associated with competitive markets. We will explore what is meant by a competitor and how a company can develop a sustainable competitive advantage over its competitors. A large part of this chapter is given to the development of brands. These form the focal point of a firm's product, pricing, promotion, and distribution plans and aim to create a distinctive position for a product. Branding lies at the heart of marketing strategy and seeks to remove a company from the harsh competition of commodity-type markets. By differentiating its product and giving it unique values, a company simplifies consumers' choices in markets that are crowded with otherwise similar products.

Introduction

Marketing is a dynamic process of ensuring a close fit between the capabilities of an organization and the demands placed upon it by its external environment. It follows that what a company offers to a market will need to evolve continually over time in order to meet changes in the company's internal objectives and in its external business environment. It is not good enough for a company to develop a marketing plan that works for a short period, but then fails to make good long-term profits for the company because the plan is not sufficiently responsive to changes in its marketing environment.

History is full of marketing plans that looked too good to be true. A company may have found a very high level of sales in the short term, but failed to earn sufficient profits over the longer term. It may be that such a company has underpriced its products, leaving it an insufficient margin to cover its fixed costs. Or it may have invested heavily in product design and promotion but failed to generate a sufficient level of sales to pay for such investment. It is not difficult to develop short-term marketing strategies that at first appear highly successful when judged by sales levels. It is much more difficult to develop a marketing strategy that is sustainable over the longer term by producing adequate levels of continuing profits. Central to this long-term strategy is the development of strong brands which can allow a company to charge premium prices for products that consistently deliver a high level of customer-defined value.

Many companies that have been hailed as successful market-led businesses have not managed to achieve a sustainable long-term success. In the UK companies such as Next, Amstrad, and Laura Ashley have risen rapidly and gained many 'Business of the Year' type of awards on the way. But each of these ended up in serious financial difficulties just a short while later. It has been noted that very few of the so-called 'excellent' companies identified by Peters and Waterman [13] in their book *In Search of Excellence* were considered to be excellent 15 years later. The marketing strategy that had led to short-term success was clearly not sustainable.

Who are a company's competitors?

Any plan to develop a competitive advantage must be based on a sound analysis of just who a company's competitors are. At first sight, it may seem obvious who the competitors are, but, as Theodore Levitt pointed out [10], a myopic view may focus on the immediate and direct competitors while overlooking the more serious threat posed by indirect and less obvious sources of competition. When railway companies in the 1930s saw their main competitors as other railway companies, they overlooked the fact that the most serious competition would come from road-based transport. More recently, banks have been made to realize that their competitors are not just other banks, or even other financial services organizations, but any organization that has a strong brand reputation and customer base. Through these, supermarkets, airlines, and car companies have all developed various forms of banking services which now compete with mainstream banks.

Even without considering the possibility of new market entrants appearing, it is possible to identify direct and indirect competitors. *Direct competitors* are generally similar in form and satisfy customers' needs in a similar way. *Indirect competitors* may appear different in form, but satisfy a fundamentally similar need. Consider the examples of prod-

Product	Typical underlying need	Direct competitors	Examples of indirect competitors
Overseas holiday	Relaxation	Rival tour operators	Garden conservatories
Restaurant meal	Social gathering	Other restaurants	Ready-prepared gourmet meals for home consumption
Television programme	Entertainment	Other television programmes	Internet service providers
Rolex watch	Social status	Other watches	Armani suit; Gucci handbag

Figure 6.1 Underlying needs, direct and indirect competitors for selected products

Figure 6.2 What business is the Parker Pen company in? At first sight, the company may appear to be in the pen business, or possibly the 'writing implement' or maybe even the 'communication' business. In fact, the company understands that the majority of its sales are made for gift giving. Gifts can be personal (e.g. to mark a relative's personal achievement or anniversary) or corporate (as when companies give away free pens as a sales incentive to reward a new order). The company is essentially in the 'gift' business, so its competitors are not just other pens, but any gift. Within this broad definition, CDs, alarm clocks, and overnight bags could all be regarded as competitors.

ucts and underlying needs shown in Figure 6.1. The table shows, for each product, possible direct and indirect competitors.

A sound analysis of the direct and indirect competitors of a firm is crucial in defining the business mission of an organization. (This is discussed further in Chapter 12.)

A useful framework for analysing the competition facing a company in a market has been provided by Michael Porter [14]. His model illustrates the relationship between existing competitors and potential competitors in a market and identifies five forces requiring evaluation:

1. the threat of new entrants;
2. the threat of substitute products;
3. the intensity of rivalry between competing firms;

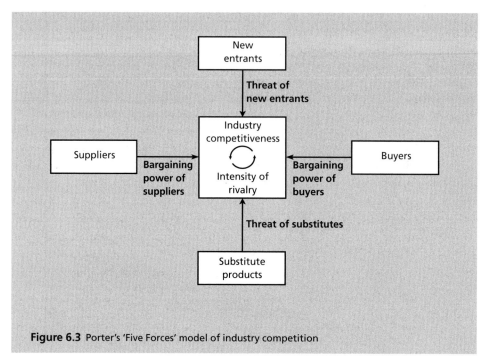

Figure 6.3 Porter's 'Five Forces' model of industry competition

4. the power of suppliers;

5. the power of buyers.

Understanding the structure of competition within a market is a vital prerequisite for developing a strategy to develop a sustainable competitive advantage. The model is shown in Figure 6.3 and the nature of these five forces are discussed below.

The threat of new entrants

The threat of new entrants is greatest where there are low barriers to entry. New entrants may already be active in a similar market sector, but in another geographic market. The threat becomes reality when a company that is strong in one geographical market decides to exploit other geographical markets. As an example, the full service airlines have been challenged on many routes by newer low-cost 'budget' airlines. Having established a base, these airlines have often gone on to further challenge the established airlines by creating new operating bases. (For example, the budget airline Ryanair has posed a new threat to Belgian and German carriers after expanding to those countries from its UK and Irish bases)

Alternatively, new entrants may arrive from outside the industry. BIC, whose technology base was plastic moulding, was well established in the disposable ballpoint pen market. They were able to diversify successfully into the wet shave razor market with plastic disposable razors, thereby challenging established market leaders such as Gillette and Wilkinson in their core business.

The threat of substitute products

Substitute products are likely to emerge from alternative technologies, particularly as the economics of production change. Initially the new technology may have high costs associated with it and serve only small niche markets. As the technology and experience develop, the level of investment rises and production volumes increase, resulting in economies of scale that are associated with falling production costs. Many products have been consigned to obscurity by the development of new technologies; for example, the market for typewriters has been considerably reduced by the development of personal computers, and the market for sugar has been reduced by the development of artificial sweeteners. These substitutes may change the whole economics of an industry and threaten the survival of manufacturers of the traditional product.

Intensity of rivalry between competing firms

The intensity of rivalry may be high if two or more firms are fighting for dominance in a fast-growing market. For example, this occurred in the UK mobile phone market during the mid-1990s and in the fight to establish the dominant format for the domestic VCR player during the early 1980s between three competing technologies—VHS, Betamax, and U-matic. A company needs to become established as the dominant technology or brand before the industry matures, because entering the market later may require considerably greater investment (although the costs of early mistakes may be avoided). In a mature industry, particularly if it is characterized by high fixed costs and excess capacity, the intensity of competitive rivalry may be very high. This is because manufacturers or service providers need to operate at or near maximum capacity in order to cover their overhead costs. As the industry matures, or at times of cyclical downturn, firms fight to maintain their maximum level of sales. Price cuts and discounting may become commonplace and profits eroded. Low-cost producers with high brand loyalty have the best chance of survival.

The power of suppliers

The power of suppliers is likely to be high if the number of suppliers is small and/or the materials, components, and services they offer are in short supply. The suppliers of silicone chips and patented medicines have at times held a powerful market position as a result of their dominance of technology and the high demand for their products.

The power of buyers

Buyers' power is likely to be high if there are relatively few buyers, if there are many alternative sources of supply, and if buyers incur only low costs in switching between suppliers. During the past couple of decades, Britain's grocery retailing sector has become increasingly dominated by a small number of very large organizations. According to the Nielsen Grocery Service (Nielsen [12]), Asda, Co-operative Stores, Iceland, Safeway, Sainsbury, Somerfield, and Tesco held over three-quarters of UK grocery market share by turnover in 2000. Power in the marketplace has shifted away from the manufacturers of grocery products to the retailers, seven of whom may buy around three-quarters of many manufacturers' total output.

▉ Branding

Traditional economic theory has been based on assumptions of perfectly competitive markets in which a large number of sellers offer for sale an identical product. All suppliers' products are assumed to be perfectly substitutable with each other and, therefore, through a process of competition, prices are minimized to the level that is just sufficient to make it worthwhile for suppliers to continue operating in the market. (Price determination in competitive markets is discussed further in Chapter 8.)

Perfect competition may at first sight appear very attractive for the welfare of society as a whole, but it can pose problems for sellers. In a perfectly competitive market, an individual firm is subject to considerable direct competition from other firms and must take its selling price from the market. An implication of perfect competition is that firms will be unable to make a level of profits that is above the norm for their market. If they did achieve higher-than-normal profits, this would act as an invitation to new market entrants, whose presence would eventually increase the level of competition in the market and drive down profits to the minimum level that makes it attractive for firms to continue in the market.

To try to avoid head-on competition with large numbers of other suppliers in a market, companies seek to differentiate their product in some way. In doing so, they create an element of monopoly power for themselves, in that no other company in the market is selling a product identical to theirs. To some people, the point of difference may be of great importance in influencing their purchase decision, and they may be prepared to pay a price premium for the differentiated product. Nevertheless, such buyers remain aware of close substitutes that are available, and may be prepared to switch to these substitutes if the price premium is considered to be too high in relation to the additional benefits received. The co-existence of a limited monopoly power with the presence of many near substitutes is often referred to as *imperfect competition*. (We will come back to this again in Chapter 8.)

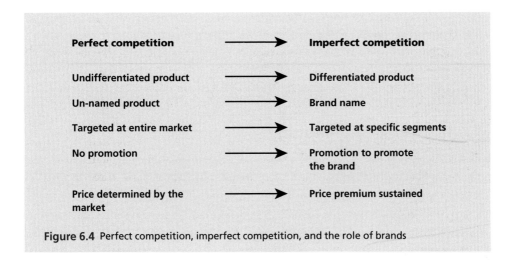

Figure 6.4 Perfect competition, imperfect competition, and the role of brands

For a marketing manager, product differentiation becomes a key to gaining a degree of monopoly power in a market. It must be remembered, however, that product differentiation alone will not prove to be commercially successful unless the differentiation is based on satisfying clearly identified consumers' needs. A differentiated product may have significant monopoly power in that it is unique, but if it fails to satisfy consumers' needs, its uniqueness has no commercial value.

Out of the need for product differentiation comes the concept of branding. A company must ensure that customers can immediately recognize its distinctive products in the marketplace. Instead of asking for a generic version of the product, customers should be able to ask for the distinctive product that they have come to prefer. A brand is essentially a way of giving a product a unique identity which differentiates it from its near competitors. The means by which this unique identity is created are discussed in this chapter.

Summarizing previous research, Doyle [5] has described brand building as the only way to create a stable, long-term demand at profitable margins. Through adding values that will attract customers, a company can provide a firm base for expansion and product development and protect itself against the strength of intermediaries and competitors. There has been much evidence linking high levels of advertising expenditure to support strong brands with high returns on capital and high market share.

Branding through product differentiation may not be possible in all markets. Where products involve consumers in low levels of risk and there are few opportunities for developing a distinctive product, competitive advantage may be based on cost leadership rather than brand development. Examples of commodity strategies are evident in many low-value consumer and industrial markets where a significant segment of customers seek a product with a basic and substitutable set of characteristics. Milk and cheese are everyday items of consumer purchase where manufacturers' brands have had relatively little impact and most consumers are happy to buy the generic milk or cheese offered by a retailer.

The history of branding

The term 'branding' pre-dates modern marketing and is generally believed to have originated in agricultural practices of the Middle Ages. Farmers who allowed their cattle to graze on open common land needed some means of distinguishing their cattle from those that were owned by other farmers sharing common grazing rights. They therefore 'branded' their animals with a branding iron, leaving an indelible mark which would clearly identify the owner of a particular animal. The role of a brand in identifying products with a particular source is shared by the medieval farmer and the modern corporation.

Economies in an early stage of development are characterized by small-scale production processes and relatively local markets. Where there are few opportunities for economies of scale in production, brands had only a limited role to play. With poor transport facilities and few opportunities to profitably expand business beyond the immediate area of production, consumers could readily identify the source of goods. In early nineteenth-century Britain, most communities had their own baker, brewer, and carpenter. None had developed the ability to achieve competitive advantage through economies of scale, while poor road and rail transport would have prevented their goods being exported to neighbouring communities. People in local communities knew where their goods had come from and were not confused by competing products from distant towns. Buyers were able to learn through personal experience of the abilities, consistency, and reliability of a supplier, while suppliers were able to adapt simple production methods to the needs of individual customers who were known personally. Through personal knowledge and trust, a supplier was likely to be able to judge the creditworthiness of each customer.

In the UK, the industrialization that occurred in the nineteenth century meant that many goods could now be produced efficiently in centralized factories rather than in small cottage industries. An efficient centralized factory could produce more output than could be consumed by the local community. Furthermore, improvements in transport infrastructure allowed the surplus production to be shipped to markets around the country. What one company could do efficiently in one factory, another company could probably do equally as well in another factory elsewhere. Therefore, firms became involved in competition in distant markets. This, however, led to a problem for buyers, whose buying process was now made more complicated. Instead of having just the local brewer's products available, they now had a range of beers to

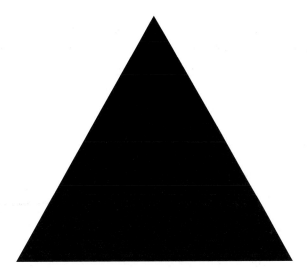

Figure 6.5 In early nineteenth-century England, consumers of beer may have had little knowledge about the quality of beer from the expanding industrialized breweries. Many brewers were reputed to add salt to their beer, in order to make the drinker thirstier, so that he would buy more beer—by which time he wouldn't notice any impurities. One of the growing brewers of the time, Bass, developed what is acknowledged to be one of the earliest brand logos in order to provide reassurance of quality to a segment of the market that was more discerning. The logo was simply a plain triangle, and essentially the same logo is still in use today

choose from. Buyers probably had little knowledge of the distant firms who were now supplying their market, or of the quality and consistency of their products. Branding emerged essentially to simplify the purchase processes of buyers who faced competing sources of supply.

In impersonal mass markets, consumers who cannot judge a product on the basis of a trusted personal relationship with a supplier instead seek reassurance through other means. The brand emerged as a means of providing reassurance of consistent quality to spatially dispersed customers who, because of the use of intermediaries, had no direct relationship with the consumers of their products. In a market characterized by choice, a brand was used by buyers to select a product they had come to trust and which satisfied their needs through its particular benefits.

Where competitive advantage for firms is gained by operating at a large scale, branding has been the traditional route by which firms have sought to reassure distant customers of consistent product quality. However, technological developments in the areas of database and production management now give large-scale producers an ability to keep in touch with customers and thereby recapture something of the relationships that brand development has provided a surrogate for. The question remains, however, whether direct marketing organizations can profitably build sales without the development of a strong brand.

MARKETING and the INTERNET

E-brands?

Can a brand be created solely through use of the internet, and is there such a thing as an e-brand? During the early days of development of the internet, there was great excitement that the internet would allow companies—including small-scale entrepreneurs—to create brands without the need for expensive mass media advertising. Have these aspirations been realized? Was there ever any chance that the new technology alone would have been able to change the basic principles of brand-building?

The late 1990s saw a spate of entrepreneurs seeking to establish new internet-based businesses. Many started on a small scale, often operating from a garage or a spare room at home, and were propelled by a seemingly limitless amount of risk capital that investors were prepared to pour into start-up companies. Some of these start-ups expanded rapidly to exploit online niches in markets as diverse as travel, fast food delivery, and gambling. The dot.com boom burst in 2000, and within a couple of years it has been estimated that about three-quarters of all new start-ups had either gone out of business or were in serious financial difficulty.

One of the fundamental problems of many start-ups was their underestimation of the costs of creating a unique identity for their business and securing trust from customers. Paradoxically, many of the start-ups focused on highly intangible services, such as travel and financial services, which are also the most susceptible to fraud or non-delivery by producers—in other words, the circumstances in which buyers are most likely to seek out trusted brands. Creating a unique and trusted brand proved to be a far more expensive task than many entrepreneurs had initially estimated, and they were not helped by the large number of online companies that were often competing for the same customers. In the case of online air ticket sales, one estimate at the height of the dot.com boom counted over 200 companies targeting UK travel buyers. How could any company hope to become distinctive and get to the top of a buyer's consideration set? Online travel retailers were in danger of becoming a highly commoditized service, with buyers simply searching for the cheapest fare. Even getting to the top of the consideration set was expensive, requiring heavy investment in banner ads, sponsored links, and efforts to improve search engine rankings.

The most successful online travel retailers emerged as those who had invested heavily in developing their brands off-line. Among the 'pure' internet based travel agents, Lastminute.com and Opodo.com spent heavily on newspaper and poster advertising and sponsorship to raise awareness of their distinctive qualities. Others, such as Thomascook.com and the airline operators' own websites, capitalized on their established brand names, which provided immediate recognition and reassurance.

The advocates of e-brands pointed to the success of direct sell companies such as Betterware and Avon Cosmetics, which had succeeded on the basis of one-to-one communication and without the need for mass advertising to develop their brand names. However, these companies had often spent several decades in which their reputation grew by satisfied customers coming back for more and recommending the company to others; internet entrepreneurs may have hoped that this process could be achieved almost instantly. The technology of the internet may have speeded up communication, but trust in a brand can still take a long time to develop. More frustrating to many internet entrepreneurs was the realization that the internet is generally an additional channel of communication, rather than the sole means by which individuals come to value brands.

Key characteristics of a brand

A brand is essentially a way of distinguishing the products of one company from those of its competitors. To have value, a brand must have consistency, reduce buyers' level of perceived risk, and offer a range of functional and emotional attributes that are of value to buyers.

Consistency

Consistency is at the heart of branding strategy. To have value in simplifying buyers' purchasing processes, consumers must come to learn that a brand stands for the same set of attributes on one purchase occasion as on all subsequent and previous occasions. Consider a brewery offering draft bitter to the market. The distinctive characteristics of the beer that contribute towards its brand values may be described as:

- taste: light hop flavour;
- strength: above-average gravity;
- appearance: clear light colour.

Consumers come to prefer the particular taste/strength/appearance of beer that is described in shorthand by a brand name. If the taste of a brand varies between one pint and the next, the ability of the brand name to act as a shorthand description of a whole bundle of attributes is significantly weakened. Next time the buyer may not bother sticking with the brand, which it does not now trust, if it has just as much chance of achieving the desired bundle of attributes from another product.

The ability of a company to secure consistency of product delivery is crucial to the development of branding. This helps to explain why branding was fastest to develop for those products that were produced using factory techniques in which quality control procedures could be used to ensure consistent standards every time. Soap powders, cigarettes, and soft drinks were all examples of products for which manufacturers developed an ability to control production standards and were early adopters of brands.

Figure 6.6 Many of our most familiar fast-moving consumer goods brands have a long history.
Typhoo tea, which can trace its origins back to 1820, is typical of a brand that has been associated with
consistency in its appeal. Despite numerous changes in ownership of the brand and many new
product formulations (such as different shapes of tea bags), many consumers remain loyal to the
Typhoo brand, and this loyalty is often passed down through generations of families

Brands have been relatively slow to develop in the services sector, partly because of the difficulty of maintaining consistent standards. Some service sectors have successfully taken on board the 'industrialization' of their production processes to ensure that a service delivered on one occasion is very similar to that delivered on all previous and subsequent occasions. Fast food restaurants have been notable in this field, and have been associated with the development of many strong international brands. On the other hand, many one-to-one services such as those provided by hairdressers, solicitors, and dentists have difficulty in 'industrializing' their service offer, and consequently corporate brands have had much more limited impact; the brand identity is essentially limited to the individual performing the service.

The term 'consistency' was noted above as an important attribute of a brand. As well as referring to specific product attributes (as in the case of the beer described earlier), consistency can refer to more general values about a producer or its range of products. As an example, the Co-operative brand name has been associated with ethical values, and these values have been applied consistently across the UK organization's activities, including retailing, banking, and travel services.

Risk reduction

In simple economies where buyers personally knew the producers of the goods and services they bought, the personal relationship helped to manage the buyer's exposure to risk. In the absence of that relationship, a brand acts as a substitute in managing buyers' exposure to risk. Branding simplifies the decision-making process by providing a sense of security and consistency for buyers which may be absent outside of a relationship with a supplier.

A brand addresses a number of dimensions of purchase risk, which have been identified as:

- physical (will the product cause me harm?)
- psychological (will this product satisfy my need for peace of mind?)
- performance (does the product work in accordance with my requirements?)
- financial (will this product provide adequate performance within my budget?)

Risk levels are perceived as being higher for products that fulfil important needs and for which there is a high level of involvement by the consumer.

Functional and emotional attributes

There have been many conceptualizations of the unique qualities of brands. These usually distinguish between dimensions that can be objectively measured (such as taste, shape, reliability) and the subjective values that can be defined only in the minds of consumers (such as the perceived personality of a brand). In an early study, Gardner and Levy [6] distinguished between the 'functional' dimensions of a brand and its 'personality'. Similar attempts to distinguish the dimensions of brands have been made by others—e.g. utilitarianism versus value expressive (Munson and Spivey [11]), need satisfaction versus impression management (Solomon [15]), and functional versus representational (de Chernatony and McWilliam [4]). It has been suggested that brands need to be positioned somewhere in a 'brand space', defined by the degree of abstraction (whether the brand has become independent from its associated product) and the degree of enactment (whether the brand focuses more on the meaning of a product or its functionality) (Berthon, Holbrook, and Hulbert [2]). With increasing affluence, the emotional or non-functional expectations of brands have become more important.

A number of dimensions of a brand's emotional appeal have been identified, including trust, liking, and sophistication, and it has been shown that products with a high level of subjective emotional appeal are associated with a greater level of customer involvement than a product that provides essentially objective benefits. This has been demonstrated in the preference shown for branded beer as opposed to a functionally identical generic beer (Allison and Uhl [1]), and in the way that the emotional appeal of brands of analgesics contributed significantly in relieving headaches (Branthwaite and Cooper [3]). As consumers buy products, they learn to appreciate their added value and begin to form a relationship with them. For example, there are many companies selling petrol and credit cards, but individual companies such as Shell and American Express have sought to create brands with which customers develop a relationship and which guide their choice in a market dominated by otherwise generic products.

There is an extensive literature on the emotional relationship consumers develop between a brand and their own perceived or sought personality. Brands are chosen when the image they create matches the needs, values, and life-styles of customers. Through socialization processes, individuals form perceptions of their self, which they attempt to reinforce or alter by relating with specific groups, products, and brands. There is evidence that branding plays a particularly important role in purchase decisions where the product is conspicuous in its use and in situations where group social acceptance is a strong motivator.

MARKETING in ACTION

Can a university be branded?

Are universities unique places of learning, or brands to be marketed just like any other product? The language of brand management has been entering the vocabulary of university vice chancellors throughout the UK. 'Good' universities have known for some time that they have their reputation to preserve, but more recently many universities have begun talking about 'managing brand values'. Research among applicants to UK universities has consistently shown that prospective students have very poor knowledge about the actual facilities on offer, such as the standards of teaching, accommodation, and library facilities. However, some universities have come to be rated more highly than others, often on the basis of non-academic information, such as the triumphs of the university's sports teams or the nightlife in town.

Many of the UK's 'new' (post-1992) universities have made a priority of developing a strong brand image with which to challenge the established universities. Even students feel it is important to have a degree from a university that has a 'good' name, in the same way as people have always wanted to belong to 'good' clubs. The view has spread that a university's 'good' name needs to be nurtured and maintained in just the same way as any fast-moving consumer product. Simply having technical excellence is not good enough.

De Montfort University has been one of the pioneers in university brand building, supporting its efforts with television advertising. It undertook research among current students which showed, perhaps surprisingly, that many preferred limited university funds to be spent on a brand building advertising campaign than on improvements in academic facilities, such as additional books for the library. Graduating from a known rather than an unknown university was seen as being important to many students.

Cynics have been quick to criticize efforts to market universities as brands. How can any brand be sustained over the long term if the infrastructure and facilities of a university are under pressure from ever diminishing resources?

Creating a distinctive brand

Branding creates a product with unique physical, functional, and psychological values and can help to transform commodities into unique products. To be successful, a brand must have a competitive advantage in at least one aspect of marketing, such that it meets the complex needs of consumers better than competitors. This section discusses the strategic issues involved in creating a strong and distinctive brand.

Choice of name

A brand is more than a name. Nevertheless, a name is usually vital to the identity of a brand and can be the most difficult to change. Many products have been redesigned and relaunched as they have gone through their life-cycle, yet their brand name has remained unchanged. In the car market, Volkswagen introduced its first Golf model in 1974. Since then, the car has gone through four completely new body designs, three new series of engines, and countless minor modifications to styling, features, engine ranges, and colours. The Golf of 2003 is larger and much better equipped than its predecessor of a quarter of a century ago. Yet the brand name remains the same. Instead of symbolizing a set of narrowly defined product characteristics, the name 'Golf' has come to stand for reliable, mid-size, safe, value-for-money motoring. These values have been essentially unchanged for thirty years. The public has come to learn what is associated with the name 'Golf', and therefore new model launches do not have to start from scratch in explaining what the car stands for.

Companies frequently engage specialist firms to develop brand names for their new products. This is often a wise investment, in view of the possible downside costs of getting a name wrong and the difficulties of subsequently changing it. A brand naming team may be made up of linguists, psychologists, sociologists, and media analysts, among others. The following are some of the factors that previous experience shows should lead to a brand name being successful.

- The name should have positive associations with the benefits and features of the product (e.g. 'Bostik' suggests adhesive qualities; 'Flash' sounds like it will clean thoroughly and quickly).

- There should be no negative associations with words that sound similar. (For example, Volkswagen had to think long and hard about the wisdom of using the name 'Sharan' in the UK for a new model. Although the name worked well in other countries, it sounded too similar to Sharon, a girl's name which at the time had been much maligned in the media.)

- The name should be memorable and easy to pronounce. (There is research evidence to suggest that names including the letter 'x' are particularly memorable, such as Andrex, Durex, Radox, etc.)

- The name must be in a tone of language that is understood and appreciated by the product's target market.

- The name must be checked my legal experts to ensure that it does not infringe on another company's brand name.

- In the age of the internet, a company must ensure that the product's name is available as a domain name. Ideally, it should also be able to register all similar sounding domain names in order to prevent unauthorized sites appearing.

Despite these guidelines, brand names exist which appear to break all the rules and would almost certainly not have been chosen today. In a world that is sceptical of offal from animals, who would have named a range of meat products 'Brains'?

MARKETING in ACTION

A Bum name or a Sic brand?

Getting a brand name wrong can cost a company dearly. For a major brand, re-tooling to change product formulations can be a relatively minor matter compared with the costs of changing a brand name. Sometimes brands fail because the underlying product has failed to meet customers' expectations. At other times a brand fails because its name was chosen with insufficient care. Occasionally, the world outside a brand name changes in a way that destroys the appeal of a once well liked name; for example, the slimmers' biscuits called Aids had to be renamed in the light of HIV scares.

With increasing globalization of markets, firms have to be careful that a brand name is capable of translation into overseas languages without causing offence or ridicule. The following brand names may have been well thought out in their own home market, but they failed to take account of local interpretations in potential overseas markets:

- General Motors may have wondered why its Nova car wasn't selling well in Spain, then realized that in the local language the brand name suggests that the car 'doesn't work'.

- British visitors to Spain are often amused to find 'Bum' crisps on sale—they probably wouldn't go down too well in an English speaking market.

- Similarly, the French drink 'Sic' wouldn't be easy to export to Britain.

Care must also be taken in choosing a corporate brand name. Corporate mergers and restructuring during the 1990s spawned numerous abstract names, many of which promptly had to be changed following public ridicule. Royal Mail should have had one of the most sought-after corporate brand names in the world, but nevertheless it decided to change the company's name to 'Consignia'. Public ridicule led it to abandon this name in 2002 and revert to its original name. There was incredulity in 2002 when the accounting firm Price Waterhouse Cooper proposed changing its name to 'Monday'. One financial analyst calculated that, during the period 1997–2000, just under half of all FTSE 100 companies that had taken on a new abstract corporate name were ejected from the FTSE 100 list within two years.

Distinctive product features

Sometimes the distinctive features of a product don't really require a brand name to prompt immediate recognition. Distinctiveness can be based on the physical design of a product (e.g. the distinctive shape of Toblerone chocolate); distinctive packaging (e.g.

Figure 6.7 The packaging of some products is so distinctive that a brand is recognizable even without a name or logo. The chocolate bar Toblerone has a distinctive shape which differentiates it from competitors and which the company guards against imitators

the lemon-shaped container used to package Jif lemon juice) or distinctive service processes (e.g. the manner in which waiting staff in a TGIFridays restaurant serve customers). Companies make great efforts through the use of patents to protect the distinctive characteristics of their products from competition, although this can be much more difficult in the case of intangible service processes.

Creation of a distinctive brand personality

It will be recalled that a brand possesses functional and emotional attributes. The emotional attributes are of particular importance in contributing to a brand's personality. This can best be described as the psychological disposition that buyers have towards a particular brand. Brands have been variously described as having personalities that are 'fun', 'reliable', 'traditional', and 'adventurous'. The Virgin group has evolved a personality for its brand which can be described as reliable, slightly offbeat, and value for money. This personality has been developed consistently across the group's product ranges, from air travel to banking and investment services.

There has been some debate about whether the emotional aspects of a brand are becoming more or less important in consumers' overall evaluation of a product. One argument is that consumers are becoming more 'marketing literate' and increasingly sceptical of firms' attempts to create abstract images that are not underpinned by reality. On the other hand, there is no doubt that, as consumers become more affluent, they buy products to satisfy a much wider and more complex range of needs, which they seek to satisfy with distinctive brands. (Refer back to the discussion of needs in Chapter 3.) A brand personality can help an individual reinforce her own self-identity, for example in the way that clothes are worn bearing brand names that have a personality of their own. An individual who wears a Gap sweatshirt is probably identifying herself with the personality that Gap has created for its brand.

Distinctive visual identity

Companies often go to great lengths to invest their brands with a distinctive visual identity. Sometimes this can be achieved simply on the basis of a colour. Within the cigarette market, Silk Cut came to 'own' the colour purple, with the result that an advertisement need not mention a brand by name, but the presence of the colour will achieve association with the brand. The importance of colour was demonstrated in 1996 when Pepsi Cola sought to adopt the colour blue in the UK cola market to distinguish itself from its predominantly red competitors. The fact that the change appeared to result in no short-term increase in sales provides a reminder that buyers may not be influenced simply by a superficial change which does not increase the product's perceived value. This may be especially true for low-involvement products such as soft drinks. One of Pepsi's arch rivals, Virgin, exploited the opportunity by stating in advertisements that it pays more attention to the *contents* of the can than to its colour.

The extent to which a company can legitimately 'own' an identifying colour is questionable. Many suppliers of generic products have copied the colours used by their branded competitors; for example, many supermarkets' own brands of coffee share a very similar colour scheme to that of the market leader, Nescafe. This has frequently led to allegations that they are 'passing off' their goods as if they were the branded product, especially where the packaging and typography are also used to imitate the brand leader. The owner of EasyJet successfully challenged the owner of easyRealestate.co.uk which had used EasyJet's colour, orange. A court held that, by using a similar name and colour, the company had sought to wrongly imply an association with EasyJet.

Colours have often come to be associated with certain product features. Bright reds and yellows are often used to signify speed (e.g. fast food, one-hour film developing), and white is often associated with purity (low fat, additive-free foods). However, the meaning of colours has to be seen in their cultural context—although white may be associated with purity in most western countries, in some other countries it is associated with bereavement.

To achieve maximum effect, corporate visual identity should be applied consistently. For a typical service based company, this would mean applying a design and colour scheme to the company's advertising, buildings, staff uniforms, and vehicles.

MARKETING in ACTION

Logos get a makeover

Many companies have rulebooks stating quite precisely how their logo should be applied. But could this consistency be counterproductive and result in the organization's being seen by its customers as boring and lacking in creativity? Research carried out for British Airways in the mid-1990s showed that its brand image was seen as stuffy and British. In an increasingly global market for airline services, it needed to shed this image, yet at the same time continue to stand for something in the eyes of customers throughout the world. The solution adopted by BA was to develop multiple identities based on ethnic art from around the world. The designs were applied in a highly visible manner to such items as aircraft tail fins, baggage labels, and furnishings in airport lounges. Traditionalists were horrified at the changes, especially, it seemed, BA's premium fare business passengers. Not long after the launch of its multi-ethnic tail fins, BA's revenues and profits began to fall. Of course, many factors contributed to this, especially a deepening world recession and the after-effects of the 11 September 2001 terrorist attacks. But the ethnic visual identities were made a scapegoat, and—possibly to deflect criticism from wider corporate problems—the company decided to restore a stylized Union Jack motif to the tail fins of half of its fleet.

BA was not alone in trying to make its visual corporate identity more stylish. The BBC, similarly regarded as stuffy, developed a playful series of images for its BBC2 television channel. The theme was the figure 2, with interpretations including rubber ducks, a fly killer, and a toy car. How many more companies would benefit from a loosening of logo designs? Against this, how does a company maintain some degree of consistency in its brand values?

Logos are an important part of corporate visual identity. The aim of a logo is to encapsulate the values of a brand and to provide an immediate reminder of the brand each time it is seen by customers and potential customers. A good logo should:

- give some indication of the business which a company is in, or the product category to which its output belongs (e.g. the logo for many water utility companies include stylized waves of water);

- stress particular advantages of a product or organization (e.g. the most advanced, the fastest, most caring, longest established);

- not be over-complicated. The simplest logos tend to stand the test of time best;

- be updated to keep it in tune with styles and fashions of the time (for example, the Shell oil company's logo has gone through numerous minor styling changes during its 70 year history, which have retained the central theme of a shell, but adapted the shape and the emphasis on particular details.

MARKETING in ACTION

Towns as logos?

Logos are often used by public and not-for-profit sector organizations, and here the public often expects to have its views about what is an acceptable logo taken into account. How far should an organization go in meeting the needs of its wider public stakeholders rather than those of its target customers?

Like many areas seeking to promote inward tourism, Leicester sought a logo for the city. The local tourism promotion company carried out research and decided that a logo featuring a fashion-clad ethnic dancer was ideal for promoting some of the key tourism benefits of Leicester: a lively city with a lot of night life, the centre of the fashion industry, and a multi-ethnic choice of artistic events and restaurants. Faced with this new logo, the immediate reaction of many long-standing Leicester residents was 'Where's the Clock Tower?' (a well known landmark in the centre of the city and a traditional symbol of the city). The marketers had rejected the use of this symbol in the city's tourism logo because it conveyed nothing of the special attributes of the city. The Clock Tower may be an important reference point for *local* residents, but would tourists from outside really identify with it and be induced to visit the city?

▌ Branding strategy

Once a firm has decided on a distinctive brand identity for a product, the next issue is to have a strategy for developing the brand. In this section, a number of alternative strategic routes are explored which each lead to a company differentiating its products from those of its competitors. One strategy is to develop a single strong brand. As an alternative, differentiated brands or brand families may be developed (Figure 6.9).

Figure 6.8 These logos are so powerful that most people could readily identify with the 'true' owner, despite the use of a false name

Finally, once a strong brand has been developed, companies are often keen to extend its use.

Development of a single strong brand

One approach to branding is to apply the same brand name to everything that a company produces. The big advantage of this approach is the economies of scale in promotion that this can bring about. Instead of promoting many minor brands through small campaigns, a company can concentrate all of its resources on one campaign for one brand. This approach has been used successfully by many large multinational companies, such as IBM, Kodak, and Cadburys, who, with a few exceptions, put their single brand name on everything they sell.

The main disadvantage of this approach is that it can pose significant risks of confusing the values of a brand. If a company positioned its product range as premium priced, top quality, confusion may arise in consumers' minds if it applied the same brand name to a budget version of its product—does the brand still stand for top quality?

Worse still for a company, a poorly performing product carrying its brand can tarnish all products carrying that name. This is a particular problem for new product launches which are of unproven reliability. (For example, the Virgin group's reputation for dependable, no-nonsense service undoubtedly suffered when it applied its brand name to train services with a very poor reliability record.)

A final problem of the strong single corporate brand is that it can make it more difficult for a company to dispose of the manufacture and marketing of products that no longer fit in its corporate plan. Very often, the main value of the products to a corporate buyer is their brand name, so the company may be forced into a monitoring agreement to protect its brand name from abuse by a company that has acquired the right to use it. Because of changes in corporate strategy, many of the products carrying the Cadburys and Virgin brand names are not in fact made or sold by these companies, yet they still need to preserve the values that the names stand for.

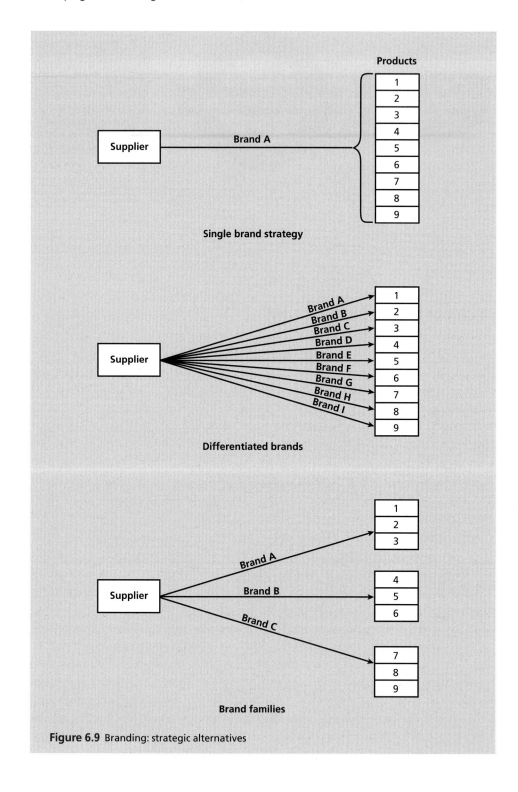

Figure 6.9 Branding: strategic alternatives

Differentiated brands

To overcome the problem of confused brand values, firms often develop different brand names to serve different market segments. In this way, the clothing retailer Arcadia uses a number of different brand names to target different segments of the clothes buying market in terms of buyers' age, disposable income, and life-style. So Top Shop serves a price conscious young female segment, while Top Man serves a similar, but male, segment; the company's Dorothy Perkins and Burtons brands target older segments, female and male respectively. The company also operates a number of other store brands which target segments that are different in terms of their age/income/fashion consciousness/price sensitivity.

Brand families

A brand family occurs where a company uses a number of brand names, but identifies each product range or market segment served with a different brand name. The range is then developed to include a line of products. In this way, the Colgate Palmolive company has developed a number of product ranges, including soap, shampoos, and toothpaste, each with its own brand name. Within each range are a number of variants; for example, Colgate toothpaste comes in original, baking soda, and total protection formats, among others.

Very often, companies promote brand names at a number of levels. As well as the corporate brand name, the name of the product category might be promoted. In addition, a special package offer within the basic product category may be developed with its own brand name. British Airways has developed a corporate brand (British Airways), brands for Club Class and its Executive Club, and brands for special offer tickets (e.g. World Savers). The danger of brand proliferation is confusion in the minds of consumers about what each brand stands for.

Brand extension

Where a company has invested heavily in a brand so that it has many positive attributes in the minds of buyers, it may feel tempted to get as much as possible out of its valuable asset. Given the increasing costs of developing strong brands, many companies have attempted to extend their brand to new product ranges. The attraction is quite clear. Rather than having to start from scratch with a new product and a new name, the company can at least start with a name whose values buyers are familiar with. So if a manufacturer of chocolate has developed a brand that stands for good taste and consistency, those values will be immediately transferred to a new range of ice cream products that the company may consider adding to its range.

Of course, extending a brand to new products poses dangers as well as opportunities. If the extension goes too far into unrelated product areas, the core values of the brand may be undermined. Consider the case of BP oil, which introduced a line of dishwashing detergent to the private consumer market. How could consumers avoid the feeling that the detergent was oily? The line was subsequently withdrawn. Considerable research has been undertaken to assess the effects of brand extensions on consumers' perceptions of a brand (e.g. Grime, Diamantopoulos, and Smith [7]).

Co-branding

Opportunities often arise for the owners of two quite different brands to work together jointly to develop a new product that carries the brand name of both partners, resulting in an otherwise unattainable gain to both. Co-branding is increasingly common in the food sector, where, for example, a branded manufacturer of meat products may develop a 'beef and ale pie' in which it co-brands the product with its own brand name and that of the beer brand that makes up one of the ingredients. The owner of the beer brand gets exposure and distribution through a new channel, while the pie brand owner adds to the distinctiveness and perceived value of its pies. As with any brand extension (see above), co-branding presents dangers where expectations of each brand are not met. A previously loyal customer of the beer brand used in the pie may have his faith in the brand reduced if the process of incorporating it into the beer leaves a nasty taste.

Protecting a brand

Once they have been created, brands can become very valuable assets to the companies that own them. Attempts to value brands usually try to estimate the price premium they command in their market, multiplied by estimated sales. A discounted cash flow calculation takes into account the value of earnings in future years. The enormous value of brands such as Coca Cola is a reflection of the significant price premium they can command and their enormous annual sales worldwide.

Like any asset of value, criminals will be tempted to appropriate the asset for themselves. If somebody else has developed a strong brand name, why not 'borrow' it to promote your own goods? The result is counterfeit goods, which carry all the superficial manifestations of brand identity, but may fail to deliver the performance that has come to be expected with the brand. Counterfeiting of goods with false brand names has been found in products as diverse as beverages, perfumes, watches, computer chips, and aircraft engine components. Sometimes consumers may be quite happy buying a low priced branded product knowing that it is a counterfeit copy—this is especially true of goods bought for conspicuous consumption, such as the fake Rolex watches that many tourists bring back from the Far East for just a few pounds. At other times buyers may be defrauded into thinking that they have bought the genuine brand, often with dangerous consequences where the integrity of the product has safety implications.

Recent research has suggested that one in five UK consumers have bought 'look-alikes' by mistake. More worryingly, about 40% expected look-alike brands to be just as good as the real product—because they thought that they are made by the same people (Jacques [8]). CDR International, a brand protection consultant, carried out research in 1998 to assess just how desirable some of our favourite brand names are. When shown a white T-shirt, consumers said they would, on average, pay a premium of 33% if it carried a designer label. This premium was even higher (at 37%) for those in the 16–35 age group, or in the C1 socio-economic group (members of which would be prepared to pay 42% more). Protecting a brand name against illegal counterfeiting is always a challenge, and over half of respondents in CDR's survey claimed that they would be happy to buy good counterfeits. Which brands were considered the most desirable by carrying the highest price premium? The top brand was Nike, followed by Calvin Klein, Rolex, Adidas, and Levi Strauss.

For the owner of a brand, counterfeit copies hit it in two ways. First, it loses sales to counterfeiters which it would probably have made itself. Second, and more importantly, buyers may come to mistrust the brand. How can they be sure that they are buying the genuine article? Firms often go to great lengths to stay one step ahead of counterfeiters, for example by regularly introducing new designs which are hard to copy.

Brand owners resort to the law to protect their assets. In the UK, the common law provides a general remedy against companies seeking to 'pass off' counterfeit products as though they were the real thing. 'Passing off' can include attempts to copy any of the distinctive brand characteristics discussed above. As an example, a bus operator was accused of passing off by painting its buses a similar colour to those of its main competitor and running on a similar route. It had been relying on public confusion to pass off its service as the one people had been expecting. Further protection is provided by legislation. The Trade Marks Act 1994, which implements the EU Trade Marks Harmonization Directive no. 89/104/EEC), provides protection for trademarks, which are defined as any sign that can be represented graphically which is capable of distinguishing goods or services of one undertaking from those of other undertakings (Trade Marks Act 1994, s. 1(1)). Where a company has a patent for a product, the Patents Act 1977 provides protection against unauthorized copying of the product specification during the currency of the patent.

■ The changing role of branding

The philosophy and practices of branding have seen a number of developments in recent years. Many have argued that brands no longer have a role in an age of greater public awareness of product characteristics and increased scepticism about brands. At the same time, many intermediaries have taken on board the practices of branding, frequently challenging manufacturers at their own game.

The end of branding?

There have been many suggestions that the processes of branding are in retreat. When the manufacturer of Marlboro cigarettes cut the price of its main brand to beat off competition from the rapidly advancing generic competitors, many began to write the obituaries for brands as we have come to know them.

Both the functional and emotional dimensions of brands have come under increasing pressure. Research has suggested that consumers are becoming increasingly critical of the messages of brand building advertising, especially those aimed at creating abstract brand personalities. Naomi Klein [9] painted a picture of a 'brandscape' in which she made a call to arms to fight the dominance and abuses of multinationals. To her, brands such as Nike, Shell, Wal-Mart, Microsoft, and McDonald's have become metaphors for a global economic system gone awry. It is also claimed that consumers are becoming increasingly confident, ready to experiment and to trust their own judgement and less tolerant of products that do not contribute to their own values.

The traditional functional qualities of a brand have also come under pressure from increasing levels of consumer legislation. Characteristics such as purity, reliability, and durability may have traditionally added value to a brand, but these are increasingly enshrined in legislation and therefore are less capable of being used to differentiate one product from another. An example of the effects of legislation on brand loyalty can be observed in the taxi market by contrasting buyer behaviour in areas with strict licensing (e.g. London) with areas where a relatively unregulated market exists. In London legislation has reduced the product to a commodity meeting strictly specified standards, whereas in the other towns customers are more likely to seek the reassurance of a branded operator.

Defenders of brands argue that much of the success of generic products during the 1990s can be attributed to periods of economic recession rather than to any fundamental change in attitude by consumers. As household disposable incomes decline during a recession, many households cut back on items of optional expenditure, which could mean substituting a premium priced brand with a cheaper generic product. By this analysis, expenditure on branded products would be expected to rise as household incomes recover. More importantly, there is strong evidence that many segments of buyers are becoming increasingly brand conscious, and advocates of branding point to the appearance of 'designer' drink brands and coffee bars to support this. In an age where individuals are less likely to develop a personal identity for themselves through traditional means such as the family and social groups that they associate with, brands have an important role to play. Brands make important statements about an individual's sought identity.

The emergence of retailers' own brands

More significantly, it has been argued that declining sales of manufacturers' branded products have in fact been offset by a growth in retailers' branded products. The concept of branding is alive and well, but is now more in the hands of retailers. Through continued investment in product improvement, retailers have been able to develop products that have comparable functional qualities to manufacturers' branded products. In many cases, customers trust a retailer more than they trust manufacturers. In the UK Marks & Spencer has long recognized this point, and more recently Tesco has gone out of its way to present itself as a caring, trustworthy retailer that always offers value for money.

With improved product ranges and corporate image strategies, intermediaries have sought to extend the functional aspects of their branding (e.g. quality of products, range of products) with the emotional appeal of the corporate brand. The use of distinctive colour schemes and alignment with good causes can help to develop an emotional relationship between the store and its customers.

The organization as a brand

The traditional role of a brand has been to differentiate a product from competing products and to create a liking of it by target customers. The process of branding has been increasingly applied to organizational image, too. This has been particularly important for services, where the intangibility of the product causes the credentials of the provider to be an important component of consumers' choices. The notion of an emotional relationship to a product has been extended to develop an emotional relationship between an organization and its customers.

Many service organizations have found the development of brands to be attractive where their service offer is highly complex and consumers find the offer mentally as well as physically intangible. In the UK the pensions industry has found it difficult to explain its products to an audience that is not receptive to technical details of a product, but nevertheless may consider a pension to be a vital provision for old age. Furthermore, the Financial Services Act 1986 limits the ability of companies to promote their pensions in creative ways. (For example, companies may quote only standard industry-wide expected rates of return.) This has led many companies to embark on comprehensive brand building programmes which say very little about the details of the products on offer, but a lot about the nature of the company offering them. The Prudential Assurance Company has built its brand image on the superior life-style that can result from dealing with the company, while Legal and General used the brand image of an umbrella as the symbol of a protective company.

It is not only in the service sector that brand building has been refocused from the product to the organization. During the 1990s, many companies moved expenditure from 'above the line' brand building activities to 'below the line' product support by means of direct marketing activities. In one notable case, the Heinz company decided to cut the money it spent on advertising individual product brands and instead to promote the Heinz brand for core values of tradition and wholesomeness. Individual products were supported by point-of-sale material, direct marketing, and a reduced amount of advertising. The company, rather than individual products, then becomes the dominant brand, and brand equity is based on customers' willingness to pay premium prices for the company's products.

The development of global brands

With the volume of international trade growing at around four times the rate of world Gross Domestic Product, companies are increasingly having to include exports as part of their marketing plan. It follows therefore that the process of branding should be considered in global terms. Economies of scale can be achieved by developing a global brand; for example, visitors from overseas can automatically recognize a McDonald's restaurant, giving it an advantage over a local branded restaurant which starts with no overseas name recognition.

There are many pitfalls in the development of brands that work in overseas markets as well as the domestic one. There is an argument that individuals' need for cultural identity is making it more difficult to justify the cost of developing a global brand (Williams [16]). This chapter has highlighted some of the problems that occur with an inappropriate choice of name. We will return to the subject of global brands in Chapter 14.

MARKETING and SOCIAL RESPONSIBILITY

Can brands be socially divisive?
Some of the healthiest food products we could buy are inexpensive but are shunned because they are not supported by brand building activities, in contrast to possibly more harmful and expensive alternatives which have the power of branding behind them. Consider the following examples.

- The market for bottled water in the UK has increased markedly during the past couple of decades, helped by the development of strong brands including Perrier, Highland

Spring, and Volvic. This is despite repeated analyses suggesting that filtered domestic tap water is purer and more beneficial than most bottled water, yet is a fraction of the cost. The water supply utility companies have not marketed the benefits of their water, partly held back by a regulatory system that prevents them raising prices for the water they supply. Meanwhile, bottled water suppliers have promoted their product, increasingly relying on 'life-style' associations to command ever-higher prices.

- Children are exposed to a vast amount of advertising for snack foods, and peer group pressure leads them to demand 'cool' brands of drinks and snacks. Meanwhile, fresh fruit—which is considered by nutritionists to be much more beneficial to children—is overlooked as it lacks strong brand building support. A fragmented industry made up of countless growers and importers and a generic range of products that cannot generally be protected by patent have resulted in very little investment being made available for brand building. Support is generally limited to national growers' associations promoting a national product, with little effort to develop life-style brands. Would children eat more apples and fewer crisps if apples were supported by a multi-million advertising campaign to portray them as a 'cool' brand?

- Consumers' Association tests have suggested that retailer's own brand training shoes costing around £10 are just as hard wearing and beneficial to children's' feet as top brand shoes advertised using sports heroes, but costing over £60. Critics have accused branded sports shoes companies of exploiting the children's susceptibility to peer group pressure and their consequent desire to be seen in only the coolest brand of sports shoes.

Are brands a form of exploitation which creates social divisiveness? Critics of branding in particular, and the capitalist system in general, have argued that brands contribute towards a division in society between the 'haves' and 'have-nots', with ostentatious displays of brands creating a feeling of grievance among those who aspire for brands but cannot afford them. Brands particularly appeal to less secure individuals as a means of establishing an identity for themselves, yet these are often the people who can least afford to pay for premium brands.

Would life be better without brands? Buying would certainly be a lot more difficult without the power of identification that a brand gives to buyers. As far as life-style brands are concerned, haven't all societies had some means of differentiating individuals within the society? Maybe we don't have the tribal dresses that have been used in the past by individuals to give them identity and therefore brands are a contemporary response to a need for identity.

■ Positioning the brand

Positioning strategy for a brand is a crucial part of developing a sustainable competitive advantage for the brand. Positioning puts a firm in a sub-segment of its chosen market, and so a firm that adopts a product positioning based on 'high reliability/high cost' will appeal to a sub-segment that has a desire for reliability and a willingness to pay for it.

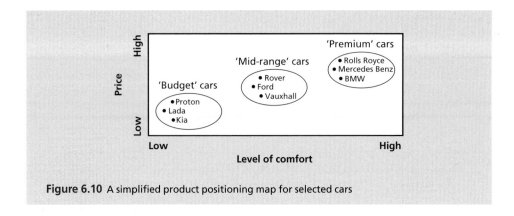

Figure 6.10 A simplified product positioning map for selected cars

For some marketers, positioning has been seen as essentially a communications issue, where the nature of the product is given and the objective is to manipulate consumers' perceptions of it. However, others have pointed out that positioning is more than merely advertising and promotion, involving the management of the whole marketing mix. Essentially, the mix must be managed in a way that is internally coherent and sustainable over the long term. A marketing mix positioning of high quality and low price may attract business from competitors in the short term, but the low prices may be insufficient to cover costs of delivering high quality, and therefore profits may be unsustainable over the long term.

A company must examine the strengths and weaknesses of its brands within their marketplace and the opportunities and threats that they face. From this, its brands take a position within their marketplace. A position can be defined by reference to a number of scales, such a price, quality, availability, durability, etc. Level of comfort and price are two dimensions of positioning that are relevant to cars. It is possible to draw a *position map* in which the positions of key players in a market are plotted in relation to these criteria. A position map plotting the positions of selected cars in respect of their price and level of comfort is shown in Figure 6.10. Both scales run from high to low, with price being a general indication of price levels charged relative to competitors and level of comfort being a subjective evaluation of features provided with the car. The position map shows that most cars lie on a diagonal line between the high comfort/high price position adopted by Mercedes Benz and Lexus and the low price/low comfort position adopted by Proton and Lada. Points along this diagonal represent feasible positioning strategies for car manufacturers. A strategy in the upper left quadrant (high price/low quality) can be described as a 'cowboy' strategy and generally is not sustainable. A position in the lower right area of the map (high quality/low price) may indicate that an organization is failing to achieve a fair exchange of value. Of course, this two-dimensional analysis of the car market is very simplistic, and buyers make judgements based on a variety of criteria. Low levels of comfort may be tolerated at a high price, for example if a car carries a strong, aspirational brand name.

The example of cars used two very simplistic positioning criteria. Wind ([17], pp. 79–81) has suggested six generic scales along which all products can be positioned. These are examined below by reference to the positioning opportunities of a leisure centre.

- **Positioning by benefits or needs satisfied**: The leisure centre could position itself somewhere between meeting pure physical recreation needs and meeting pure social needs. In practice, positioning may combine the two sets of needs, for example by giving up gym space to allow the construction of a bar.

- **Positioning by specific product features**: For example, the leisure centre could promote the fact that it has the largest swimming pool in the area, or the most advanced solarium.

- **Positioning by usage occasions**: The centre could be positioned primarily for the occasional visitor, or the service offer could be adapted to aim at the more serious user who wishes to enter a long-term programme of leisure activities.

- **Positioning by user categories**: A choice could be made between a position aimed at satisfying the needs of individual users and one aimed at meeting the needs of institutional users such as sports clubs and schools.

- **Positioning against another product**: The leisure centre could promote the fact that it has more facilities than its neighbouring competition.

- **Positioning by product class**: Management could position the centre as an educational facility rather than a centre of leisure, thereby positioning it in a different product class.

Of all the position possibilities open to a company, which position should it adopt? Selecting a product position involves three basic steps (illustrated in Figure 6.11).

1. **Undertake a marketing audit to analyse the position opportunities relative to the company's strengths.** A SWOT analysis should be undertaken to assess the opportunities and threats in a marketplace and the strengths and weaknesses of the company in meeting opportunities as they arise. An important consideration is often the position that customers currently perceive a company as occupying. If a company is perceived as being 'down-market', this may pose a major weakness in exploiting opportunities arising for more 'up-market' products. An organization that is already established in a particular product position will normally have the advantage of customer familiarity to support any new product launch. A car manufacturer such as Mercedes Benz, which has positioned itself as a high quality/high price producer, can use this as a strength to persuade customers to pay relatively high prices for a new product range, in this case a small compact car. Sometimes a

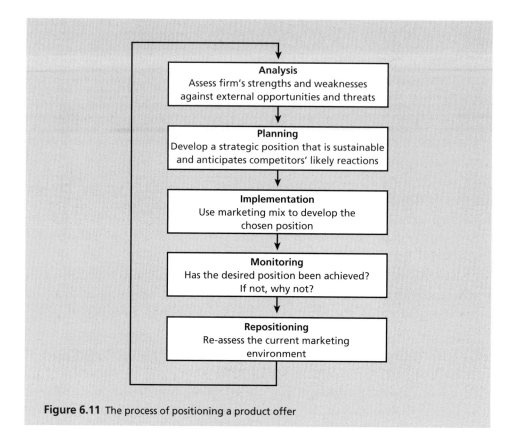

Figure 6.11 The process of positioning a product offer

weakness can be turned into a strength for positioning purposes; for example, the Avis car rental chain has stressed that, by being the number two operator, it has to try harder.

It often happens that opportunities are greatest in budget range, low-quality, low-price positions. If a company has established a position as a premium position supplier, should it seek to exploit a lower market position when the opportunity arises? It must avoid tarnishing its established brand values by association with a lower quality product. One solution is to adopt a separate identity for a new product which assumes a different position. In this way, the Volkswagen car group offers three different price/quality positions with its Volkswagen, Audi, and Skoda brands.

2. **Evaluate the position possibilities and select the most appropriate.** In undertaking a SWOT analysis, a number of potential positions may have been identified, but many may have to be discarded if they result in uneconomically small market segments, or are too costly to develop. Other positions may be rejected as being inconsistent with an organization's image. Selection from the remaining possibilities should be on the basis of the organization's greatest differential advantage in areas

that are most valued by target customers. When it entered the Indonesian market, the UK retailer Marks & Spencer realized that its UK positioning would be unsustainable against low-cost local competition. It therefore adopted a much more exclusive position, with smaller shops, limited product ranges, and relatively high prices.

3. **Use the marketing mix to develop and communicate a position.** Organizations must develop programmes to implement and promote the position they have adopted. If a car manufacturer seeks to adopt a position as a supplier of premium quality cars at premium prices, it must have in hand production facilities for ensuring consistently high quality. It must also effectively communicate this quality to potential customers in order to justify their paying premium prices.

Repositioning

Markets are dynamic, and what was once an appropriate position for a company may eventually cease to be so. A company's environmental monitoring should identify any factors that may call for a repositioning. Repositioning could become necessary for a number of reasons.

- The original positioning may have been based on an overestimation of a company's competitive advantage or of the size of the sub-segment to which the positioning was intended to appeal. Positioning strategy could have become untenable.

- The nature of customer demand may have changed, for example in respect of preferences for high quality rather than low price. It has, for example, been suggested that UK customers' attitudes towards package holidays changed during the 1990s, away from an emphasis on low price towards greater emphasis on high quality standards. Many tour operators accordingly repositioned their offering to provide higher standards at higher prices.

- Companies often try to build upon their growing strengths to reposition towards meeting the needs of more profitable high-value sub-segments. In many sectors, companies start life as simple, no-frills, low-price operations, subsequently gaining a favourable image which they use to 'trade up' to relatively high quality/high price positions. This phenomenon is well established in the field of retailing and has become known as the 'Wheel of Retailing'. This contends that retail businesses start life as cut-price, low-cost, narrow-margin operations which subsequently 'trade up' with improvements in display, more prestigious premises, increased advertising, delivery, and the provision of many other customer services which serve to drive up expenses, prices, and margins. Eventually retailers mature as high-cost, conservative, and 'top-heavy' institutions with a sales policy based on quality goods and services rather than price appeal. This in turn opens the way for the next generation of low-cost innovatory retailers to find a position vacated by maturing firms.

◼ The marketing mix

The marketing mix has already been mentioned a number of times in this book. In the following chapters we will look in detail at how companies go about using the marketing mix in order to build brands that satisfy consumers' needs and at the same time allow the company to make a sustainable level of profits.

So what exactly is the marketing mix? You may recall from Chapter 1 that the marketing mix is not a scientific theory, but merely a conceptual framework that identifies the principal decisions marketing managers make in configuring their offerings to suit customers' needs. The tools play a pivotal role in developing the sustainable competitive advantage which has been discussed in this chapter. The tools of the marketing mix can be used both to develop long-term strategies and short-term tactical programmes.

There has been a lot of debate in identifying the list of marketing mix elements. The traditional marketing mix has comprised the four elements of product, price, promotion, and place. A number of people have additionally suggested adding people, process, and physical evidence decisions. There is overlap between each of these headings, and their precise definition is not particularly important. What matters is that marketing managers can identify the actions they can take that will produce a favourable response from customers. The marketing mix has merely become a convenient framework for analysing these decisions. Some would go further and argue that the concept of a marketing mix is harmful because it encourages managers to take a narrow and compartmentalized approach to each of the mix elements. By this argument, customers buy the whole product offer and are not concerned about how decisions relating to individual components are arrived at—just so long as the total product offer is coherent and creates value in their eyes. Many critics of the marketing mix see the move towards relationship marketing (Chapter 3) as a move towards a focus on customers' holistic values and away from a narrower obsession with management of a producer-defined marketing mix.

The following chapters have been arranged in accordance with traditional definitions of the marketing mix elements, but it must never be forgotten that each element is closely related to all other elements.

◼ Chapter summary and key linkages to other chapters

Developing a sustainable competitive advantage involves a sound understanding of a firm's strengths and weaknesses relative to the opportunities and threats in its marketing environment. Research into buyer behaviour and appropriate targeting, issues discussed in previous chapters, provides input to the development of a distinctive marketing mix, discussed in the following chapters. A crucial link between the needs of customers and the capabilities of a firm is the development of a brand. The process of branding allows a company to develop a distinctive identity and position for itself and its products, so as to differentiate its products from those of competitors. By doing this, a company can avoid the worse excesses of price competition. We will look in more detail at how a company uses the marketing mix to develop a distinctive brand in the following chapters.

KEY PRINCIPLES OF MARKETING

- An overriding aim of marketing is to develop a sustainable competitive advantage for an organization.
- Competitors for a firm's products can be direct or indirect. Indirect forms of competition are more difficult to identify.
- A brand is a means of identifying one company and its products from otherwise similar products supplied by other companies.
- The functional role of a brand should be distinguished from its emotional role.
- Brands are created through the management of the marketing mix. The marketing mix is merely a convenient listing of interrelated decisions to be taken by managers.

CASE STUDY

Fairy's brand bubble never seems to burst

The detergent market is often regarded as one of the early pioneers of modern marketing. Differentiating one product from another in the minds of consumers can be extremely difficult, with one packet of detergent looking very much like another, and in many cases also performing similarly. It is often said that aspiring marketers who can succeed in the detergents market can go on to successfully market any product.

In 1960 Proctor & Gamble launched Fairy Liquid in the UK market. At that time the market for washing-up products was still in its infancy, with only 17% of households using a liquid and the rest using soap powder or soap. The first task of Procter & Gamble was therefore to educate the public of the benefits of using washing-up liquid. As market leader, Procter & Gamble stood to gain most from a change in consumers' habits. The launch of Fairy involved distributing 15 million trial bottles to about 85% of households in the UK.

Creating early awareness and trial of the product led to Fairy's gaining a market share of 27% by 1969. Strong promotional support was, and remains, a key to the brand's success. Since its launch, promotional messages have focused consistently on the mildness of the product, its long-lasting suds, and a proud positioning as a slightly more expensive product which is better value and worth paying the extra for. Mother and child images have been used extensively in advertising. This helps to create brand values of a soft, caring, homely image. Messages have been adapted around this core theme in response to changing attitudes; for example, a commercial in 1994 used a father instead of a mother at the kitchen sink. Various celebrities have been used to endorse the brand's values, including a lengthy spell of endorsement by the actress Nanette Newman. The consistency of the brand's message has been reinforced with a promotional jingle that has been modified only slightly since it was first introduced in 1960.

During the first twenty years of the brand's life, product innovation had been relatively modest. However, since then an increasingly competitive market and more discerning customers have forced the company to innovate in order to maintain and strengthen its market share. With the emergence of many 'me-too' competitors from supermarkets, Fairy needed to offer additional unique advantages to supplement its long-lasting suds.

In 1984/5 the company introduced a lemon variant of Fairy and its total market share increased to 32%. By 1987 the market share had increased to 34% with the newly introduced lemon variant accounting for one-third of sales. In 1988 a new formulation was launched, offering '15% extra mileage', as well as more effective grease eradication.

In 1992 the original Fairy Liquid was replaced with Fairy Excel, which claimed to be '50% better at dealing with grease'. This helped to increase the market share to 50%. In the following year a concentrated version of Fairy Excel Plus was launched, with the slogan 'The power of four for the price of one'. The company launched this low-bulk, high-concentration product with one eye to retailers, who were tiring of filling their valuable shelf space with more and more variants of basically low-value products. Excel Plus offered supermarkets more cost-effective and profitable use of their shelf space.

During the lifetime of Fairy Liquid, the market for detergents in different European countries has gradually converged. As a result, Excel Plus was launched simultaneously in the UK, Belgium, Denmark, Finland, Germany, Holland, Ireland, and Sweden.

In what other ways could Fairy evolve to retain its brand leadership? Preferences for new scents of detergent are continually emerging and provide an opportunity for innovation. Following a series of food safety scares, some observers of the market have pointed to a potential market for anti-bacterial food washes which would satisfy consumers' increasing concern over residues on the surface of fruit and vegetables.

Case study review questions

1. How would you explain the success of the Fairy brand?

2. How do you think Procter & Gamble has been able to increase its market share at a time when competition from supermarkets' own-label brands has intensified?

3. To what extent can the principles and practices of brand management used for Fairy Liquid be applied to other goods and services, such as televisions and package holidays?

CHAPTER REVIEW QUESTIONS

1. In the context of a sustainable competitive advantage, what is meant by customer value? How can a company ensure that it continues to deliver value?

2. What factors might explain why so many of the firms in Peters and Waterman's [13] study of excellent US firms had been eclipsed a few years later?

3. Critically evaluate the factors in the marketing environment that are crucial to the development of strong brands within a market sector.

4. With increasing levels of consumer protection legislation designed to protect buyers from faulty products and misleading advertising claims, do we still need brands? How can brands adapt to increasing levels of legislation?

5. What factors should be taken into consideration by a travel agency seeking to position its chain of outlets?

6. Using examples, discuss the problems that are likely to result from a firm seeking to reposition its product offer.

REFERENCES

[1] Allison, R., and Uhl, K. (1964), 'Influence of Beer Brand Identification on Taste Perception'. *Journal of Marketing Research*, 1(3): 36–9.

[2] Berthon, P., Holbrook, M. B., and Hulbert, J. M. (2003), Understanding and Managing the Brand Space. *MIT Sloan Management Review*, 44(2): 49–55.

[3] Branthwaite, A. and Cooper, P. (1981), 'Analgesic Effects of Branding in Treatment of Headaches'. *British Medical Journal*, no. 282 (16 May): 1576–8.

[4] de Chernatony, L. and McWilliam, G. (1990), 'Appreciating Brands as Assets through Using a Two-Dimensional Model'. *International Journal of Advertising*, 9(2): 111–19.

[5] Doyle, P. (2000), *Value-Based Marketing: marketing strategies for corporate growth and shareholder value'*. Chichester: John Wiley.

[6] Gardner, B. and Levy, S. (1955), 'The Product and the Brand'. *Harvard Business Review*, 33 (Mar./Apr.): 33–9.

[7] Grime, I., Diamantopoulos, A., and Smith, G. (2002), 'Consumer Evaluations of Extensions and their Effects on the Core Brand: key issues and research propositions'. *European Journal of Marketing*, 36: 1415–28.

[8] Jacques, E. (2002), 'The Traps and Pitfalls of Rip-Off Marketing'. *Daily Telegraph*, 9 May: 66.

[9] Klein, N. (2001), *No Logo*. London: Flamingo.

[10] Levitt, T. (1960), '*Marketing Myopia*', Harvard Business Review, Sept–Oct, pp 41–52.

[11] Munson, J.M. and Spivey, W.A. (1981), 'Products and Brand Users: stereotypes among social classes'. In K. Munroe (ed.), *Advances in Consumer Research*. Ann Arbor, Mich.: CAR.

[12] AC Nielsen (2001), *The Retail Pocket Book*. London: NTC.

[13] Peters, T. J., and Waterman, R. H. (1982), In Search of Excellence: lessons from America's best run companies. New York: Harper & Row.

[14] Porter, M. E. (1980), *Competitive Strategy: techniques for analysing industries and competitors*. New York: Free Press.

[15] Solomon, M. (1983), 'The Role of Products in Social Stimuli: a symbolic interactionism perspective'. *Journal of Consumer Research*, 10: 319–29.

[16] Williams, L. (2002), 'Pursuit of Holy Grail Comes with Global Warning: the jury is out on whether the cost of creating a world brand is worth it'. *Daily Telegraph* (London), 14 Nov.: 6.

[17] Wind, Y. J. (1982), Product Policy: concepts, methods and strategy. Reading: Addison-Wesley.

SUGGESTED FURTHER READING

The following provide insights into competitor analysis:

Hooley, G, Saunders, J. and Piercy, N. (1998), *Marketing Strategy and Competitive Positioning*, 2nd edn. Hemel Hempstead: Prentice-Hall.

Hussey, D. (2000), *Competitor Analysis: turning intelligence into success*. New York: John Wiley.

Porter, M. E. (1980), *Competitive Strategy: techniques for analysing industries and competitors*. New York: Free Press.

Ries, A. and Trout, J. (2001), *Positioning: the battle for your mind—how to be seen and heard in the overcrowded marketplace*. New York: McGraw-Hill.

The underlying theory and practice of branding are discussed in the following:

Aaker, D. A. and Joachimsthaler, E. (2002), *Brand Leadership*. New York: Free Press.

de Chernatony, L. (2001), *From Brand Vision to Brand Evaluation*. London: Butterworth-Heinemann.

Keller, K. L. (2001), *Strategic Brand Management*, 2nd edn. Englewood Cliffs, NJ: Prentice-Hall.

The importance of a brand's visual identity are discussed in the following:

Balmer, J. M. T. (1998), 'Corporate Identity and the Advent of Corporate Marketing'. *Journal of Marketing Management*, 14: 963–96.

Howard, S. (1998), *Corporate Image Management: a marketing discipline for the 21st century*. Oxford: Butterworth Heinemann.

Schmidt, K. and Ludlow, C. (2002), *Inclusive Branding: the why and how of a holistic approach to brands*. Basingstoke: Palgrave Macmillan.

USEFUL WEB LINKS

Visit the companion website to this book, with lots of interesting additional material and links for each chapter:

www.oup.com/uk/booksites/busecon/

The following sites provided by advertising agencies give an insight into the services they offer clients to create strong brands:

Altus Group Communications

www.altus-group.com

Cogbox

www.cogbox.com

Lyon Advertising

www.lyonadvertising.com

KEY TERMS

- Brand extension
- Brand family
- Brand personality
- Brands
- Co-branding
- Commodity
- Counterfeiting
- Differentiation
- Direct competitors
- Five Forces model
- Global brands
- Indirect competitors
- Own brands
- Patent
- Perfect competition
- Positioning
- Repositioning
- Trademark
- Visual identity

Developing the product

CHAPTER OBJECTIVES

The product is at the heart of a company's marketing mix planning. Customers buy a firm's products in order to satisfy their needs as cost-effectively as possible. This chapter begins by discussing the nature of the product offer. Products comprise complex bundles of attributes which must be translated into benefits for customers. Companies typically offer a range of products, each of which can be expected to go through some form of life-cycle.

Product mix planning is discussed in the context of the product life-cycle. This chapter explores the methods used by companies to keep their product ranges up to date. Innovation is an important differentiating factor for many firms, and this chapter explores methods by which innovative products can be developed, tested, and brought to market. When products approach the end of their life-cycle, it is important that they are deleted in a rational and cost-effective manner.

■ What do we mean by a product?

Products are the focal point through which companies seek to satisfy customers' needs. Most people, when they consider the marketing of products, tend to think of fast moving consumer goods such as soap powder or chocolate bars. In fact, the term 'product' can mean many things. In this chapter a 'product' is any tangible or intangible item that satisfies a need. A product can be any of the following:

- a material good
- an intangible service
- a combination of the above
- a location

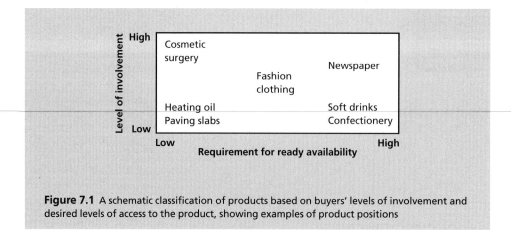

Figure 7.1 A schematic classification of products based on buyers' levels of involvement and desired levels of access to the product, showing examples of product positions

- a person
- an idea

It must be remembered that people do not buy products as an end in themselves. Products are only bought for the benefits they provide. In other words, a product is of value to someone only as long as it is perceived as satisfying some need.

It is useful to begin this chapter by identifying the wide range of products that exist. Although a truly marketing-oriented company will focus on customers, it is important to understand how product characteristics affect a company's marketing efforts. Within the different categories of products that are described below, some broad similarities in marketing requirements can be identified. Figure 7.1 attempts to classify products according to two important dimensions:

1. the level of involvement required on the part of the purchaser (e.g., the purchase of sugar calls for only very low levels of emotional involvement by the buyer, whereas in the case of fashion clothing involvement may be very high);

2. the level of availability that is typically required by purchasers (e.g., a buyer will expect a can of soft drink to be available immediately and without having to travel to get it, whereas she would be prepared to travel further, and possibly wait, to purchase some hi-fi equipment).

These are just two dimensions that contribute towards the design of an appropriate marketing mix. Others could include buyers' price sensitivity, brand loyalty, frequency of purchase, etc. The idea of placing products somewhere on a position map is introduced at this stage to emphasize an important reason for categorizing products in the first place: to explore whether marketers of one product can learn from the marketing of another product which may at first appear to be quite different, but is really quite similar in terms of the needs that it satisfies.

Material goods

Material goods can be classified under two major headings: consumer goods, and business-to-business goods. (The latter are also often referred to as industrial goods.)

Consumer goods

Consumer goods are those that are purchased to satisfy individual or household needs. They can be classified as follows:

- **Convenience goods**: These items tend to be relatively cheap and are purchased on a regular basis—tea, coffee, toothpaste, etc. They are often referred to as fast moving consumer goods (FMCGs). The purchase of this type of product is likely to involve very little decision-making effort on the part of the buyer, and in many cases an individual will tend to purchase a particular brand on a regular basis.

   Within the broad category of convenience goods, products as diverse as ice cream and toothpaste may at first appear to have very little in common; but in fact the marketing of them can be quite similar. Convenience goods are generally sold through many retail outlets so that buyers have easy access to the product. There is therefore a tendency to spend large amounts on advertising and on sales promotions aimed at the buyer rather than at the retailer. The packaging aspect of the marketing mix is also likely to be important, with the package acting as promotional tool in its own right. These items tend to be cheaply priced with the aim of selling high volumes at low margins.

- **Shopping goods**: Consumers generally put a lot more effort into choosing 'shopping' goods. These goods require decisions to be made about price, credit facilities, guarantees, after-sales service, etc. Examples of these would be dishwashers and freezers (which are examples of what are known as 'white goods'), DVD players, and digital cameras.

   These products are distributed through fewer retail outlets and therefore there is likely to be a higher margin for the retailer. Customers are usually more willing to travel to such an outlet to find a product, rather than expecting it to be available on their doorstep. Large amounts of money may be spent on advertising these goods and developing strong brands, and the amount of effort put into personal selling tends to be greater than for fast moving consumer goods.

- **Speciality goods**: For these products, consumers may spend a great deal of effort in the decision-making process. Speciality goods have one or more unique characteristics and are sold in relatively few outlets. A quality image is usually communicated as a result. Designer clothing would be an example of a speciality good. Such goods are bought infrequently, and tend to be expensive. Buyers may go to considerable effort to find the product of their choice.

- **Unsought goods**: Some goods initially may be considered by an individual not to be necessary, but they are nevertheless sold aggressively on the market. For many individuals, life insurance and pensions may be viewed as unsought services which they will buy only if they are legally required to do so and if the services are sold to them aggressively.

Business-to-business goods

These are purchased for use in a firm's production processes or to make other goods. Industrial goods are often bought by a large decision-making unit in which organizational as well as individuals' needs have to be satisfied (see Chapter 3).

Industrial goods can be divided into the following types:

- **Raw materials**: These are basic materials that are needed to produce a physical item, e.g. iron ore, chemicals, etc. They are often purchased in bulk and sold as a commodity, with little attempt at product differentiation which would justify a price premium.

- **Major equipment**: This category includes large machines and tools used in production processes. They tend to be expensive and are expected to last a number of years. The decision to purchase this type of equipment tends to be made at a very high level in an organization, and the purchase process can take a long time and involve a number of people. There is a need to build important relationships between buyers and sellers in this process, as it is likely to involve not only the agreement to purchase the equipment but also agreement on financing, maintenance contracts, guarantees, future purchases, etc.

- **Accessory equipment**: Accessory equipment involves those goods that are used in the production process or allied activities but are separate from the final 'product' itself. Examples of accessory equipment include computer software, tools, etc. These goods are generally cheaper than major equipment and the purchase process is less involved.

- **Component parts**: When put together, component parts produce a finished good. Buyers purchase such items according to their own requirements for quality and delivery time so that they can ensure that their own end product can be produced effectively and efficiently. Just-in-time delivery of component parts has become an important element of the total product offer.

- **Consumable supplies**: These goods help in the production process and do not become part of the product; for example, lubricating oil is vital to many production processes but does not become incorporated into the product. These items are typically purchased routinely by organizations with very little search effort.

Intangible services

Services can be described as 'products', although some people still find it amusing that bank accounts, package holidays, and even pop stars can be described as products. Although the term 'product' is traditionally associated with tangible goods, it can be more correctly defined as anything of value that a company offers to its customers. This value can take tangible or intangible forms.

There has been a big increase in recent years in service industries, which do not offer physical goods for sale but instead offer intangible benefits to buyers. A car mechanic offers her expertise in maintaining vehicles; a decorator or plumber sells his service. It is essentially their skills in performing a service process that are being offered for sale, rather than any physical good. In most western economies, services now account for around three-quarters of Gross Domestic Product.

The marketing of services can be quite different from the marketing of goods, although in practice many products are a combination of a good and a service. (For example, a meal in a restaurant combines the tangible elements of the food with the intangible service that is provided.) The distinguishing features of services, and their implications for marketing, are considered in more detail in Chapter 13. For now, it is worth noting a number of distinguishing features of products that are essentially service-based:

- **Intangibility**: Services cannot be seen, tasted, or touched. This means that it is very difficult for a customer to examine a service in advance. In fact, most material goods have some intangible service aspects to them, and likewise most services have at least some physical elements. Indeed, it is likely to be a question of degree of intangibility that will help in the identification of whether a product is a service.

- **Inseparability**: The provision of a service normally requires the involvement of both customer and service provider simultaneously. Production and consumption cannot be separated in the way that manufacturing companies are able to mass-produce their goods in a central factory and transport them to customers for consumption.

- **Variability**: As a result of inseparability, each service tends to be unique, and the standard of service delivery can vary from one occasion to the next. A consequence of this is that service quality is difficult to standardize and to guarantee. The best that can be achieved are minimum standards (e.g. answering the telephone after a stated number of rings) or standards relating to the physical aspects of the service (such as the temperature of a meal).

- **Perishability**: Services cannot be inventoried like material goods. If a service is not sold at the time it is produced, e.g. an empty airline seat after a plane has departed, then the service offer disappears for ever. This has important implications for service providers as they cannot store up services when demand is low in order to satisfy demand when it increases.

In much the same way as for goods, services can be further broken down into categories, such as consumer services, business-to-business services, and personal services. These are explored further in Chapter 13.

MARKETING in ACTION

Marketing, by appointment to Her Majesty

The principles of product marketing management have been extended to areas that would have been thought completely off-limits only a few years earlier. A sign of the times occurred during the late 1990s when the Royal Family took on board many of the principles of product management, although nobody went as far as to describe its activities by that name.

The marketing of the Royal Family begs the question of what the 'product' actually is (the Queen, the Royal Family, the institution?). Given the public's seemingly endless desire to uncover bad news stories about the Royal Family, how can marketers 'sell' the idea of a monarchy so that the public continues to value its role?

A major innovation was the establishment of the 'Way Ahead Group', which is chaired by the Queen, and attended by senior Family members and advisers. The group's primary function has been to look at the official work of the Royal Family and to make sure it is properly targeted and in tune with the needs of the country.

Many of the initiatives of the Way Ahead Group would seem to be taken straight from a textbook on product management. The research organization MORI was commissioned to ascertain the Royal Family's public image. In response to the group's research findings, a number of innovations in the 'product' were developed. Negative feelings of aloofness came through in the group's research and were overcome by developing greater informality among the Royal Family, such as a visit to a branch of McDonald's in Chester, which was given the appearance of Her Majesty just dropping in for a bite to eat. The Queen's Golden Jubilee celebrations of 2002 were carefully planned following extensive research, including focus group discussions. The idea of inviting the public into the grounds of Buckingham Palace for a rock concert might have seemed unimaginable to previous kings and queens, but it went ahead in June 2002 and proved a big hit with the public. Amidst this change in the monarchy, a communication secretary was appointed in an attempt to develop a more coherent image in the eyes of the media. Dialogue with the Royal Family was facilitated by the establishment of the Royal website, which by 2002 was receiving over 2 million hits a week.

Commercial enterprise has entered the lexicon of the Royal Family, with initiatives such as the opening of Buckingham Palace to visitors and the creation of the Royal Collection Trust, to make the Queen's world famous art and antiques collection commercially available.

Can product management be taken to these limits? And is it right to treat the Royal Family as a product to be marketed? If the approach is accepted, how do you set appropriate goals and measure the success or otherwise of such product management?

Ideas

Ideas can also be considered as 'products'. Political parties have developed marketing strategies to promote their own particular policies to the electorate, as have groups that are attempting to market particular issues, such as the environment, equal opportunities, etc. The key feature of these types of product is that they are intangible and have many similar characteristics to services. However, where an idea is the focus of marketing, it can be unclear just who the 'customer' is, and it can be difficult to conceptualize the exchange that takes place between the 'buyer' and the 'seller' of the idea.

Locations and people

The term 'product' can also be used to denote places (e.g. holiday resorts) and people (e.g. footballers, rock stars). These involve both tangible and intangible elements, and therefore the marketing mix should be configured accordingly.

Analysis of the product offer

Products can be complex entities, and it is useful to identify a number of levels of the product offer. Three levels will be identified here (see Figure 7.2):

1. **The core level**: Every product exists to satisfy a need, and therefore an individual is searching for a product that at the very least will have satisfaction of this basic need as its core benefit. The best way to think of this is to consider an item and identify the key benefit from its ownership. For example, the core benefit of buying food is to overcome hunger, and the core benefit of undertaking a marketing course is personal development.

    Every product has a core element, and it is the secondary and augmented elements that put 'flesh on the bones' and give a product an individual identity.

2. **The secondary level**: The secondary level of a product includes those physical features that the product actually possesses. Such elements include colour, design, shape, packaging, size, etc. A television, for example, may have entertainment as a core benefit but the secondary elements would include such features as the shape of the box, the type of screen, the size of screen, the quality of sound, the colour of the unit, whether there is a stand, etc.

3. **The augmented level**: It is this that differentiates a particular product from its competitors. The augmented level of a product tends to include intangible features such as pre-sales and after-sales service, guarantees, credit facilities, brand name, etc.

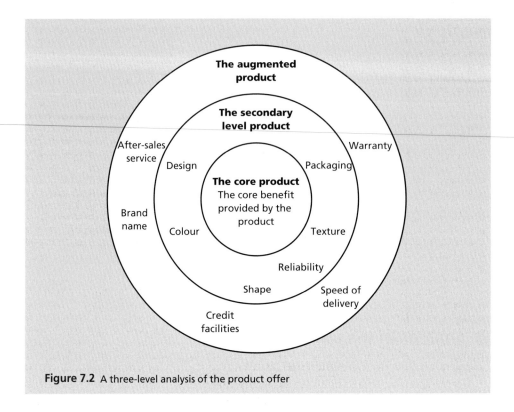

Figure 7.2 A three-level analysis of the product offer

The three-level analysis may be appropriate to tangible goods, but it has less value in the analysis of intangible services. For services, the augmented level may be the key distinguishing feature of the service. It is more appropriate therefore to talk about two levels of the product offer, with a core level representing the primary benefit and a secondary level representing the distinguishing characteristics of the service.

The product mix

The product mix comprises the complete range of products that a company offers to the market. A number of elements of a typical product portfolio can be identified and the following terms are commonly used (see Figure 7.3).

- **Product item**: This is the individual product, with its core, secondary, and augmented elements (for example, a Kodak CX4210 digital camera).

- **Product line**: This is a collection of product items that are related by the type of raw materials used, similar technology used, or merely as a common-sense grouping (e.g. a line in digital cameras). A truly effective product line should be customer-focused

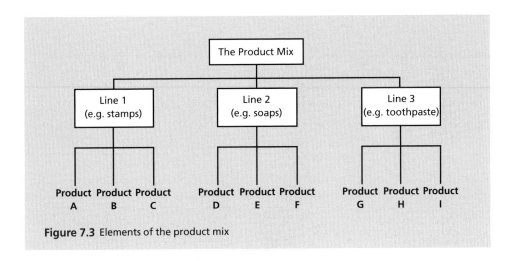

Figure 7.3 Elements of the product mix

and therefore should link to the range of needs of the particular segment/s targeted by the firm (e.g. the need for recording memories).

- **Product mix**: This is the total range of products that the company has on offer to customers and within this product mix there is what is known as the depth and the width of the product. The **depth** of the product mix refers to the number of products offered within a product line. The more products within a line, the greater the depth of the product mix. For example, the electrical retailer Dixon's has many different types of camera within its line of cameras. The **width** of the product mix refers to the number of product lines a company has, and the more lines, the greater the product mix width. Dixon's, for example, would have other lines as well as cameras, including televisions, audio equipment, computers, etc.

Quality

Quality is an important feature of a product, and buyers make choices among competing products on the basis of the ratio of quality to price. Most people would accept that a Sony CD player is of higher quality than one made by Amstrad and would be prepared to pay a higher price for it. Many will nevertheless be quite happy with the quality of the Amstrad machine, preferring its lower price.

But what do we mean by product quality? Quality is an extremely difficult concept to define in a few words. At its most basic, quality has been defined as 'conforming to requirements' (Crosby [7]). This implies that organizations must establish customers' requirements and specifications. Once established, the quality goal of the various functions of an organization is to comply strictly with these specifications. However, the questions remain: whose requirements, and whose specifications? A second series of definitions therefore state that quality is all about fitness for use (Juran[16]), a definition based primarily on satisfying customers' needs. These two definitions can be brought together in the concept of customer-perceived quality. Quality can be defined only by customers, and exists when an organization supplies goods or services to a specification that satisfies their needs and expectations.

The problem remains of identifying precisely what consumers' needs and expectations are. A company may think that it has the best-quality product based on its own criteria, but customers may have completely different criteria for judging quality. Sometimes there are benchmarks for measuring quality which can be readily agreed upon, for example that an 18 carat gold ring is better-quality than one that is only 9 carats. In the case of intangible services, it can be much more difficult to agree the criteria for assessing quality, because few tangible manifestations exist. This has led many people to draw a distinction between the technical and functional dimensions of quality.

Technical quality and functional quality

Technical quality refers to the relatively quantifiable aspects of a product, which can easily be measured by both customer and supplier. Examples of technical quality include the waiting time at a supermarket checkout and the reliability of a new car. However, consumers are also influenced by *how* the technical quality is delivered to them. This is what Gronroos [13] has described as **functional quality**, and it cannot be measured as objectively as the elements of technical quality. In the case of the queue at a supermarket checkout, functional quality is influenced by such factors as the environment in which queuing takes place and consumers' perceptions of the manner in which queues are handled by the supermarket's staff.

A lot of research has gone into trying to understand the processes by which buyers form expectations about the quality of a product. It is widely accepted that a product could be deemed to be of poor quality simply because it did not meet the buyer's expectations. A company's promotional material may have built up unsustainable expectations, resulting in perceptions of poor quality, even though an objective outside observer may have considered the technical quality to be high.

To try to provide reassurance to buyers, many companies incorporate some sort of guarantee of quality into their product offer. These can take a number of forms, including:

- The manufacturer may specify the standards in the product descriptions (e.g., bread made without preservatives; light bulbs tested for a life of 10,000 hours; clothing manufactured to be water-resistant).

- Often, product quality statements are backed up by specific guarantees of performance (e.g., the paintwork on a new car may be guaranteed to remain intact for six years).

- 'Customer charters' are often used to state the standards of service that a customer can expect. (Train operating companies have customer charters which, among other things, can provide compensation for late-running trains.)

- A company can state that its product standards are in accordance with a widely recognized general standard. Many firms proudly claim that they have been accredited with the International Standards Organization's ISO 9000 series accreditation. (ISO accreditation is granted to organizations that can show that they have in place management systems for ensuring a *consistent* standard of quality—whether this standard is high or low is largely a subjective judgement.)

Distinctive design

It has been noted many times in this book that the development of a distinctive product is the basis for strong brand development. However, distinctiveness in itself is irrelevant if buyers do not value the distinction. Marmite-flavoured lager may be distinctive, but would you buy it (Ofek and Srinivasan [23])?

A product's distinctiveness can be protected by a patent. This is a right given to an inventor which allows her exclusively to reap the benefits from the invention over a specified period. To obtain a patent in the UK, application must be made to the Patent Office in accordance with the procedure set out in the Patents Act 1977. To qualify for a patent, the invention must have certain characteristics laid down: it must be covered by the Act, it must be novel, and it must include an inventive step. In the cases of services, for which patent protection is difficult to obtain, the registration of a trademark can protect a company's distinctive identity. If a patent or trademark is infringed in any way, a successful plaintiff will be entitled to an injunction and to damages. A company can also challenge a 'copycat' product under the common law doctrine of 'passing off'.

Ownership of patents can make enormous differences to the profitability of a product range, especially within the pharmaceutical sector. The outlook for the drugs company AstraZeneca changed dramatically in 2002 when a US court extended the patent on its Losec drug (known in America as Prilosec), which is used to treat stomach ulcers. This was once the world's best-selling drug, and in 2001 it had US sales of $3.7 billion a year and worldwide sales of $5.7 billion. Granting an extension of the patent reduced the impact of generic competitors which could have copied AstraZeneca's formulation and sold their versions at a much lower price (Murray-West [22]).

Companies are often keen to imitate their rivals' successful products, and it can be difficult to define the point where a competitors' copycat product infringes on the original company's legal protection. There have been many recent examples of alleged infringement. The crisp maker Walkers challenged Tesco over what it believed to be an amazing similarity in packaging between its premium Sensations range and Tesco's Temptations crisps. Coincidentally, one of Walkers' more interesting flavours, Sea Salt and Cracked Black Pepper, also appeared in the Tesco range.

However, the ownership of patents alone may not be sufficient for market success. It has been noted that the cosmetics company L'Oreal owns over 28,000 patents for components of its cosmetics, but the main reason behind its market success is the image that it has successfully created for its products (Mills [20]).

■ Packaging

The packaging of goods performs four major functions: handling, transport, storage and the communication of product information.

Packaging is needed to ensure that a product is delivered to customers in a sound condition. The packaging should enable both distributors and end user to handle and transport the product from one place to another. In addition, packaging should also allow the product to be stored, and therefore the shape should be conducive to its being stocked on shelves and, where appropriate, in the home, office, or business. In addition to these functions, packaging should allow for the protection of the product from deterioration (in the case of perishable foods) and from breakage.

Where goods are sold to customers using self-service methods, packaging can perform an important information and promotional role. The package can inform the customer of what is inside and indeed can communicate a large amount of information directly. In addition, the package can communicate the brand name, both directly through name association and indirectly by associating the brand with a distinctive type of packaging. (For example, most people would recognize a bar of Toblerone chocolate by the shape of its packaging alone.)

The results of redesigning packaging without changing the contents can sometimes be quite dramatic. For example, Felix tripled its share of the cat food market and established itself as the number two brand following a redesign of its packaging.

MARKETING in ACTION

A pint of powder pulls a punch

The British have a long tradition of buying fresh bottles of milk delivered daily to the front door. Although today most milk is bought in plastic or cardboard containers, buying milk in a bottle still seems appealing to most people. Powdered milk had been around for a long time and, despite being nutritious, has been looked down upon by most people as an inferior product. Yet a market existed for dried milk as a 'reserve supply' of milk for those times when fresh milk was temporarily not available. But the product still had an image problem, not helped by many people's wartime memories of rations of dried milk being provided in tins and boxes. One solution identified by St Ivel was to put its dried milk in familiar shaped milk bottles. It could then sit in the fridge next to the fresh milk. The image of the product improved and sales soared.

■ 'Greening' the product range

Companies are showing increasing concern for the ecological impact that their products and production processes have on the environment. There is evidence that a growing segment of customers evaluate a product not just on the basis of traditional criteria such as quality, performance, appearance, etc., but also on the basis of its green credentials. It can be difficult for an organization to know just what is meant by the idea of being friendly to the ecological environment. Consumers may be confounded by alternative arguments about the consequences of their purchase decisions, with goods that were once considered to be environmentally 'friendly' suddenly becoming seen as enemies of the environment as knowledge and prejudice change. The following recent examples show how difficult it can be to evaluate the ecological credentials of a product.

- Recycling of old newspapers has traditionally been thought of as a 'good' thing, but recent thinking has suggested that more energy is used in collecting, transporting, and recycling used paper than is used in burning the paper and planting new trees to grow fresh materials.

- In the 1980s, diesel was seen as a relatively clean fuel because it produced fewer greenhouse gases and diesel engines were more efficient than petrol engines. By the 1990s, however, particulates released into the environment by diesel engines had become linked with increasing levels of asthma and the environmental credentials of diesel were downgraded.

- Similarly, some of the shine was taken off unleaded petrol when studies began showing that an additive of unleaded petrol—benzine—is carcinogenic.

Most members of the public are not experts on the technical aspects of a product's ecological impacts. They may therefore be easily persuaded by the most compellingly promoted argument, regardless of the technical merit of the case. Very often, a firm may have a technically sound case, but fail to win the hearts and minds of consumers, who seem intent on believing the opposite argument that is in accordance with their own prejudices. There has been considerable debate about the impact of genetically modified (GM) crops on the ecological environment. Despite a large body of 'expert' evidence that such crops will be harmless to the environment, many consumers are more convinced by vivid predictions of 'Frankenstein food'.

In addition to the actual products they sell, a company's production methods can come under scrutiny. Some companies have been accused of employing production methods that are harmful to the ecological environment (e.g. furniture manufacturers that use hardwood timber from rainforests which are not renewable; farmers who use over-intensive methods for rearing livestock). Companies that are accused of such practices may be shunned by those segments of customers who have concerns for the

Figure 7.4 Meat has traditionally been sold as a commodity-type product, with the main branding being confined to that of retailers who sell meat. Retailers from small village butchers to large grocery chains have earned the trust of customers for supplying good quality meat, but this trust has been increasingly challenged by food scares and reports of alleged inhumane treatment of animals. To provide further reassurance to meat buyers, industry bodies have developed a number of accreditation schemes. Many buyers will specifically seek out meat which carries one of these marks in the knowledge that they are buying a product which is of greater value to them than an unmarked commodity type product

ecological environment. Worse still, a company can face a campaign of boycotts and action against it, organized by pressure groups that are never likely to be customers of the company. The resulting bad press coverage from such actions has undermined the reputations of companies.

The green consumer movement can present marketers with opportunities as well as problems. Pro-active companies have capitalized on ecological issues by reducing their costs and/or improving their organizational image. The following are some examples of how firms have adapted to the green movement.

- In many markets there are segments that are prepared to pay a premium price for a product that has been produced in an ecologically sound manner. Some retailers, such as the Body Shop, have developed valuable niches on this basis. What starts off as a 'deep green' niche soon expands into a larger 'pale green' segment of customers, who prefer ecologically sound products but are unwilling to pay such a high price premium.

- Being 'green' may actually save a company money. Often, changing existing environmentally harmful practices primarily involves overcoming traditional mind-sets about how things should be done. (For example, using recyclable shipping materials may involve overcoming traditional one-way supply chain logistics operations.)

- In western developed economies, legislation to enforce environmentally sensitive methods of production is increasing. A company that adopts environmentally sensitive production methods ahead of compulsion can gain experience to its competitive advantage ahead of other companies.

MARKETING and SOCIAL RESPONSIBILITY

How green is your holiday?

Tourism is often seen as a clean industry, but marketers in the travel and tourism sector are having to address increasing concern about the environmental damage caused by tourism. Every year, 120 million glossy brochures are produced, of which an estimated 38 million are thrown away without being used. In resorts, the development of tourism frequently produces problems of waste and sewage disposal, while local residents find themselves competing for scarce water supplies. British travellers may worry about the damage that tourism causes to the environment, but recent surveys have shown that one in ten of them prefers to holiday in unspoilt or environmentally sensitive areas. Green Flag International, a non-profit-making organization, was set up to promote conservation and to persuade tour operators that being 'green' can actually save them money. Among other things, it advocates using small, privately run guest houses and hotels, shops, and public transport, and employing local people as guides. Hotels are advised on saving water and electricity, for example by not changing room towels every day. The organization also seeks to educate tourists to evaluate the environmental impact of their visit before booking a holiday, and urges tour operators to include in their brochures a statement of their environmental policies.

But why do so few people who claim to be green still seek out the cheapest package holiday, regardless of its ecological impacts? If being green doesn't always cost money, why do so many tour operators seem set in their ways? And isn't the greenest form of holiday not to travel to far-away destinations in the first place?

The product life-cycle

There is a general acceptance that most products go through a number of stages in their existence, just as humans and most living organisms go through a number of life-cycle stages. When a new product comes on to the market, there is likely to be a lot of promotional effort by a company to secure sales. It is likely that the company will have incurred high costs in the development of such a product, costs that in the early stages may not be covered by revenue. Potential customers for a new product may be few and far between and therefore sales in the early stages may be quite slow. This stage is known as the **introduction stage**.

If the new product proves popular, more people may will start to show an interest and start purchasing it. As more people buy, the firm will discover a number of cost savings

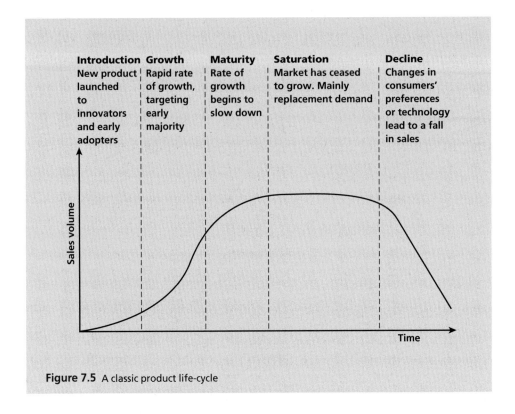

Figure 7.5 A classic product life-cycle

in producing larger quantities. Raw materials can be purchased in bulk and therefore at a cheaper cost per unit. Machinery and employees will become more efficient at producing larger quantities, resulting in economies of scale. Any initial teething problems with the product will start to be ironed out and more people will purchase the product on the basis of word of mouth rather than merely the firm's formal promotion campaign. Falling costs and rising revenues will improve profitability in what is usually referred to as the **growth stage**.

As sales of the product increase, other competitors are likely to be attracted to the market, and as a result there will be a tendency for downward pressure on prices. Promotion on the part of all competitors will tend to increase, and yet the number of customers for the product will have ceased to grow. Over a period of time, the increase in sales starts to slow down and this is known as the **maturity stage**.

As time goes by, sales start to stabilize, marking the **saturation stage**. At this point most demand is replacement demand rather than new demand, and total sales start to fall. The mobile phone market in the UK reached this point in 2002 when total sales fell for the first time (The Times [26]). Falling sales lead to the **decline stage**. Figure 7.5 displays this classical product life-cycle.

The product life-cycle fits well with the explanation put forward of how new products are adopted (Rogers [24]). Different types of customer are identified according to the speed at which a new product is adopted, and we will turn to this now.

The product life-cycle and consumer adoption processes

When an innovative product is introduced on to the market, only a small number of people will be interested in purchasing it as it is an untested item and usually quite expensive. Such people are categorized as **innovators**, and they tend to buy new products because they like to be seen owning something that is new and generally untried. People in this category are likely to have been among the first to buy mobile phones, digital cameras, and wide-screen televisions when they were launched. Despite the existence of innovators, new product launches may nevertheless be unsuccessful, as witnessed by the launch of WAP mobile phone services and the Sinclair C5 vehicle.

As the successful product begins to move to the growth stage, more people show an interest in it. The price of the product by this time has started to fall and, as innovators inform other people of the benefits of the product, more people begin to purchase it. The next wave of people to buy the product are known as **early adopters**. A key characteristic of early adopters is that they can be very influential in the groups with whom they interact, so they can be considered as opinion leaders. These individuals are generally looked on as experts in a particular field among the group, and therefore if they feel generally happy with the purchase of this relatively new product, they are likely to influence others to purchase it as well. This next group of customers are known as the **early majority**, and the product is now firmly in the growth stage of its life-cycle.

As the competition starts to enter the market and prices begin to fall ever more quickly, the next group of people start to consider purchase. These are known as the **late majority**. It is after this point that the number of potential new customers for a product starts to decline, as the product starts to move through to its maturity and saturation stages. Products are sold at lower prices as companies try and sell excess stock. The market has by now almost ceased to grow, with most demand now being replacement demand rather than new demand. There is a relatively small group of people who tend to purchase products at the end of their life-cycles, and such people are known as **laggards**. The pattern of product adoption is illustrated in Figure 7.6.

The concept of the life-cycle is useful in that any marketing activity applied to a product can be closely related to the stage in the life-cycle that the product has reached. Promotional planning, for example, can be closely related to the life-cycle. In the introductory phase emphasis will be typically placed on creating awareness through public relations activity, building on this through the growth phase with advertising. Sales promotion activity will typically be used as the market reaches maturity and

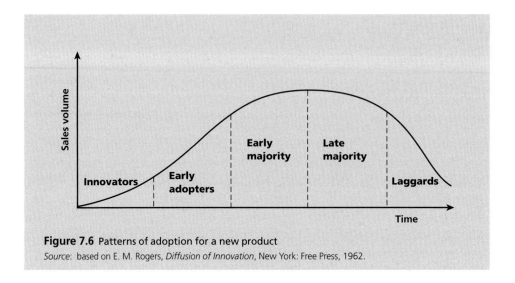

Figure 7.6 Patterns of adoption for a new product
Source: based on E. M. Rogers, *Diffusion of Innovation*, New York: Free Press, 1962.

becomes more competitive. Finally, all promotional activity may be dropped in the decline stage as the product is allowed to die naturally.

Similarly, other aspects of the marketing mix can be altered to fit the various life-cycle
stages. For example, for an innovatory product, a high price may be achievable in the
introductory stage, eventually falling as the competition gets stronger and costs fall.
Different distribution policies can be applied to the different stages.

Is there one particular pattern of product life-cycle that is applicable to all products?
In fact, different products move through the stages at different speeds, and not all
products follow the 'classic' shaped cycle. Others have an introduction stage and fail to
go any further. Others reach the growth stage and then for some reason sales fall very
rapidly. Still other products go through the introduction, growth, and maturity stages
but then stay at the maturity stage for a seemingly indefinite period. In reality, a number of different types of life-cycle can exist, and some of these can be seen in Figure 7.7.

In the first example, the product has a high level of sales at an early stage but from
then on there seems to be no change in sales. In the second example, there is a constant
increase in sales volume in each subsequent time period. The third example displays the
complete opposite: here, each subsequent period of time brings with it a fall in sales
volume after a period of initially strong sales. This could be a result of the entry of
strong and powerful competition. The fourth type of life-cycle displays the situation
where a firm actually influences the degree to which a product follows the life-cycle. In
this situation the product has been saved from decline, either through intense sales promotion activity or possibly through some form of product modification; alternatively,
external factors such as a change in customer tastes, etc., may have led to the improvement in sales. Whatever the cause, the product here displays further growth before
moving once again through to a decline phase, although sales are still higher now than

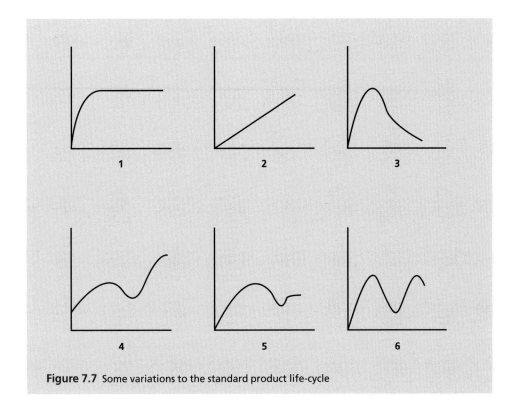

Figure 7.7 Some variations to the standard product life-cycle

they were at the original decline phase. The fifth example once again shows that the product has been saved from decline, but in this case the new cycle is at a lower stage than existed at first. The final example displays a typical life-cycle pattern for a fashion item where there is a steep drop in sales once the product is considered unfashionable, but it may subsequently become popular again.

The product life-cycle concept can play a useful role in a firm's management of its overall portfolio of products. However, it is important to be aware that there have been criticisms of the concept and its application.

Limitations of product life-cycle theory

In reality, life-cycles may look intuitively appealing when viewed with hindsight, but they are difficult to apply for short-term forecasting purposes. More fundamentally, it is difficult for marketers to identify where a product currently lies on a life-cycle. For example, if sales are stabilizing, it is difficult to ascertain whether the product has reached its peak in terms of growth and is about to decline, or whether there is just a temporary stabilization owing to external influences and that, if left alone, sales may start to increase once again in the near future. Indeed, the shape of the life-cycle can very well be

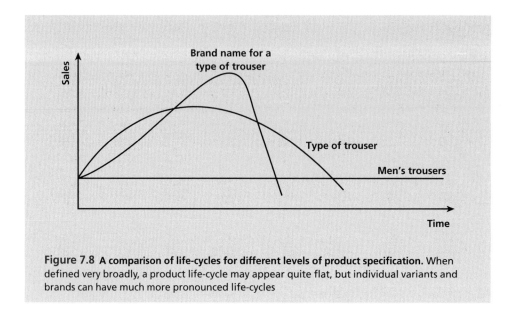

Figure 7.8 **A comparison of life-cycles for different levels of product specification.** When defined very broadly, a product life-cycle may appear quite flat, but individual variants and brands can have much more pronounced life-cycles

influenced by the actions of the marketer, and as a result there could be a self-fulfilling prophecy. For example, if there is a belief that the product is about to reach the decline phase, marketers may consciously reduce the marketing effort in response to this belief; as a result of this action, sales may fall and the product may indeed move into the decline phase!

Another observation is that the shape and duration of a life-cycle is dependent upon whether it is the product class, the product form, or a specific brand that is being considered. For example, the life-cycle of mens' trousers is quite flat, taken over a long period of time, compared with specific types of trousers (e.g. jeans, chinos), which come and go out of fashion. Within each type of trouser, brand names will go through a life-cycle of popularity. (For example, Levis rose in the 1980s but lost ground by the end of the 1990s to newer brands such as Diesel and DKNY.) These differing life-cycles are illustrated in Figure 7.8.

Innovation and new product development

We have seen how products go through a life-cycle, and that therefore most products can expect eventually to go into decline. It is therefore important for a company to develop new products to replace those that have reached the end of their life. Marketing managers must recognize the need to develop new products in response to shortening life-cycles, which in turn result from rapidly changing technology and competitive pressures.

What is innovation?

The Oxford English Dictionary defines innovation as 'making changes'. For many managers, innovation means new or better products, and innovation has often been identified as a source of a company's long-term competitive advantage. Indeed, some nations as a whole can be described as more innovative than others, and there appears to be a link between a country's spending on research and development and its economic performance.

It should be remembered that innovation is not confined to a company's product offer, but applies to all marketing functions, including distribution and promotion. Innovation must be linked to a firm's objectives, and of course must relate to customers' needs.

Many new products are merely modifications of old ones, and do not take the marketplace by storm. However, there is also a need to consider the possibilities of producing major new products in response to changing customer demands, external environmental forces, and internal strengths and weaknesses.

What are new products?

It may not be that easy actually to define what is meant by a 'new product'. Companies' routine efforts at continuous quality improvement are often closely linked to innovation, and it can be difficult to distinguish between the two (Cole [6]). New products could in fact comprise any of the following:

- improvements/revisions to existing products
- additions to existing lines
- 'new to the world' products
- new product lines
- repositioning (existing products in new segments/markets)
- cost reductions

We will consider below the distinction between product modifications and innovative products.

Product modifications

Many so-called new products are in fact modifications of existing products. Changes tend to be incremental and may include the following:

1. Minor changes can be made to how the product actually performs: this could involve the addition of new features and/or changing the packaging.

2. The quality of the basic product can be improved.

3. The style of the product can be modified, without changing its basic function. (For example, cars tend to undergo styling changes to keep in line with current design preferences.) In style-conscious industries such as fashion clothing, regularly up-dating a product's style can be crucial to continuing success. A Mintel report noted that soft drinks manufacturers have responded to consumers' desire for novelty and variety with a raft of new flavours and bottle designs (Mintel [21]).

4. Non-product attributes can be altered to produce a change of image. A change in advertising message can be used to alter the image of a product. This occurred, for example, with the change in image of Guinness from a working man's stout to a trendy social drink, and the repositioning of After Eight mints as an all-time chocolate for all ages (Mills [19]).

Innovative products

Truly new products are comparatively rare compared with product modifications, but they can be very important under certain circumstances.

- If consumer tastes are changing radically, existing products may no longer satisfy their needs. (This is often the case in many parts of the fashion clothing industry.)

- Technological change may make existing products obsolete. (For example, dot matrix printers have been made obsolete by the development of ink jet and laser printers.) However, it has been noted that new technologies need not necessarily have a better performance than those they replace (Adner [2]). For example, many professional photographers still prefer to use traditional 35 mm cameras than the newer digital cameras.

- New products may be required as a result of changes in internal processes such as accounting, office management, or labour relations. If a product becomes dangerous or illegal to produce (as has happened in the UK with many derivatives of beef products), a motivation is provided to develop a new replacement product.

- New products may be required to meet the need of intermediaries. (For example, the existing range of products may become too expensive to be handled by some distributors.)

- The social and economic environment may have changed, creating new needs in the market. For example, growing anti-American sentiment in many Muslim countries during 2002 led to the development of a range of soft drinks—such as Mecca Cola and Muslim Up—which were positioned to capitalize on this sentiment.

- If competitors are actively developing new products, a company must do likewise if it is not to lose market share.

Figure 7.9 Many people regard tea as an easily substitutable commodity product, so it can be a tough market for a company to gain a competitive advantage. Innovation has been a key to successful marketing of this age-old product. Some niche players have innovated with herbal teas, but not all innovation has been successful (for example, 'instant' powdered tea never became as popular as instant coffee). PG Tips has used innovation to gain a competitive advantage in the UK tea market. It has successfully launched new formats of tea bags which improve the taste of the tea and which are easier for consumers to use. More recently, it has capitalised on consumers' growing familiarity with cafetieres by launching 'Plunger Tea' specifically for cafetieres (Reproduced with permission of Unilever Bestfoods UK Ltd)

- New products may be developed to fill under-utilized capacity. (For example, many business hotels have filled their empty rooms at the weekend by offering innovatory weekend leisure activity breaks, such as a course in aromatherapy.)

The above analysis still does not explain the development of those major innovations, such as personal computers and mobile phones, that occur now and again and

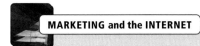

MARKETING and the INTERNET

A typist in cyberspace?

Putting the spoken word into print has seen a quickening pace with the technologies now available, which can do the job ever more speedily and accurately. The typewriter has given way to the word processor and keyboard. But what about the likely fortunes of a new speech recognition service launched at the end of the 1990s?

A UK company called Speech Machines (www.speechmachines.co.uk) uses computers to receive dictation over the telephone or as voice messages sent through the internet by e-mail. The dictation is transcribed automatically by computer with a claimed 95% accuracy. Specially written software manages the incoming dictation and automatically sends the transcribed document to one of the contract typists the company uses for checking and correction of the final manuscript. It is then sent back to the customer through the internet. The service has found a useful niche in the USA with the legal and medical professions, offering a speedy and efficient alternative to employing a secretary in-house.

But how long a life can this service expect to have before it is overtaken by increasingly sophisticated and user-friendly voice recognition software that allows users to complete the task in-house? If it is to maintain its business, how can the company offering this new service continue to develop its service offer so that it meets customers' changing needs better than any of the alternatives currently available? The benefits of the company's services were recognized by the American company MedQuist, which acquired Speech Machines in 2001. The company had already built a niche in the medical profession and added the Speech Machines service to its portfolio of document management solutions.

totally transform the marketplace. Indeed, it is highly unlikely that the use of the standard marketing approaches would have been very helpful in developing such products. If potential customers (if these could have been identified!) had been asked about their likely interest in purchasing such products, there would probably have been difficulties in using the responses given, because the major innovations would not have been heard of or understood by the respondents. The firm would have to educate customers about the new product as part of its research strategy.

Critical to the development of many new products has been a 'product champion' within an organization. A champion can continually press the case for a new product to be developed and provide the impetus for development which may be lost if responsibility is dispersed too widely. Without such people, it is likely that many innovations that we take for granted today would not have been seen through to development and launch.

Figure 7.10 The new-product development process

The new product development process

Having a formal new product development process in place is still more likely to be effective than adopting a haphazard approach to developing a product. Indeed, where costs and risks are high (as they are in many major infrastructure developments), a system needs to be in place to help keep such risks to a minimum.

It is usual to talk about a new product development process comprising a number of stages which span from having an initial idea through to the launch of the new product. We will look at each of these stages in turn, although it must be recognized that the stages often overlap each other (Figure 7.10).

Idea generation

New products come from a variety of sources rather than merely being initiated by the firm through the use of market research and the identification of untapped needs.

An important source of new product ideas is the customer. For products bought by businesses, new uses for an existing product or new ideas for a new one tend to be communicated to the sales force. For services, the important characteristic of inseparability means that there are plenty of opportunities for customers to inform service providers of new ideas or possible improvements to service processes (Alam [3]).

Another source of new product ideas is a firm's competitors. Creative imitation does not carry the same risks as developing something totally new. A consideration of the flaws that exist in a competitor's product can also produce useful ideas for new products.

Some organizations see the importance of developing new products as part of their long-term competitive strategy and try to instil an internal organizational culture hat positively thrives on new ideas. For example, Sony, the electronics company, encourages employees to move around and get involved in other departments. New perspectives and new ideas therefore come from every level of the organization, resulting in hundreds of new products every year. Similarly, 3M expects to receive new product ideas regularly from all members of staff, rather than just the Research and Development Department. Its corporate ethos has for some time included two rules: the '15% rule' and the '25% rule'. The '15% rule' states that employees should commit 15% of their time to thinking of new ideas, and the 25% rule states that every manager must ensure that at least 25% of his portfolio of products is less than five years old. A number of products that are now accepted in the marketplace have originated from this approach, e.g. Post-It notes.

Despite the need to be market-led, many new product ideas arise quite by accident in laboratory tests. As an example, the anti-impotence drug Viagra became a major commercial success when it was launched in 1998, but researchers were originally developing an anti-angina drug. Unexpected side-effects of the drug led to further development and a market opportunity.

Idea screening

Whether a firm responds positively to ideas for new products very much depends on its internal resources. As well as considering whether there are the financial resources to develop a new product (in particular, the availability of cash flow in the short term), a firm needs to consider other internal issues. For example, is there enough production capacity to cope with likely demand? Are there suitably trained personnel? Will new staff have to be recruited or present staff be retrained? In addition, the firm needs to consider the availability of the raw materials or components required to produce the new product.

Another consideration is time. New product development can take a long time from inception to final production and launch. The relevance of time depends on the type of product being developed and the market it is being developed for. Some developments can take as little as a few months whereas others can take years to come to fruition, especially where safety testing is protracted, as in the case of new drugs. The pressures of competition today mean that speed is becoming increasingly important.

Another important aspect that needs to be considered is the possibility that a new product could take sales from a product that is already in the firm's portfolio, through a process of 'cannibalization'. If this is likely to be the case, the firm needs to prepare a response to minimize this impact. Alternatively, adding a new product may help to improve the sales of existing products as the product line becomes more comprehensive.

Whether a proposed new product fits with the firm's marketing strategy must be considered. To what extent does the new product complement existing product

Figure 7.11 **Every now and again, a new product gets launched which goes on to become a high profile 'flop'.** When Clive Sinclair launched his C5 vehicle, it could have become a cult car and might have found many valuable off-road uses. But it was launched at the wrong time of year, and journalists soon got to work ridiculing the vehicle. The car was never a commercial success. But at the idea-screening stage, how could its developer have assessed whether the car would have become a premium priced cult car, or the non-selling joke that it became?

lines? Can existing distribution channels be used? Can present consumer awareness and attitudes be built upon? The new product should be consistent with the organization's existing products in terms of consumer perceptions of price and quality. Producing a lower-priced, poorer-quality product than those that already exist may be counterproductive.

Screening should ensure that the new product fits within the firm's overall corporate and marketing strategies. At this stage, many new product ideas will be dropped because they do not fit with overall marketing strategy. If the proposal passes this filter, the company can proceed to the next stage.

Although the filtering stage has been portrayed here as a rational process, there is evidence that the final selection of ideas for further development is typically affected by intuitive and political factors (Forlani, Mullins, and Walker [12]). In one investigation of scenario generation and analogical reasoning as potential sources of bias in new product forecasting, non-analytic judgement processes were found to have a significant effect on the screening process (Bolton [5]).

Concept development and testing

It is often estimated that more than 80% of new products fail, and therefore it is important that the number of potential failures is kept to a minimum. In other words, unsuccessful ideas should be eliminated as quickly as possible.

The new product concept can be tested using a number of methods, and such testing should take place before any significant amount of further investment in product development takes place. Initial market research should aim to discover potential customer attitudes to the concept and, more particularly, whether they would be interested in purchasing the product if it came on to the market. This may be quite a difficult task if the new product is a major innovation and customers have no experience of such an idea. A case in point is the experience of Barclaycard. In 1995, two cards were proposed: Barclaycard Sense, which was associated with the caring 1990s, and Barclaycard Gold, which was associated with high status. Qualitative research indicated that the Sense card would be successful and that the Gold card would fail. In this instance, the company was not convinced of the results and went ahead with both cards. Gold turned out to be hugely successful, and the Sense card underperformed.

Business analysis

A financial analysis needs to take place in order to assess whether the product concept can be made into a profitable proposition. An income and expenditure statement, together with the associated balance sheet and cash flow analysis, therefore need to be prepared. The key to this financial analysis is that the product should at least break even over a period of time. However, any financial forecasts may be based on very crude assumptions about the likely volume of sales, the selling price, distribution costs, and the cost of producing the item. Cost and revenue estimates can be closely linked with each other, so that high-volume sales results in lower unit production costs, which in turn improves profitability. This can be a very difficult and speculative part of the process. According to one estimate, 30,000 new products annually vie for the 25,000 total spots in the average supermarket. Will a new consumer product even get supermarket shelf space? Of all new package-goods products, 52% fail before their second year (Dipasquale [9]).

Because there are many unknowns in the financial analysis, a sensitivity analysis is often carried out to assess the impact on overall profitability of changes in the underlying assumptions. Would the concept still be profitable if selling prices were only half those that had been predicted?

Product development and testing

This is the translation of the idea into an actual product that can be delivered to customers. It is at this point that the decision is made to physically develop the product, and large amounts of money can be poured in at this stage. The various elements of the product have to be designed and tested. However, this testing should be more rigorous than at the concept testing stage. Customers can now see the product as it might actually look, and the company can identify possible problems that need to be resolved.

There is a need to consider the requirements for repeat purchase in addition to the single one-off purchase decision, and therefore the factors that influence trial, first purchase, adoption, and purchase frequency need to be identified. In addition, customer response to promotional material needs to be assessed.

Even given the increased rigour in this testing process, there are still difficulties. Testing consumers' responses to intangible elements of a new product is difficult. This is a particular issue when developing new services.

Market testing

A market test aims to replicate everything that is likely to exist in the entire market but on a smaller scale. Test marketing can therefore take place in a television viewing area, a test city, particular geographical regions, or, in the business-to-business context, on a sample of key customers.

Designing a market testing exercise involves making a number of decisions: Where should the test market be? What is to be tested? How long should the test last? What criteria should be used to determine success or otherwise?

Although market testing should reduce the potential risks before launch, it is important to realize that there are still potential problems. Market testing is not cheap, and in some cases can be nearly as expensive as a full-scale launch. Even a large test market is unlikely to be totally representative of the market, because in reality small test markets may lead to distortions that wouldn't be present in a national launch. Market testing is also likely to warn competitors of what is to come, and as a result the competition may act more quickly in response or may interfere with the test itself. Competitors may study the test very carefully through retail audits and their own qualitative research and may learn a lot which will allow them to launch a competitive product, but without having incurred much of the development and testing costs so far.

Product launch

How a product is launched is an important issue. Replacing an existing product with a new one tends to be a popular approach. There is likely to be an existing customer base for the new product and therefore the risks are lower, although even here mistakes can be made. When Coca Cola sought to replace its existing cola with a new formulation, it became apparent that it had misinterpreted its market research and had to reinstate the old product as 'Classic' Coke. A company may choose to sell both the old and new products simultaneously for a period of time, although this might meet with reluctance from retailers who will be required to commit twice as much shelf space to the products.

Time is a key issue. The longer a new product goes through the various developmental stages, the greater the chance that competitors will enter the market before launch. The firm can be a pioneer and enter the market first or be a follower and reduce its risks considerably. In the UK there was a race in 2003 to launch the first 'third generation' mobile phone network. The new operator Three created some publicity as the first to launch a network (on 03/03/2003), despite the fact that no handsets were available until some time afterwards (Fagan [11]). There is also the issue of stock levels—a company would normally avoid launching a new product when it had large unsold stocks of an older model that would become more difficult to dispose of after the launch of the new one.

For companies operating globally, timing of the launch in different national markets can be critical, as markets are likely to be at different stages of development and a global rollout may be inefficient for a company to manage (Wong [27]). A staggered rollout allows a company to exploit profits from one market before moving on to progressively less attractive markets, thereby maintaining a portfolio of products at different stages of market development. However, in the case of some easily transported products such as computer software, it may not be realistic to have a staged rollout, as sales would soon occur through a 'grey' market. Most launches of new products by Microsoft have involved almost simultaneous launch, demanding a high level of global commitment by the company.

MARKETING and the INTERNET

How long will the queue be at the e-bank?

The online bank Egg has now established itself as one of Europe's leading online financial services providers, with over 2.1 million customers by the end of 2002. Egg attained brand awareness with 88% of adults in the UK, which is impressive for such a young company, and acquired 600,000 new customers in 2001 alone—100,000 more than the total number of customers for its nearest UK internet rival (ABA Banking Journal [1]). But despite careful planning, the launch of Egg got off to a bumpy start.

When ATM machines first appeared a couple of decades earlier, many people thought they would never work because people liked to go into a branch and deal with a human being. Would people have the same fears about internet banking? In 1998 the internet was only beginning to catch the public's imagination, and there were still major concerns about privacy, security, download speed, and access to the internet. Would internet banking be a runaway success, or just another over-hyped new service development, of which there were many at the height of the dot.com boom?

Egg targeted busy people with neither the time nor inclination to shop around for financial services. But how many customers should the company have geared itself up to handle when it launched its new product? Launching a new product often involves a lot of guesswork. If the number is underestimated and the company doesn't have the capacity to cope with large numbers, frustration and harm to the brand reputation can soon build up.

Egg's then-parent company—Prudential—undertook the testing of its new banking service among a small group of customers. This allowed it to understand more about demand when it eventually went for a full public launch in 1998, backed by heavy online and offline advertising. Despite this, it soon became apparent that its servers could not cope, as potential customers complained of spending hours trying to log on to the bank's website. Egg's call centre was similarly overwhelmed, despite being available 24 hours a day, 7 days a week. It seemed that the bank had inadequately understood the peaked nature of demand, which meant that call centre operators might be rushed during the early evening, but idle during much of the night and early morning.

Taking a longer-term perspective, the launch of Egg was a success. It managed to gain a 'first mover' advantage in the emerging market for online banking service, something that might have been lost had it spent more time researching its market. Since launch, it has learnt a lot more about its customers and has embraced emerging technology to launch Egg TV in April 2000, which was the first interactive digital TV service from a financial services provider in Britain. But would Egg face a challenge from the High Street banks who set about reinvigorating their branches by removing glass panels and wooing customers with a coffee shop culture?

Integrating the new product development process

So far, the stages of new product development have been presented as if they are steps that necessarily have to be tackled in a sequential order. In fact, the time taken to go through this process can be considerable, allowing competitors to gain a lead. There have therefore been many attempts to carry out some of the steps simultaneously. Virtual reality systems, for example, are allowing customers to get a feel of the final product at a very early stage, allowing this to take place at the same time as concept testing and avoiding the need to wait until all steps of the process are progressed (Dahan and Hauser [8]).

The new product development process can be extremely complex, with many examples of cost overruns and delayed results (Kim and Wilemon [17]). A key to more effective new product development activity is close working relationships between marketing and manufacturing functions. In one study of 467 completed product innovation projects, increased marketing–manufacturing joint involvement was associated with better project performance (Song and Swink [25]). Even simple administrative matters such as rapid communication following the results of one stage can help to speed up the new product development process.

As can be seen, the new product development process can be time consuming and complex. This has led many companies to outsource the whole process to specialist companies who have developed an expertise in product development and market testing (Howley [14]).

Our discussion of new product development processes has focused on how large companies might typically go about the process in a logical and structured manner. There is a lot of research evidence that in smaller companies the process is much more intuitive (e.g. Enright [10]). In one study of SMEs it was found that marketing-related activities were undertaken less frequently and were less well executed than technical activities in developing new products, and the existence of a new product strategy seemed to have a significant positive impact on marketing activities (Huang, Soutar, and Brown [15]). The use of an outside consultancy can also be useful where a company's ethos is production-orientated and it seeks to bring on board broader marketing skills. It has been noted that brilliant inventors do not necessarily make good marketers of a new product (Little [18]).

■ Strategic issues in expanding the product range

Earlier in this chapter we introduced the idea of a product mix, which comprises the range of products offered by a company. Product life-cycle theory reminds us that a product mix cannot remain static, as some products will eventually cease to be profitable elements of that mix. But which direction should the new product mix take?

Product management involves ensuring that there is a succession of products available that are at different stages of their life-cycles. The planning process should involve the firm's business being managed in the same way as an investment portfolio, with attention paid to developing, maintaining, phasing out, and deleting specific elements. This process can lead management to identify where there may be market potential and therefore where investment can be most profitably made. Portfolio planning can be applied to the types of products/markets served and the stage of products in their life-cycles.

Risk spreading is an important element of portfolio planning which goes beyond marketing planning. Maintaining a balanced portfolio of activities can be just as important as earning adequate short-term profits. In this respect, a bank may be meeting a proven need by lending money to fund property purchase and earning acceptable returns from it. However, a strategic approach to portfolio management may lead it to diversify into some other activity with a counterbalancing level of cash flow and risk, turning away business that may seem attractive in the short term.

Some companies deliberately provide a range of products that—quite apart from their potential for cross selling—act in contrasting manners during the business cycle. There is a long tradition to this practice; for example, the ice cream manufacturer Walls became more sustainable as a business unit by adding sausages to its product portfolio. Sausages tended to have their highest demand in winter, counterbalancing the sharp peak in summer for ice cream. Similarly, accountancy firms have become potentially more stable units as they have amalgamated, by allowing pro-cyclical activities such as management buy-out expertise and venture capital investment to be counterbalanced by contra-cyclical activities such as insolvency work.

Sometimes statutory requirements may require a balanced portfolio of products. The Bank of England's regulation of the UK banking system, for example, imposes constraints on banks' freedom to be market-led in the pattern of their lending decisions.

For a company to put all of its efforts into supplying a very limited range of products to a narrow market segment is potentially dangerous. Over-reliance on one segment can make the survival of the organization dependent upon the fortunes of that segment and consumers' liking for its product. In any event, the fact that most markets change to some extent over time would imply that a firm's products will eventually move out of line with customers' requirements. Also, with the development of relationship marketing strategies, firms are increasingly keen to develop opportunities for offering customers a broad range of products which attract a higher share of their total expenditure. For all of these reasons, organizations seek to manage their growth in a manner that maintains a desired portfolio of products.

MARKETING in ACTION

From dairymen to hypermarket operator

Should a company 'stick to its knitting' and do what it is good at, or should it search continually for new products and new markets? Countless companies have reported disastrous results after going into areas they knew very little about. The rapid growth of Next from its core of fashion retailing to newsagents, travel, and home furnishings contributed to its near collapse in the late 1980s. WHSmith went through bad years in the mid-1990s when the newsagent's diversification into DIY retailing and television failed to work. Abbey National expanded in the late 1990s from its core of domestic mortgage lending into merchant banking and train and aircraft leasing, only to have to write off millions of pounds of losses and withdraw from these sectors in 2003.

But isn't change essential for companies, especially those facing static or declining markets for its products? One of the UK's leading grocery retailers, Asda, would not be where it is today had not the Associated Dairy Company taken a risk and set up a retailing operation. Milk was a mature market, but new opportunities for product development were available further down its distribution chain as more people sought the benefits of shopping in large supermarkets. The security services company Securicor knew that it was taking a risk when it invested in a joint venture with British Telecom to create the Cellnet (now O2) mobile phone network. And a small company manufacturing shopping baskets called WPP (standing for Wire Plastic Products) took huge risks in diversifying its product range on its way to becoming the owner of one of the world's leading advertising agencies, J. Walter Thompson.

It is fine, with hindsight, to criticize a firm's decisions about which direction its product portfolio should take. But in an uncertain world risks have to be taken. A sound analysis of a company's strengths and weaknesses and of its external environment certainly helps, but success also depends upon an element of luck.

Planning for growth

Most private-sector organizations pursue growth in one form or another, whether this is an explicit aim or merely an implicit aim of its managers. Growth is often associated with increasing returns to shareholders and greater career opportunities for managers. Growth may be vital in order to reach a critical size at which economies of scale in production, distribution, and promotion can be achieved, thereby contributing to a company's sustainable competitive advantage.

In addition to maintaining a balanced portfolio of products, total sales of all products within the portfolio must increase if a company is to grow. But where should the growth be focused? The development of new products or new markets are more risky options than simply selling more of its existing product to existing customers. More risky still is diversification into new markets and new products. The dimensions of product development and market development form the basis of the Product/Market Expansion Grid proposed by Ansoff [4]. Products and markets are each analysed in terms of their degree of novelty to an organization, and growth strategies are identified in terms of these two dimensions. In this way, four possible growth strategies can be identified. An illustration of the framework, with reference to the specific options open to a company that is currently marketing a range of organic fruit and vegetables, is shown in Figure 7.12.

The four growth options are associated with differing sets of problems and opportunities for a company. These relate to the resources required to implement a particular strategy, and the level of risk associated with each. It follows, therefore, that what might be a feasible growth strategy for one organization may not be for another. The characteristics of the four strategies are described below.

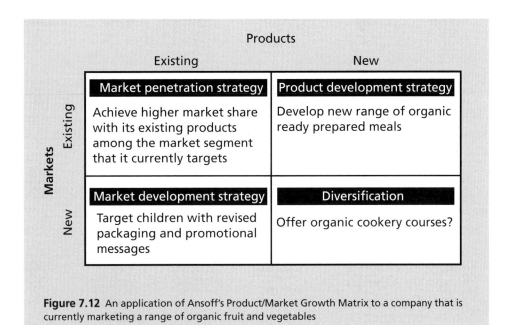

Figure 7.12 An application of Ansoff's Product/Market Growth Matrix to a company that is currently marketing a range of organic fruit and vegetables

1. **Market penetration strategies:** This type of strategy focuses growth on the existing product range by encouraging higher levels of take-up of a product among the existing target markets. In this way, a food manufacturer serving the growing market for organic produce could—all other things being equal—grow naturally, simply by maintaining its current marketing strategy. If it wanted to accelerate this growth, it could do this first by seeking to sell more products to its existing customers and second by attracting customers from its direct competitors. If the market were in fact in decline, the company could grow only by attracting customers from its competitors through more aggressive marketing policies and/or cost reduction programmes. This strategy offers the least level of risk to an organization—it is familiar with both its products and its customers.

2. **Market development strategies:** This type of strategy builds upon the existing product range that an organization has established, but seeks to find new groups of customers for them. In this way the organic foods manufacturer that had saturated its current market might seek to expand its sales to new geographical regions or overseas markets. It could also aim its marketing effort at attracting custom from groups beyond its current age/income groups—for example by targeting children with organically produced snacks. While the company may be familiar with the production side of its growth plans, it faces risks because it may have poor knowledge of different buyer behaviour patterns in the markets it is attempting to enter. For an organic food company that has built its business in south-east England, it may have little knowledge about consumer buying behaviour in northern England,

or in continental European countries, for example. It may face even greater risk in developing a marketing strategy aimed at children, whose needs it has little previous experience of satisfying.

3. **Product development strategy:** As an alternative to selling existing products in new markets, a company may choose to develop new products for its existing markets. The organic food company may add new ranges of ready meals or drinks, for example. While the company minimizes the risk associated with the uncertainty of new markets, it faces risk resulting from lack of knowledge about its new product area. Often, a feature of this growth strategy is collaboration with a product specialist who helps the organization produce the new product, leaving it free to market it effectively to its customers. Rather than setting up its own facility to produce ready prepared meals, the organic foods company may leave the specialized task of doing this and undertaking quality controls to a more experienced food manufacturer.

4. **Diversification strategy:** Here, a company expands by developing new products for new markets. Diversification can take a number of forms. The company could stay within the same general product/market area, but diversify into a new point in the distribution chain. For example, the organic food producer may move into retailing its products, rather than just selling them exclusively to wholesalers and retailers. Alternatively, it might diversify into completely unrelated areas aimed at quite different market segments, for example by offering residential cookery courses. Because the company is moving into both unknown markets and unknown product areas, this form of growth carries the greatest level of risk from a marketing management perspective. Diversification may, however, help to manage the long-term risk of the organization by reducing dependency on a narrow product/market area.

In practice, most growth that occurs is a combination of product development and market development. In very competitive markets, a company would most likely have to adapt its product slightly in order to become attractive to a new market segment.

■ Deleting products

Good portfolio management demands not only that new products are developed, but also that failing ones are deleted. Deciding when a product has reached the decline stage of its life-cycle can be quite difficult, because a downturn could simply be a temporary blip. If a downturn seems to have set in, it can sometimes be difficult to decide whether it is worth trying to revive the product, or to just let it die. Even the manner of a product's deletion requires careful thought—should it be allowed to die gradually, or suddenly killed off?

In general, there is a tendency to 'add on' rather than subtract, and therefore many products do not die but merely fade away, consuming resources of an organization which could be better used elsewhere. 'Old' products may not even cover overheads. In

Figure 7.13 Fast food was a great marketing success story of the 1980s and 1990s. Chains developed in response to changes in the pattern of family meal eating, growing levels of disposable income (especially among younger adults), a growing desire for variety seeking and increasing concern with value for money. McDonald's has a long record of innovation with the development of new menus and new formats in new countries. However, by the end of the 1990s, there was growing concern in many western countries about problems of obesity caused by eating too much high fat food. McDonald's has continued its pattern of innovation with products which address the changed needs of the early 21st century, including McCafes and here, a fruit bag which is aimed at making fresh fruit more appealing to children (and their parents) (Reproduced with permission of McDonald's Corporation)

addition, there are a number of hidden costs of supporting dying products that need to be taken into consideration; for example:

• a disproportionate amount of management time can be spent on them: this can delay the search for new products;

- short and relatively uneconomic production runs may be required where the demand for a product is small and irregular;
- they often require frequent price and stock adjustments.

Firms should have a logical planning system for deciding which products to delete. It would be naive, however, to assume that deletion is a simple process. In reality, there are a number of reasons why logical deletion procedures are not readily followed:

- Often firms do not have the information they need to identify whether a product needs to be considered for elimination. Even if an organization is aware of a potential deletion candidate, the reasons for its failure may not be known and therefore management may just leave things as they are and hope that the problem will go away by itself.
- Managers often become sentimental about products, hoping that sales will pick up when the market improves. Sometimes marketing strategy will be blamed for the lack of success, and there may be a belief that a change in advertising or pricing, for example, will improve the situation.
- Political issues within organizations may create barriers to deletion. Some individuals will have vested interests in a product and may fight elimination efforts. In fact, some individuals may hide the true facts of a product's performance to ensure that deletion is not considered at all.
- Finally, a company may fear that the sale of other products in the product range will fall if a product is deleted. With the growing importance of relationship marketing, many firms are keen to ensure that they are able to satisfy all of their target customers' needs for a particular category of product. If a product is deleted, the whole relationship may be lost.

Where weak products are identified, a number of possibilities may be open for trying to revive a product, including:

- modifying the product so that it meets changed market requirements;
- decreasing promotional expenditure, in order to minimize costs: this may be a sensible idea if there is a small loyal market;
- increasing promotional expenditure, assuming that sales are sufficiently responsive to this increased promotion;
- decreasing the price, if demand is elastic and an increase in sales revenue is likely to result;
- increasing the price, if there remains a core market that is strongly loyal to the product: by doing this, total revenue may be increased, even if sales volumes decline;
- changing the distribution system, in order to cut costs, and/or open up sales opportunities in new market segments.

If none of these options is considered feasible, the company must decide how best to delete the product. This is not always a simple task, and a number of options can be identified.

1. Ruthlessly eliminate 'overnight'. This may seem the simplest solution, but will customers take their business to other competitors? Will they take their business for other products in the company's mix with them? There may also be the problem of what to do with existing stocks of finished goods and work in progress. Sometimes a company may be contractually obliged to continue supplying a product for many years into the future, especially in the financial services sector, where products such as mortgages and pensions cannot be completely deleted until all customers' policies have reached the end of their contracted term. A sudden withdrawal of a product without notice may create bad publicity for a company, especially if customers have come to depend upon it.

2. Increase the price and let demand fade away. This may sound to many loyal customers like exploitation, but it could mean that the firm makes good profits on the product while demand lasts.

3. Reduce promotion or even stop it altogether. Again, this could increase profitability while demand lasts.

Chapter summary and linkages to other chapters

Products are the means by which a company satisfies its customers' needs. However, it must be remembered that customers seek the benefits of the product rather than the product itself. Despite this, products can be grouped according to the similarity of their marketing requirements, and a number of bases for classifying products have been suggested. Services can be described as products, but the characteristics of 'pure' services can be quite distinct from those of 'pure' goods. We will return to the distinctive characteristics of services in Chapter 13. For all products, quality is an important defining characteristic. Change in the marketing environment (Chapter 2) causes most products to go through some form of life-cycle which affects the way they are marketed.

Because most products eventually go into decline, it is important that a portfolio of established and new products is maintained in order to develop a sustainable competitive advantage (Chapter 6). This chapter has emphasized new product development as a process. The length of this process will depend upon product and market characteristics. Short new product development times can give a firm a competitive advantage, but shortening the process can also increase the risk of a failed launch.

The opposite of new product development is deletion, and a rational approach to deletion can prevent a firm becoming weighed down with a large number of minor products which consume a lot of management time but return very little, if any, profit.

Product decisions are just one element of the marketing mix, and the following chapters will discuss how price, distribution, and promotion are used to develop a distinctive and profitable market position for a product.

KEY PRINCIPLES OF MARKETING

- A customer's definition of a product focuses on the benefits provided and how the product will satisfy a need.
- A product can comprise anything that can be offered to a market. Marketers classify types of product according to the similarity of their marketing needs.
- In a dynamic marketing environment, products can expect to go through a life-cycle of development, launch, growth, saturation, and decline.
- Product life-cycle theory implies that new products will be required to replace products that go into decline.

CASE STUDY

Crossed line in new phone development

The pace of new product development in the mobile telephone sector has been quite phenomenal, especially when it is remembered that the sector hardly existed just 20 years ago. New technologies have been introduced, rapidly displacing the technology that went before them. Each leap in product development poses risks for companies, especially network operators, who must invest heavily in new capacity before they see a penny back in revenue from subscribers.

In 2000 the UK government held an auction for five new '3rd generation' (or '3G') mobile telephone licences. To the astonishment of observers, the auction raised a total of £22 billion, showing a huge act of faith by the phone companies in the new technology. To some observers, the price paid by the companies was excessive and would never be recouped, especially if another new technology came along which satisfied consumers' needs more cost effectively. Others saw '3G' technology as the key to a whole new world of mobile telephony in which the mobile phone would be positioned not just as a device for voice communication, but also as a vital business and information tool. It may take some time to tell whether the mobile phone companies' investment in 3G phones is successful, but lessons can be learnt from the launch of Telepoint services a decade earlier. The case illustrates some of the risks of new product development where technology is unproven and the political environment is uncertain.

Since the initial UK launch of cellular telephone networks in the early 1980s by Cellnet and Vodafone, the advantages of being able to make calls from any point had proved popular with the self-employed, travelling sales personnel, and business executives, among others. Beyond these segments, the service remained too expensive, and possibly over-specified, for more casual users.

In January 1989, the UK government issued licences to four companies—Zonephone (owned by Ferranti), Callpoint (owned by a consortium of Mercury Telecommunications, Motorola, and Shaye), Phonepoint (British Telecom, STC, France Telecom, Deutsche Bundespost, and Nynex), and Hutchison Telecom—to operate a network of low-cost mobile phones aimed at the mass market (commonly referred to as 'Telepoint'). These would allow callers to use a compact handset to make outgoing calls only, when they were within 150 metres of a base station, these being located in public places such as railway stations, shops, petrol stations, etc.

As in the case of many new markets that suddenly emerge, operators saw the advantages of having an early market share lead. Customers who perceived that one network was more readily available than any other would—all other things being equal—be more likely to subscribe to that network. Operators saw that a bandwagon effect could be set up, and that gaining entry to the market at a later stage could become a much more expensive market challenger exercise. With relatively low costs involved in setting up a Telepoint network, three of the four licensed operators rushed into the market, signing up outlets for terminals as well as new customers.

Such was the speed of development that the concept was not rigorously test-marketed. To many, the development was too much product-led, with insufficient understanding of buyer behaviour and competitive pressures. Each of the four companies forced through their own technologies, with little inclination or time available to discuss industry standard handsets which could eventually have caused the market to grow at a faster rate and allowed the operators to cut their costs.

Rather than thoroughly test out customer reaction to Telepoint in a small test market (as French Telecom had done with its Pointel system in Strasbourg prior to its full national launch), the operators sought to develop national coverage overnight. This inevitably led to very patchy coverage, with no outlets in some areas and heavy congestion in a few key sites. There were also the inevitable teething problems in getting the equipment to function correctly.

Worse still for the Telepoint operators, the nature of the competition had been poorly judged. Originally, a major benefit of Telepoint had been seen as removing the need to find a working telephone kiosk from which to make an outgoing call. In fact, the unreliability of public kiosks on which demand was based receded as British Telecom dramatically improved reliability, as well as increasing their availability at a number of key sites. Competition from Mercury had itself increased the number of kiosks available to users. At the top end of the Telepoint target market, the two established cellular operators had revised their pricing structure which made them more attractive for the occasional user.

The final straw for Telepoint operators came with the announcement by the government of its proposal to issue licences for a new generation of Personal Communications Networks. These would have the additional benefit of allowing both incoming and outgoing calls, and would not be tied to a limited base station range. While this in itself might not have put people off buying new Telepoint equipment, it did have the effect of bringing new investment in Telepoint networks to a halt, leaving the existing networks in a state of limbo.

Faced with the apparent failure of their new product development strategies, the Telepoint operators looked for ways of relaunching their services by refocusing their benefits to new target markets. Now that the initial target of street-based outgoing callers had all but disappeared, new ideas were developed. Hutchison Telecom, for instance, combined an outgoing handset with a paging device which would allow business and self employed people to keep in touch with base—the service was in effect being positioned as a cheap alternative to the two cellular networks. Similarly, the relaunch of Phonepoint focused on meeting the needs of three key targets: small businesses, mobile professionals, and commuters. Furthermore, the company aimed to achieve excellence within the London area—where a network of 2,000 base stations was planned—rather than spreading its resources thinly throughout the country.

Two years after its initial launch, it was estimated that no more than 5,000 subscribers in total had been signed up for Telepoint, or roughly one per base station, instead of the hundreds that were needed for viability. With hindsight, it could be argued that the launch might have been more successful had the service been more rigorously tested and developed before launch and if target markets had been more carefully selected. Moreover, many of the competitors might probably have wished that they had carried out a more rigorous environmental analysis, in which case they might have been less enthusiastic about launching in the first place.

With the arrival of 3G technology, the phone companies may have been wondering if history might be repeating itself. The scale of the risk this time round was much greater, with a huge investment needed in transmitter masts, on top of the licence fees paid to the government. In 2002 the mobile phone operator O2 launched a trial service in the Isle of Man, in an attempt to understand whether there really was a pent-up demand for mobile internet services, and the other features the technology offered. It also sought to resolve technical difficulties before a national rollout throughout the UK. This had been delayed several times.

Case study review questions

1. What lessons can the developers of 3G phones learn from the earlier experience of Telepoint?

2. In terms of a new product development process, how could the development and launch of Telepoint services have been improved in order to avoid the problems that were experienced?

3. How would the launch of Telepoint services differ in a less developed country with a less sophisticated telecommunications infrastructure?

▢ CHAPTER REVIEW QUESTIONS

1. Is there a case for considering different product strategies for each of the following types of product: material goods, services, locations, people, and ideas?

2. To what extent is the product life-cycle concept a useful tool for the marketing manager?

3 Why is it considered prudent for a firm to have a portfolio of products?

4. To what extent is the application of product portfolio analysis helpful to the marketing manager?

5. To what extent can the various stages in the new product development process be distinguished? How could they be integrated more fully?

6. With reference to specific examples, examine the practical problems of deleting products from a company's product range.

▢ REFERENCES

[1] ABA Banking Journal (2002), 'What's Egg?' *ABA Banking Journal*, 94(9): 60–1.

[2] Adner, R. (2002), 'When Are Technologies Disruptive? A demand-based view of the emergence of competition'. *Strategic Management Journal*, 23: 667–88.

[3] Alam, I. (2002), 'An Exploratory Investigation of User Involvement's New Service Development', *Journal of the Academy of Marketing Science*, 30: 250–61.

[4] Ansoff, I. H. (1957), 'Strategies for Diversification'. *Harvard Business Review*, Sept–Oct, 9: 49–62.

[5] Bolton, L. E. (2003), 'Stickier Priors: the effects of nonanalytic versus analytic thinking in new product forecasting'. *Journal of Marketing Research*, 40(1): 65–80.

[6] Cole, R. E. (2002), 'From Continuous Improvement to Continuous Innovation'. *Total Quality Management*, 13: 1051–6.

[7] Crosby, P. B. (1984), *Quality without Tears*. New York: New American Library.

[8] Dahan, E. and Hauser, J. R. (2002), 'The Virtual Customer'. *Journal of Product Innovation Management*, 19: 332–51.

[9] Dipasquale, C. B. (2002), 'Catalina Service to Track New Products'. *Advertising Age*, 73(38): 59.

[10] Enright, M. (2001), 'Approaches to Market Orientation and New Product Development in Smaller Enterprises: a proposal for a context-rich interpretative framework'. *Journal of Strategic Marketing*, 9: 301–13.

[11] Fagan, M. (2003), 'Three Launches 3 G Services—but without Handsets'. *Sunday Telegraph*, 2 March.

[12] Forlani, D., Mullins, J. W., and Walker, O. C. Jr (2002), 'New Product Decision Making: how chance and size of loss influence what marketing managers see and do'. *Psychology & Marketing*, 19: 957–81.

[13] Gronroos, C. (1984), 'A Service Quality Model and its Marketing Implications'. *European Journal of Marketing*, 18(4): 36–43.

[14] Howley, M. (2002), 'The Role of Consultancies in New Product Development'. *Journal of Product & Brand Management*, 11: 447–58.

[15] Huang, X., Soutar, G. N., and Brown, A. (2002), 'New Product Development Processes in Small and Medium-Sized Enterprises: some Australian evidence'. *Journal of Small Business Management*, 40(1): 27–42.

[16] Juran, J. M. (1982), *Upper Management and Quality*. New York: Juran Institute.

[17] Kim, J. and Wilemon, D. (2003), 'Sources and Assessment of Complexity in NPD Projects'. *R & D Management*, 33(1): 16–30.

[18] Little, G. (2002), 'Inventors Don't Always Make Great Marketers'. *Design Week*, 17(27): 15.

[19] Mills, D. (2002), 'Ad of the Week'. *Daily Telegraph*, 5 November.

[20] Mills, D. (2003), 'L'Oreal Patents: are they worth it?' *Daily Telegraph*, 18 February.

[21] Mintel (2002), *The Sports Drinks Market. London*: Mintel.

[22] Murray-West, R. (2002), 'Astrazeneca Wins Drug Patent Boost. *Daily Telegraph*, 14 October.

[23] Ofek, E. and Srinivasan, V. (2002), 'How Much Does the Market Value an Improvement in a Product Attribute?' *Marketing Science*, 21(4): 398.

[24] Rogers, E. M. (1962), *Diffusion of Innovation*. New York: Free Press.

[25] Song, M. and Swink, M. (2002), 'Marketing–Manufacturing Joint Involvement across Stages of New Product Development: effects on the success of radical *v.* incremental innovations'. *Academy of Management Proceedings*, B1–B6.

[26] *The Times* (2002), 'Mobile Phone Sales Fall'. *The Times*, 12 March: 25.

[27] Wong, V. (2002), 'Antecedents of International New Product Rollout Timeliness'. *International Marketing Review*, 19(2/3): 120–32.

SUGGESTED FURTHER READING

For a discussion on the general nature of innovation and the impact of new technologies, the following provide a useful introduction:

Cagan, J. and Vogel, C. (2001), *Creating Breakthrough Products*. Englewood Cliffs, NJ: Prentice-Hall.

Cooper, R. G. (2001), *Product Leadership: creating and launching superior new products*. Boulder, CO: Perseus Books.

Tidd, J., Pavitt, K., and Bessant, J. (2001), *Managing Innovation*, 2nd edn. Chichester: John Wiley.

New product development processes are discussed in the following:

Cooper, R. G. (2001), *Winning at New Products: accelerating the process from idea to launch*. Boulder, CO: Perseus Books.

Madhavan, R. and Grover, R. (1998), 'From Embedded Knowledge to Embodied Knowledge: new product development as knowledge management'. *Journal of Marketing*, 62(4): 1–29.

USEFUL WEB LINKS

Visit the companion website to this book, with lots of interesting additional material and links for each chapter:

www.oup.com/uk/booksites/busecon/

UK government's technology Foresight programme:

www.foresight.gov.uk

Department of Trade and Industry: 'Marketing: the way forward. Define your total product by what it does for the customer':

www.dti.gov.uk/mbp/bpgt/m9ka00001/m9ka000014.html

KEYWORDS

- **Business to Business goods**
- **Consumer goods**
- **Convenience goods**
- **Diversification**
- **Fast moving consumer goods (FMCGs)**
- **Gap analysis**
- **Innovation**
- **New product development**
- **Packaging**
- **Patent**
- **Portfolio analysis**
- **Product life-cycle**
- **Product line**
- **Product mix**
- **Quality**
- **Shopping goods**
- **Speciality goods**
- **Trademark**

8

Pricing

CHAPTER OBJECTIVES

Pricing can be a very difficult part of the marketing mix to get right, but getting it right can have a big impact on sales volumes and profitability. In the first part of this chapter we will look at the economic theory underlying price decisions. Perfectly competitive markets are introduced as one extreme in which the marketer must take prices as given from the market. From this, various other market structures are discussed and their impact on pricing decisions assessed. The second part of the chapter focuses on situations where a firm has developed some degree of uniqueness for its product, such as a brand, which sets it aside from perfectly competitive markets. Here firms have more discretion over pricing, and this chapter explores firms' objectives, strategies, and tactics in setting their prices.

Introduction

Most of the decisions made by marketing managers involve spending their company's money—on advertising, paying sales personnel, setting up distributor networks, new product development, and so on. Price is the one element of the marketing mix that directly affects the income that a company receives. In businesses with high turnover and low profit margins, a miscalculation of selling prices can have a big effect on a firm's annual profits. If the company charges too little for its products, it may find that, although it has achieved a very respectable level of sales, the low price charged is insufficient to give it any profit. Too high a price, and it may be unable to sell sufficient output to cover its fixed overhead costs. It may also end up with unsold stocks of obsolete products.

For most firms, setting prices is a difficult task which involves both scientific analysis and intuitive trial and error. This is especially true of new product launches, where a company has no historical precedent on which to base its expectations of how much customers will be prepared to pay.

In the first part of this chapter, we will look at some of the basic theory underlying firms' pricing decisions. Taking a broad perspective, firms cannot ignore market forces, so it is important to understand the relationship between market structure and the way in which prices are determined. The approach to pricing of a firm operating in a fiercely competitive market will differ quite markedly from the approach of a firm in a market where there are very few competitors.

The second part of this chapter considers more applied issues of pricing, which are applicable to companies that have some discretion in the prices they charge. (That is, they are not operating in a perfectly competitive market where prices are determined solely by the market.) Firms develop strategies in order to respond to the competitive nature of their environment; for example, they may aim to be a price leader across their range of products. For individual new product launches, a company may pursue a strategy of starting with a high price, and gradually lowering it over time. In terms of setting prices for individual products, firms pursue a variety of approaches, including basing their selling price on their production costs, on the prices that competitors are currently charging, and on customers' ability and willingness to pay.

We are living in a world in which governments increasingly seek to control the prices of key goods and services, so it is important to understand how firms can reconcile the sometimes conflicting approaches of market forces and regulation.

Of course, pricing should never be seen as an isolated element of a firm's marketing decision making. What the company is able to charge is closely related to, among other things, the quality of its products, the advertising images that it has created, and the effectiveness of its distribution strategy.

■ Effects of market structure on pricing

The market conditions facing suppliers of goods and services vary considerably. Customers of water supply companies may feel they are being exploited by high prices and poor service levels provided by companies that know that their customers have little choice of supplier. On the other hand, customers are constantly being wooed by seemingly countless credit card companies, all trying to offer deals that buyers will consider to be better than those offered by competitors. The differences in the pricing behaviour of these two groups of organizations can be related to the structure of the markets in which they operate. The term 'market structure' is used to describe:

- the number of buyers and sellers operating in a market;
- the barriers that exist to prevent new firms from entering the market (or prevent existing companies from leaving it);

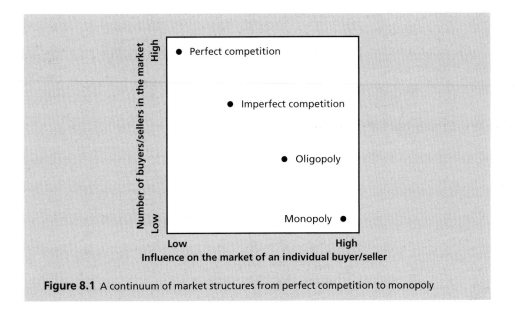

Figure 8.1 A continuum of market structures from perfect competition to monopoly

- the extent to which the supply of goods and services is concentrated in the hands of a small number of buyers (or, less frequently, the extent to which purchases are concentrated in the hands of a few buyers);
- the degree of collusion that occurs between buyers and/or sellers in the market.

An understanding of market structure underpins all pricing decisions made by marketers. Market structure influences not only the pricing decisions made by marketers within a firm, but also the nature of the response from other firms operating in the market.

Economists have developed a number of labels to describe different types of market structure. At one theoretical extreme is the model of perfect competition and at the other is pure monopoly. In practice, examples of the extremes are very rare, and most markets are referred to as being in a state of *imperfect competition* (Figure 8.1).

We are first going to spend some time looking at perfectly competitive markets. These are characterized by the following conditions.

- There are many producers supplying to the market, each with similar cost structures and each producing an identical product. No single supplier on its own can influence the market price.
- There are also many buyers in the market, none of which can, on their own, influence the market price.
- Both buyers and sellers are free to enter or leave the market; that is, there are no barriers to entry or exit.

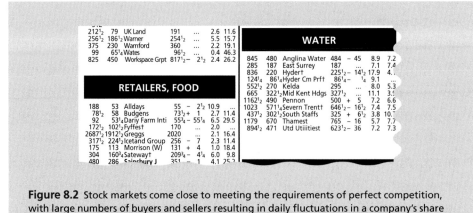

212½	79	UK Land	191	...	2.6	11.6
256½	186½	Warner	254½	...	5.5	15.7
375	230	Warnford	360	...	2.2	19.1
99	65¼	Wates	96½	...	0.4	46.3
825	450	Workspace Grpt	817½ –	2½	2.4	26.2

RETAILERS, FOOD

188	53	Alldays	55 –	2½	10.9	...
78½	58	Budgens	73½ +	1	2.7	11.4
92	53¼	Dairy Farm Inti	55¾ –	55¼	6.5	29.5
172½	102½	Fyffest	170	...	2.0	...
2687½	1912½	Greggs	2020	...	2.1	16.4
317½	224½	Icetand Group	256 –	7	2.3	11.4
175	113	Morrison (W)	131 +	4	1.0	18.4
304	160¾	Satewayt	209¾ –	4¼	6.0	9.8
480	286	Sainsbury J	351 –	1	4.1	25.2

WATER

845	480	Anglina Water	484 –	45	8.9	7.2
285	187	East Surrey	187	...	7.1	7.4
836	220	Hydert	225½ –	14½	17.9	4.
124¼	86¼	Hyder Cm Prft	86¼ –	¼	9.1	...
552½	270	Kelda	295	...	8.0	5.3
665	322½	Mid Kent Hdgs	327½	...	11.1	3.5
1162½	490	Pennon	500 +	5	7.2	6.6
1023	571¼	Severn Trentt	646½ –	16½	7.4	7.5
437½	302½	South Staffs	325 +	6½	3.8	10.7
1179	670	Thamest	765 –	16	5.7	7.7
894½	471	Utd Utiiitiest	623½ –	36	7.2	7.3

Figure 8.2 Stock markets come close to meeting the requirements of perfect competition, with large numbers of buyers and sellers resulting in daily fluctuations in a company's share price

- There is a ready supply of information for buyers and sellers, for example about competing alternatives.

These may seem quite unrealistic conditions for many markets, although a few markets do come close to meeting them (for example the 'spot' market for oil products, and stock markets where shares are bought and sold). However, the real value of studying competitive markets is that it teaches us the basic rules of supply, demand, and price determination (Figure 8.2).

The theory of supply and demand

In perfectly competitive markets, firms are price-*takers*, and their ability to set prices is limited by the level of demand and supply within the market they serve. If total demand goes up, all other things being equal, the going rate of prices in the market for their product will rise. Likewise, if there is a drop in total supply for whatever reason (for example because of bad weather), there will be further pressure for prices in the market to rise. The final price paid in the market will reflect the balance between supply-side and demand-side factors.

A market as defined here need not be a physical location where buyers and sellers meet (as happens in retail and wholesale grocery markets). A market in the economist's sense refers to all individuals and firms who wish either to buy or to sell a specified product, regardless of where they are located. A market is defined in terms of product and geographic descriptions, so the UK soft drinks market refers to all individuals in the UK who seek to buy soft drinks and the suppliers to that market.

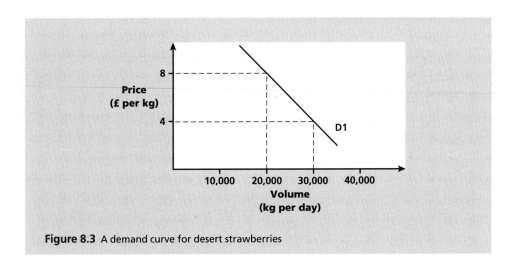

Figure 8.3 A demand curve for desert strawberries

Demand

Demand refers to how many people in a market are actually able and willing to buy a product at a given price and given a set of assumptions about the product and the environment in which it is being offered. Demand is also expressed in terms of a specified time period, for example thousands of litres of soft drinks per week. It is important to add the caveat that demand is about the quantity of a product that consumers are *willing* and *able* to buy at a specific price over a given period of time. It is important to distinguish these conditions from what people would merely *like* to buy—after all, most people would probably like to buy more expensive holidays and cars.

For most products, as their price falls, so the demand for them (as defined above) can be expected to rise. Likewise, as the price rises, demand could be expected to fall. This relationship can be plotted on a simple graph. In Figure 8.3, a *demand curve* for desert strawberries is shown by the line D1. This relates—for any given price shown on the vertical axis—the price to the volume of demand, which is shown on the horizontal axis. So at a price of £8 per kg demand is 20,000 units per period within a given area, while at a price of £4 the demand rises to 30,000 units.

The demand curve shown in Figure 8.3 refers to *total* market demand from all consumers, and is not simply measuring demand for one strawberry grower's output. The importance of this distinction will become clear later, because in imperfect markets each producer seeks to develop a unique demand function for its own differentiated product.

In drawing the price–volume relationship D1, a number of assumptions were made. These include, for example, assumptions that the price of substitutes for strawberries will not change, and that consumers will not suddenly take a dislike to strawberries.

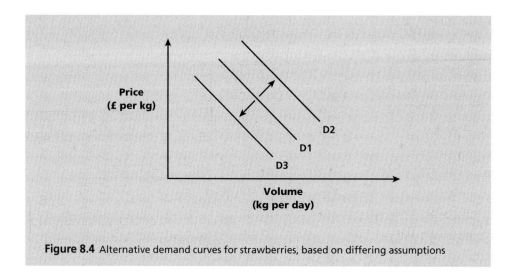

Figure 8.4 Alternative demand curves for strawberries, based on differing assumptions

Demand curve D1 measures the relationship between price and market demand for *one given set of assumptions*. When these assumptions change, a new demand curve is needed to explain the new relationship between price asked and quantity demanded.

In Figure 8.4, two sets of fresh assumptions have been made and new price–volume relationship curves D2 and D3 drawn, based on these new sets of assumptions. For new demand curve D2, more strawberries are demanded for any given price level. (Alternatively, this can be restated in terms of any given number of consumers demanding strawberries being prepared to pay a higher price.) A shift from D1 to D2 could come about for a number of reasons, including the following:

- Increased spending power available to consumers could lead to more of all goods, including strawberries, being bought.

- The demand for strawberries may be dependent upon demand for some complementary goods. For example, if demand for cream increases (perhaps because of some newly discovered health benefit), it is just possible that demand for strawberries will also rise.

- There could have been an increase in the price of substitutes for strawberries (such as peaches or raspberries), thereby increasing demand for strawberries.

- Heavy advertising of strawberries may increase demand for strawberries.

- Consumer preferences may change. This may occur, for example, if strawberries are found to have positive effects on health.

In the case of the movement in the price–volume relationship from D1 to D3, corresponding but opposite explanations can be put forward, including reduced spending power of consumers; a fall in demand for a complementary product; a fall in the price

Figure 8.5 £99.99 represents an important price point in many people's minds. Through a process of rationalization, customers of this shop may be able to justify to themselves spending £99.99 on a luxury, whereas £100.00 may be considered unacceptable. Where the market allows it, companies use various forms of psychological pricing to induce a response that would probably not be expected on the basis of assumptions about a linear demand curve (Reproduced with permission of Carphone Warehouse)

of substitutes; reduced advertising; and new evidence linking strawberries with harmful effects on health.

Most price–volume relationships slope downwards, as in Figures 8.3 and 8.4, indicating that as price rises demand falls, and vice-versa. While this is usually the case, there are exceptions. Sometimes, as the price of a product goes up, buyers are able and wiling to buy more of the product. This can occur where a product becomes increasingly desirable as more people consume it. The internet was of little value when only small numbers of people were connected to it and opportunities for buyers to communicate with others was limited. But as more customers were connected to it the value of an internet connection increased, so individuals were correspondingly willing to pay a higher price to advertise on it.

Although the price–volume relationships shown in Figures 8.3 and 8.4 are straight, this is a simplification of reality. Demand curves are usually curved, indicating that the relationship between price and volume is not constant for all price points. There may, additionally, be discontinuities at certain price points where buyers in a market have psychological price barriers (see Gourville and Soman [6]).

Drawing a conceptual diagram relating price to volume of demand is relatively easy compared with the problems of collecting data and actually measuring the relationship. The problems are both theoretical and practical.

Data can be obtained by one of two principal methods.

1. They could be collected at one point in time by comparing sales volumes in one area, at a given price, with sales volumes in another area, where a different price is

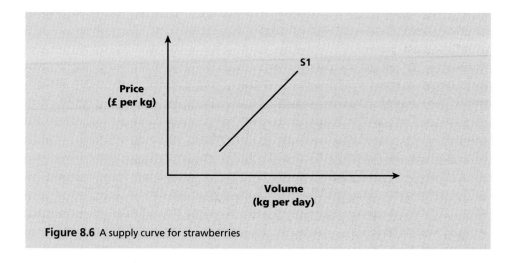

Figure 8.6 A supply curve for strawberries

charged. Retailers often experiment by charging different prices at different stores to build up some kind of picture about the relationship between price and volume. This is referred to as *cross-sectional data*. To be sure that this is accurately measuring the price–volume relationships, there must be no extraneous differences between the points of observation (such as differences in household incomes) which could partly explain differences in price–volume relationships.

2. Alternatively, a firm can change the price of a product over time and see what happens to sales volumes. This is referred to as *longitudinal data*. Again, it can be difficult to keep assumptions constant throughout the duration of the data collection, so that rising incomes or changing consumer preferences could explain sales variations just as much as changes in a product's selling price.

Supply

Firms' willingness to supply products to a market will be influenced by the prevailing price in the market. If the price they receive for selling their goods is low, they will be less willing to supply to the market than if the selling price is high. As in the case of demand, a price–volume line can be drawn, relating the market price of strawberries to volumes supplied by all farmers to the market (Figure 8.6) .

The supply curve in Figure 8.6 slopes upwards from left to right, indicating that, as the market price rises, more suppliers will be attracted to supply strawberries to the market. Conversely, as prices fall, marginal producers (such as those who operate relatively inefficiently) will drop out of the market, reducing the daily supply available.

Supply curve S1 is based on various assumptions about the relationship between price and volume supplied. If these no longer hold true, a new supply price–volume rela-

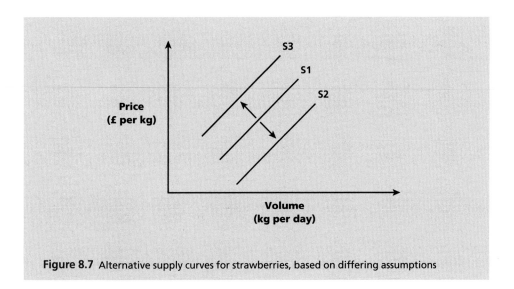

Figure 8.7 Alternative supply curves for strawberries, based on differing assumptions

tionship needs to be drawn, based on the new set of assumptions. In Figure 8.7, two new supply price–volume relationships, S2 and S3, are shown. S2 indicates a situation where, for any given price level, total supply to the market is increased. This could come about for a number of reasons, including the following:

- In the short term, extraneous factors (such as favourable weather conditions) could result in a glut of perishable strawberries which must be sold, and the market would therefore be flooded with additional supply.
- Improvements in production methods could result in suppliers being prepared to supply more strawberries at any given price (or, looked at another way, for any given volume supplied, suppliers are prepared to accept a lower price).
- Governments may give subsidies to strawberry growers, thereby increasing their willingness to supply to the market at any given price level.

New supply curve S3 indicates a situation where, for any given price level, total supply to the market is reduced. This could come about for a number of reasons, including adverse extraneous factors (e.g. bad weather for growers), increased production costs (e.g. rising wage costs), and reduction of government subsidies and/or imposition of taxes.

It should be noted that some changes in the actual volume of supply might take time to occur. So if strawberry prices went up today, it may not be until the next growing season that this results in increased planting of strawberry plants and hence a larger supply of strawberries to the market. Refer back to the discussion in Chapter 1 of the organic vegetable market and the time that it took firms to satisfy customers' demand for more organic produce.

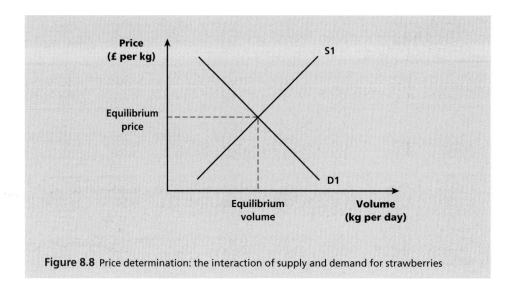

Figure 8.8 Price determination: the interaction of supply and demand for strawberries

Price determination

In competitive markets, selling prices are determined by the interaction of demand and supply. This can be illustrated by superimposing the supply curve on the demand curve (Figure 8.8).

The supply curve indicates that at lower prices fewer strawberries will be supplied to the market. But at these lower prices, customers are willing and able to buy large volumes of strawberries—more than the suppliers collectively are willing or able to supply. The demand and supply curves intersect at precisely the point where the price–volume relationship is similar for both buyers and sellers. This is the point of equilibrium where demand and supply are precisely in balance. At any lower price, there will be more demand than suppliers are willing to cater for. At any higher price, excessive supply could result in the buildup of unsold stocks.

Changes in the equilibrium market price can come about for two principal reasons.

1. Assumptions about buyers' ability or willingness to buy may change, resulting in a shift to a new demand price–volume relationship.

2. Assumptions about suppliers' ability or willingness to supply may change, resulting in a shift to a new supply price–volume relationship.

The effects of shifts in supply are illustrated in Figure 8.9. From an equilibrium price of £7 and a volume of 15,000 kg, the supply curve has shifted to S2 (perhaps in response to higher wage costs). Assuming that demand conditions remain unchanged, the new point of intersection between the demand and supply lines occurs at a volume of 12,000 kg and a price of £6. This is the new equilibrium price. A similar analysis could

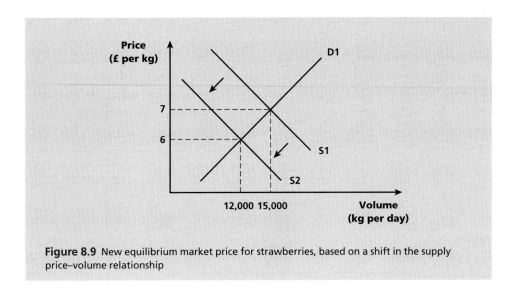

Figure 8.9 New equilibrium market price for strawberries, based on a shift in the supply price–volume relationship

be undertaken with a shift in the demand curve and noting the new point of intersection between the demand and supply lines.

Markets vary in the speed with which new equilibrium prices are established in response to changes in demand and/or supply. In pure commodity markets where products are instantly perishable, rapid adjustments in price are possible. Where speculators are able to store goods, or large buyers and sellers are able unduly to influence a market, adjustment may be slower (see Bell, Iyer, and Padmanabhan [1]). The extent of changes in price and volume traded is also dependent on the elasticity of demand and supply, which are considered later in this chapter.

Imperfections to competition

The model of perfect competition presented above is rarely seen in practice. The forces of competition may usually be ideal for consumers because of the tendency of market forces to minimize prices and/or maximize firms' outputs. But in such markets, suppliers are forced to be price-*takers* rather than price-*makers*. In a perfectly competitive market, firms are unable to use marketing strategies to affect the price at which they sell. At a higher price, buyers will immediately substitute identical products from other suppliers. Lower prices would be unsustainable in an industry where all firms had similar cost structures.

It is not surprising, therefore, that firms try to overcome the full effects of perfectly competitive markets. There are two principal methods by which a firm can seek to deviate from the workings of perfectly competitive markets to its own advantage: operating at lower costs than other firms in the market, and differentiating its products.

Operating at a lower cost

If a company operates at a lower cost than other firms, and is able to remain at a lower cost than other firms, it will be able to sustain lower prices than its competitors. In many industries economies of scale are available to firms, so that as they grow bigger their unit costs fall. This allows them to charge lower prices and still make an adequate profit. Lower prices result in a greater demand for a firm's products, which in turn can allow it to achieve even more economies of scale. This virtuous circle of lower costs leading to competitive advantage can result in a small number of firms gaining a dominant position in the marketplace, thereby violating an important assumption of perfect competition. This can lead to a situation of oligopoly or monopoly (see below), in which the dominant firms have significant power to dictate prices.

Of course, gaining a competitive advantage through economies of scale is not an option open to firms in all industries. Where production and distribution methods are simple, there may be no economies of scale available to exploit. As an example, many firms in service industries such as plumbing and decorating would find it difficult to gain a cost advantage over competitors by operating at a larger scale. Indeed, there may be diseconomies of scale associated with being too large.

Differentiating the product

We saw in the previous chapter that an entrepreneur can try to avoid head-on competition by selling a product that is somehow differentiated from competitors' products. So in the market for strawberries, a strawberry grower may try to get away from the fiercely competitive conditions that occur in wholesale fruit and vegetable markets. In such a market, the price at which a good sells is determined by the market. Instead, the supplier could try a number of differentiating strategies, including:

- concentrating on selling specially selected strawberries, for example ones that are of a particular size or ripeness;
- offering strawberries in distinctive protective packaging;
- offering a delivery service to local customers;
- offering a money-back guarantee of quality;
- offering strawberries in combination with other complementary elements of a fruit salad;
- processing the strawberries by tinning or freezing them;
- (as a result of any of the above actions) developing a distinctive brand identity for its strawberries, so that buyers don't ask just for strawberries, but for 'Brand X' strawberries by name.

In this example, the supplier has taken steps to turn a basic commodity product into something that is quite distinctive, so it has immediately cut down the number of direct competitors it faces. In fact, if its product really was unique, it would have no direct competition. (In other words, it would be a monopoly supplier of a unique product.) For some differentiated products, this may seem very true in many customers' minds; for example, some people would see a Rolex watch as being quite different to any other watch. Part of the differentiation may be only in buyers' minds, resulting from brand images and life-style associations that have been built up over time.

It must not, however, be forgotten that, although the way a supplier has presented its product may be unique, the good is still broadly similar to many competing products in terms of the ability to met buyers' basic needs. The strawberry trader therefore will still face indirect competition (from other strawberry suppliers, and from other types of fruit), just as Rolex still faces competition from other suppliers of watches.

If a supplier has successfully differentiated its product, it is no longer strictly a price-taker from the market. So the strawberry supplier that has specially selected or packaged its strawberries may be able to charge a few pence per kilogram more than the going rate for basic commodity strawberries. However, it will achieve this higher price only if customers consider that the higher price is worth paying for a better product. It will be able to experiment to see just how much more buyers are prepared to pay for its differentiated product.

Elasticity of demand

Price elasticity of demand refers to the extent to which demand changes in relation to a change in price. It is a useful indicator for business organizations because it allows them to predict what will happen to volume sales in response to a change in price.

Price elasticity of demand can be expressed as a simple formula:

$$\text{Price elasticity of demand} = \frac{(\%) \text{ change in demand}}{(\%) \text{ change in price}}.$$

Where demand is relatively unresponsive to price changes, it is said to be *inelastic* with respect to price. Where demand is highly responsive to even a small price change, it is described as being *elastic* with respect to price.

We have seen that firms face a downward-sloping demand curve for their products, indicating that as prices fall demand increases, and vice versa. By lowering its price, a firm may be able to increase its sales, but what is important to firms is that they increase their total revenue (and profits). Whether this happens depends upon the elasticity of demand for the product in question.

- If it is possible to substitute a product with another that is very similar, price elasticity is said to be high. What constitutes a similar and substitutable product can be defined only in the minds of customers. Two pairs of training shoes may seem technically similar, but their images may be so different that for many buyers they are not at all substitutable.

- The absolute value of a product and its importance to a buyer can influence its elasticity. As an example, most people would not bother shopping around for the best price on infrequently purchased boxes of matches. However, the same percentage difference in price between competing brands of television sets makes a sufficiently large difference to encourage buyers to shop around.

- It is important to understand how price cuts will be perceived by people who are the target of the cuts. A large price cut may lead some people to ask 'Why do they have to make such a cut—surely the product cannot be very good?' The consumer electronics manufacturer Amstrad had been aggressively promoting its 'e-mailer' telephone set for £99.99, so in 2003 questions were raised when, after less than a year after launch, it cut its selling price by half. To many observers the move appeared to be an act of increasing desperation and was seen as an admission by the loss-making company that the product had failed (Fletcher [5]).

A number of demand curves describing a firm's market can be described, ranging from the general product form to the specific brand, each with differing elasticity. For example, in the market for beverages the demand curve for beverages in general may be fairly inelastic, on the basis that people will always want to buy drinks of some description (Figure 8.11). Demand for one particular type of beverage, such as cola, will be slightly more elastic, as people may be attracted to cola from other drinks such as carbonated fruit juices and soda water on the basis of their relative price. Price becomes more elastic still when a particular brand of cola is considered. To many people, Coca Cola can be easily substituted with other brands of cola, so if a price differential between brands developed, switching may occur.

In general, firms will find that their products are much more inelastic to changes in price over the short term, when possibilities for substitution may be few. But over the longer term, new possibilities for substitution may appear. (For example, petrol is very inelastic over the short term but much more elastic over the long term, when motorists have a chance to adapt to less fuel-intensive cars and alternative methods of transport.) In addition to price elasticity of demand, economists measure a number of other types of elasticity that are of relevance to marketers in determining selling prices. Probably the most important of these is income elasticity of demand, which measures the responsiveness of demand to changes in buyers' incomes and can be expressed in the following way:

$$\text{Income elasticity of demand} = \frac{(\%)\ \text{change in demand}}{(\%)\ \text{change in income}}.$$

Figure 8.10 Budget airlines discovered a highly elastic demand for air services and have grown rapidly as a result. The price of a return fare from London to Glasgow can now cost less than the price of a pair of jeans and low prices have tempted more people into the airline market. For some, low prices by air meant that they switched from competing rail and road services. For others, new possibilities for taking short holidays or visiting friends were opened up which had previously not been affordable (Reproduced with permission of My TravelLite)

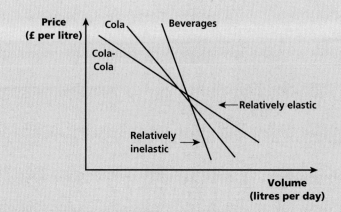

Figure 8.11 A comparison of elasticities of demand for beverages at different levels of product specificity, from a general product form to a specific brand

MARKETING in ACTION

Price alone won't sell burgers

How easily swayed are consumers of fast food by a price cut? The market for fast food in the USA and western Europe has become increasingly saturated, leading McDonald's, the market leader, to reverse its expansionary policies with a worldwide programme of branch closures in 2002. In that year it announced the first annual loss in its history. The woes of the burger market came despite vigorous price competition by the company. One campaign in the USA during 1997 cost $200 million in promotion and involved reducing the cost of a Big Mac from $1.90 to $0.55. But price alone seemed to have had little effect in the continuing war against McDonald's arch rival Burger King. The heart of the problem seemed to be that baby-boomers had got older and begun to care more about taste and healthy eating. Yet armies of fast food critics argued that McDonald's had failed to improve the taste and range of its meals in the 1990s as much as its rivals, to the point where not even price-cutting would prevent customers wandering down the road to the second rated Burger King or the third place Wendys. A Big Mac, it seemed, had become substitutable with an ever widening range of fast food, and was no longer able to command a price premium.

In general, as an individual's income rises, her demand for most products rises, giving rise to a positive income elasticity of demand. Where there is a particularly strong increase in demand in response to an increase in incomes, a product is said to have a high income elasticity of demand. This is true of luxuries such as long-haul package holidays and fitted kitchens, whose sales have increased during times of general economic prosperity but declined during recessionary periods. On the other hand, there are some goods and services for which demand goes down as income increases. These are referred to as inferior goods, and examples in most western countries include rural bus services and household coal.

Oligopoly

Imperfect competition can develop to a point where market structure can be described as **oligopolistic**. Oligopoly lies somewhere between the two extremes of perfect competition and pure monopoly. An oligopoly market is dominated by a small number of sellers that provide a large share of the total market output. The crucial point about oligopoly markets is that all suppliers in the market are interdependent. One company cannot take price or output decisions without considering the specific possible responses of the other companies.

Markets are most likely to be oligopolistic where economies of scale are significant; for example, oligopoly is typical of oil refining and distribution, pharmaceuticals, car manufacturing, and detergents. Customers of oligopoly organizations may not immediately appreciate that the products they are buying come from an oligopolist, as such firms frequently use a variety of brand names. (The detergent manufactures Unilever and Proctor & Gamble between them have over fifty apparently competing detergent products on sale in the UK.)

Oligopolists pay particular attention to the activities of their fellow oligopolists, and there is often a reluctance to upset the established order. One firm is often acknowledged as the price leader, and the other firms await its actions before adjusting their prices. In the UK household mortgage market, for example, Halifax has often been the initiator of price changes which other banks and building societies then follow. It has been suggested that firms may not match upward price movements, in the hope of gaining extra sales, but would match downward price changes for fear of losing market share.

Price wars between oligopolists can be very expensive to participants, so there is a tendency to find alternative ways to compete for customers, such as free gifts, coupons, added value offers, and sponsorship activities. This has been the norm in the UK national newspaper market, where a bewildering array of competitions, free lottery tickets and voucher offers have been used to entice readers from rival titles. However, in 2002 the owners of the *Sun* and its arch-rival the *Mirror*—each with deep pockets—engaged in a bitter price war which saw the price of each tabloid falling for a time to just 10p from its normal 32 p. This was undoubtedly expensive to both newspaper owners, especially as their advertising revenues had also been hit by a slump in advertising expenditure. After less than a year of the price war, a truce was called (*Sunday Times* [8]).

Oligopolists have often been accused of collusion and of creating barriers to entry for newcomers (such as signing exclusive distribution rights with key retailers).

Monopolistic markets

In its purest extreme, monopoly occurs where there is only one supplier to the market, perhaps because of regulatory, technical, or economic barriers to entry which potential competing suppliers would face. A pure monopoly means that one person or organization has complete control over supply to that market. A monopolist can determine the market price for its product and can be described as a 'price-maker' rather than a 'price-taker'. Where there are few substitutes for a product, and where demand is inelastic, a monopolist may be able to get away with continually increasing prices in order to increase its profits.

Sometimes monopoly control over supply comes about through a group of suppliers acting in collusion in a 'cartel'. As with the pure monopoly, companies would join a cartel in order to try and protect themselves from the harmful consequences of competition. Cartels have been suspected in many industry sectors, for example rings of cement suppliers in a region who covertly agree to share markets between themselves and not to undercut each other's prices.

A pure monopoly rarely occurs in practice. Even in the former centrally planned economies of eastern Europe, there were often active 'shadow' markets that existed alongside official monopoly suppliers. Most products have some form of substitute which reduces the monopolist's ability to set prices. Also, a firm that has significant monopoly pricing power at home may nevertheless face quite severe price competition in its overseas markets.

A company may have monopoly power over some of its users, but it may face competition if it wishes to attract new segments of users. It may therefore resort to differential pricing when targeting the two groups. As an example, many rail operators in the London area have considerable monopoly power over commuters, who need to use their train services to arrive at work by 9 a.m. on weekdays. For such commuters, the alternatives of travelling to work by bus or car are very unattractive. However, leisure travellers wishing to go shopping in London during off-peak periods may be much more price sensitive. For them, the car or bus provide realistic alternatives, and so train companies offer a range of price incentives aimed at the off-peak leisure market, while charging full fare for their peak period commuters.

In theory, a company with significant monopoly power could continually raise its prices in order to exploit its monopoly. However, marketing managers who think strategically may be reluctant to exploit their monopoly powerfully. By charging high prices in the short term, a monopolist could give signals to companies in related product fields to develop substitutes that would eventually provide effective competition. Blatant abuse of monopoly power could also result in a referral to the regulatory authorities (see below).

MARKETING in ACTION

Prices may still fly high with deregulated markets

Americans are strong advocates of the idea that air travel is cheap, following US deregulation back in the 1970s. But are low air prices in fact a myth? Is it enough to simply deregulate a market in order to ensure price competition? The theory of airline deregulation in the USA was irresistible. Any airline would be allowed to operate on any route, setting its fares as it liked. New airlines soon appeared, and initially fares were held down through competitive pressures. However, the major carriers have since acquired such a dominant position that US air fares rose on average 20% during 1997 and have risen faster than the general rate of inflation since. What went wrong?

The established airlines have managed to control 'slots' at the principal hub airports, making it difficult for new entrants to obtain entry. Many of the larger airlines have resorted to predatory pricing to keep newcomers away. This involves offering low fares on those routes and at those times that are competitive with other airlines, but charging higher fares where the airline has an effective monopoly. Some have argued that airport operators didn't want to rock the boat and were quite happy to put the interests of established carriers first, because these tended to pay higher landing fees than the low-cost 'budget' airlines. The lesson from US airline deregulation is that price competition may be expected in theory, but there are many reasons why it doesn't happen in practice.

▇ Regulatory influences on pricing

Because of the presumed superiority of competitive markets, prevailing laws in most developed countries have been used to try to remove market imperfections where these are deemed to be against the public interest. Private-sector companies must take account of various regulations in setting their prices. These can be classified as:

- direct government controls to regulate monopoly power;
- government controls on price representations.

Direct government controls to regulate monopoly power

Governments have a range of measures which can be used to prevent exploitative pricing by monopolists. At a European level, Articles 85 and 86 of the Treaty of Rome limit the ability of firms to collude with their fellow producers or distributors in fixing prices.

In the UK, the Competition Act 1998 (modified by the Enterprise Act 2002), implements European legislation.

The Act, among other things, prevents a manufacturer insisting on a price at which retailers or wholesalers must sell its products to their customers. It is illegal for manufacturers to do anything that has the effect of limiting retailers' ability to charge whatever prices they think fit; for example, it would be illegal for the manufacturer to withhold supplies unless there was another, non-price-related, reason for doing so. A firm is allowed to fix selling prices through its distribution channel only where such action can be shown to be in the public interest.

In the UK, the Director General of the Office of Fair Trading (OFT) has power to order an investigation by the Competition Commission of any anti-competitive practices that may have the effect of restricting choice or causing prices to be higher than they need be. In 2003 the OFT published the report of its investigation of alleged price fixing between the toy manufacturer Hasbro and the retailers Argos and Littlewoods. The OFT had found Argos and Littlewoods guilty of agreeing not to undercut the price of toys (including Action Man and Barbie dolls) charged by the other. The companies were fined a total of £22 million. An example of the result of this action, according to the OFT, was the inflation of the price of the board game Monopoly from £13.99 to £17.99 (*Sunday Times* [9]).

Utility companies who enjoy a monopoly position usually have their prices limited by the regulator for that industry. In the UK Ofgem, Ofwat, and Ofcom regulate certain prices of gas/electricity, water, and broadcasting telephone service providers, respectively. Governments have deregulated some utility markets, in the hope that this in itself will be instrumental in moderating price increases. (For example, numerous companies have been licensed to compete with British Telecom in the UK.) However, in many cases measures to increase competition have had only limited effect, as in the very limited competition faced by the privatized water supply companies; hence the continuing need for direct price controls. Even within the apparently more competitive telecommunications sector, the regulator has frequently intervened with instructions to operators to reduce specific categories of prices. In 2003 Oftel (a predecessor of Ofcom) published the result of an investigation by the Competition Commission into the 'termination charges' levied by mobile phone operators for calls coming in from other networks. The regulator found evidence of overcharging and ordered termination costs to be cut (White [11]).

Government controls on price representations

In any marketplace, buyers and sellers need rules to govern their conduct and prevent abuses of their respective positions. So, as well as controlling or influencing the actual level of prices, government regulation can have the effect of specifying the manner in which price information is communicated to potential customers. At a general level, the Consumer Protection Act 1987 requires that all prices shown should conform to the Code of Practice on pricing—misleading price representations which relegate details of supplementary charges to the small print or give attractive low lead-in prices for services that are not in fact available are made illegal by this Act. Other regulations affect specific industries. The Consumer Credit Act 1974 requires that the charge made for credit must include a statement of the annual percentage rate (APR) of interest. Also within the financial services sector, the Financial Services Act 1986 has resulted in quite specific requirements regarding the manner in which charges for certain insurance-related services are presented to potential customers.

Pricing objectives of companies

So far, we have considered some of the factors that underpin firms' pricing decisions. It was noted that firms seek to reduce their dependence on market forces by creating products that are distinctive in the minds of buyers, and for which there is therefore relatively little direct competition. The creation of a distinctive product clearly involves many marketing decisions, for example in relation to the design of the product, the promotional message used, and the ease with which buyers are able to get hold of it. The end result of this differentiation should be a product that buyers perceive as preferential to a basic commodity product within that product category, and for which they are prepared to pay a price premium.

We are now going to look at the decisions taken by firms that are able to act as price-*makers* rather than price-*takers*; in other words, those that have established some degree of differentiation from the rest of the market. Marketers must consider pricing not just at one point in time, but over the life of a product. So a price based on differential advantage over competitors may need to change over time as competitors gradually erode a company's differential advantage. Simplistic economic analyses of pricing also tend to overlook the complex interdependencies that can exist between different products within a firm's product range, and we will explore the subject of product mix pricing.

First, we need to consider the objectives of an organization as an important influence on its pricing decisions. Simple models of perfect competition assume that firms are motivated primarily by the desire to maximize their short-term profits. In a commodity market, where prices are taken from the market, a company cannot be expected to have any other objectives, or it would soon go out of business. However, where a company has differentiated its products to give it a degree of monopoly power, it is able to pursue a more diverse range of possible objectives. Below we consider the effects of diverse objectives on an organization's pricing policies.

Profit maximization

Economists' models of perfect competition assume that firms in a market act rationally in order to maximize their profits. In less competitive markets, the notion of profit maximization becomes much more complex to understand. The first complicating issue is the possible divergence between short-term and long-term profit objectives. A company that aims to maximize its profits over the short run may unwittingly reduce its ability to achieve long-term profit objectives. By charging high prices in a new market, it may make that market seem very attractive to new entrants. This could provide a major incentive for new competitors to appear, thereby increasing the level of competition in subsequent years, and therefore reducing long-term profitability. Drugs companies selling medicines that have just come out of their period of patent protection must decide whether to continue charging the high prices buyers have been accustomed to, or to lower the price to a point where it deters new market entrants who can no longer be sure of making a quick short-term profit.

Organizations differ in the urgency with which they need to make profits from a new product. It is frequently suggested that the open shareholding structure of UK firms makes shareholders restless for short-term profits. Managers are therefore likely to set prices to achieve these short-term objectives, even if this is at the expense of longer-term profitability. By contrast, the relatively closed capital structure of many Japanese companies has allowed them to take a longer-term view on profitability, relatively free of short-term stock market pressures. A longer-term profit objective may allow an organization to tap relatively small but high-value segments of its markets in the first year and save the exploitation of lower-value segments until subsequent years.

Finally, while it is easy to talk about maximizing profits during the present planning period, in reality many marketing managers have little understanding about the relationship between costs, sales volumes, and profitability. This can be especially true of new and emerging markets where there are few historical data on which to predict the outcome of price changes.

Sales growth

Management often does not directly receive any reward for increasing its organization's profits, so its main concern may be to achieve a *satisfactory* level of profits rather than the *maximum* possible. Managers often benefit personally where their company pursues a sales growth strategy, a point that has been made by many behaviourial studies of how managers act (e.g. Cyert and March [3]).

There are also some very good reasons why a company may benefit over the longer term by seeking to boost its short-term sales growth, even if this does mean charging very low prices in order to do so. In many industries it is essential to achieve a critical size in order to achieve economies of scale in buying, production, promotion, and dis-

Figure 8.12 Sometimes the use of advertising statements such as 'Closing Down Sale', 'Everything Must Go', and 'Stock Liquidation Sale' may be just advertising spin. Often, however, these sales reflect the fact that the company is desperately short of cash and will sell its stock at very low prices, just so that it can raise enough cash quickly enough to satisfy its creditors

tribution. On the basis of these economies of scale, a firm may be able to achieve a competitive advantage. Companies in sectors as diverse as grocery retailing, civil aviation, and publishing have used low prices to achieve short-term sales growth in the hope that this will lead to long-term profit growth.

Finally, sales growth may be an important objective, influencing pricing, because managers may have practical difficulties in establishing relationships between marketing strategy decisions and the resulting change in profitability. Going for growth may be perceived by managers to be their safest option.

Survival

For many struggling companies, the objective of maximizing profits or sales volume is quite unrealistic when they are fighting desperately to avoid bankruptcy. In these circumstances, prices may be set at very low levels, simply to get enough cash into the organization to tide it over. Many retailers have found themselves in this situation when there has been a sudden downturn in consumer demand and they are left with too much stock and expensive overheads to pay. Cash is now tied up unnecessarily in stock. In a bid to stay afloat, many desperate retailers have held stock liquidation sales, in which stocks have been sold at almost any price, just to keep cash flowing in. Even if the prices charged did not cover the original cost of goods, such pricing could satisfy managers' short-term objective of survival.

Social considerations

Talk about maximizing sales or profits may have little meaning within the public and not-for-profit sectors, where there is more emphasis on maximizing social benefits (e.g. the number of operations performed by a hospital). The price of many public services represents a tax levied by government based not on market forces, but on an individual's ability to pay, with many services being provided at no charge. In the UK, many basic health services are provided without charge to patients, and where charges are made these often reflect the ability of individuals to pay, rather than the need for the health authority to maximize its revenue (e.g. lower dental and prescription charges for disadvantaged groups).

Even where public services are provided in a more competitive market environment, pricing decisions may still be influenced by wider social objectives. As an example, Business Link organizations have been set up in the UK to offer a range of subsidized training courses to local businesses, but with the expectation that such courses should be able to charge commercial prices for their services once they have been established.

Although social objectives are normally associated with public-sector services, they are sometimes adopted by private-sector organizations also. Many companies provide goods and services for their staff (such as canteens and sports facilities) at below their market price, with the aim of adding to staffs' motivation and sense of loyalty to their organization.

Pricing strategy

Strategy is the means by which an organization seeks to achieve its objectives. Strategic decisions about pricing cannot be made in isolation from other strategic marketing decisions; so, for example, a strategy that seeks a premium price position must be matched by a product development strategy that creates a superior product and a promotional strategy that establishes in buyers' minds the value that the product offers.

The concept of positioning was discussed in Chapter 5, where it was noted that combinations anywhere along a line from high price/high quality to low price/low quality are sustainable strategic positions to adopt. A strategy that combines high price with low quality may be regarded by customers as poor value and they are likely to desert such companies where they have a choice of suppliers. For most companies such a strategy is not sustainable. A high quality/low price strategic position may appear very attractive to buyers, but it too may not be sustainable. Many companies in their public pronouncements claim this to be their strategic position, but it can pose problems for them, in the following ways.

- Are they selling themselves short and failing to recover their full costs in their bid to please customers? Unless they are operating more efficiently then other companies in their sector, there is the possibility that they will fail to make sufficient profits. In the mass market restaurant sector, for example, portion control can be quite critical to financial success. Customers may love the value offered by bigger servings, but many restaurants have gone out of business because they offered their customers too much value.

- If a company is genuinely able to offer lower prices for any given level of quality on the basis of greater efficiency, it must realize that its competitors may soon learn and copy its own levels of efficiency. Its prices will therefore no longer be the only sustainable low prices in the sector. In the European scheduled airline industry, many low-cost operators such as EasyJet and Ryanair have appeared and proceeded to undercut the established airlines. However, their competitive advantage has often been eroded when the established operators have then implemented many of the cost-cutting measures pioneered by their new competitors.

Pricing and the product life-cycle

In Chapter 7 the concept of the product life-cycle was introduced, and you will recall that many aspects of a product's marketing strategy are closely related to the position that it has reached in its life-cycle. Pricing strategy is no exception. An effective marketing strategy must identify how the role of price is to function as a product goes through different stages in its life from the launch stage through growth to maturity.

Where a company is supplying a market in which product differentiation is possible, it is able to take a long-term view on its price position. However, pressure on the product's price, and hence on its profitability, will vary during the life of the product. Figure 8.13 illustrates the typical pressures on a product's price as it progresses through its life-cycle.

Customer lifetime pricing

As well as the product life-cycle, we can also consider the customer life-cycle. You will recall from Chapter 3 that the development of ongoing buyer–seller relationships is becoming a much more important part of business strategy. Rather than bargaining over each transaction, companies are trying to view each transaction with a customer in the context of those that have gone before, and those that they hope will follow. The price offered to a prospective new client may start off relatively low and build up progressively as both buyer and seller come to recognize the value of their relationship. Think

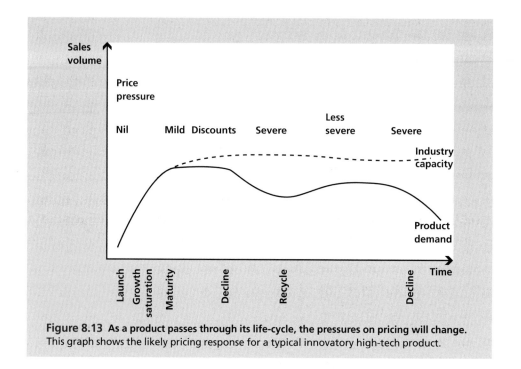

Figure 8.13 As a product passes through its life-cycle, the pressures on pricing will change. This graph shows the likely pricing response for a typical innovatory high-tech product.

back to our example in Chapter 3 of a new customer going into a restaurant. Should the profit of that individual be measured just in terms of that one meal, or in terms of the lifetime of meals it is hoped that he may buy? Viewed in the latter context, there may be scope for offering either price or non-price incentives to encourage newcomers to give the restaurant a try.

Price-skimming strategy

One approach to product life-cycle pricing is for a firm to start by charging a high price for a newly launched product, on the basis of its uniqueness. As its uniqueness is copied by other firms, the price will then have to be reduced to match those of the competitors.

This strategy is suitable for products that are genuinely innovative—the first microwave cookers in the 1970s; the first portable phones in the 1980s; the first digital cameras in the 1990s, and the first video mobile phones in the 2000s, for example. Such products are aimed initially at the segment of users who can be described as 'innovators' (discussed in Chapter 7). These are typically consumers who have the resources and inclination to be the trend-setters in purchasing new goods and services. Following these will be a group of early adopters, followed by a larger group often described as the 'early majority'. The subsequent 'late majority' group may take up the new product only when the product market itself has reached maturity. 'Laggards' are the last group to adopt a new product and would do so only when it has become commonplace and/or its price has fallen sufficiently.

The basic principle of a price-skimming strategy is to gain the highest possible price from each market segment, beginning with the highest-value segments and moving on to the next lower-value one when the purchasing ability of the first segment appears to be approaching saturation level. At this point the price level is lowered in order to appeal to the 'early adopter' segment, which has a lower price threshold at which it is prepared to purchase the product. This process is repeated for the following adoption segments.

As with so much of product life-cycle theory, identifying the points during the life-cycle at which action is needed can be very difficult, and it can also be very difficult to map out a price strategy with any degree of confidence. Consider the following problems, all of which make a price-skimming strategy difficult to formulate.

- What is the saturation level of individual market segments? At what point should the company decide to lower its prices to appeal to lower value segments?

- How long will the firm's product remain genuinely innovative in the eyes of consumers? Will the appearance of competitors diminish its uniqueness and therefore the firm's ability to charge premium prices?

- Should the firm avoid charging very high initial prices, as this may be a signal to competitors to enter the market? How strong are the barriers to entry for new competitors?

Price-skimming strategies work for consumer markets as well as business-to-business markets. Diffusion patterns for products sold mainly to business buyers can be different from those for consumer products. Business buyers generally have less of a desire to be a trend-setter for its own sake, and a different kind of rationality in purchase decisions. This limits the opportunities for price-skimming to situations where commercial buyers can use innovative products to give them a productivity advantage, which in turn will give them a competitive advantage in selling their own products to their customers at a lower price and/or a higher standard.

For many innovative products, falling prices may be further stimulated by falling production costs. Lower costs can occur because of economies of scale in production, promotion, and distribution. (For example, the cost of microwave cookers and mobile phones came down partly as a result of improved production efficiency, which itself was partly a refection of economies of scale.) Costs may also fall as a result of the **experience effect**. This refers to the process by which costs fall as experience in production is gained. By pursuing a strategy to gain experience faster than its competitors, an organization lowers its cost base and has a greater scope for adopting an aggressive pricing strategy.

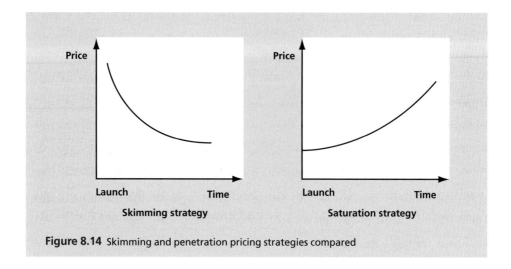

Figure 8.14 Skimming and penetration pricing strategies compared

Penetration pricing strategy

Genuinely innovative new product launches are few and far between. The vast majority of product launches are simply copies of products that consumers can already buy in substantially the same form. Consider the following product launches:

- a new television listings magazine;
- a new type of chocolate biscuit;
- a new long distance telephone service.

The principle of initially appealing to high-value segments and then dropping the price will be unlikely to work with any of these, as buyers in all segments have access to competitors' products which are essentially similar. Buyers must have a good reason for choosing to try the new product instead of sticking with the product they are currently purchasing. There are many ways in which a company can encourage trial of its product, including a product design that offers real benefits to buyers, heavy advertising, sales promotion, and sponsorship activity. One method used by many companies to encourage trial is to offer prices that are sufficiently low that a large number of buyers will switch from their existing suppliers. Sometimes the new product will even be given away, in order to get potential buyers to try it. (For example, internet service providers give away CD-ROMs with magazines to encourage free trial and takeup of their service).

Naturally, companies will not want to go on charging low prices for very long. Their hope is that, once buyers have tried and enjoyed their product, they will come back again. At this stage, the price can be raised to something that approaches competitors' price levels. The buyers no longer have to be tempted with a low price. Over time, they may even come to prefer the product over competitors', so the company may be able to charge a price premium.

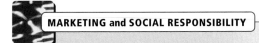

MARKETING and SOCIAL RESPONSIBILITY

One nibble and customers are nobbled

Companies use many pricing techniques to get people to try out a product and then seek to lock in the customer at ever-increasing price levels. Is this exploitation, or just good marketing? Knowing that customers who were attracted by a low price may just as easily be lost to a competitor who tries to tempt them back with low prices, companies try to lock customers in once they have tried a new product. Many new magazines launch with low prices and include series or articles which it is hoped readers will get attached to and so will carry on buying the magazine, even after the publisher has put the price up midway during the series. Many fast moving consumer goods manufacturers include competitions or gift offers with their launch sales, for which tokens need to be collected. Where the collectible items include children's toys, 'pester power' may add to the motivation to carry on buying the product. Meanwhile, the company may have taken a strategic decision to increase the price of the product while customers are part way through collecting the required number of tokens. Is this ethical?

In some cases a company can exploit the fact that customers have become physically hooked on their product. Tobacco companies have recognized the power of addiction for some time, even though they may have not publicly accepted that it happens. The effects can be seen in other products too. So with the biscuit 'Hob Nobs', a suspicion arose that individuals could become addicted to the biscuit after their initial trial, regardless of its price. Is this brilliant marketing, in that the manufacturer has perfected its product to such an extent that buyers are prepared to pay a premium price for it? Or is this an example of cynical manipulation of buyers to put them in a position of dependency?

Of course, penetration pricing strategies have their dangers. Companies often find it difficult to develop sufficient loyalty from customers that will allow them to raise prices. Customers who were attracted by low penetration prices may be just as easily lost when a competitor or another new market entrant tries offering low prices in its turn. This pricing strategy also presupposes that buyers have a high awareness of prices. Research has shown that in many markets buyers have a very poor knowledge of prices, so competing for market share on the basis of low price alone may not work.

MARKETING in ACTION

How much does a pint of beer cost?

Traditional price theory makes the assumption that there is a high level of knowledge in markets about prices charged by different competitors. In reality, this is simply not true. Many companies realize this and do not compete on price for most of their products, other than a few 'loss-leaders' for which buyers are able to make price comparisons.

The telephone company BT regularly monitors buyers' perceptions of prices of a variety of goods and services, doubtless aware that people still think of telephone charges as being very expensive. Its 1997 Business Price Perception Survey showed how knowledge of many prices was wide of the mark. Respondents gave the average price of a five-minute peak national call as £2.15, whereas in fact it was only 44p. Another sector with confusing price structures is railways. Here, respondents estimated the price of a second class return ticket from London to Edinburgh at £54, compared with the actual price of £64. In contrast to the wide variations in many service price estimates, respondents were quite accurate in their assessment of the price of a pint of beer: the average estimate of £1.73 for a pint of lager was just 2p off the true average price.

Pricing methods

Strategies need to be translated into methodologies for actually setting prices. Faced with a new product, the task of determining a selling price can sometimes appear to be quite daunting. If it is a completely new product, there may be very little historical guidance for setting prices. Companies may resort to a hunch or guesswork. However, even guesswork can be reduced to a series of rule-based decisions. Essentially, there are three questions that need to be asked when setting the price for any product:

1. How much does it cost us to make the product?

2. How much are competitors charging for a similar product?

3. What price are customers prepared to pay?

We can identify an additional factor that affects marketing managers in many public utility sectors:

4. How much will a government regulator allow us to charge customers?

The relationship between these bases for pricing is shown in Figure 8.15. Each will be considered in turn.

Cost-based pricing

The cost of producing a product sets the minimum price that a company would be prepared to charge its customers. If a commercial company is not covering its costs with its prices, it cannot continue in business indefinitely (unless, perhaps, the business has a wealthy owner and the business is kept going for reasons of prestige, as in the case of many national newspapers). The principle of a direct linkage between costs and prices

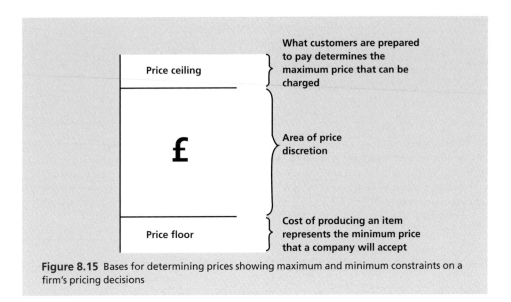

Figure 8.15 Bases for determining prices showing maximum and minimum constraints on a firm's pricing decisions

may be central to basic price theory, but marketing managers rarely find conditions to be so simple. Consider some of the problems in relating costs to prices:

- The cost of a particular product is often very difficult to calculate. This is especially true where production costs involve high levels of overhead costs which cannot easily be allocated to specific products.

- While it may be relatively easy to calculate historic costs, it is *future* costs that may be crucial in determining profitability. An office furniture manufacturer, for example, may find it difficult to set fixed prices for customers today for furniture that will be built and delivered at some time in the future. It may be difficult to predict inflation rates for labour and materials used.

- Cost-based pricing in itself does not take account of the competition that a particular product faces at any particular time, nor of the fact that some customers may value the same service more highly than others.

Despite these shortcomings, cost-based pricing is widely used in many sectors. In its most straightforward form, 'cost-plus' pricing works like this: a company calculates it total costs and divides these by the total volume of resources used, in order to determine the average cost of each unit of resource used; it then calculates a selling price by estimating the number of units of resources to be used, multiplying this by the unit cost and adding a profit margin. Cost-based pricing is widely used by solicitors, plumbers, and other labour-intensive service industries where the cost of labour is a major component of total costs. So a plumber may price a job on the basis of the total number of hours estimated to complete a job, multiplied by the historical cost per hour (including

Cost information for most recent trading year:	
Total employees' wage cost	£1,000,000
Total hours worked	70,000
Cost per employee-hour	14.28
Total other overhead costs	£600,000
Overhead cost per employee hour worked	8.57
Total chargeable amount per hour	22.85
Required profit markup	40%
Price calculation for a job requiring 100 hours of labour and £500 materials:	
100 hours @ £22.85 per hour	£2,285
Materials	500
Sub-total	2,785
Add 40% markup	1,114
Price	3,899

Figure 8.16 An example of a cost-based approach to pricing for a building contractor

overheads) of its employees, plus materials used, plus a profit margin. The principles are illustrated in Figure 8.16.

Marginal cost pricing

Another form of cost-based pricing that is widely used is referred to as marginal cost pricing. Here, a company calculates the *marginal* cost of producing one additional unit of a product (that is, the addition to the company's total costs of selling one extra item). In some industries with high levels of fixed costs, the marginal cost of producing one extra unit of output can be surprisingly small. The cost of carrying one extra passenger on an aeroplane that is about to depart with some empty seats can be little more than the cost of the airport handling charges, a meal, and marginally additional fuel. This explains why many airlines are keen to offer last-minute standby airfares, as some revenue is better than having an unsold seat, just so long as the price charged more than covers the marginal costs.

Pricing based on marginal costs may work up to a point, but companies must realize that a sufficient number of customers must be willing to pay full costs in order for others to be charged a much lower price reflecting only marginal costs. Many airlines and holiday companies have gone bankrupt because too high a proportion of their customers have been sold tickets at the marginal cost, leaving the fixed overhead costs uncovered.

Calculating marginal costs can sometimes be quite difficult. In the long term, all of a company's costs are marginal in that there is always the option to close down entire business units or even the whole company. While the marginal cost of one seat on an aeroplane may be low, if the unit of analysis is the whole journey or even the whole route, the level of marginal costs becomes much higher (see Figure 8.17).

Product	Fixed costs	Marginal costs
Meal in a restaurant	Building maintenance Rent and rates Head chef	Food
Bank mortgage	Head office staff time Building maintenance Corporate advertising	Sales commission Paper and postage
Hairdresser	Building maintenance Rent and rates	Shampoos used

Figure 8.17 **A classification of typical fixed and marginal costs for three service industries.** Note that even fixed costs could in the long term become marginal costs if the whole business unit is being evaluated

Figure 8.18 **Travel companies have for a long time used marginal cost pricing, mindful that some revenue is better than an empty plane seat or hotel room.** They have realized that some people could be tempted by low price offers to fill its spare capacity at very short notice. The online travel intermediary lastminute.com makes full use of marginal cost pricing by bringing together companies that have spare capacity with buyers who are looking for a bargain

Reproduced with permission of lastminute.com.

Competitors and pricing

Very often, a marketing manager may go about setting prices by examining what competitors are charging. But what is the competition against which prices are to be compared? From Chapter 6, you will recall that competitors can be defined at different levels:

• similar in terms of product characteristics;

or, more broadly,

• similar just in terms of the needs that a product satisfies.

As an example, a video rental shop can see its competition purely in terms of other video shops, or it could widen it to include cinemas and satellite television services, or widen it still further to include any form of entertainment.

Once it has established what market it is in and who its competitors are, a company can go about setting comparative prices. First it must establish what price position it seeks to adopt relative to its competitors. This position will reflect the wider marketing mix of the product, so if the product is perceived by buyers as being superior in quality to the competitors' products, it may justify a relatively higher price. Similarly, heavy investment in promotion or distribution channels may give it a competitive advantage which is reflected in buyers' willingness to pay relatively high prices.

MARKETING in ACTION

Lowballing among solicitors

Solicitors in the UK have traditionally enjoyed a high professional status in which high charges and slow service have become almost an expectation. However, a series of measures towards deregulation (for example the authorization of licensed conveyancers to share the solicitors' previous monopoly on house conveyancing) has led to much greater price awareness among buyers. This has been particularly true in the case of legal services provided to businesses, where many companies now routinely shop around for the lowest-priced solicitors. The old loyalty of client to lawyer has waned as clients are seduced by the lure of low fees elsewhere.

But are legal services a commodity that buyers can shop around for as and when they are required? Lawyers argue that the practice of 'lowballing' (offering very low fees to attract business) can create problems for the client as well as the lawyer. Clients may believe that, when professionals are bound to provide a competent service, they have nothing to lose by going for the cheapest possible deal. But are those practices that are willing to provide services at rock-bottom prices likely to try to achieve a profit by cutting corners? Is there a significant segment of business clients who would instead prefer value to be added to a business relationship, for example by organizing seminars on subjects of topical legal interest?

It was noted earlier in this chapter, in the discussion on market structure, that perfect competition and pure monopoly are two extremes that rarely occur in practice. In markets that show some signs of interdependency among suppliers, firms can often be described as price-makers, or price-followers. Price-makers tend to be those who, as a result of their size and power within a market, are able to determine the levels and patterns of prices, which other suppliers then follow. Within the UK insurance industry, the largest firms in the market often lead changes in rate structures. Price-takers, on the other hand, tend to have a relatively low size and market share and may lack product differentiation, resources, or management drive to adopt a proactive pricing strategy. Smaller estate agents in a local area may find it convenient simply to respond to pricing policies adopted by the dominant firms—for them to take a proactive role themselves might

Figure 8.19 The market for long distance phone calls has become increasingly competitive in the UK, and for many people price is the only means of differentiating between one supplier and another. Swiftcall is one of several companies to challenge the dominant provider, BT. Its advertising picks out a few key destinations and provides direct price comparisons with BT, providing an immediate comparison of price advantages

Reproduced with permission of Swiftcall.

bring about a reaction from the dominant firms which they would be unable to defend, because of their size and standing in the market.

Where it is difficult for a company to calculate its production costs (perhaps because of the high level of fixed costs), charging a 'going rate' can simplify the pricing process. As an example, it may be very difficult to calculate the cost of renting out a video film, as the figure will be very dependent upon assumptions made about the number of uses over which the initial purchase cost can be spread. It is much easier to take price decisions on the basis of the going rate charged by close competitors.

Many industrial goods and services are provided by means of a sealed bid tendering process where interested parties are invited to submit a bid for supplying goods or services in accordance with specifications. In the case of many government contracts, the organization inviting tenders is often legally obliged to accept the lowest priced tender, unless exceptional circumstances can be proved. The first task of a bidding company is to establish a minimum bid price based on its costs and the required rate of return, below which it would not be prepared to bid. The more difficult task is to try and put a maximum figure on what it can bid. This will be based on expectations of what its competitors will bid, based on an analysis of their strengths and weaknesses.

Demand-based pricing

What customers are prepared to pay represents the upper limit to a company's pricing possibilities. In fact, different customers often put different ceilings on the price they are prepared to pay for a product. Successful demand-oriented pricing is therefore based on effective segmentation of markets and price discrimination which achieves the maximum price from each segment.

The bases for segmenting markets were discussed in Chapter 3 and are of direct relevance in determining discriminatory prices. It was noted that, in addition to socio-economic factors, geographical location of buyers, their reason for purchase, and the time of purchase are all important bases for segmentation. Their impact on price determination is considered below.

Price discrimination between different groups of buyers

Sometimes price discrimination can be achieved by simply offering the same product to each segment, but charging a different price. This is possible with some services which are not transferrable from one individual to another. So a hairdresser can offer senior citizens a haircut that is identical to the service offered to all other customer groups in all respects except price. The justification could be that this segment is more price-sensitive than other segments, and therefore additional profitable business can be gained only by sacrificing some element of margin. By supplying more haircuts, even at a lower price, a hairdresser may end up deriving increased total revenue from this segment, while still preserving the higher prices charged to other segments.

On other occasions, however, where one segment was paying more than other segments for an identical product, price discrimination would not be sustainable. It would always be open for members of the segment being charged a higher price to try to buy the good in lower-price markets. Sometimes they will do this directly themselves, as seen by the number of British buyers who have taken advantage of lower cigarette and alcohol prices in continental Europe. Sometimes entrepreneurs will seek out goods in low priced market segments and offer them for resale in the higher-price market (a practice that retailers such as Superdrug and Tesco have carried out in respect of branded perfumes, which are sold in many overseas markets at lower prices than in the UK).

MARKETING in ACTION

Entrepreneurial senior citizens seize price discounts

Many service-sector companies have offered reduced prices for segments of senior citizens, calculating that these segments are more price sensitive than others and could usefully fill spare capacity at a profit, even at the lower prices charged. But can this apply to the sale of goods? With services, a supplier can insist that only senior citizens receive the benefit of the service they have paid for (for example by insisting on seeing proof of age during a train journey). But goods can be bought by members of a low-price segment and sold on to those of a relatively high-price one. The pitfalls of this approach to market segmentation were learnt by a German grocery retailer which offered 20% off the price of all purchases made by senior citizens. Entrepreneurial senior citizens were then seen lining up outside the supermarket offering to do other customers' shopping for them. The 20% price saving was split between the senior citizen and the person needing the goods, saving effort for the latter, providing additional income for the former—but making a mockery of the retailer's attempts at price discrimination.

To be sustainable, price discrimination is often associated with slight changes to the product offer. This can be seen in the market for air passenger services. Airlines offer a variety of fare and service combinations to suit the needs of a number of segments. One segment has to travel at short notice and is typically travelling on business. For the employer, the cost of not being able to travel at short notice may be high, so this group is prepared to pay a relatively high price in return for ready availability. A sub-segment of this market may seek extra comfort and space and is prepared to pay more for the differentiated Business Class accommodation. For non-business travellers, another segment may be happy to accept a lower price in return for committing themselves to a particular flight just two weeks before departure. Another segment with even less income to spend on travel may be prepared to take the risk of obtaining a last-minute standby flight in return for a still lower priced ticket.

Figure 8.20 It is not just large companies that practise price discrimination. Many smaller businesses, such as this hairdressing salon, charge different prices for different groups, typically offering discounts for students and senior citizens. Price discrimination would work for a haircut (unlike most goods), because one person cannot buy a cheap haircut and sell it on to another person who is not eligible for the lower price. However, even small businesses must ensure that discriminatory pricing does not create feelings of resentment from those who pay a higher price for an essentially similar service

Price discrimination by point of sale

Some companies charge different prices in different places. Hotels frequently charge much higher prices in some prime locations, despite there being little difference in facilities offered between locations. The reason for this discrimination can be a combination of cost factors (e.g. land and staff costs for a hotel are higher in central London than in northern England) and demand factors. (To large segments of potential buyers, a hotel room in central London will be considered more valuable than one located in northern England.)

Price discrimination by area is much more effective for services than for goods. Services cannot generally be transferred from the point where they are produced to another area where a buyer most wants to consume them. (For example, a Sheffield hotel room can be consumed only in Sheffield and cannot be brought to London where it would be more valuable.) Airlines often charge more at one end of a route than the other, depending on strength of demand in different national markets, and one American Express study calculated that business travellers out of the UK were being charged up to 54% more for transatlantic flights than travellers from other European cities (*Daily Telegraph* [4]). By contrast, differences between areas in the price of goods will soon be exploited by entrepreneurs who are able to buy in the lower price market and sell on in the higher price one (as has happened with cosmetics sourced from low-price Far Eastern markets and resold in the UK).

Price discrimination by type of use

A similar product can be bought by different people to satisfy quite different needs. A train journey may be perceived as an optional leisure purchase by one person, but as a means of getting work done on the way to an important business meeting by another. Train operating companies have therefore developed different fares aimed at groups with different journey purposes (e.g. off-peak fares for price-sensitive leisure travellers and first class facilities for business executives).

Even the same person may buy a product repeatedly but seek to satisfy different needs on each occasion. There are many examples of this. Most people when eating out are more likely to be price sensitive for a regular mid-day meal during their lunch hour than to a social meal with friends in the evening. Many restaurants have responded to this by offering special lunchtime menus which are very similar to meals offered in the evening, except that the price is lower.

Price discrimination by time of purchase

It is quite common for suppliers of services to charge different prices at different times of supply. Services often face an uneven demand which follows a daily, weekly, annual, seasonal, cyclical, or random pattern. At the height of each peak, pricing is usually a reflection of

- the greater willingness of customers to pay higher prices when demand is strong, and

- the greater cost that often results from service operators trying to cater for short peaks in demand.

The greater strength of demand that occurs at some points in a daily cycle can be for a number of reasons. In the case of rail services into the major conurbations, workers generally must arrive at work at a specified time and may have few realistic alternative means of getting to work. A train operator can therefore sustain a higher level of fares during the daily commuter peak period. Similarly, the higher rate charged for telephone calls during the daytime is a reflection of the greater strength of demand from the business sector during the day. Price can also occur between different periods of the week (e.g. higher fares for using many train services on a Friday evening), or between different seasons of the year (e.g. holiday charter flights over bank holiday periods).

Price discrimination by time can be effective in inducing new business at what would otherwise be a quiet period. Hotels in holiday resorts frequently lower their prices in the off-peak season to try to tempt additional custom. Many utility companies lower their charges during off-peak periods in a bid to stimulate demand—for example, lower telephone charges at weekends.

Bartering and auctions

Bartering is one of the oldest forms of price determination. It is still normal practice in many Middle Eastern and Asian bazaars, where buyer and seller go through a process of determining each others' price limits before eventually converging on an agreed price. The seller will try to establish the maximum price that an individual is prepared to pay. To western tourists visiting these markets this may seem quite daunting, but the seller has doubtless worked out in his mind principles for negotiating. From previous experience, the seller may have come to recognize that such factors as the buyers' nationality, the size of their group, the length of time that they have been in the country, and their general appearance all give clues about the sales price that could be achieved. Although bartering is associated with many less developed economies, it is typical of many high-value business-to-business sales elsewhere. There is also some evidence that it is making a resurgence in western consumer markets. It seems that individuals buying cars or hotel accommodation are increasingly prepared to haggle for a better price rather than accept the list price.

Auctions are used where it is difficult for a seller to determine the maximum price that might be achieved for a product. Unlike bartering, which is carried out on a one-to-one basis, auctions involve many people bidding against each other for an item; the seller achieves the highest price based on what the highest bidder is prepared to pay. Although traditionally auctions have been associated with high-value, difficult-to-value items, such as art and unusual houses, the internet has enabled a new generation of auctions selling relatively low-value items, such as the auction service provided by e-bay (**www.ebay.com**). As well as consumer sales, internet auctions have found a valuable role for business-to business procurement (Timmins [10]). A company can put out a tender and invite suppliers to bid, following which it chooses the lowest price bidder.

However, while bartering and auctions may seem an attractive method of extracting the maximum price from a seller, and therefore a good example of demand-based pricing, they do have problems. Price lists were developed in order to simplify the purchasing process, especially where high-volume, low-value goods are concerned. Going round Sainsbury's supermarket haggling over the price of every item of groceries would take up a lot of time and effort for buyer and seller alike. Anybody who has used an internet auction site will appreciate the uncertainty created by the buying process, in which you may not know for some time whether you have got yourself a bargain or will have to start the purchase process all over again.

MARKETING and the INTERNET

Cookies allow price discrimination at amazon.com

The internet and electronic databases have opened up vast new possibilities for companies to practise price discrimination between different groups of customers. Airlines and hotels have for some time practised revenue management techniques, designed to get the highest price possible for each unit of output. We are now all familiar with the idea that the price of a ticket for a plane journey on a specific route on a specific date at a specific time may vary—you may see it on an airline's website at one price today, but by tomorrow it may have gone up or down.

There are dangers in practising price discrimination too avidly, as the online retailer Amazon.com found to its cost. In September 2002, the company attempted to implement a differential pricing structure by tracking customers' online purchasing behaviour, in order to charge loyal customers higher prices for its DVDs. Consumers were quick to discover the price differences and complaints followed. Amazon customers on DVDTalk.com, an online forum, reported that certain DVDs had three different prices, depending on the so-called cookie a customer received from Amazon. Cookies are small files that websites transfer to customers' hard drives through the browsers they use. These files allow sites to recognize customers and track their purchase patterns. Depending on previous purchases, a DVD such as *Men in Black* could cost $33.97, $25.97, or $27.97. The list price was $39.95. One customer is reported to have ordered the DVD of Julie Taymour's *Titus*, paying $24.49. The next week he went back to Amazon and saw that the price had jumped to $26.24. As an experiment, he stripped his computer of the electronic tags that identified him to Amazon as a regular visitor, and the price then fell to $22.74. One angry message posted on DVDTalk.com stated: 'Amazon apparently offers good discounts to new users, then once they get the person hooked and coming back to their site again and again, they play with the prices to make more money' (cited in Bicknell [2]). Loyal, repeat customers were particularly incensed.

Amazon.com quickly issued reports admitting that it had been presenting different prices to different customers but denying that it had done so on the basis of any past purchasing behaviour at Amazon. A spokesman stated that the company had just been carrying out a simple price test and were not discriminating against loyal customers. However, the company later admitted that it had been carrying out discriminatory pricing, justifying its use by the fact that the practice was commonplace among both internet and bricks-and-mortar companies. Faced with vociferous criticism from its loyal customers, the company quickly ended its use of cookies to discriminate between customers and refunded the difference to customers who had paid the higher prices. Amazon.com may have had to retreat on this occasion, but the case emphasizes that traditional methods used to calculate prices are sledgehammers compared with the internet's sharp scalpel. The Web provides a continuous feedback loop in that, the more a customer buys from a website, the more the site knows about the purchaser and the weaker her bargaining position is. As one commentator put it, 'It's as if the corner drugstore saw you coming down the sidewalk, clutching your fevered brow, and then doubled the price of aspirin.' Is the use of cookies to determine prices charged to individuals an ethical practice? (Based on Bicknell [2]; Streitfeld, [7])

Pricing a product range

Most organizations sell a range of products, and the price of each individual item should recognize the pricing strategy adopted for other products in the range. Some companies may have many thousands of individual items, for each of which a price must be set.

For any given product, a company can allocate the other items in its product range to one of three categories for the purposes of pricing.

1. **Optional additional items** are those that a buyer may or may not choose to add to the main product purchased, often at the time the main product is purchased. As a matter of strategy, an organization could seek to charge a low lead-in price for the core product, but to recoup a higher margin from the additional optional items. Simply breaking a product into core and optional components may allow for the presentation of lower price indicators, which through a process of rationalization may be more acceptable to many customers. Research may show that the price of the core product is in fact the only factor that potential customers take into account when choosing between alternatives. In this way, many travel agents and tour operators cut their margins on the core holiday they sell, but make up some of their margin by charging relatively high prices for optional extras such as travel insurance policies and car hire.

2. **Captive items** occur where the core product has been purchased and the provision of additional services can be provided only by the original provider of the core product. Where these are not specified at the outset of purchasing the core product, or are left up to the discretion of the supplier, the latter is in a strong position

to charge a high price. Against this, the company must consider the effect that the perception of high exploitative prices charged for these captive items will have on customer loyalty when buyers are next considering the purchase of the core product. An example of captive product pricing is provided by many manufacturers of computer printers, which sell their printers at a low initial price, but seek to make up for this through sales of ink cartages. In 2002 the manufacturer Epson took this one stage further by fitting a chip to some of its printers which prevented users saving money by buying cheaper refill cartridges from other suppliers.

3. **Competing items** within the product range occur where a new product targets a segment of the population that overlaps the segments served by other products within the organization's mix. By a process of 'cannibalization', a company could find that it is competing with itself. In this way, a confectionary company with a large market share that launches a new chocolate bar may find that its new launch is taking sales away from its existing range of chocolate bars.

Price bundling

Price bundling is the practice of marketing two or more products in a single package for a single price. Bundling is particularly important for goods and services that have a high ratio of fixed to variable costs. Furthermore, where there is a high level of interdependency between different types of output from an organization, it may be difficult and meaningless to price each individual item. In this way, the provision of an ATM card and internet banking become an interdependent part of the current bank account offering which most UK banks do not charge for separately.

Price bundling of diverse products from an organization's product mix is frequently used as a means of building relationships with customers. In this way a health insurance policy could be bundled with a travel insurance policy or a legal protection policy. Where the bundle of service represents ease of administration to the consumer, the service organization may be able to achieve a price for the bundle that is greater than the combined price of the bundle's components.

Different groups of consumers have differing expectations about what they would expect to see in a price bundle. Car buyers in the UK, for example, expect a high level of equipment (radio, wheel trims, etc.) to be bundled in with the main price of a car, while many buyers in continental Europe would expect to pay for each item separately.

▣ The pricing of public services

Many of the pricing principles discussed above, such as price discrimination and competitor-based pricing, may be quite alien to some public services. It may be difficult or undesirable to implement a straightforward price–value relationship with individual users of public services for a number of reasons.

Figure 8.21 Companies often bundle a number of products together and charge one inclusive price. Like many seller of lunchtime snacks, the Co-op offers a discounted 'Meal Deal' to customers who buy a sandwich, a drink and selected crisps/snack bars together. For many buyers, the 'Deal' price becomes the reference price which they use to compare prices between retailers. For the retailer, a bundled price offer encourages additional spending by the customer and the discounted price of the bundle is likely to be made up from the additional margin from selling three, rather than just one item (Reproduced with permission of Oxford, Swindon and Gloucester Co-op)

Figure 8.22 Road users within the UK have not generally been charged directly for the benefits they receive from the road system, largely because of the impracticality of road pricing and issues of equity between users. Instead, users have paid for the use of roads through direct and indirect taxation. However, with improved technology and growing realization of the social and economic costs of traffic congestion, there has been a move towards pricing the use of roads. The London Congestion Charge, introduced in 2003, provides evidence that pricing a public service can change consumers' behaviour, with traffic volumes falling by about 10% since the introduction of the charge

- Pricing can be actively used as a means of social policy. Subsidized prices are often used to favour particular groups; for example, prescription charges favour the very ill and unemployed, among others. Sometimes the interests of marketing orientation and social policy can overlap. Charging lower prices for unemployed people to enter museums may provide social benefits for this group, while gaining additional revenue from a segment that might not otherwise have been able to afford a visit to the museum.

- Benefits to society at large may be as significant as the benefits received by the individual, so there may be a case for the government subsidizing low prices. Education and training courses may be provided at an uneconomic charge in order to add to the level of skills available within an economy generally.

Problems can occur in public services that have been given a largely financial, market-oriented brief, but in which social policy objectives are superimposed, possibly in conflict. Museums, leisure centres, and car park charges have frequently been at the centre of debate about the relative importance to be attached to economic and social objectives. Museums have sometimes overcome this dilemma by retaining free or nominally priced admission charges for the serious, scholarly elements of their exhibits, while offering special exhibitions which match the private sector in the standard of production and the prices charged.

Chapter summary and linkages to other chapters

This chapter began by discussing the underlying theory of price determination. Perfect competition is an idealized market structure which rarely occurs in its pure extreme, but the principles of such competition provide a relevant background to many of the pricing decisions made by marketers. Firms seek to create a distinctive product, which reduces the impact on them of intense price competition. Because imperfect markets are generally held to be against the public interest, various regulatory measures exist to improve the competitiveness of markets.

Where a company has developed a distinctive product, it becomes a price-maker rather than a price-taker. Its pricing behaviour will be influenced by its organizational objectives. Prices can be set in relation to production costs, the strength of demand, competitors' prices, or a combination of all three. Market segmentation (Chapter 5) is used to identify groups that may be able and willing to pay higher prices than average. Pricing strategy contributes towards a company's sustainable competitive advantage (Chapter 6). However, pricing must be closely related to a firm's product policy (Chapter 7), its distribution (Chapter 9), and its promotional strategies (Chapters 10 and 11) in order to create a coherent positioning for its products.

KEY PRINCIPLES OF MARKETING

- In competitive markets, prices are influenced by the interaction of supply and demand.
- Marketing seeks to develop a unique product which is subject to less direct competitive pressure and therefore allows marketers more discretion in setting prices.
- The maximum price that a company can charge is what customers are able and willing to pay (or what a government regulator will allow it to charge).
- Price should be distinguished from costs. Costs determine the minimum price that a company will charge.

CASE STUDY

A single market—so why no single price?

The laws of supply and demand imply that a price equilibrium will be reached where the quantity of a product that buyers want to buy exactly matches the quantity that sellers want to sell. Why then should this equilibrium price differ, sometimes quite markedly, between different countries?

The price charged for the same goods varies widely among European countries. A study undertaken by the Consumers' Association in 2001 showed continuing differences in the price of cars in different EU countries, with a Ford Mondeo costing almost 50% more in Germany than in Spain. For drugs, where government intervention plays a much greater part, a study by Lehman Brothers found that the difference between the cheapest and most expensive countries was as much as 300%. Part of the reason for this variation can be found in different tax rates. For example, the rate of VAT levied on some electrical goods varies between zero in Finland and over 30% in France. Transport costs can also make a big difference to bulky goods that have to be moved to areas where local production is not possible. The variability of prices around the mean tends to be relatively low for low-volume, high-value goods (e.g. computer software) which can enter international trade relatively easily.

Regional tastes can also make a difference to prices. For example, the Dutch on average eat nine times as much yoghurt as the Irish. The higher turnover of yoghurt in Dutch supermarkets results in mass-market competition which helps to drive down prices, while it remains a relatively niche market product in Ireland. The result is that yoghurt costs one-third as much in the Netherlands as it does in Ireland. Even for broadly similar products, differences in tastes may lead to reconfiguration of a product, thereby losing economies of scale and putting upward pressure on prices. As an example, the fish fingers sold in Belgium are formulated differently from those sold in the UK. Where such product differences are noticeable, the possibilities for importing goods from a low-price market to a high-price one are made more difficult.

Travel, education, and international media channels are leading to a homogenization of tastes, but regional differences remain strong and are likely to remain so. As an example, Heinz's baked bean pizza is unlikely ever to find much favour outside the UK. Differences in climate and geography will continue to result in differences between markets in the products consumers prefer to buy, so thermal underwear will remain a niche market product in Greece, but a mass-market product in Norway.

There has been hope that use of the euro will bring about some harmonization of prices throughout Europe. The theory is that, with all prices quoted in euros, consumers will be able to make immediate price comparisons and it may be difficult for sellers to maintain price differentials. Some companies, such as Mercedes Benz, have already developed a single European price list. Such an approach may be bad news for companies that have relied on high prices in some national markets to boost their global profits. The consultant McKinsey made a study of the automotive components business and calculated that a 1% change in price could result in a 10–15% change in profits.

Is a harmonization of prices across Europe inevitably going to result from the introduction of a single European currency? Evidence from the United States suggests that price differentials may still remain. There, despite the existence of a common currency, price variation around the mean is about 12%, or half the level found in Europe in 2000. Even within the UK, the universal use of sterling has not prevented the persistence of regional price discrepancies. Here, the going rate for petrol in one town can be between 5% and 10% different from that in a town just 20 or 30 miles away. This may seem remarkable, considering the mobility of buyers and the ease of shopping around for petrol. Is there any hope of a single European market harmonizing prices when there are such discrepancies of commodity type products within a single country?

Case study review questions

1. Using an analysis of supply, demand, and equilibrium price, explain why price differences for certain goods exist between different countries in Europe.

2. Using appropriate economic analysis, explain the process by which price levels are likely to become more harmonized throughout Europe as a result of the development of the euro.

3. Identify the barriers that may prevent a common price equilibrium occurring for goods and services throughout Europe.

CHAPTER REVIEW QUESTIONS

1. Critically assess methods used by companies to reduce the effects on them of intense price competition.

2. 'Elasticity of demand is a fine theoretical concept of economists, but difficult for marketers to use in practice.' Critically assess this statement.

3. What are the main challenges facing an oligopolist when determining prices? Is the task of an oligopolistic marketer more or less difficult than that of a marketing manager in a sector dominated by small businesses?

4. Using examples, compare the advantages and disadvantages of cost-plus and marginal cost pricing.

5. Using a company of your choice, critically assess how price discrimination is practised between different groups of customers.

6. What is the role of pricing for local authority services? Illustrate your answer with reference to the police or fire services.

REFERENCES

[1] Bell, D. R., Iyer, G., and Padmanabhan, V. (2002), 'Price Competition under Stockpiling and Flexible Consumption'. *Journal of Marketing Research*, 39: 292–303.

[2] Bicknell, C. (2000), *The Amazon Story*, Wired News, July 21.

[3] Cyert, R. M. and March, J. G. (1963), *A Behavioural Theory of the Firm*. Cambridge, MA: Blackwell.

[4] *Daily Telegraph* (2002), 'High-Price Airlines Fail to Get Message'. *Daily Telegraph*, 4 November: 36.

[5] Fletcher, R. (2003), 'Urgent e-mail to Sugar: nobody believes your electronic message'. *Sunday Telegraph*, 5 January.

[6] Gourville, J., and Soman, D. (2002), 'Pricing and the Psychology of Consumption'. *Harvard Business Review*, 80(9):90–6.

[7] Streitfeld, D. (2000), 'Ads on Web Don't Click', *Washington Post*, 29 October, PA1.

[8] Sunday Times (2003), '*Mirror* Prepares to End Price War'. *Sunday Times* (Business), 9 February: 3.

[9] Sunday Times (2003), 'Price Fixers Face Jail, Fines and Disqualification in Crackdown'. *Sunday Times* (Business), 23 February: 15.

[10] Timmins, N. (2003), 'A Bid to Save Money for the Government: online auctions'. *Financial Times*, 29 January: 12.

[11] White, D. (2003), 'Mobile Pricing Riles Operators'. *Daily Telegraph*, 18 January.

SUGGESTED FURTHER READING

This chapter has provided only a very brief overview of the principles of economics as they affect pricing. For a fuller discussion, the following texts provide more detailed frameworks:

Begg, D. (2002), *Economics*, 7th edn. Maidenhead, Berks: McGraw-Hill.

Chrystal, K. A. and Lipsey, R. G.(2004), *Economics*, 10th edn. Oxford: Oxford University Press.

Griffiths, A., and Wall, S. (2001), *Applied Economics*, 9th edn. Englewood Cliffs, NJ: FT Prentice-Hall.

Mankiw, N. G. (2000), *Principles of Economics*. Thomson Learning.

For an overview of pricing strategy as practised by marketers, the following provide useful insights:

Nagle, T. and Holden, R. (2001), *The Strategy and Tactics of Pricing*. Englewood Cliffs, NJ: Prentice-Hall.

Trout, J. and Rivkin, S. (1998), 'Prices: Simple Guidelines to Get them Right'. *Journal of Business Strategy*, 19(6): 13–17.

USEFUL WEB LINKS

Visit the companion website to this book, with lots of Interesting additional material and links for each chapter:

www.oup.com/uk/booksites/busecon

EuroCommerce Press Releases

www.eurocommerce.be

Trading Standards Central
   www.tradingstandards.gov.uk/business/award.htm
UK Competition Commission
   www.mmc.gov.uk
UK Office of Fair Trading
   www.oft.gov.uk

▨ KEYWORDS

- **Auctions**
- **Bartering**
- **Cannibalization**
- **Cartel**
- **Commodity market**
- **Cost-based pricing**
- **Customer lifetime pricing**
- **Demand curve**
- **Economies of scale**
- **Elasticity of demand**
- **Equilibrium price**
- **Marginal cost pricing**
- **Market structure**
- **Monopoly**
- **Oligopoly**
- **Penetration pricing strategy**
- **Perfect competition**
- **Price bundling**
- **Price determination**
- **Price discrimination**
- **Price maker**
- **Price-skimming strategy**
- **Price taker**
- **Profit maximization**

9

Distribution

CHAPTER OBJECTIVES

Most companies would encounter administrative and logistical problems if they tried to deliver their goods and services directly to each of their end consumers. Instead, companies more often than not use intermediaries to distribute their products. The first aim of this chapter is to develop an understanding of the 'place' element of the marketing mix and the role of intermediaries in marketing channels. Approaches to designing a channel of distribution and issues in the management and control of intermediaries are discussed.

The second part of the chapter considers *how* goods are physically moved between the producer and the end consumer. It seeks to develop an understanding of how efficient and effective distribution can add to a firm's competitive advantage. The chapter reviews the objectives of physical distribution management, strategic approaches to supply chain management, and the key elements of a physical distribution system. The influence of information technology (IT) on channels of distribution will become apparent as we proceed through the chapter.

■ Introduction

This chapter discusses issues concerning what is often called the 'place' (P) of the traditional marketing mix. Decisions about channel intermediaries (or 'middlemen', to use an outdated, yet user-friendly, term) and the management of physical distribution fall under this heading. 'Placing' products involves managing the processes supporting the flow of good or services from producers to consumers. The process has sometimes been described as developing the best 'routes to market' for a firm's products.

We shall examine the distribution of services later in this chapter, but most of our attention will focus on the availability of goods. Goods must be made available in the right quantity, in the right location, and at the times when customers wish to purchase them—all at an acceptable price (and cost to the producer and/or intermediary). Achieving these concurrent aims is not easy, but is essential for an organization wishing to gain a sustainable competitive advantage. There is evidence that the design of distribution channels can explain differences in marketing and sales performance (Löning and Besson [5]).

Sometimes a manufacturer will decide to dispense with intermediaries altogether. For instance, Alan Sugar, the chairman of Amstrad, was vociferous in his criticism of computer retailers when he withdrew his products from High Street outlets. Instead, Amstrad began to sell its computers to customers direct, with no 'middleman' involved. Ask yourself what the market conditions were that prompted Sugar to take such a bold decision. Such choices are not easy for manufacturers. In the following pages we will explore the complex set of issues involved in managing distribution channels in today's fast-shifting economic environment.

What is a marketing channel?

A marketing channel has been defined as 'a system of relationships existing among businesses that participate in the process of buying and selling products and services' (Bowersox and Cooper [25]). Channel *intermediaries* are those organizations that facilitate the distribution of goods to the ultimate customer. The complex roles of intermediaries, which are explored in the following section, may include taking physical ownership of products, collecting payment, and offering after-sales service. Since these activities can involve considerable risk and responsibility, it is clear that, in attempting to ensure the availability of their goods, producers must consider the needs of channel intermediaries as well as those of the end consumers. Marketing channel management refers to the choice and control of these intermediaries, although, as we shall see, the ability of manufacturers to exert influence over intermediaries such as retailers varies considerably, especially in channels for fast-moving consumer goods (FMCGs).

In addition to deciding who should be involved in a channel of distribution, it is important for marketing managers to understand the *overall* movement, storage, and availability of goods. Later in this chapter we will look at the physical distribution processes that allow goods to flow from materials suppliers to manufacturers and on to the end customer. In taking a wider perspective that extends beyond marketing channel considerations, it is common to visualize this entire 'supply chain' as a *pipeline*. The physical flow of goods *downstream* from manufacturer to consumer is frequently closely related to issues of who is involved in the channel of distribution.

■ The distribution environment

As more and more tasks are passed on to intermediaries, a company producing goods tends to lose control and power over how they are sold. A key part of channel management therefore involves the recognition that networks of intermediaries represent social systems as well as economic ones. In other words, the careful nurturing of business and personal relationships can be as important as financial considerations. This has become particularly important in the UK, where there have been many changes in the retailing environment over the last thirty years. Consumers have become more mobile, more experimental in their behaviour, and more conscious of time pressures, and they now expect products of reasonable quality, via retailers offering variety, good customer service, and easy access. The response from the retail sector has seen a transformation in shopping: you are probably aware of the trend towards out-of-town retail sites, and the decline in the number of small independent shops. You may also be aware of how some town centre intermediaries are fighting back. Yet the growth in supermarkets' market share remains inexorable: according to the Nielsen Grocery Service (ACNielsen [36]), Asda, Co-operative, Iceland, Safeway, Sainsbury, Somerfield, and Tesco held over three-quarters of UK grocery market share by turnover in 2002. These changes have meant that it is vital for brand manufacturers to maintain good relations with their retail intermediaries in order to gain access to consumers.

■ The role of intermediaries in a value chain

The *value chain* was introduced in Chapter 2; it describes the activities involved in the manufacture, marketing, and delivery of a product or service by a firm (see Figure 9.2).

Michael Porter has argued that value can be added during the movement of goods from suppliers (of raw materials or components), through the manufacturing organization, and on to the end customer, at any of the five primary activity stages shown in Figure 9.2 (Porter [34]). Marketing channels can perform an important role in the three later stages, i.e. those of outbound logistics (e.g. order processing, storage, and transportation), marketing and sales (e.g. market research, personal selling, sales promotions), and service (e.g. repair, training, spare parts). It is rare for a producer to control all these activities itself, and therefore the management of channel intermediaries, in terms of both minimizing costs and maximizing competitive advantage, plays a vital part in boosting the value added by any marketing channel. Value chains can exist in an internet environment, even though no physical goods may be directly involved, as different companies can add value to a service (e.g. by offering choice) as it passes from producer to final consumer (Porter [19]).

In order to decide whether a firm should undertake its own distribution direct to

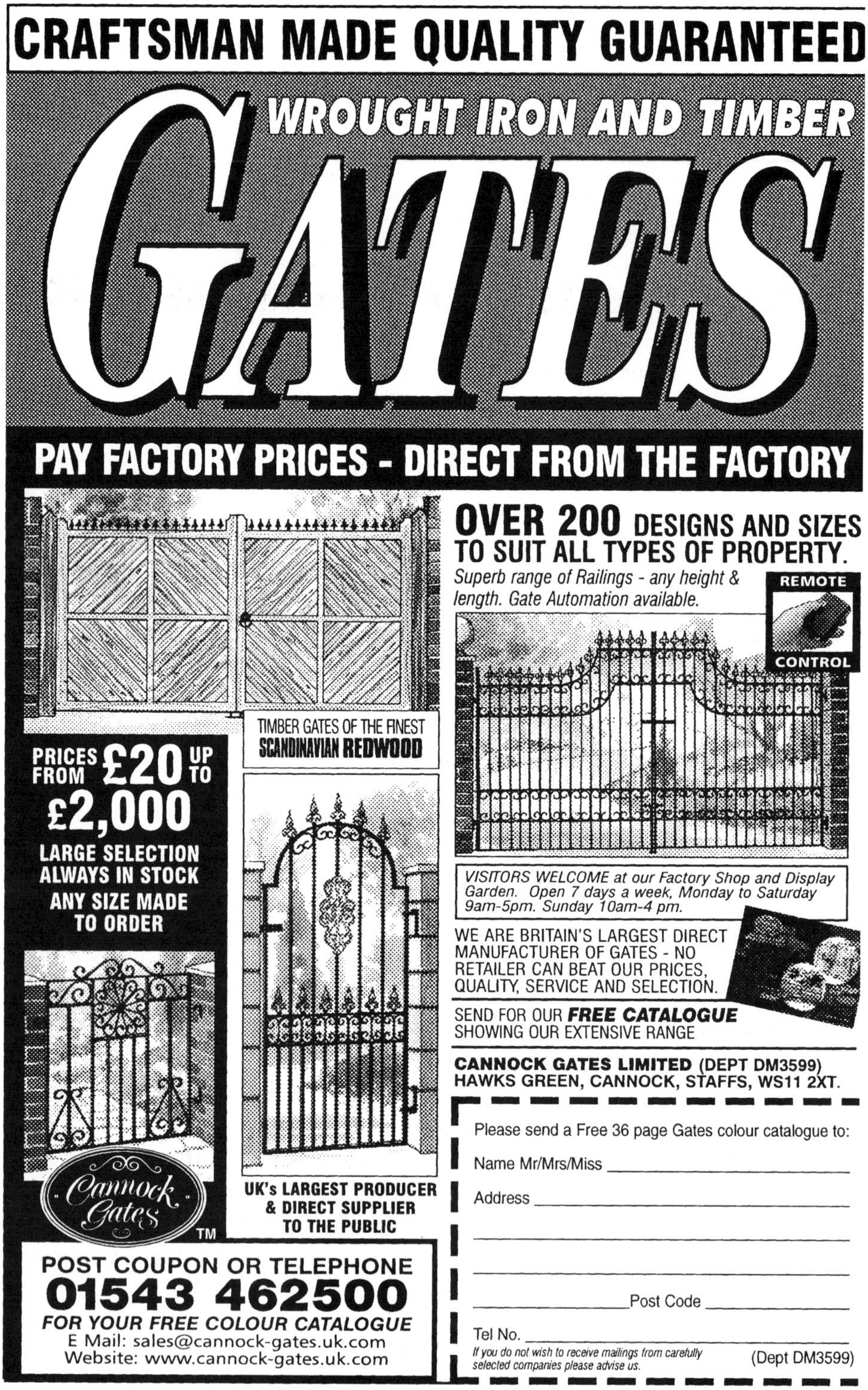

Figure 9.1 Cannock Gates serves a specialist market for gates which it feels is inadequately catered for by intermediaries. In this advertisement, which ran in the UK national press, the company stresses the price and service advantages of dealing directly with it. The fact that gates are generally made to order may make this method of distribution a sensible one, but such a strategy is less likely to succeed where the product is relatively standardized and buyers seek variety

Reproduced with permission of Cannock Gates Ltd.

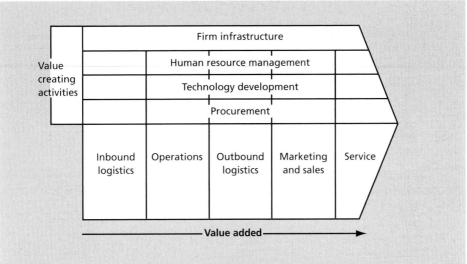

Figure 9.2 A value chain showing how value is progressively added to a product as different processes are preformed. Some of these processes may be performed more efficiently by intermediaries than by the manufacturing firm itself

consumers or whether it would be more efficient and effective to use intermediaries, it is necessary to understand the functions of these intermediaries.

Functions of intermediaries

Perhaps the most significant role of channel intermediaries is to reconcile the differing needs of manufacturers and consumers. For instance, it is typical for a fast moving consumer goods manufacturer to gain economies of scale by producing a large quantity of a limited range of goods, whereas consumers often want only a limited quantity of a wide range of goods, conveniently made available under one roof. Intermediaries can help overcome this *discrepancy of assortment* by reducing dramatically the number of contacts required between suppliers and the end customers. Distribution and selling costs are therefore reduced. This is shown in Figure 9.3. Compare the large number of channels in the first diagram with the much smaller number in the second one. By introducing one intermediary, the number of potential channels between producers and consumers has been reduced from 30 to 13.

Wholesalers can add value by breaking bulk. This might involve purchasing in large quantities from a manufacturer and then selling smaller, more manageable, volumes of stock on to retailers. *Discrepancies of quantity* are further reduced by retailers who provide consumers with individual items that suit their needs. Wholesalers can also

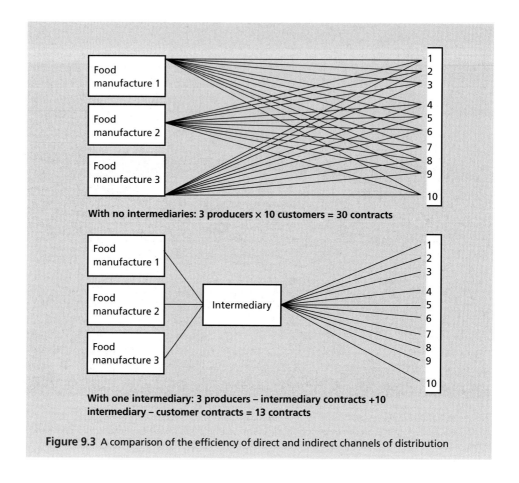

Figure 9.3 A comparison of the efficiency of direct and indirect channels of distribution

benefit small producers by combining a large number of smaller purchases from, say, agricultural smallholdings lacking the funds to deliver their goods to consumers, and then combining them into a bulk quantity for onward transport.

In many cases, intermediaries can offer superior knowledge of a target market compared with manufacturers. Retailers can therefore add value to the producer's goods by tailoring their offerings more closely to the specific requirements of consumers, for example by ensuring that goods are stocked that match the economic and life-style needs of shoppers. Think of the range of goods that Virgin Megastores offer in addition to music software.

Distributors of goods might also offer after-sales services in the form of guarantees and customer advice hotlines. If these services can be provided with a high level of expertise, then manufacturers may feel able to relinquish control of these parts of the value chain. For instance, Ahmad and Buttle [24] described the relationship between a foreign-based manufacturer of office equipment (fax machines, photocopiers, printers,

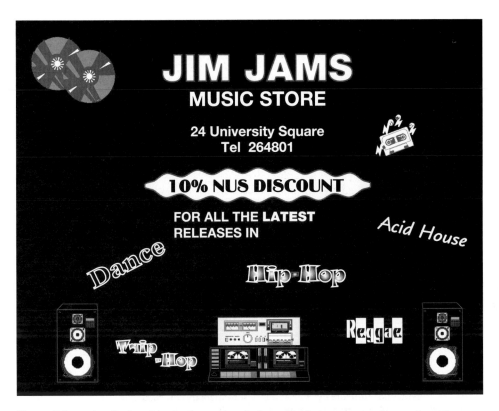

Figure 9.4 Intermediaries add value by making choice available to consumers in one place. The choice should be focused on the needs of clearly identified target markets. This music store provides an assortment of CDs which is clearly aimed at the needs of young, slightly offbeat, buyers of music

etc.) and its UK dealers. The manufacturer provides basic service training for the dealers' technical staff and allows the dealers to sell consumables such as toners. More complex repair queries, however, are handled by a head office telephone helpline for both dealers and end users.

Probably the most obvious gaps between consumers and producers in channel management are those of location and time. A *location gap* occurs owing to the geographic separation of producers and the consumers of their goods. This is rarely the case for services (see Chapter 13); nevertheless, for the vast majority of FMCGs this location gap exists, especially for companies dealing globally. A *time gap* arises between when consumers actually want to purchase products and when manufactures produce them. At the most basic level, we can see that most production facilities are at their busiest during standard working hours on Monday to Friday, while most retailers expect their daily takings to be greatest at the weekend and, increasingly, in the evenings on weekdays.

Types of intermediary

A variety of types of intermediary can participate in the value chain, or, perhaps more accurately, the supply chain. For most FMCG manufacturers, the two most commonly used intermediaries are wholesalers and retailers. These organizations are normally described as *distributors* (or 'merchants'), since they take title to products, typically building up stocks and thereby assuming risk, and then resell them. Wholesalers sell to other wholesalers and retailers; retailers sell to the ultimate consumers. Other intermediaries, such as agents and brokers, do not take title to goods. Instead, they arrange exchanges between buyers and sellers and in return receive commissions or fees. The use of agents often involves less of a financial and contractual commitment by the manufacturer and is therefore less of a risk, yet the lack of commitment to the manufacturer's goods from the agent may prove problematic.

As we mentioned earlier, retailing is an extremely high-profile area of marketing, and is worthy of further discussion. We should not, however, forget the role of *wholesalers* in marketing channels. Wholesalers are typically less obvious to us as individual consumers, but they play an important role in servicing retailers (in consumer markets) and organizational clients (in industrial or business-to-business markets). For example, it can prove prohibitively expensive for a manufacturer of industrial goods, such as a simple bolt fastening, to maintain a large sales force. In this case, access to a wide range of industrial customers may be facilitated more efficiently via a specialist wholesaler. Retailers are often serviced by wholesalers specializing in sourcing and selecting stock for a particular product line, such as greetings cards. These wholesalers can offer detailed product knowledge and in-store merchandising services to retailers, which involves maintaining their own designated selling space within a store.

Classification of retailers

Retailing represents a highly visible sector which gives us plenty of opportunities to analyse the practice of marketing theory. The consumer goods examples already discussed illustrate the significant impact that the management of marketing channels can have in the commercial environment, from the point of view of both the producers and the intermediaries themselves.

A *retailer* is simply an organization that buys products for the purpose of reselling them to consumers. Having said this, a number of different types of retailer may be identified. As the broad classifications below suggest, these store types have certain characteristics.

• **Department stores**, e.g. Debenham's. Here, we find product lines laid out into separate departments, such as ladies' and men's clothing, home furnishings, cosmetics, etc. Companies may operate as 'shops-within-shops' and pay rent as a percentage of takings to the host store.

- **Supermarkets**, e.g. Sainsbury's. These are large, self-service stores carrying a very wide range of FMCGs. They are typically located in out-of-town retail parks, although many supermarket chains have recently opened smaller city centre sites. The supermarket chains are often the first with new customer initiatives such as loyalty cards and in-store bakeries. Low prices based on large-scale efficiency are hard for smaller independent stores to match.

- **Discount sheds or 'category killers'**, e.g. Toys 'R' Us. These stores often stock bulky items such as furniture and electrical goods. The 'category killer' terminology results from the tendency of some very large specialist stores to put competing independent retailers out of business.

- **Speciality shops**, e.g. clothing (Next), music (HMV), mobile phones (Carphone Warehouse). These are typically found in central business districts of towns where prime sites are vitally important. As it is frequently only the large national chains that can afford the high rents of such sites, it might be said that many UK High Streets are now remarkably similar in the choice they offer to the shopper.

- **Convenience stores**, e.g. Spar, 7-Eleven. Geographically, and also in terms of the range of products on offer, these stores fill the gap between edge-of-town supermarkets and the 'traditional' corner shops situated close to housing estates. While independently owned convenience stores have tended to decline in number in recent years, the major UK supermarket operators have expanded into this area, as seen by Tesco's acquisition in 2002 of the T&S Stores chain and the Co-op's acquisition of Alldays convenience stores.

- **Cash and carry warehouses**, e.g. Makro. These usually offer cheaper groceries and durable goods to consumers or catering trades and small retailers.

- **Catalogue showrooms**, e.g. Argos. These stores lower their costs by maintaining only a limited display of goods, with consumers making their selection via a catalogue and collecting their purchase from a stockroom attached to the showroom site.

- **Market traders.** These remain significant outlets for many low-value products. Although they have generally declined in importance in recent years, some types of market, e.g. farmers' markets, have expanded since the late 1990s.

- **Online retailers.** Some online retailers, e.g. Amazon.com, have no physical shops that interface with the public. However, most online retailing is in fact accounted for by 'bricks and mortar' retailers. (For example, the biggest online retailer in Europe by value in 2002 was Tesco.com with sales of over £400 million.)

Within these differing types of store, we can find some interesting trends. One of the most significant changes in retailing structure has been the increased proportion of

Figure 9.5 New forms of retailing are continually emerging. One recent innovation in the UK is the outlet mall, which sells a range of brand name products at clearance prices. For shoppers, outlet malls, such as this one in Bicester, Oxfordshire, have been developed into day out attractions in their own right, attracting visitors from a wide area. For retailers and manufacturers, they provide an opportunity to sell old-season stock which would otherwise clutter their High Street outlets

trade taken by the multiple retailers (i.e. the retail chains). In the grocery sector, multiples are usually defined as retailers with over ten outlets. This change has taken place largely at the expense of independent retailers, but has also eroded the market share of the co-operatives. It is notable that, collectively, the co-operative societies represent one of the largest retailers in the country. The problem for the Co-op is that it comprises a large number of mostly autonomous societies and does not pool its buying resources into a fully integrated retailing organization. Independent retail stores are typically run by a sole trader or as a family business. Changing social trends conspire against the corner shop, which is constantly having to look for ways to differentiate itself, usually through flexible opening hours and specialist inventory. One response of independent retailers has been to form voluntary or 'symbol' groups where buying and marketing is provided centrally in return for the retailer's buying a proportion of its goods from particular wholesalers. Examples include Spar and Happy Shopper for groceries, and Unichem in the chemist sector.

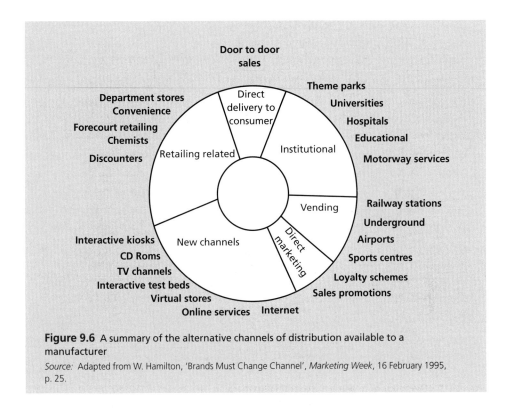

Figure 9.6 A summary of the alternative channels of distribution available to a manufacturer

Source: Adapted from W. Hamilton, 'Brands Must Change Channel', *Marketing Week*, 16 February 1995, p. 25.

Designing a channel of distribution

Manufacturers need to take a holistic view of distribution, and to adopt a 'channel vision' to maximize their opportunities to reach customers. Figure 9.6 shows the complex range of channel choices that should be considered by producers of premium branded goods. As you can see, there are many more options available than merely the traditional retail store.

Now that we are more familiar with the roles of channel intermediaries, we need to consider a producer's distribution objectives and how the selection of suitable channels might support these. *Channel objectives* should be derived from the organization's positioning strategy. The place element of the marketing mix must be consistent with the remaining marketing tools used by the marketing manager to gain a sustainable competitive advantage (see Chapter 6). This is usually achieved by considering three options:

1. **Intensive distribution**: This is generally used for FMCGs and other relatively low priced or impulse purchases. Put very simply, the more outlets are stocking your product, the greater the likelihood of its being bought. The convenience factor is often very important for these goods. An interesting development here is the increasing range of products available from petrol stations—everything from groceries

to snacks and gifts. In terms of the discrepancies of assortment and location discussed earlier, a highly intensive distribution network with wide geographical cover can prove extremely efficient. Although not a conventional 'product', look at the huge number and variety of outlets where National Lottery tickets may be bought.

2. **Exclusive distribution**: Here, distribution may be limited to a small number of intermediaries that manage to gain better margins and exclusivity. In return, the manufacturer seeks more control over how the product is marketed, and there is likely to be dedicated merchandising and sales support from the retailer. The intermediary may also agree not to stock competing lines. This is often done for expensive products with an upmarket brand image, such as Ray-Bann sunglasses or designer label clothing. Manufacturers can become upset when retailers who they see as not having the appropriate brand image attempt to stock these products or, worse, offer them at discounted prices. Witness the reaction of the perfume industry to Superdrug's stocking of fine fragrances, or Calvin Klein's protests at Tesco's carrying their underwear range.

3. **Selective distribution**: This represents a compromise between intensive and exclusive distribution. The manufacturer is looking for adequate market coverage, but still hopes to select supportive dealers. This usually occurs for 'shopping' products such as audio and video hardware.

■ Influences on channel selection

There are a number of key influences on channel selection strategies.

1. First, the expectations of the **end customer** must be addressed. This might mean taking into consideration factors such as a geographical preference to buy locally, or a tendency to feel more comfortable visiting a particular type of store (say, an independent dance-orientated music store as opposed to HMV, in order to purchase a 'house' 12 inch single), or the need for a retailer capable of offering certain after-sales services, such as washing machine repair warranties. Decisions must be made based on sound marketing research into buyer behaviour patterns (see Chapters 3 and 4). This is also true for business-to-business markets. For example, suppliers of electronic components need to determine whether business customers prefer to deal with the company's direct sales force (often the case for larger organizational clients with expert purchasing departments) or with a specialist distributor (typically used by smaller clients without this in-house expertise). In international markets, it may be essential to use an agent with an intimate knowledge of the cultural nuances of doing business in target countries (see Chapter 14).

2. **Producer-related factors** include a number of issues in addition to the distribution levels sought. An important constraint is the resources that are available to the manufacturer to bring the product to market. Some companies lack the finances to recruit and reward a sales force and so will use a wholesaler instead. This is often the case for companies making a very narrow range of products, unless the product is particularly expensive, such as a mainframe computer system. Also critical is what the manufacturer believes to be its core competence. If, for instance, this is the design and production of innovative goods, then the distribution of these goods may well be better left to a specialist channel intermediary. Another area of much contention is the desired level of channel control sought by the manufacturer. This will be discussed later in this chapter.

3. **Product attributes** can be important. Clearly, fresh produce that is highly perishable requires fairly short channels. Northern Foods, a manufacturer of chilled meals for Marks & Spencer, boasts that it takes just 24 hours from the time a fresh egg arrives at the factory to its appearance in a custard tart on the shelves of an M&S store anywhere in the country. This has implications for the storage and transportation facilities available in the channel. Heavy or large goods are frequently not suited to inner-city retail locations where consumers cannot easily drive to pick up their purchases: instead, they are often sold at out-of-town sites or are not carried by retailers at all and only sold to order via direct distribution. Some products may be so complex that personal contact between producer and buyer is essential. This can be the case for the installation of highly technical machinery, where the later stages of Porter's value chain (see above) are performed entirely by the producer, without the use of any intermediary.

4. Finally, the activities of the *competition* must be considered. If competitors have exclusive deals with certain intermediaries, then the support of other channel members with similar marketplace penetration may be sought. For instance, when Raleigh found Toys 'R' Us to be tied to an arrangement with an American supplier for young children's bicycles, it focused on alternative retailers such as John Lewis and Woolworth's for the successful launch of its 'Max 16' model. For an FMCG manufacturer, it may be crucial that a firm's product appears on the shelves of the Big Five UK supermarkets, especially if the leading competitor's brand is already there. Sometimes, of course, a brand's most significant competitor is the 'own label' product of the supermarket itself! When this happens, it can be very difficult to gain retailer support, as shown by the battles of Coca Cola to gain what it saw as adequate display space in Sainsbury's. A solution may be for the manufacturer to target convenience stores instead, or to set up alternative distribution channels such as company-owned chilled vending machines. Another solution is to set up a vertically integrated channel or a franchised operation, such as those run by many car manufacturers. These approaches will be discussed later in this chapter.

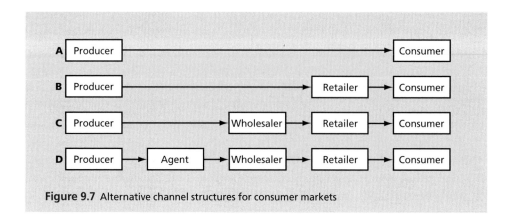

Figure 9.7 Alternative channel structures for consumer markets

Channel alternatives

Figure 9.7 shows some alternative *consumer* channels. Channel A represents a direct producer-to-consumer channel. This may involve the techniques of direct marketing or of a door-to-door sales force (e.g. Avon Cosmetics) as discussed earlier. This type of channel might include consumers who pick their own fruit from farmers' fields. Channel B represents the producer–retailer–consumer route. This is typically used by large retailers such as Sainsbury's, who have the buying power to order large quantities of goods direct from manufacturers with no need of a further middleman. The addition of the wholesaler in Channel C is more commonly used by smaller retailers with limited order quantities and, from the producer's perspective, by manufacturers of convenience goods, such as cigarettes, which need intensive distribution. The even longer structure of Channel D, via the inclusion of agents, is often used by producers entering foreign markets, where a local agent's expertise may be essential to overcome trade barriers (see Chapter 14).

A further variation in channel design occurs where one company enters into a joint distribution agreement with another company to distribute each other's products. Many mergers have occurred where two companies have sought to cross-sell their products to each other's customers. The main rationale behind the merger of the AOL and Time-Warner companies was to give Time Warner distribution access through AOL's internet service, while giving AOL substantial content for its service (Grimes [7]).

Figure 9.8 shows alternative channels used in order to reach *industrial* (business-to-business) customers. In general, these channels are shorter than those for consumer goods.

The shortest structure, that of Channel E, represents the direct manufacturer-to-customer course. This is a viable alternative for many high-value industrial products, as customer numbers here are fewer and often less geographically widespread than for

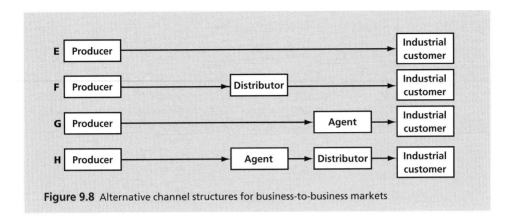

Figure 9.8 Alternative channel structures for business-to-business markets

consumer markets. Channels for large, expensive, and highly technical products such as railway engines, the development of which may require the solving of considerable mechanical problems, frequently follow this pattern.

Channel F represents the manufacturer–industrial distributor–customer route. It is used for more frequently purchased, less expensive products that are required by a wider range of industrial customers, for example tools used by garage repair workshops. The use of an agent, as in Channel G, can occur when a manufacturer chooses not to set up its own dedicated sales force, and has therefore to 'outsource' the agent's marketing and selling services. This can be a relatively quick option, but, as we have noted previously, the support offered by agents may be less than that provided by a title-taking distributor. Finally, the lengthier structure of Channel H may arise when it is found that organizational buyers in a particular market prefer to use nearby distributors. This can happen when customers need to be resupplied frequently, for instance with paper used by office photocopiers.

Multiple channels

You should be aware that some producers in both consumer and business-to-business markets use a variety of channels to distribute their goods. Think of the many different places you can purchase a can of Coca Cola, for instance.

Also, of course, some manufacturers, such as those in the personal computer sector, sell to both consumers and organizations. There is rarely one simple solution to the decision concerning which channel type should be selected by a company. Indeed, bearing in mind the power of some retailers, the problem for producers often comes down to: which channel intermediary will select *us*? This complexity is explored further in the following section.

Selecting specific intermediaries

Once a decision has been made regarding the type of channel or channels to use, it is necessary to choose individual organizations with which to work. The selection of intermediaries can have a major impact on what happens afterwards, for example the success or failure of a product launch. Ennis [23] offers a number of *criteria* that can be used to assess the relative merits of potential channel participants:

- the firm's financial position;
- depth and width of product lines carried;
- whether competitive lines are carried;
- evidence of marketing, sales, and promotional ability;
- approach to order processing and order fulfilment;
- evidence of investment in new technologies;
- reputation within industry;
- willingness to share data.

Of course, this list is by no means exhaustive. For instance, we might add market coverage, local market knowledge, and service capability. Also, the relative importance of each criterion should be considered in relation to the customer demands of the particular industry sector. Clearly, the more subjective elements in the list will be harder to evaluate.

The problem can arise of *reverse selection* in a channel of distribution. An example would be the design of an exotic ready-prepared meal recipe by a supermarket such as Safeway, which would then approach different specialist meal manufacturers for their ability to mass-produce the products to the supermarket's specification. The flexibility of such manufacturers as S&A Foods in providing Asian-style chilled meals to order, as well as in developing their own recipes, has resulted in the growth of a number of large food manufacturers whose products are sold under supermarkets' own labels, with customers completely unfamiliar with the identity of the manufacturer (e.g. Northern Foods and Samworth Brothers).

Channel conflict

If power is used in a manner believed to be unfair by one or more channel members, then conflict may arise. Conflict need not necessarily be destructive, since it can encourage managers to question the *status quo* and find ways of improving their distribution systems. Sometimes, however, strategies employed by firms can create unstable, adversarial relationships between producers and intermediaries. Magrath and Hardy [29] identified the following such behaviours:

- **Bypassing channels**: skipping established intermediaries and selling direct to the customer

- **Over-saturation**: using too many distributors within a given geographical area

- **Too many links** in the supply chain: resulting in small intermediaries having to buy from bigger dealers, who can sometimes be viewed as no better than themselves

- **New channels**: developing innovative means of distribution that pose a threat to established channels

- **Cost-cutters**: using 'discount' intermediaries alongside established dealers, thus damaging the brand image of the goods concerned

- **Inconsistency**: appearing arbitrarily to treat some intermediaries more favourably than others, for example through reward power

In recent years, power in UK distribution channels has tended to pass to a small number of dominant retailers and away from manufacturers. There is plenty of evidence of this. Following the Barclays brothers' acquisition of the Littlewoods retail chain from the Moores family in 2002, the 189-shop chain wrote to its suppliers informing them of the outcome of an 'initial trading review' which demanded a 2% price cut from all suppliers to the Littlewoods retail chain, or the loss of all future orders (Fletcher [18]). Similarly, the new owner of the Arcadia fashion chain imposed a retrospective 1.25% price cut on suppliers to the High Street group that owns Top Shop and Dorothy Perkins. With an estimated £60 million worth of outstanding invoices, the power of the retailer to make a unilateral decision and to apply the discount retrospectively netted it a 'windfall' in the region of £8 million (Fletcher [17]).

It is worth noting, of course, that some producer strategies that could be classified as contributing to conflict might just as easily be seen as legitimate attempts to fight back against growing retailer power. An example was the formation of the Consumer Needs Consortium, a marketing alliance between Unilever, Cadbury-Schweppes, Bass, and Kimberly-Clark aimed at building databases of mutual customers who can then be targeted via direct marketing initiatives, thus bypassing intermediaries.

When conflicts affecting the smooth flow of goods through the channel do arise, various methods can be used to rebuild effective relationships. From the intermediary's perspective, Narus and Anderson [31] suggest that distributors should consider the following.

- **Reach a consensus with manufacturers** on the role of intermediaries in the channel, with a view to achieving the overall channel objective of minimizing the total cost and maximizing the total value to the end customer. This may involve a recognition that, in order to accommodate developments in the marketplace (such as changes in consumer shopping habits), compromises in channel practices may be needed to maintain ultimate customer loyalty to both the product and the outlet concerned—see the discussions on Efficient Consumer Response (ECR) later.

- **Appreciate manufacturing requirements**: this can be achieved by intermediaries' visiting production plants and observing procedures for ordering and quality control. The sharing of information on likely future sales patterns can also help the manufacturer plan production schedules more accurately.

- **Fulfil commitments**: manufacturers need reassurance that intermediaries will be proficient in areas such as market penetration ability, prompt payment of bills, and product knowledge. Distributors should proactively examine their own performance levels and seek improvements where possible.

■ Channel competition

In addition to the conflict between members at different levels in the channel, we should be aware of other types of competition in marketing channels. Apart from the *vertical* competition that can develop between producer and intermediary, Palamountain [32] identified three further sorts of rivalry.

1. **Horizontal competition.** This is competition between intermediaries of the same type. The rivalries between different retailers, such as HMV and Virgin or between Body Shop and Bath & Bodyworks, serve as good examples. As discussed above, each chain seeks to develop marketing strategies that differentiates itself from its competitors.

2. **Intertype competition.** This refers to competition at the same level in the channel, but between intermediaries of different types. For example, a regulatory change in the UK in 1994 allowed for greater availability of magazines from grocery supermarkets, as a result of which the more specialist confectionists, tobacconists, and newsagents (CTN) have been challenged.

3. **Channel system competition.** This is where an entire channel is competing with a different, parallel channel. Examples are commonly found where the producer of an item itself owns the outlets of distribution for that item. This occurs not only for goods such as petrol, where oil companies such as BP control many of their petrol stations, and are in competition with supermarket garage forecourts, but also for services such as package holidays, where Thomson holidays are bookable through their own Lunn Poly outlets and also through the chain of Going Places travel agents (owned by the MyTravel group). The fact that Thomson holidays are also bookable through independent agents only makes the network of channels more complicated for the confused consumer seeking unbiased advice!

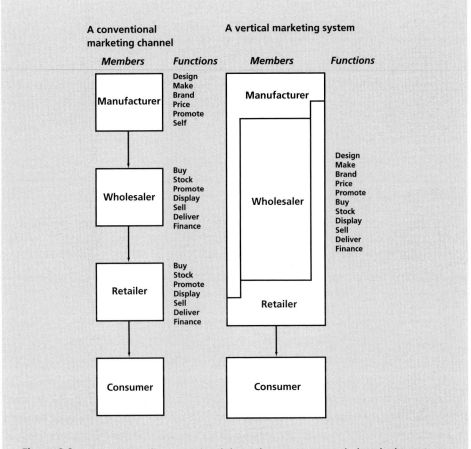

Figure 9.9 A comparison of a conventional channel structure *v.* a vertical marketing system

Source: adapted from David J. Kollat, Roger D. Blackwell, and James F. Robeson, *Strategic Marketing*, New York: Rinehart & Winston, 1972, p. 321.

Vertical marketing systems

The ownership or integration by an organization of other participants at different levels in the channel is often referred to as a vertical marketing system. These systems are seen as having several advantages over conventional marketing channels (see Figure 9.9):

- they reduce channel costs by eliminating duplication of functions;
- they minimize conflict among channel members;
- they maximize the experience and expertise of members.

There are three general types of vertical marketing system.

1. The first of these, the *corporate* system, is actually increasingly rare, since many organizations either cannot afford to, or do not wish to, invest in fixed assets or skills where they do not have a competitive advantage. An example that remains is the Dutch-based retailer C&A, which owns its own manufacturing plants and wholesale operations.

2. *Administered* systems arise when participants are financially independent but are effectively controlled by the most powerful channel member. The highly co-ordinated purchasing of a large (although declining) proportion of its goods from UK manufacturers by Marks & Spencer illustrates backward integration, whereas the management of car dealers' sale activities by BMW represents forward integration.

3. In *contractual* systems channel members' rights and obligations are defined by legal agreements. These can include collaborative agreements such as the voluntary chains discussed earlier in this chapter, where separate firms share resources and agree to joint purchasing initiatives and franchise arrangements.

Franchising systems

In a franchise system, a seller (the franchisor) gives an intermediary (the franchisee) specific services (such as marketing support) and rights to market the seller's product or service within an agreed territory. In return, the franchisee agrees to follow certain procedures and not to buy from unauthorized sellers. The franchisor also typically offers assistance in management and staff training, merchandising, and operating systems. This support is usually provided in exchange for a specified fee or royalties on sales from the franchisee. Examples of businesses that are predominantly franchised include McDonald's, Prontaprint, Benetton and Tie Rack.

Franchising offers both manufacturer/retailers and entrepreneurial intermediaries the opportunity to undertake relatively rapid market development at relatively low risk. Consequently, for many internationally operating companies franchising has become the cornerstone of their global expansion activity. Having said this, problems in controlling standards among individual franchisees can occur. This, for example, is claimed to have contributed to the failure of some of the Body Shop's outlets in France. When this takes place, the image of the franchisor can be seriously dented. From a different perspective, Benetton's franchisees in Germany were outraged at the company's controversial advertising campaigns, which they blamed for poor sales. Bitter disputes can develop where franchisor and franchisee differ in their assessment of the costs and benefits associated with their involvement in a franchise. In the UK, Esso became embroiled in a dispute over ambiguous wording of an agreement between Esso and its franchise-holders that did not make clear whether Esso or the individual franchisees should foot the bill for the gifts offered as part of Esso's 'Tiger Tokens' promotion (Lewis [9]).

Figure 9.10 Printing used to demand a high level of craft skills and specialized facilities to house printing presses. However, the development of low-cost offset litho and photocopying machines lowered the entry barriers to printing. At the same time, the structure of business was changing, with companies outsourcing much of their printing, and with a growing volume of documents needing to be copied. These conditions led to the rapid development of the fast printing sector. A number of profitable chains have grown rapidly through franchising. Prontaprint is typical in selling a franchise to people who can demonstrate commitment to high standards and profitable growth. For a small investor looking for a business of her own, a Prontaprint franchise offers the security of a brand name that customers have come to trust

Source: Reproduced with the permission of Prontaprint.

Global retailing

Chapter 14 will explore the importance of global marketing in greater detail, but we will now briefly discuss the growth of channel intermediaries across national boundaries. Pelligrini [33] suggests that retail companies have three options for growth: vertical integration, retail diversification, and internationalization. Retailing has often been slow to expand globally because of the high level of investment needed to set up in another country, especially when this involves risky acquisitions, for example the failure of Marks & Spencer to turn around the fortunes of the Brooks Brothers menswear chain in the USA. Nevertheless, because of the limited possibilities for growth in national markets, many of the more dynamic retailers have increasingly internationalized their operations.

Muniz-Martinez [30] offers an analysis of the expansion into North and South America of leading European retailers. He points out that the USA and Canada are the favoured targets, based on their cultural affinity with northern Europe, from where most leading European-based retailers originate. Moreover, the potential for profit in these relatively prosperous countries is great. Some retailers, such as Virgin Megastore and the Body Shop, have used specialization in either product sector or customer segments in order to expand. Other retailers, e.g. Carrefour, have exported a commercial concept such as the hypermarket, and adapted it to local conditions by altering the extensive ranges of food on offer to suit local consumption. This French company has also collaborated with local firms such as Gigante in Mexico. IKEA, on the other hand, remains centrally controlled, owning virtually all its stores, and deliberately tries to retain its unique 'Swedishness' without changing its product range or retailing approach to local tastes.

The internet and channel design

The trend towards direct delivery from producer to consumer has been speeded up by the growth of internet access. As a communication medium with customers, e-mail (and SMS text messaging) extends the profiling and interactivity features of direct mail. An accurate database of customers' preferences is essential if e-mail messages are not to be discarded as junk messages. The prospect of *m-mail* to individuals' mobile phones raises the prospect of a huge amount of low-cost messages being targeted at individuals, and senders of messages must ensure that their messages stand out from competitors and have immediate relevance to the recipient. Just as importantly for an organization, e-mail allows rapid internal communication between employees and members of its value chain who may be geographically quite dispersed. E-mail speeds up the process of gathering, sharing, and disseminating information about the market.

In the early stages of internet development, the technology was used to provide a modest incremental improvement on what was previously possible using voice telephone or postal services. With increasing sophistication, possibilities arise for the internet to provide additional benefits which are not possible using more traditional distribution methods. Personalization of websites can facilitate the reordering of routinely purchased services (e.g. an airline site which opens with previously recorded preferences). Many websites are now linked with other complementary value-adding services (e.g. an airline's website which has links to national and regional tourist board websites).

Some retailers have closed a number of branches or reduced their sales force and instead offered customers access to their product range via a website. Several UK suppliers of books, music, computer games, and flowers have the logistical support to develop their business on the internet. (The CD marketplace is explored in more detail in the case study at the end of this chapter.) In the longer term, it is possible that FMCG suppliers may use the internet to regain some of their lost power in channel relationships.

Figure 9.11 The internet has opened up a powerful distribution channel by which a company can communicate directly with each of its customers, providing rapid, low-cost distribution which need not involve intermediaries. The budget airline EasyJet has embraced the internet and claims to be the 'Web's favourite airline', with over three-quarters of the airline's customers using the company's website for booking their tickets. The company is proud of the fact that it does not pay commission to intermediaries, and can pass on these savings in the form of lower ticket prices

Source: Reproduced with permission of EasyJet Airline Company Ltd

Car manufacturers are recognizing the impact of the internet on their traditional dealership-based channels of distribution, with evidence that the internet is increasingly being used for selecting, negotiating, and ordering new cars. To some car buyers, the dealership has become little more than a delivery point (Morton [1]).

However, while the internet may facilitate direct communication between producers and end consumers, the chances of dialogue actually taking place are lessened by the proliferation of content on the internet, which presents a bewildering array of choice to consumers. The response has been the development of a new breed of information intermediary, or 'informediary'. This type of channel intermediary gathers information about customers and products and uses it on customers' behalf to get a better deal of some sort from a supplier. They might screen commercial messages for customers (like a specialized mailing preference service—see Chapter 11); represent their interests (say, golfing and gardening) to marketers that want access to information about them; and then find vendors that can deliver the best product at the cheapest price (perhaps in the form of a 10% discount offered by the supplier in return for access to the informediary's client list). If this happens, the informediaries can become powerful distribution channels in their own right, effectively 'selling' customers to marketers. The new generation of informediaries has effectively become a new form of value adding member in a virtual value chain (Porter [19]). Within the travel and financial services sectors, the attempts of airlines and insurance companies to create direct dialogue with customers have been overshadowed by the development of powerful informediaries such as Lastminute.com, expedia.com, and e-sure.

The advance of the internet as a distribution channel has been affected by the speed with which consumer and commercial buyers have adopted the medium. There is considerable evidence that young people have been more ready to adopt the medium than older people. In a study using a technology acceptance model, it was found that consumers' perceived ease of use was affected by a range of factors, including opinion leadership, impulsiveness, shopping orientation, and perceived web security (O'Cass and Fenech [11]).

Of course, it is not just in business-to-consumer markets that the internet is reshaping distribution channels. In business-to-business channels, the internet (and intranets and extranets) have replaced previous EDI systems for handling transactions between businesses. Government and not-for profit organizations have also incorporated the internet into their distribution channels, both for procuring purchases (Timmins [8]) and for making services available to users. (For example, NHS Direct makes medical advice available to the public through call centres and the internet.)

Despite the enormous potential of the internet to simplify communication between a company and its customers without recourse to intermediaries, problems of final delivery remain where tangible goods are involved (see Yrjölä [13]). There are also many high-involvement goods where buyers feel more comfortable being able to see and feel

---

MARKETING and the INTERNET

Low-cost cash through the internet

Banks have been at the forefront of efforts to distribute their services directly to their customers' PCs. The big four UK banks run a large and expensive branch network and have faced increased competition from new low-cost internet, telephone, and postal banking services. Many non-bank competitors have appeared, especially supermarkets, which have developed banking to complement their customer relationship building activities. A study by Ernst and Young in 1997 indicated some of the reasons why banks are keen to reduce their dependence on a large branch network. The study found that each transaction in a bank branch cost an average of 64p; by contrast, the average cost of transactions by telephone was 32p, through an ATM 27p, and through the banks' internet services just 0.5p.

But how do banks exploit the opportunities made available by the internet? Closing local branches is never popular with customers and may lead to the defection of profitable ones to competitors. Some banks have tried differential pricing by charging a fee for users of counter facilities. When Abbey National began charging its 'Instant Access' account customers £1 each time they cashed a cheque within a branch, there was understandable bad publicity. The company was clearly trying to encourage its customers to use its ATM and telephone banking facilities. But how large is the market segment that is prepared to sacrifice personal face-to-face contact for cheaper and more efficient telephone and internet-based methods of distribution? Will this eventually become the norm?

the goods before they commit to a purchase. The failed internet clothes retailer boo.com encountered the reality that many people would probably find it much easier and reassuring to try on clothes in a shop than rely on a computer image, thereby ensuring a continuing role for traditional High Street retailers (although 'bricks and clicks' retailers such as Next have quietly developed a substantial level of clothes sales via their website).

■ Physical distribution management

A channel of distribution must support the task of moving goods from the producer to the consumer so that the right goods are available to the right people in the right place at the right time. This must be done as cheaply as possible. In other words, the distribution must be both *efficient* and *effective*. Physical distribution also concerns most services organizations that have to move supporting goods (e.g. supplies of brochures for travel agents; supplies of burgers for a fast food chain). In western countries we have often come to take for granted that our favourite products will be on the shelves in a shop when we visit. Business buyers have come to depend on the prompt delivery of inputs to their production process. But when physical distribution goes wrong, customers will soon notice, and the financial effects on a company whose distribution has failed can be harsh, even threatening the survival of the company. During 2001, the children's retailer Mothercare opened a new UK distribution centre at Daventry. The aim was to increase the efficiency and effectiveness of deliveries to the company's nationwide store network. In reality, poor IT systems caused stock to be lost within its system instead of getting 'hot' products to the shelves where customers were eager to buy them. By the time they had arrived, market preferences had changed and goods had to be sold at discounted 'clearance' prices. As a direct result of its distribution problems, the company was forced to issue a series of profit warnings and its share price slumped, threatening the continued independent existence of the company (Keers [10]).

In the next few pages, as well as examining the movement of goods between producers and these downstream channel participants, we shall also be considering the flow of raw materials and components from suppliers that are *upstream* from the manufacturer. Furthermore, we shall explore the vital role played by the flow of information between supply chain members, as shown in Figure 9.12. In the figure, second-tier suppliers usually provide the raw materials (e.g. plastic resin) for first-tier suppliers to convert to component parts (e.g. steering wheels), which are then manufactured into the end product (e.g. cars) by the producer. Note that not all supply chains will contain both tiers of suppliers: we shall discuss more examples of supply chains later.

Let us begin with some definitions, and attempt to show how the terms 'physical distribution' and 'logistics' differ. *Physical distribution* refers to the movement of finished goods outward from the end of the manufacturer's assembly line to the customer, frequently via intermediaries. Functions under this heading can include warehousing,

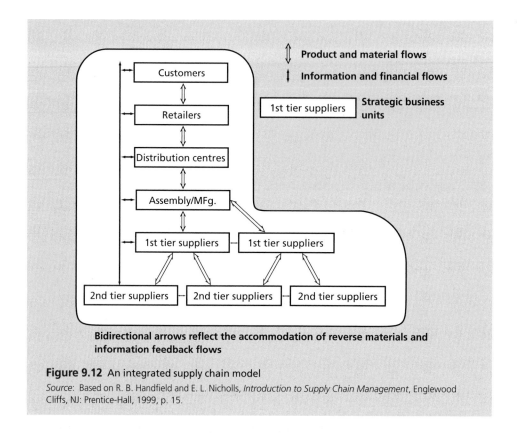

Bidirectional arrows reflect the accommodation of reverse materials and information feedback flows

Figure 9.12 An integrated supply chain model

Source: Based on R. B. Handfield and E. L. Nicholls, *Introduction to Supply Chain Management*, Englewood Cliffs, NJ: Prentice-Hall, 1999, p. 15.

transportation (often undertaken by third-party specialists), customer service, and administration. *Logistics* describes the entire process of materials and products moving into, through, and out of a firm. The US Council of Logistics Management (CLM) has defined logistics as 'the process of planning, implementing and controlling the efficient, effective flow and storage of goods, services and related information from the point of origin to the point of consumption for the purposes of conforming to customer requirements'. Physical distribution may therefore be seen as 'outbound logistics', while 'inbound logistics' covers the movement of materials from suppliers and is closely linked to the manufacturer's purchasing or procurement function. 'Materials and inventory management' typically describes the movement and stockholding of goods within a firm.

The notion of *supply chain management* is often viewed as somewhat larger than logistics, linking organizations more directly with the manufacturer's total communications network or 'supply pipeline'. The pipeline metaphor, as outlined above, helps us to picture the flows of goods and information up and down the supply chain. The 'supply chain' metaphor itself serves as a reminder that the organizations participating in the delivery of added value to the end customer must work together as 'links' in a chain of interdependent activities.

It should also be remembered that distribution is often a two-way process. Most companies have to deal with customers' returns, and a facility to move these backwards through the distribution chain should be incorporated (Nairn [6]). Increasingly, legislation is requiring companies to recycle used products, requiring collection and return services.

Physical distribution objectives

As with all elements of the marketing mix, the ultimate objective of a firm's physical distribution management is to develop a sustainable competitive advantage. However, this is becoming increasingly difficult as customers, instead of just seeking a better designed product, seek value in a much wider sense. A critical component of such customer value is *service*, and a key part of service value is *availability*. In other words, there is no value in a product until it is in the hands of the customer.

Customers often only have a *preference* for a particular brand, rather than strong brand loyalty; so when their preferred brand is not available, many customers will quite readily choose an acceptable substitute. This is equally true in both industrial and consumer markets. The choice of suppliers by a just-in-time (JIT—see later) manufacturer will be hugely influenced by delivery reliability, and not just product quality.

Companies that are responsive to customers' needs must also focus on *time* as a source of competitive advantage. Basically, the less time it takes for a company—or indeed an entire supply chain—to do things, the more flexible it can be in response to changes in the marketplace. Benetton, for instance, is able to respond to the popularity of certain colours in its ranges extremely quickly, thanks to its advanced logistics systems. Information flows from points of sale, flexible manufacturing, and global distribution all mean that Benetton's *lead times* (i.e. the time taken from receipt of a customer's order to final delivery) are shorter than clothing industry averages.

In addition to lead times, manufacturers should consider the impact of shorter life-cycles on new product development (see Chapter 7). If innovation is a company's key source of competitive advantage, then the time taken to get a new product to market will be crucial to prevent obsolescence.

Customer service in logistics

What do we mean by 'customer service'? In reality, this is a complex concept comprising a number of factors, and is an area about which academic researchers have reached different conclusions. Figure 9.13 shows schematically how logistics can contribute to customer service. From the manufacturer's perspective, customer service impacts not only on the end user but also on intermediate customers. Marketing has traditionally focused on the consumer by seeking to promote brand values and to generate a demand 'pull' within the market for a company's products. We now recognize that this by itself is often not sufficient. Because of shifts in channel power towards the retailer, it has become vital to develop the strongest possible relations with such intermediaries. In other words, marketers must design their distribution systems around the needs of both *trade* and *consumer* buyers. The benefits of both of these groups can be enhanced or diminished by the efficiency of the supplier's logistics system (see Figure 9.13). It is only when the three components are working optimally together that marketing effectiveness is maximized.

In a physical distribution context, customer service can be examined under three headings:

1. Pre-transaction elements

2. Transaction elements

3. Post-transaction elements

The evaluation of *pre-transaction* elements of customer service include companies asking themselves such questions as:

- Is our service policy communicated internally and externally?

- Are we easy to contact and to do business with?

- Is there a service management organizational structure in place?

- Can we adapt our service delivery systems to meet particular customer needs?

Transaction element issues include:

- What is the time from order to delivery?

- What is the reliability of this lead time?

- What percentage of demand can be met from stock?

- What proportion of orders are completely filled?

- How long does it take us to provide order status information?

Post-transaction element considerations include:

- What is the availability of spare parts?

- What is the call-out time for our engineers?

- Can we maintain the warranty to customers' expectations?

- How promptly do we deal with customers' complaints?

It is fair to say that some of these elements will be more important than others within different marketplaces. The key issue for marketers to grasp is that it is essential first to

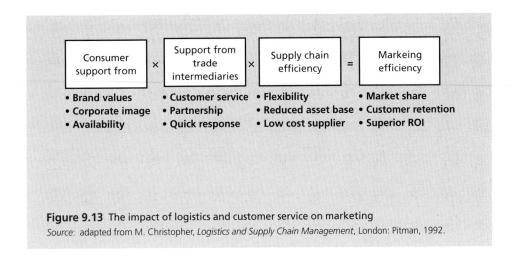

Figure 9.13 The impact of logistics and customer service on marketing

Source: adapted from M. Christopher, *Logistics and Supply Chain Management*, London: Pitman, 1992.

understand the differing requirements of different market segments (see Chapter 5), and then to tailor the company's service offering accordingly. For some customers, frequent deliveries of small quantities may be far more desirable than occasional deliveries of large volumes.

The primary objective of any logistics customer service strategy must be to reduce the customer's cost of ownership; that is, it must make the transaction more 'profitable' for the customer. For example, a delivery twice a week instead of once reduces the customer's average inventory by half and therefore cuts the cost of carrying that inventory. Similarly, reliable on-time delivery means that a retailer can reduce the need to carry safety stock, again resulting in lower stockholding costs.

Marketing logistics

In concluding our discussion of physical distribution objectives, we should quote Doyle [27], who noted that modern managers now use the concept of 'marketing logistics'. This starts by asking how customers want to receive the product (see Chapter 3 on buyer behaviour) and then works backwards to the design of the materials, final goods, inventory, transportation, warehousing, and customer service in order to meet customers' expectations. The amount of information needed by managers to make appropriate marketing logistics decisions is clearly vast. Fortunately, it is becoming increasingly available, thanks to advances in technology, and we shall discuss some of these advances in more detail at the end of this chapter.

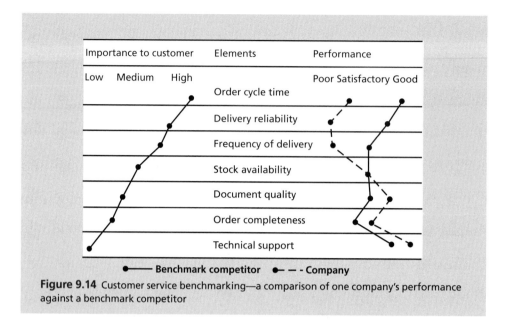

Figure 9.14 Customer service benchmarking—a comparison of one company's performance against a benchmark competitor

Identification of segments by service requirements

The marketing logistics manager first needs to determine the dimensions of service that customers most value, for example speed, reliability, or availability. Some form of marketing research is likely to be needed here (see Chapter 4). It is probable that the market will not be homogeneous: some market segments may be willing to pay high prices to obtain premium service, while others may attach greatest importance to low prices and be willing to accept minimum service levels. In attempting to meet buyers' requirements, managers must, of course, also consider cost/service trade-offs and the logistics standards set by the competition. Looking at the company's performance in relation to its main competitors is known as *benchmarking*, and allows us to identify areas for improvement. An example of a benchmarking study is shown in Figure 9.14. Which service elements do you think should be addressed by the company concerned?

Once target service levels have been identified (e.g. to deliver 95% of orders within two days; to ensure 98% availability in selected stockists of product X), the company must design a physical distribution system which can deliver them at minimum cost. The key issues for marketing logistics managers to consider include:

- How can we speed up communications and order processing?
- Where should we produce goods and store them?
- How much stock should be held?
- How can we best handle transportation?

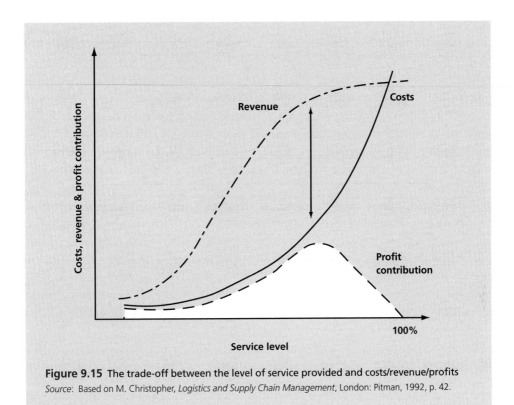

Figure 9.15 The trade-off between the level of service provided and costs/revenue/profits

Source: Based on M. Christopher, *Logistics and Supply Chain Management*, London: Pitman, 1992, p. 42.

Cost/service trade-offs

Customers will vary in the volumes of different products they purchase, but the *cost to service* ratio for these customers may also vary considerably. The Pareto Law, or '80/20 rule', will often be found to hold: roughly speaking, some 80% of a company's profits will come from only about 20% of its customers. We need to recognize that there are costs as well as benefits in providing customer service, and therefore the appropriate level of service will need to vary from customer to customer. While companies want to attract and retain customers by offering superior service to that provided by competitors, there comes a point when diminishing returns set in. For example, a chemicals supplier might continually have to keep huge stocks of a particular product because of the JIT demands of a key customer—say, an oil company. Eventually the cost of holding that inventory (perhaps in terms of storage space, or insurance bills) may force the supplier to reconsider the service levels it offers to the customer. The supplier may attempt to compromise on promises for 'next day' delivery, for example. Figure 9.15 shows the typical nature of the cost–benefit trade-offs in service-level decisions.

In Figure 9.15 Christopher [26] explains that the shape of the revenue curve is dictated by customers' response to the service level offered. The slope is initially fairly flat, since in many markets there will be a minimum threshold of acceptable service which most competitors will be providing, for example delivery within seven days. Once the threshold is passed, increasing returns to service improvements (say, getting delivery times down to five, then three, days and so on) should be achieved as customers place more orders with the company. At the top, the curve flattens out again when additional expenditure on service does not pay back. Christopher calls this 'service overkill'. The cost curve is usually a steeply rising curve, as shown, because of the need to keep high levels of inventory. By investing in IT to improve the flow of information about customer requirements, a company might, however, be able to push this curve to the right, thereby boosting overall profitability at all levels of service.

In setting physical distribution objectives, it is important for managers to understand the *total cost* of attempting to meet a specified service level. When assessing alternative approaches, the costs of some functions will increase, others will decrease, and still others may remain unchanged: the objective is to find the approach with the lowest overall cost. The concept of cost trade-offs recognizes these changing patterns, for example the 'trading' of additional information, via IT-based control systems, as an alternative to higher inventory levels; or perhaps the 'trading' of an extra regional warehouse as an alternative to a fleet of national delivery trucks.

Commercial organizations seek to maximize their ROI (return on investment) with a 'reduced asset base'. As mentioned before, the need for marketing managers to work closely with other functional areas, such as finance, is vital. An understanding of accounting should tell you that, since ROI is the product of margin and capital turnover, a company might attempt to improve this ratio by increasing sales revenue and/or reducing costs. The company may also use the leverage of improved asset turnover through lowering the value of the assets utilized. This can be achieved by a better management of inventory, thereby tying up less money in stocks. The use of JIT techniques to address this issue is discussed later in the chapter.

◾ Inventory management

You should by now be aware of the strategic importance of inventory management. Ultimately, stockholding represents costs such as storage space, obsolescence, deterioration, and interest payments. Yet, ideally, the company should carry enough stock to meet customers' orders immediately. If the desired goods are not available, then a sale may be lost, or worse—a customer may be lost to a competitor. If too much unmoved stock is held the company may find itself with large quantities of goods which it is forced to mark down. This is often the case in fashion retailing, as we saw with Mothercare. The objective of inventory management is therefore to find a balance between customer service and the cost of carrying additional stock.

A number of methods are used to achieve the desired balance in stockholding. Perhaps the most basic method is that of the *reorder point*. This approach recognizes that

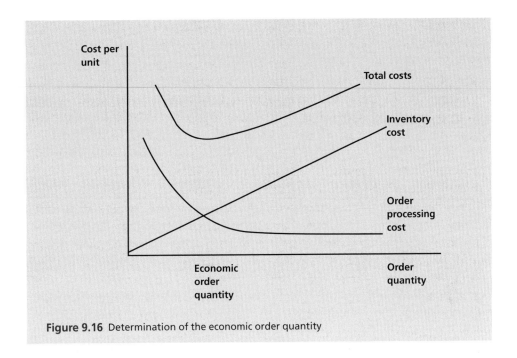

Figure 9.16 Determination of the economic order quantity

waiting to reorder stock until an extremely low level has been reached is risky, because it takes time to replenish stock. The reorder point system triggers reordering at a stock level a little higher than this 'danger' level, so that by the time new stock is received the danger level of the old stock has only just been reached. Stock is typically counted manually in small organizations, or via computerized sales systems such as 'electronic point of sale' (EPOS) (see below), which compare daily sales with starting stock levels. Safety stock levels are usually based on historical sales data. Another approach is to use the *economic order quantity* (EOQ) formula:

$$EOQ = \sqrt{2}\, do/ic,$$

where d = annual demand in units; o = cost of placing an order; i = carrying costs as a percentage of cost of one unit; and c = the cost of each unit. The principle of the EOQ model is shown in Figure 9.16. This shows an idealized theoretical relationship between order processing costs and inventory carrying costs to give the order quantity size that minimizes total costs.

Unfortunately, as with many economic models, the EOQ model does not take into sufficient account variations in customer and supplier behaviour. Where demand is unpredictable, or when stocks cannot be replenished relatively quickly, the model may be inadequate. Further, as Christopher [26] points out, the reorder quantity means that a company will be carrying more inventory than is actually required over practically the complete order cycle (the time between placing separate orders with the supplier); for example, if the EOQ is 100 units and daily usage is 10, then on the first day of the cycle the buyer would be overstocked by 90 units, on the second day by 80, and so on.

Just-in-time systems

This brings us back to the *just-in-time (JIT)* philosophy. This is based on the view, commonly attributed to the Japanese, that inventory is waste and that large inventories merely hide problems such as inaccurate forecasts, unreliable suppliers, quality issues, and production bottlenecks. The JIT concept aims to eliminate any need for safety stock, with parts for manufacture (or goods for reselling) arriving just as they are needed. As a result, small shipments must be made more frequently. Order requirements can specify the exact unloading point and time of day, with suppliers having to respond accordingly. For example, Toyota schedules its production to minimize sharp fluctuations in daily volume, and to turn out a predicted number of each model every day. Suppliers are automatically notified of orders and given a stable production schedule so they will not deliver the wrong components on the date of final assembly. This level of planning also occurs, for instance, with retailers like Marks & Spencer stipulating delivery 'windows' for its carriers, and with manufacturers such as Rover utilizing the services of third-party distributors like Exel, who consolidate and deliver quantities from several different suppliers, resulting in no congestion of delivery vehicles at the production plant. In the fast changing world of personal computers, many companies have taken the lead of Dell, which builds computers to customers' specific requirements. This reduces the risk of obsolescence, but requires carefully planned logistics if promised delivery dates are to be met.

The increasing popularity of JIT delivery among business customers clearly means that, for suppliers, the logistics service elements of availability and reliability, plus, of course, uniformly excellent product quality become paramount. Successful implementation of JIT systems relies on high levels of co-operation between supplying and buying organizations, and on the development of long-term partnerships. These closer relations can exist both upstream and downstream from the producer/manufacturer. This can affect the whole culture of an organization and the way that it goes about business. Figure 9.17 summarizes the changes within an organization as it moves from a 'Just-in-case' mentality to one of 'Just-in-time'.

The JIT concept is not without its problems. The *Financial Times* [35] reported that suppliers in the Japanese plastics industry have been in 'revolt' against JIT, claiming that it is too expensive. During the 1980s, suppliers tolerated the system because it strengthened the relationship between supplying firms and customers. Once manufacturers had become used to a steady flow of materials from one company, they were unlikely to go elsewhere. The cost to the suppliers of additional freight and stockholding

	Traditional 'just-in-case' logistics	With the development of a 'just-in-time' approach to logistics
Inventory levels	Large inventories resulting from manufacturing economies of scale and safety stock provision	Low inventories resulting from reliable, 'continuous flow' delivery
Flexibility	Minimal flexibility with long lead times	Short lead times and customer service drive flexibility
Relationships between logistics channel members	Tough, adversarial negotiations	Joint venture partnerships
Number of logistics channel members	Many, to avoid sole dependency	Fewer, but in long-term relationships
Communications	Minimal and with many secrets	Open communication and sharing of information to enable joint problem solving

Figure 9.17 The effects on organizational behaviour of the transition to a 'just-in-time' logistics system

was bearable because the Japanese plastics sector was highly profitable. However, in recent years the demand for plastics has fallen and the costs of frequent small deliveries have become insupportable: some manufacturers had been demanding three deliveries a day. Eventually, *en masse*, the Japanese petrochemicals industry association decided to tell its customers that deliveries would be limited to once a day, with additional calls available, only if paid for by the customer. Buyers were also encouraged to take larger quantities in each order. All of which is ironic, since, after all, JIT is a technique popularized by the Japanese!

Information processing

It should be clear from the previous sections that an effective and efficient supply of information is crucial to logistics management. IT is facilitating the creation of *integrated logistics systems* that link the operations of the business, such as production and distribution, with suppliers' operations on the one hand and the customer on the other. A model of information within the logistics function is shown in Figure 9.18. This shows how information about customers should drive strategic issues, such as the design of channels of distribution, through to implementation issues such as order processing and delivery.

In discussing the *value chain*, Porter [19] gives examples of how IT is transforming both the way value-creating activities are performed and the nature of linkages between

Channel member	Focus for information collection
Final customer	Preferences with respect to product configuration and delivery. Payment / order processing
Intermediaries	Availability of stocks Availability of warehouse capacity Order / delivery preferences Availability and location of transport
Manufacturer	Manufacturing schedule Raw material supplies Availability of stocks Availability of warehouse capacity Availability and location of transport

Figure 9.18 Levels of information within a logistics system
Source: based on M. Christopher, *Logistics and Supply Chain Management*, London: Pitman, 1992, p. 215.

such activities. IT is providing more information to improve management decision making. The support activities of the value chain have benefited from developments such as computerized accounting and costing procedures, electronic mail, and online ordering procedures.

We will now look at some of the impacts of IT on logistics activity.

Order processing

The physical distribution process starts when the company *receives an order*. This may be direct from the end consumer, as in the case of Dell's sales of its personal computers; it may involve a head office 'order-taker' noting a replenishment order from a major retailer; or it may be generated by an account manager visiting a major client and entering its order for some new equipment on to a laptop. Copies of this order are then usually directed to various company departments. Where relevant, this may include those responsible for inventories, purchasing, credit control, manufacturing, dispatch, warehousing, and invoicing. Customers may be serviced more efficiently if communication between these activities is speeded up. Better still, as far as is possible, the company should ensure that these activities take place *concurrently*, rather than consecutively; that is, it should try to eliminate the need to pass orders over the company's internal 'walls'.

Significant advances in IT now offer organizations the chance to reduce delays and costs in order processing. Proprietary electronic data interface (EDI) systems are now being superseded by common platform intranet, intranet, and extranet systems, allowing sales people to send order details to the relevant departments as they receive them from the customer. Using these IT systems, account managers can also provide instant status reports on the progress of their orders to customers, examining inventory levels and making recommendations for out-of-stock items as they do so. Once an order is confirmed, integrated computer systems can automatically generate orders to pick goods from warehouse shelves, to ship goods, to bill customers, to update stock records, and to confirm delivery arrangements to the customer. An integrated system can inform the production department of the potential need to make new stock, and the procurement department of the need to order new supplies, as well as warning suppliers of the producing company's imminent requirements.

Materials planning

Manufacturing resource planning (MRP) is a computer-assisted method of managing production inventory. It takes into account the producer's master production schedule (MPS), sales forecasts, existing orders, inventories, and a bill of materials (BOM) listing all the necessary inputs. It allows companies to control production inputs carefully, yet still be able to respond to most demand-driven production situations.

Delivery planning

A highly focused example of the impact of IT on physical distribution is given by the scheduling and routing of delivery vehicles. Manual methods for this process are laborious and relatively inefficient. However, it is now routine for companies to use *computerized vehicle routing and scheduling* (CVRS). This allocates vehicles to sets of delivery locations and builds routes linking these destinations. In most cases CVRS is linked to order processing systems to speed up computation and minimize errors. Other benefits to companies include: a significant overall reduction in transport costs, greater vehicle utilization, a more responsive service to customers, and the ability to ask 'what if?' questions without carrying out an expensive operational trial. More recently, CVRS systems have been linked to global positioning systems (GPS) to allow a company to identify the exact location of a consignment at any time.

IT and organizational processes

Although IT may be crucial to improving the efficiency and effectiveness of logistics systems, even the best IT system may fail when poor organizational structure and processes prevent IT being used fully. In his examination of IT in marketing, Fletcher [37] concluded that a sweeping reorganization of work practices is needed for compa-

Figure 9.19 **Some express parcel companies have extended their parcel tracking facility to allow customers to log on to the Internet to find out for themselves where an expected delivery is.** DHL, a leading express parcel and logistics company with worldwide operations, allows customers to track the status of their parcels at any time of the day, anywhere in the world. With increasing importance of Just-in-Time production methods, this valuable facility allows customers to manage their production and inventory levels more effectively (Reproduced with permission of DHL International (UK) Ltd)

nies to gain full advantage from IT. In an argument that should be familiar, he believes that this means breaking down old functional barriers and redeploying workers in new multidisciplinary ways (see also Chapter 12). This should be possible, Fletcher claims, because of the capacity of IT to provide front-line staff with the knowledge they need to act quickly and effectively via user-friendly software, hand-held terminals, and distributed information systems.

Production and warehouse location

A *warehouse* enables finished goods (as well as work in progress) to be stored and subsequently moved according to customer demands, and is therefore an important link in the supply chain. A key determinant of the availability of goods is the number and location of manufacturing facilities and warehouses. We may view decisions here in terms of the familiar 'trade-offs' concept: the greater the number of locations used, the greater the potential for rapid delivery. But more facilities will increase costs and capital employed, thus reducing ROI. As we have seen, warehouses may not necessarily be owned by manufacturers: many retailers utilize their own warehouse facilities in order to address the challenges of composite distribution and cross-docking.

Location decisions are complex because of the enormous number of potential site combinations, especially when a company is operating globally. It is increasingly common for managers to use computer-based mathematical models to aid their decision making. In doing so, however, companies must not lose sight of the trends we have already discussed, like the move towards focused factories and centralized distribution centres, and potentially conflicting views such as locating inventory locally yet controlling it centrally. Also, they should note how alternative transport arrangements (see below) might circumvent the need to invest heavily in storage facilities in the first place. For instance, the decision by Digital to cut the number of its distribution centres from 26 country locations to seven led to a large-scale, yet cost-effective, increase in the company's use of carrier services.

Regarding the logistic chain as a whole, it is also important to ask how many manufacturing plants there should be, and where they should be located. Larger factories generally achieve lower levels of cost per unit of output, but this has to be set against the cost and time involved in getting finished goods to customers. The trend in most industries has been for small manufacturing plants to be replaced by larger factories, operating at a national, European, or even world level.

Companies in fiercely competitive markets often calculate that it is cheaper to manufacture a product in a low-cost country such as China and to ship the finished product to the country where there is demand for it. Most British clothes companies now manufacture the bulk of their clothing in less developed countries where wages paid to staff can be a fraction of what would be paid to UK staff. This can more than offset higher transport costs and allow the company to compete on price, especially where there are significant price points above which buyers will not buy an item. However, locating manufacturing facilities a long way from customers extends the time between identification of a market need and the delivery of goods to meet that need. While fashion for basic underwear and socks may not change much over time, outerwear tends to be much more volatile, with preferred styles and colours changing frequently. If it takes several months to get the latest 'hot' fashion from China to Chichester, it might arrive in the shops just as customers have moved on to a new 'hot' fashion. For this reason, manufacturers supplying goods to highly volatile markets are more likely to favour manufacturing facilities closer to home. In the world of consumer electronics, Sony surprised many people when it brought production of camcorders back from China to Japan (Nakamoto [3]). Digitization had made the product life-cycle even shorter than before. Previously, because the market was growing, the company was simply able to make as many camcorders as it had capacity for. But by 2002 it had become necessary to adjust product configuration as closely as possible to market demand, something Sony felt was easier to achieve in Japan. Furthermore, this move helped to reduce the company's electronics inventory from ¥923.4 billion in the third quarter of 2000 to

¥627.5 billion in the third quarter of 2001 and again to ¥506.5 billion in the third quarter of 2002. To a company such as Sony, inventory is a business risk in a fast-changing market.

◼ Transport

The appropriate choice of transport mode is a key part of physical distribution management. This is especially important in markets where JIT delivery is the norm. A number of criteria should be used to select transport, including costs, transit time, reliability, capability (important if goods require special handling, such as chilled temperatures), security, and traceability.

Each major mode of transport has its own cost and service outcomes that must be considered by the marketing logistics manager. These are described in turn below.

Road

Road haulage has the key advantage of flexibility, with national road networks providing direct access to production facilities, warehouses, and customers. This allows lorries to transport goods from supplier to end user without unloading *en route*. The past twenty years has seen a growth in the number of dedicated contract distribution (DCD) companies such as Christian Salvesen. DCD organizations now offer both road freight transportation and warehousing to customers. For example, Exel Logistics operates a DCD arrangement to service Marks & Spencer's stores.

An issue for users of road haulage is fleet ownership versus outsourcing, and the subsequent loss of control versus flexibility. Another major issue is the increasing congestion of roads in most European countries. In 2003 the DIY chain B&Q found congestion on southern England's roads so severe that it moved its main import centre from Felixstowe and Tilbury to Humberside. Congestion (or 'southern discomfort', as the company called it), was contributing to a reported 5% or 10% failure rate at getting goods delivered on time. The company even estimated that the cost of UK road haulage was accounting for about half the cost of getting a product from the Far East into a B&Q store (*The Times* [2]).

Rail

Railways tend to be used for carrying large, bulky freight over long distances. Goods commonly carried by trains include coal, chemicals, and building aggregates. The longer the journey, the more economically competitive rail transport becomes, as can be seen in North America. A significant problem for railways, however, is the lack of flexibility in the routes. For most companies, barring those with premises directly

Figure 9.20 Suppliers of goods and services must consider the location where their products will have greatest value for end-consumers. Many supermarket operators have identified groups of consumers who would prefer to have their groceries delivered to their home rather than having to visit a supermarket to collect them. The development of the internet has resulted in home shopping for groceries being a growth area for many supermarket operators. Tesco has become one of Europe's largest online retailers, with a turnover of over £400m for its Tesco.com division in 2002. The company's logistics task must incorporate an additional link to the final consumer. Tesco serves its home delivery customers from selected individual stores, where customers' orders are assembled manually. Some companies (e.g. Ocado) have chosen instead to develop strategically located automated distribution centres specifically to serve customers requiring home delivery (Reproduced with permission of Tesco Stores PLC)

adjacent to rail yards, this means the transport of goods to and from rail depots via lorries. Because of this, the railway's share of the European transportation market has declined steadily. The opening of the Channel Tunnel has provided some benefits to UK firms, which can now move trainloads or individual containers throughout Europe without the need for transshipment.

Air

This is both the fastest and most expensive mode of transport. Its great speed over long distances means that it is often used to carry perishable goods and emergency deliveries. As international trade continues to grow, air freight should likewise grow in importance, especially in global JIT systems. Like rail, though, companies must still transport goods to and from air terminals. Air freight is eminently suited to valuable, relatively light goods such as fresh flowers, jewellery, and electronic components.

Water

This can be divided into sea and inland waterways, both of which are slow but fairly inexpensive. Ocean-going vessels carry a large variety of goods, ranging from oil shipped from the Far East to be refined in British Petroleum's Fawley coastal terminal, to basic consumer goods going to small islands like Gran Canaria. Inland water transportation, like rail, is associated with low-value, bulky commodities such as coal or steel. Its low costs mean that European rivers that are linked to canal networks, including the Rhine and the Danube, are still commonly used.

Pipeline

Pipelines are a dependable and low-maintenance form of transport for liquids and gas. They normally belong to the shipper and carry the shipper's products. The downside of this transport mode is the major investment involved in the construction of the pipeline. A good example of a logistics trade-off is given by the use of pipelines in the North Sea as opposed to oil tankers.

Global logistics

There has been a tendency for companies to market their products globally rather than just nationally or locally. We will return to the development of global brands in Chapter 14, but for now we will consider the logistical implications for a company that is considering moving from national to global marketing.

Chickens earn food miles

Do you ever wonder what is inside the 40 tonne trucks that seem to fill the motorways of Britain and most western European countries? Quite a high proportion will be carrying food of some description. The transporting of food over long distances is of course nothing new. Sir Walter Raleigh brought the first potatoes back to England from America in the sixteenth century, and the prosperity of Victorian England depended in part on the ability to import food from the colonies that couldn't be grown at home, and to export processed food back to the colonial countries. This was very much in line with ideas of comparative cost advantage—a country should concentrate on producing what it is good at and exporting its surplus, and should import products that another country is better at producing.

By 2000 Britain found itself in the apparently bizarre situation of having some of the most efficient farms in the world, but seeing its farmers going out of business despite hefty subsidies from the EU Common Agricultural Policy. At the same time, the major supermarkets were importing from around the world fruit and vegetables that have traditionally been grown in Britain. In 2002 Friends of the Earth volunteers carried out a survey by visiting 166 supermarkets, 74 greengrocers, and 48 market stalls. Even though the survey was carried out during the English apple season, the survey found that less than a third of the apples sold by the Co-op, Safeway, and Morrison's came from Britain. Only Marks & Spencer's sold more British than imported apples. Although Tesco, Safeway, and Sainsbury's sold organic apples, none of them came from Britain (Friends of the Earth [21]). By contrast, small grocery markets were much more likely to sell local apples.

The bizarre situation has occurred where the supermarkets import apples from France to be sold in Kent, the traditional home of British apple growing, plums from Spain to be sold in the traditional plum growing area of Worcestershire, and cauliflowers from Spain to replace the locally grown product in Lincolnshire. Supermarkets argue that sourcing from overseas is not just an issue of cost-saving: more importantly, the supermarkets seek a continuity of supplies from large growers who can guarantee to deliver a specified quantity at a specified time and place. The supermarkets have claimed that the fragmented nature of agricultural growers and distributors in Britain is not capable of achieving this. British supermarkets are among the most efficient in the world, and their desire to ensure that customers can always get what they want may explain the mass transport of food. Local grocery markets may sound environmentally friendly, but they rarely guarantee a continuity of supplies.

As part of their drive for efficiency, supermarkets have a tendency to move food between large warehouses and processing centres. Friends of the Earth have noted the paradox of potatoes being transported several hundred miles between distribution centres before they end up on a supermarket shelf just a few miles from where they were grown. The environmental campaigning group Sustain has estimated that the average chicken has travelled 2,000 km between the farm where it was grown and the supermarket shelf (Sustain [20]).

Are the supermarkets acting irresponsibly by denying jobs to British farmers and clogging up our roads with more heavy lorries? Or are they simply doing what we the customers expect of them? Can 'food miles' be blamed on our desire for continuous availability of products? Are we the root source of the problem by demanding foods out of season which can sensibly only be grown overseas and brought to us after a long journey? Don't we marvel at some of the exotic fruits that supermarkets' efficient distribution systems have now made available to us at affordable prices?

There are two related developments underpinning the trend towards global logistics management: the focused factory, and the centralization of inventory. *Focused factories* enable a company to gain economies of scale by limiting the range and mix of products manufactured in a single location. An obvious trade-off with this approach is the effect on transport costs and delivery lead times. Too great a focus may also reduce the flexibility of a company's production facility to respond to market trends. Focused factories can also benefit by locating in a country where production costs (e.g. through lower wage rates or taxation) can give the company a competitive advantage.

Inventory centralization has taken place as organizations steadily close national warehouses and amalgamate them into regional distribution centres (RDCs) serving a much wider geographical area. For instance, Valeo, a French automotive parts distributor, found that it was still able to maintain service levels despite merging its Belgian, German, and French warehouses into a central facility near Paris. A more recent development has been the recognition that there may be even greater gains made by not physically centralizing an inventory, but rather continuing to locate it near the customer and managing and controlling it centrally.

Going global poses a number of challenges that logistics management must seek to overcome.

- **Unreliable transit times**: In general, greater distances lead to greater transport uncertainty, increasing the need for 'buffer stocks' to be held in the supply chain. The need to obtain customs clearance can also contribute to delays and variability.

- **Extended lead times**: As the example earlier in this chapter of Sony moving its camcorder production back from China to Japan made clear, manufacturing at a distance from the market can cause problems in volatile markets. A lengthy supply chain can mean that, by the time goods finally arrive in the market, customer demand has changed.

- **Consolidation and break of bulk costs**: Breaking down bulk from a focused factory to individual national markets can be expensive. Options include shipping direct from each source to the final market in full containers, or consolidating from each source for each general geographic area, with bulk broken down into intermediate inventory ready for specific markets.

Some companies, such as the computer manufacturer Dell, have examined their value chain and calculated that there are opportunities for delaying the final configuration of a product until it is as close to the customer as possible. They can then achieve lower costs by shipping generic sub-assemblies to the local operation which typically provides finishing, local language packaging, and direct customer delivery. Dell therefore sources many of its components from China and Thailand, among other places, and serves its European markets by assembling them at a plant at Limerick, Ireland.

Trends in logistics management

In a landmark article in 1962, the management guru Peter Drucker claimed that physical distribution was the US economy's 'dark continent'. He said: 'We know little more about distribution today than Napoleon's contemporaries knew about the interior of Africa. We know it is there, and we know it is big; and that's about all' [28].

The forty years that have passed since Drucker threw down the gauntlet for companies to embrace logistics management have seen massive advances in efficiency and effectiveness in North American and European distribution. The impact of improved logistics on national economies should not be underestimated. The UK's Chartered Institute of Purchasing and Supply has claimed that even a 1% improvement in the cost of managing the supply chain can boost the bottom line of a company by as much as 15%. Logistics for the most part is an invisible part of marketing—it is unseen by the final consumer, and we tend to appreciate its significance only when things go wrong, such as a supermarket running out of potatoes, or an expected home delivery not arriving. Logistics managers deliver what other people in the marketing function promise.

So far in this chapter we have identified a number of trends that have influenced the shape of logistic systems as they are today. Now we will summarize some of the key trends for the future.

From functions to processes

Effective and efficient logistics focus on processes rather than functional responsibility. It is a challenge to overcome the problem of functional isolation in a conventional organization run by a senior manager who comes to regard his functional area as his 'territory' and who often jealously guards his own departmental budget. Typical problems include a production manager wanting to minimize costs by running large batch quantities, even though this may mean creating an inventory greater than what is needed, and a firm presenting too many faces to the final consumer, rather than the appearance of a 'seamless' organization.

The solution to these problems lies in recognizing that a customer order and its associated information flows should be at the heart of any business. This means moving from an *input-focused and budget-driven* organization to an *output-focused, market-driven* one, managing processes rather than functions; and ensuring the rapid sharing of accurate information. These are not solutions that are quick to implement.

Competition between supply networks

It is becoming too simplistic to see competition as existing between companies at just one level of the supply chain. Rather, the competition that takes place between the main UK clothing retailers should be seen as competition between integrated supply chains. The retailers may be the public face of competition to most consumers, but their source of competitive advantage lies in the networks of suppliers and distribution companies that provide the right goods at the right time for their stores, as cheaply as possible. Many commentators have pointed to weaknesses in its supply chain as a contributor to the difficulties that Marks & Spencer faced in the late 1990s, in contrast to the well-developed, flexible and low-cost distribution network developed by competitors such as George (part of Wal-Mart) and New Look.

Closer working relationships

We have seen how the need to share information has led to close working relationships becoming crucial to a successful distribution chain. In most channel relationships issues of power are never far from the surface, and they can destabilize the whole channel where one party seeks to exert power in the chain that others regard as unreasonable. Power in distribution channels has continued to move towards the retailer and away from the producer of goods.

Fewer channel members

There has been a tendency for channels to be simplified by reducing the number of members involved at each level. A good example of this is provided by the major car manufacturers, which have progressively reduced their number of component suppliers while from their remaining suppliers demanding a commitment to quality, innovation, and cost reduction.

Virtual organizations

Some people (e.g. Bowersox and Cooper [25]) have suggested that formal company structures could one day be replaced with an informal electronic network giving rise to a *virtual organization*. This would exist as a provider of integrated performance, but not as an identifiable business unit. In the case of logistics, key teams might be linked electronically to perform critical activities in an integrated fashion. 'Transparent' logistics organizations of the future would be characterized by functional disaggregation in an attempt to concentrate on work flow. Work teams could share common information regarding customer requirements and performance measures while retaining local control to achieve a high level of logistical core competency. This is essentially a form of 'electronic keiretsu'. ('Keiretsu' is a Japanese term for a loosely affiliated group of firms that share common practices and are committed to co-operation.) The fact that companies could join forces to achieve common goals and then disband presents significant challenges for the management of partnerships.

Increasingly complex consumer needs

Society is fragmenting into smaller and smaller groups with specialized interests, needs, and expectations. We saw in Chapter 5 how marketers have responded by trying to develop products that closely meet the needs of each group. This can itself create a logistical challenge, as the proliferation of variants of a basic product means higher stockholdings if buffer stocks of each product variant are to be kept. For a simple product such as Coca Cola, the product range has proliferated from one flavour, three packaging types, and three sizes in the 1970s to today's five flavours/formulations (e.g. Diet/Caffeine-free), five packaging types, and five sizes, plus special promotional packages. In order to satisfy the needs of each group that has been targeted with these differentiated products, stocks of all must be continually available.

With the development of a 24-hour society and increasingly busy life-styles, logistics management has to face the challenge of delivering goods to individual consumers' front doors not just between 9 am and 5 pm, but at other times that are convenient to consumers.

The internet

We have seen that information technology has drastically changed the nature of logistics management. It is now changing the way that consumers buy goods, with internet sales set to increase. The internet has enabled many retailers to service customers without having to maintain expensive High Street shops, but just a warehouse on a relatively low cost industrial estate (see Pitt, Berthon, and Berthon [12]; and Ranchhod and Gurău [15]). However, the delivery of goods to the final consumer has not shown the productivity gains that internet-based ordering has achieved. This is probably not surprising when it is remembered that home delivery remains a labour-intensive activity in which two of the main costs—labour and transport—are likely to continue to increase in real terms. We should not forget that in the UK the milkman has almost disappeared because efficiency of delivery cannot be improved relative to the cost of consumers' collecting milk from large, efficient supermarkets. The logistics function must also face the challenge of being able to deliver goods when somebody is at home, or of providing alternative secure storage arrangements (de Koster [14]).

Increasing public concern over the environment

This impacts upon logistics in a number of ways. An EU Directive has placed on certain manufacturers a responsibility to recycle discarded products after their use (e.g. car components that have reached the end of their life), and this calls for reverse logistics. Many distribution channels already collect waste materials for recycling (e.g. cardboard packaging) and use empty vehicles to return such material to the distribution centre where it is consolidated and forwarded to a recycling plant. Logistics managers are also likely to face growing challenges from regulators to limit the amount of environmental damage caused through distribution. We saw in the example of food miles how a section of the public (admittedly small at present) has created bad publicity for firms that move food products for miles around the country until they arrive on a supermarket shelf just a few miles from where they were produced. Over time, greater concerns with the environment are likely to lead to greater restrictions on the movements of lorries, which have become an important element of most distribution systems.

■ Chapter summary and key linkages to other chapters

The management of channel intermediaries plays a key part in a company's attempts to ensure that its goods or services are made available to the desired market segments. Making goods available where and when buyers need them is an important value adding activity which contributes towards a company's competitive advantage over rival producers (Chapter 6). Availability of a company's products must be consistent with its promotional messages (Chapters 10 and 11) and its price position (Chapter 8). The design of a marketing channel requires careful analysis and planning. For this to be done effectively, firms must be aware of the roles that intermediaries can perform and of their relative power bases.

Logistics is concerned with co-ordinating the flow of goods from suppliers to the manufacturer, through the production process, and on to the customer. In other words, it considers both 'inbound' and 'outbound' logistics (or physical distribution management), as well as the handling of inventory within companies. The overall aim of marketing logistics management is to provide customer value through service, which for many customers (both consumers and commercial) comprises the key elements of availability and timeliness. There have been numerous developments in physical distribution and logistics in the past few decades, most of which has been facilitated by advances in IT.

KEY PRINCIPLES OF MARKETING

- Value chains are at the heart of marketing. Value is added to a product as it passes through a channel of distribution.
- There is not one channel design that is appropriate in all situations; the design of an optimal channel is influenced by a range of customer, product, supplier, and competitor characteristics.
- Physical distribution may be a largely unseen activity, but it is crucial for delivering promises contained in a company's promotional messages.
- Distribution efficiency and effectiveness must be consistent with a company's product/price/promotional positioning.
- Logistics involves a series of trade-offs in order to optimize a cost/service/profit level.

CASE STUDY

Online music gives rise to distribution headaches

Who'd be the marketing manager for a music label? You might be able to rub shoulders with the stars, but once the partying is over it's time to get down to business. And 'business' is exactly what the music industry is—a very aggressive business. In 2001 the UK market for pre-recorded music was approximately £2.1 billion, at retailers' selling prices (Mintel [22]). Since 1997, retail sales value increased by 21%, although the rate of increase was beginning to slow down, largely because of the decline in the singles market and increased competitiveness in the market, which has led to the introduction of discounts and special offers. However, by 2002 the music industry appeared to be in crisis, as new forms of distribution challenged traditional retail outlets.

By 2000, CDs had become the dominant form of distributing music. Vinyl records had all but disappeared and the market share of audio cassettes had been slipping. Innovative formats had been launched but, except for mini discs, with no significant consumer impact—do you know anyone who owns a laser-disc or a DAT player? Competition within the CD marketplace is largely between major entertainment corporations who record, manufacture, and co-ordinate the distribution of products. The independent recording sector is also important as a source of new talent. The market is subject to extreme sales variation, owing to fluctuating reputations and 'hype' surrounding individual artists or related phenomena. Think of the unpredictable ups and downs in the sales of bands like Oasis and of soundtracks like The Titanic, for instance. There is also always a huge seasonal variation in volumes because of the Christmas gift-giving market. More broadly, consumer spending on recorded music forms just a part of the wider leisure and entertainment sector, which typically also includes books, magazines, sports, games, and hobby products. This means that the marketing carried out by record companies has to overcome some pretty big hurdles in order for a particular CD to enter the average consumer's consciousness.

A significant contribution to the marketing of CDs is made by distribution channels. The main intermediaries are the general High Street chains like WHSmith and Woolworth's, which sell other goods in addition to music-related products, and the specialist record chains like Virgin and HMV. The chief difference between the two types of chain is the range they stock: Woolworth's may sell more units than any other chain, but it keeps a considerably less varied list of titles on display than HMV which aims to attract the more 'knowledgeable'—and frequently higher-earning and more regular spending—music fan in addition to the chart-orientated buyer. More mature consumers tend to shop at outlets like Boots or WHSmith.

Sales in other non-traditional outlets, such as petrol stations and grocery stores, have been growing. Supermarkets in particular have moved strongly into the recorded music sector, with chains like Safeway and Sainsbury's offering a top chart selection, sometimes at discounted prices. Some chains, such as Asda, also offer singles as well as a limited 'back-catalogue' range, but these are usually mid-price or budget compilations. The number of Asda stores with record departments grew from none in 1991 to 250 by 1996. Over the same period, the number of UK independent record shops fell from nearly 2,000 to 1,500. Although record companies welcome the huge volume of sales provided by supermarkets selling music, they fear a repeat of the retail revolution in the USA which virtually wiped out the small 'indie' record shop. The music industry believes the long-term development of new bands has been harmed because the shops that used to sell debut albums are in decline. Asda's category controller for entertainment says that record companies are in a difficult position because, although publicly they feel that supermarket price promotions are devaluing music, privately they are happy to see any sector performing strongly. On the other hand, music companies are finding supermarkets, with their high expectations of marketing and merchandising support and low margins on CDs compared to groceries, much harder to deal with than specialist chains.

The grocery multiples normally buy their CDs through a wholesaler. It suits them to do so because of the hugely diverse nature of the titles available and the need for frequently changing ranges. The major wholesalers include Entertainment UK, which is part of the Kingfisher Group, and Total Home Entertainment (THE), which is part of John Menzies. The process for gaining supermarket distribution for a CD title is as follows. The major record companies present their titles to a wholesaler, which has an account with a grocery multiple. The wholesaler then recommends a selection to the retailer's buying team; it may also work out the planogram (the store shelf layout) and do the merchandising.

The internet has offered new opportunities and challenges for major labels and independent record companies to provide access to their products. Studies by Forrester Research have suggested that the sites most commonly visited by 15–24-year-olds are music related. Music is well suited to online retailing. With no need to see the actual CDs, it is easier to listen to a taster online than in a shop. Web sites can also add value by incorporating reviews, concert listings, and discographies.

However, distribution through the internet did not get off to a very good start for the music companies. Internet-based companies such as Napster.com and Aimster.com tried to get round the copyright laws by allowing 'members' to swap files with each other. This undoubtedly cost the music companies a lot of money, and they eventually succeeded through the courts in driving many of these sites out of business. But the music companies realized that new pirating sites could spring up at any time and that the internet was very difficult to police. Should they continue to rely on the courts to drive such sites out of business, or should they try to join them? The companies were aware that the internet sites were driven by energetic entrepreneurs—could the music companies harness these energies for their own benefits?

Gradually, the music companies started licensing other companies to provide mp3 format downloads using coding that prevents multiple copies subsequently being made, believing that they did not have the internet skills to set up their own distribution operations. In May 2001, the music and media giant Vivendi Universal acquired one of these sites—MP3.com—for $372 million, just six months after MP3.com had paid Vivendi $53.4 million as compensation for intentionally violating its copyrights. For MP3.com, a big attraction was having access to its new owner's back catalogue. For Vivendi, the benefit was to acquire the skills necessary to distribute through a channel it knew little about, other than as an adversary in the courts. By 2003 MP3.com had amassed 3 million users within a year of opening its European operation with a staff of just 25 (Sexton [4]). Visitors to the site enter their personal details to get access to 1.2 million songs, either as streams or downloads, depending on the content supplier. MP3.com's role as a marketing ally represented a recovery from three years previously, when the parent American website was badly wounded in the crossfire with peer-to-peer 'baddies' Napster and Aimster.

Case study review questions

1. Identify the key environmental forces that should be considered by music producers in evaluating strategies for channel design.

2. Contrast the role of a specialist music retailer with that of a grocery supermarket in the channel for CDs.

3. How would you suggest that music producers might control their marketing channels more effectively?

▢ CHAPTER REVIEW QUESTIONS

1. 'Channel intermediaries are nothing but parasites.' Why might some observers think this? Do you agree? If not, why not?

2. List the criteria you might use in selecting a channel intermediary.

3. Why does conflict so often occur between manufacturers and intermediaries? How might this conflict be resolved?

4. Contrast JIT inventory management with conventional reorder methods. Do you think the adoption of JIT techniques is viable for every sector? Where might it not be so relevant?

5. Compare the benefits and disadvantages of using road haulage and air transport for a manufacturer of valuable machine parts.

6. Giving examples from both the manufacturing and retailing sectors, discuss the effects of the internet on logistics and physical distribution management.

REFERENCES

[1] Morton, R. (2003), 'Some Pick-up in Online Sales: . . . however, most customers still prefer to buy from showrooms'. *Financial Times*, 4 March, p. 5.

[2] *The Times* (2003), 'B&Q Plans Freight Escape from Southern Route'. *The Times*, 20 January, Business, p. 4.

[3] Nakamoto, M. (2003), 'A Speedier Route from Order to Camcorder'. *Financial Times*, 12 February, p. 11.

[4] Sexton, P. (2003), 'Harmony Breaks Out: MP3.com, the internet music site, has made peace with the record companies. Now they're working together to make money'. *Financial Times*, 14 January, p. 30.

[5] Löning, H., and Besson, M. (2002), 'Can Distribution Channels Explain Differences in Marketing and Sales Performance Measurement Systems?' *European Management Journal*, 20(6): pp. 54–62.

[6] Nairn, G. (2003), 'Not Many Happy Returns: reverse logistics causes headaches and eats into already thin margins'. *Financial Times*, 5 February, p. 5.

[7] Grimes, C. (2003), 'Harry Potter and the Sales Team: the merger of AOL and Time Warner has transformed the way films are marketed'. *Financial Times*, 16 November, p. 17.

[8] Timmins, N. (2003), 'Online Auctions: e-commerce has arrived in the public sector as a way to reduce the civil procurement bill'. *Financial Times*, 29 January, p. 12.

[9] Lewis, L. (2003), 'Claws Out for Esso in War of the Tiger Tokens'. *Independent on Sunday*, 9 February, Business, p. 3.

[10] Keers, H. (2002), 'Mothercare Slips into Red as Warehouse Woes Grow'. *Daily Telegraph*, 22 November.

[11] O'Cass, A. and Fenech, T. (2003), 'Web Retailing Adoption: exploring the nature of internet users web retailing behaviour'. *Journal of Retailing & Consumer Services*, 10(2): 81–94.

[12] Pitt, L., Berthon, P. and Berthon, J. P. (1999), 'Changing Channels: the impact of the internet on distribution strategy'. *Business Horizons*, 42(2): p. 19.

[13] Yrjölä, H. (2001), 'Physical Distribution Considerations for Electronic Grocery Shopping'. *International Journal of Physical Distribution & Logistics Management*, 31(10): pp. 746–61.

[14] de Koster, R. B. M. (2002), 'Distribution Structures for Food Home Shopping'. *International Journal of Physical Distribution & Logistics Management*, 32(5): pp. 362–80.

[15] Ranchhod, A. and Gurău, C. (1999), Internet-Enabled Distribution Strategies'. *Journal of Information Technology*, 14(4): 4.

[16] Cooper, J. and Johnstone M. (1990) 'Dedicated contract distribution: An assessment of the UK market place. *International Journal of Physical Distribution and Logistics Management*, 20(1): 134–142.

[17] Fletcher, R. (2002*b*), 'Green Nets £8 million from Arcadia Suppliers'. *Sunday Telegraph*, 3 November.

[18] Fletcher, R. (2002*a*), 'Barclay Brothers to Net £15 million from Suppliers'. *Sunday Telegraph*, 24 November.

[19] Porter, M. E. (2001), 'Strategy and the Internet'. *Harvard Business Review*, March–April: 63–78.

[20] Sustain (1999), *Food Miles: still on the road to ruin*. London, Sustain.

[21] Friends of the Earth (2002), *British Apples for Sale*. London: Friends of the Earth.

[22] Mintel (2002), *CDs, Records and Tapes*. London: Mintel Group.

[23] Ennis, S. (1995), 'Channel Management'. In M. Baker (ed.), *Marketing: theory and practice*, 3rd edn. Basingstoke: Macmillan.

[24] Ahmad, R. and Buttle, F. (1998), 'Bridging the Gaps between Theory and Practice: a case of the retention of dealers of office equipment products'. In *Proceedings of Academy of Marketing Conference* (Sheffield Hallam University, 8–10 July), Sheffield Hallam University, Sheffield: pp. 16–21.

[25] Bowersox, D. J. and Cooper, M. B. (1992), *Strategic Marketing Channel Management*. New York: McGraw-Hill.

[26] Christopher, M. (1992), *Logistics and Supply Chain Management*. London: Pitman.

[27] Doyle, P. (2001), *Marketing Management and Strategy*, 3rd edn. Hemel Hempstead: FT Prentice Hall.

[28] Drucker, P. (1962), 'The Economy's Dark Continent'. *Fortune*, April: 103.

[29] Magrath, A. J. and Hardy, K. G. (1987), 'Avoiding the Pitfalls in Managing Distribution Channels'. *Business Horizons*, September–October: 29–33.

[30] Muniz-Martinez, N. (1998), 'The Internationalization of European Retailers in America: the US experience'. *International Journal of Retail & Distribution Management*, 26(1): 29–37.

[31] Narus, J. A. and Anderson, J. C. (1987), 'Distribution Contributions to Partnerships with Manufacturers'. *Business Horizons*, September–October: 34–42.

[32] Palamountain, J. C. (1955), *The Politics of Distribution*. Cambridge, Mass.: Harvard University Press.

[33] Pelligrini, L. (1994), 'Alternatives for Growth and Internationalization in Retailing'. *International Review of Retail, Distribution and Consumer Research*, 4(2): 121–48.

[34] Porter, M. E. (1985), *Competitive Advantage*. New York: Free Press.

[35] *Financial Times* (1994), 'Just-in-time now Just too much', 14 Jan, p 20.

[36] ACNielsen (2003), *The Retail Pocket Book*. Henley-on-Thames: NTC Publications.

[37] Fletcher, K. (1994), 'The evolution and use of IT in marketing', in M. Baker (ed), *The Marketing Book*, 3rd edn. Oxford: Butterworth-Heinemann, pp 333–357.

SUGGESTED FURTHER READING

For a more detailed review of the channels of distribution literature, the following develop many of the issues raised in this chapter:

Frazier, G. L. (1999), Organizing and Managing Channels of Distribution'. *Journal of the Academy of Marketing Science*, 27(2): pp. 226–40.

Löning, H., and Besson, M. (2002), 'Can Distribution Channels Explain Differences in Marketing and Sales Performance Measurement Systems?' *European Management Journal*, 20(6): pp. 54–62.

For further discussion of logistics, consult the following:

Christopher, M., and Peck, H. (2003), *Marketing Logistics and Customer Services*. Oxford: Butterworth-Heinemann.

Fawcett, S. E., and Magnan, G. M. (2002), 'The Rhetoric and Reality of Supply Chain Integration'. *International Journal of Physical Distribution & Logistics Management*, 32(5): 339–61.

USEFUL WEB LINKS

Visit the companion website to this book, with lots of interesting additional material and links for each chapter:

www.oup.com/uk/booksites/econbus

British Franchise Association:

www.british-franchise.org.uk

A discussion group for academics interested in the retail sector:

www.mailbase.ac.uk/lists/retail

Institute of Export:

www.export.org.uk

Institute of Purchasing and Supply:

www.cips.org

Southern Center for Logistics and Intermodal Transportation Georgia:

www2.gasou.edu/coba/centers/lit

Discussion group for all aspects of purchasing and supply chain management:

www.mailbase.ac.uk/lists/purchasing-supply-chain

A forum for the exchange of research ideas, developments, and findings in the fields of logistics and supply chain management, established by UK academics in conjunction with the Institute of Logistics:

www.mailbase.ac.uk/lists/logistics-research-network

KEYWORDS

- **Category management**
- **Direct marketing**
- **Distributors**
- **Economic order quantity**
- **Franchising**
- **Intermediary**

- Inventory
- Just-in-time (JIT)
- Logistics
- Marketing channel
- Middleman
- Physical distribution management
- Retailers
- Supply chain
- Value chain
- Vertical marketing system
- Virtual organizations
- Wholesalers

10

Introduction to promotion planning

CHAPTER OBJECTIVES

It is sometimes said that a well designed product, appropriately priced and distributed, should require little or no promotion. Instead, customers should be queuing to buy it. Some new products do find themselves in a seller's market, and their producers can sell all they can make without a need for promotion. But the reality of most markets is fierce competition between suppliers in which each supplier has to communicate to potential buyers the unique benefits of buying its products rather than the competitor's. This chapter aims to develop an understanding of promotion planning as an integral part of the marketing and business planning process. It then discusses the key stages of the promotion planning process, the range and variety of promotional techniques, basic models of communication, and how promotional activity can be monitored. This is the first of two chapters covering the promotion element of the marketing mix. In this chapter we will introduce general principles of communication and promotion planning; in the following chapter we will explore the elements of the promotion mix and how these are applied to achieve a company's marketing objectives.

◼ The role of promotion planning as an integral part of the marketing and business planning process

As consumers, we are surrounded and constantly bombarded by marketing communications stimuli. These stimuli reach us as a result of organizations implementing a range of promotional activity via advertising, sales promotion, public relations, selling, and direct marketing, delivered through a variety of different channels and media.

Alongside such activity, other elements of the marketing mix are also communicating to us. These include aspects of the product, pricing, and distribution, and the quality of service that we experience.

To understand fully the role of promotion planning, it is necessary to see it within the context of an organization's overall business and marketing plan, and in particular its objectives and strategy. Promotion activity generally occurs towards the end of the business and marketing planning process and should not be seen as a stand-alone series of activities which bear little relation to the organization's goals, purpose, and markets.

At its most basic, promotion planning can be visualized as a top-down process (Figure 10.1). It should be seen as one element of the business and marketing planning cycle, with the aim of ensuring that:

- the messages being communicated are consistent with an organization's corporate and marketing activity;

- promotion activity supports and adds synergy to the overall business and marketing strategy;

- consumers hear 'one voice' and not a range of disparate messages and behaviour.

Marketing and promotional objectives

Developing the 'promotional mix' entails selecting and blending different channels of communication in order to achieve the promotional objectives of the marketing mix. Specifying the objectives of a communication is important if appropriate messages are to be accurately targeted through the most appropriate channels in the most cost-effective manner possible. Typical communication objectives might be:

- to develop an awareness of an organization and its products;

- to communicate the benefits of purchasing a product;

- to build a positive image of the organization and its products;

- to influence eventual purchase of the product;

- to differentiate the company and its products from its competitors;

- to remind people of the existence of the organization and its products.

Ideally, promotional objectives should be quantified as far as possible. From the general objectives specified above, the following specific objectives are typical of those that might be set by a newly established budget airline.

- Thirty per cent of all A/B/C1 adults within the south-east region of England should be aware of the airline's brand name by the end of year 1, rising to 50% after year 2 and 70% after year 3.

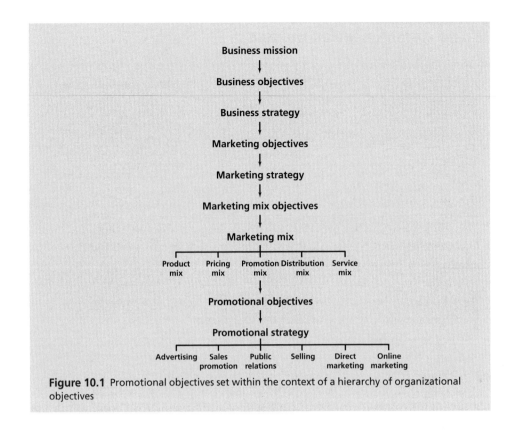

Figure 10.1 Promotional objectives set within the context of a hierarchy of organizational objectives

- Awareness levels among A/B/C1 adults who regularly fly from London area airports should be 60%, 80%, and 90% over the same time periods.
- The airline should receive 5 million hits on its website during year 1, rising to 10 million in year 3.
- By the end of year 3, the airline should be the first low-cost airline to be recalled by regular air travellers in the south-east in an unprompted survey of brand recognition.
- Ultimately, promotion effort should contribute to the sale of 1 million seats in year 1, rising to 3 million in year 3.

Promotional objectives are likely to change throughout the life-cycle of a product, as the above example would suggest. We will see later in this chapter how the promotion mix responds to changing objectives.

■ The communication process

To understand the principles of promotion planning, we first need to understand what is happening when a company sends messages to potential customers telling them about the benefits of buying its product. Some people see promotion as essentially a proactive means of persuading people to do something that they would not otherwise have done. (For example, they would not have gone to a new nightclub if they hadn't known about it.) An alternative view is that promotion is essentially a communication process which aims to remove the barriers that prevent an individual doing something. Think further about why you might not have visited a new nightclub in town:

• You may not have been aware of its existence.

• If you had known about it, you might not have had sufficient information to allow you to take action. (Where is it? What times does it open?)

• You might have wondered what benefits it would offer over the nightclub that you regularly patronize—what motivation would there be for you to break away from your present club, with which you are perfectly happy?

• You may have regarded a visit to the new nightclub as risky. (Will there be a rough clientelle? Will they rip me off for drinks prices?)

Promotional planning must address all of these issues, which are likely to vary in importance as the nightclub passes through its life-cycle. It must not be assumed that the communication process is complete once a targeted individual has become a customer. A customer is likely to need the reassurance that her chosen nightclub is the best choice, and much promotional activity is directed at reducing the cognitive dissonance that a person may have if she believes that she has made a wrong purchase decision. Furthermore, an individual may fear ridicule of her peer group if the nightclub is not continually promoted as the coolest place in town. Other nightclubs, including new challengers, may step up their promotional efforts in a bid to attract defectors from established clubs.

Communication, then, is a continual process, and we need to identify a number of elements of this process:

• The message source

• The audience to which the message is addressed

• The message itself

• The processes by which a message is encoded by the sender and decoded by the receiver, and the noise factors that may cause distortion of the message

• The channels through which the message is communicated

• The desired and actual response of the audience

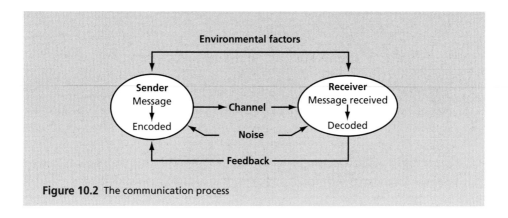

Figure 10.2 The communication process

- A feedback loop by which future communication with the target audience may be reconfigured following evaluation of the current communication.

The development of electronic channels of communication is making this process increasingly interactive, so now, instead of waiting a long time for feedback following a communication, this can often come back instantly. The elements of the process are illustrated in Figure 10.2 and are described in more detail below.

The message source

The company seeking to promote a product is the ultimate source of a message. Sometimes the identity of the source may be quite clear, but very often a company will use distinctive individuals as the apparent source of its messages. The identity of the message source can be important, because the source of a message—as distinct from the message itself—can influence the effectiveness of any communication. Aaker and Myers [8] identified three major features of sources that influence the effectiveness of any communication:

1. If a source is perceived as having power, then the audience response is likely to be compliance.

2. If a source is liked, then identification by the audience is a likely response. Important factors here include past experience and the reputation of the organization, in addition to the personality of the actual source of the communication. A salesperson, any contact personnel, a TV/radio personality, etc., are all very important in creating *liking*.

3. If a source is perceived as credible, then the message is more likely to be internalized by the audience. Credibility can be developed by establishing a source as important, high in status, power, and prestige, or by emphasizing reliability and openness. Consider the following examples of messages in which companies have selected a message source to add to the credibility of its products:

- Pharmaceutical companies frequently use doctors dressed in white coats to explain the benefits of an over-the-counter medication in their television adverts. Even if the role of doctor is played by an actor, the presence of the doctor's white coat is likely to increase the chances that we would trust the message. (Would we believe the message as much if it were communicated by a comedian?)

- Many companies seeking to stress the robust design of their product have used Germans—popularly associated with engineering superiority—to endorse the product. In one advert, the British MG Rover car company used a German voice-over to compare the build quality of its cars with those made by a leading German car manufacturer. The conclusion of many recipients of the message might have been that, if the car is good enough for the demanding Germans, it must be good enough for them.

- For many low-risk, low-involvement products, endorsement by an individual's peer group can be important. 'If people who are like me are happy with the product, then I will be happy with it as well' is a typical rationalization. A company may build on this by using an ordinary person as the message source. During 2003, the grocery retailer Tesco used an apparently ordinary (although slightly eccentric) pensioner to promote its low prices, and many similar pensioners doubtless empathized with what she was saying.

Closely related to the notion of credibility is the 'halo effect'. Coulson-Thomas [9] defined this as the 'tendency to impute to individuals and things, the qualities of other individuals and things with which they are associated'. The closer the perceived link between the 'personality' and a product, the stronger the halo effect. However, there is also a phenomenon known as the 'sleeper effect', in which the credibility of a source—and hence message retention—is built up over a period of time. The implication of this is that company and product reputation need regular reinforcement, both from formal advertising and from satisfying consumption of the product being promoted.

Celebrities are often used to endorse a product or an organization. We have a tendency to impute to the endorsed product the qualities that we have come to like about our favorite celebrity characters. There have been numerous studies of the effects of celebrity endorsement (e.g. Chung-kue and McDonald [16]). To be effective, the celebrity must be carefully chosen to match the aspirations of a product's target market. Consider the following examples of celebrity endorsement.

- Children develop a liking for television and film characters, whether they are real or inanimate. The popularity of Harry Potter books and films with children (and their parents) has led to manufacturers of products as diverse as breakfast cereals, confectionery, stationery, and computer hardware being endorsed with the character of Harry Potter (Lynch [2]).

- The TV chef Jamie Oliver has developed a loyal following among aspirational cooks which has been exploited by the grocery retailer Sainsbury's, which employed the chef to front its advertising campaign demonstrating meals made with Sainsbury's groceries.

- Companies often pay to have their products 'placed' in films. When the James Bond movie *Die Another Day* was released in 2002, 10 companies helped to pay for the film, in return for having their products included in the storylines. The list of companies included Bollinger, Philips, Sony Ericsson, Italian suit maker Brioni, Aston Martin, and Bombardier, which provided snowmobiles (Goodley [13]).

- Celebrities are often used by charities and public bodies to promote a good cause. During a 2002 advertising campaign to recruit more schoolteachers, a string of celebrities, including the Prime Minister and Lenny Henry, told viewers and readers about the important role that teachers had played in their lives.

Of course, a celebrity endorsement loses a lot of its value if the celebrity subsequently acquires a negative reputation. Naomi Campbell, for example, was notoriously dropped from her involvement in a charity campaign against wearing animal skins when she was photographed draped in fur on the catwalk. And Britney Spears was paid to promote Pepsi, only to be caught by a photographer sipping Coke (Anstead [4]).

The message

A message must be able to move an individual along a path from awareness through to eventual purchase. In order for a message to be received and understood, it must gain attention, use a common language, arouse needs, and suggest how these needs might be met. All of this should take place within the acceptable standards of the target audience. However, the product itself, the channel, and the source of the communication also convey a message, and therefore it is important that these do not conflict.

Three aspects of a communication message can be identified: content, structure, and format. It is the content that is likely to arouse attention, and change attitude and intention. The appeal or theme of the message is therefore important. The formulation of the message must include some kind of benefit, motivator, identification, or reason

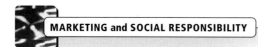

MARKETING and SOCIAL RESPONSIBILITY

Guerrilla tactics

In the world of military warfare, the most dangerous enemy is the surprise attacker, whose benhaviour is unpredictable and who can have an impact disproportionate to their efforts. So too with promotion by commercial organizations. When advertising begins to blend in with the wallpaper, it can take guerrilla tactics to grab buyers' attention.

The term 'guerrilla marketing' is not new and can be traced back to the mid-1980s. Jay Conrad Levinson describes the concept as being all about achieving conventional goals, such as increased profits, with unconventional methods, such as investing energy instead of money (Levinson [1]). Just as guerrilla warfare tactics can serve the interests of small dissident groups, guerrilla marketing is particularly suitable for the growing number of smaller businesses. Inevitably, many of the practices of guerrilla marketing can be questioned on ethical grounds.

One of the principles of guerrilla marketing is to get a message through to the target audience when the audience would least be expecting a selling message. Instead of perceptually filtering out what might be seen as a sales message, the target may be more amenable to persuasion. Drinks companies have used this in an attempt to gain acceptance among student markets. The promoters of Red Bull have used a form of viral marketing to promote their beer through students' word of mouth—after all, you are probably more likely to act on a friend's recommendation than in response to an advertisement. But is this ethical, especially if you don't realize that your friend was being paid to persuade you?

When guerrilla tactics get hooked up to the internet, the results can be even more questionable. FriendGreetings.com built up a mailing list of e-mail addresses and thousands of people followed its link to a greeting card which the company claimed was waiting for the recipient. Users were then invited to install an ActiveX control in order to view their e-card. Two lengthy end user licence agreements were displayed stating that by running the application the user is giving permission for a similar e-mail to be sent to all addresses found in the user's Outlook Express address book. Of course, most users did not bother to read the licence agreement and therefore allowed numerous unwanted e-mails to be sent from their e-mail address. Such a 'worm', which creates a flood of unwanted e-mails, can be just as much a nuisance as a virus. Guerrilla tactics had achieved their aim of attracting attention. As the message took the form of an e-card sent by somebody that the user knew, they did not suspect that clicking on to the link would result in anything untoward.

Are the practices of companies such as FriendGreetings.com ethical? Would such practices be self-defeating because the company would eventually acquire a bad reputation for itself? Is it right that 99 people should be inconvenienced so that the company can get profitable business from just 1 person out of each 100 that it targets? Is it possible to stop practices of this type? After all, users had technically given permission for a worm to get into their computer, even if the request was deviously hidden in a lengthy licence agreement!

why the audience should think or do something. Appeals can be rational, emotional, or moral.

Messages can be classified into a number of types, according to the dominant theme of the message. The following are common focal points for messages:

- **The nature and characteristics of the organization and the product on offer**: For example, television advertisements for Volkswagen have traditionally stressed their robust build quality.

- **Advantages over the competition**: Promotion by the airline Ryanair has empha-sized the low cost of its fares compared with its competitors.

- **Adaptability to buyers' needs**: Many insurance companies stress the extent to which their policies have been designed with the needs of particular age segments of the population in mind.

- **Experience of others**: Testimonials of previous satisfied customers are used to demonstrate the benefits resulting from use and the dependability of a company. (For example, Weight Watchers has used real customers to say how they successfully managed to lose weight using the company's products.)

Recipients of a message must see it as applying specifically to themselves, and they must see some reason for their being interested in it. The message must be structured accord-ing to the job it has to do. The points to be included in the message must be ordered (strongest arguments first or last) and consideration given to whether one-sided or two-sided messages should be used. Some messages use criticism of competitors' products, although there is some research evidence that negative advertising may be counter-productive (Richardson [5]). The actual format of the message will be very much determined by the medium used, e.g. the type of print if published material, type of voice if broadcast media is used, etc.

Encoding, decoding, and noise

The message that a company seeks to put across to its audience may be lengthy and in-volve a lot of technical description. However, the audience may have an attention span of only a few seconds; moreover, it is likely to be expensive to buy sufficient access to channels of communication to allow the company to put across its message in full.

Furthermore, a company may define its products in terms of their features, but it is important to remember that the audience must be *rapidly* made aware of its benefits to them. The creator of a message must therefore encode it into some acceptable form for an audience, which will then decode it.

Unfortunately, there is likely to be interference between the stages of encoding and decoding, so the message that a company sends out may not the one the audience picks up. 'Noise' occurs between the encoding and decoding of a message. Although it is dif-

Figure 10.3 This advert for De Montfort University gives very little specific information about the educational services provided by the university. However, the university successfully used a brand building promotional campaign to establish a distinctive identity which differentiates De Montfort from other 'modern' universities.

Reproduced with permission of De Montfort University.

ficult to eliminate such interference in the communication process totally, an understanding of the various elements of this 'noise' should help to minimize its effects.

Noise factors can be divided into two major types.

1. **Psychological factors**: No two individuals are the same in terms of their psychological makeup. Each person undergoes different experiences influencing his

MARKETING in ACTION

University of Fun?

How do you strike a balance between a promotional message being eye-catching and accessible on the one hand, and preserving the core values of the product on the other? Retailers, banks, and insurance companies have all encountered problems when their traditional mature audiences have been alienated by advertising that was aimed at increasing the number of younger customers. Wacky advertising may attract attention, but what does it say about the nature of the product on offer?

Liverpool-based John Moores University is one of a number of 'modern' universities that has used an unconventional approach to advertising its courses. Its 2002 undergraduate prospectus paid relatively little attention to the details of the courses on offer, but gave great emphasis to the pubs and clubs in town. It may well be that this was based on a sound analysis of the factors that influence students' choice of university. Most prospective students have only a limited ability to distinguish between the academic credentials of competing courses, whereas nightlife is an easier point of reference. But the media picked up the story, claiming that this was further evidence of 'dumbing down' in education generally, and at John Moores University in particular. Even existing students claimed that the value of their degrees would be demeaned by advertising that made their institution appear to the outside world like a 'good time university'. On the other hand, if the university went back to stuffy advertising messages and prospectuses, would it lose a point of difference with its nearby competitors?

personality, his perceptions of the world, his motives for action, and his attitudes towards people, situations, and objects. Therefore, it is not surprising to find that different people will interpret an advertisement differently.

An individual's past experience of a product or supplier is an important influence on how messages about that company's products are interpreted. Both positive and negative experiences predispose an individual to decode messages in a particular way. For example, a person may have a negative attitude towards an insurance company as a result of having previously had an insurance claim turned down by that company. This negative attitude is likely to distort her interpretation of any marketing communication from the company. In this context, therefore, the communication should involve an attempt to shift attitude as well as merely to inform.

The personality of specific members of an audience can significantly influence interpretation of a message—for example, an extrovert may interpret a message differently from an introvert. Similarly, an individual's motives can influence how a message is decoded.

A number of authors (e.g. Maslow [11]; Bayton [12]) have classified motives into those that are biological (such as the need to satisfy hunger, thirst, etc.) and those that are psychological and learned. Maslow talked of safety, social, self-esteem, and self-actualization needs, while Bayton distinguished between ego-bolstering,

Figure 10.4 **The language used in an advertisement must be in a form that is easily understood by the target market.** Compare these two styles of language. Would this advertisement for a nightclub have much impact on a target market of young people? And would the elderly market segment being targeted in this advert for bifocal glasses be alienated by its use of language?

ego-defensive, and affective needs. Both agree that in different situations one of these needs becomes dominant over the others and influences perceptions of the outside world. (The influences of motivation on buyer behaviour were discussed in more detail in Chapter 3.) As an example, an individual who has just come home from work tired and hungry and is about to eat dinner is unlikely to be amenable to an advertising phone message promoting banking services. At that moment, he is motivated by lower-order needs.

2. **Sociological factors**: In addition to the essentially personal characteristics that influence their behaviour, people are influenced by the presence of others around them. Individuals develop attitudes as a result of a conditioning process which is brought about by the culture they live in and the specific actions of family, friends, and work associates. Attitudes are learnt and are usually formed as a result of past experience. They are extremely enduring and are very influential in determining how a message is perceived.

   Attitudes are predispositions to act in a particular situation; they involve three elements:

   • The **cognitive** element of an attitude involves the knowledge and understanding of the object, person, or situation about which there is an attitude.

   • The **affective** element refers to the emotional content of an attitude and is usually expressed in terms of either positive or negative feelings.

   • The **conative** element of an attitude refers to the preparedness, on the part of the individual holding the attitude, to act positively or negatively if a particular situation involving the object or person arose.

People develop attitudes from a number of sources. In addition to the family, there are many other social groupings that influence how consumers see the world and how they decide what to purchase. Great importance is attached to the concept of reference groups. A reference group is a group with which an individual closely identifies so that they become, for her, standards of evaluation and sources of personal behavioural norms.

Reference groups can be divided into those of which an individual is a member ('membership groups') and those to which membership is aspired ('aspirational groups'). Both types of reference group influence how an individual perceives his environment and his decisions on goods and services purchases. (Think of how many people copy their best friend's or their favourite pop star's hair style or clothing.) Opinion leaders may exist who have the important task of 'trickling down' a message to other members of an audience. This type of process is most important where the cost of a product is high, the amount of information is low, the product involves significant social and symbolic value, and the purchase involves a high level of perceived risk.

Envy the girl.

Figure 10.5 **In wealthy countries, an increasing proportion of products are bought for their 'snob' value.** For example, there are many makes of music system, and the average buyer is not well qualified to distinguish between brands on the basis of their technical specification. However, Kenwood has positioned itself as an aspirational brand. By implication, somebody buying its brand will meet with social approval from their peer group.

Reproduced with permission of Kenwood Electronics.

Envy the car.

Envy the lifestyle.

NV. The system.

Perception and retention of the message

We are unlikely to remember, let alone notice, all of the messages that we come across. It was estimated by Western International Media (quoted in Southern and Johnson [23]) that every UK adult is subjected to over a thousand commercial messages in an average week. Past experience, personality, motivation, attitudes, and the influence of reference groups can all affect what we perceive and retain, leading to 'noise', which can distort an audience's perception and interpretation of a promotional message.

Individuals are likely to select only the stimuli perceived as being important to them.

- **Selective perception** occurs where communication is perceived in such a way that it merely reinforces existing attitudes and beliefs.

- **Selective reception** occurs where individuals make active decisions as to which stimuli they wish to expose themselves to. For example, a committed Conservative Party supporter may consciously avoid advertising by the Labour Party.

- **Selective retention** occurs when an individual remembers only those aspects of the message perceived as being necessary to him.

Even if an individual decides to give attention to a message, understands it, and remembers it, comprehension may still be different from what the communicator of the message expected. This perceptual distortion could be caused by those noise factors previously noted, poor encoding on the part of the communicator, or poor understanding by the audience itself. It is therefore important to pre-test all advertising before a full campaign is launched.

Noise is an extremely difficult variable to eliminate totally from any communication process. However, an understanding of its existence and its potential in hindering effective communication is vital in developing a communication strategy. The best way of minimizing such noise effects is to develop a detailed understanding of the target audience.

The target audience

The importance of market segmentation, targeting, and positioning has already been discussed in Chapter 5. Mention of this topic again here is essential when considering the principles of communication. A fundamental principle that underlies most promotional activity is that communication should be designed and placed to reach a specific type of audience. This audience represents a *market segment*. A market segment is any group of people who exhibit similar needs or demographic, social, psychological, or behavioural characteristics that will enable them to be targeted with a distinct marketing mix. Effective market segmentation presents marketers with a significant challenge. This can be demonstrated by considering the value of the traditional consumer market segmentation variables of demographics and socio-economic group against more recently developed variables such as psychographics and behavioural segmentation techniques.

Go back to Chapter 5 if you wish to review different bases for defining market segments.

Audience data

In both consumer and business-to-business markets, a challenge for marketers is to identify target markets accurately. This is increasingly being done using state-of-the-art technology to manipulate quantitative and qualitative data. The accuracy of such market information is critical for effective promotion management, especially with regard to effective use of resources and maximizing responses. The media industry has traditionally been provided with a wealth of market research data such as the Target Group Index, which mixes product usage data with demographic, socio-economic, and attitudinal data. The Broadcasters Audience Research Board (BARB) uses a panel of households to monitor television viewing data, and National Readership Surveys (NRS) provide data on newspaper and magazine readership. Alongside these data, advertising agencies and market research organizations conduct their own detailed research to provide better insights into the identification of appropriate market segmentation variables.

Of course, the importance of rigorous market segmentation and targeting varies between products and some launches succeed with only very broad definitions of their target market. One product launch that appeared to have broken all the principles of market segmentation was the UK national lottery, which gained wide market appeal with a singular message, although this has changed over time, from emphasizing winnings to emphasizing the benefits to communities that have received lottery funds. For the majority of products, however, such a homogeneous market and message is unlikely to be tenable.

Business-to-business audiences

In business-to-business markets, segmentation criteria have traditionally been based upon aggregate data such as regional location, size of organization, or Standard Industrial Classification (SIC) codes. Increasingly, however, more qualitative data are being used to identify organizations' behaviour or situations. These include such variables as the complexity of the decision-making unit, and an understanding of an individual's organization's economic situation or the benefits being sought. Generally, business-to-business markets are easier to target because of the smaller number of buying units involved, but more complex to understand and reach, particularly where the decision-making unit is complex.

MARKETING in ACTION

Magazines for men

Until a few years ago, the shelves of most newsagents would have been loaded with many general interest women's magazines (e.g. *Woman's Own*, *Women's Weekly*, *Cosmopolitan*), but very few general interest magazines aimed at men. Why? Some cynics might have argued that women were more likely to have spare time at home and could sit around reading, while 'busy' men were out at work, in the pub, or watching sport, and did not have time to read magazines. There may just have been a bit of truth in this, but the main reason has been that women's magazines have been popular with advertisers, who generally provide a high proportion of total income for a magazine publisher. In the traditional household, it has been women who have made decisions on a wide range of consumer goods purchases. Advertising the benefits of toothpaste, yogurt, or jam would have been lost on most men, who had little interest in which brand was put in front of them, and played little part in the buying process.

Take a look at the news-stand now and you will find that it carries a wide range of men's general interest magazines, such as *FHM*, *Loaded*, *Maxim*, and *Esquire*. Why have they suddenly mushroomed in number and in readership? Again, the answer lies in their attractiveness to advertisers. Talk of a male identity crisis may have spurred some sales, and it is evident that men are now involved in a much wider range of purchasing decisions than ever before. While some 'new men' may be taking a more active interest in the household shopping, many more are marrying later and indulging themselves in personal luxuries, an option that is less readily available to their married counterparts. With support from advertisers, the leading men's magazine in the UK, *FHM*, had a circulation of 570,000 copies per issue in 2001 (Audit Bureau of Circulation), overtaking the leading women's monthly magazine, *Cosmopolitan*, which had a circulation of 463,000. Advertising to men had never before looked so attractive.

Positioning in the mind of the target audience

Once the potential market segments have been identified and target audiences selected, a company will need to determine the positioning of its product in the marketplace and in the minds of consumers. It is not feasible to develop promotional plans until a clear understanding of the product positioning has been determined. Positioning was discussed in Chapter 6, but in view of its importance to promotional planning, a brief overview is provided here.

Positioning can be tangible, based upon such criteria as size, taste, quality, and price, or intangible, based upon brand image, perceptions, and value. Positioning on tangible factors will require a focus upon product and service design. For the consumer, however, it is often the intangible factors that have a significant influence on attitudes and purchase decisions. Effective management of marketing communications can enable the marketer to position a product in the consumer's mind by providing a clear brand proposition that differentiates the offer from competitive products.

A vital aspect to explore is the audience's image of an organization and its products and the degree of image consistency among the audience. An image tends to persist over time, with people continuing to see what they expect to see rather than what actually exists. The image of a firm and its products can be significantly influenced by how they are delivered, and therefore personnel who have contact with customers can play a vital role in the development of this image.

The Co-operative Bank case study (at the end of this chapter) demonstrates the importance of market segmentation, targeting, and positioning as key processes within promotion planning. Through a clear understanding of its customer base, the bank was able to deliver a relevant and distinctive message that gained immediate approval from those it targeted. Creative and media strategies were developed to gain maximum effectiveness and impact. Without such a clear understanding of the target audience, campaign effectiveness would have been significantly diminished.

Buyer readiness state

It is often important to define an audience in terms of the level of involvement of potential recipients of the communication. For example, a distinction can be made between those people who are merely aware of the existence of a product, those who are interested in possibly purchasing it, and those who definitely wish to purchase it. This is crucial, because it was noted above that the aim of communication is to move target customers through the stages from mere awareness, through liking, to eventual purchase. Segmentation of audiences does not end there, however: many communication messages are aimed at people who have already bought a product, with the aim of reducing any cognitive dissonance they may have, and encouraging them to recommend the product to their friends. A communication can sometimes succeed in targeting buyers at all stages of readiness to buy, but generally it is more likely to be focused on buyers at different stages of the process.

It is also important to note that people differ markedly in their readiness to try new products, and a number of attempts have been made to classify the population in terms of their level of risk aversity or risk-seeking inclination. For purchases that are perceived as being highly risky, customers are likely to use more credible sources of information (e.g. word-of-mouth recommendation) and to engage in a prolonged search through information sources. Rogers [10] defined a person's 'innovativeness' as the 'degree to which an individual is relatively earlier in adopting new ideas than the other members of his social system'. In each product area, there are likely to be 'consumption pioneers' and early adopters, while other individuals adopt new products only much later.

A typical adoption distribution pattern, applied to the market for mobile videophones, is illustrated in Figure 10.6. 'Innovators' are venturesome in that they are willing to try new ideas at some risk. Some people will always want to have the latest gadgets, and the promotion of new video mobile phones to this group should stress not only the technical features of the product, but also the status benefits that an early adopter of the new technology will receive. 'Early adopters' are opinion leaders in their

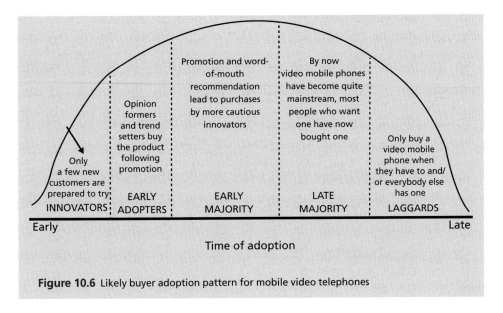

Only
a few new
customers are
prepared to try

INNOVATORS

Opinion
formers
and trend
setters buy
the product
following
promotion

EARLY
ADOPTERS

Promotion and word-
of-mouth
recommendation
lead to purchases
by more cautious
innovators

EARLY
MAJORITY

By now
video mobile phones
have become quite
mainstream, most
people who want
one have now
bought one

LATE
MAJORITY

Only buy a
video mobile
phone when
they have to and/
or everybody else
has one

LAGGARDS

Early   Late

Time of adoption

Figure 10.6 Likely buyer adoption pattern for mobile video telephones

community, adopting new products early but carefully. The 'early majority' adopt new ideas before the average person, taking their lead from opinion leaders; for this group communication should be moving towards an emphasis on the practical benefits of video mobile phones, rather than concentrating on their status benefits. The 'late majority' are sceptical, tending to adopt an innovation only after the majority of people have tried it. Finally, 'laggards' are tradition-bound, being suspicious of changes. This group adopts a new product only when it has become sufficiently widespread that it has now taken on a measure of tradition in itself. Communication aimed at them would probably emphasize low price and easy availability.

Although adoption processes for goods and services are in principle similar, differences can result from services being perceived as riskier than goods, especially where they entail a high level of personal involvement by the consumer. Evaluation of quality and value before purchase is generally more difficult, and effective promotion of services must therefore start by understanding the state of mind of potential customers and the information they seek in order to reduce their exposure to risk.

Push v. pull messages

Should a company aim its message at the final consumer who will actually use its product? We have already described the existence of a decision-making unit (DMU) and noted that the person who actually consumes a product may not be the best person to target a message at. (For example, a high proportion of men have very little influence in the purchase process for the socks that they wear.) It may also be quite futile to target a message at the person who actually goes into the shop and buys the product. (Think of 'pester power' from children.) Just as importantly, we need to consider whether messages should be aimed at the end buyer/user, or at intermediaries who will influence the purchase decisions of the end buyer/user.

This distinction forms the basis for 'push' and 'pull' models of communication (Figure 10.7). In a traditional push model, a manufacturer promotes its products heavily to wholesalers, which in turn promote heavily to retailers, which in turn use their sales skills to sell to the final buyer/user. In many markets, the end consumer may have little awareness of brands and may rely totally on what is offered to them by an intermediary. How many people visiting their dentist would specify a type of filling material by brand name that they would like the dentist to use in their filling? How many people visiting an independent financial adviser (IFA) for advice on pensions would have a preference for one pensions company rather than another? In these circumstances, a company is most likely to achieve higher levels of sales by targeting its promotional efforts at intermediaries rather than the end consumer.

The problems to a manufacturer of a 'push' approach should be apparent. In order for its message to reach the end buyer/user, it must be transmitted efficiently and effectively by each of the intermediaries who handle the message. There is a great danger that 'noise' factors could drastically change the message from what is sent out by the manufacturer to what is received by the end buyer/user. Because the manufacturer has very little control over a message as it passes through a push channel, it may seek to go over the heads of intermediaries by developing a 'pull' channel. Here, the message is aimed at the end buyer/user. If it has an effect in changing their behaviour, buyers will go into a retail outlet and demand the brand by name. The retailer will then demand a particular brand from the wholesaler, which in turn will demand the product from the manufacturer. In the field of financial services, the efforts of savings and pensions companies to develop strong brands have been designed to bring buyers to an intermediary with a prior preference for one brand over others. In computing, Intel broke with tradition by going over the heads of dealers and computer assemblers with the message to end-users that they would benefit by choosing a computer with an Intel processor.

Other important audiences for communication

It should be remembered that promotion is not always aimed solely at buyers or their immediate decision-making units. Other key audiences alongside the specific target customers should also be clearly identified in terms of their role, influence, and importance in the market place. These 'interest' groups are commonly referred to as 'stakeholders' and can include the following:

Supply chain/marketplace

- Suppliers
- Distributors/agents
- Partner organizations
- Competitors

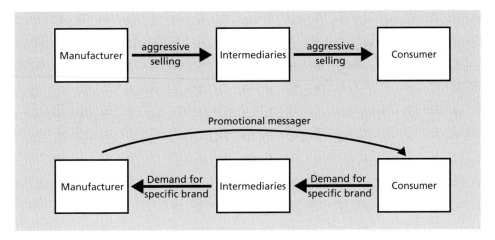

Figure 10.7 'Push' and 'pull' channels of communication compared

Figure 10.8 Most computer buyers have little knowledge about the components from which a computer is assembled. Choice is likely to be based on the ratio of readily observable benefits (e.g. speed, RAM size, DVD drive) to price. Most buyers are likely to have difficulty evaluating the quality of the processor which is at the heart of a PC, especially as new chips are continuously being developed. Intel has invested in new product development and has gained a reputation for leading edge, reliable chips. However, Intel faces challenges from other chip manufacturers whose products may be less expensive to computer assemblers, possibly allowing them to keep their selling prices below critical price points.
Intel has sought to remain not only technologically superior to its competitors, but the preference for end-consumers. The company has backed up a sophisticated quality assured supply chain network with a direct appeal to consumers about the benefits of buying a computer which incorporates an Intel processor. The brand is strengthened when end-consumers actively seek out computers which contain Intel chips (Reproduced with permission of Intel Corporation)

Political/financial bodies

- Local authorities
- Governments and international agencies
- Financial institutions

Interest groups

- Pressure groups

- Employees
- Trade unions
- Local community
- The media
- Opinion leaders

Each of these stakeholder groups at varying times can have a significant influence upon the organization in terms of its overall effectiveness, efficiency, and image. Many privatized utility companies realize that the most important target for their communication is often not the consumers who buy or use their services, but the regulators who control the prices that can be charged, or politicians who can change the legislative framework within which the utilities do business. It is often necessary to strike a balance between the short-term goals of the organization and the longer-term interests of these key groups. Communication is a vital link between the organization and its key stakeholders. Public relations is the primary tool used for communicating with such stakeholders and is discussed further in Chapter 11.

MARKETING in ACTION

Selling an organization to its employees

Although the primary target audience of an advertisement may be customers, its effects on employees should not be forgotten. This is especially true of labour-intensive services industries, where an advert can provide encouragement for front-line employees to perform their jobs with pride, as well as encouraging customers to buy. If cabin crew of British Airways see the airline's advertisements casting them in the role of helpful and friendly problem solvers, they should be able to identify with this role and carry it out effectively and with satisfaction. Employees can often become highly involved in the adverts when they are used in place of professional actors. The DIY retailer B&Q has for a long time used its own employees from different branches to promote its store offers, providing a sense of realistic credibility to customers and of involvement from employees.

Employees who have heard rumours about poor financial prospects for a company amidst talk of falling sales may have some of their confidence restored by the sight of advertisements aimed at drumming up new business.

At times, however, advertisements can serve only to demotivate staff. Advertising claims may be made which front-line staff are simply incapable of delivering, perhaps because of inadequate training or insufficient resources to keep the promises made. If employees don't believe the claims of an advert, why should customers? On occasion, adverts can actually annoy staff by casting them in a demeaning role, something the retailer Sainsbury's learnt to its cost following a series of adverts in its 'Value to Shout About' adverts. These used the actor John Cleese to promote the grocery retailer's low prices, but in doing so the scenes belittled staff and their knowledge of the new low prices. After representations from staff—and some suggestion that the campaign wasn't working with customers—the adverts were pulled.

The channel

A message must be communicated to the target audience by some means. In a very few cases, a company may be able to do the bulk of its communication face to face with its current and potential customers. A trader at a fruit and vegetable market probably has no advertising or paid promotional activity, but relies on attracting passing trade through a display of his products and face-to-face communication with each customer. Larger and more complex companies cannot rely on such simple methods. They must develop impersonal means of communication in place of face-to-face contact. We talk about communication being conducted through a *channel*, such as television, newspapers, or posters. Some of these channels may nevertheless still retain a high degree of personal contact, for example personal selling.

Channels have a tendency to distort the message that was sent. We saw earlier how messages are encoded by the sender and also by the receiver, and part of the noise that occurs between the two can be explained by the nature of the channel. Some channels are able to accommodate a lengthy message without distortion. Contrast this to a typical 30 second radio advert, where a complex message must be conveyed in a short time using only one of the senses—sound. While some channels have a facility for immediate feedback from the person receiving a message (online channels can often do this), immediate response is lacking from most channels; for example, a newspaper advert in itself doesn't allow a customer to speak back to a company that has transmitted a message through the pages of the newspaper.

Companies put a lot of effort into optimizing their use of channels so that they get the maximum number of messages through to the most number of people in their target market, at minimum cost. We will consider general approaches to evaluation later in this chapter.

We will look in more detail at the growing variety of channels available to advertisers later in this chapter under the general heading of the 'promotion mix'. In Chapter 11 we will explore in greater detail how each of these channels works.

Response: marketing communications models

Having identified the target audience and its characteristics, the communicator must consider the type of response required from it. The required response will have an influence on the source, message, and channel of communication.

It was noted above that in most cases customers are seen as going through a series of stages before finally deciding to purchase a product. It is therefore critical to recognize these buyer-readiness stages and to assess where the target audience is at any given time. The communicator will be seeking any one or more of three audience responses to the communication:

1. **Cognitive responses**—the message should be considered and understood.

2. **Affective responses**—the message should lead to some change in attitude.

3. **Behavioural responses**—finally, the message should achieve some change in behaviour (e.g. a purchase decision).

Many models have been developed to show how marketing communication has the effect of 'pushing' recipients of messages through a number of sequential stages, finally resulting in a purchase decision. The development of these communication models enables marketers to understand complex relationships, phenomena, and processes within a manageable framework. These models simplify the real world and are designed primarily to highlight specific issues. They also provide a means to explain how interrelationships between variables occur and can provide explanations of causes and outcomes of specific types of behaviour.

Communication models portray a simple and steady movement through the various stages, which should not be seen as ending when a sale is completed. It was noted in Chapter 3 that organizations increasingly seek to build relationships with their customers, so the behavioural change (the sale) should be seen as the starting point for making customers aware of other offers available from the organization and for securing repeat business. Smooth progress through these stages is impeded by the presence of 'noise' factors. The probabilities of success in each stage cumulatively decline because of noise, and therefore the probability of the final stage eventually achieving an actual purchase can be very low.

We will now look briefly at some widely used marketing communication models which seek to understand buyers' responses to communication stimuli. A range of models have been developed in the academic literature. Some of the key communication models are outlined below.

'Hierarchy of effects' models

These models propose a sequence of responses that occurs as a result of a message being received by a target audience. The two most common such models are referred to as AIDA and DAGMAR (Figure 10.9).

The principle that underlies these models is that communication acts as a stimulus which gives rise to a 'conditioned' response. Communication can therefore be developed to achieve the objective of moving people through the sequence of responses:

- To gain initial awareness of a product, advertising may be the most effective method.

- To gain liking, comprehension, and desire, brochures may provide more detail which will be needed to make a subsequent purchase decision.

- To achieve an actual sale, personal selling and sales promotion activity may be best.

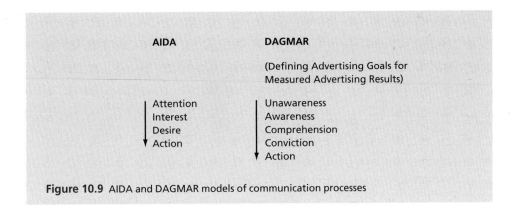

Figure 10.9 AIDA and DAGMAR models of communication processes

'Hierarchy of effects' models suggest how communications affect the mind and behaviour of the audience. The major benefit of such models is that they enable the purpose of a particular promotion to be defined and pre- and post-campaign surveys can be carried out to demonstrate the communication effect.

The models have many weaknesses, the most significant being their simplification of a complex psychological and behavioural process. The audience is seen as a passive recipient of messages as opposed to active seekers and participants in the communication process. Consumer research has shown that many consumers set predetermined parameters within which a purchase decision might be made, such as price range and style of a product. The buyer therefore selects those messages that support her in her purchase decision as opposed to being passively pulled through the sequence. These models also ignore psychological factors, such as the influence of attitudes/beliefs, motivation, and perception on behaviour. Furthermore, they assume that the sequence of response is universal, when in fact instances occur where consumption of a product may occur before any commitment to the product or service is made; similarly, awareness of, and commitment to, a product can occur at the same time as the point of purchase but with limited understanding, as happens with impulse purchases. Finally, the models ignore the effects of promotional activity that aim to limit brand switching behaviour and to promote repeat purchase.

The assumption that specific promotional effects can be measured in isolation is also a simplification of a complex communication environment. In reality, it is difficult to isolate one single cause as a communication effect. We are bombarded daily by a multitude of communication signals, each one playing its part in influencing behaviour.

Integrated models

A model that identifies and integrates psychological and behavioural elements was developed by Timothy Joyce and is shown in Figure 10.10. This model recognizes that to

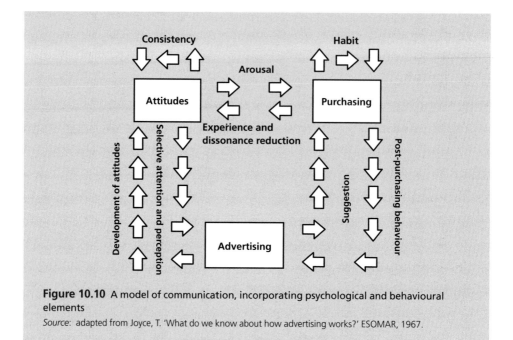

Figure 10.10 A model of communication, incorporating psychological and behavioural elements
Source: adapted from Joyce, T. 'What do we know about how advertising works?' ESOMAR, 1967.

understand how promotions work we need to understand the nature of the promotion, people's purchase behaviour, their individual psychology, and how the relationships between these factors interrelate. The effect of communication is seen not as a passive relationship but more as a continuing relationship, with habit and consistency forming an integral part of an individual's behaviour. The inclusion of perception and the selective attention to communication stimuli recognize that the consumer will not take in all of a communication message and that individuals make associations in their own minds as to the nature of the communication they have received. The model also recognizes that attitudes can be influenced by both pre- and post-purchase experience and that, while advertising might succeed in arousing interest or successfully reinforcing attitudes, post-purchase experience and dissonance may have an equal effect.

In summary, this model provides a useful framework within which to consider the complexity of the communication process. However, it does not provide a means against which promotional effects can be measured, and does not offer the simple application of the 'hierarchy of effects' models considered earlier.

Communication and buyer behaviour models

Alongside the communication models just described can be considered the buyer behaviour models, to which you were introduced in Chapter 3. These overlap with the communications models by seeking to explain the buying process. With all these models, their importance lies in their ability to help us to understand specific elements of a complex process. Despite their inherent weaknesses, they can provide useful guidelines for planning and implementing effective communication.

MARKETING in ACTION

Selling tap water

Every now and again, marketers face the challenge of promoting a product that buyers find extremely difficult to conceptualize, perhaps because they have no experience of any product that is remotely similar. It may be so novel that they cannot contemplate how the product might be able to satisfy a complex set of needs. In 2003 the UK mobile phone industry pondered how it might take consumers through the stages of adopting mobile internet services based on '3rd Generation' technology. Many cynics could not imagine a world in which users would routinely watch a video as they travelled on the tube, or turn to their phone instead of a printed map when navigating a new town. The mobile phone companies had a major awareness issue to overcome before they could go on to sell the new phones in large numbers. Perhaps they could have learnt from the experience of the UK government which in the early 1990s tried to sell to the public a 'product' which was equally difficult to comprehend.

The government's efforts to sell shares in public utilities illustrated the process of pushing the target audience through the buying process. Initial advertising was aimed at creating awareness of industries which most people took for granted. So the first adverts for the water companies' privatization used images of underground pipework to make people aware of the size and complexity of the organization that was being sold. Following this, the adverts moved towards creating a desire to become a shareholder. The British Gas adverts at this stage created the character of 'Sid', with whom people could identify as a new small shareholder. Telephone numbers given in advertisements allowed potential investors to call to obtain further information. Finally, advertising in the closing stages focused on the need to take immediate action. Newspaper adverts contained application forms and a cut-off date by which forms had to be submitted.

Was the advertising effective in taking people through the buying process? At the outset of the privatization process, cynics had claimed that very few people would want to buy shares—which they did not understand—in public utilities, whose complexities they were unaware of. In the event, shares in the privatizations were nearly all heavily oversubscribed, and much of this could be attributed to the effective multi-stage communication. The mobile phone operators faced similar levels of cynicism in 2003 with the launch of mobile internet services. Could a multi-stage communication process silence the cynics?

■ Introducing the promotion mix

Communication is received by audiences from two principal sources: those within an organization, and those external to it. The latter includes word-of-mouth recommendation from friends, editorials in the press, etc., which may have high credibility in the product evaluation process. Sources originating within an organization can be divided into those originating from the traditional marketing function (which can be divided into personal two-way channels such as personal selling and impersonal one-way channels such as advertising), and those originating from front-line production resources. In the case of services that involve consumers in the production process, the promotion mix has to be considered more broadly than is the case with manufactured goods. Front-line operations staff and service outlets become a valuable channel of communication.

The promotion mix comprises those activities that a company uses to promote its products and its corporate image to customers, potential customers, and the key stakeholder groups described above. These activities are conventionally identified by a number of headings, although they overlap. As with the marketing mix itself, definitions of the promotion mix elements are not in themselves particularly important—what is more important is to recognize the interdependencies between them. The most commonly used headings for promotion mix elements are advertising, sales promotion, selling, public relations, direct marketing, and online marketing. Within each of these categories a further range of options can be identified. (For example, advertising involves mixing a variety of media, such as newspaper, television and radio advertising.) Figure 10.11 outlines the key elements of the promotion mix.

The choice of a particular combination of communication channels will depend primarily on the characteristics of the target audience, especially its habits in terms of exposure to messages. Other important considerations include the present and potential market size for the product (advertising on television may not be appropriate for a product that has a local niche market, for example), the nature of the product itself (the more personal the product, the more effective the two-way communication channel), and of course the costs of the various channels.

An important trend affecting promotional planning is the increasing fragmentation of markets, resulting in smaller market segments, and hence smaller audiences for a highly specific message. Fortunately, this has occurred at a time of growing media availability and choice. Sophisticated database technology and the internet have opened new possibilities for communicating messages to narrowly defined audiences, while the development of the mobile internet through third generation mobile phones and global positioning systems allows targeting not only by individual, but also according to where and when a company believes that the individual will be most responsive to a message. Such fragmentation of both markets and media availability confirms the need for increased sophistication of market segmentation and targeting techniques within the promotion planning process.

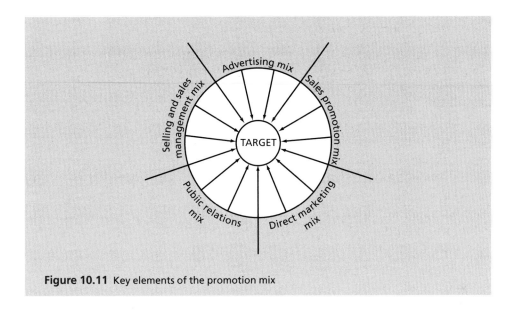

Figure 10.11 Key elements of the promotion mix

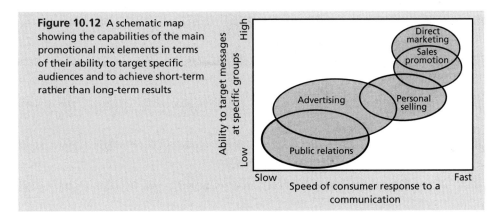

Figure 10.12 A schematic map showing the capabilities of the main promotional mix elements in terms of their ability to target specific audiences and to achieve short-term rather than long-term results

The elements of the promotion mix vary in the extent to which they can achieve the diverse communication objectives described earlier in this chapter. Advertising, for example, is generally fairly good at developing an image for a company, but is less capable of conveying complex factual information about a product. Direct marketing is much better at adapting a message to very small audiences, but is less useful for image building. Two important aspects of communication objectives are shown in Figure 10.12:

1. the extent to which a message can be adapted to the needs of a specific audience; and

2. the extent to which a message can achieve a short-term or a long-term response from the audience.

	£m
Television	4,646
National newspaper	1,711
Regional newspaper	919
Consumer magazines	591
Business & prefessional journals	758
Press production costs	702
Outdoor and transport	823
Radio	595
Cinema	128
Direct mail	2,049
Internet	155

Figure 10.13 Estimate of UK display advertising by medium, 2000

Source: based on Advertising Association estimates

In the figure a two-dimensional grid has been drawn, in which the main elements of the promotional mix have been located. The diagram shows that, while different mix elements may have distinctive functions, there is nevertheless some overlap. Some media, such as advertising, are capable of spanning a range of objectives.

Figure 10.13 gives some indication of the relative importance of the different elements of the promotion mix, as measured by expenditure. In the following section the scope of the main elements of the promotion mix are briefly discussed. More detailed discussion will follow in the next chapter.

The promotion mix and the product life-cycle

A very important consideration in arriving at a promotion mix is the stage a product has reached in its life-cycle (see Chapter 7). Advertising and public relations are more likely to form important channels of communication during the introductory stage of the life-cycle, where the major objective is often to increase overall audience awareness. Sales promotion can be used to stimulate trial, and in some instances personal selling can be used to acquire distribution coverage. During a product's growth stage the use of all communication channels can generally be reduced, as demand during this phase tends to produce its own momentum through word-of-mouth communications. However, as the product develops into its maturity stage, there may be a call for an increase in advertising and sales promotion activity. Finally, when the product is seen to be going into decline, advertising and public relations are often reduced, although sales promotion can still quite usefully be applied. Sometimes products in decline are allowed to die quietly with very little promotion. In the case of many long-life financial services, which a company would like to delete but cannot for contractual reasons, the service may be kept going with no promotional support at all.

Advertising

This is defined here as 'any paid form of non-personal communication of ideas, goods, or services delivered through selected media channels'.

This definition provides a succinct statement of advertising, from the running of adverts on prime-time television through to placing a postcard in a newsagent's window. The term 'media' simply refers to where the advert is placed. In addition to television and newspapers, a hot air balloon with an advertising message and football hoardings seen at stadiums are all different forms of media.

The selection of media is critical. In an ideal world, a specific advertisement would be seen and read by all of its intended target audience. In reality, such coverage is difficult to achieve. Different media are therefore selected to increase the probability of a member of the target audience seeing the advert at least once. The combination of types of media used for this purpose is often referred to as the *media mix*.

Advertising is defined as non-personal. Advertisements are targeted at a mass audience and not to a specific individual. One of the benefits of advertising is its ability to reach a large number of people at relatively low cost. That is not to say that advertising costs are low. If an advertiser wishes to reach a prime-time television audience or to place a full-page advert in a high-quality magazine or newspaper, then the costs will range from tens of thousands of pounds to hundreds of thousands of pounds just for one spot or insertion. When we consider the cost per 1,000 people, however, this can work out to be relatively low. With large audiences or readerships, the cost of an advertisement per 1,000 viewers or readers can often fall to just a few pence.

The decision whether or not to advertise will be determined by an organization's market situation and its objectives. In the next chapter we will be looking in more detail at the development of advertising strategy and its implementation.

Selling and sales management

A sales force provides the personal interface between a company and its customers. This contact may be face to face, by telephone, or, more recently, through the internet. The salesperson acts as a conduit through which information can be passed from an organization to its customers and vice versa. A product that is perfect in design, targeted at segments of the consumer population who crave it, and promoted with great flair and at a price structured to meet every possible combination of purchase occasion may nevertheless remain on the pallets in the warehouse if no professional selling effort is involved.

Personal selling and sales management are discussed further in the following chapter.

Sales promotion

The Institute of Sales Promotion defines sales promotions as 'a range of tactical marketing techniques designed, within a strategic marketing framework, to add value to a product in order to achieve a specific sales and marketing objective'.

Sales promotions can be targeted at consumers with the aim of pulling sales through a channel of distribution, or at the distributor with the aim of pushing products through the channel, or at a combination of both. The most common consumer sales promotion techniques include special offers—for instance price reductions or 'two for the price of one'—competitions, gifts, coupons, or incentive schemes such as air miles and retailers' loyalty cards. Sales promotions targeted at distributors include seasonal incentives and bulk purchase offers.

Traditionally, sales promotions have been used tactically to encourage brand switching, as a response to competitors' activity, or to create a short-term increase in the level and frequency of sales. Increasingly, sales promotions are now being used more strategically and are being integrated into an overall communications strategy.

Sales promotion will be discussed further in the following chapter.

Public relations

Public relations encompasses 'the deliberate, planned, and sustained effort to establish and maintain mutual understanding between an organization and its publics' (Institute of Public Relations). In recent years there has been a significant increase in both interest and expenditure on public relations activity.

The key feature of public relations (PR) is its focus on the 'public', or stakeholder, groups that have an interest in, or an influence on, an organization's activities and positioning in the marketplace. Some of the key groups were identified earlier in this chapter. As suggested in the definition, a key role of PR is to establish and maintain mutual understanding between the organization and its key stakeholder groups. If the interests and issues raised by these groups are ignored or mishandled, the resulting publicity can harm the organization's public image. The following chapter will consider this important and growing field of activity.

Sponsorship

Sponsorship does not fit neatly into a categorization of the main elements of the promotion mix. Essentially, it uses a combination of advertising, public relations, sales promotion, and direct marketing to associate a company's product or corporate image (which may be unknown or misunderstood) with the image of something that is well understood.

Direct marketing

In recent years IT developments have opened up a number of new possibilities for companies to communicate with their customers. Direct mail, telephone response media, and the internet all allow promotional messages to be tailored and targeted to individuals, having regard to their unique needs. The principles and techniques of direct marketing are discussed in the following chapter.

Online marketing

The internet has become an important element of the promotion mix and often combines a promotion function with a distribution function. Despite the importance of online media, many would argue that it has become an integrative element of the promotion mix rather than an element in its own right.

Use of online media crosses all of the other promotion mix elements; for example, a static web page meets our definition for advertising; the internet is often used as a tool of direct marketing in which a sales promotion offer is made; public relations professionals are increasingly using internet chat rooms proactively and reactively; and sales personnel are using the internet to follow up sales leads. These multi-faceted aspects of online promotion are discussed in greater detail in the following chapter.

MARKETING in ACTION

Above or below the line?

Marketing managers have for long talked about the distinction between 'above-the-line' and 'below-the-line' promotion, referring (respectively) to advertising expenditure on the one hand, and other less direct promotional expenditure such as sales promotion and direct marketing on the other. Despite recent talk of 'through-the-line' promotion and 'media neutral planning', specialists in different elements of promotion can remain dogged in their ghetto's snobbery. Advertising managers have too often been unfamiliar with the potential of direct mail as an acquisition and recruitment tool. Moreover, despite a move towards customer relationship building activity, acquisition remains the lifeblood of a competitive marketplace, and this drives many advertising campaigns. Yet integration of media is becoming increasingly evident.

Tesco provides a good example of the potential for direct marketing's ability to acquire customers and to complement other media activities. Tesco has for some time relied on advertising to communicate its core brand values of low prices, good quality products, and a wide range of services at its stores. But it has recognized the need to speak to smaller target markets using more selective media. One target the store set itself was to become the leading baby provisions supplier to the market of expectant parents. It developed a mother and baby club, which recruited nearly a quarter of a million members in just eight weeks from launch and a market share representing one-third of all UK births per year. Its award-winning campaign involved 6 million mailings of letters, collectible magazines, and product coupons, targeting its audience by using advertising in media seen by expectant parents, as well as through in-store promotion activities. Once customers had been recruited, Tesco had a valuable basis for relationship development. Inevitably, once the baby was born, the parents' needs changed, and Tesco would know about this and be able to respond with appropriate product offers.

Word-of-mouth

Of course, an organization's image can be projected through channels other than the formal communication process. There is a lot of evidence, for example, that, when differentiating between a variety of professional and personal services providers, customers prefer to be guided by information from friends and other personal contacts rather than the usual promotion mix (e.g. Susskind [20]; Walker [17]). Of course, positive word-of-mouth recommendation is generally dependent on customers having good experiences with an organization, and studies have shown how unexpectedly high standards of service from a company can promote recommendation (Derbaix and Vanhamme [15]). On the other hand, a bad experience can rapidly be spread as negative word-of-mouth discouragement (Laczniak, DeCarlo, and Ramaswami [7]). An important communication objective therefore is often to leverage this 'free' form of positive promotion and to limit the damage caused by negative word-of-mouth by encouraging dissatisfied customers to resolve their problems before they tell others. In addition to providing a good product that people would want to recommend to their friends, firms facilitate word-of-mouth recommendation through such means as customer referral cards (Figure 10.14).

Word-of-mouth recommendation has been further facilitated by the internet. As well as telling their friends, messages left with bulletin boards and chat rooms can spread a message very rapidly. Many companies have embraced the internet to develop 'viral' marketing, in which a message can be spread rapidly from one person to a handful of friends, who each in turn inform a handful of their friends (Gelb and Sundaram [21]; Welker [14]). In one case, the online marketing firm NewGate distributed advance excerpts of a new children's book to online forum leaders. When the forum leaders read the pre-released chapters they quickly spread the excitement and anticipation for the book, which ended up being on the *New York Times* bestseller list. The company had used more than 400,000 discussion boards and message forums across the net, targeting about 11 million 'e-fluentials', who in turn reached 55 million consumers by spreading the word (Cardwell [6]).

Other sources of messages

It was noted earlier that promotional messages about a company could come from many different sources within the organization, and not just the traditional promotion channels that originate in marketing departments. Service industries, in particular provide opportunities for front-line staff and service outlets to act as live advertisements for a company.

The general appearance of a shop, restaurant, or car dealership can promote the image of a service organization. A brightly coloured and clean exterior can transmit a message that the organization is fast, efficient, and well run. Outlets can be used to

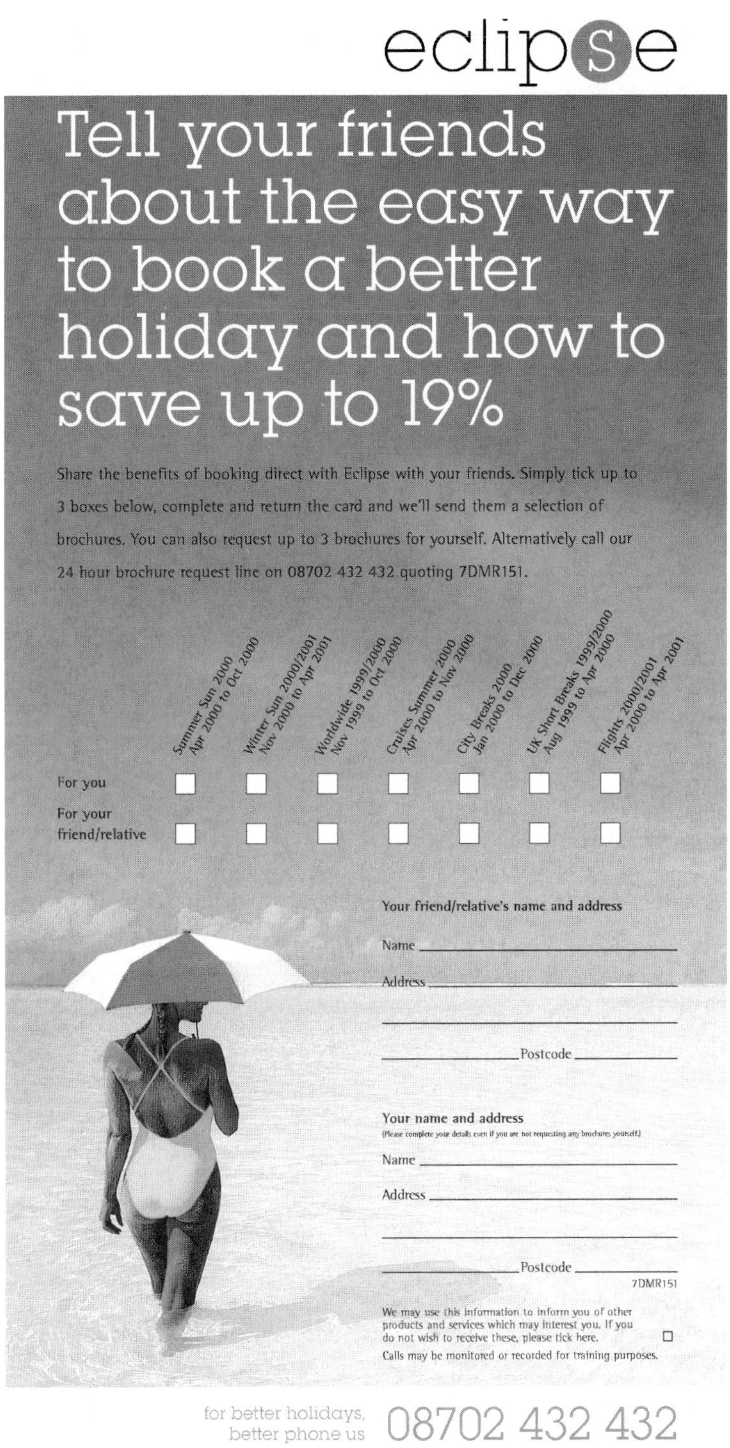

Figure 10.14 It should never be forgotten that the most powerful form of promotion is word-of-mouth recommendation. Companies go to great lengths to encourage their satisfied customers to recommend them to friends. Eclipse Holidays tries to make it easy for customers to recommend it to a friend by providing this reply-paid brochure request form

Reproduced with permission of Eclipse Holidays Ltd.

display advertising posters which in heavily trafficked locations can result in valuable exposure. Many retailers with town centre locations regard these opportunities as so great that they do not need to undertake more conventional promotion. Among the large UK retailers, Marks & Spencer until the 1990s paid for very little promotional activity, arguing that over half the population passed one of its stores during any week, thereby exposing them to powerful 'free' messages. Although the company's promotional mix now includes more paid-for advertising, store locations are still considered to be valuable promotional media.

Outlets can also provide valuable opportunities to show service production processes to potential customers, something that is much more difficult to achieve through conventional media. A restaurant displaying modern, state-of-the-art equipment and a solicitor's clean and tidy office both send out promotional messages about the organizations.

Stages of the promotion planning process

Promotional activity is unlikely to be effective unless it forms part of a cohesive and integrated promotional plan. A key element of that plan is the decision on how the elements of the promotional mix should be implemented. However, prior to such decision, analysis needs to be undertaken and objectives and strategy agreed. A useful framework within which to consider promotional planning is SOST '4Ms' proposed by Smith [22], which sees the process beginning with a general review of a company's situation, and proceeds through objectives, strategy, and tactics.

1. **Situation**

    (a) Company—sales and market share trends, summary strengths and weaknesses

    (b) Product service range—features, benefits, and Unique Selling Proposition; product positioning

    (c) Market structure—growth, opportunities and hazards, target markets and competition

2. **Objectives**: short, medium, and long-term

    (a) Marketing objectives

    (b) Communication objectives

3. **Strategy**: how the objectives will be achieved; this can be a summary of the promotional mix and can include the marketing mix (no tactical details here)

4. **Tactics**: the detailed activities to implement strategy; the detailed planning of how, when, and where various promotional activities (communication tools) occur

5. **4Ms**

(a) *Men*: men (and women!)—Who is responsible for what? Are there enough suitably experienced men and women in-house to handle various projects? Have they got spare capacity to take on extra tasks? Are outside agencies needed, or should extra permanent staff be recruited?

(b) *Money*: budget—what will it cost? Is it affordable? Is it good value for money? Should the money be spent elsewhere? Does the budget include research to measure the effectiveness of various other activities? Is there an allowance for contingencies?

(c) *Minutes*: time-scale and deadlines for each stage of each activity—proposals, concept development, concept testing, regional testing, national roll-out, European launch.

(d) *Measurement*: monitoring the results of all activities helps the marketing manager to understand what works well and what is not worth repeating in the next campaign. Clearly defined and specific objectives provide yardsticks for measurement. The monitored results also help the manager to make realistic forecasts and ultimately to build better marketing communication plans in the future.

The situation analysis should ideally be part of a comprehensive audit of an organization's competitive position. It should highlight market trends, market position, competitor activity, consumer perceptions, etc. From this analysis a clearer understanding of the situation can be obtained and appropriate objectives and strategies agreed. It is also important to conduct an internal audit of the organization to determine resource requirements and availability.

After analysing the situation, objectives can be set. Promotion mix objectives should relate to the organization's marketing and communications objectives. Marketing objectives typically refer to market share, new product development or positioning, etc. Communications objectives refer to how the total communications activity will help achieve marketing objectives. Typically models such as AIDA or DAGMAR can be used, but more individualized and specific communications objectives are likely to be identified on completion of the audit. The promotion mix objectives relate directly to what each element of the promotion mix is expected to achieve. Objectives can be set for advertising activity, sales promotions, public relations, selling, direct marketing activities, and online communication.

A mnemonic that provides a useful framework by which to formulate objectives is SMARTT. Objectives should be

• Specific
• Measurable
• Achievable

- Relevant
- Timed
- Targeted

Establishing clear objectives is an important part of the promotional planning process in providing direction and focus to promotional activity. Care should therefore be taken in ensuring that the objectives set are SMARTT.

The choice of promotional strategy will be determined by the objectives. A range of promotional options are likely to be available, and the role of the strategist is to determine which is best. Strategy is not about doing things, but about setting the direction, scope, and breadth by which things will be done, and allocating resources. The strategy document should provide guidance on the future implementation of promotional activity and its evaluation.

Implementation of the promotion mix will be the most detailed part of the promotional plan. Specific objectives, strategies, and tactics can be set for each element of the mix and timings of activities and budgets allocated. Activities can be time-scaled on a chart to form the basis of a campaign as shown in Figure 10.15.

Product X	Schedule of Promotional Activity									
	J	F	M	A	M	J	J	A	S	O
TV adverts	X	X				X	X			
Magazine adverts		X	X	X			X	X	X	
Press releases	X	X				X	X		X	X
Sales promotions			X	X	X				X	X
Trade promotions	X	X				X	X		X	X
Field sales	X	X				X	X		X	X
Telephone sales	X	X	X			X	X	X		
Sponsorship				X				X		
Exhibition				X						
Community event							X			

Figure 10.15 Developing a media-specific implementation programme

The promotion campaign

A campaign brings together a wide range of media-related activities so that, instead of being a series of unrelated activities, they can act in a planned and co-ordinated way to achieve promotional objectives. The first stage of campaign planning is to have a clear understanding of these promotional objectives (see above). Once these have been clarified, a message can be developed that is most likely to achieve the objectives. The next step is the production of the media plan. Having defined the target audience in terms of its size, location, and media characteristics, media must be selected that achieve the desired levels of exposure/repetition with the target audience. A media plan must be formulated which specifies:

- the allocation of expenditure between the different media;
- the selection of specific media components—for example, in the case of print media, decisions need to be made regarding the type (tabloid *v.* broadsheet), size of advertisement, whether or not to use a Sunday supplement, and whether there is to be national or local coverage;
- the frequency and timing of insertions;
- the cost of reaching a particular target group for each of the media vehicles specified in the plan.

The role of promotion agencies

Should a company undertake its own campaign management, or give the task to a specialist agency? There are many benefits in giving the task to an outside agency. The culture of a company, especially large ones operating in stable or regulated environments, may not be conducive to the creativity that promotion demands and therefore it may be better to leave promotional activity to an outside organization which has a more creative culture. It may be easier for an outsider to be more customer-focused and to see opportunities for promotion that are not immediately apparent to insiders who are too close to the product. A further major benefit of using an outside agency is its ability to use its expertise in developing and executing campaigns. Such agencies can usually purchase media on more favourable terms than a single company acting alone. External agencies have tended to become much broader in their abilities. While many still specialize in one type of promotion (e.g. advertising or direct mail), there has been a tendency for agencies to offer their clients a broad range of promotion management services. Clients' requirement for integrated marketing communications (sometimes referred to as 'media neutral planning') in an increasingly complex and fragmented media world has been one reason for the development of large multi-media promotion agencies. An integrated approach implies consistency in the structure of communications and the attitudes they develop (Fill [19]).

Against these benefits, external agencies are sometimes accused of losing sight of the true nature of a product and its target customers. While an agency may be free to take risky innovations, these can sometimes prove disastrous and need to be disowned by the client company. The relationship between an advertising agency and its client company is critical. There are many examples of very long-lasting relationships which have been mutually beneficial and have given the agency considerable experience in understanding the client's needs. Dissatisfaction with the relationship may result in the client company's inviting rival agencies to 'pitch' for its account. Large organizations frequently use a number of agencies to cover different product and/or geographical areas. Where a company uses the specialized services of different media agencies, there is a danger that these could seek to use more of the client's money on the medium they specialize in, rather than on the medium that is best suited to the client. A specialist advertising agency may see a direct marketing agency as a threat, rather than part of an integrated solution which would benefit the client.

■ Setting budgets for promotional activity

Promotional expenditure can become a drain on an organization's resources if no conscious attempt is made to determine an appropriate budget and to ensure that expenditure is kept within the budget. A number of methods are commonly used to determine the promotional budget.

- **What can be afforded**: This is largely a subjective assessment and pays little attention to the long-term promotional needs of a product. It regards advertising as a luxury which can be afforded in good times and cut back during lean times. In reality, this approach is used by many smaller companies to whom advertising spending is seen as the first and easy short-term target for reducing expenditure in bad times.

- **Percentage of sales**: By this method, advertising expenditure rises or falls to reflect changes in sales. In fact, sales are likely to be influenced by advertising rather than vice versa, and this method is likely to accentuate any given situation. If sales are declining during a recession, *more* advertising may be required to induce sales, but this method of determining the budget implies imposing a cut in advertising expenditure.

- **Competitive parity**: Advertising expenditure is determined by the amount spent by competitors. Many market sectors see periodic outbursts of promotional expenditure, often accompanying a change in some other element of firms' marketing mix. As an example, the manufacturers of games consoles stepped up their promotional budgets during 2002 in an attempt to become the most desired console. Microsoft, which launched Xbox in Europe in March 2002, committed a £350 million global budget for promotion, outstripping Nintendo's £61 million expenditure to promote the

European launch of its GameCube console and providing a strong challenge to Sony's best-seller, PlayStation 2 (Curtis [3]). However, merely increasing advertising expenditure may hide the fact that other elements of the marketing mix need adjusting in order to gain a competitive market position in relation to competitors.

- **Residual**: This is the least satisfactory approach, and merely assigns to the advertising budget what is left after all other costs have been covered. It may bear no relationship to promotional objectives, especially as a downturn in the business cycle may call for greater expenditure rather than less.

- **Objective and task**: This approach starts by defining promotional objectives. Tasks are then set that relate to specific targets. In this way, advertising is seen as a necessary—even though risky—investment in a brand, ranking in importance with other more obvious costs such as production and salary costs. This is the most rational approach to setting a promotional budget.

It was noted above that many of a firm's activities that communicate messages about the firm and its products do not fit neatly under the heading of 'promotion', and therefore may not be included in the promotional budget. It was noted earlier that in the past it was common to talk about 'above-the-line' and 'below-the-line' promotional activities, referring respectively to advertising and other forms of promotion. In large organizations, having separately managed budgets for different elements of the promotion mix may have served the status needs of individual managers, but the result may have been a fragmented promotion plan. With increasing emphasis on integrated communications, this distinction has become increasingly irrelevant. Also, instead of the advertising manager engaging an advertising agency and the direct marketing manager recruiting a direct marketing agency, there has been a tendency (noted above) for agencies themselves to become more multi-channel, thereby allowing a client company to hand its entire promotional planning activity over to one all-purpose agency.

There are still, however, problems in defining the true promotion budget. While there has been a tendency to bring under the budget heading some items that were previously considered outside of it (e.g. low-scale direct marketing activities), others are difficult to include. Should a company's website be included within the promotional budget, or should it be seen as part of a company's wider budget for supporting its distribution system? More seriously, how should temporary price discounts be handled? Should these be included as a promotional item of expenditure, perhaps on the basis that they are a temporary means of stimulating sales? Or should they be regarded not as a cost, but as a reduction in revenue budgets? There are also issues about the extent to which promotion managers should have budgetary responsibility for the customer-facing messages that are given out by a company's buildings and staff. Should the promotion budget for a fashion retailer include provision for a designer-look frontage to the store that conveys a message about the clothes within the store?

MARKETING and the INTERNET

Switch in Amazon promotion strategy

One of the early paradoxes of the 'new media' of the late 1990s was their reliance on 'old' media. To those that had advocated a revolution in media channels, it would seem odd that some of the biggest newspaper and television advertisers in 1999 were internet-related advertisers, with companies such as Lastminute.com, Freeserve and Yahoo! spending huge amounts to promote their internet-based services.

Among the big spenders was Amazon.com, which had soaked up billions of dollars of its investors' capital in developing a high-profile brand, backed up by high levels of service. Up until 2002, Amazon had used TV advertising both for brand-building and for driving immediate sales. The company's TV ad campaign—which in 2001 cost an estimated $50 million—focused on the advantages of shopping online versus going to a shopping mall. It had an impressive web presence which promoted the company and its products.

In 2002 Amazon decided to stop all TV advertising. Was this just another wild idea by a company whose chairman—Jeff Bezos—had ruffled the feathers of many investors through his seemingly wacky ideas? Or was the decision simply a reflection of the fact that the promotional objectives of Amazon had changed, and therefore called for new communication tools?

The company had carried out extensive research into what was now a substantial customer base. Simply encouraging existing customers to buy more (for example through new product ranges) was one way of securing additional sales. But its research also showed that shipping costs were a major point of contention with existing and would-be customers. With local High Street bookstores offering attractive prices and long opening hours, plus free ordering and collection services, people often felt miffed about having to pay a $3 shipping charge for an item that cost only $25. Although the company felt that the creative message of its TV adverts was working, it thought that free shipping and lower prices would bring an even greater return on its investment.

The company switched its advertising budget to fund a sales promotion of free shipping costs in the USA for purchases over $25. After an initial trial, the free shipping promotion was extended in 2003 to the British market for purchases over £39.

Amazon had another promotional tool up its sleeve which it planned to use fully: its network of associates who place a banner ad for Amazon on their own websites and take a small percentage of sales revenue when a visitor to their websites clicks through to Amazon and makes a purchase. The company itself was a big spender on banner adverts on other companies' sites, and it strengthened this form of promotion, helped by a slump in charges for banner ads as other dot.com advertisers were removed from the market through bankruptcy.

Stopping all television advertising is an unusual move for a major brand such as Amazon. Its brand had been built up successfully, to the extent that it scored highly in unprompted recall of booksellers' names. But could it have built the brand entirely online without television and newspaper support? Might the brand need refreshing with further TV advertising to protect it against new 'clicks and mortar' bookstores in the future?

Source: based on D. Kawamoto, 'Amazon switches off TV ads', **www.CNETNews.com**, 10 February, 2003

📖 Monitoring and evaluating the promotional effort

Evaluation of promotional activity performs an important role in the promotional plan, providing feedback to help inform future activity and to enable adjustments to be made to promotional activity if objectives are not being achieved. It is important that enough resources are allocated for evaluation of promotional activity, a point often overlooked by marketers.

It can be very difficult to assess the effectiveness of promotional activities. In respect of advertising, Lord Rothermere once famously said that half of all advertising was wasted, but the trouble was he couldn't tell which half. In one study of 135 campaigns by 40 advertising agencies, it was found that almost none of the agencies really knew, or ever could know, whether or not their campaigns were successful (Henderson [18]). However, while much evaluation relies on instinct and gut feeling, attempts at evaluation are becoming increasingly sophisticated. Databases are making it possible for marketers to track messages and the responses they generate. As we will see in the next chapter, direct marketing companies use a variety of techniques to measure the response to a message, allowing them to refine their efforts in future targeting. The development of the internet is allowing previously unimaginable levels of information about an audience's behaviour with respect to a message. Cookies embedded in an individual's computer can enable a company to learn how the viewer arrived at a company's site, the range of sites that she had previously visited, her movements around the site, how long she spent on different pages, where she went to subsequently, and whether she made a purchase/enquiry for further information.

It should not be forgotten that evaluation of communication must be made against the objectives set for that communication. A message that had the objective of creating awareness of a brand should not be criticized if it failed to achieve a short-term increase in sales. Instead, evaluation should be based on changes in the level of awareness of the brand among the target market.

In combination, a number of techniques can be used to try to assess the effectiveness of an individual advert or an advertising campaign:

- Prior to launching a message, companies use focus groups to test its effectiveness. Researchers are particularly concerned to identify memorable parts of the message and how far an individual progressed before he skipped to the next subject. Prior evaluation of an advert can help companies to avoid running adverts that subsequently turn out to be offensive or misinterpreted.

- Routine monitoring of a sample panel's television viewing is undertaken by BARB. Similar monitoring of the press is undertaken by the National Readership Survey. While such monitoring can estimate how many people see an advertisement, they provide little evidence of whether the advert was recalled or acted upon.

Figure 10.16 In a weekly telephone omnibus survey, NOP asks a national representative sample of adults aged 15+ about the adverts that they have seen recently. This table, published in *Marketing* magazine, gives some indication of levels of awareness created by individual advertising campaigns. Additional qualitative techniques are useful in order to establish the extent to which the campaigns have changed viewers' attitudes

Reproduced with permission of Haymarket Publishing

- To overcome the above problem, a number of panels are retained by market research agencies and are consulted regularly to ascertain which recent advertisements or other promotional messages they can recall, either spontaneously or with prompting. One example is the NOP weekly telephone omnibus survey carried out among 1,000 adults on behalf of sponsoring companies (Figure 10.16).

Chapter summary and links to other chapters

Very few products can be sold in competitive markets without any form of promotion. This chapter has shown how the features of a product need to be communicated to potential buyers as benefits that will satisfy a need. We saw in Chapter 3 that needs can be complex, and can change over time for an individual. Promotion can help to take people through a number of stages of the buying process, from merely being aware of a product through to committing themselves to a purchase. Messages are communicated through channels to reach a target audience. The existence of 'noise' means that the message that was encoded and sent is not the same as the one that is received and decoded.

This chapter has stressed that promotion planning is an integral part of the marketing and business planning process. The promotional message must be consistent with the positioning of a product (Chapters 6 and 7), its price position (Chapter 8), and its availability (Chapter 9). Services have special promotional needs (Chapter 13). Promotion becomes more complex where overseas markets are involved (Chapter 14).

In the following chapter we will explore the elements of the promotion mix and how these are applied to achieve a company's marketing objectives.

KEY PRINCIPLES OF MARKETING

- Promotional messages should translate product features into benefits for buyers.
- The audience for a promotional message should correspond to the target market for the product being promoted.
- There can be multiple targets involved in promoting a product, including all members of a decision-making unit and the intermediaries that handle the product.
- Communication is a process that aims to take a target through stages from awareness to action.
- The promotional objectives for a product must be related to the stage of the product's life-cycle.

CASE STUDY

Ethical values used to position bank

The Co-operative Bank evolved from its origins in 1872 as a bank of the Co-operative Wholesale and Retail Societies to become by 2003 one of the leading UK clearing banks with a network of over 100 branches. Throughout the 1980s it enjoyed steady growth as a result of several innovative new products, such as free in-credit banking, extended opening hours, and interest-bearing current accounts. However, by the end of the decade the bank found its market position being steadily eroded by increased competition from the larger clearing banks and particularly from building societies, which were by then able to enter the personal banking sector as a result of the deregulation of the banking sector. The Co-operative Bank is one of the smaller clearing banks. As a result of increased competition, it saw its market share fall from 2.7% in 1986 to 2% by 1991.

Alongside this trend, the bank faced a changing customer profile. Traditionally it had attracted a high proportion of its customers from the more affluent A/B/C1 social groups. By 1992 this was changing: an increasing number of new accounts were coming from the C2/D/E social groups, while at the same time the bank was losing its core A/B/C1 accounts. This trend was diluting its position as a more upmarket bank and reducing its potential to cross-sell more profitable financial products.

The bank's research showed that, outside of its customer base, it lacked a clear image and that what image there was showed the bank as rather staid, old-fashioned, and with left-wing political affinities. Furthermore, spontaneous recall of its name had steadily fallen, despite extensive advertising of its innovative new products.

The bank realized that immediate action was necessary to rebuild its image and stem the loss of its A/B/C1 accounts. The size of the bank and its profitability meant that the advertising budget was modest, and therefore a focused campaign with maximum effectiveness was crucial.

The advertising agency BDDH was appointed to devise a promotional campaign. The agency 'interrogated' the Co-operative Bank to identify any distinctive competencies upon which it could build a campaign. It discovered that the bank's heritage offered a unique positioning opportunity against other mainstream banks. This derived in particular from its sourcing and distribution of funds, which had been governed by an unwritten ethical code prohibiting the bank from lending money to environmentally or politically unsound organizations. BDDH set out to transform the results of its interrogation into a relevant and motivating proposition that would appeal to potential customers beyond the bank's current customer base. A key strategic decision was made to target promotional activity at the growing number of 'ethical consumers' who, importantly, were found to have a more upmarket A/B/C1 profile.

The 'ethical bank' formed the foundation on which BDDH built its campaign. Initially this was tested on its existing customer base, where it gained a high level of approval. The bank incorporated its ethical stance into its customer charter. Advertising was initially used to raise awareness of the bank's positioning. The creative work was deliberately provocative and motivating, while at the same time maintaining the bank's credentials as a High Street lender. The creative images used were often simple and stark.

The key objectives of the campaign were to:

- build customer loyalty and so stem the outflow of A/B/C1s;
- expand the customer base, targeting A/B/C1s;
- expand the corporate customer base.

National press and regional television in the bank's 'northern heartland' were the primary media used in the initial stages of the campaign. The cinema was utilized as the campaign progressed.

As a result of this promotional campaign, the marketing objectives were exceeded. The bank established a strong and differentiated brand platform which it subsequently used to launch new services, including its 'Smile' internet banking operation (**www.smile.co.uk**). The campaign's success can be put down to a clear understanding of the bank's customer base and its own unique competencies. The campaign was carefully targeted with the aim of achieving maximum impact, which enabled the message to be delivered cost-effectively.

The case clearly demonstrates how effective promotional activity, linked closely to business and marketing objectives and strategy, can provide a long-term sustainable competitive position in the marketplace.

Case study review questions

1. How can the Co-operative Bank assess whether its ethical position has been effective?

2. What dangers does the Co-operative Bank face in promoting an ethical position?

3. Critically assess the promotional positioning of other banks with which you are familiar.

CHAPTER REVIEW QUESTIONS

1. What is meant by the promotion mix?

2. Evaluate the usefulness of the hierarchy of effect models as an approach to understanding how advertising works. Select two recent advertising campaigns to illustrate your points.

3. To what extent do you think consumers have an active rather than passive role in the 'consumption' of promotions?

4. What is the difference between a promotional objective, a promotional strategy, and promotional tactics?

5. For an organization of your choice, outline its current promotional strategy. Use the SOST 4Ms framework to support your answer.

6. Show how promotional planning can be integrated into an organization's overall marketing and communications planning framework.

REFERENCES

[1] Levinson, J. C. (200), *Guerrilla Marketing for the 21st Century*.

[2] Lynch, D. (2001), 'The Magic of *Harry Potter*'. *Advertising Age*. 72(50): 26.

[3] Curtis, J. (2002), 'Playing at the Next Level'. *Marketing*, 3 July: 26–7.

[4] Anstead, M. (2002), 'The Faces that Grace a Thousand Launches: from soap stars at supermarkets to supermodels at the Tate, celebs pull crowds'. *Daily Telegraph*, 31 October: 4.

[5] Richardson, G. W. (2001), 'Looking for Meaning in All the Wrong Places: why negative advertising is a suspect category'. *Journal of Communication*, 51: 775–90.

[6] Cardwell, A. (2002), 'Subliminal Advertising'. *Ziff Davis Smart Business*, 15(3): 51–2.

[7] Laczniak, R. N., DeCarlo, T. E., and Ramaswami, S. N. (2001), 'Consumers' Responses to Negative Word-of-Mouth Communication: an attribution theory perspective'. *Journal of Consumer Psychology*, 11(1): 57–73.

[8] Aaker, D. A. and Myers, J. G. (1982), Advertising Management, Prentice Hall

[9] Coulson-Thomas, C. T. (1985), Marketing Communications, Heinemann

[10] Rogers, E. M. (1962), Diffusion of Innovation, Free Press, New York

[11] Maslow, A. (1943), 'A Theory of Human Motivation', *Psychological Review*, **50**, 4, pp. 370–396.

[12] Bayton, J. A. (1958), 'Motivation, Cognition, Learning—Basic Factors in Consumer Behavior', Journal of Marketing, 22, 3, pp 282–289.

[13] Goodley, S. (2002), 'Licensed to Make a Killing: a growing trend sees the world's best-known brands flock to air products in Bond's new romp'. *Daily Telegraph*, 28 October: 32.

[14] Welker, C. B. (2002), 'The Paradigm of Viral Communication'. *Information Services & Use*, 22(1): 3–8.

[15] Derbaix, C. and Vanhamme, J. (2003), 'Inducing Word-of-Mouth by Eliciting Surprise: a pilot investigation'. *Journal of Economic Psychology*, 24(1): 99–116.

[16] Chung-kue, H. and McDonald, D. (2002), 'An Examination on Multiple Celebrity Endorsers in Advertising'. *Journal of Product & Brand Management*, 11(1): 19–29.

[17] Walker, L. J.-H. (2001), 'The Measurement of Word-of-Mouth Communication and an Investigation of Service Quality and Customer Commitment as Potential Antecedents'. *Journal of Service Research*, 4(1): 60–75.

[18] Henderson Britt, S. (2000), 'Are So-called Successful Advertising Campaigns Really Successful?' *Journal of Advertising Research*, 40(6): 25–31.

[19] Fill, C. (2001), 'Essentially a Matter of Consistency: integrated marketing communications'. *Marketing Review*, 1(4): 409–26.

[20] Susskind, A. M. (2002), 'I Told You So! Restaurant customers' word-of-mouth communication patterns.' *Cornell Hotel & Restaurant Administration Quarterly*, 43(2): 75–85.

[21] Gelb, B. D. and Sundaram, S. (2002), 'Adapting to "Word of Mouse"'. *Business Horizons*, 45(4): 21–5.

[22] Smith, P. (2001), *Marketing Communications: an integrated approach*, 3rd edn. London: Kogan Page.

[23] Salthern, C. and Johnson, J. (1999) *Consumer Value in the future*. London: WPP, The Store, p. 10.

▨ SUGGESTED FURTHER READING

Individual elements of the promotion mix are considered in the following chapters. For a general overview of communication methods and campaign planning, the following are useful:

Fill, C. (2001), *Marketing Communications: contexts, strategies, and applications*. Hemel Hempstead: FT Prentice Hall.

Picton, D. and Broderick, A. (eds.) (2000), *Integrated Marketing Communications*. Hemel Hempstead: FT Prentice Hall.

Smith, P. (2001), *Marketing Communications: an integrated approach*, 3rd edn. London: Kogan Page.

USEFUL WEB LINKS

Visit the companion website to this book, with lots of additional material and links for each chapter:
  www.oup.com/uk/booksites/busecon
Institute of Practitioners in Advertising, Sales & Marketing Resource Directory
  www.salesdoctors.com/directory/dircos/3102i02.htm
Institute of Sales Promotion
  www.thebiz.co.uk/isp.htm
The British codes of advertising and sales promotion
  www.asa.org.uk/bcasp/bcasp.txt
Institute of Direct Marketing
  www.thebiz.co.uk/instdirm.htm
Institute of Professional Sales
  www.iops.co.uk
Institute of Public Relations
  www.ipr.org.uk
Direct Marketing Association
  www.the-dma.org

KEYWORDS

- **Advertising**
- **Buyer readiness state**
- **Channel of communication**
- **Cognitive dissonance**
- **Communication models**
- **Communication process**
- **Decoding**
- **Direct marketing**
- **Encoding**
- **Halo effect**
- **Hierarchy of effects model**
- **Noise**
- **Online marketing**
- **Promotional mix**
- **Public relations**
- **Reference group**
- **Sales promotion**
- **Selling**
- **Sponsorship**
- **Target audience**
- **Viral marketing**
- **Word of mouth**

Developing the promotion mix

CHAPTER OBJECTIVES

The previous chapter introduced general principles of promotional planning. This chapter focuses on the different elements that make up the promotion mix—advertising, selling, sales promotion, public relations, sponsorship, direct marketing, and online marketing. The characteristics of the different media that make up the promotion mix will be explored. The importance of setting promotional objectives, developing a strategy, and monitoring implementation was stressed in the previous chapter and forms a basis for discussion of individual media. In reading this chapter, you should not lose sight of the interrelationship between the different elements of the promotion mix, and indeed between the promotion mix and the wider marketing mix.

Advertising

The role of advertising in the promotion mix

Advertising is mass, paid communication which is used to transmit information, develop attitudes, and induce some form of response from the audience. It seeks to bring about a response by providing information to potential customers, by trying to modify their desires, and by supplying reasons why they should prefer that particular company's product. The different elements of the promotion mix were introduced in the previous chapter, but it must be stressed that advertising, like the other mix elements, cannot be seen in isolation. Advertising is frequently used to support sales promotion and direct marketing activity, for example.

How does advertising work?

Think back to our discussion in the previous chapter about the objectives of communication. You will recall that a message may be required to do a number of things, from simply creating awareness of a product, through to achieving a final sale. Advertising can be used to achieve a wide range of objectives, but it is generally best suited to building a longer-term image for an organization and its products. Advertising is also best at targeting broadly defined target audiences where dialogue is not called for.

The most important element of the advertising process is to identify the audience at which communication is aimed. The audience of an advertisement determines what is to be said, when it is to be said, where it is to be said, and who is to say it.

The sought response can include cognitive responses (the message should be considered and understood); affective responses (the message should lead to some change in attitude); or behavioural responses (the message should achieve some change in behaviour, such as a purchase decision).

Advertising must recognize these different possible responses and target audiences that are in a position to make the desired response. Securing an immediate purchase is only one possible response. In most cases, customers are seen as going through a series of stages before finally deciding to purchase a product. It is therefore critical to know these buyer-readiness stages and to assess the stage at which the target audience is at any given time. These are the focus of 'hierarchy of effects' models that were discussed in the previous chapter.

The role of advertising often does not end when a sale has been achieved. Advertising is often aimed at customers after they have made a purchase, to encourage them to feel that they made the correct choice (thereby reducing 'cognitive dissonance') and to foster further purchases from the company. It was noted in Chapter 3 that organizations increasingly seek to build relationships with their customers, so the behavioural change (the sale) should be seen as the starting-point for making customers aware of other offers available from the organization.

The importance of recognizing different adopter categories is reflected in advertising for mobile telephones. In the early stages, advertising stressed the benefits of flexibility and security, which appealed to some segments of more affluent private buyers and company buyers. Over time, many segments' resistance to owning a mobile phone has diminished, so by 2000 the message had changed to one of cheapness, sophistication, and lack of contractual formality.

An advertising message must be able to move an individual along a path from awareness through to eventual purchase. In order for a message to be received and understood, it must gain attention, use a common language, arouse needs, and suggest how these needs may be met. We saw in the previous chapter how the content, structure, and format of a message can be developed in order to achieve promotional objectives. We also saw how a complex message needs to be encoded before being transmitted. The

Figure 11.1 Advertisers must fight to gain the attention of an audience; simply stating the benefits of a product may be inadequate to gain attention or to create a distinctive identity. This advertisement does not say much about the product on offer and is not likely to achieve any sales in the short term, but it does raise awareness of the KitKat brand and it helps to give it a distinctive and humorous position in the competitive market for confectionery products

message that the receiver decodes may be quite different, owing to the presence of a variety of 'noise' factors.

Determining advertising objectives

Specifying advertising objectives is important if appropriate messages are to be accurately targeted through the most appropriate media in the most cost-effective manner possible.

A number of factors should guide the formulation of advertising objectives:

- They should reflect the areas of accountability for those who implement the advertising programme.
- The target audience should be defined as accurately as possible.
- There should be a clear statement of the desired response from the target audience (e.g. whether the desired response is a purchase, desire, or merely a growing awareness of the product being advertised).
- Wherever possible, goals should be expressed in quantitative terms. (For example, promotional objectives for a new type of motor insurance policy may begin with an objective to achieve awareness of the brand name by 30% within the 25–55-year-old London-based insurance-buying public within one year of launch.)
- Objectives should refer to a stated period of time.

Although it is commonplace to think that advertising can increase sales, it is extremely difficult to prove that advertising alone is responsible for a sales increase. Sales, after all, can be the result of many intervening variables, some of which are internal to the organization (e.g. public relations activity, pricing policy), while others are external (e.g. the state of the national economy). It is therefore too simplistic to set advertising objectives simply in terms of increasing sales by a specified amount. Given the existence of diverse adopter categories and the many stages in the communication process that were described earlier, more appropriate objectives can often be specified in terms of levels of awareness or comprehension.

Advertising media

Effective advertising requires a good understanding of the media habits of the target audience. If a firm's target market is not in the habit of being exposed to a particular medium, much of the value of advertising through that medium will be wasted. As an example, attempts to promote premium credit cards to high-income segments by means of television commercials may lose much of their value, because research suggests that the higher socio-economic groups tend to spend a greater proportion of their viewing time watching BBC rather than commercial channels. On the other hand, they are heavy readers of Sunday newspaper magazine supplements.

Information about target audiences' media habits is obtained from a number of sources. Newspaper readership information is collated by the National Readership Survey. For each newspaper, this shows reading frequency and average readership per issue (as distinct from circulation) broken down into age, class, sex, ownership of consumer durables, etc. Television viewing information is collected by the Broadcasters Audience Research Board (BARB). This indicates the number of people watching particular channels at particular times by reference to two types of television rating (TVR): one for the number of *households* watching a programme/advertising slot, and one for the number of *people* watching.

Using such sources of information, the media characteristics of a particular target audience can be ascertained and a media plan produced which achieves maximum penetration of the target audience.

Characteristics of advertising media

The choice of media is influenced by the characteristics of each medium and its ability to achieve the specified promotional objectives. The following are some of the most common types of media and their characteristics.

Newspapers. Daily newspapers tend to have a high degree of reader loyalty, reflecting the fact that each national title is targeted at specific segments of the population. This loyalty means that the printed message tends to be perceived by readers as having a high level of credibility. Therefore, daily papers may be useful for prestige and reminder advertising. They can be used for creating general awareness of a product or a brand as well as providing detailed product information. In this way, banks use newspapers both for adverts designed to create a brand awareness and liking for the organization, and for adverts giving specific details of savings accounts. The latter may include an invitation to act in the form of a Freepost account opening coupon.

Daily newspapers, however, are normally read hurriedly, and therefore lengthy copy is likely to be wasted. Sunday newspapers also appeal to highly segmented audiences but are generally read at a more leisurely pace than daily papers. They are also more likely to be read at home and shared by households, which may be important for appealing to family-based purchase decisions.

Local newspapers offer a much greater degree of geographical segmentation than is possible with national titles. Within their circulation areas, they also achieve much higher levels of readership penetration. In the case of free home delivered newspapers, total penetration can be achieved, although actual readership levels are more open to question. While national advertising through local newspapers is expensive and inefficient, it is useful for purely local suppliers, as well as national organizations wishing to target specific areas with local messages, or to pretest national advertising copy.

The distinction between national, regional, and local papers has become blurred as flexible printing systems and high-speed data transfer allow local editions of national and international newspapers to be produced, appealing to advertisers seeking tightly specified audiences. Many commentators have wrongly forecast the demise of newspapers in the face of competition from electronic sources of news, but newspapers have fought back and adapted. There is, however, a trend towards lower newspaper readership by some groups, especially young people (Lauf [10]).

MARKETING in ACTION

What does your newspaper say about you?
In most countries, advertisers are attracted to national newspapers by the highly segmented audience of each newspaper. Not only do we tend to be loyal to our preferred newspaper, but we may be inclined subconsciously to regard advertisements placed in it as being more believable. An individual's choice of national newspaper can say a lot about his or her values, attitudes, and life-style. Researchers have developed a number of detailed indicators of the profile of a newspaper's readership, but the following tongue-in-cheek analysis of UK newspaper readership may not be too far from the truth:
The Times is read by the people who run the country.
The Financial Times is read by the people who own the country.
The Telegraph is read by people who think that the country should be run the way that it was in the past.
The Mail is read by the wives of the people that run the country.
The Independent's readers keep an open mind about who should run the country.
Sun readers don't care who runs the country, so long as she looks good on page 3.

What does your preferred newspaper say about you?

Magazines/journals. Within the UK, and most western countries, there is an extensive selection of magazine and journal titles. While some high-circulation magazines appeal to broad groups of people (e.g. *Radio Times*), most titles are specialized in terms of their content and targeting. In this way, *What Car?* magazine may be a highly specific medium for car manufacturers, dealers, and loan companies to promote their goods and services to new car buyers. Specialist trade titles allow messages to be aimed at intermediaries; for example, manufacturers of catering equipment will gain access to an audience of key buyers through *The Caterer* magazine.

Although advertising in magazines may at first seem relatively expensive compared with newspapers, it represents good value to advertisers in terms of the high number of target readers per copy and the highly segmented nature of their audiences.

Television. This is an expensive, but very powerful, medium. Although it tends to be used mainly for the long-term task of creating brand awareness, it can also be used to create a rapid sales response. The very fact that a message has been seen on television can give credibility to the message source, and many companies add the phrase 'as seen on TV' to give additional credibility to their other media communications. The power of the television medium is enhanced by its ability to appeal to the senses of both sight and sound, and to use movement and colour to develop a sales message.

The major limitation of television advertising is its cost. For most small businesses, television advertising rates start at too high a level to be considered. The high starting price for television advertising reflects not only high production costs, but also the difficulty in segmenting television audiences, either socio-economically or in terms of narrowly defined geographical areas. Also, the question must be asked as to how many people within the target audience are actually receptive to a television advert. Is the target viewer actually in the room when an advertisement is being broadcast? If the viewer is present, is he receptive to the message? The use of video recorders and remote controls has important implications for the effectiveness of television advertising. Television advertisers must use their creative talents to ensure that a short 30 second slot creates sufficient impact that a viewer pays attention to the whole of the advertisement.

With the development of digital broadcasting and the proliferation of television channels, the ability of the medium to segment audiences is increasing. There are now numerous channels that have developed distinctive audiences, such as the Discovery Channel, MTV, and Sky Sports. With the development of interactive television, advertising can be used to elicit an immediate response. (For example, a pizza company can use an advert to create an awareness and liking of its brand, as well as offering immediate ordering and delivery of a pizza.)

Commercial radio. Radio advertising in the UK has seen considerable growth in recent years, recovering from its traditional perception as the poor relation of television advertising. The threshold cost of radio advertising is much lower than for television, reflecting much more local segmentation of radio audiences and the lower production costs of radio adverts. A major advantage over other media is that the audience can be involved in other activities—particularly driving—while being exposed to an advertisement. Inevitably, a radio message is less powerful than a television message, relying solely on the sense of sound. Although there are often doubts about the extent to which an audience receives and understands a radio message, it does form a useful reminder medium when used in conjunction with other media.

Cinema. Because of the captive nature of cinema audiences, this medium has the potential to make a major impact. It is frequently used to promote local services such as food outlets, whose target market broadly corresponds to the audience of most cinemas. However, without repetition, cinema advertisements have little lasting effect, although they do tend to be useful for supporting press and television advertising.

Outdoor advertising. This is useful for reminder copy and can support other media activities. The effect of an advertisement on television or in the national press can be prolonged if recipients are exposed to a reminder poster on their way to work the following day. If strategically placed, the posters can appeal to segmented audiences; for

Figure 11.2 Radio is a useful advertising medium for communicating with audiences when they are captive and/or open to persuasion. This advertisement demonstrates the power of radio in communicating a message about a fast-moving consumer good, just at the moment when the audience may be most receptive to a message about the product

Reproduced with permission of the Radio Advertising Bureau.

Figure 11.3 Many outdoor poster sites command high levels of passing audiences, and can be powerful where viewers are captive. This advertising message on a bus shelter makes a simple point which has not been lost on advertisers of products targeted at motorists stuck in traffic jams

example, London Underground sites in the City of London are seen by large numbers of affluent business people. The sides of buses are often used to support new products available locally (e.g. new store openings) and have the ability to spread their message as the bus travels along local routes. Posters can generally be used only to convey a simple communication rather than complex details.

Electronic media. The internet has opened up new opportunities for companies to communicate with their target markets. Much of the development in this area allows companies to enter into a one-to-one dialogue with customers, which is not strictly a form of advertising as defined here. The use of the internet for one-to-one communication and distribution is considered in more detail later in this chapter. In addition, most medium and large-sized companies now have their own websites which address mass audiences. Creating an awareness of these sites has become a major challenge for companies, with conventional media often being used to promote the website address. As a further method of attracting 'hits', companies frequently pay for hotlinks out of other companies' web sites.

Other innovative media. Advertising media can become very cluttered by the sheer volume of advertising. Companies that spot new media may avoid some of this clutter by having the field to themselves, at least until it too becomes cluttered. Innovative media that have targeted specific groups in recent years include:

- adverts on milk bottles promoting breakfast cereals;
- adverts on petrol pumps promoting car insurance;
- adverts on the sides of cows promoting ice-cream.

Media selection and evaluation

Faced with the availability of such a great variety of media, advertising managers need some criteria to assess the most effective mix of media to meet their objectives. Increasingly sophisticated computer packages are becoming available which produce a schedule of advertising activities, based on their ability to get through to the target audience cost-effectively. Such programmes are based on a number of important criteria: the impact an advertisement will have on the target audience; the extent to which the effects of a particular advertising message 'wear out' over time; and the cost of advertising through a particular medium. These are considered below.

Advertising exposure

Advertising exposure of a particular communication is determined by two factors: cover/reach, and frequency. **Cover**, or **reach**, is the percentage of a particular target audience reached by a medium or a whole campaign, while **frequency** is the number of times a particular target audience has an 'opportunity to see/hear' (OTS/OTH) an advertising message. The combination of these two factors results in an index of advertising exposure which is usually stated in terms of 'gross rating points' (GRPs). For example, if an objective is to reach 50% of the target audience three times a year, this would be stated as a GRP of 150 (i.e. 50×3).

Within a given budget, there has to be a trade-off between cover/reach and frequency. A greater emphasis on reach means less emphasis on frequency and vice versa. The actual balance at any given time will depend on advertising objectives. Frequency may be a more important objective in situations where a new brand requires increased awareness—to increase loyalty to a non-dominant brand, to match the frequency of competitors' advertising, or to increase the level of understanding of a complex message.

Advertising impact

Impact is usually more closely related to the message than the medium. If, however, the medium is the message, then advertising impact should be an important criterion for media selection. Different media can produce different levels of awareness and comprehension of an identical message. In this way, the image of a high-performance car presented via television is very much more powerful than that presented via radio.

Wearout

The concept of advertising exposure assumes that all advertising slots have equal value. However, the effect of additional slots may in fact decline, resulting in diminishing returns for each unit of expenditure. There is usually a 'threshold' level of advertising beneath which little audience response occurs. Once over this threshold, audience response tends to increase quite rapidly through a 'generation' phase until eventually a saturation point is reached. Any further advertising leads to a negative or declining response, i.e. **wearout**. Generally, wearout is more a function of the message, but if wearout for the same message does vary between media, this should be taken into account when choosing between media. Wearout may be alleviated by broadening the variety of media being used (although this is likely to increase marginal costs) or, alternatively, by incorporating a more 'creative' approach in the message. A typical relationship between advertising repetitions and audience response is illustrated in Figure 11.5.

The possibilities for overcoming the effects of wearout are dependent upon the pattern of audience responses. Two response functions over time are shown in Fig. 17.5. The 'S' shape response pattern implies that there is a need for a lot of advertising initially in order to ensure that a threshold is reached. This can be achieved by an initial 'burst' campaign, slowly reducing over time. On the other hand, the concave response pattern implies that a more regular 'drip' campaign is the most appropriate.

Cost

The cost of using different media varies markedly. A medium that at first sight appears to be expensive may in fact be good value in terms of achieving promotional objectives, so it follows that a sound basis for measuring cost is needed. There are generally two related cost criteria:

1. **Cost per gross rating point**: This is usually used for broadcast media and is the cost of a set of adverts divided by the gross rating points.
2. **Cost per thousand**: This is used for print media to calculate the cost of getting the message seen by 1,000 members of the target market.

Figure 11.4 Banner adverts have become big business as companies try to attract internet users to their own websites. Advertising on a high profile portal such as handbag.com has become the equivalent of having a poster ad in a busy High Street shopping centre and many of the old rules for selecting the best sites still apply. Advertisers will be more interested in a banner ad on busy portals, which explains why some of the largest portals have survived and prospered, while many smaller, less popular ones have gone out of business. Matching the profile of a portal with the advertiser's target market remains crucial and handbag.com has become attractive to advertisers seeking to address female audiences. However, unlike the High Street poster, internet banner ads have a lot of additional advantages. Hotlinks can take a viewer directly to further information, something that is not possible with most forms of advertising. An internet advertiser has much more information about visitors to a site than would be available to a newspaper or television advertiser. By using cookies, internet advertisers can even change the message that a person sees depending on the sites that they have previously visited (Reproduced with permission of handbag.com)

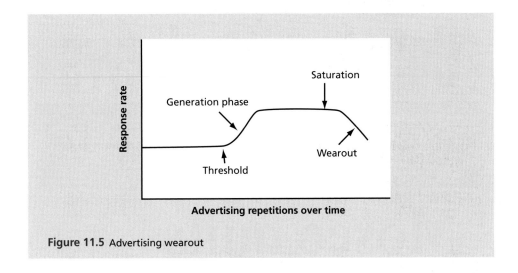

Figure 11.5 Advertising wearout

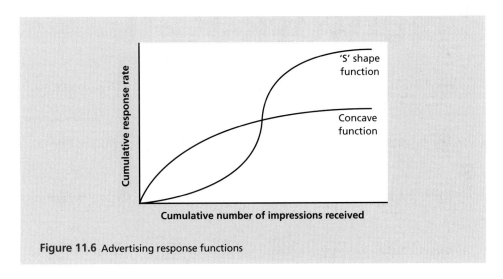

Figure 11.6 Advertising response functions

These measures can be used to make cost comparisons between different media. However, a true comparison needs to take into consideration the different degrees of effectiveness each medium has; in other words, the strength of the media vehicle needs to be considered, as does the location, duration, timing, and—where relevant—size of the advertisement, plus a variety of more complex factors. These are all combined to form 'media weights' which are used in comparing the effectiveness, of different media. Cost effectiveness, therefore, is calculated using the following formula:

$$\text{Cost effectiveness} = \frac{\text{Readers/Viewers in Target Market} \times \text{Media Weight}}{\text{Cost}}$$

Construction News

www.cnplus.co.uk   Thursday October 16 2003   Weekly £2

AGENDA

Major problems

Amicus' Paul Corby is a key player in making the Major Projects Agreement work. Pages 10-11

PILING SPECIAL

Irish challenge

Simon Bullivant tells how precast piles and foundations solved a tricky Belfast site problem. Page 52

IN THE NEWS

In the balance

Ballast Services chief Phillip Cooper in takeover talks as Dutch parent company bales out. Page 3

Rail operator under renewed pressure as its head of procurement hands in his notice

Mosco quits Network Rail

BY RUSS LYNCH

NETWORK RAIL was left reeling again this week after procurement guru Les Mosco decided to quit the company.

Mr Mosco, who joined the former Railtrack in June 2000, will leave the not-for-profit operator on October 31.

The news comes less than a week after Network Rail took a further three deals in-house following a decision by Jarvis to quit the rail maintenance sector.

A senior source at one rail maintenance contractor hinted that Mr Mosco had resigned after clashes with the Strategic Rail Authority.

He said: "He will be sadly missed, as he was very proactive and keen to talk to contractors.

"But he was being put under pressure by the SRA to deliver major projects and was trying to run a business with extremely limited resources. Les had introduced performance indicators and was working hard to make the savings but, in the end, perhaps, enough was enough."

Network Rail's cost submission to rail regulator Tom Winsor last month concluded that just £24.5 billion should be spent on the network between 2004 and 2009, compared with the £29.5 billion figure forecast in June.

But a senior Network Rail insider played down the rumours of a rift with the SRA. He said: "There is nothing going on here, it is just one of those things that happen. Supply chain director is not a board position and there was nowhere for him to go at the company, so he thought it was time to move on."

The source added that Network Rail had not yet found a replacement for Mr Mosco, even though he is due to leave two weeks tomorrow (Friday).

Mr Mosco came to Network Rail from energy company Amerada Hess, where he was executive manager of global procurement. Prior to that he ran a procurement programme for Natwest Bank.

Spokesmen for Network Rail and the Strategic Rail Authority both declined to comment on Mr Mosco's resignation.

Mr Mosco was unavailable for comment.
russell.lynch@contract.emap.com

Network Rail procurement chief Les Mosco has resigned amid rumours of a row with the Strategic Rail Authority

Kingspan wins £25m arbitration

THE FORMER president and chief executive officer of raised access flooring specialist Tate Global Corporation has been ordered to pay £25 million to Kingspan.

Daniel R Baker and fellow vendors were hit by the compensation claim following an investigation into the sale of US-based Tate to Kingspan.

A panel of independent arbitrators at the American Arbitration Association, based in Washington, USA, found Mr Baker liable for the award and breach of contract, common law fraud and federal and Pennsylvania securities law violations.

The team also found Mr Baker and the other sellers liable to interest payments of more than £3,500 per day, backdated to September 19.

The ruling centres on the purchase of Tate by Kingspan in 2000 for £80 million, which consisted of £67 million cash and £13 million to settle Tate's debt. Kingspan claimed that the
■ **See page 2**

Drivers meet on crane pay

CRANE operators held a mass meeting in east London on Tuesday night to discuss pay and conditions in the industry.

Major crane firms were expected to be present, along with officials from electrical union Amicus, who are pushing for improvements in pay to match those received by HTC Plant.

Drivers at HTC voted overwhelmingly last December in favour of an improved pay and conditions package, which saw overtime, travel and lodging allowances all go up.

The basic hourly wage increased from £7.40 to £7.72 and in August HTC also received a £3-an-hour bonus.

The union has now set its sights on a similar increase for other firms. The meeting, which
■ **See page 2**

Issue No: 6838

Dutch parent firm pulls the plug on Ballast

PANIC swept through Ballast on Tuesday when Dutch parent Ballast Nedam decided to pull financial support from its ailing subsidiary.

More than 1,000 jobs were in doubt as a war of words broke out between the British and Dutch sides of the firm.

A source at one regional office said: "It has been bedlam. We've had girls crying, people packing up stuff in boxes. We don't know what's going to happen. But I know one thing: it's parachute time."

Ballast's Dutch boss and his management team resigned on the eve of the announcement, leaving the British bosses in charge. As *Construction News* went to press UK chiefs were in crisis talks with accountants Deloitte & Touche.

A spokesman for Ballast Nedam said the British management team would decide the future of the business this week but expected it to apply for protection from creditors. He said hopes that the business could be sold were unjustified.

A UK board source said: "It is still too early to talk about applying for protection from creditors. We are still in the process of talking to our advisers and nothing will be decided until that is done."
■ **See page 3**

CONSTRUCTION'S BIGGEST SELLING NEWSPAPER

Figure 11.7 **Trade journals are particularly valuable for targeting highly specific groups of business buyers.** Construction News is the most widely circulated publication within the UK building and civil engineering sector with a total ABC average circulation figure of 27,224 (July 2001–June 2002). This makes it an ideal medium for promoting a range of construction related products, such as plant and equipment. A fuller understanding of the publication's readers is provided by an in-depth readership survey which is conducted every 2 years. Among other things, the survey has established that 4 people on average read each copy of Construction News, giving an industry-wide readership of 100,000 per week (Reproduced with permission of Construction News)

■ Constraints on advertising

Britain, like most developed countries, recognizes the possibly harmful effects that advertising can have on the values and activities of society. Advertisers therefore face a number of controls on the content and distribution of their adverts. The content of advertisements is influenced just as much by voluntary codes as by legislation, although the effect of EU legislation has been to move more towards legislation; for example, from 2003 it has been illegal to advertise tobacco products (Britt and Wentz [21]).

For printed media, the Advertising Standards Authority (ASA) oversees the British Code of Advertising Practice, which states that all advertisements appearing in members' publications must be legal, honest, decent, and truthful. The penalty for breaching the ASA code is the adverse publicity that follows, and ultimately the Authority could ban an advertisement or a business from advertising in all members' publications. In 2002 the ASA banned Yves Saint Laurent's advertisement for Opium, which featured a naked picture of Sophie Dahl. Earlier, it had required the fashion chain French Connection to submit all of its advertisements to the ASA for prior approval after the company repeatedly flouted ASA guidelines for the use of the company's FCUK acronym (*Daily Telegraph* [2]).

A stronger voluntary code is provided by the Independent Television Commission, which licenses and regulates commercially funded television services in the UK. The Broadcasting Acts have devolved to the Commission the task of developing a code for advertisers. Like the ASA code, it too is continually evolving to meet the changing attitudes and expectations of the public. In recent years, restrictions on some products have been tightened up. (For example, prior to the law banning the advertising of tobacco products, loopholes were closed that had allowed tobacco brand names to be used to promote non-tobacco products offered by the manufacturers, such as sportswear and overseas holidays.) On the other hand, advertising restrictions for some products have been relaxed in response to changing public attitudes. Adverts for condoms have moved from being completely banned, to being allowed in very abstract form, to the present situation where the product itself can be mentioned using actors in life-like situations. The ITC can fine companies that breach its code, or ban their advertisements. In 2003 the Commission fined Auctionworld, a teleshopping auction channel, £10,000 after it had received a large number of complaints from viewers claiming that their goods had not arrived within the advertised delivery period, in breach of the ITC code.

Numerous other forms of voluntary controls exist. Many trade associations have codes that impose restrictions on how their members can advertise. Solicitors, for example, were previously not allowed to advertise at all, but now can do so within limits defined by the Law Society.

🔲 Personal selling

Personal selling involves interpersonal dialogue. It requires person-to-person interaction between a prospective customer and a salesperson. Such dialogue may occur face to face or by other personal forms of communication. Personal selling is not simply about persuasion and persistence, although undoubtedly such skills and attributes do come in useful. Professional selling is more about gathering market and customer information; listening, interpreting, and understanding customer needs; managing the customer–supplier relationship interface; and communicating clearly to the customer the benefits of purchasing a particular product that meets their needs.

Selling as a profession is often devalued and misunderstood. Much of this misunderstanding comes from the activities of sectors of the profession itself, particularly the sleazy end represented by pressurized selling techniques, which traditionally were (and still commonly are) practised in several consumer service and goods industries such as double glazing, financial services, time-share property, and kitchens/bathrooms. In an industrial context, professional selling is more highly regarded. However, such regard is often as much a reflection of an organization's orientation towards sales in preference to marketing as a recognition of the role of selling within marketing. In fact, sales orientation is often evident in many industrial organizations where the sales manager/director is given prominence over most marketing functions.

The interrelationship between sales and marketing was explored by Steward [26], who suggested that to omit the importance of selling as an integral component of the marketing activities of an organization is akin to 'omitting a striker from a football team, a gun without a firing pin, a chemical formula without a catalyst and a organism without the means of reproduction'. It is not uncommon to hear of the marketing department that has launched a new product or offered a sales promotion that the sales force has heard nothing about until the customer asks about it. Similarly, the sales force may be focusing its selling activities in the wrong markets or on inappropriate products. A common complaint from marketing departments is that the sales force withholds important market information. Such inconsistencies should be avoided through proactive attention by both marketing and sales functions.

There is only limited evidence to support the view of Drucker [22], who stated that if organizations got their marketing activity right they would not need a sales force, as customers would come beating a path to their door. Such a statement is naïve and does not recognize the complex nature of many purchase decisions and the importance of human relationships and the sales function in business transactions.

A further dimension of the role of selling and sales management relates to the changing nature of how organizations are doing business, particularly with regard to the trend towards strategic partnerships, joint ventures, alliances, and the increasingly integrated nature of supply chain structures. Very few organizations can operate without considering the range of networks that have been established within industry sectors

(Christopher, Payne, and Ballantyne [1]). Being part of a network is often a prerequisite for doing business, and once in the network the maintenance and building of relationships becomes a critical aspect of an organization's marketing and sales strategy.

MARKETING in ACTION

Sales people need to sell their image

Salesmen and women are not a highly esteemed group of people in the UK. One recent survey carried out by a recruitment consultant typified many similar surveys when it put used car salesmen firmly in the bottom place of least desired professions. Doctors and the clergy—two occupations least associated with selling—scored very highly. Similar surveys in the USA have shown quite a different picture, with salesmanship being considered a great virtue. Why should there be such an apparent difference in attitudes? Maybe the British, being traditionally very reserved, don't like being sold to. Perhaps most people don't understand the wide range of tasks that a salesperson performs, especially in business-to-business selling where technical design skills may be called upon. Much of the misapprehension about selling may be due to perceived bad practices within a number of sectors. But is bad practice ultimately the salesperson's worse enemy? Is a trusted salesperson more likely to achieve not just a one-off sale, but repeat sales?

Types of selling

Selling includes activities that range from a shop assistant selling a bar of chocolate for a few pence to teams negotiating a multi-million pound contract to supply aircraft. McMurry [24] provides a standard classification of roles associated with different selling situations:

- **Deliverer**: The salesperson's job here is mainly concerned with delivering the product, e.g. milk, beer, bread, etc. She possesses little in the way of selling responsibilities. Increases in sales are more likely to stem from a good service and a pleasant manner.

- **Inside order taker**: The salesperson is predominantly an inside order taker, e.g. the sales assistant in a retail outlet. Opportunities to sell are rather limited, as customers have in many cases already made up their minds.

- **Outside order taker**: The salesperson is predominantly an order taker but works in the field and is sometimes able to negotiate additional sales. Selling is usually done by senior executives at head office. The field salesperson simply records and processes the customers' orders and makes sure that the customer is carrying sufficient stock. Good service and a pleasant personality may lead to more orders, but the salesperson has only limited opportunity for creative selling.

- **Missionary selling**: The salesperson does not actually take orders but rather builds up goodwill, educates the actual or potential user, and undertakes various promotional activities, e.g. a salesperson for a pharmaceutical company who makes doctors and pharmacists aware of the benefits of prescribing a new drug.

- **Technical selling**: Many companies in business-to-business markets use sales engineers or salespeople with technical knowledge where product and application knowledge is a central part of the selling function.

- **Creative selling**: This involves creating a favourable impression of a product and can be applied to both tangible goods and intangible services. Services tend to be more difficult because the product cannot easily be demonstrated.

Many of these roles are still evident within organizations, but the list does not do justice to the role of a modern professional field salesperson, which involves significantly greater responsibilities and more complex roles than McMurry's list gives him credit for.

Tasks of a salesperson

A number of tasks typically undertaken by a salesperson can be identified:

- **Prospecting**: searching for prospects or leads
- **Targeting**: deciding how to allocate time among prospects and customers
- **Communicating**: skilfully communicating information about the company's products and services
- **Selling**: knowing the art of sales—approaching, presenting, answering objections, and closing
- **Servicing**: providing various services to customers—consulting on their problems, rendering technical assistance, arranging financing, and expediting delivery
- **Information gathering**: conducting market research and intelligence work and filling in call reports
- **Allocating**: deciding which customers will get scarce products during product shortages

The range of these roles and responsibilities will vary between organizations and sectors, particularly in terms of the level of complexity. For a retail salesperson the primary role is to meet customers who enter the shop and through dialogue to encourage purchase of a product. Such a salesperson may also be responsible for maintaining the appearance of the stock on the shelf and providing support and advice to customers. A telephone salesperson requires a different range of skills, often following a predetermined and well-tested script.

Such lists provide some value in identifying the traditional role of a salesperson, but they can be criticized for their transactional orientation, which does not recognize the importance of the ongoing relationship between the buyer and the seller. Modern sales personnel are as much, if not more, interested in the process that maintains a delighted and loyal customer as they are in achieving the current sales transaction (Egan [23]). The salesperson's primary role then becomes one of managing the relationship rather than just handling the transactions that take place within the relationship. This requires a range of new skills from the salesperson, but alongside these personal skills there needs to be a range of support mechanisms and processes provided by the organization.

Principles of personal selling

Selling techniques can be placed on a continuum from a high-pressured, sales-orientated approach to a softer solutions-based, customer-orientated approach. As indicated earlier, much of the blame for selling's low professional esteem lies in its reputation for sleazy hard sell. Such a reputation does not do justice to the sales profession, and therefore a clearer identification of the skills that lead to effective and professional sales performance need to be considered.

- **Selling skills**: A professional salesperson will require extensive training in sales and negotiation techniques. Other important skills are time management, area management, and report writing.

- **Company and product knowledge**: A salesperson must have extensive and up-to-date knowledge of both the company he represents and the products it offers. Knowledge of the company should include a clear understanding of its mission and purpose, its key personnel, its operations and support functions, and its manufacturing and service processes. The salesperson must have knowledge of the products and services he can offer and their applications. While a salesperson may have sound technical knowledge, it is equally critical that such knowledge can be explained to the customer in terms of benefits and not just features. Every product feature or performance attribute will accrue some benefit to a customer, and it is the salesperson's role to sell the benefits (e.g. time saving, efficiency/cost gains, performance improvements, etc.). A salesperson cannot afford to make promises that the organization does not have the competence or capacity to meet.

- **Market and customer knowledge**: The salesperson will be closer to the customer than most other personnel in the organization. A key part of his role is likely to be as the 'eyes and ears' of the organization. The salesperson should act as a communication conduit to the marketing department, providing detailed information on competitor activities, market trends, customer requirements, changes in key personnel, etc. This is often a neglected part of a salesperson's role, and yet the benefits that can accrue from having accurate and timely information justify attention to this aspect of the role.

- **Time management and area management**: Careful management of time and planning of calls can generate opportunities for the salesperson to make extra sales visits

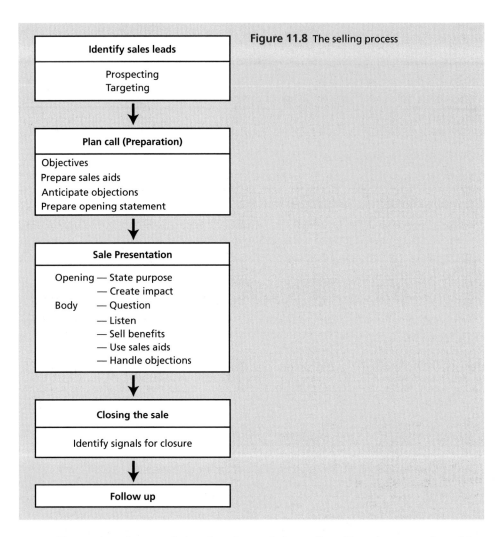

Figure 11.8 The selling process

or gather and analyse market and customer information. If a salesperson is making three sales calls per day over 300 days, this would generate 900 sales visits per annum. If 20% of these visits generated a sale, 180 sales would be achieved. One extra sales call per day would generate 300 extra opportunities to sell a product or service. If 20% of these calls were successfully turned into orders, this would represent 60 extra sales, a 33% increase in sales to that salesperson. Spending more time with customers normally generates more business for the organization, and therefore a salesperson should be trained in time management so that less time is spent travelling or waiting.

Elements of the selling process

Selling is essentially a process, and most analyses of selling identify a number of key stages in the selling process (Figure 11.8).

Figure 11.9 The barriers facing a salesperson are well illustrated in this message used in an advertisement by the publisher of *Business Week*, McGraw-Hill

I don't know who you are.
I don't know your company.
I don't know your company's products.
I don't know what your company stands for.
I don't know your company's customers.
I don't know your company's record.
I don't know your company's reputation.
Now—What was it you wanted to sell me?

Prospecting and targeting

A key function of a salesperson is to assist in the process of identifying and generating sales leads in conjunction with marketing. Unsophisticated prospecting involves door knocking; searching through telephone directories, trade directories, and other general listings of companies; etc. The probability is that only a small percentage of those contacted will be interested in what the organization has to offer. The generation of sales leads from referrals by customers, suppliers, or other business/social contacts will usually provide better prospects. Similarly, leads generated by exhibitions, conferences, seminars, and responses to advertisements will prove to be 'warmer' leads. Databases and the internet are increasingly being used to develop and refine lists of prospects (Grewal, Levy and Marshall [19]).

Having established a customer prospect list, the salesperson should conduct some form of evaluation of each potential buyer in terms of her business, markets, products and probability of purchase. Those prospects that appear to offer the most potential can then be shortlisted for contact.

Preparation

Before contacting potential customers, a good salesperson will obtain as much insight as possible into the organization's history and current business situation and strategy. Much of this information can be gleaned from contacts within the industry or by analysing annual reports and other company publications. Preparation can be as simple as knowing the key contact's name and how long he has been at the organization and in his current role. Clear sales objectives should be set before approaching the customer. Without objectives, the call can become just a chat and nothing will be achieved.

The sales presentation

This will vary in style depending upon the product/service and the nature of the relationship established with the prospective customer. What follows is the general framework and guidelines that a good salesperson will follow when presenting a standard sales pitch to the client.

- **Create impact**: In the opening minutes of a sales call, the salesperson should endeavour to create interest and develop a rapport with the buyer. There is evidence that the first impressions of a salesperson can have a significant impact on the final outcome (Sparks and Areni [17]). It is only once a rapport has been established that the salesperson should commence the next stage of the sales presentation.

- **Asking questions and listening**: By asking questions, the salesperson aims to ascertain the exact nature of the customer's needs, concerns, issues, and possible objections to making a purchase. Asking questions also has the benefit of keeping control of the sales interview. The salesperson's ability to listen to what has been said is a critical skill; often the buyer will provide clues as to his interest or needs or potential objections that can be missed if the buyer is not listening.

- **Selling the benefits**: Once the salesperson has clarified the client's needs and answered his concerns, the next stage of the selling process is to sell a product's benefits. Customers buy benefits, not features, and are interested in what the product or service can do for them or their organization. The presentation may involve a demonstration or use of visual props.

- **Buying signals**: Signs of interest are called 'buying signals'. A question from the buyer asking for more details is a buying signal. A comment such as 'that's interesting' is a very strong buying signal. All buying signals should be closed by the salesperson.

- **Closing the sale**: This refers to the salesperson's technique of asking the buyer for an order. Asking for the order should come naturally when a salesperson knows that she has clarified a customer's needs and key concerns, answered all his questions, and handled potential reasons not to buy to the satisfaction of the customer.

- **Follow-up**: The follow-up is another important relationship-builder and can signal the opportunity for potential future repeat business. The follow-up may take the form of a letter confirming the issues discussed or a telephone call to ensure the buyer is satisfied.

Business-to-business selling: the complex sale

In a business-to-business context the sales presentations may cover a period of many weeks and months and involve a number of individuals. Commercial goods and services are often purchased by professional buyers who are highly trained managers responsible for significant levels of expenditure. These buyers will not be working in isolation but may be part of a project team or committee that is evaluating alternative suppliers. While knowledge of these teams/committees is important, the seller also needs to be aware of the different purchase roles that are evident within industrial/business purchase decisions. The concept of a decision-making unit was introduced in Chapter 3, and you should be aware of the individuals, or groups of individuals, who

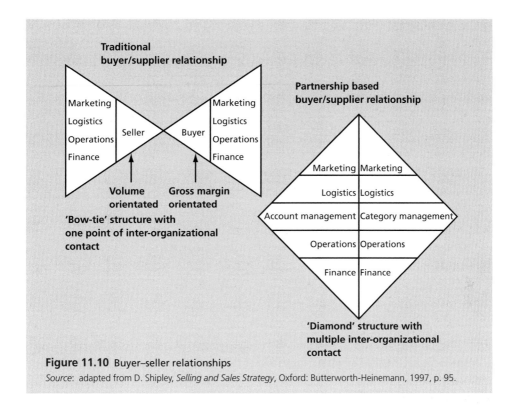

Figure 11.10 Buyer–seller relationships

Source: adapted from D. Shipley, *Selling and Sales Strategy*, Oxford: Butterworth-Heinemann, 1997, p. 95.

may need to be approached by the salesperson—the buyer; the user; the decision maker; the approver; the influencer; and the gatekeeper. The salesperson must understand the different sets of needs of each of these groups and adapt her sales message accordingly.

A common purchasing technique is to use a tender document requesting specifications and quotes; this is sealed, and is considered by the buying centre but with no salesperson present. Some contracts/projects take several years before decisions are made.

Key account management

In response to the trend away from transaction-based marketing and towards ongoing buyer–seller relationships (Chapter 3), organization structures are being developed with new roles such as category managers, customer relations managers, business development managers, and key account managers. While the traditional buyer–seller relationship would have been one of contract/price and volume negotiation, the new relationship approach involves multifunctional levels of interaction with the key account manager role requiring a greater range of skills than was necessary under the traditional buyer–seller relationship model (Figure 11.10).

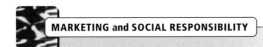

		Company sales orientation	
		Transaction	Relationship
	The Sale	Account opener	'Have a nice day'
Salesperson's primary concern	Customer	Account keeper	Key account manager

Figure 11.11 Supplier sales and marketing approaches *Source*: adapted from D. Shipley, *Selling and Sales Strategy*, Oxford: Butterworth-Heinemann, 1997, p. 92.

MARKETING and SOCIAL RESPONSIBILITY

Over-enthusiastic selling of pensions

Can a salesperson be too successful? Many sales personnel have responded vigorously to bonus or other incentives offered by their employers to achieve sales that looked good at the time, but later came back to haunt the company. One of the key characteristics of a good salesperson is her ability to listen and to gain a good understanding of a buyer's needs. But what happens when the customer doesn't really have a very good understanding of his own needs? Furthermore, what happens when you couple this with a salesperson who would rather earn her sales commission as easily as possible than probe the true needs of the customer? The result has been a series of mis-selling scandals that have tarnished the reputation of a number of business sectors, especially financial services.

The term 'caveat emptor' ('let the buyer be aware') has been used to excuse the situation where a salesperson has sold an individual an item that was not very good, or not suited to his needs: it implies that it was the buyer's fault for buying wrongly, rather the seller's fault for selling wrongly. The balance is now tilting in the consumer's favour as society's expectations of sellers is rising. This has been demonstrated through the mis-selling of a range of financial services during the 1980s and 1990s. Perhaps the most serious occurred where sales personnel employed by the big UK pensions companies persuaded employees to cash in the pension schemes they had with their own employers and to take out a new personal pension scheme with the salespersons' company. By 2003 the value of personal pensions had fallen sharply following a fall in stock market prices.

Why did so many people give up a good employer's pension scheme for a much more dubious personal pension scheme? Many may have been tempted by a one-off payment from the government, and the salesperson may have been tempted to sell personal pensions too aggressively by a hefty commission payment on the sale. The customer may have thought he was buying into a good deal, but most buyers were not able to understand the complexities of a personal pension scheme. In most cases the customer was badly advised and found that the pension he had bought into was worth much less than the employer's pension he had given up. The over-enthusiastic selling resulted in the big pensions companies being reprimanded by their industry watchdog and forced to pay millions of pounds in fines and compensation to customers. They were forced to rethink the way they managed their sales personnel; but much of the change simply involved going back to traditional best practice—ensuring that the sales force would listen to the customer and understand what he really needed; training the sales force to have greater product knowledge; and structuring salespeople's rewards to recognize a balance between the need for short-term incentives and long-term relationships.

MARKETING in ACTION

Is there a return on tea and biscuits?

Talk about the importance of relationship building may be fine, but can it ever be a complete substitute for the hard skills of selling? In all too many companies, it seems that sales and service people see their task as 'account managing' and 'relationship building', and abhor the idea of selling.

Every salesperson knows the importance of human relations, interpersonal skills, and having a positive attitude towards the job of selling. But is this enough to make a good salesperson? Unfortunately, when combined with the theory of self-motivation and the setting of clearly defined objectives, it can produce an adverse reaction in some individuals, who then spend so much of their day trying to persuade themselves that they feel great, reciting self-motivators like 'Success is achieved by those who try and keep trying', or 'When the going gets tough the tough get going' and 'I'm going to be top salesperson this year!' that they forget that their real task is to locate decision makers and persuade them to buy. Pontificating about success is fine, but at the end of the day, salesmen must make it happen!

One of the popular tactics of such people is to show up unannounced at a customer's home or place of work and invite themselves in for tea and biscuits (T&B). They see tea and biscuits as a good method of building personal relationships. But is such relationship-building actually sought by customers? Many claim to hate such intrusions and prefer to be left to get on with their work. Although the salesperson's product may be vital to their business, they often do not welcome the pressure from 'T&B' reps for a personal relationship—they may just want a business relationship.

One further thought about the emergence of relationship managers: how can a company tell whether its relationship managers are performing effectively? How many 'T&B' visits does it take before you would expect evidence of results in the form of a sale? Could relationship management be just an invitation for soft management when what is really needed is a hard sell?

With key account management, the salesperson and the organization are committed to building long-term, ongoing relationships with key account customers. The orientation and structure of the organization is such that cross-functional support and adequate resources are committed to enable the 'key account' manager to succeed.

The salesperson's role under the key account management approach shifts from a transactional to a relationship orientation; therefore a new set of skills and knowledge is required. Shipley [25] suggests that a range of generic sales/marketing approaches exists for suppliers to select from. Figure 11.11 summarizes these different approaches using two axes, with the sales and marketing approach on the horizontal axis and the salesperson's primary concern on the vertical axis. It is suggested that the concern of the salesperson is positioned along a continuum running from concern for getting the sales to concern for managing the well-being of the customer. The salesperson's style will be influenced by whether her organization has a transactional or relational orientation, for instance in terms of how performance is evaluated and rewarded, time-scales for achievement of goals, etc.

■ Sales promotion

Sales promotion involves those activities—other than advertising, personal selling, and public relations—that stimulate customer purchase and the effectiveness of intermediaries. The Institute of Sales Promotion defines sales promotions as

a range of tactical marketing techniques designed within a strategic marketing framework, to add value to a product or service in order to achieve a specific sales and marketing objective.

Although sales promotion activity can be used to create awareness, it is usually used for the later stages of the buying process, that is to create interest and desire, and—in particular—to bring about action. Sales promotion can quite successfully complement other tools within the promotion mix, for example by reinforcing a particular image or identity developed through advertising.

Over the last few years there has been a rapid increase in the use of sales promotion, for a number of reasons.

- There has been a greater acceptance of the use of sales promotion by top management, and more people are now qualified to use it. In addition, there is greater pressure today to obtain a quick sales response, something that sales promotion can be good at achieving.

- Markets have become increasingly competitive, and there is evidence that customers have become less loyal to brands and are prepared to go for the best deal on offer. Sales promotion is often used to break brand loyalty.

- As advertising channels proliferate, audiences have become saturated with messages and advertising efficiency has declined because of increasing costs and media clutter.

- New technology in targeting has resulted in an increase in the efficiency and effectiveness of sales promotion.

Planning for sales promotion

Effective sales promotion involves an ongoing process with a number of stages.

1. **Establishment of objectives.** If the target is the customer, objectives could include the encouragement of increased usage or the building of trial among non-users or other brand users. For intermediaries, objectives could be to encourage off-season sales, or offsetting competitive promotions. While sales promotion can be used merely to gain attention for a product, a more likely aim is to provide an incentive incorporating an offer that represents value to the target audience. It can also act as an invitation to make a purchase now rather than later. Sales promotion activity is often aimed at attracting brand switchers but is unlikely to turn them into loyal brand users without the use of other elements of the promotion mix. In fact, sales promotion is generally used to break down brand loyalty, whereas advertising is used to build it up (Low and Mohr [18]). Sales promotion can gain new users or encourage more frequent purchase, but it cannot compensate for inadequate advertising, poor delivery, or poor product quality.

2. **Planning the sales promotion programme.** The major decisions that need to be made when designing the sales promotion programme relate to the timing of the promotion and how long the sales promotion tool is to be used. Also important are the size of the incentive, rules for entry, and the overall budget for the promotion.

3. **Selection of promotion tools.** Promotional objectives form the basis for selecting the most appropriate sales promotion tools. The cost and effectiveness of each tool must be assessed with regard to achieving these objectives in respect of each target market. The tools available to the service marketer are described in more detail below.

4. **Pre-testing.** This should be undertaken in order to ensure that potentially expensive problems are discovered before the full launch of a promotion. Testing in selected market segments can highlight problems of ambiguity and response rates, and give an indication of cost effectiveness.

5. **Implementation.** The programme for implementation must include two important time factors. First, it must indicate the 'lead time'—the time necessary to bring the programme up to the point where the incentive is to be made available to the public. Second, it must indicate the 'sell-in time', which is the period of time from the date of release to when approximately 90% of incentive material has been received by potential customers.

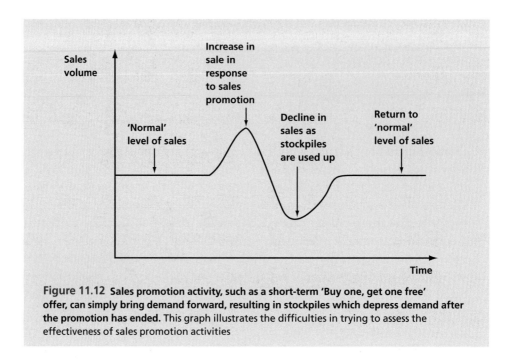

Figure 11.12 Sales promotion activity, such as a short-term 'Buy one, get one free' offer, can simply bring demand forward, resulting in stockpiles which depress demand after the promotion has ended. This graph illustrates the difficulties in trying to assess the effectiveness of sales promotion activities

6. **Evaluation.** The performance of the promotion needs to be assessed against the objectives set. If objectives are specific and quantifiable, measurement would seem to be easy. However, extraneous factors can account for the apparent success of many sales promotion activities; for example, competitive actions or seasonal variations may influence customers' decision making. It can also be extremely difficult to separate out the effects of sales promotion activity from other promotional activity—or indeed from other marketing mix changes, such as a lower price. A further problem is that sales promotion activity may simply bring demand forward, resulting in buyers building up stockpiles which then depresses demand for the product in future periods. This is especially true of products that are of low value and have a long shelf-life. This effect is illustrated in Figure 11.12.

Sales promotion tools

A wide and ever increasing range of sales promotion tools are available to marketers. Some of the more commonly used tools aimed at the final consumer include the following.

- **Free samples/visits/consultations:** These encourage trial of a product and can be valuable where consumers are currently loyal to another supplier. They could, for ex-

Figure 11.13 Coupons have been used by marketers for a long time to promote sales. They allow groups of prospective or actual customers to be targeted with an incentive to encourage them to become a new customer, or to become a bigger spending customer. By restricting the distribution of coupons to those who it is most interested in, a company avoids giving a price reduction to everybody, including those who are loyal and probably find its prices good value. More recently, the internet has allowed electronic coupons to be distributed efficiently and effectively. By studying site visitors' previous behaviour, unique coupons can be generated. These can either be used online or printed for use elsewhere. The online retailer Amazon.com has made extensive use of coupons to promote sales, such as this one, which is configured according to the information that the company has available about specific targets. Combined with a carefully planned Internet based promotion programme and an active affiliates programme, Amazon has become the leading online book retailer in the UK. (Reproduced with permission of Amazon.com.)

ample, be used by a breakfast cereal manufacturer to entice potential customers to try their brand. In the case of new products which are perceived as being expensive and of poor value to a consumer, they can encourage trial. Satellite television companies, for example, have often used this approach with free trial offers. For established products, the excessive offering of free samples can demean the value of the product on offer and buyers may become reluctant to pay for a product that they have seen being given away freely.

- **Money-off price incentives:** Price incentives can be used tactically to try to counteract temporary increases in competitor activity. They can also be used to stimulate sales of a new product shortly after launch or to stimulate demand during slack periods where price is considered to be a key element in a customer's purchase decision. Price incentives tend to be an expensive form of sales promotion, as the incentive is given to customers regardless of its motivational effect on them. A restaurant reducing its prices for all customers is unable to extract the full price from those customers who may have been willing to pay the full price. There is also a danger that price incentives can become built into consumers' expectations so that their removal will result in a fall in business.

- **Coupons/vouchers:** These allow holders to obtain a discount off a purchase and can be targeted at quite specific groups of users or potential users, often combined with the direct marketing techniques discussed later in this chapter. To encourage trial by potential new users, vouchers can be distributed to non-users who fit a specified profile. In this way, a manufacturer of cosmetics may provide a voucher with a women's magazine whose readership corresponds with the manufacturer's target market. To encourage repeat usage, vouchers can be given as a loyalty bonus. Voucher offers tend to be much more cost-effective than straight price incentives because of their ability to segment markets. As an example, a tourist attraction can recognize that visitors from overseas might see the full price as being only a small part of their total holiday cost and representing good value, while a local family might need an incentive to make more frequent visits to the attraction.

- **Gift offers:** Companies often provide the incentive of a gift to encourage short-term sales. Gifts can take many forms, such as a Marks & Spencer gift token or a T-shirt, and

MARKETING in ACTION

Assaulting our senses to secure a sale

Background music in retail stores may be dismissed by some as mere 'muzac', while to others it may be deeply irritating. But does it make any difference in bringing about a sale?

Techniques to match music with retail environments are becoming increasingly sophisticated. AEI, a US-based company specializing in designing music for retailers, has devised a system whereby tracks can be beamed into a store via satellite, allowing the selection of music to be controlled remotely. The company begins by analysing the environment of a store, including the demographics of customers, store layout, lighting, and pattern of demand throughout the day. As an example of music selection, the company chose mellow jazz for the cosmopolitan and slightly off-beat coffee and sandwich shop Pret à Manger. Contemporary jazz with hints of ethnicity was chosen for Habitat, supposedly to support traditional craft products.

We may not be aware of these assaults on our senses, but controlled experiments have shown that they can influence our buying behaviour. Using another of our senses—smell—the retailer Woolworth's has claimed that the smell of mulled wine increased its overall sales during the Christmas shopping period. Supermarkets routinely pump recirculated smells of bread and coffee through their stores, but exclude others such as fish and soap powder.

Gone are the days of a tape recorder under the manager's desk and the odd air freshener. To be effective, sales promotion techniques must gain a detailed understanding of what motivates a customer to buy. Very often, the most effective techniques are the ones that we are not even conscious of.

Figure 11.14 **In many markets where products are perceived by buyers as being basically similar, it may be necessary to offer an incentive in order to initiate a dialogue.** Eager to enter buyers' choice set, many insurance companies, such as this one, provide a token gift in order to generate an initial response. Many firms offer further incentives following a completed purchase. Sales promotion activities of this type may be particularly important where consumers' ability to differentiate between competing products is low and an incentive offers a tangible basis for differentiation

Reproduced with permission of Lloyds TSB Insurance Services Ltd.

FREE Parker Pen when you call for a quote!

Find out how much you could save with The Insurance Shop. Call us now for a free quote without obligation, and we'll send you a free Parker Pen by way of a thank you.

FREE Up to £30 worth of Marks & Spencer Gift Vouchers when you take out home insurance

That's right, just take out a building or contents insurance policy with The Insurance Shop, and we'll send you Marks & Spencer Gift Vouchers worth £15. Or £30 if you take out both.

the insurance shop

can encourage immediate and/or repeated purchase. The gift can satisfy a number of objectives. In order to promote initial enquiry, many firms offer a gift for merely enquiring about their products. This provides an opportunity to submit, with the gift, samples and brochures of the firm's products. A gift can also be used to bring about immediate action—for example a free clock radio if a purchase is made within a specified period. For existing customers, gifts can be used to develop and reward loyalty. Many consumer goods companies encourage customers to collect tokens which can be redeemed against selected promotional merchandise.

Sometimes, a company might charge a small amount for a 'gift', making the gift offer self-financing. Or the gift could be inscribed with a message, which will be seen by the user and others for some time to come. Some petrol retailers and breakfast cereal manufacturers, among others, sell ranges of promotional clothing, paid for by a combination of vouchers and cash. Some gifts are provided collaboratively between companies with quite different product ranges. For example, a grocery retailer may give rewards of money-off vouchers at a chain of restaurants, satisfying the promotional criteria of the retailer (rewarding loyalty) and the restaurant (encouraging trial).

- **Competitions:** The offer of a competition adds to the value of the total offer. Instead of simply buying an insurance policy, a customer buys the policy plus a dream of winning a prize to which she attaches significance. Competitions can be used both to create trial among non-users and to encourage loyalty among existing customers (e.g. a competition for which a number of proofs of purchase are necessary to enter).

Sales promotion tools aimed at *intermediaries* include the following.

- **Short-term sales bonuses:** These can be used to stimulate sales during slack periods or to develop loyalty from intermediaries in the face of competitor activity.

- **Competitions and gifts:** These can be aimed at sales personnel working for intermediaries and can serve to increase awareness of a brand and, if entry to the competition is conditional upon achieving sales targets, encourage additional sales.

- **Point of purchase material:** To stimulate additional sales, a supplier can provide a range of incentives to help intermediaries. Many consumer goods suppliers offer retailers and field sales staff a range of eye-catching displays to demonstrate the benefits of their product at the point of purchase.

- **Co-operative advertising:** Suppliers can agree to subscribe to local advertising by an intermediary, for instance when a car manufacturer promotes the location of its dealers as well as the core benefits of its cars. Co-operative advertising is often undertaken in conjunction with a significant event, such as the opening of a new outlet by the intermediary, or the launch of a new product.

Public relations

The role of public relations in the promotion mix

Public relations (PR) is used to establish and enhance a positive image of an organization and its products among its various publics. It is defined by the Institute of Public Relations as

the deliberate, planned and sustained effort to establish and maintain mutual understanding between an organization and its publics.

The words 'deliberate', 'planned', and 'sustained' are crucial here, as companies cannot simply 'do a bit of PR' in isolated bursts and hope for the type of result that comes from a more concerted effort. Public relations as a professional activity is treated with suspicion by many people, but this probably reflects a perception of a short-term opportunistic activity, rather than the long-term commitment advocated by public relations professionals. A good long-term PR strategy will make it much easier for a company to use PR tools when it has a real emergency and needs to communicate with its audience. As an example, a food manufacturer that has carefully used PR to develop a good mutual understanding between itself and its principal publics will be better placed to use PR to counter a food safety incident than a manufacturer that uses PR tools only as and when needed.

Because public relations is involved with more than just customer relationships, it is often handled at a corporate level rather than at the functional level of marketing management, and it can be difficult to integrate public relations fully into the overall promotional plan. For many companies, public relations covers communication with investor and community groups, among others.

Public relations and corporate reputation

Public relations is very important for maintaining a firm's reputation, especially where it is facing a crisis. In the UK, various rail operators have faced numerous challenges following accidents. The good public relations activity of Railtrack following the Paddington train crash in 1999 has been contrasted with the relatively weak and tardy response of the rail maintenance contractor Jarvis when its slack working practices were accused of causing a major rail crash at Potters Bar in 2002.

A potentially even bigger crisis faced the Mercedes Benz company when its newly launched A-Class overturned during a test drive with journalists in Sweden. The reputation of Mercedes' eagerly awaited new car was at stake as critics accused the German company of producing an unsafe car (Ihlen [9]). Like many companies presented with such a crisis, Mercedes faced a dilemma of whether to stand its ground and claim that there was nothing wrong, or openly admit to its problems. By standing its ground, the problem might just have gone away; but if it had persisted the company's image would have been tarnished not only by its building an unsafe car, but additionally by having been dishonest about it in its earlier statements.

With the development of a 24/7 media environment, companies' reputations can be destroyed more quickly and easily than ever before. It took very little time for the accountancy firm Arthur Andersen to be brought down from having a multi-million-pound income with blue-chip clients and an international network, to being picked over by competitors and deserted by long-term clients. By all accounts, Anderson was still doing good work at its offices in Singapore and Auckland, but its involvement with just one client—Enron—had changed the public's perceptions of the company to the point where business leaders were going out of their way not to be associated with it. The pervasiveness of present-day news media meant that what could have been a local difficulty had led to a multi-national organization being brought down (*The Times* [12]).

Establishing and maintaining corporate reputation is a discipline with a lot of components, including issues of brand development, crisis management, public affairs, and relations with the City. High-profile resignations of chief executives, succession vacuums, and aborted merger talks have put the value of corporate reputations into perspective. A company must communicate well beyond its customers to all stakeholders, including employees, suppliers, financial backers, and the media.

The characteristics of public relations

As an element within the promotion mix, public relations presents a number of valuable opportunities as well as problems. Some of its more important characteristics are described below.

- **Relatively low cost:** The major advantage of public relations is that it tends to be much cheaper, in terms of cost per person reached, than any other type of promotion. Apart from nominal production costs, much PR activity can be carried out at almost no cost, in marked contrast to the high cost of buying space or time in the main media. To make the most use of this apparently free resource, many companies retain outside PR consultants who can prove themselves to be cost-effective in developing these opportunities.

- **Can be targeted:** Public relations activities can be targeted to a small specialized audience if the right media vehicle is used.

- **Credibility:** The results of PR activity often have a high degree of credibility, compared with other promotional sources such as advertising. This is because the audience may regard such a message as coming from an apparently impartial and non-commercial source. Where information is presented as news, readers or viewers may be less critical of it than if it is presented as an advertisement, which they may presume to be biased.

- **Relatively uncontrollable:** A company can exercise little direct control over how its public relations activity is subsequently handled and interpreted. If successful, a press release may be printed in full, although there can be no control over where or when it is printed. At worst, a press release can be misinterpreted and the result can be very unfavourable news coverage. This is in contrast to advertising, where an advertiser can exercise considerable control over the content, placing, and timing of an advert.

- **Saturation of effort:** The fact that many organizations compete for a finite amount of media attention puts pressure on the public relations effort to be better than that of competitors. There can be no guarantee that PR activity will have any impact on the targets at whom it is aimed.

The publics of public relations

Public relations can be distinguished from customer relations because its concerns go beyond the creation of mutually beneficial relationships with actual or potential customers. The following additional audiences for public relations can be identified.

- **Employees:** It may be important to communicate with employees on such issues as job security, working conditions, and the state of the market. Staff will inevitably hear things that may affect them from other sources, and public relations can seek to provide an authoritative view on these issues, through the use of in-house publications, newsletters, and employee recognition activities.

- **Suppliers:** These may need assurances that a company is a credible one to deal with and that contractual obligations will be met. Highlighting favourable annual reports and drawing attention to major new developments can help to raise the profile and credibility of a company in the eyes of its suppliers.

- **Intermediaries:** These may share many of the same concerns as customers and need reassurance about a company's capabilities. Are a firm's intermediaries showing commitment to a particular line of business? What new product developments are being considered that may raise the morale of intermediaries?

- **Government:** In many cases, actions of government can significantly affect the fortunes of an organization, and therefore relationships with government departments—at local, national, and supranational level—need to be carefully developed. This can include lobbying of members of Parliament, and communicating the company's views to government inquiries and civil servants.

- **Financial community:** This includes financial institutions that have supported, are currently supporting, or may in future support the organization. Shareholders, both private and institutional, form an important element of this community and must be reassured that the organization is going to achieve its stated objectives.

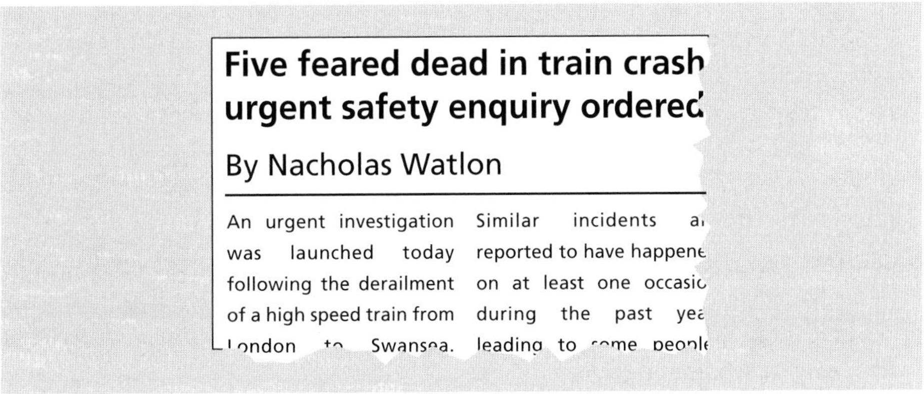

Five feared dead in train crash urgent safety enquiry ordered

By Nacholas Watlon

An urgent investigation was launched today following the derailment of a high speed train from London to Swansea. Similar incidents are reported to have happened on at least one occasion during the past year leading to some people

Figure 11.15 A crisis can hit even the best run company, with events such as contaminated food, wrongdoings of its directors, and industrial accidents undoing its hard-earned good reputation. Cultivating a good image with the public in general can help to protect a company's image from such shocks. Close relations with the media, built up over a period of time, can ease the process of restoring a company's reputation. Many of the best run companies practise their response to a simulated crisis, so that when one occurs their response can be fast and co-ordinated

- **Local communities/pressure groups:** It is sometimes important for an organization to be seen as a 'good neighbour' in its local community. The organization can enhance its image through the use of charitable contributions, sponsorship of local events, being seen to support the local environment, and so on.

- **The media:** As powerful opinion-formers, members of the media represent an important audience. Public relations activity seeks to create a favourable predisposition by this group, which will then be passed on to the other audiences identified above. The use of the media to convey an organization's message is considered below.

The tools of public relations

A wide range of tools is available to the PR practitioner, and the suitability of each tool is dependent upon the promotional objectives at which it is directed. In general, the tools of public relations are best suited to creating awareness of an organization and its products, or a liking for them. Public relations tends to be less effective in directly bringing about action in the form of purchase decisions.

Some of the important tools of public relations are described below.

- **Press releases:** A press release can be defined as a communication that seeks to secure *editorial* space in the media, as distinct from paid-for advertising space. Because of its important contribution towards the promotion mix, this tool is considered in more detail later.

- **Lobbying:** Professional lobbyists are often employed by a company in an effort to inform and hence influence those key decision makers who may be critical to its success. Lobbying can take place at a local level (e.g. a fast food company seeking to convince members of a local authority about the benefits of allowing them to locate in a sensitive area); at a national level (e.g. lobbying by UK brewers to bring UK tax on beer down to the lower levels of many other European countries); and at a supranational level (e.g. the lobbying by herbal remedy companies in 2003 against planned new EU regulations which would require expensive product testing).

- **Education and training:** In an effort to develop a better understanding—and hence liking—of an organization and its products, many firms aim education and training programmes at important target groups. In this way, food manufacturers frequently supply schools and colleges with educational material that will predispose recipients of the material to their brand. Open days are another common method of educating the public by showing them the complex processes that occur 'behind the scenes' in order to ensure a high quality of output for customers.

- **Exhibitions and trade shows:** Most companies attend exhibitions not with the intention of making an immediate sale, but to create an awareness of their organization which will result in a sale over the longer term. Exhibitions offer the chance for potential customers to talk face to face with representatives of the organization and to sample products. Exhibitions are used to target both consumer and commercial audiences. Many trade shows are important events in their respective business sectors, where a high proportion of key decision makers are likely to be present. The annual World Travel Market in London, for example, is an ideal opportunity for travel-related organizations to communicate with their key business customers. The absence of a company at such key exhibitions may lead to concern among some visitors about why they have chosen not to be there.

- **In-house journals:** The number of in-house magazines produced by companies is now huge, with examples spanning sectors from airlines to banks and supermarkets. By adopting a news-based magazine format, the message becomes more credible than if it were presented as a pure advertisement. Often, outside advertisers contribute revenue which can make such journals self-financing. Travel operators often publish magazines that are read by a captive travelling public.

- **Sponsorship:** There is argument about whether this strictly forms part of the public relations portfolio of tools. It is, however, being increasingly used as an element of the promotion mix and is described in more detail later in this chapter.

Press relations

The aim of press relations is to create a long-term sense of mutual understanding between an organization and the media. This understanding with the media is developed by means of:

Figure 11.16 Faced with a news story that the media wishes to cover, a newspaper or radio station may seek specialists within an industrial sector who are knowledgeable on the issues involved. A local tour operator may be asked by a local newspaper to comment upon the consequences of a natural disaster in an overseas resort. This helps both the reporter and the tour operator in question, whose representative is fielded as an expert

- **Press releases:** This is the most frequent form of press relations activity and is commonly used to announce new product launches, new appointments, or significant achievements.
- **Press conferences:** These are used where a major event is to be announced and an opportunity for a two-way dialogue between the organization and the media is considered desirable.

Press relations activity has the advantage of being relatively inexpensive to use and being able to reach large audiences with a high degree of credibility. Against this, a major disadvantage is the lack of control that the generator of a press release has over how it is subsequently handled, in terms of appearance, timing, and content. (It is likely to be edited.) Because of the competition from other organizations for press coverage, there can be no guarantee that any particular item will actually be used. Indeed, it is often suggested that over 90% of press releases sent to media editors end up in the bin without being used.

An important element of press relations is the avoidance of negative publicity. For highly variable goods and services (such as airline and train services), there is always the possibility that the media will pick up one bad incident and leave their audience thinking that this is the norm for a particular organization. This is particularly a problem for highly visible public or quasi-public services, about which readers enjoy reading bad news stories to confirm their own prejudices. Media editors have a tendency to write stories that they believe their audiences would like to hear, so if a bad news story about a train company can be assured of a sympathetic hearing it will most likely be run. It would take a great deal of effort by train operators to prove to editors that they are out of touch with the reality facing their readers or viewers.

External events sometimes lead to bad publicity for an organization, as where increased air traffic congestion leads to stories of major delays for airline passengers. Sometimes the negative actions of other organizations within the same sector may lead to a generally poor reputation for the sector as a whole. In all situations, an organization needs to establish contingency plans to minimize any surprise and confusion resulting from such bad publicity. Bad publicity is more likely to be managed effectively if an organization has invested time and effort in developing mutually supportive relations with the media.

Evaluating public relations activity

It has traditionally been argued that the results of public relations could not be measured. Furthermore, this did not really matter, because PR was relatively inexpensive anyway and it was clearly a good thing to be doing. Such an attitude is now much less acceptable, and there is a growing demand for tools to measure and evaluate PR properly.

Media content analysis and press cuttings are the most commonly used evaluation techniques, but a range of confusing alternatives has appeared, including 'advertising

MARKETING in ACTION

Advertising + PR = More impact per pound

How can an advertising manager make his adverts go further? One solution is to get the media to talk about the ads, so that they are given free editorial coverage. This is where advertising must work closely with public relations, and managers must bear in mind that, as in all PR, control over actual media coverage may be quite limited.

That outrageous adverts have ended up being talked about in the media is exemplified by Club 18–30 Holidays, which has acquired notoriety for its saucy adverts on billboards and in newspapers. A turning-point, however, came with the deliberate integration of advertising and PR. A pioneer in this was the 'Hello Boys' advertising campaign for Wonderbra, which featured posters of the supermodel Eva Herzigova. Advertising agency TBWA worked closely with PR consultancy Jackie Cooper to secure media coverage of the advertising campaign, which it achieved, for example, by arranging media interviews with the supermodel Herzigova and putting out quirky stories about the advertising posters being stolen by collectors. Another example of this close integration was undertaken for an advert for the Renault Clio, which featured comedians Vic Reeves and Bob Mortimer at Nicole's wedding. Beer Davies Publicity sent 3,000 wedding invitations to national and local press, asking journalists to join 'Papa' at the wedding of his beloved daughter, 'Nicole'. It also invited them to attend a pre-wedding breakfast at the Savoy Hotel the day before, where the advert was unveiled. As a result, the story featured in most of the UK national newspapers. Some of the papers even covered the news that members of Nicole's internet fan club attended the launch event carrying banners urging Nicole 'Don't do it!'

But securing PR coverage for an advert is not always easy. Journalists may get wise to advertisers' tactics and take no interest in the story. PR must be innovative in giving an editor a story that his audience will want to hear about. There is also a problem when an advert generates negative publicity, something that happened with Help the Aged in an advertising campaign featuring elderly people in a morgue. It may have gained attention by using shock tactics, but did this really help to advance its cause?

value equivalents' and 'opportunities to see'. Innovations in computer software are providing new tools which can allow for rapid tracking of media coverage and a calculation of the likely audience. In addition to measuring volume and circulation figures, national readership data are used to calculate reach and frequency, and occasionally gross rating points. While clients may wish to know that their money has been spent effectively, PR consultants are keen to show the high impact achieved by PR in comparison with a similar budget advertising campaign.

Another important aspect of PR evaluation is the pre-testing of messages. According to the Institute of Public Relations, only 3% of consultants have ever pre-tested their messages, despite the possibilities of misinterpretation that may subsequently arise.

Who should do the PR evaluation? Many PR consultancies provide an evaluation service to their clients using agreed criteria. Meanwhile, many specialist evaluation companies have emerged that may be contracted directly by the client, or subcontracted by a consultant to provide detailed evaluation.

◼ Sponsorship

Sponsorship does not fit neatly into a categorization of the main elements of the promotion mix. Essentially, it uses a combination of advertising, public relations, sales promotion, and direct marketing to associate a company's product or corporate image that may be unknown or misunderstood with the image of something that is well understood. As the general clutter of media advertising has increased in recent years, sponsorship has come to play a progressively important role in the promotion mix. With consumers becoming increasingly critical of organizations' societal credentials, sponsorship has been seen by many organizations as a cost-effective means of enhancing their image.

Sponsorship involves a company's investment in events or causes in order to achieve objectives such as increased awareness levels, enhanced reputation, etc. Sponsorship activities include a brewer sponsoring tennis matches (e.g. the Stella Artois tournament) and an organization sponsoring specific television programmes (such as Cadbury's sponsorship of *Coronation Street*).

As with promotional planning in general, segmentation is crucial to successful sponsorship. A company must have a good definition of the audience to which it wishes to communicate its message, and must then seek sponsorship vehicles whose audiences match that target market. As an example, the tour operator Kuoni Travel's sponsorship of Classic FM programmes matches Kuoni's target market with Classic FM's audience. Sponsorship often takes place at a local level; for example, an estate agency moving into an area may seek to increase awareness of it by sponsoring a school fete or a local theatrical group.

It is difficult to evaluate sponsorship activities because of the problem of isolating the effects of sponsorship from other elements of the promotion mix. Direct measurement is likely to be possible only if sponsorship is the predominant tool. Sponsorship should therefore be seen as a tool that complements other elements of the promotion mix.

◼ Direct marketing

Defining direct marketing

Direct marketing has become very important to marketing managers during the past couple of decades and there is every indication that it will continue to become increasingly significant in the future. Direct marketing essentially entails companies opening up a dialogue directly between themselves and the end consumers of their products, thereby avoiding the need to communicate through indirect media such as press and television advertising. It can also allow a firm to communicate directly with its customers without having to go through retail or wholesale intermediaries. However, it must be emphasized that the direct marketing activities described in this section are

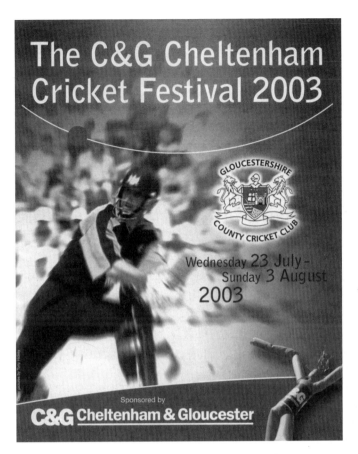

Figure 11.17 Sponsorship of sporting events allows a company's brand name to be seen by viewers of the event and to associate the brand with the values of the sport concerned.
Cheltenham & Gloucester is the third largest provider of household mortgages in the UK, and has to compete with dozens of other banks and building societies for buyers' attention. By sponsoring a public activity, the brand name is exposed to potential buyers, especially, in this case, cricket fans, for whom C&G may be high on the list of brands which are spontaneously recalled. The company's financial services products are also likely to be attributed with some of the characteristics of cricket—traditional, very English, reliable etc (Reproduced with permission of Cheltenham &Gloucester)

often used to support other elements of the promotion mix and should therefore not be seen in isolation.

There is no universally agreed definition of what constitutes direct marketing, but we will begin with the definition used by the UK Direct Marketing Association. It defines direct marketing as:

Communications where data are used systematically to achieve quantifiable marketing objectives and where direct contact is invited or made between a company and its customers.

We will refine this definition of direct marketing a little later and explore the different ways in which organizations have interpreted the basic concept.

MARKETING in ACTION

Sponsoring yesterday's star?

Using celebrities to endorse brands can work wonders. Walkers Crisps' use of Gary Lineker and Michael Owen proved particularly successful, with sales of 'Salt 'n' Lineker' branded crisps increasing by 60% over their previous salt and vinegar equivalent. French Connection's sponsorship of Lennox Lewis exposed worldwide audiences to Lewis in the ringside wearing a 'fcuk fear' hat for his world championship fight against Evander Holyfield, and was regarded as highly cost-effective.

Despite these successes, sponsors must be extremely careful about which celebrities they choose to sponsor. Relying on just one famous celebrity is a risk because there is always an element of the unknown. It is essential to analyse the qualities that an individual brings to a brand—merely having celebrity status is not on its own sufficient. There is a lengthy catalogue of celebrity sponsorships that have gone wrong. Pepsi aimed for maximum appeal among children by sponsoring Michael Jackson, until damaging allegations about his sex life were reported extensively in the media. Prior to the 2002 World Cup, sponsors of the England football team took a gamble on whether the team would make it to the final or be knocked out at an early stage.

Another danger is that the sponsored celebrity doesn't truly believe in the product that she is endorsing, and makes this known to the public. Actress Helen Bonham-Carter might have appeared to be the ideal face to promote Yardley beauty products, but much of the benefit of her sponsorship was undone when she admitted to the media that she didn't wear makeup.

How can a sponsor avoid such problems? Careful analysis of the risks beforehand is essential. Placing too much emphasis on just one celebrity can increase risks. Companies are increasingly seeking opt-out clauses in sponsorship contracts that allow them to pull out if a celebrity does anything that may harm the sponsor's brand.

Direct marketing is growing very rapidly. The UK Direct Marketing Association regularly makes estimates of total expenditure by firms on direct marketing in the UK and has estimated that total direct marketing expenditure grew by 80% in the period 1996–2001, rising from £6.1 billion to £11.14 billion (Direct Marketing Association [27]). As a further indicator of its significance to the marketing community, the Institute of Direct Marketing has estimated that 10% of all new graduates entering marketing careers begin in direct marketing.

There continues to be debate among academics and practitioners about what distinguishes direct marketing from relationship marketing (discussed in Chapter 5). To many, the two are indistinguishable. An alternative view, which is adopted here, is that relationship marketing should be seen as more embracing than direct marketing, often incorporating relationships among multiple levels of a supply/distribution chain. Viewed in this way, direct marketing can be seen as a process of simplifying distribution and communication channels, whereas relationship marketing often involves structuring complex networks of interrelationships between organizations at different points in a value chain.

We discussed the tendency towards direct channels of distribution in Chapter 9. Before the industrial revolution of the nineteenth century, most communication channels were direct. Centralized factory production and the need to develop brands in dispersed markets led to indirect forms of communication becoming predominant. Today, information technology is allowing many companies to go back to dealing with their customers on a one-to-one basis. Consider the factors that have helped to bring this about:

- Modern databases can now allow a company to have immediate access to information about all of its customers. Some sellers of high-value goods and services have always been able to keep records of each individual customer (e.g. banks and sellers of industrial capital equipment). Today, the opportunities for sellers of relatively low-value, high-volume goods to collect, store, analyse, and retrieve information about their customers is continually increasing.

- Computer-assisted manufacturing systems are allowing products to be produced economically in very short runs, in some cases a run of one, tailored to the specific needs of individual customers. The services sector has led the way in being able to tailor products precisely to customers' needs (e.g. a tour itinerary packaged specifically by a tour company to meet the needs of one individual). Manufacturing companies are now catching up with flexible manufacturing systems. Individually designed products call for one-to-one communication of the unique benefits to an individual.

- Developments in technology have allowed order processing and delivery systems to become more efficient, allowing large centralized manufacturers to deal directly with large numbers of geographically dispersed customers.

Key features of direct marketing

The terms used by industry and academics to define direct marketing remain fragmented.

- **Direct response marketing (DRM)** is a term used to encompass marketing activities that are designed to induce a direct response from mail order, direct mail, direct response advertising, and telemarketing. These activities have developed rapidly and have been reliant on the production of mailing lists. As the use of computers has expanded, so has the production, sale, and purchase of lists.

- **Database marketing (DBM)** is an interactive approach to customer contact management relying on the maintenance of accurate customer and prospective customer information, competitor information, and internal company information. The database is used to provide computer-aided sales support for direct response marketing, and to support customer information and service systems (Hartley and Starkey [28], p. 158).

- **Computer-aided sales support (CASS)** involves a company's field sales, sales support, and telemarketing teams' having direct access to the organization's customer database via desktop or portable computers. Through this, they can access customer/prospective customer information, competitor information, and company information. When they are working effectively, such systems can allow a company's sales personnel to identify and pursue prospects in a much more coherent and targeted manner, compared with lone sales personnel, whose information may be incomplete and out of date.

Finally, direct marketing is not just about recruiting new customers. It is also concerned with creating loyalty among existing customers and retaining their business. So many companies include a customer information and service (CIS) system within their direct marketing efforts. Customer helplines are becoming an important feature of many companies in both the goods and services sectors.

In recent years, the term 'customer relationship management' (CRM) has become popular, and is used to describe the processes by which a company seeks to integrate all of the 'touch points' that a customer has with an organization into one central database (Ragins and Greco [03]). Customers increasingly expect a company to be able to answer their questions immediately and in a seamless manner which does not involve being transferred between numerous operators.

On the other side of the profit equation, many organizations see the development of databases as an opportunity to gain competitive advantage through cost-cutting, where the use of databases reduces the cost of maintaining face-to-face dialogue through a sales force. Sellers of high-value, low-volume industrial products were early users of database marketing. Within consumer markets, the use of database marketing has expanded from high-value financial service sectors to low-value fast moving consumer goods.

Figure 11.18 The use of consumer freephone helplines is becoming an increasingly important element of communication. Some helplines are aimed mainly at answering questions before a buyer commits to a purchase, perhaps by giving expert technical advice that a store assistant might not have been able to do. At other times, the ability quickly to resolve problems with a purchase can turn a customer from a dissatisfied grumbler to one who is enthusiastic and will recommend a company to their friends

The development of customer databases

At the heart of companies' direct marketing efforts is a database identifying prospective customers, current customers, and lapsed customers. The effectiveness of direct marketing is critically dependent on the quality of customer details held on the database. To many people, direct marketing has become synonymous with 'junk mail'. But mail becomes junk in the hands of the recipient only if it has been poorly targeted so that it does not meet the needs of the person to whom it has been sent. Consider the following cases:

- A company selling bulbs and shrubs for domestic gardeners sent its catalogues to people living in upstairs flats in an inner-city area of London.
- A bank that had just refused a loan to an individual shortly afterwards sent out a mailing to that same customer enclosing details of its loans and an application form.
- A company manufacturing baby nappies sent promotional material and a trial offer for its products to a resident of a retirement home.

In each of these cases, it is just possible that the companies concerned had carefully studied their target market and made a decision that successfully hit their target market, even though it seemed intuitively ridiculous. (For example, the firm supplying bulbs and shrubs may have identified a group of flat dwellers who went away to their country cottages at the weekend.) However, the above examples serve only to show that the individual dialogue that is a defining characteristic of direct marketing cannot exist where a company is speaking to people who have no motivation whatsoever to enter into a dialogue.

So how does a company develop a database that at least allows it to enter into an appropriate dialogue with the right people? We will consider a number of aspects of database management: using all internal leads possible to build up a database of prospective customers; buying in mailing lists to supplement these sources; and updating the list so that it continues to be relevant to the needs of the company and its customers.

Developing a database from internal leads

Companies typically let a lot of information about prospective and actual customers pass them by—or at least, if they have it they do not make use of it. Consider the following sources of information to which companies typically have access, and which, with careful management, can be usefully added to a database:

- **Routine customer enquiries.** Many companies simply send out sales literature when an enquirer gives their name and address. Increasingly, companies are taking the postcode element of an enquirer's address very seriously. By analysing postcodes using a geodemographic procedure such as MOSAIC, a lot can be learned about the background of an enquirer. At the very least, a careful analysis of postcodes tells the company something about the geographical spread of its enquiries, something that may be vital to planning future marketing efforts. It should also be able subsequently to identify which postcode areas result in the highest 'conversion' rate (that is, in a sale). Companies often go beyond asking for an enquirer's name and address. Typical additional questions include: Where did you see the advertisement? (helps monitor the effectiveness of the firm's advertising); When do you intend to buy? (helps the company follow up an enquiry at a later date if the purchase intention is not immediate); Do you currently own a specified item? (can help to distinguish first-time purchasers from replacement purchasers who may approach the purchase decision in quite different ways); and basic demographic details, such as age group and marital status (helps to develop a profile of an enquirer's needs specifically, and a profile of enquirers generally).

Of course, companies can go too far in the information they collect from a casual enquiry and risk alienating the enquirer. There is also a danger that a firm's intermediaries may be suspicious of its opening a dialogue directly with what they regard as their own customers. Where a company intends to retain a dealer network to distribute its goods, a direct marketing approach can be of mutual benefit where the information captured is passed on to dealers, so that they are better informed about prospects for the firm's products.

- **Customer orders.** An efficient company will capture information from enquirers, analyse it to create a profile of its prospects, and assess which sources of enquiry result in the most profitable business. Once a prospect has become an actual customer, a company can track subsequent purchases, building up a more refined profile of the customer's needs. From this it should spot opportunities for opening a dialogue to sell related or replacement products.

Buying in mailing lists

Very often a company will have few opportunities to build up its own database of prospective customers, or else it would be extremely costly and time-consuming to do so. An alternative is to buy in an existing mailing list. Leasing mailing lists has become a major industry in its own right, with numerous organizations such as ICD and Experian offering mailing lists tailored to the needs of individual client companies. These list brokers gather information from multiple sources, including:

- the electoral register, to which everybody resident in the UK over the age of 18 must give their details (although, from 2002, individuals can opt out of the list that is made available for use by commercial organizations);
- companies that have recently supplied particular categories of goods or services to their customers;

- directories, such as Yellow Pages;

- surveys specially commissioned by the list broker (e.g., ICD regularly distributes a questionnaire to households, asking the recipients to complete information about themselves and their buying habits, in return for an incentive reward);

- surveys bought in from other companies which had used the survey to research their own customers.

The extent to which companies can trade personal details of individuals is limited in the UK by the Data Protection Act 1998. In general, individuals have the right to prevent a company from passing on their details to organizations other than the one to which they initially gave the information. The direct marketing industry has become concerned at the rising number of people who choose not to allow their details to be passed on to other organizations. While the volume of junk mail has been reduced by better targeting by companies, junk e-mail ('spam') is a growing problem. Many people are reluctant to pass on their e-mail address for fear of receiving large volumes of 'spam' mail, which may cost almost nothing for a sender to send, but can be very annoying to the recipient. There are similar concerns relating to the use of databases of mobile phone numbers which can be used to crudely target large numbers of individuals with SMS messages. Such concerns have led many people to use their legal rights to opt out of being included in databases, making some people difficult to identify (Milne and Rohm [14], Gaskill *et al.* [16]).

Lists can become out of date very rapidly, so some mailing lists may be of dubious reliability. People moving house, deaths, and companies going out of business are typical reasons for a name on a mailing list no longer being a prospect. The better suppliers of mailing lists use multiple sources of information to confirm the existence of an individual on the list and to delete any if they have not had a recent positive confirmation of their existence. To illustrate the multiple sources of information that can be used to build a picture of an individual, ICD has estimated that, for each person on its National Consumer Database, it has an average of 72 separate pieces of information.

Merging multiple lists can be a highly complex task, with electronically stored lists coming in a variety of formats. In many direct marketing organizations, individuals with a sound understanding of relational databases (that is, databases relating to a number of sources of information) are a valuable resource in short supply.

Maintaining a database

Once a prospective customer has become an actual customer, a company can enter into a more personal dialogue than when dealing through the medium of bought-in lists. Companies should try to collect information from customers that is relevant to an understanding of their needs and future purchase intentions. The following are examples of simple questions that a company might ask its customers in order to obtain basic information about product requirements and delivery details:

- For what purpose are you buying this item (e.g. for gift or self-use)?

- How many of this type of product do you buy in a year? (gives some indication of the purchasing potential of this customer)

- How frequently do you buy a related product item? (indicates opportunities for broadening the relationship between the company and its customers)

- From which source do you normally obtain this type of product? (can give an indication of the buying behaviour, e.g. normally buy from upmarket specialist stores or general purpose stores)

- When do you intend to make your next purchase of this or a related product? (allows the company to target the customer at a time when they are most receptive)

In addition, the company should seek to fill in gaps in its knowledge abut the demographic and socio-economic profile of its customers. Companies often seek additional information about a customer in fairly low-key ways, for example when completing a guarantee registration card or when entering a prize draw/competition. Many online traders seek to gather information about a customer when she is placing an order. However, too much information collection may be seen by the customer as an unnecessary invasion of privacy and she may just click to another site to place her order. A company must always consider whether it can profitably use the information that it has collected from its customers. For many low-value goods and services, the benefits may be low compared with the costs of collection.

If a company has maintained its database effectively, it should instantly be able to build up a picture of each of its customers. So when a customer calls in with an enquiry, any individual within the company taking the call should have available full details of the enquirer's recent transactions, notes about his particular preferences, and any problems that he might have encountered in the past. Companies that have managed to make up-to-date information available to all of their front-line employees are recreating in these individuals the ability to have the one-to-one dialogue that the owner of a small business used to be able to have with each of the customers who was personally known to him. When systems are working well, customers can be awestruck with the attention to detail shown by the company and the feeling that the company has put them uniquely at the centre of all its attention. When companies fail to update their customer database, the results can be disastrous for developing ongoing relationships. Consider the following problems that customers frequently encounter.

- One employee alone does not have access to sufficient information to allow her to resolve an issue, so a customer is referred to numerous other employees, often having to explain afresh the problem that he is seeking to resolve.

- Data are incorrectly entered, resulting in incorrect records (e.g., the wrong telephone number is recorded for the customer).

- The company fails to note customers' preferences, resulting in the wrong goods and services being delivered, despite these preferences having been previously specified (e.g., a customer of a telephone company requests the option of monthly billing but instead is billed quarterly).

- The company does not record details of problems that the customer has had in previous dealings, thereby preventing employees who have future contact with customer from being sensitive to the customer's perceptions of the company.

- Individuals are sent information that is completely irrelevant to their needs (e.g., a customer of a car manufacturer is sent promotional material for special offers on new cars for several months right after they have in fact bought a new car from the company).

Profiling and targeting

With direct marketing, a company can use its database to develop a profile of who its best customers are. Consider the case of a direct response company advertising in the national press to promote a mobile phone incorporating a video camera, a product it has no previous experience in selling. It would probably have a reasonable idea of its target market from previous related experience, and may choose to advertise in national newspapers and magazines whose audience closely matches its own target market. Prospective customers would be invited to return a coupon or telephone for further information about the offer. In both cases, the company would obtain two vital pieces of information from the initial enquiry:

1. The postcode of all respondents, which can yield a lot of information about their demographic profile. Linked to an analysis programme such as MOSAIC, a company can learn a lot about the profile of individuals responding to its advertisements. Companies therefore go to great lengths to ensure that people disclose their postcode.

2. Where the respondent saw the advertisement, which is vital for future campaign planning. Very often, codes are used in firms' return addresses to identify the source of the advertisement. At other times more subtle efforts are made to identify the source, such as the use of different response telephone numbers in different advertisements.

From its initial response, a company can get a reasonable idea of what type of person is showing most interest in its product. This indicates market potential, but the company needs to go one step further and analyse which of its callers actually becomes a customer. A further analysis is made to establish which types of respondent are the most

GUARANTEE REGISTRATION CARD

Name   Mr/Miss/Mrs/Other _____ First Name _____ Surname _____

Address   _____

Postcode   _____

Model No. of product purchased   HN_____

Where did you buy this product? _____

Which of the following best describes your reason for purchase?

Gift_____
Replacement for existing equipment_____
Purchase of addition equipment_____
First time purchase of this type of product_____

What is your age group?   Under 18 ☐   18–25 ☐   25–35 ☐

                               36–45 ☐   46–55 ☐   56–65 ☐

                               65+ ☐

Male or female?   Male ☐   Female ☐

Your occupation_____

Please tell us whether you own, or are considering buying, the following:

	Already own	Considering buying
Mobile telephone	☐	☐
Widescreen television	☐	☐
Home computer	☐	☐

Tick this box if you would NOT like to be informed from time to time of new products and special offers. ☐

THANK YOU

Now return this card to the address shown overleaf.
You will also be entered in our monthly prize draw.

Figure 11.19 Guarantee registration cards can say a lot about an individual. Cards such as this one offer consumers who complete it a number of benefits, such as priority attention in the event of a safety recall of the product and entry into a prize draw. But the main beneficiary is the manufacturer, who gets to learn a lot about the profile of the buyer and his reasons for buying its products

successful prospects in terms of conversion to paying customers. Very often a company may find that a high level of initial enquiry among one segment is matched by a below-average level of conversions. Where this is the case, the company needs to examine the appeal of the offer to this segment. Was the product appropriately specified? Was it overpriced? Were the benefits of ownership stressed sufficiently?

For the initial enquirers who were converted into customers, the company can seek to obtain further information at the time of ordering (e.g. what type of phone do they currently own, how often do they renew their phone, whether the purchase was for their personal use, business use, or a gift for someone else). If the company is offering credit facilities, this gives a further legitimate reason to collect more information to build up a profile customers wishing to buy on credit.

Having started out with only a general idea about who constitutes its target market, the company now has a fairly detailed profile of who its customers are. If it is offering a range of phones and accessory products, it would be able to identify who the most profitable customers will be in terms of the total value of their orders. Armed with this more refined profile of its target market, the company can seek these people out using direct methods of communication. Newspaper advertising may have been appropriate when the nature of its target market was poorly understood; it may also have had value in its own right for raising general levels of awareness of the company. But now the firm can look through its own customer records and pick out all of those customers who meet the profile of its most likely profitable customers. It can supplement this list by buying in lists based on the characteristics of prospects who it now knows are most likely to buy innovative consumer technology.

The company can then go on to track the purchases of those customers it had attracted with its initial phone offer. It may find that some converts went on to become regular customers not only of its phones, but of its related product offers. These represent particularly attractive customers for the company, and it would seek to establish whether frequent buying is associated with any particular combination of an individual's demographic characteristics (e.g. aged under 30, living in a better residential area, and reading *FHM* magazine). The company may make particular efforts to obtain an initial purchase from this group, in the knowledge that there is a high probability of such buyers' going on to become regular, profitable customers. It may calculate that targeting this group with an introductory subsidized incentive offer is justified in terms of the probable payback from future orders, whereas such an incentive might be unjustified when targeted at a segment for whom an analysis of buying behaviour showed that they only ever made one purchase from the company.

Finally, a profile analysis of an organization's customers may suggest that some are not at all profitable and are unlikely to ever become profitable. Just as a company requires a means of adding new prospects to its database, it requires a means of 'exiting' those who have not responded profitably to its attempts to create a dialogue. Many companies determine a period of time after which a customer will be deleted from their

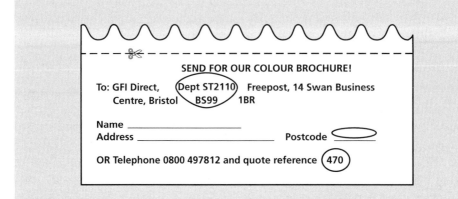

Figure 11.20 Even a simple response form such as this one in a newspaper can give a company a lot of valuable information. A code helps to assess the effectiveness of specific media, while the respondent's postcode helps to build up a profile of enquirers and subsequent purchasers

active database if she has not placed an order. If a company has carried out a thorough profile analysis of its customers, it may decide that some groups should be given more latitude than others—analysis may suggest that, although a particular customer has not placed an order for a considerable time, this category of customer has a tendency to place very profitable orders when it does eventually buy. Companies may adopt a graduated process of removing individuals from their active database. They may invite individuals to confirm that they want to continue mailings or reduce the frequency of mailings.

Companies are amassing increasing volumes of data with which to profile their customers and prospective customers. However, it is felt by many that the ability of companies to use such data effectively is lagging behind the growth in volume of data. Techniques such as Artificial Intelligence, Fuzzy Logic, and Neural Networks have been used to find patterns in large databases, and in particular to identify those variables that are most closely associated with sales and profitability (Ratner [13]). The use of 'cookies' to send back data from users' computers has add to the weight of data to be analysed, but has created major concerns over the ethics of the processes by which data are gathered, analysed, and distributed (Morse and Morse [11]).

Direct marketing media

One of the problems in defining and quantifying direct marketing is that it uses a wide range of media. So advertising could be used as part of traditional mass marketing strategy, or it could be used to try and initiate a direct dialogue between a company and its

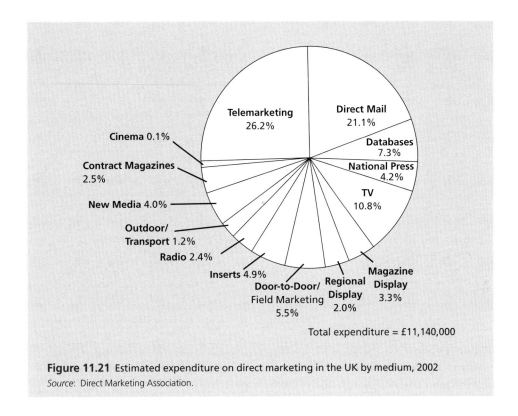

Figure 11.21 Estimated expenditure on direct marketing in the UK by medium, 2002
Source: Direct Marketing Association.

prospective customers. It is therefore difficult to get anything better than rough estimates of how much is spent on direct marketing on the various communication media.

Of the estimated £11 billion spent on direct marketing in 2002, the largest proportion was accounted for by direct mail and telemarketing (Figure 11.21). The main media used by direct marketers are described below.

Direct mail

To many people, direct mail and direct marketing are synonymous. In fact, the former is just one of numerous media used by companies to communicate directly with prospective and existing customers.

Direct mail is able to communicate details of product features that would be difficult to achieve in a 30-second television commercial, or even a whole-page newspaper advertisement. Many companies therefore use their mass media advertising to develop strong brand images, direct mail to provide product particulars, and a personal call to take immediate action. Within the financial services sector, companies have often used television advertising to present abstract images of themselves, while confining details

New Email Old Email Sent Email

Sele	Ty	Date	Email Address	Subject
☐	⊗	08-07-03	d4gtmldn2@abso.com	Growth Company BSSM is gaining exposure ....
☐	⊗	08-07-03	k9gpw3hx2d@ma.hw....	"I promise you will lose weight with HGH" mtigf
☐	⊗	08-07-03	p18pbfli@hotmail.com	RE:Try neglected and lonely h o u s e w i v e s! ....
☐	⊗	08-07-03	541jmn@hotmail.com	Prescriptions written and filled online! US doctors and ...
☐	⊗	08-07-03	brtnj75d@hotmail.com	World's smallest Digital Camera
☐	⊗	07-07-03	rohit21@ivoicedat...	Confirmed: Compelling News on Your Mortgage Application
☐	⊗	07-07-03	rfjv5bdq34@action...	"No dieting and lose weight with HGH" ou
☐	⊗	07-07-03	0ewu0zost@brighto...	great free offer for hgh.................... cf_iyeuyf
☐	⊗	07-07-03	annacam6@yahoo.com	lets party!
☐	⊗	07-07-03	v7ccgubsy@hotmail...	Want a natural "bulge?"......................................
☐	⊗	07-07-03	annacam18@ljf.com	lets party!
☐	⊗	07-07-03	cgreenford2giok@y...	start the summer off right
☐	⊗	07-07-03	nycmbB32PtV5C3P1@...	Lowest Mortgage Rates in 50 Years - Gone Tomorrow! .DHDI
☐	⊗	07-07-03	qu7qppjlor@wonder...	how to look young again, try hgh!.................. ems...
☐	⊗	07-07-03	0005644986vdpv@al...	hi
☐	⊗	07-07-03	samuntiro@runbox.com	Viagra, Soma, Fioricet, Prescribed Online for Free, Shipp...
☐	⊗	07-07-03	q4ddopcygm5a@surf...	Order Diet Pills, Viagra & Other Drugs Online! No Prior ...
☐	⊗	07-07-03	MoGeorge41	-=Reduce Your Debt By 50% or More! No Hassle & Nothing to...
☐	⊗	06-07-03	08uwe4jjjk@cricke...	You Can Order Pain Relief, Weight Loss & Anti-Depressant ...
☐	⊗	06-07-03	g52ycbggdtv@gekko...	Order Diet Pills, Viagra & Other Drugs Online! No Prior ...
☐	⊗	06-07-03	savertovqklpt@dis...	Xenical, Phentermine, Viagra & many others prescribed on...
☐	⊗	06-07-03	t5cxjbhia@yahoo.com	Size DOES matter! Enlarge your penis NOW! sc mhf
☐	⊗	05-07-03	za0rneyu@hotmail.com	You can order Anti-depressants, weight loss meds,and pain...
☐	⊗	05-07-03	Kittietwci@vigrex...	Don't over-pay for viagra our customers save 80%!
☐	⊗	05-07-03	marty65peterxbn@w...	Low Cost Prescriptions Overnighted To Your Doorstep piftz

Figure 11.22 Direct mail becomes junk mail if it is not properly targeted. With the development of e-mail, many companies are trying to replace conventional direct mail with e-mail, saving production costs and allowing more effective communication of their product proposition. Evidence of this is seen in a report that business mail volumes handled by the Royal Mail fell by 1.5% in 2002, some of which was doubtless attributable to displacement by e-mail. However, it remains a challenge for a company's e-mails to grab the attention of recipients when their mailbox may be full of 'spam' mail

of such things as interest rates, loan terms, and notice periods to direct mailshots. More recently, this tendency has spread to the fast moving consumer goods sector.

Direct mail is gradually losing its image as junk mail, and surveys have shown that many people actually like to receive direct mail. Among advertising agencies, direct mail is no longer seen as the Cinderella it once was, and greater creative effort is put into designing effective direct mail materials. Increasingly, advertising agencies are seeing direct mail and mass media advertising as two parts of a single creative effort.

Telemarketing

The cost of communicating by telephone has fallen relative to the cost of mail services, because of increasing competition and cost savings brought about by new technology. Furthermore, there is the suggestion that we are all becoming more accustomed to using the telephone, although differences do occur between individuals in how they relate to the telephone; for example, it is suggested that females are better able to hold telephone conversations than males.

Telemarketing can be divided into inbound and outbound operations. The former is concerned with handling the incoming calls that result from a company's promotion of a telephone number for sales enquiries. With the use of mass media to promote such numbers, companies can be swamped with calls immediately following the launch of an advert. This is especially true of freephone telephone numbers that are shown on television during peak times. Companies need to be able to handle such surges; otherwise the cost of generating leads is wasted and prospective customers who cannot get through may form such a bad impression of the company that they will not bother calling back. Research by Mintel into 2,000 users of call centres found that by far the biggest complaint when telephoning a call centre was the time spent waiting on hold, with some 60% complaining about this. Those aged between 25 and 34 were the least tolerant towards call centres with around 35% abandoning calls. Just 5% of consumers had never experienced a problem with a call centre (Mintel [7]).

Large companies often use agencies to handle their incoming calls; using the latest switching technology, calls can then be routed throughout the country to operators who are free. Increasingly, companies based in the UK are routing their calls to be answered by operators located in distant countries such as India. This can greatly reduce costs of running a call centre and can lessen staff turnover problems. Careful use of 'time shifting' can allow calls to be answered during the working day in the country where the call centre is located, corresponding with a peak in enquiries that occur in the evening in the customer's country. Also, by staggering advertisements (e.g. by showing an advert in different television regions at different times of the day), problems created by surges in incoming calls can be reduced. Many inbound telemarketing agencies have developed automated answering systems, in which callers give answers to a series of automated question prompts. Such systems can be very efficient at handling sudden surges in incoming calls and may be quite adequate for simple requests for brochures. However, many callers remain reluctant to use such systems and may become exasperated when the rigidity of a machine-based system does not allow for their specific needs to be addressed.

Outbound telemarketing involves a company using the telephone to contact potential or existing customers with a sales offer. Telephone selling has a very bad image in the UK, generating thoughts of poorly timed calls which disturb an individual with a sales offer in which they have no interest. As with direct mail, better targeting has reduced the nuisance value of receiving telephone calls that are of no interest to the receiver of the call. The increasing number of private households that prefer to go 'ex-directory' poses further problems for outbound telemarketing.

Newspaper/magazine/television advertising

Where advertising is used to encourage an immediate and direct response, firms are able to monitor the effectiveness of individual advertisements. It was noted above that the use of codes can identify the level of new enquiries generated by each advertisement, and the proportion of these that went on to become actual customers. However, as with the assessment of all advertising effectiveness, it can be difficult to isolate completely the effects of extraneous factors. A direct response advertisement may achieve a high level of response only if potential customers see it in the context of the brand-building advertising that has gone before it.

Door-to-door

The traditional mass media have developed methods of delivering their messages to progressively smaller audiences. Local editions of newspapers and cable television channels are evidence of this trend. One form of printed media that can deliver a message to a narrowly targeted audience is door-to-door leaflet distribution. Companies deliver promotional material to a block of addresses in a locality, either directly by themselves, through companies specializing in door-to-door distribution of leaflets, through inserts in local newspapers, or through block distribution agreements with the Post Office. Door-to-door distribution has traditionally been seen as the poor relation of the main advertising media, but it has seen a resurgence in recent years. Developments in information technology now allow for the controlled distribution of promotional material to be undertaken more cost-effectively. The method can also enable product samples to be delivered to selected households.

Electronic media

The range and sophistication of electronic media available to direct marketers has increased markedly in recent years. This increasingly important area of online marketing is considered in more detail below, but here we briefly note the wide range of electronic media that are used by direct marketers to communicate—using text, images, and voice—with customers and potential customers:

- Electronic media first came to prominence in the business-to-business sector with the use of proprietary Electronic Data Interchange (EDI) systems. These were essentially used to improve distribution efficiency, and promotion was a secondary consideration of such systems.

- The telephone developed beyond a basic voice medium to allow additional text based interaction. Telephone banking allows a bank to communicate with its customers using automated procedures linked to databases. Many companies use automated telephone response systems to provide personalized information to callers based on the response the callers keyed in.

- The internet is now used extensively for communicating with customers and potential customers (see next page).

- Global positioning systems have the potential to target buyers depending upon their location.

The development of electronic media has witnessed a merging of technologies and an integration of communication solutions available to marketers. For example, television has become more interactive and now shares some characteristics of the internet. CD-ROMs are often distributed to potential buyers and allow the recipient to read the message contained in them, and also to update the message by using links to the internet that are embedded in the CD.

MARKETING and the INTERNET

They've bought the hardware—now target them with software

How does a retailer strong on selling computer hardware overcome its relative lack of success in getting customers to buy its software? The electrical retailer Comet claims to be one of the top three UK retailers of games console hardware. However, although its out-of-town store format has appealed to people looking for special offers on its hardware, it is not as well suited to competing with the major High Street stores for follow-up software sales. Customers find browsing for a new game title easier in the High Street than making a special journey to one of Comet's out-of-town sites. The solution? Comet set to work building up a database of games console owners from its own sales records and bought-in lists. It then set about using this list to extend the relationship with its hardware customers. A direct marketing initiative featured new game show previews, competitions, in-store promotions, and money-off vouchers for games. Initially, mailshots were used, but the company gradually built up a record of customers' e-mail addresses. This was a natural development, given the high likelihood that games players would also be intensive internet users. Sending messages by e-mail had the advantage that Comet could provide hyperlinks to websites where new games could be demonstrated, something that was not possible with printed media. Use of the internet allowed the company to track the transactions of its customers much more efficiently, and the use of cookies could allow the company to learn which other sites its shoppers were visiting. By being seen to be giving special benefits to its hardware customers, it aimed to entice previous customers back and to extend its relationship with them in a cost-effective manner.

Limitations to the development of direct marketing

Although direct marketing has become an important part of many companies' marketing efforts, there are limits to its application. Here we summarize some of the more important constraints on direct marketing.

Cost effectiveness

An important advantage of direct marketing is that it can target segments as small as one. This is fine for companies that produce high-value goods and services that are tailored to the needs of specific customers. It helps to explain the popularity of direct marketing in such sectors as computer hardware and motor insurance. However, many goods and services are capable of appealing to large groups of customers in their 'standard' form without any attempt at differentiation. Where the value of the goods is low and volume sales are high, the cost of attempting to communicate directly with each individual customer may be prohibitive. Furthermore, the advantage of being able to tailor a product to customers' precise needs may be largely irrelevant where the product presents little opportunity for differentiation. The Heinz company made a highly publicized attempt to develop a database to communicate directly with the consumers of its products, but quietly reverted back to traditional mass media. There was evidently little scope for differentiating its low-value, low-involvement products to a fairly homogeneous market.

Legislative constraints

Effective direct marketing requires companies to handle large amounts of information about prospective, actual, and lapsed customers. The manner in which companies buy and sell information about individuals raises a number of ethical issues. Should a customer of a company have a right to consider the dialogue she enters into with the company to be private between the two parties? Is it then unethical for the company to sell on information about its customers to third-party companies? How can an individual prevent damage being done to their reputation by incorrect information being distributed within and outside of a company? How can whole communities (e.g. in postcode areas with a poor credit rating) avoid being discriminated against?

Direct marketing has sought to put its own house in order with voluntary codes of conduct, in an attempt to deflect the call for greater legislation. In the UK, the Mailing Preference Service (which allows individuals to opt out of receiving direct mail) is an example of this approach. However, the direct marketing sector remains fragmented, and it is very difficult to enforce a code of conduct that respects the concerns of society as a whole. Legislation has therefore been introduced to further safeguard ethical standards. The 1998 Data Protection Act (based on an EU Directive) sets out rules by which companies can record and disseminate information about their customers.

There has been much talk of 'permission marketing', in which dialogue is based on buyers' giving permission for a company to communicate with them (Tezinde, Smith, and Murphy [20]). This puts greater control of marketing communications in the hands of the buyer, and technology is increasingly facilitating buyers' ability to be selective in what communications they choose to receive (Graeff and Harmon [15]). The introduc-

ers and TiVo, a personal television programming and recording
how technology is providing people with the means to control
ges.

edia have a tendency to go through a life-cycle. This typically
begins when a new medium appears; at first it is uncluttered, and users of it have
relatively few other messages to compete with. Over time, the medium becomes more
popular with advertisers, resulting in individual adverts having diminishing impact on
their target audiences. This leads to an opportunity for new media to develop, offering
innovative advertisers the chance to have maximum impact in an as yet uncluttered
medium. There is debate about where direct marketing currently is in its life-cycle. The
use of direct mail and telemarketing is certainly more mature in the USA than in
Europe, with the result that many question its current effectiveness in the USA.

■ Online marketing

Online business passes under a number of names, and terminology is constantly changing as technology develops and managers and academics from differing functions interact. It is useful to define the terms 'e-business' and 'e-commerce'. **E-business** has
been defined as:

the ability to integrate local and wide area networks through the use of internet protocols to
effectively remove the barriers between businesses, their customers and their suppliers in global
markets. (National Computing Centre [32])

This is a broader definition than that usually attributed to the narrower function of e-
commerce, which has been defined as

transactions of goods or services for which payment occurs over the internet or other wide area
networks. (Chaffey [29])

The internet has emerged as a versatile element of the promotion mix which often
combines a promotional function with a distribution function. In the early days of
online marketing, there were many claims that the way organizations do business with
their customers would change dramatically and for ever. In the brave new online world,
shops would gradually disappear as we began to communicate extensively through the
medium of the internet. Of course, many people's early hopes for the internet have
since been moderated, and it may be more realistic to regard online marketing not as a
stand-alone activity, but just as one component of a company's integrated marketing
communications. The number of 'pure' internet-based companies is very small in

relation to the total number of companies using the internet. Even dedicated online organizations such as Amazon.com and Esure.com make extensive use of non-internet based communication methods, further emphasizing that online marketing must be seen in the context of a company's overall communications strategy.

We have already mentioned some of the advantages of online marketing in our previous discussion of the elements of the promotion mix and have noted the overlap between promotion mix elements:

- Our definition of advertising includes web pages that broadcast to large numbers of people but are not interactive.

- Personal selling is relying increasingly on online communication to support the efforts of sales personnel.

- Public relations professionals have come to understand the impact of chat rooms and dissident websites on a company's reputation and have developed web-based tools of their own.

- Online media have become an integral element of direct marketing by opening up an additional channel through which a company can enter into an interactive dialogue with its customers.

Objectives and development of online media

Communication using online media involves a number of stages of development. At the most basic level, a company's website can simply give additional information about its services; for example, many hotels have websites that give information about their location and the facilities available. At this stage of development, the internet is being used simply as an online form of the traditional printed brochure. Although a static, one-to-all website may now seem quite unadventurous, we should nevertheless recognize the advantages that it has over traditional printed brochures:

- It is much less expensive to produce.

- It can be updated very rapidly (e.g. in response to a price change) without having to destroy existing stacks of brochures.

- Information can be provided immediately to prospective customers anywhere in the world, without the delay inherent in a postal delivery.

- Comprehensive information can be provided within the site—more than could realistically be provided within the confines of a printed brochure.

- Links can be provided to other related information; for example, a hotel can include a hyperlink to local tourist attractions.

The second stage of online development allows some degree of interactive dialogue between a company and visitors to its website. At its simplest, this can take the form of a facility for visitors to enter a dialogue with the company by e-mail, perhaps to find out further information. Interactivity could be added by creating a script that allows the visitor to ask simple questions and for the site to generate answers that are of direct relevance to the visitor. This could take the form of a simple ready reckoner type of calculator to allow the user to calculate the monthly repayments on a mortgage, in which he is invited to enter various loan amounts and repayment periods. More complex interactivity can be developed by linking the customer's request to a database of information. This is used by railway operators (e.g. **www.nationalrail.co.uk**) to provide precise information on possible rail journeys in response to a customer's request for information on train times between two specified points at a specified time.

Many online retailers used targeted e-mail services to encourage customers to visit their sites. The travel and leisure retailer Lastminute.com, for example, claims to send more than 2 million e-mails to customers every week. The content of the e-mail is tailored to fit the recipient's age, life-style and other factors (Kirchgaessner [4]).

The third stage of online development is to allow immediate fulfilment of a request, such as confirmation of a hotel booking or reservation of a plane ticket. By linking a customer's online request to a real-time database of availability, the company can immediately communicate a specific price/product offer. Many airline and hotel companies have used the principles of yield management to change their price and product offer continually to reflect the changing balance between supply and demand; so the message that it sends to a site visitor may be quite different from one that it sent even just half an hour earlier.

The internet is used extensively for comparison shopping, and a lot of research has gone into understanding which sites produce the best results in terms of moving an individual through the stages of purchase. A regularly updated site that contains information of direct relevance to a user and is fast to download has become a minimum requirement for most users of the medium.

In the case of tangible goods, immediate fulfilment of an order is not possible in the way that it is with airline reservations or the sale of data services. Companies therefore seek to integrate online communication with other forms of communication. Very often, a website is used to provide background information about a product and to guide the site visitor to a dealer's premises. The car maker Vauxhall launched its internet site in 1999 with the aim of offering restricted models—known as VIP models (Vauxhall internet price)—at special prices. Vauxhall has since moved its complete range online. The company claims that, although actual sales completed through its website are low—about 1,000 a year—the site does create a lot of interest, generating an estimated 70,000 dealer sales leads in 2002 (Morton [5]).

Online communication is particularly attractive for many services, such as travel and financial services, where the costs of delivering bulky objects is not a major constraint. Many people had become used to buying these services by telephone, and online services offer an opportunity to provide buyers with more information and a speedier re-

Figure 11.23 Companies have taken on board the basic functions of SMS text messaging to target customers and potential customers. For example, during 2002 Allied Domecq sent out several thousand SMS text messages as part of a campaign for its Tia Maria brand (Rubach [8]). SMS text messages allow only a very short message to be communicated, and to be effective these need to be linked to other methods of demographic data collection and profiling. Early experience of mobile internet facilities through Wireless Application Protocol (WAP) technology was disappointing, but the development of 'Third Generation' mobile telephony offers new opportunities for interactive dialogue at any location. By linking wireless access to Global Positioning Systems (GPS), individuals can be targeted with information that is relevant to their immediate needs. Examples include restaurants seeking to fill spare capacity by sending messages to mobile phone users who are in the area at a time the restaurant has spare capacity

sponse. It has been predicted that by 2010 the majority of package holidays will be bought through the internet and High Street travel agencies will serve only a small niche market. According to Forrester Research (in Flood [30]), worldwide internet airline ticket sales topped $7 billion in 2000 and US online hotel bookings were over $2 billion. Although research estimates and forecast sales vary widely, most surveys agree that travel is the largest e-commerce sector by value.

Other sectors to benefit from e-commerce are music/books/video, PCs/software, small electronic products, clothing, and food. According to a survey by Ernest & Young covering 12 countries and 4,000 consumers (Wheeler [31]), the most frequently purchased goods are CDs and books. In fact, there are no surprises in their list (Figure 11.24). The top five product categories have been served by direct marketing channels for years, initially by catalogue and mail, then by telephone, and now by the internet.

In most western countries, the majority of the population now has access to the internet, either at home, at work, or at their place of study. The internet is now firmly established as a communication medium in most organizations, and in a growing proportion of households use of the internet is becoming as commonplace as switching on the television. An important consideration to marketers is that those households who have internet access tend to be the higher-income households and opinion leaders that companies are particularly keen to target (Kwak, Fox, and Zinkhan [6]). The development of high-capacity fibre optic lines will increase the amount of data that can be

Figure 11.24 Percentage of UK internet users who have purchased selected products, 2000

Source: Ernst & Young; in E. Wheeler, 'Online Shopping is Tough for Pure Players', Computing (UK), 1 February 2001, pp. 40–1.

Category	%
CDs & music	67
Books	65
PCs	53
Tickets	39
Videos and film	36
Small electronic	30
Clothing	28
Food & drink	23
Toys	15

transmitted through the internet, thereby reducing the problems of slow download speed which have inhibited e-commerce.

Viral marketing

Because of the low cost and high speed with which messages can be created and communicated, online media have become important tools in what has come to be known as 'viral marketing'. This involves a message being targeted at one person who then passes it on to a number of her friends, each of whom in turn passes it on. In February 2003, immediately prior to the UK ban on tobacco advertising, the makers of Hamlet cigars capitalized on the nostalgia attached to its TV ads, which had ended with the tagline 'Happiness is a cigar called Hamlet'. Visitors to its site could download the ads to view or e-mail them to a friend. To help boost the viral campaign for the UK's best-selling cigar, registered visitors who sent an ad to a friend were entered in a drawing for £500 (Britt and Wentz [21]).

Website evaluation

Similar to traditional promotional media, it can be difficult to make a company's website stand out in a crowded environment. With literally millions of communication messages seeking to find a web surfer, companies must develop a strategy for promoting their web presence. Without heavy promotion of a website address through conventional media, or paying for a 'hotlink' via a network portal, a company's website may remain unseen in cyberspace. Many companies have applied their website addresses to ancillary materials such as carrier bags, time-tables, and price lists, in much the same way as they would promote their telephone numbers. A lot of money has been spent by companies on advertisements in the traditional media drawing attention to their website. Buying access to target customers on the internet has become an important activity, with portals such as Yahoo! charging for the use of banner advertisements on their popular websites. A number of companies, such as Doubleclick.com, exist to collect information about individuals' usage patterns with a view to improving the targeting of advertisements through paid-for websites.

Limitations of online media

Online media have developed rapidly over the last decade and have provided benefits to buyers and sellers that previously would have been almost unimaginable. Rapid growth inevitably brings developmental problems, some of which are summarized as follows.

- For many types of goods, customers may place great value on being able to inspect goods physically prior to purchase—something that will never be completely possible with 'virtual' representation of goods through electronic media. Online media are unlikely in the near future to be able to communicate using the senses of touch and smell. Even the two-dimensional representation of images may be a poor substitute for a three-dimensional representation of a product in real life. Many buyers would prefer the availability of these additional sensory stimuli when selecting clothes, fresh vegetables, and soft furnishings, which helps to explain why these sectors have been relatively slow to adopt online communication. There are also many high-involvement goods where buyers feel more comfortable being able to see and feel the goods before they commit to a purchase. The failed internet clothes retailer Boo.com encountered the reality that many people would probably find it much easier and more reassuring to try on clothes in a shop than to rely on a computer image, thereby ensuring a continuing role for traditional High Street retailers.

- Many buyers, especially private buyers, retain doubts about the security of financial transactions carried out through the internet, which has lagged behind the levels of security achieved by the banks' own closed Electronic Funds Transfer at Point of Purchase (EFTPOS) systems. There are also concerns that personal information collected through an interactive dialogue with a company may inadvertently be disclosed elsewhere. While stories of online customers' credit card details being accidentally shown to other website users achieve headline news, in reality privacy tends to be greater using online media than in the typical offline situation, where a customer discloses personal information through the post or a telephone call. Again, these problems are likely to be resolved over time, increasing the potential role of the internet as a marketing medium.

- Systems often require high capital outlay, and there may be a slow return on such investment. Compatibility within the technological architecture can be a further limitation, with new technologies continually requiring additional investment from companies. In the early days of the 'dot.com' boom investors were eager to invest in new technology—unwisely, as it turned out. Given a previous history of failed web initiatives, raising capital for next-generation technology can be a challenge.

- As use of the internet as a communication medium has increased, it has become increasingly cluttered. This effect has been experienced during the development of all media, and companies using the internet have faced increasing challenges in drawing people to their website. Getting a high ranking in search engines has become a critical skill, and specialist companies will seek to raise a client's rankings. From being a very cheap source of messages, companies are having to spend increasing amounts of money promoting their web presence, both online and offline. A new generation of 'informediaries' has appeared to simplify communication between online buyers and sellers.

- Many companies have been keen to move communication with customers to the internet and away from other more expensive media. Research undertaken by Oxford Associates in a number of US-based industries suggested that most companies achieved a 20–40% reduction in transaction costs when selling through distributors and partners, 40–45% when selling through call centres, and over 50% when selling over the internet. However, they warned against following a cost reduction strategy that does not take account of buyer behaviour. A company could too easily lose key customers as it cuts back its sales force and call centres, hoping that buyers will migrate to the internet. There have been many cases of online systems that have faced lengthy teething problems, costing a lot in lost customer goodwill.

◾ Chapter summary and linkages to other chapters

This chapter has reviewed the elements of the promotion mix. Although each element of the mix has a different role to play, they are very much interdependent. The headings this chapter has used to define the elements of the promotion mix are to some extent arbitrary, and we have seen, for example, how advertising is often an important part of sales promotion and direct marketing activity. The usefulness of each mix element varies at different stages in the communication process. All elements of the promotion mix share a similar process of setting objectives, developing a strategic and tactical plan, implementing the plan, and then evaluating the results. We have seen how evaluation is becoming increasingly comprehensive with direct marketing and online media. It is very difficult to separate the contribution to sales of each promotional activity from other elements of the marketing mix. If the other elements of the marketing mix are not correct, promotion alone is unlikely to make customers buy the product. You should recall from the previous chapter that the different elements of the promotion mix are brought together in a campaign, which should be united by a common message.

KEY PRINCIPLES OF MARKETING

- Definitions of the elements of the promotion mix are not water-tight and all elements overlap with each other.
- The effects of any promotional medium will be greater if its message is integrated with other media.
- All elements of the promotion mix involve a process of analysis, objective setting, development of strategies, implementation, and evaluation.
- Objectives set for individual elements of the promotion mix must be consistent with overall marketing objectives.

CASE STUDY

Free flights promotion ends in disaster

The Hoover company's attempts to sell more white goods by offering an incentive of free flights has become a legendary disaster in the field of sales promotions. An examination of the case is useful for highlighting some of the problems of planning, implementing, and monitoring sales promotions.

During the early 1990s, Hoover was faced with a period of economic recession in which discretionary expenditure on consumer durables was held back. In these conditions, most vacuum sales were replacements for worn-out machines or first-time buys for people setting up home. The challenge was to increase the sales of machines bought to upgrade existing equipment.

The company came up with the idea of offering free airline tickets to America for anybody buying one of its vacuum cleaners or other white goods. For many people, a holiday in the USA may have been perceived as an unnecessary and unaffordable luxury during a period of recession, but one that might be justified if it came free with the purchase of an 'essential' vacuum cleaner.

The immediate result of the sales promotion was to boost the company's sales of vacuum cleaners to more than double the level of the previous year. So far so good. But then serious problems set in. The first problem occurred when Hoover could not satisfy demand for its vacuum cleaners and had to resort to paying its staff overtime rates of pay in order to increase supply. It should be remembered that the initial objective of the promotion was to utilize existing spare capacity in the firm rather than add to that capacity. The company had carried out insufficient research prior to launching its incentive. Had it done so, it might have reached the conclusion that the incentive was too generous and was likely to create more demand than the company could cope with.

A second problem occurred during subsequent periods when sales fell to below their pre-incentive levels. Many people had simply brought forward their purchase of a vacuum cleaner, washing machine, or whatever. Worse still, many people had bought their product simply to get the free tickets, which at £70 for a cleaner with a free £250 ticket made sense. These people frequently disposed of the cleaners as they had no need for them. The classified ads of local newspapers contained many adverts for 'nearly new, unused' vacuum cleaners at discounted prices, and this further depressed sales of new machines once the sales promotion had come to an end.

A third and more serious problem occurred when large numbers of buyers tried to use their free flight vouchers. All sales promotions are based on an assumption of take-up rates, which can be as low as 5–10%. Anything higher, and the cost of the incentives actually given away can wipe out the benefits arising from increased sales. In this case, Hoover had carried out insufficient pre-testing of the sales promotion in order to assess the likely take-up rate and was surprised by the actual take-up which subsequently occurred. In an attempt to control costs, the company became notorious for its attempts to 'suppress' take-up of free flights. Many claimants complained that telephone lines were constantly busy and, when they did get through, they were offered the most unattractive flights possible. It was reported that claimants from the south-east of England were offered only flights departing from Scotland and those from Scotland offered only flights from London, in order to reduce the attractiveness of the free offer. These activities attracted high levels of coverage in the media and left a once highly respected brand with a perception of mistrust. Five years after the initial débâcle, the Hoover Holiday Pressure Group continued to be an awkward reminder for the company.

The free flights promotion eventually cost Hoover a reported £37 million in redemption charges, without bringing about any long-term growth in sales. With appropriate pre-testing, these costs could have been foreseen. Worse still, the company's brand image had been tarnished in a way that would take many years—if ever—to recover from.

Case study review questions

1. What are the inherent problems for a company such as Hoover in assessing the effectiveness of sales promotion activity?

2. Identify a programme of research that Hoover could have undertaken in order to avoid the costly failure of its free flights promotion.

3. What alternative methods of promotion might have been more suitable to achieve Hoover's objective of utilizing spare capacity during a period of economic recession?

▢ CHAPTER REVIEW QUESTIONS

1. To what extent is it possible, or desirable, to identify advertising as a distinct element of the promotion mix?

2. To what extent is it true to say that advertising builds brands, while sales promotion undermines them? Is there any overlap or convergence of the two functions?

3. Advise a company selling stairlifts for elderly and disabled people on the sponsorship opportunities that it may be able to exploit successfully.

4. What is the relationship between selling and marketing?

5. Critically evaluate the steps that companies can take to ensure that their direct mail does not become 'junk' mail.

6. Is there a role for mass media advertising in the new age of direct marketing? In what circumstances does advertising have a particular advantage over direct communication?

▢ REFERENCES

[1] Christopher, M., Payne, A., and Ballantyne, D. (2002), *Relationship Marketing: creating shareholder value*. Oxford: Butterworth-Heinemann.

[2] *Daily Telegraph* (2003), 'The Verdict? FCUK just isn't shocking'. *Daily Telegraph*, 13 March, p. 22.

[3] Ragins, E. J. and Greco, A. J. (2003), 'Relationship Management and E-business: more than a software solution'. *Review of Business*, 24(1): 25–30.

[4] Kirchgaessner, S. (2003), 'Need Inflatable Sheep, Fast? Lastminute.com: speed and reliability are essential ingredients for online success'. *Financial Times*, 5 February, p. 4.

[5] Morton, R. (2003), 'Some Pick-up in Online sales: however, most customers still prefer to buy from showrooms'. *Financial Times*, 4 March, p. 5.

[6] Kwak, H., Fox, R. J., and Zinkhan, G. M. (2002), 'What Products Can Be Successfully Promoted and Sold via the Internet?' *Journal of Advertising Research*, 42(1): 23–38.

[7] Mintel (2002), *Optimising the Power of Call Centres*. London: Mintel.

[8] Rubach, E. (2002), 'Domecq Adds SMS Blitz to £18 million Tia Maria Offensive'. *Precision Marketing*, 6–14 June, p. 3.

[9] Ihlen, O. (2002), 'Defending the Mercedes A-Class: combining and changing crisis-response strategies'. *Journal of Public Relations Research*, 14(3): 185–206.

[10] Lauf, E. (2001), 'The Vanishing Young Reader'. *European Journal of Communication*, 16(2): 233–44.

[11] Morse, J. and Morse, S. (2002), 'Teaching Temperance to the "Cookie Monster": ethical challenges to data mining and direct marketing'. *Business & Society Review*, 107(1): 76–97.

[12] *The Times* (2002), 'Media Age Poses Threat to Reputations'. London: *The Times* (Business), 1 May, p. 29.

[13] Ratner, B. (2001), 'Finding the Best Variables for Direct Marketing Models'. *Journal of Targeting, Measurement & Analysis for Marketing*, 9(3): 270–96.

[14] Milne, G. R. and Rohm, A. J. (2000), 'Consumer Privacy and Name Removal across Direct

Marketing Channels: exploring opt-in and opt-out alternatives'. *Journal of Public Policy & Marketing*, 19(2): 238–49.

[15] Graeff, T. R. and Harmon, S. (2002), 'Collecting and Using Personal Data: consumers' awareness and concerns'. *Journal of Consumer Marketing*, 19(4/5): 302–16.

[16] Gaskill, S., MacIntyre, P., Malcolm, W., and Hackett, A. (2001), 'Consent to Direct Marketing in the Financial Services Sector'. *Journal of Financial Services Marketing*, 5(4): 356–40.

[17] Sparks J. R. and Areni, C. S. (2002), 'The Effects of Sales Presentation Quality and Initial Perceptions on Persuasion: a multiple role perspective'. *Journal of Business Research*, 55(6): 517–28.

[18] Low, G. S. and Mohr, J. J. (2000), 'Advertising vs Sales Promotion: a brand management perspective'. *Journal of Product & Brand Management*, 9(6): 389–404.

[19] Grewal, D., Levy, M. and Marshall, G. W. (2002), 'Personal Selling in Retail Settings: how does the internet and related technologies enable and limit successful selling?' *Journal of Marketing Management*, 18(3–4): 128–35.

[20] Tezinde, T., Smith, B. and Murphy, J. (2002), 'Getting Permission: exploring factors affecting permission marketing'. *Journal of Interactive Marketing*, 16(4): 28–36.

[21] Britt, B. and Wentz, L. (2003), 'Tobacco Ads Go Out with Bang in UK'. *Advertising Age*, 74(7): 16.

[22] Drucker, P. (1973), *Management: tasks, responsibilities and practices*. New York: Harper & Row.

[23] Egan, C. (1997), *The CIM Handbook of Selling and Sales Strategy: a practical guide to selling and implementing effective sales strategies*. London: Chartered Institute of Marketing.

[24] McMurry, R. N. (1961), 'The Mystique of Super Salesmanship', *Harvard Business Review*, 26(March–April): 114–32.

[25] Shipley, D. (1997), *Selling and Sales Strategy: selling to and managing key accounts*. Oxford: Butterworth-Heinemann.

[26] Steward, K. (1993), *Marketing Led, Sales Driven: professional selling in a marketing environment*. Oxford: Butterworth-Heinemann.

[27] Direct Marketing Association (2002), *Census of the UK Direct Marketing Industry*. London: Direct Marketing Association.

[28] Hartley, B. and Starkey, M. (1996), *The Management of Sales and Customer Relations: book of readings*. London: International Thompson Business Press.

[29] Chaffey, D. (ed.), (1999), *Business Information Systems: technology development and management*. London: Pitman.

[30] Flood, G. (2001), 'Online Travel Businesses Fly High on the Net'. *Computing (UK)*, 8 March: 48–9.

[31] Wheeler, E. (2001), 'Online Shopping is Tough for the Pure-Players'. *Computing (UK)*, 1 February: 40–1.

[32] National Computing Centre (2001), *The People Implications of Efective E-Business.* Guideline No. 257. London: National Computing Centre.

▣ SUGGESTED FURTHER READING

For general reading on the principles of promotion planning, refer back to the suggested further reading in Chapter 10. For more detailed coverage of specific elements of the promotion mix, the following provide a good introductory overview:

Beck-Burridge, M. and Walton, J. (2001), *Sports Sponsorship and Brand Development*. Basingstoke: Palgrave Macmillan.

Chaffey, D. and Smith, P. R. (2001), *E-marketing Excellence*. Oxford: Butterworth-Heinemann.

Cheverton, P. (2001), *Key Account Management*. London: Kogan Page.

Cummins, J. and Mullin, R. (2002), *Sales Promotion: how to create, implement and integrate campaigns that really work*. London: Kogan Page.

Jefkins, F. and Yadin, D. (2000), *Advertising*, 4th edn. Hemel Hempsted, NJ: Prentice Hall.

Oliver, S. (2001), *Public Relations Strategy: a guide to corporate communications management*. London: Kogan Page.

Tapp, A. (2001), *Principles of Direct and Database Marketing*, 2nd edn. Hemel Hempstead, NJ: Prentice Hall.

▣ USEFUL WEB LINKS

Visit the companion website to this book, with lots of interesting additional material and links for each chapter:
www.oup.com/uk/booksites/busecon

Institute of Practitioners in Advertising
www.ipa.co.uk/contents.html

Advertising Association (UK)
www.adassoc.org.uk

Advertising Standards Authority
www.asa.org.uk

Independent Television Commission
www.itc.org.uk

Newspaper Readership Survey
www.inma.org/reading.html

American Association of Advertising Agencies
www.aaaa.org

European Association of Advertising Agencies
www.eaaa.b

Institute of Professional Sales
iops.co.uk

National Alliance of Sales & Marketing Executives (USA)
www.nasme.com/nasme_inside.html

Institute of Sales Promotion
isp.org.uk

Institute of Public Relations
www.ipr.org.uk

Institute of Direct Marketing
  www.theidm.co.uk
Direct Marketing Association (UK)
  www.dma.org.uk
Direct Marketing Association (USA)
  www.the-dma.org
American Telemarketing Association
  www.ataconnect.org
Association for the Advancement of Relationship Marketing
  www.aarm.org
Links to direct marketing associations throughout the world
  www.one1.com.sg/Resource/DMAssns.htm
Direct Mail Information Service (a UK site sponsored by Royal Mail providing detailed statistics about the UK and comparative European information)
  www.dmis.co.uk

KEYWORDS

- **Advertising exposure**
- **Advertising impact**
- **Advertising response functions**
- **Customer relationship management**
- **Database marketing**
- **Direct mail**
- **Direct marketing**
- **Door-to-door**
- **Electronic media**
- **Key account management**
- **Lobbying**
- **Mailing lists**
- **Online marketing**
- **Personal selling**
- **Press conference**
- **Press release**
- **Profiling**
- **Prospecting**
- **Public relations**
- **Sales promotion**
- **Sponsorship**
- **Telemarketing**
- **Voluntary codes**
- **Wearout**

PART 4

Bringing it together

Managing the marketing effort

CHAPTER OBJECTIVES

This chapter brings together the theory of the previous chapters in a framework that can be implemented by marketing managers. Too many marketing plans fail to be implemented effectively, and this chapter explores the bases for effective marketing management. Marketing management involves a never-ending process of analysis, planning, implementation, and control. Timely and relevant information, acted upon by appropriately structured and motivated management, is crucial to success.

Introduction

A frequently heard comment about some aspects of marketing is that it is 'fine in theory, but doesn't work in practice'. This book has presented a lot of the theory that underlies marketing management decisions, but theory and good ideas alone will not create long-term profitability. Nor is it good enough just to have the right product at the right time. Good management is crucial to bringing about *sustainable* success.

Most people will have had experience of companies that do not appear to have the management capabilities necessary for success. At the operational level, inadequate investment in staff training and a distribution system that results in the wrong products being delivered late to the wrong place are signs of bad management. At a strategic level, poor management can be seen by a preoccupation with declining products at the expense of new opportunities and a lack of information about current market conditions.

There is an ongoing debate about whether management is an art or a science. Those who advocate a scientific approach set great value in structured procedures, for example in the way information is routinely collected and analysed. Rationality and safety underlie the scientific approach. Most of the top 100 UK companies have systematic procedures for management which make them a safe bet for investors, even if they lack the occasional sparkle of smaller and more volatile companies.

Advocates of a creative arts approach would argue that the business environment is changing rapidly and therefore a scientific framework, which worked in the past, may no longer be valid in the future. Furthermore, under the scientific approach it may take a long time to reach a decision, putting a firm at a competitive disadvantage in a fast-moving market. By taking a scientific approach, managers often end up breaking a large problem down into component sub-problems, and fail to take a holistic overview. If all other firms are following a similar scientific approach, for example using similar business models, they may all end up with 'me-too' strategies. A more creative approach is likely to encourage unique solutions which may either succeed spectacularly or fail miserably. Later in this chapter we will explore how different management structures and processes can either help or hinder the process of developing a sustainable competitive advantage.

Information is a key element of the marketing management process. We saw in Chapter 4 how, in large organizations, information is a medium for keeping in touch with customers, employees, suppliers, and intermediaries. Getting the right information to the right people at the right time is crucial if the management of a company is to be able to develop and implement a strategy. Without appropriate information, strategy formulation can become guesswork and the implementation of that strategy may be half-hearted. Inadequate monitoring may not warn of problems until it is too late to do anything about them.

■ The marketing management process

Marketing management can be seen as a continual process. This section identifies the key elements of the process, although just who should be responsible for each element is a subject that will be returned to later in a discussion on marketing management organization.

There are five key stages in the marketing management process (Figure 12.1).

1. **Where are we now? Analysis of the organization's current market position.** A vital starting-point for marketing planning is an analysis of a company's current marketing environment, often undertaken by means of a SWOT analysis or a marketing audit. A **marketing audit** is a relatively new concept and has been defined as:

a systematical, critical and unbiased review and appraisal of the environment and of the company's operations. A marketing audit is part of the larger management audit and is concerned with the marketing environment and marketing operations. (McDonald [9])

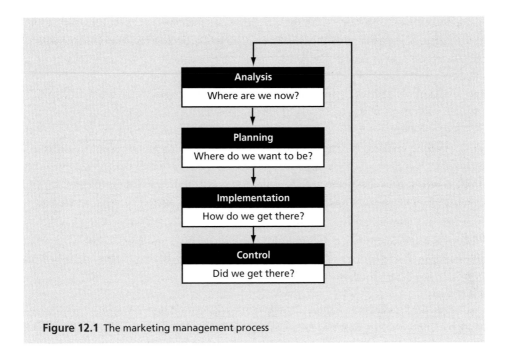

Figure 12.1 The marketing management process

A marketing audit typically includes analysis of the organization's current market share, the size and nature of its customer base, customer perceptions of the organization's output, and the internal strengths and weaknesses of the organization in terms of production, personnel, and financial resources. A marketing audit addresses these issues using both quantitative and qualitative methods where appropriate. But what information should be collected? A company's mission statement can provide its employees with guidance about what is relevant and irrelevant in analysing its current position.

How much analysis of the current situation should a company undertake? While it is nearly always true that a sound analysis of the current situation is an essential prerequisite to developing a marketing plan for the future, excessive preoccupation with the current situation can have its costs. Analysis on its own will not provide the management decisions that are necessary for defining the future marketing plan. A 'paralysis by analysis' can occur in organizations that avoid making hard decisions about the future by continually seeking more information about the present. A plateau is usually reached at which little additional information is any longer available that will improve the quality of marketing plan decisions. Worse still, in markets that are fast changing, excessive analysis of the current position can put a company at a competitive disadvantage to firms that are more willing to take a risk and exploit a market opportunity ahead of its competitors.

2. **Where do we want to be? Setting marketing objectives.**   Without clearly specified objectives, marketing management can drift aimlessly. Objectives have a number of functions within an organization:

- They add to the sense of purpose within the organization, without which there would be little focus for managers' efforts.

- They help to achieve consistency between decisions made at different points within the organization; for example, it would be inconsistent if a production manager used a production objective that was unrelated to the marketing manager's sales objective.

- Objectives are used as motivational devices and can be used in a variety of formal and informal ways to stimulate increased performance by managers.

- Objectives allow for more effective control within an organization. Unless clear objectives have been set at the outset, it is very difficult to know whether the firm has achieved what it set out to achieve, and what corrective action to take if its efforts seem to be going adrift during the plan period.

To be effective, objectives must be capable of realistic achievement and must be accepted as such by the people responsible for acting on them. If objectives are set unattainably high, the whole process of planning can be brought into disrepute by the company's employees. Wherever possible, objectives should be quantified and should clearly specify the time period to which they relate. Inconsistency between objectives should be avoided. This sometimes occurs, for example, where sales objectives can be achieved only by reducing selling prices, thereby making it impossible to achieve a profitability objective.

3. **How can we get there? Developing a marketing strategy.**   There are usually many ways in which marketing objectives can be achieved. For example, a financial return objective could be satisfied equally well by a high sales volume/low price strategy or a low volume/high price strategy. Identifying the strategic alternatives open to an organization relies on interpreting data and evaluating a number of possible future scenarios. Within this evaluation, factors such as the likelihood of success, the level of downside risk, and the amount of resources required to implement a strategy need to be taken into consideration. What may be an appropriate strategy for one company may be quite inappropriate for another, on account of differences in financial resources, past history, and personnel strengths, among other things.

It often happens that the objectives set for the planning period are greater than what could be achieved if growth occurred at the historic trend rate. Where such a 'planning gap' exists, the aim of the planning process is to develop a strategy that will close this gap. This can be done either by reducing the original objective downward to a level that is more realistic, given the historical pattern, or by accelerating the trend rate from its historical pattern to a higher level by means of marketing strategy. In practice, the planning gap is reduced by a combination of revising objectives and amending marketing strategies (Figure 12.2).

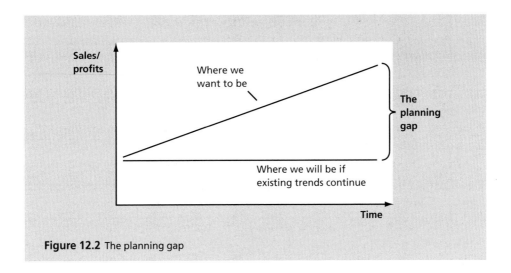

Figure 12.2 The planning gap

There have been many prescriptions for developing marketing strategies, some of which were discussed in Chapter 6 in the context of the development of a sustainable competitive advantage.

4. **How will we implement the strategy?** Having chosen a strategy, the next step is to implement it. This is usually done through a 12-month marketing plan which sets out programmes for, among other things, the timing and costing of promotional programmes, pricing plans, and the recruitment and payment of distributors. These detailed programmes should flow directly from the marketing strategy, which itself starts from marketing objectives. Too many companies develop a strategy that sounds fine, but they fail to think through fully the detail of implementation.

5. **Did we get there? Monitoring and controlling the marketing programme.** Marketing plans are of little value if they are to be implemented only half-heartedly. An ongoing part of the marketing management process is therefore to monitor the implementation of the plan and to seek an explanation of any deviation from it.

Effective control systems demand timely, accurate, and relevant information about an organization's operations and environment. Control systems require three underlying components to be in place:

1. the setting of targets or standards of expected performance;
2. the measurement and evaluation of actual performance;
3. the corrective action to be taken where necessary.

Many control systems fail because employees within an organization have been given inappropriate or unrealistic targets. Even where targets are set and appropriate data are collected, control systems may fail because of a failure by management to act on the information available. Control information should identify variances from target and should be able to indicate whether the variance is within or beyond the control of the person responsible for meeting the target. If it is beyond that person's control, the issue should become one of revising the target so that it once more becomes achievable. If the variance is the result of factors that are subject to a manager's control, a number of measures can be taken to try to revise their behaviour, including incentive schemes, training, and disciplinary action.

Strategic, tactical, and contingency planning

From the above description, marketing planning is best viewed as a continuous process. However, it is necessary to produce periodic statements of a plan which all individuals in an organization can work towards. Three types of periodic plan can be identified.

1. The **strategic** element of a marketing plan focuses on the overriding direction that an organization's efforts will take in order to meet its objectives.

2. The **tactical** element is more concerned with plans for implementing the detail of the strategic plan.

The division between the strategic and tactical elements of a marketing plan can sometimes be difficult to define. Typically, a strategic marketing plan is concerned with mapping out direction over a five-year planning period, whereas a tactical marketing plan is concerned with implementation during the next 12 months. Many business sectors view their strategic planning periods very differently, and in the case of large-scale infrastructure projects such as airports or railways, the strategic planning period may be very long indeed. On the other hand, many small-scale, low-technology businesses may find little need for a strategic plan beyond the immediate operational period.

3. A **contingency** plan seeks to identify scenarios where the assumptions of the position analysis on which strategic decisions were based turn out to be false. For example, a food manufacturer might have assumed that there would be no significant change in consumers' attitudes towards a particular category of food. However, the possibility of a food scare, such as those associated with salmonella in chickens and BSE in beef, could seriously affect the implementation of a marketing plan. A contingency plan would allow a firm to react quickly to such a scenario, for example by increasing its promotional expenditure and cutting back on production capacity.

The dynamic marketing environment

In developing a marketing plan, it can be very easy to assume a stable market. In Chapter 6 we saw that, in reality, most markets are dynamic and a marketing plan needs to take account of not just competitors' current strategies, but also their likely future strategies. If a market appears attractive to one organization, then it probably appears equally attractive to others as well. These other organizations may possess equal competitive advantage in addressing the market. If all such firms decide to enter the market, oversupply results, profit margins become squeezed, and the market becomes relatively unattractive. This could be observed in the semi-conductor market, which in the mid-1990s looked highly attractive, with a rapid growth in demand and a shortage of supply. This was the signal for many companies to enter the market, with the result that by 2000 oversupply had resulted, the price of semi-conductors had fallen from over £4 to less than 50p, and many manufacturing operations had become unprofitable.

Marketing planning and corporate planning

Marketing management is just one of the specialist management functions that can be identified within most commercial organizations. What is the relationship between marketing management and corporate management? At one extreme, the two can be seen as synonymous. If an organization stands or falls primarily on its ability to satisfy customer needs, then it can be argued that marketing planning is so central to the organization's activities that it becomes corporate planning. The alternative view is that marketing is just one of the functions of an organization that affects its performance. Marketing takes its goals from corporate plans just as the personnel or production functions of the organization do. In business sectors where customers have relatively little choice and production capacity is limited, the significance of the marketing plan to the corporate plan will be less than for a company facing fierce competition. Many public-sector service organizations claim to go through the marketing planning process when in fact, although the term 'marketing planning' may be referred to by name, it is given much less significance than the development of production plans to serve a stable market.

The relationship between the processes of marketing and corporate planning can be two-way, again reflecting the importance of marketing to the total planning process. Marketing information is fed into the corporate planning process for analysis and formulation of the corporate plan in a process sometimes referred to as 'bottom-up planning'. In a 'top-down' process, the corporate plan is developed and functional objectives are specified for marketing.

■ Planning as an inter-functional integrator

The marketing planning process helps to integrate the efforts of a diverse range of people throughout an organization. The plan allows everybody to 'sing from the same hymn sheet'. Without the plan, individuals may end up doing things that are in direct conflict with their colleagues.

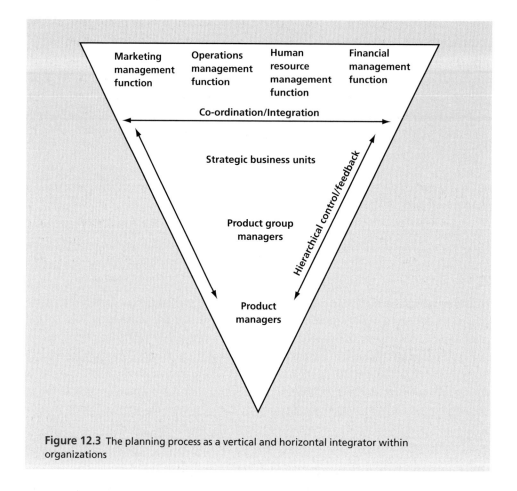

Figure 12.3 The planning process as a vertical and horizontal integrator within organizations

Corporate and marketing planning processes act as integrators in horizontal and vertical dimensions (see Figure 12.3).

- **In the horizontal dimension**, the planning process brings together the plans of the specialized functions that are necessary to make the organization work. Marketing is just one function of an organization which generates its own planning process. Other functional plans found in most organizations are financial plans, personnel plans, and production plans. The components of these functional plans must recognize their interdependencies if they are to be effective. For example, a car manufacturer's marketing strategic plan which anticipates a 20% growth in sales of its cars over a five-year planning period should be reflected in a strategic production plan that allows for output to increase by a similar amount, as well as a financial plan that identifies strategies for raising the required level of finance for new investment and work in progress and a personnel plan for recruiting additional staff. Within the marketing department, a plan helps to ensure that the activities of advertising personnel are mutually supportive of the activities of sales and market research staff, for example.

- **In the vertical dimension**, the planning process provides a framework for decisions to be made at different levels of the corporate hierarchy. Objectives can be specified in progressively more detail, from the global objectives of the corporate plan, to the information required to operationalize these objectives at the level of individual operational units (or strategic business units) and—in turn—for individual products.

The mission statement

A corporate mission statement provides a focal point for the marketing planning process. It can be likened to a hidden hand which guides all employees in an organization in developing and implementing marketing plans. Drucker [4] identified a number of basic questions that management needs to ask in drawing up a mission statement:

- What is our business?
- Who is the customer?
- What is value to the customer?
- What will our business be?
- What should our business be?

By forcing management to focus on the essential nature of the business it is in and the nature of customer needs it seeks to satisfy, the problem of 'marketing myopia' identified by Levitt [7] can be avoided. Levitt argued that, in order to avoid a narrow, short-sighted view of their business, managers should define their business in terms of the needs that they fulfil rather than the products they produce. In the classic example, railway operators lost their way because they defined their output in terms of the *technology* of tracked vehicles, rather than in terms of the core benefit of *movement* that they provided. They lost out to the development of cars and buses, which provided similar benefits using different technologies.

The nature of an organization's mission statement is a reflection of a number of factors, including the organization's ownership (e.g. public-sector *v.* private-sector statements); the previous history of the organization; the resources available; and major opportunities and threats faced by the organization.

In services organizations where the interface between consumers and production personnel is often critical, communication of the values contained within the mission statement can be very important. The statement is frequently repeated by organizations in staff newsletters and in notices at the place of work. An example of a mission statement that is widely communicated to the workforce—as well as to customers—is shown in Figure 12.4.

Statement of Purpose

Figure 12.4 An example of a mission statement. Reproduced with permission of British Gas

We aim to be...
a world class energy company and the leading international gas business

by...

▶ running a professional gas business providing safe, secure and reliable supplies

▶ actively developing an international business in exploration and production of oil and gas

▶ making strategic investments in other energy-related projects and businesses world wide

▶ satisfying our customers' wishes for excellent quality of service and outstanding value

▶ constantly and energetically seeking to improve quality and productivity in all we do

▶ caring for the environment

▶ maintaining a high quality workforce with equal opportunities for all

▶ cultivating good relations with customers, employees, suppliers, shareholders and the communities we serve and thereby improving returns to shareholders.

British Gas

Organizing the marketing management function

It was noted earlier that the principles of marketing might be fine in theory, but they are difficult in practice. The same can be said for the process of marketing planning. The process may look fine in theory, but it needs the right people to implement the process and make it a success. There have been too many cases of marketing planners developing a plan for which the operational implications have not been fully thought through and which therefore fails to deliver value to customers and profits to the company.

A frequent problem occurs where the marketing planning function becomes cut off from other functional departments. The whole issue of organizing a company so that it has a company-wide focus on marketing is considered in a later section. Here we look inwardly at the marketing department and ask how it can best be organized in order to meet marketing objectives.

Responsibilities given to the marketing department vary from one organization to another, reflecting the competitive nature of a company and also its traditions and organizational inertia. Within marketing departments, four basic approaches to allocating these responsibilities are identified here—although, in practice, most marketing

MARKETING and the INTERNET

Small entrepreneurs soon eclipsed by larger rivals

What type of marketing management has won out in the battle to exploit the capabilities of the internet? How has the lone maverick entrepreneur, devoid of any marketing planning processes, fared against larger organizations with more formalized marketing planning processes? The early days of the internet were dominated by stories of 'nerds' beavering away in a spare room at home to develop a website. This was a classic approach of the very small business, which had previously seen low-cost, innovative individuals exploit new opportunities in mobile phone retailing and video rental, among many other fields. Free of any bureaucracy, entrepreneurial small businesses could single-mindedly pursue their dream of a 'new economy' in which any small business was able to communicate with the whole world from a humble makeshift office.

The smaller business soon began to lose out in the competitive stakes, as larger companies rapidly became the driving force in the internet era. Belying their image as lumbering dinosaurs, the corporate giants adopted e-commerce, evolving their working practices and supply chains to gain substantial benefits. The advantages held by these established bricks-and-mortar companies over the upstart dot.com entrepreneurs included industry depth, a strong brand identity, and customer trust. They also had good access to capital, and expertise in managing their existing businesses.

Meanwhile, what of the small business owners who were the pioneers of the internet? Many of their businesses grew rapidly to establish a position in the marketplace; for example, Lastminute.com started on a very limited budget but by 2003 had become a mainstream business with public limited company (plc) status. Other entrepreneurs could not keep up with the pace of competition and either sold out to larger, better resourced rivals (e.g. Jungle.com sold out to the GUS group), or went into receivership through lack of funds (e.g. Boo.com).

With hindsight, could the respective roles of small entrepreneurial businesses and large corporate organizations have been predicted? Was it only to be expected that small businesses would be the early innovators, to be rapidly overtaken by larger companies when their markets became mainstream? Would a formalized marketing planning system have helped or hindered the smaller traders whose main strength was often their owners' impulsive enthusiasm? Was equity capital invested in larger companies in safer hands, or had these companies' sometimes bureaucratic marketing planning processes led them to miss out on opportunities? Or should those processes have been even more rigorous to prevent the losses incurred by many companies such as Marconi following the bursting of the dot.com bubble in 2000?

departments show more than one approach. The four approaches allocate marketing responsibilities by: functions performed, geographical area covered, products or groups of products managed, and market segments managed.

The great diversity of organizational structures highlights the fact that there is no one unique structure that is appropriate to all firms, even within the same business sector.

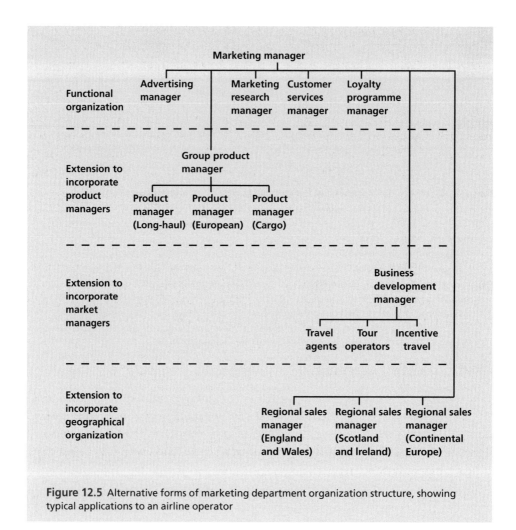

Figure 12.5 Alternative forms of marketing department organization structure, showing typical applications to an airline operator

Overall, the organization of a marketing department must allow for a flexible and adaptable response to customers' needs within a changing environment, while aiming to reduce the level of confusion, ambiguity, and cost inherent in some structures. An illustration of the four approaches to marketing management structures is shown in Figure 12.5 using the example of an airline.

Management by functional responsibility

A traditional and common basis of organizing a marketing department is to divide responsibilities into identifiable marketing functions. Typically, these functions may be advertising, sales, research and development, marketing research, and customer services. The precise division of the functional responsibilities will depend upon the nature of the organization. Buying and merchandising are likely to be important features in a retailing organization, while research and development will be important for an electronics company.

The main advantage of a functional organization lies in its administrative simplicity. Against this, there can be a tendency for policy responsibility on specific products or markets to become lost between numerous functional specialists. There is also the possibility of destructive rivalry between functional specialists for their share of marketing budgets—for example rivalry between an advertising manager and a sales manager for a larger share of the promotional budget.

Management by geographical responsibility

Companies selling a product nationwide usually organize some of their marketing functions, especially the sales function, on a geographical basis. For companies operating internationally, there is usually some geographical basis to organization in the way the marketing activities are organized in individual national markets.

Management by product type

Where a company produces a variety of products, it is quite common to appoint a product manager to manage a particular product or product line. This form of organization does not replace the functional organization, but provides an additional layer of management which co-ordinates the functional activities. The product manager's role includes a number of key tasks:

- Developing a long-range strategy and short-term annual plan for a product or group of products
- Working with internal and external functional specialists to develop and implement marketing programmes, for example in relation to advertising and sales promotion
- Monitoring the performance of the product and noting changes in the marketing environment which may pose opportunities or threats

In theory, a product manager can react more quickly to changes in the product's marketing environment than would be possible if no one had specific responsibility for the product. Although product management structures can allow for a focused strategy to be developed in respect of individual products, there are nevertheless some shortcomings. The most serious one arises when a product manager is given a lot of responsibility for ensuring that objectives for the product are met, but relatively little control over the resource inputs he has at his disposal. Product managers typically must rely on persuasion to get the co-operation of advertising, sales, and other functional specialist departments. Confusion can arise in the minds of staff within an organization as to whom they are accountable to for their day-to-day actions—the product manager, or a functional specialist such as a sales manager? Product management structures can lead to larger numbers of people being employed, resulting in a higher cost structure, which may put the organization at a competitive disadvantage in price-sensitive markets.

Management by market segment

Many companies sell basically similar products to different types of customer who vary significantly in their needs. For example, an airline provides services targeted at leisure travellers, business travellers, tour operators, and freight forwarders, among others; each of these groups has differing requirements in terms of speed, reliability, price, etc., and a market segment manager can become expert in understanding these needs and developing an appropriate product offer for each group. Instead of being given specific financial targets for their products, market managers are usually given growth or market share targets.

The main advantage of this form of organization is that it allows marketing activity to be focused on meeting the needs of distinct and identified groups of customers— something that should be at the heart of any truly marketing-oriented organization. Also, new products are more likely to emerge within this structure than where an organization's response is confined to traditional product management boundaries. Market management structures are also arguably more conducive to the important task of developing relationships with customers, especially in business-to-business markets. Where an organization has a number of very important customers, it is common to find the appointment of key account managers to handle relationships with those clients in order to exploit marketing opportunities that are of mutual benefit to both (discussed in Chapter 11).

Many of the disadvantages of the product management organization are also shared by market-based structures. There can again be a conflict between responsibility and authority, and this form of structure can also become expensive to operate.

Integrating marketing management with other management functions

Should an organization actually have a marketing department? The idea is becoming increasingly popular that the existence of a separate marketing department may in fact hinder the development of a true customer-centred marketing orientation. By placing all marketing activity in a marketing department, non-marketing staff may consider that responsibility for getting new or repeat business is nothing to do with them, but should be left to the marketing department. While it is becoming fashionable to talk

MARKETING and SOCIAL RESPONSIBILITY

Should insurance companies build Chinese walls?

The conventional wisdom is that product managers in service firms should work together to put their customers' needs above internal management demarcations. But could there sometimes be an ethical case against too much sharing of information by product managers?

Consider the case of merchant banks offering investment management and capital raising services. In a proposed take-over bid, it is often necessary for those involved in raising the capital required by a client to work very discreetly for fear of prematurely raising the share price of the target company. If this information were available to staff working in investment management, it would give them an unfair advantage over the market generally, allowing them to build up a shareholding in the target company ahead of the announcement of a take-over bid. Merchant banks have sought to build 'Chinese walls' around their operations where this risk is present, and the adoption of a product marketing management structure can allow greater effective separation of functions. Numerous other service industries can be identified where similar ethical problems can be lessened by the adoption of a product management structure. The problem has become particularly acute in the accounting sector, where a firm of accountants may sell both auditing services and management consultancy services to a company. There have been many allegations that accountants have been too ready to accept compromises in their auditing function in order to pick up lucrative management consultancy business. The investigation of the accountant Arthur Anderson's involvement with the failed energy company Enron in 2002 revealed evidence of unethical practice in the way that the firm had mixed accountancy and consultancy activities, and led to renewed debate about the ethics of 'one-stop' accountancy/consultancy businesses.

How do large diversified services firms convince their customers that information given in confidence to one section of the organization will not be used against them in another section? And how can society generally be confident that organizations that should be acting as a gamekeeper are not also acting as a poacher?

about everybody becoming a 'part-time marketer' (see Gummesson [5]), a marketing department is usually required in order to co-ordinate and implement those functions that cannot sensibly be delegated to operational personnel. Advertising, sales management, and pricing decisions, for example, usually need some central co-ordination by a marketing department. The importance that a marketing department assumes within any organization is a reflection on the nature of its operating environment. An organization operating in a fiercely competitive environment would typically attach great importance to its marketing department as a means of producing a focused marketing mix strategy by which it could gain competitive advantage over its competitors. On the other hand, a company operating in a relatively stable environment would be more likely to allow strategic decisions to be taken by personnel who were not marketing strategists—for example, pricing decisions may be taken by accountants with less need to understand the marketing implications of price decisions.

In a marketing-oriented organization, customers are at the centre of all of the organization's activities. Customers are the concern not simply of the marketing department, but of all the production and administrative personnel whose actions may directly or indirectly impinge upon the customers' service. In the words of Drucker [4],

Marketing is so basic that it cannot be considered to be a separate function. It is the whole business seen from the point of view of its final result, that is, from the customer's point of view.

The activities of a number of functional departments can impinge on customers' perceptions of the value they get from a company.

- Personnel plans can have a crucial bearing on marketing plans. The selection, training, motivation, and control of staff cannot be considered in isolation from marketing objectives and strategies. Possible conflict between personnel and marketing functions may arise where, for example, marketing demands highly trained and motivated staff, but the personnel function pursues a policy that emphasizes cost reduction and uniform pay structures.

- Marketing managers may try to respond as closely as possible to customers' needs but encounter opposition from production managers, who argue that a product of the required standard cannot be achieved. A marketing manager may want large numbers of product variants in order to satisfy market niches, whereas a production manager may seek large production runs of standardized products.

- Ultimately, finance managers assume responsibility for the allocation of the funds that are needed to implement a marketing plan. At a more operational level, finance managers' actions in respect of the level of credit offered to customers, or towards stockholdings, can also significantly affect the quality of service and the volume of customers that the organization is able to serve.

The problem of how to bring people in an organization together to act collectively, while also being able to place responsibility on an individual, is one that continues to generate considerable discussion. Two recent developments in this debate are noted here: matrix organization structures, and the idea of business process re-engineering.

The matrix approach to management

The essence of a matrix type of organization is to allow individuals to concentrate on a functional, product, or market specialization and to bring them together in task force teams to solve problems, taking an organizational view rather than their own narrow specialist view. Product managers can concentrate on excellence in production, while market managers focus on meeting consumer needs without any preference for a particular product (see Figure 12.6).

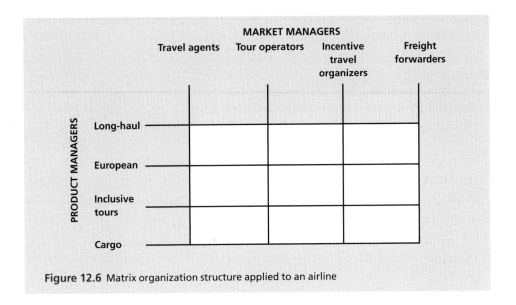

Figure 12.6 Matrix organization structure applied to an airline

The most important advantages of matrix structures are that they can allow organizations to respond rapidly to environmental change. Short-term project teams can be assembled and disbanded at short notice to meet changed needs. Project teams can bring together a wide variety of disciplines and can be used to evaluate new products before full-scale development is undertaken. A grocery retailer exploring the possibility of developing internet-based home shopping might establish a team drawn from staff involved in distribution, advertising, market research, and technology-based research and development.

The flexibility of matrix structures can be increased by bringing temporary workers into the structure on a contract basis as and when needed. There has been a trend for many companies to lay off significant numbers of workers—including management—and to buy these back when needed. As well as cutting fixed costs, such 'modular' organizations have the potential to respond very rapidly to environmental change.

High levels of motivation can be present in effectively managed teams within matrix structures. Against this, matrix organizations can have a number of drawbacks. Most serious is the confused lines of authority that often result. Staff members may not be clear about which superior they are responsible to for a particular aspect of their duties, resulting in possible stress and demotivation. Where a matrix structure is introduced into an organization with a history and culture of functional specialization, it can be very difficult to implement effectively. Members of staff may be reluctant to act outside a role that they have traditionally defined narrowly and guarded jealously. Finally, matrix structures invariably result in more managers being employed within an organization. At best this can result in a costly addition to the salary bill; at worst, the existence of additional managers can also slow down decision-making processes where the managers show a reluctance to act outside a narrow functional role.

Business process re-engineering

All of the management structures described so far have a tendency to grow incrementally, adding and subtracting bits in a pragmatic way. The result is often an illogical structure that is largely a result of historical accident. A more radical approach to integrating marketing with other functions is to start with a clean sheet of paper and ask: 'How would we design this business if we were starting from scratch today?' The term 'business process re-engineering' has been commonly applied to this approach, although 'radical restructuring' and 'zero based plans' can mean very much the same thing. The underlying principle here is to design an organization around key value-adding activities. Essentially, it is about radically redesigning the processes by which an organization does business in order that it can achieve major savings in cost, or improvements in output, or both.

To be effective, re-engineering needs to be led by strong individuals who have the authority to oversee implementation from beginning to end. They will need to overcome fear, resistance, and cynicism which will inevitably slow the task down. At first sight, though, this approach to reorganization would appear to be in conflict with participative approaches to management, such as total quality management, that stress employee involvement in change. Successful companies therefore seek to involve their employees in the detail of implementation, even if the radical nature of the agenda is not negotiable.

◼ Marketing management and smaller businesses

Much of what has been written so far in this chapter about marketing management processes and structures might sound fine for larger organizations, but what about smaller businesses where the very idea of a 'management structure' and a formalized marketing planning system may seem quite alien?

The term 'small business' (or SME, standing for Small and Medium-sized Enterprise) is difficult to define. In an industry such as car manufacture, a firm with 100 employees would be considered very small, whereas among solicitors, a practice of that size would be considered large. The term 'small business' is therefore a relative one, based typically on some measure of numbers of employees or capital employed. Within the European Union, the Eurostat definition of small companies is often used:

- Micro-organizations: 0–9 employees
- Small organizations: 10–99 employees

MARKETING in ACTION

The 'wideboys' of British business?

How is the marketing manager seen within an organization? One message of this book is that in increasingly competitive markets marketing can be fundamental to success, and this should be reflected in the status of that department within an organization. But this does not stop many companies looking suspiciously on their marketing managers.

Marketing managers have been described as the 'wideboys' of British business—never in the office, always over budget, and not properly accountable. A survey undertaken in 1998 by the Chartered Institute of Marketing highlighted the apparent problem when it found that 80% of senior managers claimed there was a cultural prejudice in their companies against marketing managers; 38% named marketing as the most important factor in business success, although marketing managers appeared to be under-represented on companies' boards of directors—while 51% of companies had a marketer on the board, finance directors were represented on 88% of boards. Relatively few chief executives have a background in marketing. The marketing department is often the first to feel the effects of recession.

Is this apparent prejudice within organizations against marketing justified? Have marketers concentrated too much on short-term gimmicks and too little on long-term strategy? Or have marketers simply failed to promote their own reputations within the organizations in which they work? And is this apparent anti-marketing mentality a peculiarly British phenomenon where marketing and selling are often viewed with suspicion?

- Medium-sized organizations: 100–499 employees
- Large organizations: 500+ employees

Despite the tendency of firms to grow, there has been renewed interest in the role of small businesses within the economy. It has been suggested that many of Britain's competitors, including many of the Far Eastern economies, have attributed their growth to a strong small business sector. In recent years developed economies have seen a significant increase in the number of small businesses, especially in the expanding services sector. It should not be forgotten that in the UK, SMEs account for 99% of all businesses, 45% of non-government employment, and 40% of turnover (excluding the finance sector). By contrast, the 7,000 largest businesses accounted for 43% of non-government employment and 46% of turnover (Department of Trade and Industry). In the UK there are 3.7 million small businesses, of which 2.7 million are 'size class zero' businesses, made up of sole traders or partners without any employees.

The change in the structure and organization of industry and commerce, the growing emphasis on specialized services, and the application of new technology have tended to encourage small businesses. Flexible manufacturing systems are increasingly able to allow a business to function at a much lower level of output than previously. An example is printing, where new production processes have allowed entrepreneurs to undertake small print runs on relatively inexpensive machinery. The success of the small printer has been further encouraged by the proliferation of small business users of printed material requiring small print runs and a rapid turn-round of work. The tendency for large companies to subcontract functions such as cleaning and catering in order to concentrate on their core business has also given new opportunities to the small business sector.

In terms of marketing management, SMEs have a number of important characteristics.

1. They generally offer much greater adaptability than larger firms. With less bureaucracy and fewer channels of communications, decisions can be taken rapidly. A larger organization may be burdened with constraints which tend to slow the decision-making process, such as the need to negotiate new working practices with trade union representatives, or the need to obtain the board of directors' approval for major decisions. As organizations grow, there is an inherent tendency for them to become more risk-averse by building in systems of control that make them slower to adapt to changes in their business environment.

2. Small businesses tend to be good innovators. This comes about through their greater adaptability, especially where large amounts of capital are not required. Small firms can also be good innovators where they operate in markets dominated by a small number of larger companies and the only way in which a small business can gain entry to the market is to develop an innovatory product aimed at a small niche. The soap powder market in Britain is dominated by a small number of large producers, yet it was a relatively small company that identified a niche for environmentally friendly powders and introduced innovatory products to the market.

It is not only small entrepreneurs who have been creating new small businesses. Many larger organizations have also recognized their value and have tried to replicate them at a distance from their own structure. Many large manufacturing organizations operating in mature markets have created autonomous new small business units to serve rapidly developing or specialist niche markets, free of the bureaucratic culture of the parent organization. In the education sector, many universities have established small research companies at arm's length from the universities' organizational structures.

While small businesses have certainly seen a resurgence in recent years, it should also be recognized that they have a very high failure rate. Conclusive evidence of the failure rate of small businesses is difficult to obtain, especially in view of the problem of identifying new businesses that do not need to register in the first place. However, one indication of failure rates comes from an analysis of VAT (value added tax) registrations, which show that during the 1990s only about one-third of businesses set up ten years previously were still registered.

MARKETING in ACTION

Are entrepreneurs born or bred?

Is there such a thing as an 'entrepreneurship gene'? Further developments in the science of genetics may one day add some evidence to the debate about whether entrepreneurs are born or bred. But what about students leaving university today? Evidence abounds of students who are attributed with an 'entrepreneurship' gene. As an example, a company called Innocent was set up by in 1999 by three entrepreneurial Cambridge University graduates—Adam Balon, Richard Reed, and Jon Wright—to produce fresh fruit smoothies. By 2002 the company was already producing 200,000 smoothies a week with an annual sales turnover of £7 million. The budding entrepreneurs initially tested their dream by buying £500 of fresh fruit and selling their smoothies at a stall during a weekend jazz festival in London.

Of course, for every entrepreneurial success story there are scores of failures, and it is commonly estimated that a third of new entrants to self-employment leave within three years—even more in periods of economic recession. Very often, an entrepreneur can be good at creating a business, but much less good at handling the procedures that are necessary to keep a larger organization on track. Typical of this tendency is Michelle Mone, inventor of the cleavage enhancing Ultimo bra. She launched her business, MJM International, in 1996 and enjoyed an annual turnover of more than £1 million within just a few years. Her products went on to achieve global fame when Julia Roberts wore an Ultimo bra for her role in the Oscar-winning film *Erin Brockovich*. In 2001 turnover reached £3 million, and Mone announced plans to float her company. But when the planned float failed to take off, her fortunes seemed to unwind. The bank called in the company's overdraft, she began experiencing problems with designers, and a department store cancelled its order, leaving her business with 15,000 unsold bras. It seemed that designing stylish bras for the rich and famous was one thing, but handling relationships with large retail buyers was quite another. Mone pulled her products out of department stores in 2001 to sell direct to the public via an internet site, but sales have remained static.

So what are the characteristics of an entrepreneur? Most authorities agree that a willingness to take risks is crucial—it really does seem to be necessary to speculate in order to accumulate. Of course, taking risk implies that, while some entrepreneurs will succeed beyond their wildest dreams, many will fail. Good entrepreneurs are able to pick themselves up quickly following a failure. Being optimistic and spotting opportunities is important, as is the ability to work long hours, and to have a belief in yourself and your ideas.

It would seem that many would-be entrepreneurs don't set out on the road to entrepreneurship because they have a fear of failure. Some cultures condemn individuals who have failed, but in other countries, such as the United States, there is an environment in which failure is recognized as a sign of a well-intentioned individual who hit a bit of bad luck, and success is about more than having a bit of undeserved good luck. Can this difference in cultural values explain why some countries seem to have a larger number of entrepreneurial companies?

■ Internal market places

Every organization can be considered to be a marketplace consisting of a diverse group of employees engaging in exchanges between one another. These internal exchanges include relationships between customer-contact staff and the backroom staff, managers and the customer-contact staff, managers and the backroom staff, and, for large organizations, between the head office and each branch. In the most general sense, employees have been seen by some as 'consumers' of services provided by their employer, such as a pleasant working environment, provision of a pension scheme, and good facilities for performing their tasks.

Increasingly, organizations are asking internal service departments, such as information technology, human resources, accounting, and media services, to be more accountable and to put in bids to provide services, in competition with external providers. This has resulted in employees' effectively trading services with other employees within their organization. In a growing number of instances, organizations have out-sourced the services traditionally provided by such internal departments, resulting in extended 'network' or 'virtual' organizations.

The internal trading of services is closely related to the idea developed in the total quality management literature of 'Next operation as a customer' (NOAC) (Denton [3]). NOAC is based on the idea that each group within an organization should treat the recipients of its output as an internal customer and strive to provide high-quality outputs for them (e.g. Lukas and Maignan [8]). Through this approach, quality will be built into the product delivered to the final customer. This concept of an internal market of buyers and suppliers is closely related to the concept of the value chain (Porter [13]). A modified value chain in terms of internal suppliers is shown in Figure 12.7.

There are, however, problems in drawing analogies between internal and external markets for goods and services. External customers can usually take their business elsewhere if they are not satisfied with the service provided, while internal customers may be required to use a designated service unit within their organization. Consequently, the internal customer is frequently a captive customer. Employees as customers may be tied to employment contracts with little short-term prospect of 'buying' employment elsewhere. Many studies of internal marketing that focus on internal customers and suppliers have not differentiated between the different types of internal customer that may exist within the firm and their differing internal service expectations. This would appear to be no more marketing-oriented than a marketing plan that treats all external customers as homogeneous.

There is a widely held view that, if employees are not happy with their jobs, external customers will never be uppermost in their minds. This is especially true for services that involve direct contact between employees and customers. Nevertheless, many have recognized that there is a three-way fight between the firm, the contact personnel, and the customer. To give an example, it may sound like a good idea to give employees

Figure 12.7 A modified value chain for internally produced goods and services

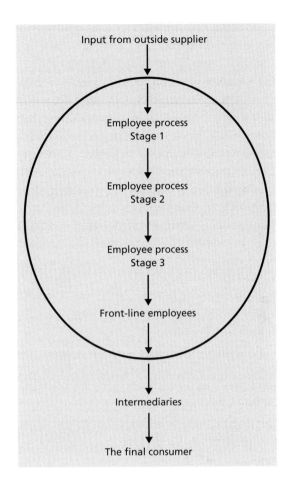

Input from outside supplier

Employee process
Stage 1

Employee process
Stage 2

Employee process
Stage 3

Front-line employees

Intermediaries

The final consumer

longer rest breaks because this satisfies their needs as internal 'customers'. But longer rest breaks may result in greater waiting time for external customers, as fewer staff are now available to serve them. A fine balance has to be drawn, and there is no conclusive proof that in all situations happier employees necessarily result in happier external customers and a more profitable service operation.

▇ Leadership

Many of the most successful market-led companies, such as Virgin Group, J. D. Weatherspoon, and Dell Computers, attribute their success in part to the quality of leadership within their organizations. The results of poor leadership are evident in many failing service organizations. Many commentators attributed the decline in fortunes of Marks & Spencers and Sainsbury's to leadership rifts within their senior managements.

What is good leadership for one organization need not necessarily be so for another. Organizations operating in relatively stable environments may be best suited with a leadership style that places a lot of power in a hierarchical chain of command. In the UK, many banks until recently had leadership styles that were drawn from models developed in the armed forces, as evidenced by some managers having titles such as 'superintendent' and 'inspector'. Such rigid, hierarchical patterns of leadership may be less effective where the marketing environment is changing rapidly and a flexible response is called for (as has happened in the banking sector).

What makes a good leader of a marketing-oriented company? And are leaders born, or can individuals acquire the skills of leadership? On the latter point there is little doubt that development is possible, and successful companies have invested heavily in leadership development programmes. As for what makes a successful leader of people, there have been many suggestions of desirable traits, including:

- Setting clear expectations of staff
- Recognizing excellence appropriately and facilitating staff in overcoming their weaknesses
- Leading by example
- Being able to empathize with employees
- Showing adaptability to changing circumstances

In too many companies, bad leadership is characterized by:

- 'Management by confusion', in which expectations of staff are ambiguously stated and management actions are guided by a secretive 'hidden agenda'
- Reward systems that are not based on performance and are perceived as being unfair
- The deliberate or inadvertent creation of an 'us-and-them' attitude
- Failure to understand the aspirations of employees
- Failure to take the initiative where environmental change calls for adaptation

Managing information

We saw in Chapter 4 how information represents a bridge between an organization and its environment. It is the means by which a picture of the changing environment is built up within the organization. Marketing management is responsible for turning information into specific marketing plans. The marketing management function of any organization requires a constant flow of information for two principal purposes:

1. to provide information as an input to the planning of marketing activities;
2. to monitor the implementation of marketing programmes and allow corrective action to be taken if performance diverges from target.

MARKETING in ACTION

Managing by example

Beginning with a small shop in Dundalk in 1960, the Irish grocery retailer SuperQuinn has grown to a successful chain of 12 shops and seven shopping centres employing over 2,000 people throughout Ireland. A large part of this success has been attributed to the leadership style of the company's founder, Feargal Quinn, and the emphasis on linking employees' activities to excellence in service quality. But what makes such leadership style distinctive?

An important principle is that managers should lead by example and should never lose contact with the most important person in the organization—the customer. It is the task of a leader to set the tone for customer-focused excellence. To prevent managers losing sight of customers' needs, Quinn uses every opportunity to move them closer to customers, including locating their offices not in a comfortable room upstairs, but in the middle of the sales floor. Managers regularly take part in customer panels where customers talk about their expectations and perceptions of SuperQuinn. Subcontracting this task entirely to a market research agency is seen as alien to the leadership culture of the company. The company requires its managers to spend periods doing routine front-line jobs (such as packing customers' bags), a practice that has become commonplace in many successful services organizations. This keeps managers close to the company and improves their ability to empathize with junior employees.

Does this leadership style work? Given the company's level of growth, profits, and rate of repeat business, it must be doing something right, contradicting much of the scientific management theories that management is a specialist task which can be separated from routine dealings with customers and employees.

A timely supply of appropriate information provides feedback on an organization's performance, allowing actual performance to be compared with target performance. On the basis of this information, control measures can be applied which seek—where necessary—to put the organization back on its original targets. Organizations also learn from the past in order to understand the future better. For making longer-term planning decisions, historical information is supplemented by a variety of continuous and *ad hoc* studies, all designed to allow better informed decisions to be made.

Marketing information cannot in itself produce decisions: it merely provides data which must be interpreted by marketing managers. As an inter-functional integrator, marketing information draws data from all functional areas of an organization, which in turn use data to focus on meeting customers' needs more effectively.

You will recall from Chapter 4 that, to be useful to management, information should be collected from a variety of sources in a systematic manner and turned into knowledge that can be shared throughout the organization and acted upon. An important task of marketing management is to plan the collection, analysis, and dissemination of information in a way that balances the costs of collecting the information against the costs of a poor decision based on inadequate information. A number of factors will determine the efficiency and effectiveness of these activities.

- **The accuracy with which the information requirements have been defined:** It can be very difficult to identify what information should be of relevance in a company's information gathering activities and to separate relevance from irrelevance. This is a particular problem for large multi-output firms expanding into new markets/products. The mission statement of an organization may give some indication of the boundaries for its information search.

- **The extensiveness of the search for information:** A balance has to be struck between the need for information and the cost of collecting it. The most critical elements of the marketing environment must be identified and the cost of collecting relevant information weighed against the cost that would result from a poorly informed management decision.

- **The appropriateness of the sources of information:** Information for decision making can usually be obtained from numerous sources; for example, customers' attitudes towards a product can be measured using a variety of quantitative and qualitative techniques. Companies often rely on the former when more qualitative techniques are really called for. Successful companies use a variety of sources of information.

- **The speed of communication:** A marketing manager must facilitate rapid communication of information to the people capable of acting on it. Deciding what information to withhold from an individual and the concise reporting of relevant information can be as important as deciding what information to include if information overload is to be avoided.

Of course, information itself will not produce decisions, and it was noted earlier that a preoccupation with data collection and analysis can lead to a 'paralysis by analysis'. A crucial skill of management is to interpret information, and a variety of quantitative and qualitative techniques are used to support management decisions. We have seen in previous chapters how rules-based systems have been used to help decisions in relation to such issues as retail location and the allocation of advertisements between different media. Rules-based techniques often need to be supplemented with the intuition and experience of the marketing manager. Rules-based systems for decision support may be fine in stable and predictable environments, where historically collected data may be a good guide to the future. They can be of much less value where the environment is changing and the old 'rules' are no longer appropriate. Many successful entrepreneurs have spotted such changes and, using a combination of intuition, experience, and analysis, have exploited new opportunities.

Using information for control

So far, we have looked at information primarily as a means of improving planning for the future. But it must not be forgotten that marketing managers have a control function as well as a planning function. Indeed, many people have criticized the marketing profession for being good on planning, sometimes lacking in implementation skills, but much worse at monitoring and evaluating their efforts. Control is an important and often overlooked function of marketing, and the key to effective control is to give the right information to the right people at the right time. Providing too much information can be costly in terms of the effort required to assemble and disseminate it and can also reduce effective control where the valuable information is hidden among information of secondary importance. A control system will show variances between budgeted performance and actual performance, and will highlight those differences that are beyond a specified zone of tolerance. An analysis of variance from target should also indicate whether the variance is within or beyond the control of the person responsible for meeting the target. If it is beyond her control, the issue should become one of revising the target so that it becomes once more achievable. If the variance is the result of factors that are subject to an individual's control, a number of measures can be taken to try to revise behaviour.

The following are some of the things that most organizations will need information on if they are to monitor adequately the implementation of their marketing plan:

- Financial targets—sales turnover/contribution/profit margin, disaggregated by product/business unit
- Market analysis, e.g. market share
- Effectiveness of communication—productivity of sales personnel, effectiveness of advertising, effectiveness of sales promotion
- Pricing—level of discounts given, price position
- Personnel—level of skills achieved by employees, survey of customer comments on staff performance
- Quality levels achieved—e.g. reliability, complaint level

Where performance is below target, the reasons may not be immediately obvious. A comprehensive marketing information system can allow an organization to analyse variance. A uniform fall in sales performance across the organization, combined with intelligence gained about the state of the market, would suggest that remedial action aimed at improving the performance of individual sales personnel may not be as effective as a reassessment of targets or strategies in the light of the changed sales environment.

Successful control mechanisms require three underlying components to be in place:

1. The setting of targets or standards of expected performance
2. The measurement and evaluation of actual performance
3. The means to take corrective action where necessary

The Marketing Metrics research project, sponsored among other organizations by the Chartered Institute of Marketing, set out in 1997 to look at real-world marketing performance assessment. It found that only a small minority of UK firms fully assess their marketing performance, despite most of them thinking that they do so adequately. Nearly all firms compare actual sales with sales targets, and there is an increasing focus on shareholder value, but relatively few measure customer value. The 1999 Marketing Forum, comprising leading UK marketers, found that those claiming to measure marketing expenditure effectiveness grew from 75% to 83% between 1995 and 1997, but of those, only 14% growing to 21% had conducted measures of brand equity—an important outcome of marketing activity.

A number of reasons were identified by Ambler [1] of why firms may be unwilling or unable to measure their marketing effectiveness.

- The board is not marketing or customer oriented, and has no senior marketing representation on it. Little board agenda time is made available to discuss marketing issues.

- Determination and effort may be considered more important than objectivity. To use an analogy, the First World War would never have been won if the soldiers had known the score—it was won by sheer determination.

- Some company boards believe that accountants should be solely responsible for accounting for all that matters. Internal measures maybe interpreted as navel gazing, and are no substitute for measuring sales and market share.

- Marketers may argue against having their effectiveness measured too closely by pointing out that marketing is the business of the whole company, and so they cannot be held specifically accountable.

- Marketers are often too busy fighting the next battle and feel that this should take priority over worrying about the last one.

- In reality, the status of a marketer is determined by the size of the department's marketing budget. Size of budget, which can be measured, looks more credible on a CV than subjective outcomes.

- Marketing effectiveness may be perceived as something essentially unmeasurable, which should be assessed by more subjective 'feel good' or 'good news' aspects.

- Marketers may argue that past experience has shown that marketing expenditure cannot be related to sales and profits; i.e., profit and loss account measures do not work.

- The environment changes too fast, so results need to be judged by the new realities, not those in place or forecast when the plan was drawn up.

- Creating new measurement systems takes too long—the current marketing team will have moved on by the time the report comes out.

It is important to note that measuring overall marketing performance is not the same as measuring marketing expenditure effectiveness. Some marketing-led organizations, such as Marks & Spencer, have managed with only minimal marketing expenditure budgets. More importantly, the effectiveness of the marketing expenditure budget cannot be assessed without measuring the change in the asset of brand equity.

Brand equity is fundamental to assessment. The results of marketers' actions should live on after the current financial period. You will recall from Chapter 6 that this corresponds to the premium that buyers are prepared to pay for a specified brand rather than a generic product. There is plenty of evidence of organizations whose marketing is ineffective and who have seen their brand equity diminish. Banks who were once trusted institutions have caused anger among many of their customers through perceptions of overcharging, incorrect debits, and poor communication. One result has been that many customers have shifted their bank accounts and credit cards to supermarkets and other rivals to banks, which have achieved high levels of brand equity. Many of these misgivings about banks can be attributed to operational functions, but this only serves to emphasize the point that marketing should be a company-wide integrator. Customers may not care who in the bank is the source of their grievance, but the result is the same: the value they place on a bank's brand is lower than it was before.

Improving organizational effectiveness for marketing

What makes some organizations more effective at marketing than others? And what practical steps can a company take to become one of the best at marketing? One widely used framework for analysis—The McKinsey 7S framework developed by Peters and Waterman [10]—identified seven essential elements for a successful business, based on a study of the most successful American companies. The elements are broken down into the hardware (Strategy, Structure, and Systems) and the software (Skills, Staff, Styles, and Shared values). Formalized strategies, structures, and systems on their own were not considered to be sufficient to bring about success—these could be operationalized only with appropriate intangible 'software'. In other words, the quality of management, in terms of leadership and working with people to achieve stated goals, is critical.

At a strategic level, companies have used a number of methods to try to develop a pervasive marketing orientation throughout their organization:

- In-house educational programmes can aim to train non-marketing employees to empathize with customers' expectations. Some organizations have tried 'job swops', in

MARKETING in ACTION

How do patients measure up?

The UK's National Health Service (NHS) has increasingly been driven to meet higher 'customer service' standards, in addition to the standards of clinical excellence that have traditionally been expected from health care professionals. Starting with the publication of a 'Patients' Charter' in the mid-1990s, governments have steadily increased the targets placed on health care administrators, often linking funding to the achievement of targets. But, like many performance targets, their value in the NHS has been questioned by many.

The idea of introducing targets that relate mainly to customer handling rather than to clinical issues has been dismissed by many as mere window dressing. But even the meaning of these non-clinical statistics is open to doubt, as hospitals find ways of making their performance look good on paper, if not in practice. For example, Accident and Emergency (A and E) departments use triage nurses to assess new patients upon arrival, thereby keeping within their Patients' Charter target for the time taken to see a new patient initially. However, A and E departments may be slower in providing actual treatment. In 2003, a number of ambulance services were reprimanded for trying to make their response times appear better than they actually were by measuring the response time from when an ambulance set out, rather than when a call for help was received.

Even the whole value of publishing performance indicators for hospitals has been questioned by many. What does it mean if a consultant or a department has a long waiting time for appointments? Rather than being an indicator of inefficiency, could it be that a long waiting list is an indicator of a consultant who is very popular with patients? And doesn't the very fact that performance indicators are published push up users' expectations of service delivery, so that in the end they may become more dissatisfied even though actual performance has improved?

which backroom production people spend time at the sharp end of their business, in front of customers and learning about their needs.

- By appointing senior managers who have experience of marketing, marketing values may permeate throughout an organization in a top-down manner.

- The introduction of outside consultants is sometimes used as an external change agent. Consultants can impartially apply their previous experience of introducing a marketing culture to an organization.

- Getting top management to empathize with customers, to understand what they value in a brand, is generally not a problem for small businesses, but formal or informal processes, such as 'Management by Walking About', can help managers in larger organizations to gain the necessary understanding.

- A commonly used method of making management think in marketing terms is to introduce a formal market-oriented planning system. When proposing any initiative, managers must work through a list of market-related headings, such as an analysis of the competitive environment and an identification of market opportunities when developing their annual plans. This prevents a myopic focus on the product alone.

- It was noted above that building brand equity is a primary function of marketing management and is likely to be developed by using brand equity as a basis for rewarding managers.

The overall result of these activities should be to develop a customer-focused marketing culture within an organization. Within many organizations, it has proved very difficult to change cultural attitudes when the nature of an organization's operating environment has changed significantly, rendering the established culture a liability in terms of strategic marketing management. As an example, the cultural values of UK clearing banks have for a long time continued to be dominated by prudence and caution, when in some product areas, e.g. insurance sales, a more aggressive approach to marketing management is called for.

As an organization develops, it is essential that the dominant culture adapts. While a small business may quite successfully embrace a centralized power culture, continued growth may cause this culture to become a liability. There are many cases of businesses, such as the electronics company Amstrad, that have reportedly failed to make the cultural transition from small entrepreneur to large corporate entity. Similarly, the privatization of many public utilities called for a transformation from a bureaucratic role culture to a task-oriented culture (see Handy [6]).

■ Chapter summary and key linkages to other chapters

This chapter has provided a brief overview of marketing management. There are now many books about how marketing management can be improved, and this chapter has only been able to provide a summary of the main issues involved. Planning and control is central to marketing management. However, marketing plans do not develop by accident, so it is essential that an organization has a structure that facilitates the development of a strategy and its implementation. Marketing management cannot be separated from other business functions, especially finance, production management, and human resource management. Numerous approaches to improving the effectiveness of an organization's marketing implementation have been discussed, and the importance has been stressed of focusing around key processes that create customer value.

There are close links between this chapter and Chapter 6, where we looked at how companies can develop a sustainable advantage through the management of the marketing mix (Chapters 7–11). Information is crucial to management (Chapter 4) in order that it can build a better picture of its operating environment (Chapter 2). It is the task of a marketing manager to ensure sustainable competitive advantage through such means as new product development (Chapter 7) and the development of appropriate distribution channels (Chapter 9).

CASE STUDY

Marketing a tourism destination: an organizational challenge for local authorities

----

It is often said that a graduate who has been trained in the marketing department of one of the 'blue chip' fast moving consumer goods companies such as Procter & Gamble has handled the ultimate marketing challenge. It is often claimed that, if they can succeed in such a competitive market, they will be able to market anything. But could they market a tourist destination?

Local authorities have increasingly been taking an active role in promoting inward tourism to their area, in order to generate local economic development. The tourism 'product' being marketed is a combination of elements from both the private and public sectors—the private sector is responsible for tourist attractions operating to narrow commercial criteria, while the public sector has responsibility for infrastructure and planning policies that affect tourism. But how can local authorities with a traditional bureaucratic culture match the entrepreneurial skills of the private sector? Moreover, how do they avoid duplicating the efforts of the private sector they are helping to promote?

Tourism marketing management poses a number of problems for local authorities. Many of the facilities that impact on tourists' enjoyment of an area—such as car parking, cleanliness, planning, and conservation policies—have traditionally operated in a bureaucratic planning culture rather than a marketing culture. In marketing an area, local authorities are often constrained by bureaucratic culture and political pressure to meet the needs of their own residents as well as those of potential visitors. But against this, the visitors who the local authority is seeking to attract are becoming increasingly selective in the face of competition from many areas. In short, local authorities have had to become very customer-centred in their attempts to attract visitors. How does a marketing manager of a tourism destination handle the possible conflict that may occur between meeting the needs of tourists and those of residents? In some 'honeypot' tourism hotspots, such as Bath and Cambridge, reconciling the needs of both groups has proved to be a difficult task.

An approach adopted in many tourist areas is co-operation between all parties involved in tourism. In an attempt to combine the need for centrally administered marketing of an area with the dynamism of the private sector, local collaborative marketing ventures have become common in this field. Examples include the Birmingham Visitor and Convention Bureau and the Greater Glasgow and Clyde Valley Tourist Board. Co-operative tourism marketing organizations typically comprise district and county councils, regional development agencies, local landowners, hotel owners, and operators of tourism attractions. Partners contribute funds to support items of expenditure that in their own right might not yield a return, but could result in more tourist spending across the area as a whole. Most of these organizations have been incorporated as formal limited companies, providing an organizational structure that is separately accountable and is attractive to private-sector partners.

The creation of tourism development companies has helped to bring the dynamism of private-sector type organizations to a framework in which strategic marketing decisions and action programmes can be developed. Examples of successful collaboration include the development of conference centres, which bring together private-sector conference and hotel developers, transport operators, and local authorities. A local authority's objectives (such as creating employment or eliminating eyesores) can often be achieved more effectively by delivering its services—e.g. signposting, car park provision, and land use planning—within the framework of a marketing strategy developed jointly with the private sector. Having a strategic overall plan can be crucial to success—after all, if the local authority built a conference centre but the private sector did not build hotels to accommodate conference delegates, the chances of the conference centre's succeeding would be reduced.

The development of electronic commerce now offers new opportunities for collaboratively marketing tourism destinations. There is the potential to create 'virtual co-operation', whereby potential tourists can browse through websites of individual facilities at a destination and develop a coherent picture of the destination experience on offer. The creative linking of websites facilitates the profiling of enquiries in a way that allows potential tourists to develop their own package of experiences from a visit to a destination.

Case study review questions

1. Contrast the objectives of public and private-sector organizations that are involved in tourism.

2. Summarize the benefits of collaboration between public and private-sector organizations in the tourism sector.

3. Identify the main problems of collective marketing of a tourism destination, compared with the marketing of an individual hotel.

☐ CHAPTER REVIEW QUESTIONS

1. What is the difference between marketing planning and corporate planning? Should they be considered synonymous?

2. 'Mission statements are the result of senior managers' undertaking management development courses. They may have the language, but mission statements are invariably ignored by the very people who they are aimed at.' Is this a fair statement?

3.   Do you agree with the notion that a marketing department can actually be a barrier to the successful development of a marketing orientation? Give examples.

4.   What is the value of contingency planning? Identify one sector where the production of contingency plans is likely to have significant marketing benefits, and the factors that need to be taken into account.

5.   Every now and again management gurus develop new ideas for managing organizations, such as business process re-engineering and customer relationship management. Is there too much hype in such prescriptions?

6.   What are the main differences in implementing a market-oriented management structure within the public as opposed to the private service sector?

REFERENCES

[1]   Ambler, T. (1998), 'Why is Marketing not Measuring Up?' *Marketing*, 24 (September): 24–5.

[2]   Bateson, J. E. G. (1989), *Managing Services Marketing: text and readings*, 2nd edn. Forth Worth, Texas: Dryden Press.

[3]   Denton, D. K. (1990), 'Customer Focused Management'. *HR Magazine* (Lexington, Mass.), August: 62–7.

[4]   Drucker, P. (1973), *Management: tasks, responsibilities and practices*. New York: Harper & Row.

[5]   Gummesson, E. (2001), *Total Relationship Marketing*. Oxford: Butterworth-Heinemann.

[6]   Handy, C. (1994), *Understanding Organizations*, 4th edn. Harmondsworth: Penguin.

[7]   Levitt, T. (1960), 'Marketing Myopia', *Harvard Business Review*, 38(4): 45–56.

[8]   Lukas, B. A. and Maignan, I. (1996), 'Striving for Quality: the key role of internal and external customers'. *Journal of Market Focused Management*, 1: 175–97.

[9]   McDonald, M. (2002), *Marketing Plans: how to prepare them; how to use them*, 5th edn. Oxford: Butterworth-Heinemann.

[10] Peters, T. J., and Waterman, R. H. (1982), *In Search of Excellence: lessons from America's best run companies*. New York: Harper & Row.

[11] Reynoso, J. F. and Moores, B. (1996), 'Internal Relationships'. In F. Buttle, (ed.), *Relationship Marketing: theory and practice*. London: Paul Chapman, pp. 55–73.

[12] Varey, R. J. (1995), 'Internal Marketing: a review and some interdisciplinary research challenges'. *International Journal of Service Industry Management*, 6(1): 40–63.

[13] Porter, M. (1980), *Competitive strategy: Technique for analyzing industries and competitors*. Free Press: New York.

SUGGESTED FURTHER READING

There are many texts on the subject of marketing management which focus on how an organization can implement measures to respond to a changing external environment. The following are useful:

Baker, M. J. (2000), *Marketing Strategy and Management*, 3rd edn. Basingstoke: Palgrave Macmillan.

Doyle, P. (2001), *Marketing Management and Strategy*, 3rd edn. Englewood Cliffs, NJ: Prentice Hall.

Kotler, P. (2002), *Marketing Management: analysis, planning, implementation and control*, 11th edn. Englewood Cliffs, NJ: Prentice-Hall.

Piercy, N. (2001), *Market-Led Strategic Change*, 3rd edn. Oxford: Butterworth-Heinemann.

McDonald, M. (2002), *Marketing Plans*, 5th edn. Oxford: Butterworth-Heienemann.

USEFUL WEB LINKS

Visit the companion website to this book, with lots of interesting additional material and links for each chapter:
www.oup.com/uk/booksites/busecon

Chartered Institute of Marketing
www.cim.co.uk

British Institute of Management
www.inst-mgt.org.uk

Institute of Management and Administration (US source of business and management information)
www.ioma.com

Inc. magazine, Small Business Resource Index
www.inc.com/idx/idx_t_Sb.html

Strategy & Business: articles, book reviews, and special features for business leaders (sponsored by Booz Allen and Hamilton)
www.strategy-business.com

Manager's Daily: news and reports for management
www.dma.net/managers

A discussion group for academics engaged in research into what constitutes organizational effectiveness and how this may be achieved and maintained in contemporary business:
www.mailbase.ac.uk.lists.org-effectiveness

KEYWORDS

- **Contingency planning**
- **Control systems**
- **Corporate planning**
- **Entrepeneurship**
- **Internal markets**
- **Leadership**
- **Matrix organizations**
- **Mission statement**
- **Planning gap**
- **SMEs**
- **Strategic business units**

The marketing of services

CHAPTER OBJECTIVES

Services now form the dominant sector of most western economies, yet marketing theory still tends to be oriented towards the goods sector. The aim of this chapter is to identify the distinguishing characteristics of services and the effects these have on marketing. Key topics of intangibility, inseparability, variability, and perishability are introduced. It is noted that most products we buy have a combination of goods and services characteristics and it may be more appropriate to talk about a goods–service continuum than to make a clear distinction between the two. An extended marketing mix is developed, in which the importance of people management is emphasized.

Introduction

The literature on marketing theory and applications has been dominated by the manufactured goods sector. This is probably not surprising, because marketing in its modern form first took root in those manufacturing sectors that faced the greatest competition from the 1930s onwards. However, the service sector has continued to grow in industrialized economies where it now forms the dominant part of many national economies. In growing, the service sector has become more competitive and has taken on board the principles of marketing. Deregulation of many services and rising expectations of consumers have had a dramatic effect on marketing activities within the sector.

But can we simply apply the established body of marketing knowledge, which is based on manufactured goods, to the service sector? Is the marketing of services fundamentally different from the marketing of goods? Or is it just a special case of general marketing theory?

This chapter discusses the distinctive characteristics of services and the extent to which these call for a revision to the general principles of marketing. While many of the general principles can be applied to services, there are areas where a new set of tools needs to be developed. Of particular importance are the effects of service intangibility on buyers' decision-making processes, the effects of producing services 'live' in the presence of the consumer, and the crucial role played by an organization's employees in the total product offer.

The importance of the services sector

Although we have seen recent rapid growth in the service sector, the sector itself is not new. There are numerous biblical references to innkeepers, money lenders, and other service providers. Even the so-called 'Industrial Revolution' can more accurately be described as a service revolution, for it could not have taken place without the development of crucial service sectors. For example, without the development of railways, goods could not have been distributed from centralized factories to geographically dispersed consumers and many people would not have been able to get to work. Investment in new factories called for a banking system that could circulate funds at a national rather than a purely local level. A service sector emerged to meet the needs of manufacturing, including the needs of intermediaries who were essential for the distribution and transportation of manufacturers' goods to increasingly dispersed markets. Today, we continue to rely on services to exploit developments in the manufacturing sector.

There is little doubt that the service sector has become a dominant force in developed economies, accounting for about three-quarters of all employment in the USA, the UK, Canada, and Australia. Between 1970 and 1997, it is reported that the EU created about one and a half million new jobs per year in the service sector—twice the average for the rest of the economy (Eurostat [3]). There appears to be a close correlation between the level of economic development in an economy (as expressed by its GDP per capita) and the strength of its service sector. There is a two-way relationship between services and economic development.

Producer services help a country by providing inputs to production processes. Producer services have had a major impact on national economies, and many service industries have facilitated improved productivity elsewhere in the manufacturing and agricultural sectors. As an example, transport and distribution services have often had the effect of stimulating economic development at local and national levels (e.g. following the improvement of rail or road services). One reason why Russian agriculture has not been fully exploited has been the ineffective distribution system available to food producers.

Consumer services, on the other hand, consume wealth rather than create it. As national economies become more prosperous, we have a tendency to increase our consumption of a wide range of consumer services, such as holidays, entertainment, and eating out.

What are services?

It can be difficult to define just what is meant by a service because most products we buy contain a mixture of goods elements and service elements. A meal in a restaurant contains a combination of goods (the food) and service (the manner in which the food is served). Even apparently 'pure' goods such as timber often contain service elements (e.g. the service required in transporting timber from where it was produced to where a customer requires it).

Modern definitions of services focus on the fact that a service in itself produces no tangible output, although it may be instrumental in a process leading to the production of some tangible output. We can define a service as:

any activity or benefit exchanged between individuals or organizations which is essentially intangible and does not result in the ownership of anything. A service may exist in its own right or may form part of a tangible product.

In a more tongue-in-cheek manner, services have been described as 'anything which cannot be dropped on your foot'.

'Pure' services have a number of distinctive characteristics that differentiate them from goods and have implications for the way in which they are marketed. These characteristics are often described as intangibility, inseparability, variability, perishability, and the impossibility of being owned.

Intangibility

A pure service cannot be assessed using any of the physical senses. It is an abstraction which cannot be directly examined before it is purchased. A prospective purchaser of most goods is able to examine the goods for physical integrity, aesthetic appearance, taste, smell, etc. Many advertising claims relating to these tangible properties can be verified by inspection prior to purchase. By contrast, pure services have no tangible properties that can be used by consumers to verify advertising claims before the purchase is made. The intangible process characteristics that define services, such as reliability, personal care, attentiveness of staff, friendliness of staff, etc., can be verified only once a service has been purchased and consumed.

Measuring quality for services can be very different compared with goods. Goods generally have tangible benchmarks against which quality can be assessed (e.g. durability,

Figure 13.1 A holiday is a highly intangible product and this advert of Orlando Tourism Bureau emphasizes the fact that customers buy into a dream which cannot be directly assessed at the time of purchase. Consumers of services typically seek to trduce their risk by comsulting multiple sources of information, especially word of mouth recommendation from friends who have previously used the service. Orlando's many tourist facilities have a long history of providing high quality aattractions and customer service, giving rise to widespread word-of-mouth recommendation. However, it should not be forgotten that if any service company fails to deliver its promised dream, it would not be able to rely on future word of mouth recommendation (Reproduced with permission of Orlando Tourism Bureau)

reliability, taste). In the case of services, these benchmarks can often be defined only in the minds of consumers. So, while there may be little doubt that a car that does 40 miles per gallon of fuel is better than one that does only 30, the same quality judgement cannot be made between, say, a restaurant meal that lasts one hour and another that lasts two hours. In the latter case, the expectations of diners are crucial to an understanding of their perceptions of service quality, which may not be the same as the judgements of an outside observer.

Where goods form an important component of a service offer, many of the practices associated with conventional goods marketing can be applied to this part of the service offer. Restaurants represent a mix of tangibles and intangibles, and, in respect of the food element, fewer of the particular characteristics of services marketing are encountered. The presence of a tangible component gives customers a visible basis on which to judge quality. While some services (such as restaurants) are rich in such tangible cues, other services (e.g. life insurance) provide relatively little tangible evidence.

Intangibility has a number of important marketing implications. The lack of physical evidence that it implies increases the level of uncertainty a consumer faces when choosing between competing services. An important part of a services marketing programme will therefore involve reducing consumers' uncertainty by such means as adding physical evidence and the development of strong brands. It is interesting to note that pure goods and pure services tend to move in opposite directions in terms of their general approach to the issue of tangibility. While service marketers seek to add tangible evidence to their product, pure goods marketers often seek to augment their products by adding intangible elements such as after-sales service and improved distribution.

Inseparability

The production and consumption of a tangible good are two separate activities. Companies usually produce goods in one central location and then transport them to the place where customers most want to buy them. In this way, manufacturing companies can achieve economies of scale through centralized production and can maintain centralized quality control checks. They can also produce their goods at a time that is convenient to their factories and staff, then make them available to customers at times that are convenient to customers. Production and consumption are said to be separable. The consumption of a service, on the other hand, is said to be inseparable from its means of production. Producer and consumer must interact in order for the benefits of the service to be realized. Both must normally meet at a time and a place that is mutually convenient in order that the producer can directly pass on service benefits. In the extreme case of personal care services, the customer must be present during the entire production process. A surgeon, for example, cannot provide a service without the involvement of a patient. For services, marketing becomes a means of facilitating complex producer–consumer interaction, rather than merely a medium of exchange.

Figure 13.2 We are all familiar with buying clothing and shoes made in countries such as China and India where production costs are much lower. The production of goods in a low-cost country can be separated from their consumption in a high-income country. This opportunity for separation has not generally been possible for services, as the consumer and producer normally need to interact with each other. The development of telecommunications is allowing new opportunities for lessening the effects of service inseparability. Many service companies have located call centres in low-cost countries such as India, and customers may be quite unaware that their call is being answered several thousand miles away (Reproduced with permission of Iserve Systems Ltd)

Inseparability occurs whether the producer is human—as in the case of health care services—or a machine (e.g. a bank ATM machine). The service of the ATM machine can be realized only if the producer and consumer interact. In some cases, it has been possible geographically to separate service production and consumption, especially where there is a low level of personal contact. This has happened, for example, in the banking sector, where many banks have replaced local branches (where there is face-to-face interaction between producer and consumer) with centralized telephone call centres (where interaction takes place through the medium of the telephone) or internet banking.

Inseparability has a number of important marketing implications for services. To begin with, whereas goods are generally first produced, then offered for sale, and finally sold and consumed, inseparability causes this process to be modified for services. They are generally sold first, then produced and consumed simultaneously. Second, while the method of goods production is to a large extent (though by no means always) of little importance to the consumer, production processes are critical to the enjoyment of services.

In the case of goods, consumers are not a part of the process of production, and, in general, so long as the product they receive meets their expectations, they are satisfied. (However, there are exceptions—for example where the ethics of production methods cause concern, or where quality can be assessed only with a knowledge of production stages that are hidden from the consumer's view.) With services, the active participation of the customer in the production process makes the process as important as the end benefit. In some cases, an apparently slight change in service production methods may totally destroy the value of the service being provided. A person buying a ticket for a concert by Cliff Richard may derive no benefit at all from the concert if Richard has to cancel and the gig is performed by Ossie Osmond instead.

Variability

Most manufactured goods can now be produced with high standards of consistency. However, when asked about the consistency of services such as trains, restaurant meals, or legal advice, most people would probably say that they have experienced high levels of variability. For services, variability impacts upon customers not just in terms of outcomes, but also in terms of processes of production. It is the latter point that causes variability to pose a much greater problem for services than for goods. Because consumers are generally involved in the production process for a service at the same time as they consume it, it can be difficult to carry out monitoring and control to ensure consistent standards. The opportunity for pre-delivery inspection and rejection that is open to the goods manufacturer is not normally possible with services.

Variability in production standards is of greatest concern to service organizations where customers are highly involved in the production process, especially where production methods make it impractical to monitor service production. This is true of many labour-intensive personal services provided in a one-to-one situation, such as personal health care. Some services allow greater scope for quality control checks to be undertaken during the production process, allowing an organization to provide a consistently high level of service. This is especially true of machine-based services; for example, telecommunication services can typically operate with very low failure rates.

The tendency today is for equipment-based services to be regarded as less variable than those involving a high degree of personal intervention in the production process. Many service organizations have sought to reduce variability—and hence to build strong brands—by adopting equipment-based production methods. Replacements of human telephone operators with computerized voice systems and branch-based banking with internet banking are typical of this trend. Sometimes reduced personnel variability has been achieved by passing on part of the production process to consumers, in the way that self-service petrol filling stations are no longer dependent on the quality of service of forecourt staff.

The variability of service output can pose problems for brand building in services compared with tangible goods. For the latter it is usually relatively easy to incorporate monitoring and quality control procedures into production processes in order to ensure that a brand stands for a consistency of output. The service sector's attempts to reduce variability concentrate on methods used to select, train, motivate, and control personnel. In some cases, service offers have been simplified, jobs have been 'deskilled', and personnel replaced with machines in order to reduce human variability and hence build more consistent brands.

Perishability

Unlike most goods, services cannot be stored. Most goods manufacturers that are unable to sell their current output can carry forward stocks for future sale. The only significant costs are storage, financing, and the possibility of loss through wastage or obsolescence. By contrast, the producer of a service that cannot sell all of its output produced in the current period gets no chance to carry it forward for sale in a subsequent period. A train operator that offers seats on the 8.10 a.m. train from Leeds to Bradford cannot sell any empty seats once the train has departed: the service offer disappears, and spare seats cannot be stored to meet a surge in demand which may occur later in the day.

Very few services face a constant pattern of demand through time. Many show considerable variation, which could follow a daily (e.g. city centre sandwich bars at lunchtime), weekly (the Friday evening peak in demand for railway travel), seasonal (shops at Christmas time), cyclical (mortgages), or unpredictable pattern of demand (emergency building repair services following heavy storms).

The perishability of services results in greater attention having to be paid to the management of demand by trying to even out peaks and troughs in demand and by scheduling service production to follow this pattern as far as possible. It is not good enough to ensure that supply and demand are matched overall in the long term: they must

WHITEHEAD TRAVEL

LATE AVAILABILITY OFFERS

21 June Gran Canaria	14 nights H/B	£259
21 June Crete	7 nights B/B	£159
22 June Palma	7 nights B/B	£139
24 June Orlando Fly/Drive	14 nights	£339

All flights from Gatwick

Figure 13.3 **Services are instantly perishable, and when the capacity of a service process is not used, it is lost for ever.** A package holiday that is not sold by the departure date is lost for ever—the empty aircraft seat and hotel room cannot be stored for sale at a later date. Offers such as these last-minute deals emphasize the perishable nature of services

match for each minute and for each place that service is offered. Pricing and promotion are two of the tools commonly adopted to resolve demand and supply imbalances.

Impossibility of being owned

This feature is related to the characteristics of intangibility and perishability. In purchasing goods, buyers generally acquire titles to the goods in question and can subsequently do as they wish with them. On the other hand, when a service is performed, no ownership is transferred from the seller to the buyer. The buyer is merely buying the right to a service process, such as the use of a car park or an accountant's time. A distinction should be drawn between the inability to own the service act, and the rights that a buyer may acquire to have a service carried out at some time in the future. (A theatre gift voucher, for example, only gives rights to the service.)

The inability to own a service has implications for the design of distribution channels, so a wholesaler or retailer cannot take title, as is the case with goods. Instead, direct distribution methods are more common and, where intermediaries are used, they generally act as a co-producer with the service provider.

Goods and services compared

Most of the products we buy are a combination of goods and services. For example, although cars have traditionally been considered examples of pure goods, today most cars are sold with considerable service benefits, such as an extended warranty, a maintenance contract, or a financing facility. In fact, many car manufacturers now see themselves as service providers in which a lease contract provides all the services necessary to keep a car maintained, insured, financed, and replaced. The idea of a manufacturer selling a tangible item (the car) and then not having any dealings with the customer until he is ready to replace it is a rapidly disappearing approach to the marketing of cars. (See Case Study at the end of this chapter.)

Just as many pure goods may in reality be quite service-like, so many apparently pure services contain substantial goods elements. A package holiday may seem like a pure service, but it includes tangible elements in the form of the airplane, the hotel room, and the transfer coach, for example. This has led some people to argue that we do not really need a separate theory of marketing for services. In the words of Theodore Levitt,

there is no such thing as service industries. There are only industries where service components are greater or less than those of other industries. (Levitt [6])

Others have pointed to the distinctiveness of services, which makes the application of traditional marketing principles inappropriate. Examples of early work that sought to define the nature of services is provided by Gronroos [4], Lovelock [7], and Shostack [10].

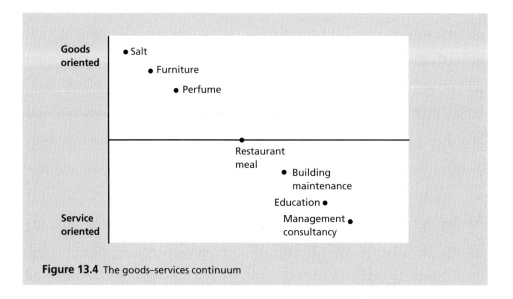

Figure 13.4 The goods–services continuum

Pure goods and pure services are hypothetical extremes, but they are nevertheless important to note because they help to define the distinctive characteristics of goods and services marketing. In between the extremes is a wide range of products which are a combination of tangible goods elements and intangible service elements. It is therefore common to talk about a goods–services continuum along which all products can be placed by reference to their service or goods dominance (see Figure 13.4).

The five characteristics of intangibility, inseparability, perishability, variability, and lack of ownership are not entirely exclusive to services, as they are shared by many manufactured goods. For example, on the subject of variability, there are some non-service industries—such as tropical fruits—that have difficulty in achieving high levels of consistent output, whereas some service industries such as car parks can achieve a consistent standard of service in terms of availability, cleanliness, etc. Similarly, many tangible goods share the problem of intangible services in being incapable of full examination before consumption. It is not normally possible, for instance, to judge the taste of a bottle of wine in a supermarket before it has been purchased and (at least partially) consumed. Figure 13.6 illustrates the points of convergence between goods and services.

Classifying services

Because the service sector accounts for about three-quarters of economic activity in developed countries, it is unlikely that one body of marketing theory will be applicable to all services, from a jobbing electrician to a multinational airline.

We deliver it. We plant it.

We email advice on it.

It's a wonder we don't come round

and tuck it in at night.

At Crocus, our trained gardeners will deliver* weekends, mornings or until 8 in the evening.
We'll even plant for you if you like. And after a fond farewell, we'll send your plants a
regular email to make sure they're alright.

*Service only available in certain parts of the country.

crocus.co.uk
GARDENERS BY NATURE

Figure 13.5 Plant growing has traditionally been firmly rooted in the horticultural sector. However, by recognizing trends in technology and social attitudes, this company has spotted a new opportunity to add services to its product offer. The company doesn't just grow and sell plants, but offers a complete service to busy people by delivering and planting them. It has embraced the new technology by e-mailing plant owners periodic advice about what they should be doing to keep their plants in top condition

Reproduced with permission of crocus.co.uk.

Intangibility	Goods are increasingly augmented with intangible services (e.g. insurance, credit facilities) Services are augmented with tangibles (e.g. staff uniforms, brochures)
Inseparability	Goods are increasingly produced in the presence of customers (e.g. while-you-wait tailoring) Services consumption is increasingly separated from production (e.g. telephone banking)
Perishability	Goods are now more likely to be supplied using 'just-in-time' principles of the service sector Tangible components of the service offer can be stored. Improved management of supply and demand patterns reduces problem of perishability.
Variability	Industrialization of services allows levels of reliability to be achieved that match those of goods
Lack of ownership	Goods increasingly comprise service elements that cannot be owned Services often comprise tangible elements that can be owned (e.g. a telephone 'calling card')

Figure 13.6 Points of convergence between goods and services

The goods sector has traditionally developed classifications to describe the marketing needs of different groups of goods. You may recall from Chapter 7 that terms such as fast-moving consumer goods, shopping goods, speciality goods, white goods, brown goods, etc., are widely used and convey a lot of information about the marketing requirements of products within a category, for example with respect to buying processes, methods of promotion, and distribution. Something similar is needed for the service sector.

Traditional production-based methods of classifying services are not particularly useful for marketers. Small guest houses and international hotels may fall within the same sector, but their marketing needs are very different. The international hotel may in fact share more in common with an airline in terms of customers' expectations and a peaked pattern of demand.

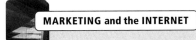

MARKETING and the INTERNET

New service sector in data processing emerges

Improvements in technology and changes in users' needs can transform a nation's service sector. A study of a number of less developed economies illustrates how a new service sector, data processing, has emerged in what have traditionally been largely agricultural economies.

Data processing emerged almost from nowhere during the 1980s and 1990s as organizations of all kinds found increasing need to enter data into computerized databases—records of customer sales, of services performed, details of rolling stock movements, to name but a few. Many organizations were just beginning to appreciate the huge amount of data they were letting slip by, instead of analysing it to build up customer databases or to analyse performance levels, etc. In the early days, most firms regarded this as a back room function that they could perform most cost effectively by using their own staff on their own premises. With time, an increasing volume of data to be processed and the growing sophistication of data analysis systems, many service companies emerged to take the burden of data processing off the client companies.

At first, most data processing companies operated close to their clients—closeness was demanded by the limitations of data communication channels. However, by the 1990s the rapid developments in telecommunications—especially the development of satellites and fibre optic links—allowed large volumes of data to be transmitted over long distances much more cheaply and reliably than ever before.

One company—US-based Saztec—operates data processing centres in the Philippines and includes the UK's Home Office among its customers. Its Philippines employees are reported to earn an average of $50 per month—one-fifth of the salary paid to the company's staff in Kansas. Staff turnover, at less than 1%, is much lower than the 35% annual rate at its Kansas base. Furthermore, the company is able to obtain a higher quality of output by the military style organization and control of its staff—something that would not be accepted in the USA.

Other countries have developed strong service sectors based on data processing, including Jamaica, which, in addition to exploiting its low labour costs, offers the advantages of a sophisticated infrastructure—such as satellite links—and generous tax incentives. Ireland, by contrast, exploited the fact that it has a relatively highly educated and English speaking workforce who earn less than their counterparts in the USA or the UK.

More recently, internet service providers have used skilled low-cost staff in less developed countries to establish customer service centres. Many companies such as AOL have established service support centres in the Indian city of Bangalore, where enquiries coming in via e-mail and telephone are handled. A customer in the UK may call a freephone number with an enquiry about her account and be unaware of the fact that the call is being routed to India. Users of the company's internet services will probably never know that much of the maintenance of its website is carried out a long way from home.

Western countries went through their service revolution many years ago. The development of the internet now allows less developed economies to strengthen their service sectors and thereby increase their GDP.

The following sections identify some of the more commonly used bases for classifying services. It should be noted that many of these bases derive from the five fundamental characteristics of services that were noted earlier.

Degree of intangibility

Intangibility goes to the heart of most definitions of services. It was noted earlier that intangibility has consequences for the way in which buyers perceive risk in a purchase decision. The task of providing evidence that a service will deliver its promises becomes more difficult where the service is highly intangible. As a classification device, degree of intangibility has many uses, and this will be returned to later in the context of the management of the services marketing mix.

Producer *v.* consumer services

Consumer services are provided for individuals who use up the service for their own enjoyment or benefit. No further economic benefit results from the consumption of the service. By contrast, producer services are bought by a business in order that it can produce something else of economic benefit. An industrial cleaning company may sell cleaning services to an airport operator in order that the latter can sell the services of clean terminal buildings to airline operators and their customers.

Status of the service within the total product offer

Many services exist to add value to the total product offer, for example where a goods manufacturer augments its core tangible product with additional service benefits such as after-sales warranties. At other times, the service is sold as a separate product which customers can purchase to add value to their own goods (a car valeting service, for instance, purchased to add to the resale value of a used car). A further group of services may add value to a product more fundamentally by making it available in the first place (e.g. distribution and financing services).

Extent of inseparability

Some services can be provided only in the presence of customers. For example, the production of personal care services cannot be separated from their consumption. Other services are better able to separate production from consumption—for example, a listener to a radio station does not need to interact with the staff of the radio station. Customer involvement in production processes is generally lower where the service is carried out on their possessions, rather than on their mind or body directly.

The marketing of highly inseparable services calls for great attention to the processes of production, with fewer opportunities for 'back-room' quality control checks before service delivery takes place.

Pattern of service delivery

At one extreme, some services are purchased only when they are needed as a series of one-off transactions. This is typical of low-value, undifferentiated services that may be bought on impulse or with little conscious search activity (e.g. taxis and snacks in cafes). It can also be true of specialized, high-value services that are purchased only as required. For example, funeral services are generally bought as one-off transactions only when needed.

By contrast, for some other services it is impractical to supply the service on a one-off basis because of the production methods involved—for instance, it is impractical to provide a telephone line to a house only when it is needed, so the line itself is supplied continuously—or where the benefits of a service are required continuously (e.g. insurance policies).

Extent of people orientation

By far the most important means by which consumers evaluate some services is the quality of the front-line staff who serve them; this is important for sectors as diverse as hairdressing, accountancy, and law. At the other extreme, many services can be delivered with very little human involvement—a pay-and-display car park involves minimal human input in the form of checking tickets and keeping the car park clean. The management and marketing of people-based services can be very different from those based on equipment.

Significance of the service to the purchaser

Some services are purchased frequently, are of low value, low involvement, are consumed very rapidly, and are likely to be purchased on impulse with very little pre-purchase activity. Such services may represent a very small proportion of the purchaser's total expenditure and correspond to the goods marketer's definition of fast-moving consumer goods (FMCGs). The casual purchase of a lottery ticket would fit into this category. At the other end of the scale, long-lasting services may be purchased infrequently, and when they are, the decision-making process takes longer and involves more people. Life insurance and package holidays fit into this category.

Marketable v. unmarketable services

Finally, it should be remembered that many services are still considered by some cultures to be unmarketable. Many government services are provided for the public benefit with no attempt made to charge users of the service. This can happen when it is impossible to exclude individuals or groups of individuals from benefiting from a service. (For example, it is not possible in practice for a local authority to charge individuals for the use of local footpaths.) Many of the services provided within private households (e.g. child care) are considered by many cultures to be unmarketable.

Multiple classifications

The great diversity of services have now been classified in a way that focuses on their marketing needs rather than on their dominant methods of production. It will be apparent that within any sector there are likely to be major sub-categories of services which have distinctive marketing needs, and which may share a lot with other sectors. This commonality of marketing needs has provided great opportunities for companies that have extended their product range into services that are basically similar in their marketing needs if not in their production methods. Many of the UK grocery retailers have considered that the way people open savings accounts is similar to the way that they select groceries, so have extended their marketing expertise by applying it to the savings and investment market.

Although a number of bases for classifying services have been presented in isolation, in practice, services like goods are classified by a number of criteria simultaneously. There have been several attempts to develop multi-dimensional approaches for identifying clusters of similar services.

🔲 An extended marketing mix for services

The marketing mix is not based on any theory, but on the need for marketing managers to break down their decision making into a number of identifiable and actionable headings. The familiar 4Ps marketing mix, firmly based on the needs of the manufactured goods sector, has given us the four familiar Ps of Product, Price, Promotion, and Place. These 4Ps have been found to be too limited in their application to services. Particular problems that limit their usefulness to services include the following.

- The intangible nature of services is overlooked in most analyses of the mix. For example, the product mix is frequently analysed in terms of tangible design properties which may not be relevant to a service. Similarly, physical distribution management may not be an important element of place mix decisions.

- The promotion mix of the traditional 4Ps fails to recognize the promotion of services that takes place at the point of consumption by the production personnel, unlike the situation with most physical goods, which are normally produced away from the consumer so that production personnel have no direct involvement in promotion to

MARKETING and SOCIAL RESPONSIBILITY

Clean and green services?

Service industries are often seen as 'clean' industries, good for the ecological environment. Compared with traditional manufacturing industries such as car production and chemical processing, we might think that financial services and tourism look very clean and benign to the ecological environment. But services can nevertheless have quite harmful impacts which consumers may be quite unaware of.

Governments in many parts of the world have tried to attract tourists to their area, believing that this is a much cleaner way of creating new employment than manufacturing industries. But consider the following ecological impacts of a typical holiday:

- Merely travelling to a tourist destination creates harmful pollutants in the atmosphere. The advent of budget airlines may have brought tourists flocking to previously underdeveloped areas, but an effect of increased flying is to release 'greenhouse gases' into the atmosphere. For example, it has been estimated that half a billion tonnes of carbon dioxide was emitted by aircraft into the atmosphere in 2002.

- Within destination resorts, development has led to the loss of many species of wildlife and many more have been threatened; for example, the breeding habits of the loggerhead turtle on the Greek island of Zakynthos has been threatened by intensive development of beaches for recreational purposes.

- The influx of tourists puts pressure on limited natural resources. In dry regions, the summertime arrival of tourists can put great pressure on water resources. Should local residents be rationed in order that tourists can have their towels washed each day?

- Tourists create rubbish which has to be dispose of in an environmentally sensitive manner. What happens to all of those fast food packages and discarded drinks cans?

Some tour operators have tried to recognize the potentially harmful impacts of their holidays. British Airways Holidays has drawn up a 'green list' of environmentally friendly hotels in the Caribbean. British Airways decided to follow a number of German tour operators by using a survey of 100 hotels carried out by the International Hotels Environment Initiative (IHEI) and the Caribbean Hotel Association. Thirteen hotels which were identified as having the best environmental practices, achieving at least a 75% 'pass rate' in key areas, were given an eco-logo in British Airways brochure.

British Airways may be following public sentiment, but will its eco-friendly labels significantly influence buyers' choices? Do most tourists really take much interest in the local ecological impacts of their holiday? Would most bargain-seeking holiday makers be prepared to pay even a small amount more in order to stay at an ecologically benign hotel?

the final consumer. For a bank clerk, hairdresser, or singer, the manner in which the service is produced is an essential element of the total promotion of the service.

- The price element overlooks the fact that many services are produced by the public sector with no price charged to the final consumer.

These weaknesses have resulted in a number of attempts to redefine a marketing mix for the service sector. The expansion by Booms and Bitner [2] provides a useful framework for the service sector. It should be stressed that this is not an empirically proven theory of services marketing, but an analysis of the decisions that services marketers take in developing services to satisfy customers' needs. In addition to the four traditional elements of the marketing mix, it is common to recognize the importance of People and Processes as additional elements. Booms and Bitner also talk about Physical evidence making up a seventh P.

Decisions on one element of the extended marketing mix can be made only by reference to other elements of the mix in order to give a sustainable product positioning. The importance attached to each element of the extended marketing mix will vary between services. In a highly automated service such as vending machine dispensing, the people element will be a less important element of the mix than a people-intensive business such as a restaurant.

A brief overview of the extended services marketing mix elements is given below. In the case of the four traditional Ps, emphasis is on distinguishing their application in a services rather than a goods context.

Products

Marketing mix management must recognize a number of significant differences between goods and services. In Chapter 7 a model was described comprising various levels of product definition. The model starts from the 'core' level (defining the basic needs that are satisfied by the product), and progresses through a 'tangible' level (the tangible manifestation of the product), to an 'augmented' level (the services that are added to the product). While this analysis is held to be true of products in general, the problems of inseparability and intangibility make application of the three generic levels of product offer less meaningful to the service offer. Instead, the product offer in respect of services can be more usefully analysed in terms of two components:

1. the core service, which represents the core benefit; and
2. the secondary service, which represents both the tangible and augmented product levels.

The secondary service can be best understood in terms of the manner in which a service is delivered. For example, Little Chef and Brewers Fayre restaurants both satisfy the same basic need for fast, economical, hygienic food, but they do so in differing ways. This is reflected in different procedures for taking and delivering orders, the differences in menus, and the ambience of the restaurants.

Services tend to be relatively easy to copy and cannot generally benefit from patent protection, as is often the case with goods. New product development often occurs in

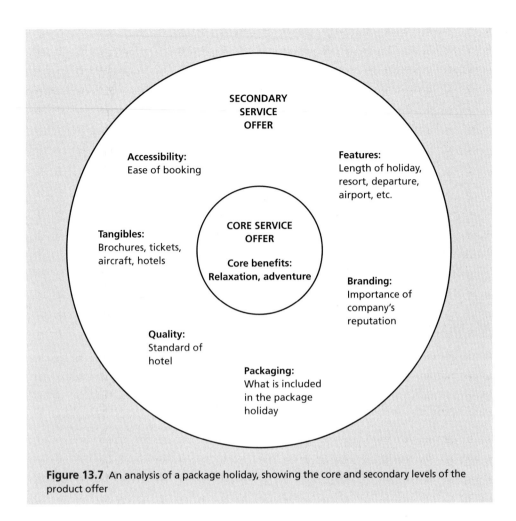

Figure 13.7 An analysis of a package holiday, showing the core and secondary levels of the product offer

an incremental fashion, with a lot of variants of a basic service. The proliferation of mortgage products by a building society, all with slightly differing terms and conditions but basically similar in their function, is an example of this.

Pricing

A number of points of difference with respect to services pricing must be noted here.

- The inseparable nature of services makes the possibilities for price discrimination between different groups of users much greater than is usually the case with most manufactured goods, which can easily be purchased by one person, stored, and sold to another person.

- A second difference between goods and services pricing is based on the high level of fixed costs that many service providers experience. The marginal cost of one additional telephone call, one additional seat on an airplane, or one additional place in a cinema is often very low. This can give service suppliers a lot of scope for charging different prices for what is basically a similar product offer.

- In the absence of tangible evidence, the price alone of a service may be a very important indicator of quality. (For example, you might presume that a hairdresser charging £20 is better than one charging £10.)

- Services are more likely than goods to be made available in distorted markets, or in circumstances where no market exists at all. Public services such as museums and schools that have sought to adopt marketing principles often do not have any control over the price element of the marketing mix. The reward for attracting more visitors to a museum or pupils to a school may be additional centrally derived grants, rather than income received directly from the users of the service.

Promotion

Although the principles of communication discussed in Chapter 10 are similar for goods and services, a number of distinctive promotional needs of services can be identified, deriving from the distinguishing characteristics of services. The following are particularly important.

- The intangible nature of the service offer often results in consumers perceiving a high level of risk in the buying process, which promotion must seek to overcome. A number of methods are commonly used to remedy this, including the development of strong brands; encouragement of word-of-mouth recommendation; promotion of trial usage of a service; and the use of credible message sources in promotion (especially through public relations activity).

- Promotion of a service offer cannot generally be isolated from promotion of the service *provider*. Customers cannot sensibly evaluate many intangible, high perceived risk services, such as pensions and insurance policies, without knowing the identity of the service provider. In many cases the service may be difficult to comprehend in any case (this is certainly true of pensions for most people), so promotion of the service provider becomes far more important than promotion of individual service offers.

- Visible production processes, especially service personnel, become an important element of the promotion effort. Where service production processes are inseparable from their consumption, new opportunities are provided for promoting a service. Front-line staff can become sales people for an organization. The service outlet can become a billboard that people see as they pass by.

- The intangible nature of services and the heightened possibilities for fraud result in their promotion being generally more constrained by legal and voluntary controls than is the case with goods. Financial services and overseas holidays are two examples of service industries with extensive voluntary and statutory limitations on promotion.

Place

Decisions concerning place refer to the ease of access that potential customers have to a service. For services, it is more appropriate to talk about *accessibility*, rather than place, as a mix element.

The inseparability of services makes the task of passing on service benefits much more complex than is the case with manufactured goods. Inseparability implies that services are consumed at the point of production; in other words, a service cannot be produced by one person in one place and handled by other people to make it available to customers in other places. A service cannot therefore be produced where costs are lowest and sold where demand is greatest—customer accessibility must be designed into the service production system.

Place decisions can involve physical location decisions (as in deciding where to place a hotel), decisions about which intermediaries to use in making a service accessible to a consumer (e.g. whether a tour operator uses travel agents or sells its holidays direct to customers), and non-locational decisions (such as the use of internet delivery systems). For pure services, decisions about how physically to move a good are of little strategic relevance. However, most services involve the movement of goods in some form. These can be materials necessary to produce a service (such as travel brochures and fast food packaging material), or the service can have as its sole purpose the movement of goods (e.g. road haulage, plant hire).

People

For most services, people are a vital element of the marketing mix. It can be almost a cliché to say that for some businesses the employees *are* the business—if these are taken away, the organization is left with very few assets with which it can seek to gain competitive advantage in meeting customers' needs. For some organizations, the management of personnel can be seen as just one other asset to be managed. For others, human resource management is so central to the activities of the organization that it cannot be seen as a separate activity.

Where production can be separated from consumption—as is the case with most manufactured goods—management can usually take measures to reduce the direct effect of people on the final output as received by customers. In service industries, all employees are what Gummeson [5] has called 'part time marketers', in that their actions have a much more direct effect on the output received by customers.

Figure 13.8 In labour-intensive industries where employees must carry out their tasks 'live' in front of customers, the performance of employees can have a major impact on service quality. In this advertisement, British Airways stresses the importance of the 'people' element of its marketing mix in giving it a competitive advantage
Reproduced with permission of British Airways plc.

People planning in its widest sense has impacts on a firm's service offer in three main ways.

1. Most service production processes require the service organization's own personnel to provide significant inputs to the service production process, both at the front-line point of delivery and in those parts of the production process that are relatively re-moved from the final consumer. In the case of many one-to-one personal services, the service provider's own personnel constitute by far the most important element of the total service offering.

2. Many service processes require the active involvement of consumers of the service, and consumers therefore become involved as co-producers of the service. At its sim-plest, this can involve consumers' merely presenting themselves or their objects to the service provider in order for the service to be provided—for example, a customer might deliver her car to the garage rather than have it collected by the garage. In the

case of services performed on the body or mind, the consumer must necessarily be designed into the production process.

3. Other people who simultaneously consume a mass-produced service can affect the benefits an individual receives from the service in a number of ways. First, the characteristics of other users of a service can affect the image of the service (in much the same way as owners of certain brands of goods can lend them some degree of 'snob' appeal). In this way, a nightclub can build up an exclusive image on account of the high-spending, high-profile users who patronize it. Second, the presence of other consumers in the service production–delivery process means that the final quality of the service that any customer receives is dependent on the performance of other consumers. In effect, the *other* customers become co-producers of the service offering. Fellow consumers often have an important role to play in enhancing the quality of the service offering, as where a full house in a theatre creates an atmosphere for all customers to enjoy. On other occasions, fellow consumers can contribute negatively to the service production process, as where rowdy behaviour in a pub or smoking in a restaurant detracts from the enjoyment of an event for other customers.

Processes

Production processes are usually of little concern to consumers of manufactured goods, but they can be of critical concern to consumers of 'high contact' services where the consumer can be seen as a co-producer of the service. Customers of a restaurant can be deeply affected by the manner in which staff serve them and the amount of waiting that is involved during the production process. Issues arise as to the boundary between the producer and consumer in terms of the allocation of production functions—for example, a restaurant might require customers to collect their meals from a counter, or to clear away their own rubbish. With services, a clear distinction cannot be made between marketing and operations management.

A lot of attention has gone into the study of 'service encounters', defined by Shostack [11] as 'a period of time during which a consumer directly interacts with a service'. Among the multiplicity of service encounters, some will be crucial to successful completion of the service delivery process. These are often referred to as critical incidents and have been defined by Bitner, Booms, and Tetreault [1] as 'specific interactions between customers and service firm employees that are especially satisfying or especially dissatisfying'. While their definition focuses on the role of personnel in critical incidents, they can also arise as a result of interaction with the service provider's equipment.

Where service production processes are complex and involve multiple service encounters, it is important for an organization to gain a holistic view of how the elements of the service relate to each other. 'Blueprinting' is a graphical approach proposed by

Shostack [10], designed to overcome problems that occur where a new service is launched without adequate identification of the necessary support functions. A customer blueprint has three main elements:

1. All of the principal functions required to make and distribute a service are identified, along with the responsible company unit or personnel.

2. Timing and sequencing relationships among the functions are depicted graphically.

3. For each function, acceptable tolerances are identified in terms of the variation from standard that can be tolerated without adversely affecting customers' perception of quality.

Services are, in general, very labour intensive, and they have not witnessed the major productivity increases seen in many manufacturing industries. Sometimes service processes have been 'industrialized' and deskilled by the process of simplifying employees' tasks and reducing their scope for judgement and error.

As real labour costs have increased and service markets become more competitive, many service organizations have sought to pass on a greater part of the production process to their customers in order to try to retain price competitiveness. At first, customers' expectations may hinder this process, but productivity savings often result from one segment taking on additional responsibilities in return for lower prices. This then becomes the norm for other follower segments. Examples where the boundary has been redefined to include greater production by the customer include supermarkets that have replaced checkout operators with customer-operated scanners, and restaurants where waiter service has been replaced with self-service.

While service production boundaries have generally been pushed out to involve consumers more fully in the production process, some service organizations have identified segments that are prepared to pay higher prices in order to relieve themselves of parts of their co-production responsibilities. Examples include fast food firms that avoid the need for customers to come to their outlet by offering a delivery service.

Physical evidence

The intangible nature of a service means that potential customers are unable to judge a service before it is consumed, increasing the riskiness of a purchase decision. An important element of marketing planning is therefore to reduce this level of risk by offering tangible evidence of the promised service delivery. This evidence can take a number of forms. At its simplest, a brochure can describe and give pictures of important elements of the service product—a holiday brochure gives pictorial evidence of hotels and resorts for this purpose. The appearance of staff can give evidence about the nature of a service—a tidily dressed ticket clerk for an airline gives some indication that the airline operation as a whole is run with care and attention. Buildings are frequently used to give evidence of service characteristics. Fast food and photo processing outlets often use red and yellow colour schemes to convey an image of speedy service.

■ Chapter summary and linkages to other chapters

The service sector is now a dominant part of the economies of most developed countries. However, defining just what is meant by a service has caused some debate, and this chapter has reviewed some of the bases for classifying services into categories that are useful for the purposes of marketing management. Pure services are distinguished by the characteristics of intangibility, inseparability, perishability, variability, and a lack of ownership. Increasingly, however, goods and services are converging in terms of these characteristics. Few products can be described as pure goods or pure services—most are a combination of the two. There has been considerable debate about whether a new set of principles of marketing is required to understand services, or whether the established basic principles merely need adapting to the needs of services. The traditional marketing mix of the 4Ps which has been described in Chapters 7–11 has been found to be inadequate for managers in the service sector, and this chapter has discussed an alternative extended marketing mix of 7Ps, which also recognizes the importance of personnel, processes and physical evidence.

▢ KEY PRINCIPLES OF MARKETING

- Pure services are intangible, making assessment of product attributes difficult prior to consumption.
- The production of services cannot generally be separated from their consumption.
- Services are instantly perishable—stocks of services cannot be stored.
- All products contain a combination of goods and services attributes.

CASE STUDY

Ford cars go in for a service

To many people, cars come pretty close to the goods-dominant extreme of a goods–services continuum. They are produced in factories from the combination of thousands of components, and to most people the physical properties of a car can readily be assessed. But recent experience from the car sector suggests that car manufacturers may now be rather more enthusiastic to describe themselves as service-oriented companies.

The days are long gone when a car manufacturer would sell a car on the strength of its design features and then forget about the customer until the time came to replace the car three (or more) years later. Car manufacturers have realized that car buyers seek more than the tangible offering—important though that is. Over time, they have moved increasingly into services in an attempt to gain a larger share of car buyers' wallets.

In the UK, Ford has led the way in many aspects of this increasing service orientation. It saw an opportunity in the 1970s, with the liberalization of consumer credit regulations, to offer car buyers loan facilities with which to make their car purchase. Not only did this make it easier for middle-income groups to buy its cars, it also allowed Ford to retain the margins that would otherwise have gone to banks, which were the main alternative source of car loan finance. Ford Motor Credit has become a licensed credit broker and a major profit centre within the company.

The next major attempt to gain a greater share of car buyers' wallets came through offering extended warranties on the cars it sold. Traditionally, new cars had come with just 12 months' warranty, but Ford realized that many buyers wanted to buy peace of mind in the assurance that they were not going to face unexpected repair bills after their initial warranty had expired. Increased competition from Japanese importers, and the improving reliability of Ford's new cars, encouraged this development.

By the mid-1990s, Ford came round to the view that many of its customers were buying mobility services, rather than a car *per se*. So it came up with schemes where customers paid a small deposit, followed by a fixed amount per month, in return for which they received comprehensive finance and warranty facilities; in addition, it promised that the company would take back the car after three years and replace it with a new one. Marketed under the 'Options' brand name, Ford was soon selling nearly half of its new cars to private buyers using this method. Over time the scheme was developed to include facilities for maintaining and insuring the car.

Repairs and maintenance have always been important in the car sector, but manufacturers tended to lose out on much of the benefits of this because of a fragmented dealership network. Separate customer databases for maintenance and new car sales often did not meet, and Ford found that it had very little direct communication with the people who had bought its cars. By the 1990s the dealership network was becoming more closely integrated with Ford's operations, and new opportunities were seized for keeping new car buyers within the Ford dealership system. Recent buyers could be alerted to new services available at local dealers, using a database managed centrally by Ford. Numerous initiatives were launched, such as Ford's own mobile phone service. Ford sought to make it easy for customers to get back on the road when their own cars were taken in for servicing, so the provision of car hire facilities contributed to the service ethos. In 1996 the company linked up with Barclaycard to offer a Ford branded credit card, and Ford then found itself providing a service to its customers that was quite removed from the tangible cars it sold (although points that accrued through use of the card could be used to reduce the price of a new Ford car).

By 2000, volume car manufacturers had ceased to make big profits in the UK. In 2002, Ford, with 18% of the market, made just £8 million in profits on its European operations. Falling profit margins on the sale of new cars were partly offset by profits made on service-based activities. In the same year, the company made £1.38 billion worldwide from its credit arm, which arranged finance for about 40% of all new cars that it sold. But adding services is not a guaranteed route to increased profitability. Ford's acquisition of the KwikFit tyre fitting chain failed to be a success, and it was later sold back to its founder at a price well below what Ford had paid for it. Could this have been a warning that Ford's core competencies lie in engineering and design, rather than in running labour-intensive service operations?

Case study review questions

1. Given the evidence of Ford, is it still appropriate to talk about the goods and services sectors being quite distinctive?

2. What business is Ford in? What business should it be in?

3. Discuss the view that Ford should do what it is good at—designing cars—and leave services to other companies.

CHAPTER REVIEW QUESTIONS

1. With the service sector now accounting for over three-quarters of GDP in western countries, is it still sensible to talk about services as a special case of marketing, rather than treating goods as the special case?

2. Critically assess the effects of service inseparability on marketing management.

3. How can you explain the fact that some countries (e.g. the USA) seem to be particularly good at producing services, whereas others with a similar level of education and GDP (e.g. Germany) are viewed as relatively inferior? Does national culture affect the performance of service organizations?

4. Many in the UK have associated service with servitude. Is there any continuing basis for regarding services as somehow a second-class type of activity?

5. Critically examine the advantages and disadvantages, to a company producing packaging machinery for the food industry, of its recruiting a marketing manager whose experience has been in service sector companies.

6. Discuss the view that the extended marketing mix of seven 'P's may go some way towards overcoming shortcomings of the traditional marketing mix, but is still unsuitable compared with a holistic customer-focused approach which starts from the needs of the customer, rather than the marketing agenda of the supplier.

REFERENCES

[1] Bitner, M. J., Booms, B. H., and Tetreault, M. S. (1990), 'The Service Encounter: diagnosing favorable and unfavorable incidents'. *Journal of Marketing*, 54(January): 71–84.

[2] Booms, B. H. and Bitner, M. J. (1981), 'Marketing Strategies and Organization Structures for Service Firms'. In J. H. Donnelly and W. R. George (eds.), *Marketing of Services*. Chicago: American Marketing Association, pp. 51–67.

[3] Eurostat (1998), *Services in Europe: key figures*. Luxembourg: Office for Official Publications of the European Communities.

[4] Gronroos, C. (1978), 'A Service Oriented Approach to Marketing of Services'. *European Journal of Marketing*, 12(8): 588–601.

[5] Gummeson, E. (2001), *Total Relationship Marketing*. Oxford: Butterworth-Heinemann.

[6] Levitt, T. (1972), 'Production Line Approach to Service'. *Harvard Business Review*, 50(September/October): 41–52.

[7] Lovelock, C. (1981), 'Why Marketing Needs to be Different for Services'. In J. H. Donnelly and W. R. George (eds.), *Marketing of Services*. Chicago: American Marketing Association.

[8] Sasser, W. E., Olsen, R. P., and Wyckoff, D. D. (1978), *Management of Service Operations: texts, cases, readings.* Boston: Allyn & Bacon.

[9] Shostack, G. L. (1977), 'Breaking Free from Product Marketing'. *Journal of Marketing*, 41: 73–80.

[10] Shostack, G. L. (1984), 'Designing Services that Deliver'. *Harvard Business Review*, January/February: 133–9.

[11] Shostack, G. L. (1985), 'Planning the Service Encounter'. In J. A. Czepiel, M. R. Solomon, and C. F. Suprenant (eds.), *The Service Encounter*. Lexington, Mass.: Lexington Books, pp. 243–54.

SUGGESTED FURTHER READING

There are now numerous texts which deal specifically with the marketing of services and the following are among recent works which provide a comprehensive coverage.

Palmer, A. (2001), *Principles of Services Marketing*, 3rd edn. Maidenhead, Berks: McGraw-Hill.

Lovelock, C., Lewis, B., and Vandermerwe, S. (1999), *Services Marketing*. Hemel Hempstead: Prentice-Hall.

Zeithamal, V., and Bitner, J. (2002), *Services Marketing*. New York: McGraw-Hill.

A number of articles appeared towards the end of the 1970s seeking to identify the nature of services and their distinctive marketing needs. The articles by Lovelock (1981), Sasser, Olsen, and Wyckoff (1978), and Shostack (1977) referred to above are worth revisiting. In addition, the following are still worth reading because they establish many of the basic principles of services marketing:

Bateson, J. (1977), 'Do We Need Service Marketing?' In *Marketing Consumer Services: New Insights*, Report 77–115. Boston: Marketing Science Institute.

Berry, L. L. (1980), 'Service Marketing is Different'. *Business*, 30(3): 24–9.

Levitt, T. (1981), 'Marketing Intangible Products and Product Intangibles'. *Harvard Business Review*, 59: 95–102.

Zeithamal, V. A. (1981), 'How Consumers Evaluation Processes Differ between Goods and Services'. In J. H. Donnelly and W. R. George (eds.), *Marketing of Services*. Chicago: American Marketing Association, pp. 186–90.

A number of these articles can be found in the following books of readings:

Bateson, J. and Hoffman, K. D. (1999), *Managing Services Marketing: text and readings*. Hinsdale, Ill.: Dryden Press.

Gabbott, M. and Hogg, G. (1997), *Contemporary Services Marketing Management: a reader.* London: Dryden Press.

USEFUL WEB LINKS

Visit the companion website to this book, with lots of interesting additional material and links for each chapter:

www.oup.com/uk/booksites/busecon

A forum to discuss research, trends, and best practices for excellence in customer service. List members are encouraged to discuss practical business issues as well as academic research:

www.mailbase.ac.uk/lists/customer-service

KEYWORDS

- **Blueprinting**
- **Critical incidents**
- **Inseparability**
- **Intangibility**
- **Perishability**
- **Service encounter**

14

Global marketing

CHAPTER OBJECTIVES

Markets are becoming increasingly global, and the aim of this chapter is to understand the main challenges facing a company setting out to develop foreign markets. The chapter begins by discussing in general terms the reasons why international trade takes place. For a company that has decided to expand overseas, careful market analysis is necessary to avoid failure. A product may need to be adapted to suit the needs of a local market. Distribution is crucial, and this chapter discusses alternative approaches to gaining access to customers in foreign markets.

Introduction

Few firms can afford to think of marketing purely in terms of their domestic market. To survive and prosper, they must increasingly look to the world as their market. Foreign countries pose opportunities as well as threats. The opportunities for a firm come from its being able to sell its products in a market where it may have a competitive advantage over domestic producers. The problems arise where those foreign producers possess competitive advantages that challenge a firm in its own domestic market.

The global marketing environment is changing rapidly, and understanding that environment calls for a great amount of research. The impact of improving international communications and cultural convergence are just two dynamic factors at work in shaping the global marketing environment. The failure of a company to understand these dynamic forces has often resulted in its lack of success in seeking to exploit foreign markets, as the following examples illustrate.

- British Airways (BA) failed in its attempts to enter the North American market through its investment in the ailing airline USAir. BA had difficulties in overcoming trade union objections to changes in working practices, among other things, which led the company eventually to pull out of its involvement with USAir.

- The mobile phone company MM02 invested over £1.5 billion in the Dutch mobile phone operator Telfort but failed to achieve higher than fifth ranking in the Dutch market. In April 2003 the company admitted defeat and sold the entire Dutch operation for just £16 million.

- Even the fast food retailer McDonald's initially failed to make profits when it entered the UK market in the 1970s and had to adjust its format rapidly in order to achieve profitability.

New challenges face the international marketer. According to Naomi Klein [5], Nike, Shell, Wal-Mart, Microsoft, and McDonald's have become metaphors for a global economic system gone awry, evidenced by growing concern about the pay and conditions of Third World workers. Klein believes that brands and their multinational owners, rather than governments, will increasingly become the target for activists.

For firms that persevere, the benefits of developing international markets can be a quite significant contribution to a company's overall profitability. Consider the following cases.

- Although McDonald's may have had difficulties in the early stages of developing many of its foreign markets, these markets now account for the bulk of the company's sales turnover and profits. Had it confined itself to its domestic American market, saturation and increased levels of competition within that market would have severely limited its future profit growth.

- The German yogurt brand Müller was little known in the UK a decade ago, but by successfully exploiting a market niche and rapidly developing its product portfolio, it has now become the leading yoghurt brand in Britain.

- The retailer Tesco has steadily developed markets in eastern Europe and the Far East, and although profits were slow to begin with, overseas expansion has lessened the company's dependence on the increasingly saturated UK market.

Fundamentally, the task of marketing management in foreign markets is similar to the task in domestic markets. Customers' needs remain the driving force of marketing efforts and a company promotes the benefits to customers of buying its products, which are produced as efficiently as possible, distributed through the most appropriate channels, and priced according to local market conditions. The major challenge to exporting companies lies in sensitively adapting marketing strategies that have worked at home to the needs of foreign markets whose environments may be totally different from anything previously experienced. 'Global strength and local adaptability' form the basis of many firms' mission statements in relation to foreign markets.

This chapter begins by exploring the reasons why firms should seek to develop foreign markets in the first place. Once a firm has decided to operate at an international rather than a local level, it must go about assessing possible markets, and the bases for such assessments are discussed. If it decides to enter a market, a firm must consider how its product offer might need to be adapted to meet local sensitivities. Most firms enter international markets with the help of partners of some kind, and this chapter concludes with a discussion of market entry strategies.

Why export?

There is clear evidence that the volume and value of international trade have been rising in recent years faster than domestic growth. Taking the UK as an example, while the value of GDP increased by 21% between 1995 and 2002, the value of exports increased by 31%. This growth can be understood from two perspectives: from the perspective of national economies, and from that of individual trading organizations.

National reasons for trade occurring

From the perspective of national economies, there are many reasons for the increasing importance of international trade.

- Goods and services are traded between economies in order to exploit comparative cost advantages. This means that an economy will export those goods and services that it is particularly well suited to producing, and will import those for which another country has an advantage. A simple example can illustrate this point. Imagine two countries, country A which has ideal conditions for the mining of minerals but a climate that is inhospitable to agriculture, and country B, which is ideally suited for agriculture, but has mineral resources that are expensive to exploit. It would make little economic sense for country A to try to develop its agricultural sector when its output would be much more expensive than for it to buy from country B. Likewise, it may be uneconomic for country B to develop its mining industry. In both cases, it would almost certainly be better for each country to concentrate on what it is good at producing, and to export the surplus in exchange for goods and services that other countries can produce more efficiently.

- Although the theory of comparative cost advantage sounds fine in principle, many countries try to protect their own industries, however inefficient they are, against foreign competition with tariff barriers. The removal of many restrictions on international trade (such as the creation of the Single European Market) has allowed countries to exploit their comparative cost advantages. Nevertheless, many distortions to international trade remain, especially concerning agricultural products.

- Rising disposable incomes have resulted in greater consumption of many types of goods and services that can only be provided by foreign suppliers—for example overseas tourism and the consumption of exotic fruit and vegetables. (On the other hand, many developing economies that previously imported specialist goods and services can now produce these items domestically.)

- Homogenization of international market segments has resulted from cultural convergence, which itself has been encouraged by improved communications and increasing levels of overseas travel. Combined with the decline in trade barriers, convergence of cultural attitudes towards many products has allowed many companies to regard parts of their foreign markets as though they are part of their domestic market.

Firms' reasons for developing foreign trade

For an individual company, the development of foreign markets can be attractive for a number of reasons. These can be analysed in terms of 'pull' factors, based on the attractiveness of a potential foreign market, and 'push' factors, which make an organization's domestic market appear less attractive.

- Foreign markets represent new market segments which a firm may be able to serve with its existing range of products. In this way, a company can stick to making products that it is good at.

- By expanding overseas, a company that has developed a strong brand can stretch the coverage of that brand. By developing in a foreign market, the company will start with the advantage that some visitors from its domestic market will already understand what the brand stands for. Similarly, for residents of the new market, many may have already become familiar with the brand during visits to the manufacturer's home market. In short, there are economies of scale in promoting a brand in multiple markets simultaneously.

- Saturation of its domestic market can force a company to seek foreign markets. Saturation can come about where a product reaches the maturity stage of its life-cycle in the domestic market, while being at a much earlier stage of the cycle in less developed foreign markets. As an example of this, the market for fast food restaurants is approaching saturation in a number of western markets—especially the USA—but fast food represents relatively new opportunities in many eastern European countries that are in the early stages of development.

- Spreading risk is an important motivation for foreign expansion, and can allow a company to reduce its dependence on one geographical market.

- The nature of a product may require an organization to become active in a foreign market. In the case of scheduled international air services, an airline flying an overseas route will inevitably become involved in marketing at the foreign end of its routes.

- Some companies supply goods and services to business buyers who themselves operate internationally. Such large customers may demand that one single supplier meets their needs in all of the international markets in which they operate. This means that a supplying company has to become involved in international trade. As an example, many multinational businesses seek to engage an advertising agency that can organize a global campaign to launch in all of their international markets.

- There are also many cases where private consumers demand that goods and services be internationally available. An example is the car hire business, where customers often need to be able to book a hire car in one country for collection and use in another. To succeed in attracting these customers, car hire companies need to operate internationally.

- Some products are highly specialized, and the domestic market is too small to allow economies of scale to be exploited. Foreign markets must be exploited in order to achieve a critical mass which allows a competitive market positioning. Aircraft engine maintenance and oil exploration services fall into this category.

- A company may have developed a product that is not suited to its domestic market, so that exporting is the only option for exploiting the product. As an example, domestic legislation may make the market for drugs, alcohol, or tobacco related products less attractive than foreign markets where more liberal legislation exists.

▪ A note on exporting of services

Export of manufactured goods can be represented by stocks of goods moving in one direction, and payment (in cash or in goods) moving in the other. However, the intangible nature of most services gives a different meaning to the export of services. Any analysis of international trade in services is complicated by the diverse nature of producer–supplier interaction, stemming from the inseparability of service production/ consumption processes.

International trade statistics for services hide the fact that trade can take a number of forms. Sometimes credits (or 'exports') are earned by customers from overseas travelling to an organization's domestic market in order to consume a service (e.g. a foreign patient visiting a doctor in the UK). On other occasions credits are earned by domestic producers taking their production processes to customers in foreign markets (e.g. a builder travelling to do a job in a foreign country). Sometimes production and consumption of services can be separated, as in the case of electronic information services, avoiding the need for buyer and seller to meet for international trade to occur.

MARKETING and SOCIAL RESPONSIBILITY

Saturated burgers for less saturated markets

A saturated domestic market is often the spur for companies to seek new foreign markets. But is there a moral case against companies seeking to promote a western style of consumption in countries with well-established and sustainable life-styles?

Cigarette companies have attracted criticism by trying to make up for falling cigarette sales in the west by developing the emerging markets of Asia. Fast food companies have stepped up their efforts to develop new foreign markets as western markets for fast food have become saturated. Is it responsible to promote burgers that are high in saturated fats to people whose diets are inherently healthier? Is it right that fast food companies should develop low-fat burgers for the American market, partly out of fear of litigation, while selling higher-fat burgers to less developed countries, where legislation and consumers' awareness of health issues are more lax? Defenders of fast food companies point to the fact that they are providing hygienic food prepared in conditions that may be far superior to the norm in many developing countries. They have offered jobs to individuals which can be the envy of their peer groups. Should the solution be greater education of consumers in healthy eating, rather than more regulation? Is greater education a realistic prospect in a culture where fast food has become a cultural icon?

■ Analysing foreign marketing opportunities

Foreign markets can present very different opportunities and threats compared with those a company has been used to in its domestic market. Before a detailed market analysis is undertaken, a company should consider in general terms whether the envisaged environment of a market is likely to be attractive. By considering in general terms such matters as political stability or cultural attitudes, the company may screen out potential markets for which it considers further analysis cannot be justified by the likelihood of success.

The PEST framework is useful for analysing foreign marketing opportunities. This is a starting point for analysis, but it should be recognized that international expansion can take place for a variety of idiosyncratic reasons. (For example, the owner of a business may have enjoyed holidays in a country and chosen that country to set up a foreign venture.)

Political factors

Government and quasi-government organizations influence the legislative and economic frameworks within which organizations trade.

At a national level, individual governments can influence marketing opportunities in a country in a number of ways.

- **Unstable political systems** are often very unattractive to companies considering foreign expansion. For example, the instability of some central and eastern European governments has posed unacceptable risks for firms considering committing resources to an overseas market.

- **Regulations governing product standards** may require an exporter to reconfigure its products expensively for a foreign market.

- **Legislation** may be used by governments to try to protect domestic producers against foreign competition.

- Sometimes governments impose **import controls** or simply make the task of getting clearance for imports very difficult.

- Where a company is planning to set up a production facility overseas, legislation on **health and safety standards** as well as minimum wages and welfare provision may add to a firm's costs.

- **Restrictions on currency movements** may make it difficult to repatriate profits earned from a foreign operation.

- **Legislation protecting trademarks** varies between companies—in some countries, such as Thailand, a trademark owner may find it very hard to protect itself legally from imitators.

Exporters also need to consider the political significance of regional trading blocs. The European Union (EU) is an example of a trading bloc that seeks to create favourable trading conditions for companies located within the bloc, regardless of the national borders within the bloc. For companies seeking to develop within one of those countries, the existence of trading blocs creates problems and opportunities. The problems occasionally arise where tariffs or other restrictions are placed on goods and services imported from outside the bloc. The biggest opportunity is that, once an exporter is inside one member country, the process of expansion to other bloc member countries can be made very much easier through the harmonization of standards and dismantling of internal borders. Within the EU, monetary union has also reduced obstacles to international trade posed by the volatility in exchange rates. Fluctuating exchange rates can make it difficult for sellers to predict the value of their future foreign sales in terms of their own domestic currency.

The development of the EU has been paralleled by the development of a number of other regional trading blocs, most notably the ASEAN group of South-East Asian countries and the NAFTA grouping of the USA, Canada, and Mexico.

There have been many attempts to liberalize world trade. Members of the World Trade Organization (WTO) seek greater international economic prosperity by exploiting fully the comparative cost advantages of nations by reducing the barriers that inhibit international trade. Members agree not to increase tariffs or quotas on imports, except in permitted circumstances. However, many critics of the WTO have accused it

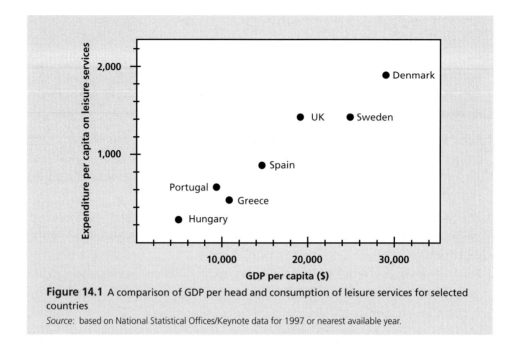

Figure 14.1 A comparison of GDP per head and consumption of leisure services for selected countries

Source: based on National Statistical Offices/Keynote data for 1997 or nearest available year.

of pursuing a western capitalist agenda for trade liberalization which less developed economies have little realistic prospect of exploiting. As an example, the Indian Post Office may in theory be able to benefit from the liberalization of trade in services by being able to set up an operation in the United States; but in practice, it is much more likely that Federal Express will challenge the Indian Post Office in its domestic market.

Economic factors

All other things being equal, an exporter would target prosperous foreign markets. A generally accepted measure of the economic attractiveness of a foreign market is the level of GDP per capita. The demand for most goods and services increases as this figure increases (Figure 14.1). However, intending exporters should also consider the distribution of income within a country, which may identify valuable niche markets. As an example, Indonesia has a relatively low GDP per head, but this still allows for a small but wealthy segment of society which has the desire and ability to pay for luxury western goods.

An exporter should consider economic prosperity not only as it is today, but also as it is likely to develop in the future. While the market for some goods and services in the west may be saturated, less developed economies may be at the start of a growth phase. The level of competitive pressure within the economy must also be considered—again, not just as it is now, but how it is likely to be in the future.

Social factors

An understanding of a society's cultural values is crucial for an exporter. Individuals from different cultures not only buy different products, but also may respond in different ways to the same product. Examples of differing cultural attitudes and their effects on international trade include the following.

- Some goods and services may be rendered obsolete by different types of social structure. As an example, extended family structures common in some countries have the ability to produce a wide range of services within the family unit, including caring for children and elderly members.
- A product that is taken for granted in the domestic market might be seen as socially unacceptable in a foreign market. (Loans charging interest may be regarded as unacceptable in Muslim communities.)
- Buying processes vary between different cultures—for example, the role of women in shopping for certain types of product may differ in foreign markets compared with the domestic market.

It has been common to talk about cultural convergence, implying that individuals are becoming more alike in the way they think and behave. Advocates of the concept of cultural convergence remind us that needs are universal and therefore there should be no reason why satisfaction of those needs should not also be universal. If a Big Mac satisfies a New Yorker's need for hygienic, fast, and convenient food, why should it not satisfy those similar needs for someone in Cairo? Against this, many observers have noted individuals' growing need for *identity* in a world that is becoming increasingly homogenized. Support for regional breakaway governments (e.g. by the Kurdish and Basque people) may provide some evidence of this. During the buildup to the Iraq war in 2003, many consumers in Arab countries used purchases of Muslim products such as Mecca Cola to identify themselves with an anti-American cause. Banks in many Muslim country have reported increased interest in syariah-based banking products (*Business Times* [3]).

It is also important to consider the demographic structure of a foreign market. Within the EU countries, the total population in recent times has increased at a natural rate of about 1.0 per 1,000 population. (That is, for every 1,000 deaths, there are 1,001 births.) However, this hides a range of rates of increase, with, at each extreme, Ireland having a particularly high birth rate and Germany a particularly low one. This has major implications for future age structures and consumption patterns. By 2030, people over 65 in Germany will account for almost half the adult population, compared with just one-fifth in 2000. And, unless that country's birth rate recovers from its present low of 1.3 per woman, over the same period its population of under-35s will shrink about twice as fast as the older population will grow. The net result will be that the total population, now 82 million, will decline to 70–73 million. The number of people of working age will fall by a full quarter, from 40 million today to 30 million. In Japan, the world's second-largest economy, the population will peak in 2005, at around 125 million. By 2050, according to the more pessimistic government forecasts, the population will have shrunk to around 95 million. Long before that, around 2030, the share of the over-65s in the adult population will have grown to about half (*Economist* [4]).

Much faster population growth has occurred outside the developed countries. Between 1960 and 1994, the population of Africa rose by 150% and Latin America by 100%, compared to just 17% in EU countries. More importantly, these trends seem set to continue.

Marketers are concerned with the rise in immigration to western developed countries, and the resulting ethnic diversity in these countries has presented challenges and opportunities. For an exporter, identifying significant ethnic groups within a country may be an important part of the evaluation of potential export markets.

Technological factors

An analysis of the technological environment of potential foreign markets is important for companies that require the use of a well-developed technical infrastructure. Communications are an important element of the technological infrastructure. For example, poorly developed telephone and postal communications may inhibit attempts to respond rapidly to customers' requests. Ireland has attracted many high-technology companies on the strength of the country's commitment to broadband internet access and its emphasis on training in IT. Where there is only a low level of skills among the population, the ability to produce goods and services in the local market, or to offer back-up support, may be limited.

MARKETING in ACTION

A hotel for lunatics?

Hilton International, owner of many of the world's most prestigious hotels, has joined the race to build the first hotel on the moon. It has developed a project called the Lunar Hilton, which would comprise a complex with 5,000 rooms. Powered by two huge solar panels, the resort would have its own beach and sea as well as a working farm. Experts disagree on the practicalities of life on the moon, but barriers seem to be diminishing as new discoveries are made.

'Space tourism' received a boost in April 2001, when the determined multi-millionaire Dennis Tito paid $20 million for a roundtrip ticket to the International Space Station. Such is the interest in exploiting the moon for tourism that there is now a Space Tourism Association, and a lot of national pride is at stake. Russians launched the first spaceship and now the first tourist in space. In Japan, the Kinki Nippon Tourist (KNT) Company, the country's second largest wholesale tour operator, set up a space travel club in 2002. Back in 1998 KNT helped a Japanese Pepsi franchisee launch a sweepstakes for a suborbital flight. The company received 650,000 applications for five tickets, each going for $98,000. The company is convinced that excursion-class spaceships will become a driving force for the travel industry in the twenty-first century.

Three Japanese companies have between them already spent £25 million on development work for their own moon projects. Compared with this, Hilton's expenditure to date of £100,000 looks quite modest. Is the company mad in believing that people will want to visit the moon? Or is this just the kind of long-term strategic thinking that so many businesses lack? With the world becoming smaller and increasingly saturated with goods and services, does the moon offer a unique opportunity for expansion?

A more detailed analysis of potential markets

A rough environmental analysis along the lines discussed above would have reduced the number of possible foreign markets. At this stage the method of analysis is very qualitative, and is often based on the 'gut feeling' of a company's senior management. Very often, the list of potential markets is reduced through idiosyncratic factors, such as personal links between senior managers and their friends and family in a country. Senior management has been known to target a market for apparently personal reasons, such as the opportunity to get away to enjoy good golf courses. Where the business potential of prospective markets is otherwise fairly indistinguishable, such personal factors may sway the final choice. However, if they are a starting point for a decision, with no underlying business assessment, a foreign venture could be doomed.

Once a company has developed a shortlist of foreign markets, it can set about the task of collecting more detailed information about each of them. The methods used to research a potential foreign market are in principle similar to those used to research the domestic market. Research would normally begin by using secondary data about the potential foreign market, which are available at home. Sources that are readily accessible through specialized libraries, government organizations, and specialist research organizations include Department of Trade and Industry information for exporters, reports of international agencies such as the Organisation for Economic Co-operation and Development (OECD), chambers of commerce, and private sources of information such as that provided by banks. Details of some specific sources are shown in Figure 14.2.

Secondary research at home will often be followed up with further desk research of materials available locally within the shortlisted markets. This is most likely to be carried out by appointing a local research agency. Its brief may include a review of reports published by the target market's own government and by specialist locally based market research agencies.

Government agencies
    Department of Trade and Industry market reports
    Foreign governments—e.g. USA
        Department of Commerce
    Foreign national and local development agencies

International agencies
    European Union (Eurostat, etc.)
    Organization for Economic Co-operation and
        Development (OECD)
    World Trade Organization
    United Nations
    World Bank
    International Monetary Fund
    World Health Organization

Research organizations
    Economist Intelligence Unit
    Dun and Bradstreet International
    Market research firms

Publications
    Financial Times country surveys
    Business International
    International Trade Reporter
    Banks' export reviews

Trade associations
    Chambers of trade and commerce
    Industry specific associations

Online resources
    Eurostat
    Mintel online
    FT online, etc.

Figure 14.2 Sources of secondary information on foreign markets

Secondary data have their limitations in assessing the attractiveness of a foreign market. Problems are compounded by the greater difficulty in gaining access to data, possible language differences, and problems of definition.

Primary research would be undertaken in a foreign market when a company has become happy about the general potential of a market, but is unsure about a number of issues that would be critical for success. These might include whether intermediaries would be willing and able to handle their product, or whether traditional cultural attitudes would prevent widespread adoption of it. Prior to commissioning its own specific research (or instead of doing its own research), a company may go for the lower-cost option of undertaking research through an omnibus survey. These are surveys regularly undertaken among a panel of consumers in foreign markets (e.g. the Gallup European Omnibus) which carry questions on behalf of a number of sponsors.

A local agency would better understand attitudes towards privacy and the level of literacy that might affect response rates for different forms of research. Language barriers would be reduced but not eliminated, as the problem of comparability between markets remains. For example, when an American respondent claims to 'really like' a product, the meaning may be comparable to a German consumer who claims to 'quite like' the product. It would be wrong to assume on the basis of this research that the product is better liked by American than German consumers.

MARKETING in ACTION

Is the glass half full or half empty?
The chairman of Bata, the shoe manufacturer, is famously quoted for his analysis of a foreign market for his firm's shoes. Two employees were dispatched to a potential market in Africa and noticed that very few people were wearing shoes. 'No hope here—the people don't wear shoes' was the response of one. But the other saw it quite differently 'What an opportunity—just think what this market will be worth when these people start wearing shoes!' Facts alone will not make a market entry decision: the facts must be interpreted, and this interpretation can lead to quite diverse conclusions.

▇ Adapting the product offer to foreign markets

'Global strength and local adaptability' are the stated aims of many successful companies that operate in international markets. But how can such local adaptability be achieved? And how can a company ensure that the benefits of economies of scale that derive from global size are not undermined by the cost of adapting to each individual market? Too many companies have failed overseas because they did not fully take into account local sensitivities to their products. For example, attitudes towards promotional programmes differ between cultures. The choice of colours in advertising or sales outlets needs to be made with care because of symbolic associations. (For example, the colour associated with mourning/bereavement varies across cultures.) Also, what is considered to be an acceptable method of procuring a sale varies between cultures. In Middle Eastern markets, for example, a bribe to a public official may be considered essential, whereas in most western countries this is unacceptable.

A crucial task of overseas marketing management is the design of a marketing programme that is sensitive to local needs. The following sections examine the extent to which adaptation of the marketing mix to local needs is either desirable or possible. In particular, should a company seek to develop one globally uniform product offer, or make it different in each of the foreign markets which it serves? Sometimes a company may simply change the promotion of its product, while keeping the product itself the same in all markets. Five types of strategy can be identified, based on the extent to which product and promotion decisions vary from the global norm.

MARKETING in ACTION

Miniaturized hotels for miniaturized people?

How does a large American hotel chain adapt its service offer to the Japanese market? Hotels operated by Hilton International in the USA have bedrooms that, to many visitors from overseas, are surprisingly large. But what would an American think of a typical Japanese hotel? Land prices in America are generally fairly low outside of the main metropolitan areas, hence the relatively spacious facilities offered. But in Japan space is at a premium, and this has given rise to all sorts of miniaturized hotel formats, aimed at keeping prices at an affordable level. How could Hilton International remain affordable yet retain its generic brand values? Following extensive research, the company developed a hotel format that was appropriate to the Japanese market. To avoid the problem of visitors from America being shocked by the relatively cramped spaces, Hilton International developed applied a separate brand format, 'Wa No Kutsurogi' ('Providing Comfort and Service the Japanese Way').

1. **Maintain a uniform product and promotion worldwide**: This approach develops a global marketing strategy as though the world were a single market. The benefits of this approach are numerous. Customers travelling from one market to another can immediately recognize a brand and the values it stands for. If, instead, the product were different in a foreign market, a traveller purchasing it overseas might come away confused about the qualities of the brand. If Coca Cola tasted too different in foreign countries, could this detract from individuals' perceived value of the brand when they got back home?

   Product standardization can also yield benefits of economies of scale. As well as lowering the unit costs of production, economies can extend to the collection of market research, the design of buildings and uniforms, etc. The use of a common brand name in foreign markets also benefits from economies of scale. Travellers to foreign markets will already be familiar with the brand's values as a result of promotion in the domestic market. However, care must be taken in selecting a brand name that will have no unfortunate connotations in foreign markets. There are many legendary cases of brand names that have not worked in foreign markets; for example,

Figure 14.3 With a name like 'Pschitt', would you buy this product? As the markets for many products become increasingly global, companies are going to greater lengths to ensure that the name chosen for a new product will work in all of the markets the company is likely to operate in. Pschitt is now owned by Perrier and has, not surprisingly, decided against exporting this product to its English speaking markets. Had it been developing the product today, it would almost certainly have chosen a different brand name. Creative agencies that develop brand identities for clients are themselves having to work at a global level in order to satisfy the needs of their global clients

Opel's Corsa car translated into 'won't go' in Spain and many English speaking people are left wondering about the likely taste of 'Bum' crisps or 'Pschitt' soft drinks. There can also be problems where legislation prevents an international slogan being used. In Quebec, for example, companies have been fined for using standard anglicized advertising material without changing it to French as required by the province's legislation.

2. **Retain a uniform product formulation, but adapt promotion**: This strategy produces an essentially uniform global product, but adapts the promotional programme to local markets. The manner in which brand values are communicated in advertisements is a reflection of the cultural values of a society. For this reason, a snack food manufacturer may use a straightforward, brash, hard-sell approach in its American market, a humorous approach in its British market, and a seductive approach in its French market, even though the product offer is essentially the same in each market. Some images and symbols used to promote a product in the domestic market might fail in a foreign market. Animals, which are often used to promote a range of home-based goods and services, present a caring and comfortable image in Britain, but in markets such as Japan animals are seen as unclean, disgusting objects.

Bombs or bouquets for Belfast?

How do you promote the image of a tourist destination in foreign markets? The destination itself cannot be adapted to suit the needs of individual markets. The Tower of London will always be the same for tourists, whether they are from Manchester, Madras, or Melbourne. But the promotional message can be fine-tuned to stress the aspects on which different markets place high value.

Take the case of the Brand Ireland campaign, a joint effort by the Northern Ireland Tourist Board and Bord Failte to increase the number of visitors to Ireland, north and south. Several hours of footage was filmed featuring tourist attractions around Ireland. This was reduced to a series of 15 and 30-second television commercials, but a different cut was made for each of the major markets targeted by the campaign. The German cut stressed the wild, rugged nature of the country, the Italian cut stressed the romance of the island, the American cut stressed Ireland's history, and the English cut stressed that Ireland is so close, but so different. The strap line 'Live a different life' worked well in most markets, but had to be changed in the USA after focus groups identified unfortunate associations with cross-dressing.

3. **Adapt the product offer only**: This may be done in order to meet specific local needs or legislation, while retaining the benefits of a global image. For example, flavourings and colourings used in confectionery may be illegal in some foreign markets, requiring reformulation of the product. Exporters must continue to track changes in consumers' tastes as they become more used to a product. For example, in 2002 the Dutch brewer Heineken changed its UK product offer to a more alcoholic brew after market research suggested the standard lager market was losing its appeal. The company phased out its Cold Filtered and Export products and replaced them with Heineken premium lager, the 5% alcohol content product now sold in 170 countries (Batt [2]).

4. **Adapt both product and promotion**: In practice, most companies undertake a combination of product and promotion modification in order to meet local market needs, while still trying to stay true to their global brand values and worldwide economies of scale.

5. **Develop new products**: Sometimes markets emerge for which a company has no product offering that can be easily adapted. In order to gain access to a foreign market, it may be necessary to develop new products. Western financial services companies entering Muslim countries have developed new forms of loans which don't charge interest but pay back a higher amount in capital. The firms may have had no similar product in their domestic market, but development of a new product has been necessary to gain acceptance from significant segments in Muslim

markets. This option compounds the risk of a new market with the risk of a new product.

Pricing in foreign markets

The issue of whether to globalize or adapt to local conditions arises again in respect of pricing decisions. On the one hand, it might be appealing to customers if a company charged a standard price for a product regardless of where in the world it was purchased. Customers would then always have an idea of how much the product would cost, and this would help to develop a long-term relationship between the company and its customers. However, the reality is that a variety of factors cause global companies to charge different prices in the different markets in which they operate:

- A brand that is highly valued at home may be unheard of in a foreign market, and therefore unable to command its accustomed price premium.

- Competitive pressure varies between markets, reflecting the stage of market development that a product has reached and the impact of regulations against anti-competitive practices.

- Where it is difficult to make a product at home and export it to the foreign market, a company will face cost levels that may be significantly different from those applying to the domestic market. For services that use people-intensive production methods, which cannot be 'exported' from a company's domestic base, variations in wage levels between countries will have a significant effect on total costs, and hence will influence pricing. Personnel costs may also be affected by differences in the welfare provisions that employers are required to pay for. Other significant cost elements that often vary between markets include the level of property prices or rental costs.

- Taxes vary between different markets—for example, the rate of value added tax (or its equivalent sales tax) can be as high as 38% in Italy compared with $17\frac{1}{2}$% in the UK. There are also differences between markets in the manner in which sales taxes are expressed. In many markets taxes are fully incorporated into price schedules, although in others (such as in the USA) it is more usual to price a service exclusive of taxes, with the amount of tax added in small print on the line below.

- Local customs influence customers' expectations of the way in which a product is priced. While customers in the domestic market might expect to pay for bundles of products, in a foreign market consumers might expect to pay a separate price for each component of the bundle, or vice versa. It has been noted, for example, that UK car buyers prefer to pay an all-inclusive price for new cars, while buyers in continental Europe prefer to pay a low base price, but to be able to add features to their own specification.

- Formal price lists for a product may be expected in some markets, but in others individual bartering may the norm. Having a published price list which it sticks to may put a firm at a competitive disadvantage.

- Government regulations can limit price freedom in foreign markets. In addition to controls over prices charged by public utilities, many governments require that 'fair' prices be charged in a wide range of goods and services—e.g. tourism-related services—and that the prices charged be clearly publicized. Retailers that use 'Buy one, get one free' offers in the UK have found this type of price promotion illegal in Germany.

The development of the single European market has tended to reduce price differences between member states, although significant differences remain for many products (refer back to Chapter 8). If wide differences in the pre-tax price of goods emerge between countries, it is open to entrepreneurs to buy goods in the lower priced market and sell them in the higher priced market. The 'grey' market in perfume imported from the Far East to western Europe is evidence of this. Because of their inseparability, it is much more difficult, and often impossible, to transfer a service from a low priced market to a high priced one.

Distributing goods and services in foreign markets

Getting distribution strategy right is crucial to success in foreign markets (as indeed it is in the domestic market). The cost of making goods and services readily available to consumers can be quite daunting, and for this reason many exporters choose to go into partnership with companies that are already established in a market. The whole issue of market entry strategy is considered in more detail later in this chapter. Many exporters have failed because they had not fully thought through the costs and barriers of getting their products to the final consumer.

Although the principles of distribution planning in foreign markets are similar to those for the domestic market, the following potential differences should be noted and accommodated:

- Consumer behaviour may differ significantly in foreign markets. What is a widely accepted outlet in one country may be regarded with suspicion in another. For example, buying cosmetics in a supermarket is now accepted as normal in the UK, but may meet resistance in some other countries.

- Consumers vary in the extent to which they are prepared to travel to obtain a product. In less developed economies where transport and refrigeration equipment are less readily available, consumers may seek very local access to intermediaries to replenish their stocks of perishable products. In car-based economies such as the USA, intermediaries may be selected by consumers on the basis of their range of choice and easy access by car.

Figure 14.4 National Car Rentals sought to simplify its pricing structure and strengthen its brand position by offering one price throughout Europe. Inevitably there is some risk inherent in this approach, as taxes and competitive pressures differ throughout Europe. In non-euro countries there is also the potential problem of currency fluctuations. To try and limit these risks, the company has restricted the single price offer according to the type of car and type of customer
Reproduced with permission of National Car Rental

- Differences in the social, economic, and technical environments of a market can result in the existence of different patterns of intermediaries. As an example, the interrelatedness of wholesalers and retailers in Japan can make it much more difficult for a foreign retailer to get into that market than into some other foreign markets. In some markets there may be no direct equivalent of a type of intermediary found in the domestic market. (For example, estate agents on the UK model are often not available in many foreign markets.)

- The law of a country can restrict the use of intermediaries which would otherwise be commonplace in the domestic market. Governments of many countries restrict the sale of alcohol, financial services, and gambling services—among others—to a much narrower set of possible intermediaries than may be the case in the domestic market.

People decisions

Should a company employ local or expatriate staff? The latter may be preferable where a company is providing a highly specialized product and may be useful in adding to the global uniformity of the product offer. In some service industries, the presence of front-line expatriate serving staff can add to the appeal of a service; for example, a chain of traditional Irish pubs established in mainland Europe may add to their appeal by employing authentic Irish staff.

For relatively straightforward goods and services, however, a large proportion of staff is likely to be recruited locally, leaving just senior management posts to be filled by expatriates. Sometimes an extensive staff development programme may be required to ensure that locally recruited staff perform in a manner that is consistent with the company's global image. This can often be quite a difficult task. A company moving into a previously centrally planned economy may have difficulty developing values of customer focus among staff members who have been accustomed to taking instructions from above.

■ Market entry strategies

Although new foreign markets provide a company with opportunities, they can also present high levels of risk. A company's market entry strategy should aim to balance the opportunities with the risks involved.

The main issues here are:

- How rapidly should a company commit itself to a foreign market?

- Who, if anybody, should the company work with in developing a foreign market?

Time scale for foreign market development

Should a company move as quickly as possible to develop a foreign market when the opportunity arises? This approach may have some merit, as being first can give long-term advantages. The market leader's product could become the benchmark by which consumers subsequently judge all products within its class. An early developer could also tie up key distribution outlets, making it difficult for a subsequent competitor to move into the market.

While there may be long-term benefits from being the first company to develop a new category of product in a foreign market, there are also risks. If development is hurried and a product is launched before quality can be guaranteed to live up to an organization's international standards, the company's long-term image can be damaged, both in the new foreign market and in its wider world market. In the turbulent marketing environment of eastern Europe in the late 1980s, two of the world's principal fast food retailers—McDonald's and Burger King—pursued quite different strategies. McDonald's waited until political, economic, social, and technological conditions allowed it to launch a restaurant that could meet its global standards. Burger King, however, in its desire to be first in the market, got in quickly but was able to offer only a sub-standard service, giving it an image from which it has subsequently struggled to recover.

Risk can be minimized by gradually committing more resources to a market, based on experience to date. Temporary facilities can be established which have low start-up and close-down costs and where the principal physical and human assets can be transferred to another location. Rather than setting up its own distribution system, a company can buy in distribution services from another company, with relatively low close-down costs should the venture fail.

A good example of risk reduction through the use of temporary facilities was found in the pattern of retail development throughout eastern Germany following reunification. Foreign companies were initially reluctant to commit themselves to building stores in specific locations in a part of the country that was still economically unstable and where patterns of land use were rapidly changing. The solution adopted by many companies was to set up branches in temporary marquees or mobile vehicles. These could move in response to the changing pattern of demand. While the location of retail outlets remained risky, this did not prevent retailers from establishing their networks of distribution warehouses, which could respond more flexibly to the changing pattern of retail location.

Who should be involved in foreign market development?

An assessment of risk is required in deciding whether an organization should enter a foreign market on its own, or in association with another organization. Going in alone increases the strategic and operational control that the organization has over its foreign operations. However, it exposes it to the greatest risk where the foreign market is relatively poorly understood. A range of market entry possibilities are considered below.

Exporting directly to customers overseas

This involves producing goods at a firm's domestic production facilities and shipping them to the foreign market. Choosing to sell directly to customers can be an extremely expensive task where the product in question is low in value and high in volume. Direct exporting is therefore limited to companies who sell specialized, high-value products. In the case of intangible services, it is possible to sell directly to consumers in foreign markets, but a company may find its task made much easier by using some form of information intermediary (see below).

Exporting through an export/import agent

Because of the difficulty in obtaining access to foreign customers, many first-time exporters choose to use an import or export agent. In return for a fee or commission, the agent uses its contacts to exploit distribution opportunities in a foreign market. Agency agreements vary in their time scale and responsibilities. At one extreme, an agent can be casually recruited to sell a batch of items on a no-sale, no-fee basis. At the other extreme, an agent may agree to develop a market and be given sole rights to sell the company's product in that market for a number of years.

Direct investment in a foreign subsidiary

Very often it is difficult for an exporter to serve a market from its home base. The cost of transporting goods to foreign markets may put it at a competitive disadvantage. It may even face tariff barriers levied on imported goods. The use of an import or export agent can leave an exporter with very little control over its foreign market.

Direct investment in a foreign subsidiary gives a company maximum control over its foreign operations, but can expose it to a high level of risk where it has only a poor understanding of the foreign market. A company can either set up its own foreign subsidiary from scratch (as many UK hotel companies have done to develop hotels in foreign markets), or it can acquire control of a company that is already trading. When Heineken sought to gain a larger market share in the Islamic market, it acquired the Egyptian brewer Ahram's, whose popular Fayrouz line of non-alcoholic flavoured beers had acquired respectability by being certified by Al Azhar, a prestigious Sunni Islam body, as *halal*, and permitted for consumption by Muslims (Allam [1]).

Where the nature of the product offer differs very little between national markets, or where it appeals to an international market (e.g. hotels), the risks from creating a new subsidiary are reduced. Where there are barriers to entry and the product is aimed at a distinctly different local market with its own preferences, the acquisition of an established subsidiary may be preferred. Even the latter course of action is not risk-free, as was illustrated by the problems encountered by Marks & Spencer following its acquisition of the American Brooks Brothers clothing chain, which it eventually sold in 2002 following losses.

Direct investment in a foreign subsidiary may also be made difficult by legislation restricting ownership of certain services by foreigners. Many developing countries have complex requirements which allow a foreign investor to acquire only a minority stake in a company.

Licensing/franchising

Rather than setting up its own operations in a foreign market, a company can license a local company to provide a product. A licence allows the local licensee to manufacture and sell the product as if it were made by the licensor itself. The licensee pays an agreed amount to the licensor for the right to sell its products (usually on the basis of turnover or volume of sales) and agrees to maintain specified quality standards. Licensing is widely used for low-value, high-volume products such as soft drinks. The Coca Cola company licenses local bottlers around the world to produce and sell its drinks.

In the case of services, it is necessary for a licensor to retain greater control over the processes of production, and not just the tangible outcome. Licensing or franchising in a foreign market can take a number of forms. Sometimes the franchisor enters into a direct franchising relationship with each individual franchisee. The difficulty in this approach lies in monitoring and controlling a possibly large number of franchisees in a country far from home. To overcome some of these problems, the franchisor normally establishes its own subsidiary in the foreign territory which negotiates and monitors franchisees locally. Alternatively, it could grant a master franchise for an area to a franchisee where the latter effectively would become the franchisor in the foreign country.

Franchising can allow an organization to expand rapidly overseas with relatively low capital requirements. However, it is subject to the same issues of control that affect domestic franchise agreements. (These were discussed in Chapter 9.)

Joint ventures

International joint ventures involve two or more firms' sharing their competencies to develop a market. Usually one of the partners will be a local company in the target market with detailed knowledge of that market, while another will be a company 'back home' with technical and/or financial competencies but little knowledge of the market. Joint ventures can balance a company's desire for control with risk minimization, and can be attractive in many situations.

Venture partners	% holding	Subsidiary/purpose
GfK	40	Creation of ORG-GfK Marketing Services, based in
ORG-Marg	60	Bangalore, India, to monitor monthly retail sales in retail outlets for the consumer technology markets
Siemens AG	50	Creation of enterprise to deliver converged voice and data
3M Corp	50	products to businesses
International Power	20	Operation of gas-powered electricity generation in Malaysia
Malakoff	80	
Prudential	50	Creation of Prudential Assicurazione to provide insurance
Inholding (Italy)	50	services in Italy

Figure 14.5 Examples of international joint ventures

- A joint venture with an organization already based in the proposed foreign market makes the task of collecting information about the market, and responding sensitively to it, relatively easy.

- A joint venture can spread risk where the initial capital requirement threshold is high.

- Where foreign governments restrict the rights of foreign companies to set up business on their account, a partnership with a local company—possibly involving a minority shareholding—may be the only means of entering the market.

- There may be significant barriers to entry which a company already based in the foreign market could help to overcome. A common barrier to entry is access to a comprehensive network of intermediaries.

- There may be a reluctance on the part of consumers to deal with what appears to be a foreign company. A joint venture can allow the operation to be fronted by a domestic producer with which customers can be familiar, while allowing the foreign partner to provide capital and management expertise.

- Taxation of company profits may favour a joint venture rather than outright purchase of a foreign subsidiary.

Joint ventures are an important feature of many business sectors where the benefits listed above can be achieved. They have assumed particular importance in the car manufacturing, airline, and financial services sectors. Some recent examples of joint ventures are shown in Figure 14.5.

Strategic alliances

Strategic alliances have become an important form of joint venture in international business. They comprise agreements between two or more organizations where each

Figure 14.6 With the globalization of markets, strategic alliances are becoming increasingly crucial to facilitate overseas growth. In the airline sector, an alliance such as Oneworld allows an airline's services to be marketed by all other alliance members. To its customers, British Airways is able to offer 'seamless' travel around the globe on services of fellow alliance members. For the company, there are opportunities to rationalize operations in foreign countries

Reproduced with permission of Oneworld Alliance

partner seeks to add to its competencies by combining its resources with those of a partner. A strategic alliance generally involves co-operation between partners rather than joint ownership of a subsidiary set up for a specific purpose, although it may include agreement for collaborators to purchase shares in the businesses of other members of the alliance.

Strategic alliances allow individual companies to build upon the relationship that they have developed with their clients by allowing them to sell on services which they do not produce themselves, but instead are produced by another member of the alliance. This arrangement is reciprocated between members of the alliance. Strategic alliances have become important within the airline industry, where operators share their route networks through 'code-sharing', thereby increasing the range of origin–destination opportunities that can be provided with a through ticket. Some strategic alliances of airlines, such as the 'Oneworld' alliance comprising British

Airways, Aer Lingus, Qantas, Cathay Pacific, American Airlines, and Canadian Airlines, allow an extensive range of 'seamless' travel possibilities, to the mutual advantage of all members of the alliance.

Global e-commerce

The internet is changing the landscape of global competition. In theory, a company can use its website to promote its products around the world very cost-effectively. A buyer in one country can surf the World Wide Web to find the best combination of product and price available to it, regardless of where in the world a supplier is based. The transparency of prices and the apparent easy availability of products from overseas suppliers has forced many organizations to see their markets at a global rather than a purely local level.

Although e-commerce has created a lot of interest as a means of opening up world trade, its limitations must be noted. Buyers are still likely to be cautious about dealing with a foreign company that they have not heard of. If it is difficult enough for a foreign supplier of television sets to establish itself in the UK market when it has real products available for inspection in local shops, how much harder is it going to be for a foreign-based internet company? Can the buyer trust an unknown brand to perform as promised? What will happen about after-sales service? Who can the buyer complain to if things go wrong? There is also the question of actually distributing the product (see Randall and Harrison-Walker [6]). This has been overcome with some services. (For example, electronic ticketing has created more efficient and effective competition between airlines.) But for bulky goods, the sometimes difficult reality of global physical distribution has to be balanced against the simplicity of global promotion through a website.

The internet is undoubtedly offering new opportunities for firms to enter foreign markets. However, basic rules of foreign market entry still apply, and many of the successful uses of global e-commerce have involved more traditional approaches based on joint ventures and strategic alliances. A number of global internet intermediaries (or informediaries) such as Amazon.com and Yahoo! have emerged as internationally respected brands. For many suppliers entering a foreign market, it may be safer and more cost-effective to work through these, rather than acting alone.

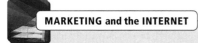

MARKETING and the INTERNET

How do you find a needle in an international haystack?
In the early days of the internet, many people assumed, perhaps naively, that international markets could be opened up through the internet at very little cost. An entrepreneur with a bright idea and a good product proposition would no longer need

to distribute expensively printed brochures around the world or employ a network of agents. With direct communication through the internet, a buyer seeking supplies of fasteners or needles could trawl the internet for the best source of supplier. The supplier just had to have a website, and buyers would come. Of course, life is not so simple, and one of the biggest challenges is to simply get a potential customer to your site. In the case of many consumer goods and services, the only sensible solution may be to pay one of the many information intermediaries who act as a cyber exchange between often geographically separated buyers and sellers.

But what about the case of specialized business-to-business sales where intermediaries may be few and far between? Here, the importance of getting a high ranking in search engines becomes even more important. It is claimed that there are over 20,000 search engines available to internet users, but the reality is that the top 10 search engines account for over 90% of all searches. Being close to the top of these search engines has become an important part of marketing strategy. Consider the case of a company that specializes in buying redundant manufacturing machinery from factories that have closed down, and reselling it to buyers looking for second-hand equipment. Addressing global markets is often key to success here. After all, if a shoe factory that has just closed down in Leicester is selling off its injection moulding equipment, it is unlikely that there will be many potential buyers for the equipment in Leicester, or indeed the UK—if one company in the UK couldn't profitably use the equipment, then it is likely that no UK companies will be able to. But the equipment may be just what an entrepreneur in Romania is looking for.

How can a UK-based trader in second-hand equipment get its site top of the list that the Romanian is looking at? Relying on searches for 'machinery' or even 'second-hand machinery' is unlikely to be very fruitful—after all, there are likely to be thousands of sites in this category across the world. But including market-specific terms such as 'injection moulding' and 'shoes' in the web page text and meta-tags will help to put a company's site higher in a specialized search category. Having several pages with different titles, text, and meta-tags provides more opportunities to target specific international market segments. And there's another trick that many companies use to get overseas buyers to their site. It costs relatively little to produce a foreign-language version of the main pages of a company's site. If a Romanian entrepreneur entered 'πρεψηψφορμα βπρςλψκη' in a search engine instead of 'injection moulding' or 'shoes', the seller's site would probably come very close to the top of the search results.

⬛ Chapter summary and key linkages to other chapters

Few firms can afford to define their marketing environment only at the national level. Markets are becoming increasingly global in nature, presenting opportunities for expansion overseas, but also the threat of new entrants from overseas in the domestic market. Many foreign ventures undertaken by firms fail, suggesting the need for a rigorous appraisal of potential new markets. Many of the principles of researching markets that were discussed in Chapter 4 apply equally to research in foreign markets. Companies must make a careful study of how buyer behaviour may differ in a foreign market

(Chapter 3). If a decision is made to enter a foreign market, care must be taken to be sensitive to local needs by carefully adapting the marketing mix (Chapters 7–11). A balance has to be made between local sensitivity and maintaining the strength and economies of scale of a global brand. Entering a new market involves a high level of risk, and firms often seek to minimize this by sharing risk with other companies, although this can result in a loss of control.

KEY PRINCIPLES OF MARKETING

- The basic principles of marketing apply whether a firm is dealing with its domestic market or a foreign market.
- The competing demands of global standardization and local adaptation must be reconciled.
- Understanding the effects of cultural differences on buyer behaviour is crucial to successful overseas marketing.

CASE STUDY

The Czech beer market—a bittersweet venture for Bass

Why should one of the UK's leading brewers choose to develop the market for beer in a country that is already saturated with famous beers at rock-bottom prices? To lovers of real ale, the Czech Republic is probably a heaven. But to Bass Breweries (as it was then known), the Czech market represented an opportunity waiting to be developed. However, a study of the Bass venture into the Czech Republic illustrates that understanding the environment of an emerging market can involve a lot of risks, and in Bass's case the company ultimately failed to achieve its ambitions.

Eastern Europe, and the Czech Republic in particular, has one of the world's highest rates of per capita consumption of beer, which in 1997 stood at 160 litres per person, double the rate of most western European countries. The Czech Republic has a long tradition of brewing, with some of the world's oldest and most respected beers, including the Staropramen, Ostravar, and Vratislav brands. One of the reasons for the high consumption of beer has been its high quality and low price. The price of a litre of beer in 1997 was typically less than a quarter of what a comparable litre would have cost in the UK, the low price reflecting low taxes and low margins for producers.

So, in a country of high-quality beers and low prices, what could Bass have hoped to add to the market? When it first looked at the beer market in the Czech Republic, it saw a fragmented market where marketing was just emerging after decades of centralized planning. Beer drinkers had become used to a mentality of taking what was available, rather than seeking the best product to suit their needs. Bass saw that the fragmented market was ripe for consolidation. In 1997 the three largest breweries held only 55% of the market, with another 25% held by small regional brewers, none of which had a national market share of over 3%. Even Budwar, possibly the best known Czech beer in the UK, accounted for just 3% of the Czech domestic market. Many of the Czech Republic's near neighbours had similar structural problems and opportunities in their beer sector, and, along with other western investors, Bass saw the country as a platform for expansion into the rest of eastern Europe.

In addition to exploiting the Czech market, Bass also saw an opportunity to develop global markets for the high-quality beers that were currently confined to the domestic Czech market. Bass could use its global distribution network to exploit the brands in a way that would be impossible for domestic companies.

Bass first invested in the Czech Republic in 1994, with a 34% stake in Prague Breweries, which it later increased to 46%. This brought Bass three Prague-based breweries which would have seemed quite small and unsophisticated by UK standards. In 1995 it bought 78% of Vratislavice nad Nisou (with two breweries in North Boherrda) and 51% of Ostravar, a brewery in North Moravia. In 1996 Bass acquired a controlling interest in Prague Breweries when it increased its stake to 51%. In 1997 the three companies in which it had invested were merged under the name Prague Breweries, in which Bass has a 55% stake. This made Prague Breweries the second-biggest brewer in the Czech Republic, but it still had only a 14% market share. The market leader, Prazdroj, had 27%. Bass had started the process of consolidation in the industry, but it still had a long way to go if it was to match progress in western Europe.

The merger of the three breweries started the process of reducing competition in the sector. It also provided an opportunity to begin cutting costs, by disposing of some of its capacity. Bass decided early on that its core business was brewing and subsequently sold its acquired soft drinks businesses to Corona.

A further approach to making the Czech market profitable was the development of strong brands which could be sold at decent margins. By 1997 Bass had four national and three regional brands, but it took a pragmatic approach to retaining the long-established regional brands—they would be kept as long as people continued to buy them. Doubtless Bass was mindful of the short-sightedness of UK brewers' attempts to suppress regional brands a couple of decades earlier, only to see them find a new valuable role a few years later as 'real ale'.

Bass's first new product development in the Czech Republic was a premium lager called Velvet, developed and brewed locally but with the help of Bass in the UK. From the beginning, Bass sought to position Velvet as something quite different from commodity beers. It had a distinctive smooth, creamy head, and Bass commissioned special glasses for it to be served in. To add to its differentiation, Bass provided training for bar staff on how to pour and serve it. Velvet was aimed at high-income consumers and was promoted through bars and restaurants with targeted tastings. Promotional support was provided by advertising in *Elle, Harper's Bazaar* and *Esquire*, and by a dedicated sales team. Despite the conservatism of Czech drinkers, Bass had successfully found a niche market—the emerging middle classes in stylish bars.

Bass's strategy was to invest heavily in brands for the long term. When developing a brand, the company would start with a market research programme carried out among consumers to learn more about their beer needs, and their perceptions of competing brands. It would then undertake life-style segmentation, something previously unheard of.

Another strength of Bass in its home market was distribution, and this represented another opportunity in the Czech market. By the end of 1997, a new sales, marketing, and distribution structure was in place, making it possible to distribute national brands efficiently and effectively. The structure included national marketing, key account, and business development teams, along with a unified sales force and distribution network. In three years, one result of this reorganization was to increase penetration of the company's products from 50% to 80% of all retail outlets in the Czech Republic.

Overcoming cultural barriers of the Czech people proved to be one of the biggest challenges for Bass. It seemed that many people found the change to a market-based system difficult to cope with, after 40 years of centralized planning. The whole idea of customer focus seemed to lack credibility among employees who had been used to customers' having no choice. While Bass might have been expert at brewing, branding, and distribution issues, it underestimated how much time it would have to spend on change management issues and instilling western values into staff. Problems were encountered in getting people to make decisions, motivating them to act on their decisions, and then checking that agreed actions were actually being undertaken. Recruitment, appraisal, and reward increasingly stressed a number of key attitudes of mind: being customer focused, results-driven, and innovative; behaving with integrity; treating people with respect; showing respect for the community. As an example of the problems that had to be overcome, salesmen had a pride, fostered by years of production orientation, that prevented them from listening to retailers.

Bass never managed to achieve profitability in the Czech market. Despite being an early mover in the consolidation of the Czech beer market, it was increasingly threatened by other international brewers who had gone through the same process of evaluating overseas markets and had decided to enter the Czech market.

The biggest threat came from the Japanese investment bank Nomura International, which was battling with Bass's Czech brands to dominate the country's beer market. Nomura had acquired Radegast and Pilsner, giving it 44% of the Czech beer market, and observers claimed that it was using its marketing muscle to win exclusive contracts with pubs and restaurants, keeping beer prices down. Bass, along with many of the smaller brewers, contended that Nomura was illegally abusing its dominant position, and formally complained to the Czech government's Office for Economic Competition. This government regulator originally blocked the Radegast–Pilsner marketing merger to protect small brewers, but reversed its decision in 1999, citing a technicality. Bass had argued that in the Czech Republic beer was a loss-making industry, and the current practices of Nomura were just giving the market leader a chance to squeeze everyone else out in due course.

Back home, all of the major UK breweries were undertaking reviews of what business they should be in, and Bass decided that its future should lie in the growing leisure sector (where it owned restaurants, hotels, and fitness centres), rather than brewing. It came to an agreement whereby the Belgian brewer Interbrew SA acquired all of Bass's brewing operations. Although the take-over of Bass's UK operations was blocked by the Department of Trade and Industry on competition grounds, Interbrew's acquisition of Bass's non-UK businesses was cleared by the European Commission. Bass was subsequently renamed Six Continents and in 2003 split its pub operations into a new company, Mitchells and Butler.

Interbrew already had a significant part of its business in central and eastern Europe, with operations in Russia, Ukraine, Hungary, Croatia, Romania, Bulgaria, Montenegro, and the Czech Republic. It had a long-term vision for Bass's brands and, following the acquisition of Bass's Czech assets, earmarked 3 billion Czech koruna for the development of Prazske Pivovary. Could it succeed where Bass had not been able to earn a profit?

Case study review questions

1. Review the alternative market entry strategies that were open to Bass in 1994 and assess each for its level of risk.

2. Identify the principal barriers Bass faced in developing a marketing culture in its Czech operations. How could it overcome these barriers?

3. Critically assess the problems and opportunities for Interbrew's investment in the Czech Republic arising from further integration of the country into the European Union.

CHAPTER REVIEW QUESTIONS

1. Examine the reasons why a UK-based furniture retailer should seek to expand into continental Europe.

2. What cultural differences might cause problems for a fast food chain developing outlets in India?

3. How might a UK clothing manufacturer go about researching market potential for its products in Germany?

4. In what circumstances is a global, rather than a localized, marketing strategy likely to be successful?

5. Suggest methods by which a firm of building contractors can minimize the risk of proposed foreign expansion.

6. What is meant by a strategic alliance, and why are they of importance to the services sector? Give examples of strategic alliances.

REFERENCES

[1] Allam, A. (2003), 'Making Near Beer Acceptable in Near East'. *New York Times*, 4 January, p. C3.

[2] Batt, C. (2002), 'Heineken Pumps Up the Volume'. *Daily Telegraph* 17 August, p. 29.

[3] Business Times (2002), 'More Local Banks Now Offer Islamic Products, Services'. *Business Times*, 14 February, p. 12.

[4] *The Economist* (2001), 'The New Demographics'. *The Economist*, 11 March, Special Section, pp. 5–8.

[5] Klein, N. (2000), *No Logo*, London: Flamingo.

[6] Randall, E. J. and Harrison-Walker, L. J. (2002), 'If You Build It, Will They Come? Barriers to international e-marketing'. *Journal of Marketing Theory & Practice*, 10(2): 12–21.

▣ SUGGESTED FURTHER READING

The following references offer a general review of the factors that influence firms' foreign expansion decisions:

Czinkota, M. R. (2001), International Marketing. London: International, Thomson Learning.

Doole, I, (2001), *International Marketing Strategy: analysis, development and implementation*. London: Thomson Learning.

Keegan, W. J. and Green, M. C. (2001), *Global Marketing Management*, 7th edn. Englewood Cliffs, NJ: Prentice Hall.

Steenkamp, J. B. E. M. and Ter Hofstede, F. (2002), 'International Market Segmentation: issues and perspectives'. *International Journal of Research in Marketing*, September: pp. 72–79.

For a general overview of trends in international business, consult the following:

Economic Trends: a monthly publication of the UK Office for National Statistics which includes statistics relating to international trade performance.

Overseas Trade: a DTI–FCO magazine for exporters published ten times per year by Brass Tacks Publishing Co., London.

World Trade Organization Annual Report, published annually.

World Trade Organization *Trade Policy Review* (serial).

Overseas Direct Investment: detailed breakdown of UK overseas direct investment activity, outward and inward, by component, country, and industry (Office for National Statistics)

▣ USEFUL WEB LINKS

Visit the comparion website to this book, with lots of interesting additional material and links for each chapter:

www.oup.com/uk/booksites/busecon

Overseas Trade Statistics

www.ons.gov.uk

EmuNet: the online gateway to Europe

www.euro-emu.co.uk

OECD International Trade: Statistics on international transactions

www.oecd.org/std/serint.htm

US International Trade Statistics
   www.census.gov/ftp/pub/foreign-trade/www
International Business Resources on the WWW: Statistical data and information resources
   www.ciber.msu.edu/busres/statinfo.htm
University of Massachusettes database of international business periodicals, economic surveys, country factbooks, export/import information, statistical compilations, and guides to government contacts and trade associations
   www.lib.umb.edu/reference/int_buss.html
World Trade Organization: This site provides information on international trade developments, statistics, WTO documents and policies
   www.wto.org
Trade Partners UK: Advice and information from the Department of Trade and Industry for exporters. Provides information on overseas markets by region
   www.tradepartners.gov.uk
International Monetary Fund: Site contains IMF news, publications, and international economic information
   www.imf.org
Economist Intelligence Unit: Selected free access to global business intelligence reports
   www.eiu.com
World Link: The online magazine of the World Economic Forum, with a searchable archive
   www.worldlink.co.uk
EU Euro website: The official EU website on the euro includes documents, legislation, links to other websites, and a search engine. It provides access to basic information and documentation on the euro
   europa.eu.int/euro/html/entry.html
Infonation: An interactive statistical database for the member states of the United Nations
   www.un.org/Pubs/CyberSchoolBus/infonation/e_infonation.htm
Annual Barclays Country Reports: Country reports containing data on market analysis, economic policy, the political environment, recent trends and outlooks
   www.corporate.barclays.com/go/cms.nsf/lookup
Country Risk Analysis: A rich source of historical data about world trading markets. Discusses economic, financial, and political events that impact on international trade.
   www.duke.edu/~charvey/Country_risk/couindex.htm
Financial Times: The newspapers archive, including country reports
   www.ft.com
CIA World Publications, *The World Fact Book*: Published by CIA World Publications, this website gives access to facts and statistics on more than 250 countries and other entities
   www.odci.gov/cia/publications/factbook/index.html
UK overseas trade statistics: The site includes a summary of recent trade statistics
   www.statistics.gov.uk
US International Trade Statistics: US oriented, but contains a lot of data on world markets
   www.census.gov/ftp/pub/foreign-trade/www/
Organisation for Economic Co-operation and Development (OECD) International Trade: The OECD's database on international trade shows the value of each member country's exports and imports of goods and services by type
   www.oecd.org/std/serint.htm

International Business Resources on the WWW: Michigan State University's site provides many useful links to statistical data and information resources
www.ciber.msu.edu/busres/Static/Statistical-Data-Sources.htm

KEYWORDS

- **Export/import agents**
- **Exporting**
- **Global e-commerce**
- **Global marketing**
- **Joint ventures**
- **Strategic alliances**

Glossary of marketing terms

- **Above-the-line** Expenditure on paid-for advertising
- **ACORN** ('A Classification of Residential Neighbourhood') a widely used geodemographic database of residential locality types
- **Adoption process** Rate at which individuals start buying a product
- **Advertising** The process by which an advertiser communicates with target audiences through paid-for messages
- **Advertising agency** An organization which specialises in communication on behalf of clients
- **Advertising campaign** A coherent and planned approach to communication over a specified period of time
- **Advertising media** Communication channels such as radio, television and newspapers
- **Agent** An individual or company acting in a capacity on behalf of a principal (e.g. a sales agent). An agent does not generally take ownership of goods
- **AIDA model** (Attention, Interest, Desire, Action) A mnemonic used to describe the process of communicating a series of messages
- **Augmented product** The core product offer with the addition of differentiating benefits, e.g. additional services
- **Awareness** The proportion of a target audience who have heard of a particular product of service (either 'prompted' or 'unprompted')
- **Banner advertisements** Paid for advertisements on other companies' websites
- **Barriers to entry** Obstacles facing a company when it wishes to enter a market
- **Below-the-line** Expenditure on promotional activities which involves non-commission paying media
- **Benchmarking** Setting performance goals for an organization based on those achieved by its competitors
- **Branding** The process of creating a distinctive identity for a product which differentiates it from its competitors
- **Brand equity** The capitalised value of price premiums that customers are prepared to pay for a brand, compared with a similar generic product
- **Budget** The amount of money scheduled to be spent or received in future periods
- **Business cycle** Fluctuations in the level of activity in an economy, commonly measured by employment levels and aggregate demand
- **Business-to-business marketing** Targeting goods and services at businesses who use the products to add value in their own production processes, as distinct from consumers who are the final consumers of the product
- **Buying behaviour** The way in which customers act, and the processes involved in making a purchase decision

- **Cannibalization** Occurs where one product within a company's range reduces sales of other products in its range
- **Cartel** An association of suppliers which seeks to restrict costly competition between its members
- **Cognitive dissonance** Mental discomfort that occurs following a purchase decision which the buyer may subsequently believe to have been a poor decision
- **Communication mix** The various media and messages which are used to communicate with a target audience
- **Competitive advantage** A firm has a marketing mix that the target market sees as meeting its needs better than the mix of competing firms
- **Cookies** A small programme embeded in a computer which collects information that can be forwarded and interrogated by a remote computer
- **Consumer** The final user of a good or a service
- **Consumer goods** Goods or services which are targeted at private individuals, rather than at organizations
- **Consumer panel** Research involving a group of consumers who report on their purchases over a period of time
- **Contingency plan** An alternative plan which can be rapidly implemented if the asumptions underlying the original plan turn out to be false
- **Core product** The essential benefit provided by a good or service
- **Corporate planning** Planning which involves all functions within an organization
- **Cost per thousand** Used in advertising as a measure of cost per thousand people viewing or reading an advertisement
- **Cost plus pricing** A pricing method in which a percentage 'mark-up' is added to the costs of producing a product
- **Coverage** The percentage of a targeted audience that have an opportunity to see a particular advertisement
- **Culture** The whole set of beliefs, attitudes and ways of behaving shared by a group of people
- **Customer** People who buy a firm's products (although customers may not be the actual consumers of the product)
- **Customer Relationship management (CRM)** A process of intergating the multiple contacts which a customer may have with an organization to create a shared knowledge base about the customer's history, preferences and likely future needs
- **DAGMAR model** (Defining Advertising Goals for Measured Advertising Results) An acronym for a model of the communication process
- **Database Marketing (DBM)** The use of a list of customers (potential and actual) which drives communication between an organization and its customers
- **Decision Making Unit (DMU)** The group of individuals who are involved in making a purchase decision
- **Decision support system** Models which are used to inform management decisions on the bases of available data
- **Demand** The willingness and ability of buyers to buy a particular product at a particular time at a given price
- **Demography** The study of population characteristics, e.g. relating to broad population statistics, such as age, sex, household composition

- **Desk research** Research which uses existing (secondary) sources of information
- **Differentiation** Creating a product which is different in some way from its main competitors, in the eyes of the target market
- **Diffusion** The rate at which new products are adopted by different customer adoption categories
- **Direct mail** A form of below-the-line promotion, which uses personalised communication, sent directly from the advertiser to potential and actual customers
- **Direct marketing** Direct communication between a seller and individual customers using a promotion method other than face-to-face selling. Direct mail is one communication channel used by direct marketing
- **Discriminatory pricing** Selling a product at two or more prices, where the difference in prices is not based on differences in costs
- **Distributor** A person or organization who assists in the task of making goods and services available to end-users. Distributors of goods generally take ownership of goods from suppliers and are responsible for collecting payments
- **Diversification** Broadening the spread of markets served and/or products supplied by a business
- **E-Business** The ability to integrate local and wide area networks through the use of Internet protocols to effectively remove the barriers between businesses, their customers and their suppliers in global markets
- **E-Commerce** Transactions of goods or services for which payment occurs over the Internet or other wide area networks
- **Economies of Scale** Costs per unit fall as total output increases
- **Elasticity of demand** Responsiveness of customer demand to changes in price or some other variable
- **Entrepreneur** An individual who takes risks with a view to profitably exploiting business opportunities
- **Environmental set** The elements within an organization's environment which are currently of major concern to it
- **Environment** Everything that exists outside the boundaries of a system
- **Ethics** Statements of what is right and wrong
- **Ethnographic research** Interpreative research which seeks a greater understanding from the perspectives of the value systems of those being researched
- **Exchange rate** The price of one currency expressed in terms of another currency
- **Experimental research** A research approach which evaluates alternatives within a controlled framework
- **Exploratory research** Initial marketing research used to review a problem in general before committing larger expenditure to a study
- **Fast-moving consumer goods** (fmcgs) Frequently purchased products, usually of low value
- **Field research** Primary research, not using existing published sources
- **Fixed costs** Costs that do not increase as total output increases
- **Focus group** A qualitative research technique in which groups of consumers are brought together to discuss their views and attitudes to a specific topic
- **Franchising** An agreement where a franchisor develops a product format and marketing

strategy and sells the right for other individuals or organizations ('franchisees') to use that format

- **Gatekeepers** Members of a decision making unit who control access to information about available choices
- **Geodemographic analysis** The analysis of markets using a combination of geographic and demographic information
- **Global brands** Goods and services which can have universal appeal and are marketed in numerous countries with little modification to product or image
- **Guerrilla marketing** The use of unconventional promotion tactics which are unexpected by the target audience
- **Hierarchy of needs** A model of consumer motivation proposed by Maslow
- **Horizontal integration** Merging of firms' activities at a similar point in a value chain
- **Image** The perceptions of a product, brand, or company
- **Industrial goods** Goods which are bought by industrial organizations. Often also referred to as Business-to-business goods
- **Imperfect market** A market in which the assumptions of perfect competition are violated
- **Income elasticity of demand** A measure of the responsiveness of demand for a product to changes in household incomes
- **Industrialisation of services** The process of standardising and mass producing services
- **Inseparability** The inability to separate consumption of a service from its production
- **Intangibility** The inability to assess to service using any tangible evidence
- **Intermediaries** Individuals or organizations who are involved in transferring goods and services from the producer to the final consumer
- **Internal marketing** The application of the principles and practices of marketing to an organization's dealings with its employees
- **Internet marketing** Use of the world wide web to communicate with customers and potential customers with a view to making a sale
- **Intranet** a restricted access, local internet communication channel
- **Joint venture** An agreement between two or more firms to exploit a business opportunity, in which capital funding, profits, risk and core competencies are shared
- **Just-in-time production** Reliably producing goods and getting them to customers just before customers need them
- **Key client** A customer who is particularly important to an organization
- **Ladder of loyalty** A representation of the stages a buyer goes through in the process of becoming a committed and loyal customer of a supplier
- **Learning organization** An organization wide sharing of knowledge which leads to better decisions being made by the organization
- **Life cycle** A phenomenon that exhibits cyclical patterns (e.g. in respect of products, markets and buyer-seller relationships)
- **Loyalty** Non-random repeat purchasing from a seller, with behavioural and attitudinal dimensions
- **Macro-environment** The general external business environment in which a firm operates
- **Marginal cost** The addition to total cost resulting from the production of one additional unit of output

- **Market development** A strategy used by an organization to increase sales by offering its existing products in new markets
- **Market leader** The organization which has the greatest share of sales in a given market
- **Market penetration** A strategy used by an organization to increase sales by trying to sell more of its current range of products to its current target customers
- **Market research** Activity to acquire knowledge of external factors relating to an organization's marketplace
- **Market research agencies** Organizations employed by client companies to collect information about the client company's market place (although market research agencies do not strictly act in an 'agency' capacity)
- **Marketing research** Distinguished from market research because marketing research is concerned with research into all of a company's marketing functions (e.g. research into pricing and distribution effectiveness)
- **Matrix organization structure** An organization structure which relies on coordination of management through cross-functional group leaders
- **Media** Channels of communication, e.g. television, radio, newspapers, etc
- **Mission statement** A means of reminding everyone within an organization of the essential purpose of the organization
- **Model of buyer behaviour** A simplified representation of the processes that buyers go through in making a purchase decision
- **Monopoly** A market in which there is only one supplier. Rarely achieved in practice, as most products have some form of substitute
- **Mystery shoppers** An observational form of marketing research
- **Needs** The underlying forces that drive an individual to make a purchase which will remove a feeling of deprivation
- **New product development** The process of identifying, developing and evaluating new product offers
- **Niche** A small sub-segment of a market which can be targeted with a distinct marketing strategy
- **Noise** Factors that distort the flow of communication between sender and receiver
- **Market segmentation** A process of identifying groups of customers within a broad product market who share similar needs and respond similarly to a given marketing mix formulation
- **Market share** One company's sales value (or volume) as a proportion of the total sales (or volume) for that market
- **Market** A group of potential customers with similar needs who are willing to exchange something of value with sellers offering products that satisfy their needs. Economists define a market more widely by including sellers who interact with buyers, either in a tangible market (e.g. Covent Garden vegetable market), or a conceptual market (e.g. the UK market for vegetables)
- **Marketing** The management process which identifies, anticipates and supplies customer requirements efficiently and profitably (Chartered Institute of Marketing definition)
- **Marketing audit** A systematic review of a company's marketing activities and of its marketing environment
- **Marketing environment** The social, economical, legal, political, cultural and technological factors, external to the marketing function of an organization which affect its actions

- **Marketing information system** A systematic way of collecting, analysing and disseminating information which is relevant to a company's marketing
- **Marketing intelligence** Relatively unstructured information about trends and events in a company's marketing environment
- **Marketing mix** A series of convenient headings for decisions to be made by marketing managers in eliciting a profitable consumer response
- **Marketing planning** A systematic process of analysing a company's environment, then developing objectives, strategies and action which are appropriate to the company's resources
- **Non-price competition** Non-price benefits such as warranties or additional features, or merchandising which can give a company's product a competitive advantage
- **Objective** A target to work towards
- **Observational research** Research which studies customers' reactions and behaviour without any direct interaction
- **Oligopoly** A market dominated by a few interdependent suppliers
- **Omnibus survey** A regular questionnaire undertaken on behalf of multiple clients, usually involving very large samples
- **Organic growth** A 'natural' form of growth in which a company's growth rate is influenced by its previous success rate
- **Perfect competition** An ideal type market in which there are no barriers to entry, no one firm can dominate the market, there is full information available to all buyers and sellers, and all sellers sell an undifferentiated product
- **Permission marketing** Communication by a company with customers and potential customers which is based on consent to receive communications
- **Perishability** Services perish instantly, as the service offer cannot be stored for sale at a future time
- **Personal selling** A face-to-face communication between an organization and its customers, with a view to achieving a sale
- **PEST analysis** (or 'STEP' analysis) Elements of the macro marketing environment, comprising political/legal, economic, social/cultural and technological environments
- **Physical Distribution Management** The process of ensuring that the right goods get to the right place at the right time, cost effectively
- **Place** The point where a product is to be made available to consumers
- **Point-of-sale (or Point of Purchase)** In retail, the area where customers make their final decision to buy
- **Positioning** Decisions about how the marketing mix for a company's product should be developed in comparison to the marketing mix of competing products
- **Press release** News story written for, and distributed to the news media with a view to inclusion in media editorial
- **Pressure group** A group which is formed to promote a particular cause
- **Price elasticity of demand** A measure of the responsiveness of demand for a product to change in the price of the product
- **Primary data** New, original data obtained from field research
- **Product life cycle** The different stages through which a product develops over time, reflecting different needs, sales levels and profitability

- **Product line** A number of related products offered by a supplier, which often cover a broadly similar type of need
- **Product mix** The total range of goods and services offered by an organization
- **Production orientation** Where the focus of an organization is on production capability rather than consumers' needs
- **Productivity** The efficiency with which inputs are turned into outputs
- **Profiling** A description of the characteristics of actual or target customers, based on data analysis
- **Profit** The excess of revenue over costs (although it can be difficult to calculate costs for particular products, and therefore their profitability)
- **Promotion mix** The combination of media and messages which a company uses to communicate with actual and potential customers
- **Prospecting** Techniques to identify potential new customers
- **Psychographics** A basis for segmentation derived from attitudinal and behavioural variables
- **Public Relations** A deliberate and planned effort to create mutual understanding between an organization and its various publics
- **Pull strategy** A marketing strategy in which the manufacturer promotes directly to the final customers, who then demand products from intermediaries, who in turn 'pull' goods from the manufacturer
- **Push strategy** A marketing strategy in which the manufacturer promotes primarily to intermediaries, relying on them to promote to their customers
- **Qualitative research** Research which produces essentially attitudinal, non-numerical data
- **Quantitative research** Research based on large samples, but which may be lacking in interpretation. Sometimes called 'hard data'
- **Quality** The standard of delivery of goods or services, often expressed in terms of the extent to which they meet customers' expectations
- **Questionnarie** A set of questions used to obtain information from a respondent
- **Quota sample** A sampling method where those questioned are numerically in proportion to pre-defined characteristics, e.g. sex, age, occupation
- **Random sample** A sampling method where everyone in the population has an equal chance of being included in the sample
- **Relationship marketing** A means by which an organization seeks to maintain an ongoing relationship between itself and its customers, based on continuous patterns of service delivery, rather than isolated and discrete transactions
- **Repositioning** The development of a new marketing mix relative to that of competitors, to replace the existing mix
- **Sales orientation** The focus of an organization is on selling its products more aggressively, while probably not fully understanding the needs of customers and the types of products they would prefer to buy
- **Sales promotion** Techniques and incentives used to increase short-term sales
- **Segment** A grouping of customers who have similar needs and respond in a similar way to a given marketing stimulus
- **Segmentation** The process of identifying groups of customers who have similar needs and respond in a similar way to a given marketing stimulus

- **Scientific approach** Using the rules of scientific procedure in order to develop objectivity and repeatability
- **Sealed bid pricing** Submission of a price quotation for supplying goods or services, in which the identity or price of competing bids is not known
- **Secondary research** Using previously conducted research data
- **Services** products which are essentially intangible and cannot be owned
- **Social responsibility** Accepting corporate responsibilities to customers and non-customers which go beyond legal or contractual requirements
- **Societal marketing** Marketing which attempts to improve social benefits
- **Socio-economic groups** A grouping of the population based on occupation
- **Spam** unsolicited e-mail
- **Speciality goods** Consumer goods for which buyers are prepared or make an effort to acquire
- **Sponsorship** Payment by a company to be associated with a particular event or activity
- **Stakeholder** Any person with an interest in the activities of an organization (e.g. customers, employees, government agencies, and local communities)
- **Strategic alliances** Agreements between organizations which are based on a long-term recognition that they could each benefit by co-operating on some aspect of their marketing
- **Strategy** The overall, long-term direction or approach which a company aims to follow, in order to achieve its objectives
- **SWOT analysis** An acronym for strengths and weaknesses, opportunities and threats and used to assess the internal strengths and weaknesses of an organization against its external threats and opportunities
- **Tactics** Operational activities that put into effect a company's marketing strategy
- **Target market** The segment of a market at which a marketing mix is aimed
- **Test marketing** A trial launch of a product into a limited area to test its marketing mix prior to a full national launch
- **Telemarketing** Sales activity which focuses on the use of the telephone to enter into a two way dialogue with present and potential customers
- **Unique selling proposition (USP)** A selling claim based on a differentiated product feature or unique element of the marketing mix
- **Value chain** The sequence of activities and organizations involved in transforming a product from one which is of low value to one that is of high value
- **Vertical integration** The extension of a firm's activities to previous or subsequent points in a value chain
- **Vertical marketing systems (VMS)** The integration of intermediaries at different levels of a distribution chain to improve efficiency and effectiveness of the chain as a whole
- **Viral marketing** Encouraging recommendation of a company or its products through word of mouth
- **Wholesaler** An intermediary which buys products in bulk and resells them in smaller quantities to retailers
- **Word-of-mouth promotion** The act of recommendation by existing customers to their friends
- **Yield management** Using variable pricing to maximize the earnings from fixed resources, e.g. hotel rooms, airline seats

Subject index

Index of authors cited in text

Index of Organizations and Brands cited in text